University Casebook Series

December, 1982

ACCOUNTING AND THE LAW, Fourth Edition (1978), with Problems Pamphlet (Successor to Dohr, Phillips, Thompson & Warren)

George C. Thompson, Professor, Columbia University Graduate School of Business.

Robert Whitman, Professor of Law, University of Connecticut.

Ellis L. Phillips, Jr., Member of the New York Bar.

William C. Warren, Professor of Law Emeritus, Columbia University.

ACCOUNTING FOR LAWYERS, MATERIALS ON (1980)

David R. Herwitz, Professor of Law, Harvard University.

ADMINISTRATIVE LAW, Seventh Edition (1979), with 1983 Problems Supplement (Supplement edited in association with Paul R. Verkuil, Dean and Professor of Law, Tulane University)

Walter Gellhorn, University Professor Emeritus, Columbia University.

Clark Byse, Professor of Law, Harvard University.

Peter L. Strauss, Professor of Law, Columbia University.

ADMIRALTY, Second Edition (1978), with Statute and Rule Supplement

Jo Desha Lucas, Professor of Law, University of Chicago.

ADVOCACY, see also Lawyering Process

AGENCY, see also Enterprise Organization

AGENCY—PARTNERSHIPS, Third Edition (1982)

Abridgement from Conard, Knauss & Siegel's Enterprise Organization, Third Edition.

ANTITRUST AND REGULATORY ALTERNATIVES (1977), Fifth Edition

Louis B. Schwartz, Professor of Law, University of Pennsylvania.

John J. Flynn, Professor of Law, University of Utah.

ANTITRUST SUPPLEMENT—SELECTED STATUTES AND RELATED MATERIALS (1977)

John J. Flynn, Professor of Law, University of Utah.

BUSINESS ORGANIZATION, see also Enterprise Organization

BUSINESS PLANNING (1966), with 1982 Supplement

David R. Herwitz, Professor of Law, Harvard University.

BUSINESS TORTS (1972)

Milton Handler, Professor of Law Emeritus, Columbia University.

CHILDREN IN THE LEGAL SYSTEM (1983)

Walter Wadlington, Professor of Law, University of Virginia.

Charles H. Whitebread, Professor of Law, University of Southern California.

Samuel Davis, Professor of Law, University of Georgia.

CIVIL PROCEDURE, see Procedure

CLINIC, see also Lawyering Process

COMMERCIAL AND CONSUMER TRANSACTIONS, Second Edition (1978)

William D. Warren, Dean of the School of Law, University of California, Los Angeles.
William E. Hogan, Professor of Law, Cornell University.
Robert L. Jordan, Professor of Law, University of California, Los Angeles.

COMMERCIAL LAW, CASES & MATERIALS ON, Third Edition (1976), with 1982 Supplement

E. Allan Farnsworth, Professor of Law, Columbia University.
John Honnold, Professor of Law, University of Pennsylvania.

COMMERCIAL PAPER, Second Edition (1976)

E. Allan Farnsworth, Professor of Law, Columbia University.

COMMERCIAL PAPER AND BANK DEPOSITS AND COLLECTIONS (1967), with Statutory Supplement

William D. Hawkland, Professor of Law, University of Illinois.

COMMERCIAL TRANSACTIONS—Principles and Policies (1982)

Alan Schwartz, Professor of Law, University of Southern California.
Robert E. Scott, Professor of Law, University of Virginia.

COMPARATIVE LAW, Fourth Edition (1980)

Rudolf B. Schlesinger, Professor of Law, Hastings College of the Law.

COMPETITIVE PROCESS, LEGAL REGULATION OF THE, Second Edition (1979), with Statutory Supplement and 1982 Case Supplement

Edmund W. Kitch, Professor of Law, University of Chicago.
Harvey S. Perlman, Professor of Law, University of Virginia.

CONFLICT OF LAWS, Seventh Edition (1978), with 1982 Supplement

Willis L. M. Reese, Professor of Law, Columbia University,
Maurice Rosenberg, Professor of Law, Columbia University.

CONSTITUTIONAL LAW, Sixth Edition (1981), with 1982 Supplement

Edward L. Barrett, Jr., Professor of Law, University of California, Davis.
William Cohen, Professor of Law, Stanford University.

CONSTITUTIONAL LAW: THE STRUCTURE OF GOVERNMENT (Reprinted from CONSTITUTIONAL LAW, Sixth Edition), with 1982 Supplement

Edward L. Barrett, Jr., Professor of Law, University of California, Davis.
William Cohen, Professor of Law, Stanford University.

CONSTITUTIONAL LAW, CIVIL LIBERTY AND INDIVIDUAL RIGHTS, Second Edition (1982)

William Cohen, Professor of Law, Stanford Law School.
John Kaplan, Professor of Law, Stanford Law School.

CONSTITUTIONAL LAW, Tenth Edition (1980), with 1982 Supplement

Gerald Gunther, Professor of Law, Stanford University.

CONSTITUTIONAL LAW, INDIVIDUAL RIGHTS IN, Third Edition (1981), with 1982 Supplement (Reprinted from CONSTITUTIONAL LAW, Tenth Edition)

Gerald Gunther, Professor of Law, Stanford University.

UNIVERSITY CASEBOOK SERIES—Continued

CONTRACT LAW AND ITS APPLICATION, Second Edition (1977)

The late Addison Mueller, Professor of Law, University of California, Los Angeles.

Arthur I. Rosett, Professor of Law, University of California, Los Angeles.

CONTRACT LAW, STUDIES IN, Second Edition (1977)

Edward J. Murphy, Professor of Law, University of Notre Dame.

Richard E. Speidel, Professor of Law, University of Virginia.

CONTRACTS, Fourth Edition (1982)

John P. Dawson, Professor of Law Emeritus, Harvard University.

William Burnett Harvey, Professor of Law and Political Science, Boston University.

Stanley D. Henderson, Professor of Law, University of Virginia.

CONTRACTS, Third Edition (1980), with Statutory Supplement

E. Allan Farnsworth, Professor of Law, Columbia University.

William F. Young, Professor of Law, Columbia University.

CONTRACTS, Second Edition (1978), with Statutory and Administrative Law Supplement (1978)

Ian R. Macneil, Professor of Law, Cornell University.

COPYRIGHT, PATENTS AND TRADEMARKS, see also Competitive Process

COPYRIGHT, PATENT, TRADEMARK AND RELATED STATE DOCTRINES, Second Edition (1981), with Problem Supplement and Statutory Supplement

Paul Goldstein, Professor of Law, Stanford University.

COPYRIGHT, Unfair Competition, and Other Topics Bearing on the Protection of Literary, Musical, and Artistic Works, Third Edition (1978)

Benjamin Kaplan, Professor of Law Emeritus, Harvard University,

Ralph S. Brown, Jr., Professor of Law, Yale University.

CORPORATE FINANCE, Second Edition (1979), with 1982 New Developments Supplement

Victor Brudney, Professor of Law, Harvard University.

Marvin A. Chirelstein, Professor of Law, Yale University.

CORPORATE READJUSTMENTS AND REORGANIZATIONS (1976)

Walter J. Blum, Professor of Law, University of Chicago.

Stanley A. Kaplan, Professor of Law, University of Chicago.

CORPORATION LAW, BASIC, Second Edition (1979), with Documentary Supplement

Detlev F. Vagts, Professor of Law, Harvard University.

CORPORATIONS, see also Enterprise Organization

CORPORATIONS, Fifth Edition—Unabridged (1980)

William L. Cary, Professor of Law, Columbia University.

Melvin Aron Eisenberg, Professor of Law, University of California, Berkeley.

CORPORATIONS, Fifth Edition—Abridged (1980)

William L. Cary, Professor of Law, Columbia University.

Melvin Aron Eisenberg, Professor of Law, University of California, Berkeley.

UNIVERSITY CASEBOOK SERIES—Continued

CORPORATIONS, Second Edition (1982)

Alfred F. Conard, Professor of Law, University of Michigan.
Robert N. Knauss, Dean of the Law School, University of Houston.
Stanley Siegel, Professor of Law, University of California, Los Angeles.

CORPORATIONS, THE LAW OF: WHAT CORPORATE LAWYERS DO (1976)

Jan G. Deutsch, Professor of Law, Yale University.
Joseph J. Bianco, Professor of Law, Yeshiva University.

CORPORATIONS COURSE GAME PLAN (1975)

David R. Herwitz, Professor of Law, Harvard University.

CORRECTIONS, SEE SENTENCING

CREDIT TRANSACTIONS AND CONSUMER PROTECTION (1976)

John Honnold, Professor of Law, University of Pennsylvania.

CREDITORS' RIGHTS, see also Debtor-Creditor Law

CRIMINAL JUSTICE, THE ADMINISTRATION OF, Second Edition (1969)

Francis C. Sullivan, Professor of Law, Louisiana State University.
Paul Hardin III, Professor of Law, Duke University.
John Huston, Professor of Law, University of Washington.
Frank R. Lacy, Professor of Law, University of Oregon.
Daniel E. Murray, Professor of Law, University of Miami.
George W. Pugh, Professor of Law, Louisiana State University.

CRIMINAL JUSTICE ADMINISTRATION, Second Edition (1982)

Frank W. Miller, Professor of Law, Washington University.
Robert O. Dawson, Professor of Law, University of Texas.
George E. Dix, Professor of Law, University of Texas.
Raymond I. Parnas, Professor of Law, University of California, Davis.

CRIMINAL LAW, Second Edition (1979)

Fred E. Inbau, Professor of Law Emeritus, Northwestern University.
James R. Thompson, Professor of Law Emeritus, Northwestern University.
Andre A. Moenssens, Professor of Law, University of Richmond.

CRIMINAL LAW (1982)

Peter W. Low, Professor of Law, University of Virginia.
John C. Jeffries, Jr., Professor of Law, University of Virginia.
Richard C. Bonnie, Professor of Law, University of Virginia.

CRIMINAL LAW, Third Edition (1980)

Lloyd L. Weinreb, Professor of Law, Harvard University.

CRIMINAL LAW AND PROCEDURE, Fifth Edition (1977)

Rollin M. Perkins, Professor of Law Emeritus, University of California, Hastings College of the Law.
Ronald N. Boyce, Professor of Law, University of Utah.

CRIMINAL PROCEDURE, Second Edition (1980), with 1982 Supplement

Fred E. Inbau, Professor of Law Emeritus, Northwestern University.
James R. Thompson, Professor of Law Emeritus, Northwestern University.
James B. Haddad, Professor of Law, Northwestern University.
James B. Zagel, Chief, Criminal Justice Division, Office of Attorney General of Illinois.
Gary L. Starkman, Assistant U. S. Attorney, Northern District of Illinois.

CRIMINAL PROCEDURE, CONSTITUTIONAL (1977), with 1980 Supplement

James E. Scarboro, Professor of Law, University of Colorado.
James B. White, Professor of Law, University of Chicago.

CRIMINAL PROCESS, Third Edition (1978), with 1982 Supplement

Lloyd L. Weinreb, Professor of Law, Harvard University.

DAMAGES, Second Edition (1952)

Charles T. McCormick, late Professor of Law, University of Texas.
William F. Fritz, late Professor of Law, University of Texas.

DEBTOR–CREDITOR LAW, Second Edition (1981), with Statutory Supplement

William D. Warren, Dean of the School of Law, University of California, Los Angeles.
William E. Hogan, Professor of Law, New York University.

DECEDENTS' ESTATES (1971)

Max Rheinstein, late Professor of Law Emeritus, University of Chicago.
Mary Ann Glendon, Professor of Law, Boston College.

DECEDENTS' ESTATES AND TRUSTS, Sixth Edition (1982)

John Ritchie, Emeritus Dean and Wigmore Professor of Law, Northwestern University.
Neill H. Alford, Jr., Professor of Law, University of Virginia.
Richard W. Effland, Professor of Law, Arizona State University.

DECEDENTS' ESTATES AND TRUSTS (1968)

Howard R. Williams, Professor of Law, Stanford University.

DOMESTIC RELATIONS, see also Family Law

DOMESTIC RELATIONS, Third Edition (1978), with 1980 Supplement

Walter Wadlington, Professor of Law, University of Virginia.
Monrad G. Paulsen, Dean of the Law School, Yeshiva University.

ELECTRONIC MASS MEDIA, Second Edition (1979)

William K. Jones, Professor of Law, Columbia University.

EMPLOYMENT DISCRIMINATION (1983)

Joel W. Friedman, Professor of Law, Tulane University.
George M. Strickler, Professor of Law, Tulane University.

ENERGY LAW (1983)

Donald N. Zillman, Professor of Law, University of Utah.
Laurence Lattman, Dean of Mines and Engineering, University of Utah.

ENTERPRISE ORGANIZATION, Third Edition (1982), with 1982 Corporation and Partnership Statutes, Rules and Forms Supplement

Alfred F. Conard, Professor of Law, University of Michigan.
Robert L. Knauss, Dean of the Law School, University of Houston.
Stanley Siegel, Professor of Law, University of California, Los Angeles.

ENVIRONMENTAL POLICY LAW (1982)

Thomas J. Schoenbaum, Professor of Law, Tulane University.

EQUITY, see also Remedies

UNIVERSITY CASEBOOK SERIES—Continued

EQUITY, RESTITUTION AND DAMAGES, Second Edition (1974)
Robert Childres, late Professor of Law, Northwestern University.
William F. Johnson, Jr., Professor of Law, New York University.

ESTATE PLANNING, Second Edition (1982), with Documentary Supplement
David Westfall, Professor of Law, Harvard University.

ETHICS, see Legal Profession, and Professional Responsibility

ETHICS AND PROFESSIONAL RESPONSIBILITY (1981) (Reprinted from THE LAWYERING PROCESS)
Gary Bellow, Professor of Law, Harvard University.
Bea Moulton, Legal Services Corporation.

EVIDENCE, Fourth Edition (1981)
David W. Louisell, late Professor of Law, University of California, Berkeley.
John Kaplan, Professor of Law, Stanford University.
Jon R. Waltz, Professor of Law, Northwestern University.

EVIDENCE (1968)
Francis C. Sullivan, Professor of Law, Louisiana State University.
Paul Hardin, III, Professor of Law, Duke University.

EVIDENCE, Seventh Edition (1983) with Rules and Statute Supplement (1981)
Jack B. Weinstein, Chief Judge, United States District Court.
John H. Mansfield, Professor of Law, Harvard University.
Norman Abrams, Professor of Law, University of California, Los Angeles.
Margaret Berger, Professor of Law, Brooklyn Law School.

FAMILY LAW, see also Domestic Relations

FAMILY LAW (1978), with 1983 Supplement
Judith C. Areen, Professor of Law, Georgetown University.

FAMILY LAW AND CHILDREN IN THE LEGAL SYSTEM, STATUTORY MATERIALS (1981)
Walter Wadlington, Professor of Law, University of Virginia.

FEDERAL COURTS, Seventh Edition (1982)
Charles T. McCormick, late Professor of Law, University of Texas.
James H. Chadbourn, Professor of Law, Harvard University.
Charles Alan Wright, Professor of Law, University of Texas.

FEDERAL COURTS AND THE FEDERAL SYSTEM, Hart and Wechsler's Second Edition (1973), with 1981 Supplement
Paul M. Bator, Professor of Law, Harvard University.
Paul J. Mishkin, Professor of Law, University of California, Berkeley.
David L. Shapiro, Professor of Law, Harvard University.
Herbert Wechsler, Professor of Law, Columbia University.

FEDERAL PUBLIC LAND AND RESOURCES LAW (1981)
George C. Coggins, Professor of Law, University of Kansas.
Charles F. Wilkinson, Professor of Law, University of Oregon.

FEDERAL RULES OF CIVIL PROCEDURE, 1982 Edition

FEDERAL TAXATION, see Taxation

UNIVERSITY CASEBOOK SERIES—Continued

FOOD AND DRUG LAW (1980), with Statutory Supplement
Richard A. Merrill, Dean of the School of Law, University of Virginia.
Peter Barton Hutt, Esq.

FUTURE INTERESTS (1958)
Philip Mechem, late Professor of Law Emeritus, University of Pennsylvania.

FUTURE INTERESTS (1970)
Howard R. Williams, Professor of Law, Stanford University.

FUTURE INTERESTS AND ESTATE PLANNING (1961), with 1962 Supplement
W. Barton Leach, late Professor of Law, Harvard University.
James K. Logan, formerly Dean of the Law School, University of Kansas.

GOVERNMENT CONTRACTS, FEDERAL (1975), with 1980 Supplement
John W. Whelan, Professor of Law, Hastings College of the Law.
Robert S. Pasley, Professor of Law Emeritus, Cornell University.

INJUNCTIONS (1972)
Owen M. Fiss, Professor of Law, Yale University.

INSTITUTIONAL INVESTORS, 1978
David L. Ratner, Professor of Law, Cornell University.

INSURANCE (1971)
William F. Young, Professor of Law, Columbia University.

INTERNATIONAL LAW, see also Transnational Legal Problems and United Nations Law

INTERNATIONAL LAW IN CONTEMPORARY PERSPECTIVE (1981), with Essay Supplement
Myres S. McDougal, Professor of Law, Yale University.
W. Michael Reisman, Professor of Law, Yale University.

INTERNATIONAL LEGAL SYSTEM, Second Edition (1981), with Documentary Supplement
Joseph Modeste Sweeney, Professor of Law, Tulane University.
Covey T. Oliver, Professor of Law, University of Pennsylvania.
Noyes E. Leech, Professor of Law, University of Pennsylvania.

INTERNATIONAL TRADE AND INVESTMENT, REGULATION OF (1970)
Carl H. Fulda, late Professor of Law, University of Texas.
Warren F. Schwartz, Professor of Law, University of Virginia.

INTRODUCTION TO LAW, see also Legal Method, On Law in Courts, and Dynamics of American Law

INTRODUCTION TO THE STUDY OF LAW (1970)
E. Wayne Thode, late Professor of Law, University of Utah.
Leon Lebowitz, Professor of Law, University of Texas.
Lester J. Mazor, Professor of Law, University of Utah.

JUDICIAL CODE and Rules of Procedure in the Federal Courts with Excerpts from the Criminal Code, 1981 Edition
Henry M. Hart, Jr., late Professor of Law, Harvard University.
Herbert Wechsler, Professor of Law, Columbia University.

vii

UNIVERSITY CASEBOOK SERIES—Continued

JURISPRUDENCE (Temporary Edition Hardbound) (1949)

Lon L. Fuller, Professor of Law Emeritus, Harvard University.

JUVENILE, see also Children

JUVENILE JUSTICE PROCESS, Second Edition (1976), with 1980 Supplement

Frank W. Miller, Professor of Law, Washington University.
Robert O. Dawson, Professor of Law, University of Texas.
George E. Dix, Professor of Law, University of Texas.
Raymond I. Parnas, Professor of Law, University of California, Davis.

LABOR LAW, Ninth Edition (1981), with Statutory Supplement

Archibald Cox, Professor of Law, Harvard University.
Derek C. Bok, President, Harvard University.
Robert A. Gorman, Professor of Law, University of Pennsylvania.

LABOR LAW, Second Edition (1982), with Statutory Supplement

Clyde W. Summers, Professor of Law, University of Pennsylvania.
Harry H. Wellington, Dean of the Law School, Yale University.
Alan Hyde, Professor of Law, Rutgers University.

LAND FINANCING, Second Edition (1977)

Norman Penney, Professor of Law, Cornell University.
Richard F. Broude, Member of the California Bar.

LAW AND MEDICINE (1980)

Walter Wadlington, Professor of Law and Professor of Legal Medicine, University of Virginia.
Jon R. Waltz, Professor of Law, Northwestern University.
Roger B. Dworkin, Professor of Law, Indiana University, and Professor of Biomedical History, University of Washington.

LAW, LANGUAGE AND ETHICS (1972)

William R. Bishin, Professor of Law, University of Southern California.
Christopher D. Stone, Professor of Law, University of Southern California.

LAWYERING PROCESS (1978), with Civil Problem Supplement and Criminal Problem Supplement

Gary Bellow, Professor of Law, Harvard University.
Bea Moulton, Professor of Law, Arizona State University.

LEGAL METHOD (1980)

Harry W. Jones, Professor of Law Emeritus, Columbia University.
John M. Kernochan, Professor of Law, Columbia University.
Arthur W. Murphy, Professor of Law, Columbia University.

LEGAL METHODS (1969)

Robert N. Covington, Professor of Law, Vanderbilt University.
E. Blythe Stason, late Professor of Law, Vanderbilt University.
John W. Wade, Professor of Law, Vanderbilt University.
Elliott E. Cheatham, late Professor of Law, Vanderbilt University.
Theodore A. Smedley, Professor of Law, Vanderbilt University.

LEGAL PROFESSION (1970)

Samuel D. Thurman, Dean of the College of Law, University of Utah.
Ellis L. Phillips, Jr., Professor of Law, Columbia University.
Elliott E. Cheatham, late Professor of Law, Vanderbilt University.

UNIVERSITY CASEBOOK SERIES—Continued

LEGISLATION, Fourth Edition (1982) (by Fordham)

Horace E. Read, late Vice President, Dalhousie University.
John W. MacDonald, Professor of Law Emeritus, Cornell Law School.
Jefferson B. Fordham, Professor of Law, University of Utah.
William J. Pierce, Professor of Law, University of Michigan.

LEGISLATIVE AND ADMINISTRATIVE PROCESSES, Second Edition (1981)

Hans A. Linde, Judge, Supreme Court of Oregon.
George Bunn, Professor of Law, University of Wisconsin.
Fredericka Paff, Professor of Law, University of Wisconsin.
W. Lawrence Church, Professor of Law, University of Wisconsin.

LOCAL GOVERNMENT LAW, Revised Edition (1975)

Jefferson B. Fordham, Professor of Law, University of Utah.

MASS MEDIA LAW, Second Edition (1982)

Marc A. Franklin, Professor of Law, Stanford University.

MENTAL HEALTH PROCESS, Second Edition (1976), with 1981 Supplement

Frank W. Miller, Professor of Law, Washington University.
Robert O. Dawson, Professor of Law, University of Texas.
George E. Dix, Professor of Law, University of Texas.
Raymond I. Parnas, Professor of Law, University of California, Davis.

MUNICIPAL CORPORATIONS, see Local Government Law

NEGOTIABLE INSTRUMENTS, see Commercial Paper

NEGOTIATION (1981) (Reprinted from THE LAWYERING PROCESS)

Gary Bellow, Professor of Law, Harvard Law School.
Bea Moulton, Legal Services Corporation.

NEW YORK PRACTICE, Fourth Edition (1978)

Herbert Peterfreund, Professor of Law, New York University.
Joseph M. McLaughlin, Dean of the Law School, Fordham University.

OIL AND GAS, Fourth Edition (1979)

Howard R. Williams, Professor of Law, Stanford University.
Richard C. Maxwell, Professor of Law, University of California, Los Angeles.
Charles J. Meyers, Dean of the Law School, Stanford University.

ON LAW IN COURTS (1965)

Paul J. Mishkin, Professor of Law, University of California, Berkeley.
Clarence Morris, Professor of Law Emeritus, University of Pennsylvania.

PERSPECTIVES ON THE LAWYER AS PLANNER (Reprint of Chapters One through Five of Planning by Lawyers) (1978)

Louis M. Brown, Professor of Law, University of Southern California.
Edward A. Dauer, Professor of Law, Yale University.

PLANNING BY LAWYERS, MATERIALS ON A NONADVERSARIAL LEGAL PROCESS (1978)

Louis M. Brown, Professor of Law, University of Southern California.
Edward A. Dauer, Professor of Law, Yale University.

PLEADING AND PROCEDURE, see Procedure, Civil

UNIVERSITY CASEBOOK SERIES—Continued

POLICE FUNCTION, Third Edition (1982)

Reprint of Chapters 1–10 of Miller, Dawson, Dix and Parnas' Criminal Justice Administration, Second Edition.

PREPARING AND PRESENTING THE CASE (1981) (Reprinted from THE LAWYERING PROCESS)

Gary Bellow, Professor of Law, Harvard Law School.
Bea Moulton, Legal Services Corporation.

PREVENTIVE LAW, see also Planning by Lawyers

PROCEDURE—CIVIL PROCEDURE, Second Edition (1974), with 1979 Supplement

James H. Chadbourn, Professor of Law, Harvard University.
A. Leo Levin, Professor of Law, University of Pennsylvania.
Philip Shuchman, Professor of Law, University of Connecticut.

PROCEDURE—CIVIL PROCEDURE, Fourth Edition (1978), with 1982 Supplement

Richard H. Field, late Professor of Law, Harvard University.
Benjamin Kaplan, Professor of Law Emeritus, Harvard University.
Kevin M. Clermont, Professor of Law, Cornell University.

PROCEDURE—CIVIL PROCEDURE, Third Edition (1976), with 1982 Supplement

Maurice Rosenberg, Professor of Law, Columbia University.
Jack B. Weinstein, Professor of Law, Columbia University.
Hans Smit, Professor of Law, Columbia University.
Harold L. Korn, Professor of Law, Columbia University.

PROCEDURE—PLEADING AND PROCEDURE: State and Federal, Fourth Edition (1979), with 1982 Supplement

David W. Louisell, late Professor of Law, University of California, Berkeley.
Geoffrey C. Hazard, Jr., Professor of Law, Yale University.

PROCEDURE—FEDERAL RULES OF CIVIL PROCEDURE, 1982 Edition

PRODUCTS LIABILITY (1980)

Marshall S. Shapo, Professor of Law, Northwestern University.

PRODUCTS LIABILITY AND SAFETY (1980), with Statutory Supplement

W. Page Keeton, Professor of Law, University of Texas.
David G. Owen, Professor of Law, University of South Carolina.
John E. Montgomery, Professor of Law, University of South Carolina.

PROFESSIONAL RESPONSIBILITY, Second Edition (1981), with Selected National Standards Supplement

Thomas D. Morgan, Dean of the Law School, Emory University.
Ronald D. Rotunda, Professor of Law, University of Illinois.

PROPERTY, Fourth Edition (1978)

John E. Cribbet, Dean of the Law School, University of Illinois.
Corwin W. Johnson, Professor of Law, University of Texas.

PROPERTY—PERSONAL (1953)

S. Kenneth Skolfield, late Professor of Law Emeritus, Boston University.

PROPERTY—PERSONAL, Third Edition (1954)

Everett Fraser, late Dean of the Law School Emeritus, University of Minnesota. Third Edition by Charles W. Taintor, late Professor of Law, University of Pittsburgh.

PROPERTY—INTRODUCTION, TO REAL PROPERTY, Third Edition (1954)

Everett Fraser, late Dean of the Law School Emeritus, University of Minnesota.

PROPERTY—REAL AND PERSONAL, Combined Edition (1954)

Everett Fraser, late Dean of the Law School Emeritus, University of Minnesota. Third Edition of Personal Property by Charles W. Taintor, late Professor of Law, University of Pittsburgh.

PROPERTY—REAL PROPERTY AND CONVEYANCING (1954)

Edward E. Bade, late Professor of Law, University of Minnesota.

PROPERTY—FUNDAMENTALS OF MODERN REAL PROPERTY, Second Edition (1982)

Edward H. Rabin, Professor of Law, University of California, Davis.

PROPERTY—PROBLEMS IN REAL PROPERTY (Pamphlet) (1969)

Edward H. Rabin, Professor of Law, University of California, Davis.

PROSECUTION AND ADJUDICATION, Second Edition (1982)

Reprint of Chapters 11–26 of Miller, Dawson, Dix and Parnas' Criminal Justice Administration, Second Edition.

PUBLIC REGULATION OF DANGEROUS PRODUCTS (paperback) (1980)

Marshall S. Shapo, Professor of Law, Northwestern University.

PUBLIC UTILITY LAW, see Free Enterprise, also Regulated Industries

REAL ESTATE PLANNING (1980), with 1980 Problems, Statutes and New Materials Supplement

Norton L. Steuben, Professor of Law, University of Colorado.

REAL ESTATE TRANSACTIONS (1980), with Statute, Form and Problem Supplement

Paul Goldstein, Professor of Law, Stanford University.

RECEIVERSHIP AND CORPORATE REORGANIZATION, see Creditors' Rights

REGULATED INDUSTRIES, Second Edition, 1976

William K. Jones, Professor of Law, Columbia University.

REMEDIES (1982)

Edward D. Re, Chief Judge, U. S. Court of International Trade.

RESTITUTION, Second Edition (1966)

John W. Wade, Professor of Law, Vanderbilt University.

SALES (1980)

Marion W. Benfield, Jr., Professor of Law, University of Illinois.
William D. Hawkland, Chancellor, Louisiana State University Law Center.

SALES AND SALES FINANCING, Fourth Edition (1976), with 1982 Supplement

John Honnold, Professor of Law, University of Pennsylvania.

UNIVERSITY CASEBOOK SERIES—Continued

SALES LAW AND THE CONTRACTING PROCESS (1982)

Reprint of Chapters 1–10 of Schwartz and Scott's Commercial Transactions.

SECURITIES REGULATION, Fifth Edition (1982), with 1982 Selected Statutes, Rules and Forms Supplement

Richard W. Jennings, Professor of Law, University of California, Berkeley.
Harold Marsh, Jr., Member of the California Bar.

SECURITIES REGULATION (1982), with 1983 Supplement

Larry D. Soderquist, Professor of Law, Vanderbilt University.

SENTENCING AND THE CORRECTIONAL PROCESS, Second Edition (1976)

Frank W. Miller, Professor of Law, Washington University.
Robert O. Dawson, Professor of Law, University of Texas.
George E. Dix, Professor of Law, University of Texas.
Raymond I. Parnas, Professor of Law, University of California, Davis.

SOCIAL WELFARE AND THE INDIVIDUAL (1971)

Robert J. Levy, Professor of Law, University of Minnesota.
Thomas P. Lewis, Dean of the College of Law, University of Kentucky.
Peter W. Martin, Professor of Law, Cornell University.

TAX, POLICY ANALYSIS OF THE FEDERAL INCOME (1976)

William A. Klein, Professor of Law, University of California, Los Angeles.

TAXATION, FEDERAL INCOME (1976), with 1982 Supplement

Erwin N. Griswold, Dean Emeritus, Harvard Law School.
Michael J. Graetz, Professor of Law, University of Virginia.

TAXATION, FEDERAL INCOME, Fourth Edition (1982)

James J. Freeland, Professor of Law, University of Florida.
Stephen A. Lind, Professor of Law, University of Florida.
Richard B. Stephens, Professor of Law Emeritus, University of Florida.

TAXATION, FEDERAL INCOME, Volume I, Personal Income Taxation (1972), with 1982 Supplement; Volume II, Taxation of Partnerships and Corporations, Second Edition (1980)

Stanley S. Surrey, Professor of Law, Harvard University.
William C. Warren, Professor of Law Emeritus, Columbia University.
Paul R. McDaniel, Professor of Law, Boston College Law School.
Hugh J. Ault, Professor of Law, Boston College Law School.

TAXATION, FEDERAL WEALTH TRANSFER, Second Edition (1982)

Stanley S. Surrey, Professor of Law, Harvard University.
William C. Warren, Professor of Law Emeritus, Columbia University.
Paul R. McDaniel, Professor of Law, Boston College Law School.
Harry L. Gutman, Instructor, Harvard Law School and Boston College Law School.

TAXATION OF INDIVIDUALS, PARTNERSHIPS AND CORPORATIONS, PROBLEMS in the (1978)

Norton L. Steuben, Professor of Law, University of Colorado.
William J. Turnier, Professor of Law, University of North Carolina.

TAXES AND FINANCE—STATE AND LOCAL (1974)

Oliver Oldman, Professor of Law, Harvard University.
Ferdinand P. Schoettle, Professor of Law, University of Minnesota.

TORT LAW AND ALTERNATIVES: INJURIES AND REMEDIES, Second Edition (1979)

Marc A. Franklin, Professor of Law, Stanford University.

TORTS, Seventh Edition (1982)

William L. Prosser, late Professor of Law, University of California, Hastings College.
John W. Wade, Professor of Law, Vanderbilt University.
Victor E. Schwartz, Professor of Law, American University.

TORTS, Third Edition (1976)

Harry Shulman, late Dean of the Law School, Yale University.
Fleming James, Jr., Professor of Law Emeritus, Yale University.
Oscar S. Gray, Professor of Law, University of Maryland.

TRADE REGULATION (1975), with 1979 Supplement

Milton Handler, Professor of Law Emeritus, Columbia University.
Harlan M. Blake, Professor of Law, Columbia University.
Robert Pitofsky, Professor of Law, Georgetown University.
Harvey J. Goldschmid, Professor of Law, Columbia University.

TRADE REGULATION, see Antitrust

TRANSNATIONAL LEGAL PROBLEMS, Second Edition (1976) with 1982 Case and Documentary Supplement

Henry J. Steiner, Professor of Law, Harvard University.
Detlev F. Vagts, Professor of Law, Harvard University.

TRIAL, see also Evidence, Making the Record, Lawyering Process and Preparing and Presenting the Case

TRIAL ADVOCACY (1968)

A. Leo Levin, Professor of Law, University of Pennsylvania.
Harold Cramer, of the Pennsylvania Bar.
Maurice Rosenberg, Professor of Law, Columbia University, Consultant.

TRUSTS, Fifth Edition (1978)

George G. Bogert, late Professor of Law Emeritus, University of Chicago.
Dallin H. Oaks, President, Brigham Young University.

TRUSTS AND SUCCESSION (Palmer's), Third Edition (1978)

Richard V. Wellman, Professor of Law, University of Georgia.
Lawrence W. Waggoner, Professor of Law, University of Michigan.
Olin L. Browder, Jr., Professor of Law, University of Michigan.

UNFAIR COMPETITION, see Competitive Process and Business Torts

UNITED NATIONS IN ACTION (1968)

Louis B. Sohn, Professor of Law, Harvard University.

UNITED NATIONS LAW, Second Edition (1967), with Documentary Supplement (1968)

Louis B. Sohn, Professor of Law, Harvard University.

WATER RESOURCE MANAGEMENT, Second Edition (1980), with 1983 Supplement

Charles J. Meyers, Dean of the Law School, Stanford University.
A. Dan Tarlock, Professor of Law, Indiana Unversity.

WILLS AND ADMINISTRATION, Fifth Edition (1961)

Philip Mechem, late Professor of Law, University of Pennsylvania.
Thomas E. Atkinson, late Professor of Law, New York University.

WORLD LAW, see United Nations Law

University Casebook Series

EDITORIAL BOARD

COMMERCIAL PAPER

By

ROBERT L. JORDAN

Professor of Law
University of California, Los Angeles

and

WILLIAM D. WARREN

Professor of Law
University of California, Los Angeles

Mineola, New York
THE FOUNDATION PRESS, INC.
1983

Reprinted in part from Jordan and Warren's Commercial Law © 1983
By The Foundation Press, Inc.

Library of Congress Catalog Card Number: 83–80652

ISBN 0–88277–129–9

J. & W. Comm.Paper UCB

PREFACE

We offer this book for use in courses in commercial paper or negotiable instruments of from 30 to 45 class hours. We cover in depth Articles 3 and 4 of the Uniform Commercial Code. We also include materials on documentary sales, documents of title, and letters of credit. Throughout the book we track negotiable instruments issues with parallel developments with respect to credit cards and electronic fund transfers.

In selecting cases, we have favored recent cases that discuss trends in commercial paper decisions. The large number included that are less than five years old demonstrates the vitality of this field of law. Alas, clients stubbornly persist in their refusal to litigate some of the most interesting issues of the UCC. We make up for their lack of cooperation in this regard by including a large number of problems throughout the book that are analytical excursions into areas of the UCC as yet unexplored by the courts. Other problems are closely based on the facts of actual cases; their inclusion serves to give breadth to the course without undue length.

Our thrust is rigorous statutory analysis. We have designed the book to serve the needs of differing pedagogical styles. In using these materials we expect to discuss in class most of the principal cases and many of the problems. Other teachers may wish to spend virtually all of their class time either on the cases or on the numerous problems.

We find that students more easily learn a technical course like commercial paper if they are given some background in the field by way of text discussion. Hence, one of our major efforts has been to include text notes throughout the book designed to prepare students for coming to grips with the cases and problems.

We are particularly indebted to Marilyn Schroeter who bore the major burden of typing and preparing the manuscript for publication. Her unerring efficiency and attentiveness to detail greatly eased our task. We also want to thank Mary Portanova who aided in the typing of the manuscript.

ROBERT L. JORDAN
WILLIAM D. WARREN

April, 1983

*

SUMMARY OF CONTENTS

*

TABLE OF CONTENTS

TABLE OF CONTENTS

TABLE OF CASES

The principal cases are in italic type. Cases cited or discussed are in roman. References are to Pages.

TABLE OF CASES

*

COMMERCIAL PAPER

*

Chapter 1

INTRODUCTION TO NEGOTIABLE INSTRUMENTS AND THE CONCEPT OF NEGOTIABILITY

―――

A. INTRODUCTORY NOTE

―――

1. TYPES OF NEGOTIABLE INSTRUMENTS

In order to understand negotiable instruments it is essential to understand its terminology. This note explains some of the basic vocabulary.

Negotiable instruments are obligations to pay money and they fall into two principal categories: promises to pay money and orders to pay money. A promise to pay, or promissory note, in its most simple form might read as follows:

> I promise to pay on demand $1,000 to the
> order of Richard Roe.
>
>   John Doe

The principal example of an order to pay is an ordinary check. It is addressed to a bank and states:

> Pay to the order of Richard Roe $1,000.
>
>   John Doe

At the time of issuance of a promissory note it has at least two parties. One party is the obligor or "maker" who promises to pay. The other party is the person to whom payment is to be made, or the "payee." A check, on issuance, has three parties. The depositor who orders payment is the "drawer." The bank, to whom the order is directed, is the "drawee." The person entitled to payment pursuant to the order of the drawer is the "payee."

1

2. INSTRUMENTS TO ORDER OR TO BEARER; INDORSEMENT

To qualify as a negotiable instrument, a note or check must be made payable "to order" or "to bearer" UCC § 3–104(1)(d). UCC § 3–110 tells when an instrument is payable to order and UCC § 3–111 states when an instrument is payable to bearer. The terms "to order" and "to bearer" relate to how we determine who is entitled to payment of the instrument. If a note is payable "to the order of John Doe" the maker of the note agrees to pay the amount of the note to anyone designated by John Doe, i.e., according to John Doe's order. John Doe communicates his order to the maker either by presenting the note in its original form to the maker and demanding payment to himself, or by writing his order on the note. This written order, which must include Doe's signature, is known as an indorsement and is usually made on the back of the instrument. An indorsement is most commonly made as part of a transfer of the instrument. John Doe can transfer the note to Jane Doe by delivering it to her after writing "Pay to the order of Jane Doe" on the back of the note and signing his name. John has made what is known as a special indorsement, UCC § 3–204(1), and he has become party to the note in a new capacity—that of indorser. "Pay to Jane Doe" and "I hereby assign my rights in this instrument to Jane Doe" are other examples of special indorsements and are identical in legal effect to "Pay to the order of Jane Doe." UCC § 3–204(1), § 3–202(4) and Comment 5 to § 3–202. As an indorser, John may have certain liabilities. UCC § 3–414. John is also the transferor of the note and in that capacity he may have separate liabilities. UCC § 3–417(2). We will consider these liabilities in detail in Chapter 6. After John's indorsement the note is payable according to Jane's order. UCC § 3–204(1). Jane has also replaced John as the "holder" of the note. UCC § 1–201(20). The identity of the holder of the note is of great importance because with few exceptions only the holder of a negotiable instrument may enforce its payment. UCC § 3–301.

To change the facts somewhat suppose that John had ordered payment by simply signing his name on the back of the note without designating to whom the note was to be payable. This is known as a blank indorsement and its effect is to make the note payable to bearer, i.e., anyone in possession of it. UCC § 3–204(2). "Pay to bearer" or "pay to cash" would be other examples of blank indorsements. If the note indorsed in blank is delivered by John to Jane, she becomes the bearer of the note, UCC § 1–201(5), as well as its holder. UCC § 1–201(20).

If John's rights in the note are transferred to Jane by a process which results in Jane's becoming a holder of the note we say that John has "negotiated" the note to Jane. UCC § 3–202. If the note is transferred from John to Jane in some other way, e.g., a delivery of the note without John's indorsement, no negotiation has occurred, Whether a negotiation occurred is of great importance. As we shall see, if John negotiates the note to Jane she may have remarkably greater rights to collect on the instrument than does John.

To test your understanding consider the following: Suppose John indorses the note to the order of Jane and delivers it to her. Jane then indorses the note by simply signing her name and delivers the note to Richard Roe. Is Roe the holder of the note? Is he the bearer? Has the note been negotiated? Suppose John doesn't indorse the note at all and he delivers it to Jane. Has John transferred the note? Has he negotiated it? Who is the bearer of the note? Who is the holder of the note?

3. LIABILITY ON PROMISES TO PAY AND ORDERS TO PAY; ACCEPTANCE AND CERTIFICATION

The promissory note is the most simple kind of negotiable instrument. The person primarily obligated to pay is the maker who has expressly agreed to do so. The person entitled to payment is the holder of the note. UCC § 3–301. The order to pay is more complex. Somebody has been ordered to pay the instrument but nobody has expressly agreed to pay it. Orders to pay are called "bills of exchange" or in more modern usage "drafts." A check is a demand draft drawn on a bank. UCC § 3–104(2). A draft normally arises out of a pre-existing debtor-creditor relationship. For example, suppose that in a sales transaction a seller provides goods to the buyer and is a creditor for the sales price. Pursuant to pre-existing agreement the seller (the drawer) draws a draft which orders the buyer (the drawee) to pay to a named payee a sum of money which represents the purchase price. The draft is then delivered by the drawer to the payee. The payee, or a subsequent holder, presents it to the drawee for payment. By paying the draft the drawee discharges the debt owed to the drawer. Later we will examine in detail these sales transactions. This kind of transaction is essentially similar to the more common check transaction. Depositor (drawer), who is a creditor of his bank in the amount of his deposit balance, draws a check on the debtor bank (drawee) ordering the bank to pay money to the order of the payee named in the check. In both examples the drawee has no contract relationship to the payee or other holder and it has made no promise to pay that can be enforced by the holder. UCC § 3–409. Whether the drawee pays the draft depends upon its obligation to the drawer. If by express or implied contract (the sales agreement or the bank-depositor agreement) the drawee has agreed to pay properly presented drafts, a failure to pay would be a breach of contract with the drawer, but the holder acquires no rights against the drawee. Before codification of negotiable instruments law by the Uniform Negotiable Instruments Law (NIL) in the late 19th century a minority of states took the view that a check created a direct liability on the part of the drawee bank to the holder. The theory was that a check amounted to an equitable assignment of the drawer's funds on deposit, but NIL § 189 took the majority view that the check is not itself an assignment. UCC § 3–409 follows the NIL in that respect.

Let us look at situations in which the drawee incurs a legal obligation to the holder of the draft to pay it when properly presented. Drafts used in sales and some other commercial transactions can be of two types. One type, and the most common, is the demand draft or "sight draft." It contemplates that the amount of the draft be paid by the drawee upon presentation or "on sight." If the drawee refuses to pay, it is said that the draft has been "dishonored." UCC § 3–507(1). Upon dishonor of the draft the holder may have rights of recourse against the drawer or others even though he has no rights against the drawee. UCC § 3–413(2) and § 3–414. A check is an example of a demand draft. Another type of draft, called a "time draft" does not contemplate immediate payment by the drawee. For example, suppose the draft reads as follows: "Pay $1,000 to the order of Jane Doe sixty days after presentment of this draft." Here, two steps are contemplated. Jane Doe, or some subsequent holder, will initially present the draft to the drawee to start the running of the 60 days, and when they have passed, a second presentment will be made for payment. But the holder at the time of the initial presentment is entitled to know whether or not the drawee is agreeable to honoring the draft. If the drawee does not "accept" the draft a dishonor of the draft occurs. UCC § 3–507(1). "Acceptance" is the agreement by the drawee that it will pay the draft. UCC § 3–410. This acceptance is signified by the drawee's signing of the draft with or without the word "accepted." The date of acceptance is also normally included but is not required. UCC § 3–410. The drawee's acceptance is a promise to pay the draft to the holder of the draft. The drawee's obligation on the draft as "acceptor" is similar to the obligation of the maker of a promissory note to pay the holder. UCC § 3–413(1). A more common example of acceptance is the certified check. If the payee of an ordinary check wants assurance of payment, one way of getting it is to insist that the drawee bank accept the check before it is presented for payment. This is done by the drawee bank's signing the check in much the same way as described in the case of the time draft. Only the terminology differs. The bank's signature is commonly called "certification" but it is identical to acceptance. UCC § 3–411. Certification is normally obtained by the drawer prior to delivery of the check to the payee, but sometimes the holder of an uncertified check may prefer to obtain the drawee bank's agreement to pay rather than payment itself. This can be done by having drawee bank certify the check. Sometimes, the drawee will obligate itself to pay the draft by a separate agreement with, or for the benefit of, the holder. The most common example is the letter of credit issued by drawee banks which we will examine in a later chapter. A failure to honor the draft results in a breach of the separate agreement. UCC § 3–409(2).

PROBLEM

Buyer offered Dealer his check for $1,100 in partial payment for a used car. Before taking the check, Dealer telephoned Buyer's bank and asked whether there were funds in Buyer's account to cover the check and made inquiries into Buyer's reputation for credit-worthiness. An officer of the bank stated that Buyer's account was ample to cover the check and that Buyer had had no overdrafts in his account at that bank. In finishing his telephone conversation with the bank representative, Dealer said: "Well, thanks for the information. I appreciate your help very much. Now my understanding is that Buyer has the money in your bank to pay this check and that if we take this check you will pay it when it is presented. Right?" The bank representative replied: "Sure, it will be paid. We've never had any trouble with Buyer."

Dealer closed the deal and deposited Buyer's check the next day. When the check was presented to Buyer's bank, payment was refused because other checks on the account which cleared after the telephone conversation depleted the account to a balance of only $375. What are Dealer's rights against the bank?

What are Dealer's rights if the bank representative had been mistaken about the balance of Buyer's account at the time of the call and the correct balance at that time had been only $375?

B. THE CONCEPT OF NEGOTIABILITY

1. NEGOTIABILITY OF INSTRUMENTS: HISTORICAL ORIGINS

Professor Gilmore sketches the background of negotiable instruments law in the following quotation from his article "Formalism and the Law of Negotiable Instruments," 13 Creighton L. Rev. 441, 446–450 (1979)*

Our law of negotiable instruments dates from the late eighteenth century. * * * Lord Mansfield and his colleagues in the late eighteenth century were faced with radically new problems for which they devised radically new solutions.

The radically new problems all stemmed from the industrial revolution and the vastly increased number of commercial transactions which it spawned. When goods were shipped, they had to be paid for. The idea that the payments could be made in metallic currency, chronically in short supply, was ludicrous. The primitive banking system could not cope with the situation: the bank check which—a hundred years later—became the universal payment device was unknown. In effect the merchants and the bankers invented their own paper currency. The form which they used was an old one: the so-called bill of exchange which was an order issued by one person (the drawer) to a second person (the drawee) directing the drawee to pay a specified sum of money at a specified time to a third person (the holder). Frequently these bills, drawn by sellers on buyers, represented the purchase price of goods sold. In a more sophisticated and somewhat later variant a mercantile banking house issued what came to be called a letter of credit to a customer. The letter authorized the customer to draw on the bankers for the purchase price of goods which he intended to buy: Through the first half of the nineteenth century Yankees trading out of Boston, armed with their letters of credit

* Reprinted with permission of the Creighton Law Review.

which were frequently issued by English houses, roamed the Far East assembling their precious and fabulously profitable cargoes of silks and teas and spices, paying for them with drafts on London. For half a century these bills or drafts were an indispensable supplement to the official currencies and were indeed used as currency: the bills which showed up in litigation had, as the case reports tell us, passed from hand to hand in a long series of transactions. And a draft on a ranking London house was a much safer as well as a much more convenient thing to have than a bag-full of clipped Maria Theresa dollars. These bills moved in a world-wide market, typically ending up in the possession of people who knew nothing about the transaction which had given rise to the bill, had no way of finding out anything about the transaction and, in any case, had not the slightest interest in it.

Against that background, the courts, English and American, put together, in not much more than half a century, the law of negotiable instruments almost exactly as we know it today. Indeed anyone who has mastered the current American formulation of the subject in Article 3 of the Uniform Commercial Code will have a startling sense of *déjà vu*—I suppose this is *déjà vu* in reverse—if he then goes back to the mid-nineteenth century treatises: time seems to have been suspended, nothing has changed, the late twentieth century law of negotiable instruments is still a law for clipper ships and their exotic cargoes from the Indies. The *déjà-vu* is false, a sort of floating mirage—but I will return to that later.

In putting together their law of negotiable instruments, the courts assumed that the new mercantile currency was a good thing whose use should be encouraged. Two quite simple ideas became the foundation pieces for the whole structure. One was the good faith purchase idea. The stranger who purchased the bill in the market was entitled to do so without inquiry into the facts of the underlying transaction or of previous transfers of the bill and without being affected by them: if he bought the bill for value, in good faith and in the ordinary course of business, he held it free both of underlying contract defenses and of outstanding equities of ownership. The other idea which, the first time you run into it, sounds like nonsense—the legal mind at its worst—was even more basic to the structure and indeed was what gave the completed edifice its pure and almost unearthly beauty. That was the idea that the piece of paper on which the bill was written or printed should be treated as if it—the piece of paper—was itself the claim or debt which it evidenced. This idea came to be known as the doctrine of merger,—the debt was merged in the instrument. At one stroke it drastically simplified the law of negotiable instruments, to the benefit of both purchasers and the people required to pay the instruments. Under merger theory the only way of transferring the debt represented by the bill was by physical delivery of the bill itself to the transferee. The courts also worked out an elaborate set of rules on when the transferor was required to endorse, as well as deliver, the bill and on what liabilities to subsequent parties he assumed by endorsing. When these formalities—delivery and endorsement—had been accomplished—but not until then—the transfer became a negotiation and the transferee a holder. Only the holder— the person physically in possession of the bill under a proper chain of endorsements—was entitled to demand payment of the bill from the party required to pay it; only payment to such a holder discharged the bill as well as the underlying obligation. Merger theory was also of immense importance from the point of view of the paying party: not only did he know whom he was supposed to pay—the holder—but, under another aspect of the theory, he was entitled to pay (and get his discharge) even if he knew, to state an extreme case, that the holder he paid had acquired the bill by fraud or trickery from a previous holder. Parties with claims adverse to the holder were required to fight their own battles; they could not involve the payor by serving notice on him not to pay.

———

The "radical new solutions" that Professor Gilmore speaks of were reached in two seminal cases. The first, Miller v. Race, 1 Burr. 452, 97 Eng.Rep. 398 (K.B. 1758), presented the question of title to a stolen promissory note issued by the Bank of England for the payment of 21 pounds ten shillings to "William Finney or bearer, on demand." (For the effect of this term see UCC § 3–108 and § 3–111(b).) On December 11 Finney mailed the note to one Odenharty but that night the note was stolen from the mails by a robber. The next day, in the words of Lord Mansfield, "an inn-keeper took it, bona fide, in his business from a person who made an appearance of a gentleman. Here is no pretence or suspicion of collusion with the robber: for this matter was strictly inquired and examined into at the trial; and is so stated in the case 'that he took it for a full and valuable consideration, in the usual course of business.' Indeed if there had been any collusion, or any circumstances of unfair dealing; the case had been much otherwise. If it had been a note for 1000 [pounds] it might have been suspicious: but this was a small note for 21 [pounds] 10 [shillings] only: and money given in exchange for it." On December 13 Finney, having learned of the robbery, "applied to the Bank of England 'to stop the payment of this note:' which was ordered accordingly, upon Mr. Finney's entering into proper security 'to indemnify the bank.' " Plaintiff then delivered the note for payment to defendant, a clerk of the Bank of England. Defendant refused to pay or to redeliver the note to Plaintiff. In an action in trover judgment for the amount of the note was given to Plaintiff. Lord Mansfield in holding that Plaintiff, the good faith purchaser, had acquired good title to the note superior to that of Finney said "A banknote is constantly and universally, both at home and abroad, treated as money, as cash; and paid and received, as cash; and it is necessary, for the purposes of commerce, that their currency should be established and secured."

Notes of the kind involved in Miller v. Race were the ancestors of modern English currency and similar in form. A modern ten-pound note reads as follows "I promise to pay the bearer on demand the sum of ten pounds." The promise to pay is signed by the Chief Cashier of the Bank of England "For the Governor and Company of the Bank of England." Commercial transactions would be seriously impeded if money, or its equivalent, could not be accepted without question as to whether the taker was acquiring good title to it. The rule of Miller v. Race might have been explained as being simply a recognition of this fact in the case of certain bank obligations which, de facto, were taken as the equivalent of money. But the rule was also applied to the obligations of individuals to which the rationale of "money equivalent" was less persuasive.

The second case, Peacock v. Rhodes, 2 Doug. 633, 99 Eng.Rep. 402 (K.B. 1781), involved a bill of exchange, payable on issue to "William Ingham, or order", and subsequently indorsed by Ingham in blank. Neither the drawer nor the drawee was a bank. The bill, indorsed in blank, was stolen and negotiated to plaintiff, a mercer who "received the bill from a man not known, who called himself William Brown, and, by that name, indorsed the bill to the plaintiff, of whom he bought cloth, and other articles in the way of the plaintiff's trade as a mercer, in his shop at Scarborough, and paid him that bill, the value whereof the plaintiff gave to the buyer in cloth and other articles, and cash, and small bills."

Lord Mansfield stated that the case was within the rule of Miller v. Race. "The holder of a bill of exchange, or promissory note, is not to be considered in the light of an assignee of the payee. An assignee must take the thing assigned, subject to all the equity to which the original party was subject. If this rule applied to bills and promissory notes, it would stop their currency. The law is settled, that a holder, coming fairly by a bill or note, has nothing to do with the transaction between the original parties; unless, perhaps, in the single case (which is a hard one, but has been determined) of a note won at play. I see no difference between a note indorsed blank, and one payable to bearer. They both go by delivery, and possession proves property in both cases. The question of mala fides was for the consideration of the jury. The circumstances, that the buyer and also the drawers were strangers to the plaintiff, and that he took the bill for goods on which he had a profit, were grounds of suspicion, very fit for their consideration. But they have considered them, and have found it was received in the course of trade, and, therefore, the case is clear, and within the principle of * * * Miller v. Race * * * " *Consequences of negotiability*

(1) Miller v. Race and Peacock v. Rhodes state the first consequence of negotiability—that the holder of a negotiable instrument taking the instrument as a good faith purchaser for value takes title to the instrument free of the claim that another person owns the instrument. A good faith purchaser to qualify for this right must be a "holder in due course" which is defined in UCC § 3–302. It is vital to understand that a holder in due course must first of all be a "holder" of the instrument. UCC § 1–201(20). For example, the transferee of an unindorsed instrument payable to order cannot be a holder in due course because he is not the holder of the instrument. UCC § 3–305(1) states the rule of Miller v. Race in modern terms.

(2) The second consequence of negotiability is that the holder in due course takes the instrument free of most defenses on the instrument. UCC § 3–305(2). The following are examples: Case 1. The maker paid the holder of a negotiable promissory note payable on demand but did not take possession of the note nor indicate on its face that it had been paid. UCC § 3–505(1)(d). The maker's payment to the holder discharged his obligation on the note, UCC § 3–603(1), and was a defense to any future demand for payment by that holder. Comment 2 to UCC § 3–601.

But a subsequent holder in due course could enforce the note against the maker free of the defense of discharge. UCC § 3–602. Case 2. Buyer paid for goods purchased from Seller by giving his promissory note payable to the order of Seller. Seller refused to deliver the goods promised. Seller as holder of the note cannot enforce the note against Buyer. Failure of consideration is a valid defense. But Buyer cannot assert this defense against a holder in due course to whom the note might be negotiated. UCC § 3–305(2).

2. NEGOTIABILITY OF INSTRUMENTS: MODERN APPLICATIONS

One cannot appreciate how harsh the concept of negotiability is until we see it in the context of modern sales transactions. We will go into more detail about consumer transactions in Chapter 3, but for now consider the consequences of protecting the finance company in the following case against the defense of fraud.

UNIVERSAL C.I.T. CREDIT CORP. v. INGEL

Supreme Judicial Court of Massachusetts, 1964.
347 Mass. 119, 196 N.E.2d 847.

SPIEGEL, JUSTICE. This is an action of contract on a promissory note by the assignee of the payee against the maker. The case was first tried in the District Court of Fitchburg, to which it had been remanded by the Superior Court. There was a finding for the plaintiff in the sum of $1,630.12. At the request of the defendants, the case was retransferred to the Superior Court for trial by jury. Upon conclusion of the evidence the court allowed a motion by the plaintiff for a directed verdict to which the defendants excepted. They also excepted to the exclusion of certain evidence.

At the trial the plaintiff introduced in evidence the note, a completion certificate signed by the defendants, and the District Court's finding for the plaintiff. The defendants admitted the authenticity of the signatures on the note and the completion certificate. As a witness for the defendants, one Charles D. Fahey testified that he was the plaintiff's Boston branch manager at the time the defendants' note was purchased, and that the plaintiff purchases instalment contracts regarding automobile and property improvement purchases. He described the procedures by which purchases of commercial paper are arranged by the plaintiff; these procedures included a credit check on the "customer," i.e., the maker of the note which the plaintiff is planning to purchase. The defendants attempted to introduce through Fahey a credit report obtained by the plaintiff on Allied Aluminum Associates, Inc. (Allied), the payee of the note. The defendants excepted to the exclusion of this evidence. They offered to prove that the excluded report, which was dated "3–31–59," contained the following statement: "The subject firm is engaged in the sale of storm windows, doors, roofing, siding, and bathroom and kitchen remodeling work. The firm engages a crew of commission salesmen and it is reported they have been doing a good volume of business. They are reported to employ high pressure sales methods for the most part. They have done considerable advertising in newspapers, on radio, and have done soliciting by telephone. They have been criticized for their advertising methods, and have been accused of using bait advertising, and using false and misleading statements. The Boston Better Business Bureau has had numerous complaints regarding their advertising methods, and have reported same to the Attorney General. *FHA has had no complaints other than report of this from Better Business Bureau and have warned the firm to stop their practice.*"

The defendants excepted to the exclusion of testimony by the defendant Dora Ingel concerning certain of her negotiations with Allied. An offer of proof was made which indicates that this testimony might have been evidence of fraud or breach of warranty on the part of Allied. They also excepted to the exclusion of a letter [2] from the plaintiff to the defendant Albert.

2.

"October 27, 1959
Identification
'B'

Mr. Albert Ingel
115 Belmont
Fitchburg, Massachusetts

Re: 200–12–51767

Dear Sir.

We are sorry to learn that the Aluminum Siding on which we hold your promissory note, is giving you cause for complaint. Our part in the transactions consisted of extending the credit which you desired, and arranging to accept prepayment of the advance on terms convenient to you. We did not perform any of the work, and any questions in connection with materials and workmanship should be adjusted with the dealer from whom you made your purchase. Therefore, we have passed your report along to Allied Aluminum and we are confident that everything reasonably possible will be done to correct any faulty conditions which may exist.

In the meantime, we shall appreciate your continuing to make payments on your note as they fall due so that your account may be kept in current condition.

Very truly yours,
UNIVERSAL C.I.T.
CREDIT CORPORATION
C. KEVENY
Collection Man"

I.

The defendants contend that the note was nonnegotiable as a matter of law and, therefore, any defence which could be raised against Allied may also be raised against the plaintiff. * * *

[The court concluded that the note was a negotiable instrument.]

II.

The finding of the District Court which the plaintiff offered in evidence is, under G.L. c. 231, § 102C, prima facie evidence upon such matters as are put in issue by the pleading at the trial in the Superior Court. Lubell v. First Nat. Stores, Inc., 342 Mass. 161, 164, 172 N.E.2d 689. The defendants' answer denies that the plaintiff is "a holder in due course" of the note on which the action is brought; accordingly, this must be regarded as a matter "put in issue by the pleadings." We are satisfied that the finding of the District Court was prima facie evidence that the plaintiff took the note for value and without notice, and notwithstanding the provisions of [UCC §] 3–307(3), the burden was on the defendants to rebut the plaintiff's prima facie case. See Cook v. Farm Service Stores, Inc., 301 Mass. 564, 566, 17 N.E.2d 890.

III.

The trial judge correctly excluded the evidence offered by the defendants to show that the plaintiff and Allied had worked together on various aspects of the financing and that the plaintiff was aware of complaints against Allied by previous customers. We are of opinion that there was nothing in this evidence by which the plaintiff had "reason to know" of any fraud.[8] The letter of October 27, 1959, from the plaintiff to the defendant Albert was also properly excluded; it is immaterial that the

---

8. [UCC] § 3–302(1) states: "A holder in due course is a holder who takes the instrument * * * (c) without notice that it is overdue or has been dishonored or of any defense against or claim to it on the part of any person." "Notice" is defined in [UCC] § 1–201(25) as follows: "A person has 'notice' of a fact when (a) he has actual knowledge of it; or (b) he has received a notice or notification of it; or (c) from all the facts and circumstances known to him at the time in question he has reason to know that it exists."

plaintiff may have found out about Allied's allegedly fraudulent representations after the note had been purchased.

Exceptions overruled.

———

Whether the doctrine of negotiability in all its vigor is necessary or desirable when applied to modern negotiable instruments—promissory notes and checks—has been challenged. See Gilmore, The Good Faith Purchase Idea and the Uniform Commercial Code: Confessions of a Repentant Draftsman, 15 Ga.L. Rev. 605 (1981). Consider the following observations of Dean Albert J. Rosenthal taken from his article, Negotiability—Who Needs It? 71 Colum.L.Rev. 375, 378–385 (1971)*:

A. *Promissory Notes*

* * *

The negotiable promissory note of today is quite a different instrument, serving different purposes, and the consequences of its negotiability are quite different in impact. By far the most commonly employed variety of the species today is the note given by the installment purchaser of goods to reflect the unpaid portion of the purchase price. Typically, such a note is transferred just once, from the dealer to the lender (usually either a finance company or a bank), and thereafter remains in the possession of the latter or its lawyers until it is either paid off or offered in evidence in court. Its negotiable character is of no importance with respect to claims of ownership, as it is unlikely to be lost or stolen. Even if it is, the last indorsement will have been a special indorsement to the order of the lender; without the genuine further indorsement of the latter there can be no subsequent holder, much less a holder in due course.

The only significant consequence of the negotiability of such a note is that it cuts off the defenses of the maker. If, for example, the purchaser gives the note in payment for a refrigerator, the finance company is entitled to full payment regardless of whether the refrigerator fails to work or whether its sale was accomplished through fraudulent misrepresentations or, indeed, whether it was ever delivered at all. And it may be small comfort to the buyer, forced to pay the finance company in full, to know that he has a cause of action against the seller, which may at best be collectible with difficulty and may in many cases be worthless because the seller is insolvent or has left town.

A promissory note of this kind, and a consequence of negotiability that works in this fashion, are a far cry from the stolen Bank of England note, and the protection accorded its purchaser, in Miller v. Race. Whether the finance company should be allowed to prevail free of the maker's defenses raises questions that ought to be decided on their own merits, and not merely through the absent-minded application of a doctrine created to meet an entirely different situation.

The social evils flowing from negotiability in this circumstance have become manifest, and there has been a clear trend in both the courts and the legislatures toward amelioration of its consequences. In particular, the unfairness to the poorest members of the community of the law governing consumer installment purchases has generated a reaction that is giving rise to a major alteration in it. This departure is being accomplished, not by modification of the provisions of Article 3 of the Code, but by legislative action forbidding the use of negotiable instruments in consumer installment transactions and by judicial attempts to stretch the facts to deny holder in due course status to finance companies. Since the installment buyer can be similarly harmed even without a negotiable instrument if there is a clause in his purchase contract waiving, as against an assignee of his obligation, any defenses on the contract that he may have, legislatures and courts have also been moving in the direction of declaring such clauses invalid.

It is not clear whether the apparent weakness in the opposition to these changes springs from a lack of genuine need on the part of sellers or lenders for continuation of the power to cut off buyers' defenses. While there has been ground to believe that where this protection is denied, credit nevertheless will remain available, a recent study suggests that this may not be so.

If an exception is carved out, should it be limited to consumer paper, or should it be applied to promissory notes across the board? Thus far, the demand for reform has been confined largely to the former. While there may be small commercial purchasers also in need of similar protection, and while there may be other situations in which unfair advantage seems to be taken of makers of promissory notes, there does not appear in such cases to be a resulting social problem of comparable dimension. On the other hand, we need to know more about the range of other uses to which promissory notes are put in today's economy, and about the circumstances in which the cutting off of claims and defenses in connection with such notes serves legitimate needs or works undue hardship.

* * *

B. *Checks*

* * *

To begin with, negotiability normally plays almost no part with respect to checks. While some checks are cashed at a grocery store or across the counter at a bank, the overwhelming majority of checks are deposited by the payee for collection at his own bank, which, acting merely as the depositor's agent for that purpose, sends the check through banking channels to the drawee bank where it is presented for payment. If paid, the check is so marked and is ultimately returned to the drawer along with his monthly statement; if the check is dishonored, a slip setting forth the reason is attached to it and goes with it back through banking channels to the payee.

There is no holder in due course (except perhaps the payee himself) of such a check since, even though such other requirements as good faith and lack of notice may be met, the bank would not have given value for the check. Any dispute between drawer and payee will, therefore, simply be between themselves, with no one else in a position to assert special rights.

Let us now modify the case of a relatively poor buyer purchasing a refrigerator on installments, and substitute a middle-class consumer paying for it with his personal check. If the refrigerator fails to work properly, if its defect is immediately apparent, if the buyer's attempts to get redress from the seller prove unavailing, and if the buyer moves with sufficient alacrity, he can often stop payment on his check before it has cleared through his own bank. The buyer and seller will then be in a position themselves to resolve their dispute on the merits, with the buyer having the tactical advantage that the seller will have to bring suit in order to collect if the matter cannot be resolved without litigation.

Suppose, however, the bank in which the seller-payee deposits the check allows him to draw against it before it has been collected. This is not standard practice, but it does occur with some frequency. When the check is presented to the drawee bank for payment, it is dishonored because of the stop payment order. This time, however, the depositary bank is given the status of holder in due course "to the extent to which credit for the item has been withdrawn or applied," or "if it makes an advance on or against the item." To this extent, the drawer cannot assert against the bank the defense that the sale of the refrigerator was fraudulent. Although the stop payment order is effective, its utility to the drawer is defeated, since he is liable to the depositary bank.

*   *   *

If the depositary bank were to grant credit to the payee by allowing withdrawals before collection, and if it were to do this in reliance upon its knowledge of the *drawer's* financial standing or reputation, there might be good reason to protect the depositary bank in this fashion. Typically, however the depositary bank pays no attention to the identity of the drawer; in fact, it does not even know whether the drawer's signature is genuine. It will often allow or refuse to allow withdrawals against the check before collection solely on the basis of its relations with and knowledge of the creditworthiness of its own customer, the payee. If payment is stopped, and the depositary bank cannot recover its advances by charging the amount back against the payee's account, but is permitted to hold the drawer liable, the bank receives a windfall: in such cases, it picks up the liability of the drawer, which by hypothesis it had not counted upon when it made its decision to allow withdrawals before collection.

The fact that the depositary bank would not normally be relying upon the drawer's credit may be seen in the improbable combination of circumstances that have to coincide for the drawer's liability to matter. First, the bank's customer, the payee, must have allowed his account to drop to the point at which some of his withdrawals cannot be charged against other funds in the account but must be regarded as advances against the uncollected check. Second, the payee must be insolvent, or at least his assets must not be readily amenable to collection. Third, the drawer has to be solvent and available, and his signature genuine. Fourth, the check must be dis-

honored. Finally, for the doctrine to make any ultimate difference, the drawer must have a legitimate defense on the
check that is good against the payee, but is not of a type that
can be asserted against a holder in due course. Only if all of
these elements coincide is the bank's position improved by
virtue of its becoming a holder in due course. It must therefore be a rare case indeed in which the bank's decision to extend credit before the check is collected can be regarded as
having been made in reliance upon its ability to cut off the
defenses of the drawer. Neither banks specifically, nor commerce in general, seem to need the rule declaring the bank to
be a holder in due course. Where the bank relies entirely on
the identity and credit of the payee in allowing withdrawals,
it should shock no one's conscience if the bank were limited
to the payee as a source of reimbursement.

* * *

3. FORMAL REQUISITES OF NEGOTIABLE INSTRUMENTS

UCC § 3–104(1) adopts the basic requirements for negotiability that had been worked out at common law and codified in Brit-
ain by Chalmers in the Bills of Exchange Act (1882) and in this
country by Crawford in the Uniform Negotiable Instruments
Law (1896). The elements of negotiability are treated in more
detail in the following sections: unconditional promise or order
(Section 3–105); sum certain (Section 3–106); payable in money
(Section 3–107); payable on demand (Section 3–108); definite
time (Section 3–109); payable to order (Section 3–110); payable
to bearer (Section 3–111); terms and omissions not affecting negotiability (Section 3–112); the seal (Section 3–113); and antedat-
ing and postdating (Section 3–114).

Is the Code's treatment of negotiability inconsistent? As we
shall see, the benefits of negotiability (in a limited form) are conferred upon the buyer of goods "entrusted" to the seller by the
owner only in the commercial setting (Section 2–403(2) and (3)),
that is, when the purchase is made from a dealer. Under Sections 7–501(4) and 7–502, a holder of a document of title enjoys
negotiability only if he takes it in the regular course of business.
Under Section 8–102(a)(ii) a security is an instrument of a kind
commonly dealt with in securities exchanges or commonly recognized as a medium for investment; Section 8–105 makes such an
instrument negotiable. But the Code continues to use the formalities for creating and transferring an instrument as the

screening device for selecting the purchasers to be protected, and it is noteworthy that in doing so the Code draftsmen did not substantially lessen the formal requirements for creating negotiability. Under the Code the function of the instrument—whether it is used in a commercial transaction or not—is quite beside the point. An instrument meeting the technical requirements of Section 3–104(1) is negotiable even though its use falls wholly without the mainstream of commerce.

Acceptance by the UCC draftsmen of the same basic formal prerequisites to negotiability as existed under the NIL is persuasive that these matters have a continuing function. What is it? It is hard to maintain any longer that such traditional formal requirements as certainty of time and sum, unconditional promises, and the presence of words of art like "order" or "bearer" are essential to the currency of instruments in commerce. The willingness of the courts during the NIL years to erode, in response to the needs of the commercial community, the strict formal requirements of negotiability demonstrates that perhaps the only formal attribute of an instrument that has real effect on its currency is its ultimate status of negotiability. Why then leave the formal requirements of negotiability as a trap for the unschooled? Why not prescribe that an instrument is negotiable which contains this legend: "This instrument is a negotiable instrument."? Is a possible justification for the Code's rejection of this the view that to adopt consensual negotiability would lower the bars of negotiability too much and extend that harsh doctrine too far into noncommercial situations? Is it that to some extent at least, the ancient, if somewhat irrelevant, formalities of negotiability keep negotiable instruments in the hands of professionals and thus usually in the commercial process? Or is the decision of the Code draftsmen to keep the old formal requirements for negotiability attributable to nothing more than the fact that, after all, the old system worked pretty well?

4. NEGOTIABILITY OF GOODS

Miller v. Race recognized the principle that a purchaser of a note from a thief with no title to the note could under some circumstances acquire good title to the note superior to that of the owner who lost the note by theft. This principle does not apply to goods. There is, however, a doctrine of good faith purchase applicable to goods that allows a purchaser to acquire a better title to the goods than the seller had. For example, if X, through fraudulent representations, induced Y to transfer title of goods to X, traditional legal analysis was that X had legal title to the goods but that Y had a right recognized in equity to rescind the transaction and revest title in himself. X's imperfect legal title was referred to as "voidable title." But if X sold the goods to a bona fide purchaser for value without notice of Y's claim to them, the BFP got good title free of Y's claim. The transaction of sale between X and the BFP resulted in passage of the legal title to the BFP. Since in equity there was no basis for choosing between the two innocent parties, Y and BFP, BFP's legal title was left undisturbed. Y had rights only against X. This easily stated rule proved very difficult to apply, as is demonstrated by Phelps v. McQuade set forth below. UCC § 2–403(1) which is a modern application of the rule has resolved little of the difficulty. Under the traditional rule the BFP could win only if his seller had a legal title that could be conveyed. Thus the rule fell far short of the doctrine of Miller v. Race. But in some cases it is possible for a purchaser of goods to acquire good title when his seller had no title whatsoever. Porter v. Wertz explores UCC § 2–403(2) and (3) which set forth this concept.

For an excellent treatment on the subject of the negotiability of goods, see Gilmore, The Commercial Doctrine of Good Faith Purchase, 63 Yale L.J. 1057 (1954). Later Professor Gilmore revised his views on the matter in The Good Faith Purchase Idea and the Uniform Commercial Code: Confessions of a Repentant Draftsman, 15 Ga.L.Rev. 605 (1981).

PHELPS v. McQUADE

Court of Appeals of New York, 1917.
220 N.Y. 232, 115 N.E. 441, 1918B, L.R.A. 973.

ANDREWS, J. One Walter J. Gwynne falsely represented to the appellants that he was Baldwin J. Gwynne, a man of financial responsibility, residing at Cleveland, Ohio. Relying upon the truth of this statement the appellants delivered to him upon credit a quantity of jewelry. Gwynne in turn sold it to the respondent, who bought it without notice, express or implied, of any defect in title, and for value. Learning of the deception practiced upon them, the appellants began an action in replevin to recover the goods.

The only question before us is whether under such circumstances, the vendor of personal property does or does not retain title thereto after he has parted with possession thereof.

The learned Appellate Division rested their decision upon the definition of common-law larceny, holding that where such larceny had been committed the thief acquired no title by his crime; where it had not, at least a voidable title passed. We agree with that statement of the law. But we should prefer to define the rule in another form. Where the vendor of personal property intends to sell his goods to the person with whom he deals, then title passes, even though he be deceived as to that person's identity or responsibility. Otherwise it does not. It is purely a question of the vendor's intention.

The fact that the vendor deals with the person personally rather than by letter is immaterial, except in so far as it bears upon the question of intent.

Where the transaction is a personal one, the seller intends to transfer title to a person of credit, and he supposes the one standing before him to be that person. He is deceived. But in spite of that fact his primary intention is to sell his goods to the person with whom he negotiates.

Where the transaction is by letter the vendor intends to deal with the person whose name is signed to the letter. He knows no one else. He supposes he is dealing with no one else. And while in both cases other facts may be shown that would alter the rule, yet in their absence, in the first, title passes; in the second, it does not. Two cases that illustrate the distinction are Edmunds v. Merchants' Despatch Transportation Company, 135 Mass. 283, and Cundy v. Lindsay, 3 App.Cas. 463.

In Edmunds v. Merchants' Transportation Company a swindler, representing himself to be one Edward Pape, personally bought goods of the plaintiff on credit. The court held that the title passed. "The minds of the parties met and agreed upon all the terms of the sale, the thing sold, the price and time of payment, the person selling and the person buying. The fact that the seller was induced to sell by fraud of the buyer made the sale voidable, but not void. He could not have supposed that he was selling to any other person; his intention was to sell to the person present, and identified by sight and hearing; it does not defeat the sale because the buyer assumed a false name, or practiced any other deceit to induce the vendor to sell."

Cases of the same type are Perkins v. Anderson, 65 Iowa 398, 21 N.W. 696, and Hickey v. McDonald, 151 Ala. 497, 44 So. 201, 13 L.R.A.,N.S., 413.

In Cundy v. Lindsay one Blenkarn, signing himself Blenkiron & Co., bought goods by letter of Lindsay & Co. The latter

shipped the goods to Blenkiron & Co. They knew of the firm of
Blenkiron & Son; believed the letter came from that firm and
that the goods were shipped to it. Blenkiron & Son were the
persons with whom Lindsay & Co., intended to deal and supposed they were dealing. Under those circumstances it was held
that, although Blenkarn obtained possession of the goods, he
never acquired title thereto.

A similar case is Mercantile Nat. Bank, N. Y. v. Silverman,
148 App.Div. 1, 132 N.Y.S. 1017.

Another class of cases such as Hentz v. Miller, 94 N.Y. 64,
and Consumers' Ice Company of Buffalo v. Webster, Son & Co.,
32 App.Div. 592, 53 N.Y.S. 56, illustrate the rule under different
circumstances. In them, persons falsely stating that they are
the agents or representatives of others fraudulently obtained
possession of goods under a pretense of sale to such others.
There is no intention on the part of the vendor to sell to the
pretended agent or representative and no title passes.

In indictments for larceny, before the definition of that crime
was changed by statute, this question of the passing of title was
material; and, therefore, discussions as to whether an indict-
ment or conviction could be sustained were relevant in cases
where the question was whether or not the title had in fact
passed. But in cases of each class the intention of the person
having title to the goods and delivering them to another was the
ultimate matter to be decided. And although it might be said in
the one class of cases that where title did not pass there was no
larceny, and in the other that where there was larceny the title
did not pass, yet in both the test to be applied was this same
intention on the part of the owner of the property.

The judgment of the Appellate Division must be affirmed,
with costs.

HISCOCK, C. J., and CHASE, COLLIN, CARDOZO, and POUND,
JJ., concur. McLAUGHLIN, J., not sitting.

Judgment affirmed.

NOTES

1. In Rogers v. Dutton, 182 Mass. 187, 65 N.E. 56 (1902),
Simmons fraudulently represented to Seller that he was Buyer's
agent and that Buyer wanted to purchase some hay. Induced
by these misrepresentations, Seller agreed to sell Buyer the hay
and delivered it to Buyer's place of business. Simmons told
Buyer that the hay belonged to Simmons. Simmons sold it to

Buyer, received payment, and absconded. Seller was allowed to recover the hay. Holmes, C. J., stated: "It is evident on these facts that there was no sale and that plaintiff never parted with his title." 182 Mass. at 188–189, 65 N.E. at 56.

2. How would UCC § 2–403 apply to the face-to-face impersonation in *Phelps*, the impersonation by letter referred to in *Phelps*, and the misrepresentation of agency in *Rogers*?

3. The third sentence of UCC § 2–403(1) provides that when goods have been delivered under a "transaction of purchase" the purchaser has the power to transfer good title to a good faith purchaser for value in four cases: deception as to identity, receipt of a bad check, cash sale and fraudulent delivery. Was the use of the quoted phrase a drafting error which might frustrate the purpose of the third sentence? That is, if a jurisdiction's pre-Code case law is that of *Phelps*, has the property been delivered to the defrauder pursuant to a "transaction of purchase" if the seller did not intend to pass title? See the definition of "purchase" in UCC § 1–201(32).

PORTER v. WERTZ

Court of Appeals of New York, 1981.
53 N.Y.2d 696, 439 N.Y.S.2d 105, 421 N.E.2d 500.

[The following facts are taken from the opinions of the trial court and of the Appellate Division, 68 A.D.2d 141, 416 N.Y.S.2d 254. Plaintiff, Samuel Porter, owned a Maurice Utrillo painting entitled "Chateau de Lion-sur-Mer." He had several dealings with an art dealer that he knew by the name "Peter Wertz" including one in the spring of 1973 for the sale by Porter of a painting by Childe Hassam for $150,000, payable $50,000 in cash and $100,000 in promissory notes. At about the same time the dealer expressed an interest in buying the Utrillo painting. Porter agreed to let him have it temporarily for hanging in the dealer's house pending his decision whether to buy the painting. In June 1973 Porter sought return of the painting but was unable to find the dealer. In July 1973 Porter made two sad discoveries. First, he found out that "Peter Wertz" was in reality named Harold Von Maker who had a long record of unsatisfied judgments, arrests for the crimes of possession of obscene literature, false pretenses and theft of checks, and convictions for various crimes including a scheme to defraud the Chase Manhattan Bank. Second, the promissory notes that Porter had taken for the Hassam painting were returned dishonored when they were presented for payment. Porter's attorney communicated with Von Maker's attorney and, in August 1973, an agreement was signed. Von Maker agreed to either return the Utrillo paintings or pay Porter $30,000. As security for Von Maker's agreement, Porter was given the option, in the event of Von Maker's default, to seize a painting deposited by Von Maker in escrow with Von Maker's lawyer. Von Maker did not return the painting or pay the $30,000. When Porter seized the escrowed painting, it turned out to be a forgery.

At the time of making the agreement with Porter, Von Maker had already disposed of the Utrillo painting. He did so through the efforts of the real Peter Wertz, an employee of a Madison Avenue gourmet grocery where he worked as a "seller of caviar and other luxury food items." Von Maker had delivered the Utrillo painting to Wertz who appeared with it at the art gallery of defendant Feigen. There was disputed testimony that Feigen thought that Wertz was an art dealer. Feigen had a buyer for the Utrillo painting in defendant Brenner. The painting was transferred to Brenner who then sold it to someone who took the painting to South America. Porter sued Feigen and Brenner, among others, for conversion.]

OPINION OF THE COURT

MEMORANDUM. The judgment appealed from and order of the Appellate Division brought up for review should be affirmed, 68 A.D.2d 141, 416 N.Y.S.2d 254, with costs. We agree with the Appellate Division's conclusion that subdivision (2) of section 2–403 of the Uniform Commercial Code does not insulate defendants from plaintiff Porter's lawful claim to the Utrillo painting. Subdivision (2) of section 2–403 of the Uniform Commercial Code provides: "Any entrusting of possession of goods to a merchant who deals in goods of that kind gives him power to transfer all rights of the entruster to a buyer in ordinary course of business." The "entruster provision" of the Uniform Commercial Code is designed to enhance the reliability of commercial sales by merchants (who deal with the kind of goods sold on a regular basis) while shifting the risk of loss through fraudulent transfer to the owner of the goods, who can select the merchant to whom he entrusts his property. It protects only those who purchase from the merchant to whom the property was entrusted in the ordinary course of the merchant's business.

While the Utrillo painting was entrusted to Harold Von Maker, an art merchant, the Feigen Gallery purchased the painting

not from Von Maker, but from one Peter Wertz, who turns out
to have been a delicatessen employee acquainted with Von Maker. It seems that Von Maker frequented the delicatessen where
Peter Wertz was employed and that at some point Von Maker
began to identify himself as Peter Wertz in certain art transactions.   Indeed, Von Maker identified himself as Peter Wertz in
his dealings with Porter.

Defendants argued that Feigen reasonably assumed that the
Peter Wertz who offered the Utrillo to him was an art merchant
because Feigen had been informed by Henry Sloan that an art
dealer named Peter Wertz desired to sell a Utrillo painting.   Feigen therefore aruges that for purposes of subdivision (2) of section 2–403 of the Uniform Commercial Code it is as though he
purchased from a merchant in the ordinary course of business.
Alternatively, he claims that he actually purchased the Utrillo
from Von Maker, the art dealer to whom it had been entrusted,
because Peter Wertz sold the painting on Von Maker's behalf.
Neither argument has merit.

Even if Peter Wertz were acting on Von Maker's behalf, unless he disclosed this fact to Feigen, it could hardly be said that
Feigen relied upon Von Maker's status as an art merchant. It
does not appear that the actual Peter Wertz ever represented
that he was acting on behalf of Von Maker in selling the painting.

As to the argument that Feigen reasonably assumed that Peter Wertz was an art merchant, it is apparent from the opinion
of the Appellate Division that the court rejected the fact finding
essential to this argument, namely, that Peter Wertz had been
introduced to Feigen by Henry Sloan as an art merchant.   The
court noted that in his examination before trial Richard Feigen
had testified that he could not recall whether Henry Sloan had
described Peter Wertz as an art dealer and concluded that this
substantially weakened the probative force of Feigen's trial testimony on this point.   Indeed, Peter Wertz testified that Von
Maker had not directed him to the Feigen Gallery but had simply
delivered the painting to Wertz and asked him to try to find a
buyer for the Utrillo.   Wertz had been to several art galleries
before he approached the Feigen Gallery.   Thus, the Appellate
Division's finding has support in the record.

Because Peter Wertz was not an art dealer and the Appellate
Division has found that Feigen was not duped by Von Maker
into believing that Peter Wertz was such a dealer, subdivision (2)
of section 2–403 of the Uniform Commercial Code is inapplicable

for three distinct reasons: (1) even if Peter Wertz were an art merchant rather than a delicatessen employee, he is not the same merchant to whom Porter entrusted the Utrillo painting; (2) Wertz was not an art merchant; and (3) the sale was not in the ordinary course of Wertz' business because he did not deal in goods of that kind (Uniform Commercial Code, § 1–201, subd. [9]).

Nor can the defendants-appellants rely on the doctrine of equitable estoppel. It has been observed that subdivision (1) of section 2–403 of the Uniform Commercial Code incorporates the doctrines of estoppel, agency and apparent agency because it states that a purchaser acquires not only all title that his transferor had, but also all title that he had power to transfer (White & Summers, Uniform Commercial Code, § 3–11, p. 139).

An estoppel might arise if Porter had clothed Peter Wertz with ownership of or authority to sell the Utrillo painting and the Feigen Gallery had relied upon Wertz' apparent ownership or right to transfer it. But Porter never even delivered the painting to Peter Wertz, much less create apparent ownership in him; he delivered the painting to Von Maker for his own personal use. It is true, as previously noted, that Von Maker used the name Peter Wertz in his dealings with Porter, but the Appellate Division found that the Feigen Gallery purchased from the actual Peter Wertz and that there was insufficient evidence to establish the claim that Peter Wertz had been described as an art dealer by Henry Sloan. Nothing Porter did influenced the Feigen Gallery's decision to purchase from Peter Wertz a delicatessen employee. Accordingly, the Feigen Gallery cannot protect its defective title by a defense of estoppel.

The Appellate Division opined that even if Von Maker had duped Feigen into believing that Peter Wertz was an art dealer, subdivision (2) of section 2–403 of the Uniform Commercial Code would still not protect his defective title because as a merchant, Feigen failed to purchase in good faith. Among merchants good faith requires not only honesty in fact but observance of reasonable commercial standards. (Uniform Commercial Code, § 2–103, subd. [1], par. [b]). The Appellate Division concluded that it was a departure from reasonable commercial standards for the Feigen Gallery to fail to inquire concerning the title to the Utrillo and to fail to question Peter Wertz' credentials as an art dealer. On this appeal we have received *amicus* briefs from the New York State Attorney-General urging that the court hold that good faith among art merchants requires inquiry as to the ownership of an *object d'art*, and from the Art Dealers Association of America, Inc., arguing that the ordinary custom in the art business is not to inquire as to title and that a duty of inquiry would cripple the art business which is centered in New York. In view of our disposition we do not reach the good faith question.

COOKE, C. J., and JASEN, GABRIELLI, JONES, WACHTLER, FUCHSBERG and MEYER, JJ., concur.

Judgment appealed from and order of the Appellate Division brought up for review affirmed with costs, in a memorandum.

PROBLEMS

1. Suppose Feigen had purchased the painting directly from Von Maker. How would the court have decided the case?

2. Plaintiff was the owner of a diamond watch. Plaintiff borrowed $1,000 from Pawnbroker and left the watch as a pledge securing the loan. The next day Pawnbroker sold the watch for $1,800 to Defendant who saw it displayed for sale in the pawnshop. Defendant bought in good faith and without knowledge of Plaintiff's claim to the watch. Assume that the applicable law provides that a pawnbroker may sell the goods pledged only after default by the borrower and the passage of a period of time during which the borrower may redeem the goods by paying the amount owed to the pawnbroker. The sale by Pawnbroker violated this law because Plaintiff was not in default. Did Defendant acquire good title to the watch by virtue of UCC § 2–403(2) and (3)? How does this case compare with the case stated in Problem 1?

3. Consider the following cases:

Case 1. Plaintiff gave possession of a diamond watch to Jeweler on the following terms: Jeweler was to exhibit it for sale in his retail store at a price of $2,000; in the event that Jeweler found a purchaser he was to inform Plaintiff; no sale was to be made without Plaintiff's prior consent; in the event of sale Jeweler was to remit the proceeds of sale, less a 25% commission, to Plaintiff.

Case 2. Plaintiff gave possession of the diamond watch to Jeweler for the purpose of having certain alterations made to it.

Case 3. Thief stole the diamond watch from Plaintiff and then sold it to Jeweler for $1,000.

In each case assume the following: Jeweler sold the watch for $1,800 cash to Defendant, an ordinary retail customer who bought in good faith without any notice of Plaintiff's rights in the watch; Plaintiff had no prior knowledge of the sale and did not consent to it; Jeweler failed to remit any part of the proceeds of sale to Plaintiff; Jeweler is insolvent and completely without assets.

What are the rights of Plaintiff under UCC § 2–403(2) and (3) in each case if Plaintiff brings an action for conversion against Defendant? UCC § 2–403 represents a balancing of the interests of Plaintiff and Defendant, both of whom are the victims of the dishonesty of a third party. How is the balancing done in each case? Are the equities the same in each case? How does the policy underlying UCC § 2–403 differ from the policy stated in Miller v. Race?

4. Suppose in Case 1 of Problem 3 Jeweler pawned the diamond watch as security for a loan obtained from Pawnbroker. Pawnbroker believed that the watch was owned by Jeweler and had no notice of Plaintiff's claim to the watch. Jeweler defaulted on the loan. What are the rights of Pawnbroker and Plaintiff to the watch under UCC § 2–403(2) and (3)? Does UCC § 2–403(1) apply to this case? Does UCC § 2–326 apply? See Maurice Shire, Inc. v. Gerald Modell, Inc., 19 U.C.C. Rep. 1096 (N.Y.Sup.Ct.1976).

5. NEGOTIABILITY OF DOCUMENTS OF TITLE

Goods are frequently held by commercial bailees who are either transporting or storing the goods. These bailees issue a document which evidences the fact that the goods are held by the bailee and which sets forth the bailment contract. Documents issued by these bailees are known as documents of title and are governed by Article 7 of the UCC and by various Federal statutes. The two principal documents of title are the bill of lading and the warehouse receipt. A bill of lading, defined in UCC § 1–201(6), is issued by a person called the carrier engaged in the business of transporting or forwarding goods. A warehouse receipt, defined in UCC § 1–201(45), is issued by a person known as a warehouseman (UCC § 7–102(h)) engaged in the business of storing goods for hire. Documents of title can be either negotiable or non-negotiable, and negotiability is determined by the form of the document as in the case of negotiable instruments. UCC § 7–104(1) and (2). When a document of title is transferred the transfer may in some cases result in a transfer of title to the document and also a transfer of title to the goods for which the document was issued. And, in some cases, a transferor without good title to either the document or the goods is able to transfer a good title to his transferee. Negotiability as applied to documents of title borrows some elements from the law applicable to negotiable instruments and some elements from the law applicable to goods. First read UCC § 7–501, § 7–502, and § 7–503 and § 7–504. Then read the excerpt from the Warren article reproduced below. Finally, consider the problems that follow the Warren article.

WARREN, CUTTING OFF CLAIMS OF OWNERSHIP UNDER THE UCC

30 U. of Chi.L.Rev. 469, 482–487 (1963).*

III. DOCUMENTS

There is a dual problem in treating claims of ownership in documents of title, for consideration must be given to claims in the goods represented by the documents as well as claims in the documents themselves. First, claims in the documents will be considered.

As late as 1879, the Supreme Court could say, without appearing to be particularly wrong-headed, that a statute declaring that bills of lading "shall be negotiable and may be transferred by indorsement and delivery" meant simply to prescribe the *manner* of negotiation and not its effect.[65] The Court said:

> Bills of lading are regarded as so much cotton, grain, iron, or other articles of merchandise. * * * They are, in commerce, a very different thing from bills of exchange and promissory notes, answering a different purpose and performing different functions. It cannot be, therefore, that the statute which made them negotiable by indorsement and delivery, or negotiable *in the same manner* as bills of exchange and promissory notes are negotiable, intended to change totally their character, put them *in all respects* on the footing of instruments which are the representatives of money, and charge the negotiation of them with all the consequences which usually attend or follow the negotiation of

* Reprinted with permission of the publisher.

65. Shaw v. Railroad Co., 101 U.S. 557, 562 (1879).

bills and notes. Some of these consequences would be very strange if not impossible.[66]

The strange and impossible consequences of which Mr. Justice Strong wrote with such distaste, that is, full negotiability, were only a generation or so away when the words were written. But the day of full negotiability of documents was to be preceded by an interim period during which documents were more negotiable than goods but less negotiable than instruments. The Uniform Sales Act and the Uniform Warehouse Receipts Act were products of this intermediate period, and under their provisions claims of ownership in a document were cut off only when the owner had entrusted it to another who then sold to a good faith purchaser.[67] In the case of theft of a document, in a form negotiable by delivery, the owner could successfully assert his claim against the good faith purchaser. Scarcely was this halfway position codified in the Sales Act and Warehouse Receipts Act when it was abandoned in the later Uniform Bills of Lading Act which tersely provided: "A negotiable bill may be negotiated by any person in possession of the same, however such possession may have been acquired. * * * "[68]

The Code draftsmen seemed to have an easy task in this area; all they had to do was to follow the route laid out for them in the Bills of Lading Act and make documents as negotiable as instruments. This they declined to do. Under section 7–501, claims of ownership in the document are cut off only when the document is "duly negotiated," that is, negotiated in the regular course of business or financing.[69] Hence, in the beginning docu-

---

66. Id. at 565. (Emphasis in original.)

67. Uniform Sales Act § 32; Uniform Warehouse Receipts Act § 40.

68. Uniform Bills of Lading Act § 41. Some states changed the Uniform Sales Act and Uniform Warehouse Receipts Act to conform to the Uniform Bills of Lading Act. See Uniform Sales Act § 32, statutory notes, 1 Uniform Laws Ann. (1950); Uniform Warehouse Receipts Act § 40, statutory notes, 3 Uniform Laws Ann. (1959), for listings of the states that have adopted the amendment.

69. Section 7–501(4) provides that a document is not "duly negotiated" where "it is established that the negotiation is not in the regular course of business or financing or involves re-

ceiving the document in settlement or payment of a money obligation." California Senate Preprint Bill No. 7 (1963), the version of the Code submitted to the California Legislature in 1963, omits the requirements contained in the quoted language that a due negotiation must be in the regular course of business and must not involve receiving a document in settlement or payment of a money debt. The Report of California Senate Fact Finding Committee on Judiciary, the Uniform Commercial Code 526 (1961) explains the omission: "[The regular course of business requirement] in our opinion would seriously impair the negotiability of documents of title and their value for use as collateral and in other aspects of trade and commerce. So far as we know, the proponents of

ments and goods were treated alike—neither was negotiable—and now in the Code they are again accorded somewhat similar treatment in that each is negotiable only in essentially commercial transactions. Of course, goods are at a more rudimentary stage of development and are not given full negotiability even in the commercial setting.

When we come to non-negotiable documents, further analogizing to goods becomes idle, for section 7–504 provides that the transferee of a non-negotiable instrument acquires only the interests his transferor had or had the *actual* authority to convey. Claims of ownership that the buyer of goods might take free of by raising an estoppel argument will, under this section, prevail over a good faith purchaser of the non-negotiable document.[70] Not only is the buyer of a non-negotiable document subject to claims in the document that arose before he took the document, but he is also vulnerable to claims in the goods that his transferor may create after taking the document. Thus, the transferor may sell the goods covered by the document to a buyer in ordinary course of business and this party can cut off the transferee's claims in the goods by either obtaining the goods from the bailee or notifying the bailee before the transferee does so.[71] The transferee of a non-negotiable instrument is at the mercy of his transferor until he has either notified the bailee or obtained possession of the goods. Professor Williston quietly observed: "[D]ocuments of title unless negotiable in form are not proper subjects for commercial dealings."[72]

Nor is the lot of one who takes a negotiable document through other than due negotiation a happy one. He, too, takes only what rights his transferor had or had the actual authority

the Code have offered no proof that this radical new concept is necessary to correct any particular evil which has arisen under the Uniform Acts. Rather, it seems to be concerned with the hypothetical classroom situation where a professor negotiates a document of title covering hides belonging to a tramp. [See note 50 supra.] Nor can we see any reason to deny the status of a holder in due course to a person who receives a document in 'settlement of payment' of an obligation, whereas a person who takes a document as *security* for an obligation, even a pre-existing obligation, is granted that status. Furthermore under this provision, if a person holding

documents as security and who was a holder in due course agreed to accept them in settlement of the same obligation, he would thereupon lose that status. This result is irrational. But that, of course, would be the most common case where a document would be received in settlement or payment of an obligation."

70. See Uniform Commercial Code § 7–504, comment 1.

71. Uniform Commercial Code § 7–504(2)(b). See the comment on this section in Braucher, op. cit. supra note 24, at 73–75.

72. 2 Williston 556.

to convey.[73] The official comments explain his plight by saying that if purchasers in the regular flow of commerce are to be protected, then, it follows—and the commentator apparently believes that it follows as the night follows the day—that purchasers outside the regular course of dealings are not to have the benefits of negotiability and must take fewer rights than if they had purchased the goods themselves.[74]

With regard to claims of ownership in documents, we see the Code enforcing the mercantile doctrine with vengeance. Purchasers in the regular course of dealings are protected; those outside the pale are treated with but scant civility. In the words of the song, "you're in or you're out of the money."

Documents of title, unlike bills of exchange, are related to specific goods and their validity depends upon the extent to which they represent the goods behind them. We must, therefore, examine claims of ownership in the goods themselves and note in what degree purchasers of the documents covering the goods take free of these claims. The simple rule adopted by the early uniform acts was that a good faith purchaser of a negotiable document received such title as the person who bailed the goods had in the goods or had the ability to convey to a good faith purchaser of the goods themselves.[75] A thief or a mere bailee could not sell the goods directly and cut off claims of ownership, nor could he improve his position by bailing the goods, obtaining a document of title and selling that document.[76] On the other hand, a fraudulent vendee or an agent with indicia of ownership could sell the goods to a good faith purchaser free of claims of ownership and could accomplish the same result by obtaining a document and negotiating it.[77]

---

73. Uniform Commercial Code § 7–504(1).

74. Uniform Commercial Code § 7–504, comment 1.

75. Uniform Sales Act § 33; Uniform Bills of Lading Act § 32; Uniform Warehouse Receipts Act § 41.

76. W. S. Brown Mercantile Co. v. Yielding Bros. Dep't Store, Inc., 200 Ala. 412, 76 So. 4 (1917) (crop subject to chattel mortgage bailed and warehouse receipts sold to good faith purchaser; mortgagee held to have cause of action against purchaser); see also Kendall Produce Co. v. Terminal Warehouse Co., 295 Pa. 450, 145 Atl.

511 (1929) (bailee); Gazzola v. Lacy Bros. & Kimball, 156 Tenn. 229, 299 S.W. 1039 (1927) (bailee); Dunagan v. Griffin, 151 S.W.2d 250 (Tex.Civ. App.1941) (bailee).

77. Standard Bank of Canada v. Lowman, 1 F.2d 935 (W.D.Wash.1924) (apparent authority); Luhrs v. Valley Ranch Co., Inc., 27 Ariz. 206, 232 Pac. 1014 (1925) (apparent authority); Baldwin v. Childs, 249 N.Y. 212, 163 N.E. 737 (1928) (fraudulent vendee); Lippencott Distrib. Co. v. Peoples Commercial & Sav. Bank, 137 Ohio St. 399, 30 N.E.2d 691 (1940) (consignment).

The extent to which a document represented the goods and could be negotiated free of claims of ownership in the goods was, then, determined by looking to the law of the good faith purchase of goods. It is not surprising that rules developed by courts to cut off or to honor claims of ownership in goods failed to cover some situations—and produced some unfortunate results in others—that arose when negotiable documents came on the scene.

The problem was that—at least after the arrival of the UBLA—the commercial doctrine of the good faith purchaser was completely accepted as to documents and largely rejected as to goods. Hence, if the owner of goods gave a negotiable bill of lading covering the goods, the recipient could cut off prior claims of ownership by transferring it. But if the owner gave possession of the goods themselves, the recipient could, in theory, not cut off the claims. What were the courts to do with the cases where the owner of goods entrusted them to another with the authority to obtain a document of title, or with the expectation that the party entrusted would obtain a document, or knowing of the likelihood that he would obtain a document of title? Should some or all of these situations be treated as though the owner had entrusted the other person with the document itself?[78] Moreover, what disposition was to be made of cases where the owner entrusted the other party with a document and the recipient used the document to obtain the goods, let us say from a carrier, then took the goods and bailed them with a warehouse, and negotiated the warehouse receipt obtained thereby to a good faith purchaser?[79] Even here one case treated this as

---

78. The question is nicely raised in the sharecropper cases; there the landlord is paid by taking a share of the crop and has a lien on the crop to this extent. The landlord leaves the crop in the possession of the tenant with the authority to deal with the crop as owner and knowing of the likelihood that the crop will be warehoused. Courts have often protected purchasers of the resulting warehouse receipts: Salt River Valley Water Users' Ass'n v. Peoria Ginning Co., 27 Ariz. 145, 231 Pac. 415 (1924); Grauman v. Jackson, 216 Ark. 326, 225 S.W.2d 678 (1950); Commodity Credit Corp. v. Usrey, 199 Ark. 406, 133 S.W.2d 887 (1939) (landlord held to know of custom that cotton ginners did not long retain the physical prop-

erty but either sold it or stored it in a warehouse); Buelow v. Abell, 9 La. App. 624, 121 So. 657 (1928); McGee v. Carver, 141 Miss. 463, 106 So. 760 (1926). Contra, Purity Feed Mills Co. v. Moore, 152 La. 393, 93 So. 196 (1922); Phillips v. Box, 204 Miss. 231, 37 So.2d 266 (1948).

79. In Commercial Nat. Bank of New Orleans v. Canal-Louisiana Bank & Trust Co., 239 U.S. 520 (1916), *O* pledged bills of lading representing cotton to *A* Bank which then entrusted the bills to *O* on trust receipts; *O* surrendered the bills to the carrier, took possession of the cotton and warehoused it receiving warehouse receipts; the receipts were pledged to *B* Bank. The courts held for *B* Bank,

though the recipient had originally been entrusted with the goods themselves and refused to protect a good faith purchaser of the negotiable warehouse receipt.[80]

Section 7–503 of the Code evinces recognition of the fact that documents of title raise some problems that do not appear with respect to either goods alone or instruments alone. The section reads in part:

(1) A document of title confers no right in goods against a person who before issuance of the document had a legal interest or a perfected security interest in them and who neither

(a) delivered or entrusted them or any document of title covering them to the bailor or his nominee with actual or apparent authority to ship, store, or sell or with power to obtain delivery under this Article (Section 7–403) or with power of disposition under this Act (Sections 2–403 and 9–307) or other statute or rule of law; nor

(b) acquiesced in the procurement by the bailor or his nominee of any document of title.

This is a difficult section to construe, but it is subject to this interpretation: If the owner of the goods entrusts a negotiable document of title representing the goods to a second party, this party can obtain the goods from the bailee (for example, a railroad) thereby discharging the document, bail the goods again and negotiate the second document, a warehouse receipt, to a good faith purchaser free of any claims of ownership on the part of the original owner without regard to the original purpose of the entrusting. If goods are entrusted by the owner to a second party, the latter can obtain a document of title and negotiate it free of any claims of ownership if the goods were entrusted to

---

reasoning that had *O* pledged to *B* the original bills of lading, *B* would clearly prevail and that the same result should follow because *A* must have contemplated that *O* would take the bills to the carrier, obtain the goods and then warehouse them.

80. Gazzola v. Lacy Bros. & Kimball, 156 Tenn. 229, 299 S.W. 1039 (1927). Here *O* mailed bills of lading representing cotton to *F*, a factor, with orders not to sell the cotton until further notice; *F* used the bills to obtain possession of the cotton and warehoused it, negotiating the ware-

house receipts to *A* Bank in pledge. The court held for *O* and said that since the bills were not immediately exchanged for the warehouse receipts, the latter could not be considered as derivative of the former. Thus the case is treated as though *O* entrusted mere possession of the cotton to *F* with authority only to store it. The custom of cotton factors in Memphis to warehouse all cotton sent to them for any purpose and to take out negotiable warehouse receipts to facilitate the handling of the goods was ignored by the court.

him with either the actual or apparent authority to sell, ship or store them. Moreover, if goods are entrusted to one who deals in goods of that nature (whatever the purpose of the entrusting), the recipient has the power to bail the goods and negotiate the resulting document of title to a good faith purchaser free of claims of ownership.

But the Code does not stop there; the acquiescence subsection is added. Anyone who has ever had to defend the Code in a legislative hearing knows that at some point during the discussions on Article 7, some opponent of the Code will refer to the acquiescence subsection, and with the gleam of anticipated triumph in his eye, say: "Now, what does *that* mean?" If one understands the issues facing the draftsman of section 7–503 he will appreciate the formidable drafting problem involved. The draftsman has attempted to meet this problem by providing that any time the owner of goods allows a document of title representing those goods to get into the flow of commercial transactions anyone taking the document in the regular course of business takes free of claims of ownership. The subsection covers the situation in which the facts do not fit well into any of the categories of subsection (a) but the owner of the goods knew the party to whom he entrusted the goods was likely to bail them and obtain a negotiable document of title. Subsection (b) provides that if he has this knowledge and does nothing about it, he should be treated as though he started the document itself in the commercial stream.

PROBLEMS

The following sections of the UCC are relevant to the solution of these problems: § 2–403, § 7–104, § 7–403, § 7–404, § 7–501, § 7–502, § 7–503, § 7–504, and § 7–603. - *Conflicting Claims; Interpleader*

1. O, a cotton producer, stored cotton in Public Warehouse which issued to O a warehouse receipt which provided that the cotton was deliverable to the bearer of the warehouse receipt. X, an employee of O, stole the warehouse receipt from O and sold and delivered it to Y, a cotton merchant who knew that the warehouse receipt had been stolen. Y then sold and delivered the warehouse receipt to BFP, another cotton merchant who purchased in good faith and without notice that the document was not the property of Y. O later learned all the facts and brought an action against BFP to recover the warehouse receipt and against Public Warehouse for delivery of the cotton repre-

sented by the warehouse receipt. Decide the merits of the two actions brought by O.

2. O, a cotton producer, stored cotton in Public Warehouse which issued to O a warehouse receipt in bearer form. X, an employee of O, stole the warehouse receipt from O and sold and delivered it to Y, a cotton merchant who knew that the warehouse receipt had been stolen. Y then obtained delivery of the cotton from Public Warehouse upon presentation and surrender of the warehouse receipt. Y then sold the cotton to BFP, a cotton merchant who purchased in good faith without any notice of O's claim to the cotton. O, upon learning the facts, brought an action against BFP for conversion of the cotton. Decide the merits of the action.

3. O, a cotton producer, was the owner of cotton that was being transported in O's truck to O's customer. X, a hijacker, stole O's truck and the cotton that it contained. X delivered the cotton to Public Warehouse which issued to X a warehouse receipt in bearer form. X sold and delivered the warehouse receipt to Y, a cotton merchant who knew that the warehouse receipt was stolen. Y then sold and delivered the warehouse receipt to BFP, another cotton merchant who purchased in good faith and without notice that the document was not the property of Y. BFP then obtained delivery of the cotton from Public Warehouse upon presentation and surrender of the warehouse receipt. O later learned all of the facts and brought an action against BFP and Public Warehouse for conversion of the cotton. Decide the merits of the two actions brought by O. Suppose Public Warehouse had not yet delivered the cotton to anyone. If both O and BFP demand delivery, to whom is Public Warehouse required to deliver? What should Public Warehouse do to protect itself?

4. O, a cotton producer, was the owner of cotton. O, not having any space on his premises to store the cotton, asked Y, a cotton merchant, for permission to store the cotton on Y's premises for a few days while O found a buyer for it. Y agreed and the cotton was delivered to Y. Y received no consideration for storing O's cotton and was not engaged in the business of storing goods for hire. Assume the following two alternative fact situations:

(a) Y, without O's permission or knowledge, sold the cotton to BFP, a cotton merchant who bought the cotton in good faith believing that it was the property of Y.

(b) Y, without O's permission or knowledge, delivered the cotton to Public Warehouse which issued to Y a warehouse receipt in bearer form. Y then sold and delivered the warehouse receipt to BFP, a cotton merchant, who bought in good faith and without notice of O's claim to the cotton. BFP then obtained delivery of the cotton from Public Warehouse upon presentation and surrender of the warehouse receipt.

(c) Assume all facts set forth in (b) except that the warehouse receipt involved was non-negotiable.

In each case O, upon learning the facts, brought an action against BFP for conversion of the cotton. Decide the merits of the actions.

6. LOST OR STOLEN CREDIT CARDS

Credit cards are not transferred in the manner of instruments or documents of title; nor are they sold as goods are. But they are frequently lost or stolen, and the problem of their fraudulent use has perplexed courts and legislatures for many years. By one theory or another most decisions resulted in imposing the liability resulting from the unauthorized use of credit cards on the card issuer. See Annotation, Liability of Holder of Credit Card or Plate for Purchases Made Thereon by Another Person, 15 A.L.R.3d 1086 (1967). The *Sears* case set out below is one of the more favorable decisions to card issuers. In fact credit card issuers for the most part adopted the practice of absorbing losses resulting from lost or stolen credit cards without attempting to shift losses to their cardholder customers.

During the 1960's a number of states enacted legislation limiting the liability of cardholders, and in 1970 Congress enacted legislation banning unsolicited issuance of credit cards and placing a $50 limit on a cardholder's liability for unauthorized use of credit cards. Pub. Law 91–508 (Title V), 84 Stat. 1126–1127. Portions of this statute are set out after *Sears*. For a thorough discussion of the federal legislation, see Weistart, Consumer Protection in the Credit Card Industry: Federal Legislative Controls, 70 Mich.L.Rev. 1476 (1972).

SEARS, ROEBUCK AND CO. v. DUKE

Supreme Court of Texas, 1969.
441 S.W.2d 521.

REAVLEY, JUSTICE.   Sears, Roebuck and Co. sued Waldo Duke for the price of merchandise sold to an imposter using the Sears credit card issued to Duke.   The purchases were made within two weeks following Duke's loss of the card, and two weeks before either he or Sears had knowledge of its loss.   After the jury absolved both parties of negligence, the trial court entered judgment for Sears.   The Court of Civil Appeals ordered a new trial on the ground that Sears failed to offer sufficient proof of the exercise of care, on the occasion of each sale, to ascertain the identity of the credit card user.   433 S.W.2d 919. We hold that the Court of Civil Appeals imposed an incorrect duty on Sears, that Sears was entitled to rely upon the card alone as identification unless circumstances presented cause for further inquiry; and we remand the case to that court for reconsideration of points before it.

Duke and his wife lived in Lubbock, Texas and did business with the Sears store located there.   In 1960 he signed a "Sears Revolving Charge Account Agreement" which began as follows:

"In consideration of your selling merchandise to me on Sears revolving Charge Account, I agree to the following regarding all purchases made by me or on my Sears revolving Charge Account identification   *   *   *"

Two credit cards were issued with the account number and the name, Waldo N. Duke, on the front of the cards.   There is no question raised at any point in this record but that the credit cards were the Sears "identification" to which the credit agreement refers.   No additional terms of agreement appear on the back of the card, but there is a statement saying that the card is the property of Sears and its loss or theft should be reported. Mrs. Duke signed as "authorized purchaser" and used one of the cards.   The second card, unsigned, was carried by Duke with a number of other credit cards.

Duke was in New York on a business trip during the week of December 12, 1965, and he left his credit cards in a suitcase in his hotel room.   Apparently the thief took the Sears card and a Sinclair Refining Company card, made a note of Duke's home address and signed "Waldo N. Duke" in his own handwriting on the Sears card.   Presumably the card was taken December 13, and over $1,200 in merchandise was purchased in various Sears stores in the New York area within the following two weeks. On January 12, 1966, the credit department of the Sears store in Lubbock received notice of the unusual number of charges on the Duke account, and an inquiry was made to Mr. and Mrs. Duke. It was then that all of the parties first realized that the card was missing.

Duke has taken the position that he is not liable for the unauthorized use of his credit card, or for sales made by Sears to a stranger. There is no basis here for tort liability against Duke. The evidence clearly supports the findings of the jury to the effect that Duke was not negligent in the loss of his card or in the failure to report the loss to Sears. The jury has found that Duke was not negligent in failing to sign his card, and no point in that connection is presented to us. The question then is his contractual obligation, and this turns upon the construction of the words of the credit agreement set forth above. By that agreement Duke did more than promise to pay for merchandise he purchased. He promised to pay for "all purchases made on my Sears revolving Charge Account identification." The meaning we give to these words is that Duke will pay for *all* sales made by Sears to a purchaser identifying himself by the use of the credit card, which was issued by Sears upon receipt of the executed credit agreement.

Duke says that his obligation does not cover the sale to a person who is not in fact authorized to use the card or to make a purchase on Duke's credit. But this is precisely the purpose of this card: to satisfy the question of identity and of authorization. It is the reason why Duke was called upon to sign an agreement to pay not only for his purchases from Sears but for those made on the issued identification as well.

Duke further argues that if Sears wanted the agreement to have so drastic an effect as to bind him to pay for unauthorized purchases, Sears should have expressly so stated on either the agreement or the credit cards. We believe this to be the meaning of the agreement, and we do not regard this result to be so surprising in this credit card age. When Duke himself made a purchase and presented his credit card, he would not expect to be questioned. He should not expect the disguised thief to be.

The convenience of the credit card to both issuer and holder presents both with attendant risks. In general, and subject to contrary agreement by the parties, the one who can best control the risk should assume it. Thus, the issuer who puts a card into the mail without prior agreement with its intended holder should assume the larger part of the risk of improper use. After a holder accepts the card or agrees to pay for purchases made through its use, the risk of misuse is his unless and until he notifies the issuer otherwise. The holder can destroy his card if he feels that this is too great a burden. But if he is to carry it about, he must guard it as he does his currency if he is to avoid the expense of use by an imposter. If it is lost or stolen, by notifying the issuer, the holder shifts the risk of misuse back to the one who created the device. Texaco, Inc. v. Goldstein, 34 Misc.2d 751, 229 N.Y.S.2d 51 (N.Y.Mun.Ct.) aff'd 39 Misc.2d 552, 241 N.Y.S.2d 495 (App.Div., 1962).

The issuer of the card, or the seller of the goods, cannot ignore suspicious circumstances when selling to an imposter. The holder's liability has its limitations whether it be said that the issuer cannot avoid liability for his own negligence, or that the promise of the holder should be construed as being conditional upon the merchant's fulfillment of his obligation. See Comment: The Tripartite Credit Card Transaction: The Legal Infant, 48 Calif.L.R. 459, 483 (1960). In Gulf Refining Co. v. Williams Roofing Co., 208 Ark. 362, 186 S.W.2d 790, 158 A.L.R. 754 (1945), the holder of the card had printed "GOOD FOR TRUCK ONLY" on the face of the credit card. It was held that the seller was required to observe the limitation. In an often cited Oregon case, the address on the credit card of the holder was shown to be in Oregon, while Idaho license plates were on the car used by the imposter when the purchases were made. This was held to raise a fact question as to the seller's care. Union Oil Co. of California v. Lull, 220 Or. 412, 349 P.2d 243 (1960).

The cases differ as to the nature of the issuer-seller's duty of care, and as to the burden of proof. We hold that the seller need not demand more identification than the credit card as a matter of normal procedure. This is the function of the credit card, and it should be considered satisfactory evidence of identity of the holder or authorized user, unless the appearances or circumstances would raise a question in the mind of a reasonable seller. Proof that the seller did fail to use ordinary care in this respect is a defense to the liability of the holder of the card, and the burden of proof should be placed upon him.

The Court of Civil Appeals has ruled that the jury finding in favor of Sears, as to its care in ascertaining the identity and authority of the persons using the credit card, was not supported by sufficient evidence. However, that court has incorrectly placed the burden of proof upon Sears and has further enlarged the burden on Sears by holding that it could not discharge its duty of care by accepting the credit card as the only proof of identity. The judgment must therefore be reversed. We are unable to render judgment here in favor of Sears by holding, as Sears urges, that there was no evidence of its lack of care. Many purchases were made in the same stores, and one New York area store inquired of the Lubbock store as to Duke's credit standing in connection with one large purchase without any question being raised about the irregularity. The case must be remanded to the Court of Civil Appeals for reconsideration of the points of factual insufficiency to support the jury finding, which is a matter solely within that court's jurisdiction.

The judgment is reversed and the cause is remanded to the Court of Civil Appeals for further proceedings consistent with this opinion.

Question of Sear's lack of care

rev'd + rem'd

NOTE

See generally, Bergsten, Credit Cards—A Prelude to the Cashless Society, 8 B.C.Indus. & Com.L.Rev. 485 (1967); Macaulay, Private Legislation and the Duty to Read—Business Run by IBM Machine, The Law of Contracts and Credit Cards, 19 Vand. L.Rev. 1051 (1966).

CONSUMER CREDIT PROTECTION ACT

41 - 52

[15 U.S.C. § 1601 et seq.]

§ 1602. Definitions and rules of construction

* * *

(j) The term "adequate notice", as used in section 1643 of this title, means a printed notice to a cardholder which sets forth the pertinent facts clearly and conspicuously so that a person against whom it is to operate could reasonably be expected to have noticed it and understood its meaning. Such notice may be given to a cardholder by printing the notice on any credit card, or on each periodic statement of account, issued to the cardholder, or by any other means reasonably assuring the receipt thereof by the cardholder.

(k) The term "credit card" means any card, plate, coupon book or other credit device existing for the purpose of obtaining money, property, labor, or services on credit.

(*l*) The term "accepted credit card" means any credit card which the cardholder has requested and received or has signed or has used, or authorized another to use, for the purpose of obtaining money, property, labor or services on credit.

(m) The term "cardholder" means any person to whom a credit card is issued or any person who has agreed with the card issuer to pay obligations arising from the issuance of a credit card to another person.

(n) The term "card issuer" means any person who issues a credit card, or the agent of such person with respect to such card.

(o) The term "unauthorized use", as used in section 1643 of this title, means a use of a credit card by a person other than the cardholder who does not have actual, implied, or apparent authority for such use and from which the cardholder receives no benefit.

* * *

§ 1643. Liability of holder of credit card

(a)(1) A cardholder shall be liable for the unauthorized use of a credit card only if—

"(A) the card is an accepted credit card;

"(B) the liability is not in excess of $50;

"(C) the card issuer gives adequate notice to the cardholder of the potential liability;

"(D) the card issuer has provided the cardholder with a description of the means by which the card issuer may be notified of loss or theft of the card, which description may be provided on the face or reverse side of the statement required by section 1637(b) of this title or on a separate notice accompanying such statement;

"(E) the unauthorized use occurs before the card issuer has been notified that an unauthorized use of the credit card has occurred or may occur as the result of loss, theft, or otherwise; and

"(f) the card issuer has provided a method whereby the user of such card can be identified as the person authorized to use it.

"(2) For purposes of this section, a card issuer has been notified when such steps as may be reasonably required in the ordinary course of business to provide the card issuer with the pertinent information have been taken, whether or not any particular officer, employee, or agent of the card issuer does in fact receive such information."

(b) In any action by a card issuer to enforce liability for the use of a credit card, the burden of proof is upon the card issuer to show that the use was authorized or, if the use was unauthorized, then the burden of proof is upon the card issuer to show that the conditions of liability for the unauthorized use of a credit card, as set forth in subsection (a), have been met.

(c) Nothing in this section imposes liability upon a cardholder for the unauthorized use of a credit card in excess of his liability for such use under other applicable law or under any agreement with the card issuer.

(d) Except as provided in this section, a cardholder incurs no liability from the unauthorized use of a credit card.

§ 1645.   **Business credit cards; limits on liability of employees**

The exemption provided by section 1603(1) of this title does not apply to the provisions of sections 1642, 1643, and 1644 of this title, except that a card issuer and a business or other organization which provides credit cards issued by the same card issuer to ten or more of its employees may by contract agree as to liability of the business or other organization with respect to unauthorized use of such credit cards without regard to the provisions of section 1643 of this title, but in no case may such business or other organization or card issuer impose liability upon any employee with respect to unauthorized use of such a credit card except in accordance with and subject to the limitations of section 1643 of this title.

MARTIN v. AMERICAN EXPRESS, INC.

Court of Civil Appeals of Alabama, 1978.
361 So.2d 597.

BRADLEY, JUDGE.   This appeal is the result of an order by the Circuit Court of Montgomery County granting appellee's (American Express, Inc.) motion for summary judgment.

In the summer of 1972 appellant (Robert A. Martin) applied for and was issued an American Express credit card. Approximately three years later, in April of 1975, Martin gave his credit card to a business associate named E. L. McBride. The reason for this action by Martin was apparently to enable McBride to use the card for the purpose of a joint business venture into which the two men had entered. Martin claimed that he orally authorized McBride to charge up to $500 on the credit card. However, in June of 1975 Martin received a statement from American Express which indicated that the amount owed on his credit card account was approximately $5,300. Martin denied that he had signed the credit card invoices which demonstrate that an amount has been charged to the cardholder's account. Upon learning of Martin's refusal to pay the charges incurred through the use of his credit card, American Express filed suit against Martin to obtain the money which it claimed Martin owed.

As the suit proceeded, American Express deposed Martin. In his deposition Martin admitted that he had given his credit card to McBride for use in a joint venture. Martin further stated that he did not know McBride very well, but that he (Martin) was not concerned about that fact because he told McBride not to charge more than $500 to his (Martin's) credit card account. Martin was also relying on a letter which he had sent to American Express prior to giving his card to McBride. Martin testified that in this letter he asked American Express not to allow the total charges on his account to exceed $1,000. Moreover, in his deposition Martin indicated that McBride subsequently returned the credit card to him (Martin) and shortly thereafter disappeared.

On the basis of this deposition American Express moved for a summary judgment pursuant to Rule 56, ARCP. The trial court granted this motion and Martin filed an appeal to this court.

We believe that the trial court properly entered an order granting a summary judgment in favor of American Express and therefore affirm the trial court's action.

Despite the various arguments presented by the attorneys in this case, we perceive only one issue before us on this appeal. That issue is whether the use of a credit card by a person who has received the card and permission to utilize it from the cardholder constitutes "unauthorized use" under the Truth in Lending Act, 15 U.S.C.A. § 1602(o) and § 1643(a). We hold that in instances where a cardholder, who is under no compulsion by fraud, duress or otherwise, voluntarily permits the use of his (or her) credit card by another person, the cardholder has authorized the use of that card and is thereby responsible for any charges as a result of that use.

Section 1643(a), which is of principal concern in this case, limits a cardholder's liability to $50 for the "unauthorized use of a credit card." However, the statutory limitation on liability comes into play only where there is an "unauthorized use" of a credit card. Credit Card Service Corp. v. Federal Trade Comm'n, 161 U.S.App.D.C. 424, 495 F.2d 1004 (1974). And section 1602(*o*) defines "unauthorized use" as the "use of a credit card by a person other than the cardholder [a] who does not have actual, implied, or apparent authority for such use, and [b] from which the cardholder receives no benefit."

American Express argues that the actions of Martin in giving McBride the credit card clearly demonstrated that Martin was not entitled to rely on the $50 limitation for unauthorized use of a credit card. Conversely, Martin relies on the familiar principle of agency law that a principal has the right to presume that his agent will act only within the sphere of his authority, and that in the absence of circumstances sufficient to place him on notice, a principal will not be held liable for his failure to ascertain that his agent is acting beyond the scope of his authority. University Chevrolet Company v. Bank of Moundville, 25 Ala.App. 506, 150 So. 557, cert. den. 227 Ala. 516, 150 So. 560 (1933). Thus, Martin submits that he cannot be held liable for the acts of his agent in that the latter was authorized to charge only $500 to Martin's American Express account, yet exceeded his authority by charging in excess of that amount.

We fail to see the applicability of common law principles regarding agents and the scope of their authority to the statutory provisions in question. The Truth in Lending Act is to be liberally construed in favor of the consumer. Irvin v. Public Finance Company of Alabama, Ala.Civ.App., 340 So.2d 811 (1976). And its terms are to be strictly enforced. Irvin v. Public Finance Company of Alabama, supra. However, it is a well-settled rule of statutory construction that the plain language of a statute offers the primary guidance to its meaning. American Airlines, Inc. v. Remis Industries, Inc., 494 F.2d 196 (2d Cir. 1974). Accordingly, where the language found in the statute is clear and unambiguous and the words used therein plainly and distinctly demonstrate the intent of the framers of the statute, there is no occasion to resort to any other means of interpretation or to interject common law principles into the statutory provisions in question. See American Airlines, Inc. v. Remis Industries, Inc., supra.

 We believe Congress clearly indicated that "unauthorized use" of a card would occur only where there was no "actual, implied or apparent authority" for such use by the cardholder. In the present case Martin maintains that the actual, implied or apparent authority given by him to McBride was limited to the $500 amount which Martin told McBride not to exceed. Thus, Martin says he gave no authority for McBride to charge the large sum which eventually resulted in this suit. Furthermore, Martin asserts that prior to giving the card to McBride, he (Martin) wrote American Express and requested that its employees not allow the amounts charged to his credit card account to exceed $1,000. And since no such action was taken, Martin argues that any sum charged in excess of $1,000 constituted an "unauthorized" charge on his credit card.

We cannot accept either of the above contentions. McBride was actually authorized by Martin to use the latter's card. Martin admitted this fact. And the authority to use it, if not actual, remained apparent even after McBride ignored Martin's directions by charging over $500 to Martin's credit card account. Consequently, Martin was not entitled to rely on the provisions contained in section 1643(a) and he must be held responsible for any purchases made through the use of his card.

Nor are we aware of any requirement, either by statute, contract or trade usage, which would compel a credit card issuer to undertake a policy whereby the issuer would see to it that charges on a cardholder's account do not exceed a specified amount. Such a policy would place a difficult and potentially disastrous burden on the issuer. We know of no authority which requires a card issuer to perform services of this nature and Martin has provided us with none. Rule 28(a)(5), ARAP.

The express intent of Congress in enacting the Truth in Lending Act was to protect the consumer or cardholder against charges for the unauthorized use of his or her credit card and to limit his or her liability for such unauthorized use to a maximum of $50 providing, however, that the conditions set forth in the statute are complied with. First National City Bank v. Mullarkey, 87 Misc.2d 1, 385 N.Y.S.2d 473 (1976). We believe that § 1643(a) clearly indicates that such protection is warranted where the card is obtained from the cardholder as a result of loss, theft, or wrongdoing.[2]   However, we are not persuaded that section 1643(a) is applicable where a cardholder voluntarily and knowingly allows another to use his card and that person subsequently misuses the card.

Were we to adopt any other view, we would provide the unscrupulous and dishonest cardholder with the means to defraud the card issuer by allowing his or her friends to use the card, run up hundreds of dollars in charges and then limit his or her liability to $50 by notifying the card issuer.[3]   We do not believe such a result was either intended or sanctioned by Congress when it enacted section 1643(a).

Based on the pleadings and deposition before it, the trial court concluded that there was no genuine issue as to any material fact and that the moving party (American Express) was entitled to a judgment as a matter of law.   The court did not err in reaching such a conclusion.   Accordingly, the judgment of the trial court granting American Express's motion for summary judgment is affirmed.

Affirmed.

7.   ELECTRONIC FUND TRANSFERS

Electronic fund transfers are governed by the Electronic Fund Transfer Act, 15 U.S.C. § 1693 et seq.   We set forth after the following problem certain provisions of Regulation E that implements this Act.   *Start 1/27/87*

PROBLEM

Bank maintains automated teller machines (ATMs) for the convenience of its customers.   At an ATM a cardholder may withdraw funds from his bank account, make deposits in his account, and engage in other banking transactions.   A cardholder activates an ATM by inserting his plastic access card into the

---

2.   This construction is supported by two of the conditions for limitation of liability in unauthorized use situations under § 1643(a).   Those conditions are: (1) that the card issuer has provided the cardholder with a self-addressed, pre-stamped notification to be mailed by the cardholder in the event of *loss or theft* of the credit card; and (2) that the unauthorized use occurs before the cardholder has

notified the card issuer that an unauthorized use of the credit card has occurred or may occur as the result of *loss, theft* or otherwise.

3.   By this statement we do not mean to imply that Martin acted dishonestly or deceitfully in this matter. Indeed, he appears merely to be the victim of his own generosity.

terminal and entering his personal identification number (PIN) on the keyboard.

What is the liability of Cardholder in the following cases under Regulation E? See Penney & Baker, The Law of Electronic Fund Transfer Systems ¶ 6.03 (1980).

Case 1. Cardholder carried his access card and PIN in different compartments of his wallet. Thief stole the wallet and immediately used the card and PIN to withdraw $100 from Cardholder's account at one of Bank's ATMs.

Case 2. Bank sent Cardholder his access card and PIN in the same envelope. Thief stole the envelope from Cardholder's mailbox and immediately used the card and PIN to withdraw $100 from Cardholder's account at one of Bank's ATMs.

Case 3. Bank places its ATMs in pairs with an adjacent telephone for use by customers to report a defective machine. When Cardholder approached ATM #1 he found a man on the telephone dressed as a repairman who told him that #1 was broken and that he was on the line to the Bank trying to solve the problem. Cardholder then inserted his access card in ATM #2 and the "repairman" was able to observe him punching in his PIN. The "repairman" then asked Cardholder to help him test #1 by inserting his access card. After Cardholder complied with this request and departed, the "repairman" then used Cardholder's PIN and withdrew $200. When Cardholder found that his account was charged for an additional $200, he complained to Bank only to learn that the "repairman" was an imposter with no connection to Bank. See Mortimer, Electronic Fund Transfers, 37 Bus.Law. 1327, 1332–33 (1982).

REGULATION E

[12 C.F.R. Pt. 205 et seq.]

§ 205.2 Definitions and rules of construction.

For the purposes of this regulation, the following definitions apply, unless the context indicates otherwise:

(a)(1) "Access device" means a card, code, or other means of access to a consumer's account, or any combination thereof, that may be used by the consumer for the purpose of initiating electronic fund transfers.

(2) An access device becomes an "accepted access device" when the consumer to whom the access device was issued:

(i) Requests and receives, or signs, or uses, or authorizes another to use, the access device for the purpose of transferring money between accounts or obtaining money, property, labor or services;

(ii) Requests validation of an access device issued on an unsolicited basis; or

(iii) Receives an access device issued in renewal of, or in substitution for, an accepted access device, whether such access device is issued by the initial financial institution or a successor.

(b) "Account" means a demand deposit (checking), savings, or other consumer asset account (other than an occasional or incidental credit balance in a credit plan) held either directly or indirectly by a financial institution and established primarily for personal, family, or household purposes.

* * *

(g) "Electronic fund transfer" means any transfer of funds, other than a transaction originated by check, draft, or similar paper instrument, that is initiated through an electronic terminal, telephone, or computer or magnetic tape for the purpose of ordering, instructing, or authorizing a financial institution to debit or credit an account. The term includes, but is not limited to, point-of-sale transfers, automated teller machine transfers, direct deposits or withdrawals of funds, and transfers initiated by telephone. The term does not include payments made by check, draft, or similar paper instrument at an electronic terminal.

(h) "Electronic terminal" means an electronic device, other than a telephone operated by a consumer, through which a consumer may initiate an electronic fund transfer. The term includes, but is not limited to, point-of-sale terminals, automated teller machines, and cash dispensing machines.

* * *

(l) "Unauthorized electronic fund transfer" means an electronic fund transfer from a consumer's account initiated by a person other than the consumer without actual authority to initiate the transfer and from which the consumer receives no benefit. The term does not include any electronic fund transfer (1) initiated by a person who was furnished with the access device to the consumer's account by the consumer, unless the consumer has notified the financial institution involved that transfers by that person are no longer authorized, (2) initiated with fraudulent intent by the consumer or any person acting in concert with the consumer, or (3) that is initiated by the financial institution or its employee.

§ 205.6 Liability of consumer for unauthorized transfers.

(a) *General rule.* A consumer is liable, within the limitations described in paragraph (b) of this section, for unauthorized electronic fund transfers involving the consumer's account only if:

(1) The access device used for the unauthorized transfers is an accepted access device;

(2) The financial institution has provided a means (such as by signature, photograph, fingerprint, or electronic or mechanical confirmation) to identify the consumer to whom the access device was issued; and

(3) The financial institution has provided the following information, in writing, to the consumer:

(i) A summary of the consumer's liability under this section, or under other applicable law or agreement, for unauthorized electronic fund transfers and, at the financial institution's option, notice of the advisability of promptly reporting loss or theft of the access device or unauthorized transfers.

(ii) The telephone number and address of the person or office to be notified in the event the consumer believes that an unauthorized electronic fund transfer has been or may be made.

(iii) The financial institution's business days, as determined under § 205.2(d), unless applicable State law or an agreement between the consumer and the financial institution sets a liability limit not greater than $50.

(b) *Limitations on amount of liability.* The amount of a consumer's liability for an unauthorized electronic fund transfer or a series of related unauthorized transfers shall not exceed $50 or the amount of unauthorized transfers that occur before notice to the financial institution under paragraph (c) of this section, whichever is less, unless one or both of the following exceptions apply:

(1) If the consumer fails to notify the financial institution within 2 business days after learning of the loss or theft of the

access device, the consumer's liability shall not exceed the lesser of $500 or the sum of

(i) $50 or the amount of unauthorized electronic fund transfers that occur before the close of the 2 business days, whichever is less, and

(ii) the amount of unauthorized electronic fund transfers that the financial institution establishes would not have occurred but for the failure of the consumer to notify the institution within 2 business days after the consumer learns of the loss or theft of the access device, and that occur after the close of 2 business days and before notice to the financial institution.

(2) If the consumer fails to report within 60 days of transmittal of the periodic statement any unauthorized electronic fund transfer that appears on the statement, the consumer's liability shall not exceed the sum of

(i) The lesser of $50 or the amount of unauthorized electronic fund transfers that appear on the periodic statement or that occur during the 60-day period, and

(ii) The amount of unauthorized electronic fund transfers that occur after the close of the 60 days and before notice to the financial institution and that the financial institution establishes would not have occurred but for the failure of the consumer to notify the financial institution within that time.

(3) Paragraphs (b)(1) and (2) of this section may both apply in some circumstances. Paragraph (b)(1) shall determine the consumer's liability for any unauthorized transfers that appear on the periodic statement and occur before the close of the 60-day period, and paragraph (b)(2)(ii) shall determine liability for transfers that occur after the close of the 60-day period.

(4) If a delay in notifying the financial institution was due to extenuating circumstances, such as extended travel or hospitalization, the time periods specified above shall be extended to a reasonable time.

(5) If applicable State law or an agreement between the consumer and financial institution imposes lesser liability than that provided in paragraph (b) of this section, the consumer's liability shall not exceed that imposed under that law or agreement.

(c) *Notice to financial institution.* For purposes of this section, notice to a financial institution is given when a consumer takes such steps as are reasonably necessary to provide the financial institution with the pertinent information, whether or not any particular officer, employee, or agent of the financial institution does in fact receive the information. Notice in writing is considered given at the time the consumer deposits the notice in the mail or delivers the notice for transmission by any other usual means to the financial institution. Notice in writing is considered given at the time of receipt or, whether or not received, at the expiration of the time ordinarily required for transmission, whichever is earlier. Notice is also considered given when the financial institution becomes aware of circumstances that lead to the reasonable belief that an unauthorized electronic fund transfer involving the consumer's account has been or may be made.

Chapter 2

LIABILITY OF PARTIES TO NEGOTIABLE INSTRUMENTS

A. LIABILITY OF SECONDARY PARTIES FOR NON-PAYMENT. PRESENTMENT, DISHONOR AND NOTICE OF DISHONOR

The holder of an uncertified check cannot be certain that the check will be paid when presented. He takes the minimal risk of insolvency of the drawee bank, but runs the far greater risk that the check will not be paid either because the drawer does not have sufficient funds on deposit with the drawee bank or because the drawer has stopped payment. A check is simply an order to pay and that order can be countermanded by the drawer. The drawee is obliged to honor any timely stop payment order received before the drawee has paid the check or has taken other action with respect to the check equivalent to payment. UCC § 4–403 and § 4–303. This right to stop payment is very important to the buyer of goods or services who has paid by check but who has second thoughts about the transaction shortly after payment. It can be used by a defrauded buyer as well as by a buyer trying to avoid a just obligation.

As you might expect, the holder of a dishonored check has a cause of action against the defaulting drawer for the amount of the check, UCC § 3–413(2), and he has a similar action against any indorser. UCC § 3–414(1). The drawer is treated by UCC § 3–102(1)(d) as a secondary party along with indorsers. This terminology simply recognizes that a check is normally paid by the drawee. If the check is not paid recourse can be made to the drawer or to indorsers, but the ultimate liability rests with the drawer. If a note is not paid by the maker indorsers are liable as in the case of nonpayment of a check.

Liability against secondary parties is conditional upon (1) presentment of the instrument to the drawee or maker, (2) dishonor, (3) notice of dishonor, and (4) protest in the case of a draft which on its face appears to be drawn or payable outside of the United States. Study the relevant UCC provisions: § 3–501 through § 3–508 and § 3–511. UCC § 3–503(1)(c) retains the rigorous rule that presentment of a note due on a fixed date must be made on the exact date or indorsers are released under UCC § 3–502(1)(a). But § 3–503 is subject to contrary agreement and the rule is avoided by the inclusion in most promissory note forms of a clause stating in substance the following "The maker and the indorsers and guarantors of the note waive presentment, notice of dishonor, and protest of the note." Thus, as a practical matter the technicalities of presentment, dishonor and notice of dishonor have importance primarily in the case of checks. Since presentment, dishonor and notice of dishonor are important in determining the liability of drawers only in the relatively rare case of insolvency of the drawee bank, this technical law has most importance in determining the liability of indorsers of checks, and even with respect to them there is very little litigation. Most checks are deposited by the payee with a depositary bank which will collect the check for the depositor by having it presented for payment. The depositary bank gives the depositor credit for the check which is conditional upon the check's being paid when presented. This conditional credit is called "provisional settlement" in bank collection terminology. UCC § 4–104(j) and Comment 6 to § 4–104. Upon dishonor of a check for which a provisional settlement has been made, the "depositary bank" or "collecting bank" (UCC § 4–105(a) and (d)) has a right to revoke the settlement if it acts promptly. UCC § 4–212(1). Normally the depositary bank will use this remedy rather than the remedy provided by UCC § 3–414(1). The two remedies are not identical. Sometimes an indorser or depositor is liable under both provisions. Sometimes only one of the provisions applies. We will examine the depositary bank's remedies under Article 4 of the UCC in Chapter 5 as part of our study of the bank-collection process.

PROBLEMS

1. Buyer gave Seller a check drawn by Buyer on Drawee, an out-of-state bank. Seller learned shortly thereafter that Buyer had a long record of writing bad checks. Seller, fearing that Buyer was about to abscond, immediately brought suit against Buyer for the amount of the check. Seller never presented the check for payment, but in fact Buyer did not have sufficient funds in his account to cover the check. Was the check dishonored? Is Buyer liable under UCC § 3–413(2)?

2. A check is drawn by Drawer on Drawee Bank and is delivered to Payee on February 1. At all times Drawer had sufficient funds in his account to cover the check.

Case 1. Drawee Bank failed on February 25. The check was never presented for payment.

Case 2. Drawee Bank failed on March 10. The check was presented for payment on March 11 and payment was refused because of Drawee Bank's insolvency. Drawer's account is fully insured by the Federal Deposit Insurance Corporation but payment to depositors was not made by FDIC until about six months after the bank's failure.

State in each case what if any liability Drawer has to the holder of the check if suit is brought on March 15.

B. STOP PAYMENT ORDERS REGARDING CERTIFIED OR CASHIER'S CHECKS

We have seen that a seller who takes an uncertified check in payment has a cause of action against the buyer as drawer of the check if the check is dishonored, but this right is of small solace to the seller if the buyer has no money in his account or stops payment. A wise seller dealing with an untrustworthy buyer will insist on receiving an instrument which a bank is obliged to pay. Usually, the seller will ask for a certified check or an instrument usually called a cashier's check. The latter instrument is in form a check drawn by a bank on itself as drawee. The cashier's check is not specifically dealt with by the UCC and does not fit very well into either of the two categories of notes or drafts. UCC § 3–118(a) states that "a draft drawn on the drawer is effective as a note," but courts commonly speak of a cashier's check as a check "accepted by the act of issuance." In most cases it will not make any difference whether the issuing bank is treated as maker or acceptor because the two liabilities are similar. UCC § 3–413(1). To the extent, however, that some sections of the UCC apply only to acceptors, liability on a cashier's check may be influenced by whether the issuing bank is treated as an acceptor or as the maker of a note. The following case discusses the power to stop payment of bank obligations such as certified or cashier's checks.

DZIURAK v. CHASE MANHATTAN BANK, N.A.

Supreme Court of New York, Appellate Division, Second Department, 1977.
58 A.D.2d 103, 396 N.Y.S.2d 414.

COHALAN, JUSTICE PRESIDING. The sole question on this appeal is whether a bank depositor to whom an "official bank check" has been issued (and by him endorsed to the order of a third party), can legally stop payment thereon, in the absence of a court order or an indemnification bond. An official bank check is commonly referred to as a "cashier's check." Trial Term held. it could be stopped. We disagree.

A recitation of the facts is necessary to place the problem in proper focus.

The plaintiff currently holds a judgment against the defendant Chase Manhattan Bank (Bank) in the amount of $17,000, plus interest and costs.

During the year 1973 Dziurak maintained a savings account with "Branch # 40" of the Bank in the sum of $18,000. He was cozened by an acquaintance named Staveris into a proposal whereby, for $22,000 cash, he could acquire a one-third interest in a corporation whose sole asset was a going restaurant. There was nothing in writing to bind the bargain. Dziurak paid Staveris $5,000 down. He then went to the Bank and, through the assistant manager, arranged for the proper withdrawal. He asked for a "check" to be drawn to the order of Staveris. Monaco, the assistant manager, advised him to have the check drawn to himself as payee. A further bit of advice by Monaco was for Dziurak to go to his attorney, who would instruct him how to endorse the check.

The $17,000 was transferred to the Bank's coffers and Dziurak's savings account was debited accordingly. A cashier's check was then issued to the order of "Francis A. Dziurak."

Plaintiff ignored the suggestion that he consult with his attorney. Instead he wrote on the back of the instrument "Francis Dziurak. Pay to order Mario Staveris" and delivered the item to Staveris. The latter, instead of depositing the check into the corporate restaurant account, deposited it in his own savings account.

Before he learned of Staveris' perfidy and before the cashier's check had cleared, Dziurak belatedly sought the advice of a local attorney. Very properly, the attorney advised him to try to stop payment on the cashier's check.

Back went Dziurak to the Bank. He saw Monaco and asked him if the check had cleared. It had not, but had arrived at the Bank that morning.

While plaintiff was with him, Monaco telephoned the Bank's attorneys and was advised that the check could not be stopped, absent a court order. He so advised the plaintiff and while Dziurak was still with him he telephoned the plaintiff's attorney to advise him to the same effect. The attorney said he was aware that a court order could effectively produce a stop of the payment.

This action was started against the Bank after judgment was first taken against Staveris, and after execution was returned unsatisfied.

As to the law, the controlling statutes are contained in several sections of the Uniform Commercial Code (hereafter UCC) which, in turn, are fleshed out in reported decisions of nisi prius and appellate courts.

We begin with subdivision (1) of section 4–403 of the UCC ("Customer's Right to Stop Payment; Burden of Proof of Loss"):

> "A customer may by order to his bank stop payment of *any item payable for his account* but the order must be received at such time and in such manner as to afford the bank a reasonable opportunity to act on it prior to any action by the bank with respect to the item described in Section 4–303" (emphasis supplied).

As to this section (4–403) we part company with Trial Term, which held that the $17,000 represented by the cashier's check was actually Dziurak's money and not that of the Bank. As noted in Wertz v. Richardson Hgts. Bank & Trust, 495 S.W.2d 572, 574 [Tex.]:

> "A cashier's check is not one payable for the customer's account but rather for the bank's account. It is the bank which is obligated on the check".

The reference in section 4–403 more properly fits the situation where the depositor, as drawer, issues his own check on his own bank, as drawee. Such a check can be stopped if reasonable notice is given.

> "A cashier's check is of a very different character. It is the primary obligation of the bank which issues it (citation omitted) and constitutes its written promise to pay upon demand (citation omitted). It has been said that a cashier's check is a

bill of exchange drawn by a bank upon itself, accepted in advance by the very act of issuance" (Matter of Bank of United States [O'Neill], 243 App.Div. 287, 291, 277 N.Y.S. 96, 100).

This exposition of the law has been followed consistently. * * *

No decisions holding to the contrary have been unearthed.

But to go on. Subdivision (1) of section 4–303 of the UCC ("When Items Subject to   *   *   *   Stop-Order") states, in part:

"Any   *   *   *   stop-order received by   *   *   *   a payor bank, whether or not effective under other rules of law to terminate   *   *   *   the bank's right or duty to pay an item   *   *   *   comes too late to so terminate   *   *   *   if the   *   *   *   stop-order   *   *   *   is received   *   *   *   and a reasonable time for the bank to act thereon expires   *   *   * after the bank has done any one of the following:

"(a) accepted or certified the item."

The next section to consider is 3–410

("Definition and Operation of Acceptance"):

"(1) Acceptance is the drawee's signed engagement to honor the draft as presented. It must be written on the draft, and may consist of his signature alone. It becomes operative when completed by delivery or notification."

At this point we can refer back to annotation 5 in the Official Comment under section 4–403 of the UCC (McKinney's Cons. Laws of N.Y., Book 62½, Part 2, p. 611):

"There is no right to stop payment after certification of a check or other acceptance of a draft, and this is true no matter who procures the certification. See Sections 3–411 and 4–303. The acceptance is the drawee's own engagement to pay, and he is not required to impair his credit by refusing payment for the convenience of the drawer."

Thus, the Bank's one signature on the instrument constitutes both a drawing and an acceptance and makes the Bank a drawer and a drawee. (See Matter of Bank of United States [O'Neill] supra).

In the recitation of the facts, mention was made that the local attorney for the plaintiff remarked to Monaco that he was aware that a court order (presumably one of a court of competent jurisdiction) could have acted as a "stop payment" order. The statute providing for such an order is section 3–603 of the

UCC. It is headnoted "Payment or Satisfaction" and, pertinently, reads:

"(1) The liability of any party is discharged to the extent of his payments * * * to the holder even though it is made with knowledge of a claim of another person to the instrument unless prior to such payment * * * *the person making the claim either supplies indemnity deemed adequate by the party seeking the discharge* or enjoins payment or satisfaction by order of a court of competent jurisdiction in an action in which the adverse claimant and the holder are parties" (emphasis supplied).

The fact that the attorney for the plaintiff was aware that a court order could effect a stop payment presupposes that he also knew he could file an indemnity bond to protect the Bank, since both options are included in subdivision (1) of section 3–603 of the UCC.

Viewed in retrospect, the Bank, as a practical matter, could quite safely have stopped payment on its cashier's check and, by interpleader, have paid the money into court. Staveris could not have established himself as a holder in due course (see UCC, § 3–302). But, if the Legislature laid upon a bank the onus of questioning the reason for the issuance of all cashier's checks it would destroy the efficacy of such instruments, which, for all practical purposes, are treated as the equivalent of cash (Goshen Nat. Bank v. State of New York, 141 N.Y. 379, 387, 36 N.E. 316, 317).

To do justice to the Bank, it is only fair to observe that the entire brouhaha was occasioned by the intransigence of Dziurak. Had he followed the advice of Monaco to consult his own attorney, the situation in which the parties are now involved would have been averted. It was well said in National Safe Deposit, Sav. & Trust Co. v. Hibbs, 229 U.S. 391, 394, 33 S.Ct. 818, 57 L.Ed. 1241, wherein the doctrine of equitable estoppel was invoked for dismissing the complaint and cited with approval in Bunge Corp. v. Manufacturers Hanover Trust Co., 31 N.Y.2d 223, 228, 335 N.Y.S.2d 412, 415, 286 N.E.2d 903, 905:

"That where one of two innocent persons must suffer by the acts of a third, he who has enabled such third person to occasion the loss must sustain it."

Dziurak provoked the issue; Dziurak should shoulder the blame.

There is a profusion of cases to the effect that a cashier's check, once issued and in the possession of a third party, cannot legally be stopped except as provided by statute (see UCC, § 3–603). One of the leading cases of recent vintage is Kaufman v. Chase Manhattan Bank, Nat. Ass'n, D.C., 370 F.Supp. 276.

There, in an opinion by Chief Judge Edelstein, plaintiff Kaufman was granted summary judgment. In that case the bank, at the request of a depositor, drew a cashier's check to plaintiff as payee. When it was presented for payment the bank refused to honor it. Chief Judge Edelstein wrote that (p. 278):

"A cashier's check   *   *   *   is a check drawn by the bank upon itself, payable to another person, and issued by an authorized officer of the bank. The bank, therefore, becomes both the drawer and drawee; and the check becomes a promise by the bank to draw the amount of the check from its own resources and to pay the check upon demand. Thus, the issuance of the cashier's check constitutes an acceptance by the issuing bank; and the cashier's check becomes the primary obligation of the bank."

A reference to subdivision (1) of section 3–410 of the UCC was contained in a footnote to the opinion with respect to acceptance upon issuance.

Contrary to Trial Term's opinion, the statute makes no distinction between a cashier's check presented for payment by a payee or one presented by an endorsee of the payee. (See Moon Over Mountain Bank v. Marine Midland, 87 Misc.2d 918, 386 N.Y.S.2d 974, supra, and the cases therein cited.) It engages to pay on demand to the person who presents the check unless he falls within either of the categories listed in subdivision (1) of section 3–603 of the UCC (theft or restrictive endorsement).

From all that has been stated, and harsh as it may appear, it follows that the judgment must be reversed and the complaint dismissed, with costs.

Whether future remedies are available to persons situated as is the plaintiff at bar must be left to the discretion of the State Legislature.

*   *   *

NOTES

1. In the principal case Dziurak was payee of the check. His claim was that he was fraudulently induced to transfer the check to Staveris. This fraud could be used as a basis of rescinding the transaction of transfer. If Bank is bound by Dzi-

urak's claim, of which it had notice prior to payment, it could not safely pay Staveris. Bank has no way of determining whether the claim of Dziurak is meritorious or not and has no interest in the dispute. Two provisions of the UCC protect Bank in this case. The last sentence of UCC § 3–306(d) provides that Bank may not assert the claim of Dziurak against Staveris. Thus, payment by Bank to Staveris is not wrongful. UCC § 3–603(1), relied on by the Court, is consistent. Payment to Staveris discharges any liability Bank may have had on the instrument to Dziurak. The remedy under both sections is for Dziurak to assume the burden of litigating the claim with Staveris and holding Bank harmless. Dziurak must either obtain an injunction against payment, or if Bank is cooperative, can indemnify Bank and defend Bank's refusal to pay. This remedy is a substitute for the right to stop payment, but it applies only to cases in which there is a claim to ownership of the check. See Note, Personal Money Orders and Teller's Checks: Mavericks Under the U.C.C., 67 Colum.L.Rev. 524, 543–546 (1967). Suppose the check had been issued in the name of Staveris as payee and delivered to Dziurak. Is this case covered by UCC § 3–306(d) and § 3–603(1)? In this situation Dziurak is a "remitter." He has purchased the check but is not a party to it. He has no rights on the check itself and therefore there is no liability to him by Bank that is discharged by payment to the holder, Staveris. Should this affect his ability to prevent payment to Bank?

2.   Some courts treat the obligation of the issuer of a cashier's check as an absolute obligation to pay the instrument in accordance with its terms at the time the issuer became obligated on it. Consider State ex rel. Chan Siew Lai v. Powell, 536 S.W.2d 14 (Mo.1976). In connection with a proposed purchase and sale of fertilizer, Kin Tak, a resident of Hong Kong, was alleged to have fraudulently induced Gunn, a resident of the United States, to purchase from Issuing Bank a cashier's check for $150,000 payable to Kin Tak, which was delivered to Kin Tak. As a result of the alleged fraud Gunn would receive nothing for the $150,000. When Gunn learned of the fraud he obtained a temporary injunction against Issuing Bank's paying the cashier's check. In his petition Gunn stated that if the check were paid Gunn would have no effective remedy because "all potential defendants are nonresidents of [this country] and [because of] the tremendous expense, delay and difficulty in the institution of [suits in] courts wherein the laws may not be the law under which these parties contracted." 536 S.W.2d at 15. Issuing Bank did not oppose issuance of the injunction. After issu-

ance of the injunction, Chan intervened seeking to dissolve the injunction. Chan alleged that he was the holder of the check and entitled to receive payment. The judge issuing the injunction decided to continue the injunction in force. The Supreme Court of Missouri by writ of prohibition in effect ordered that the injunction be dissolved. It held that Gunn had no authority to stop payment citing UCC § 4–303. It went on to say that because cashier's checks are accepted as a substitute for cash, public policy does not favor a rule that would permit the nonpayment of them. It stated that Gunn's allegations of fraud in his petition, even if true, afforded no grounds for relief and went on to say that Gunn could not state any facts by amendment of his petition that would allow him the remedy asked. The lower court was held to have exceeded its jurisdiction in granting the injunction. Gunn was left with an action against Kin Tak, presumably in Hong Kong, as his sole remedy. The court did not discuss at all the question of how Chan became holder, whether or not Chan was acting for Kin Tak, and whether Chan had notice or knowledge of the fraud. Apparently, Chan would have won even if he had been a holder not in due course with full knowledge of the fraud. The court did not cite UCC § 3–603. Professor Lawrence in his article, Making Cashier's Checks and Other Bank Checks Cost-Effective: A Plea for Revision of Articles 3 and 4 of the Uniform Commercial Code, 64 Minn.L.Rev. 275 (1980), argues that the UCC should be amended to make it clear that the issuer of a cashier's check has an absolute liability to pay in a case such as Chan Siew Lai. Do you agree? This case is reminiscent of Miller v. Race, supra p. 7, in which the result was also based on the notion that the instrument involved was a substitute for cash. Would plaintiff in Miller v. Race have won if he had taken the bank note from the robber knowing that the bank note had been stolen? Note that in both cases nonpayment of the instrument is not based on any defense of the obligor, but rather is based on the claim of a third party. UCC § 3–603(1) and § 3–306(d).

C. INSTRUMENTS AS CONDITIONAL PAYMENT. RIGHTS ON THE INSTRUMENT AND ON THE UNDERLYING TRANSACTION

The buyer's obligation arising from a sale is commonly "paid" by the seller's receipt of the buyer's note or check. Implicit in the transaction is the understanding that if the note or check is not paid when due buyer's obligation on the sale has not been satisfied and seller, therefore, should be able to enforce it. Thus, the cases usually say that the instrument is taken as "conditional payment." A complication arises, however, because the transaction gives rise to a second obligation of the buyer, as maker or drawer, on the instrument itself. UCC § 3–413(1) and (2). This obligation is distinct from the underlying obligation of the buyer to pay for whatever was purchased. Whether the seller sues for the unpaid price or the amount of the dishonored instrument is normally not important. There are some procedural advantages to suing on the instrument but in substance the two causes of action are the same. The parties, if they had thought about the matter at all, would probably have agreed that the seller should be entitled to enforce either obligation. UCC § 3–802, which is designed to carry out the likely understanding of the parties in cases in which no understanding was expressed by them, reflects this view. But what UCC § 3–802 actually says is somewhat different, and the language of the section can provide some unexpected results. Consider the next two cases.

LAKEWAY CO. v. BRAVO

Court of Civil Appeals of Texas, Tyler, 1979.
576 S.W.2d 926.

SUMMERS, CHIEF JUSTICE. This appeal is from a summary judgment granted in favor of appellees.

Appellees, Sr. and Sra. Bravo, Citizens of Mexico, brought suit against appellant, Lakeway Company, for specific performance of a contract for sale of land, that is for delivery of a deed to the property in question, and Lakeway Company counterclaimed for $8,188.45, the balance which it alleged was due as purchase money under the contract.

Both appellees and appellant filed their respective motions for summary judgment. The trial court granted the appellees' motion for summary judgment and denied the appellant's motion, from which action appellant has appealed. We affirm.

By a written contract (drawn by Lakeway and executed in both Spanish and English versions) dated July 31, 1976, the Bravos contracted to buy and Lakeway Company agreed to sell a certain Lakeway lot located in Travis County, Texas. The contract stipulated the total purchase price in the following manner "US$25,820.00 (MEX$322,750.00)." The down payment was described to be "US$5,000.00 (MEX$62,500.00)." At the time the contract was signed, the Bravos paid, by check, the down payment of 62,500 Mexican pesos which was equivalent to $5,000.00 (U.S.). This down payment in pesos was accepted by Lakeway.

On August 18, 1976 (which was a Saturday), Lakeway received Mr. Bravo's check drawn on Banco National de Mexico payable to Lakeway Company in the amount of 260,250 pesos, at that time the equivalent of U.S. $20,820.00. This was for the second and final payment under the contract. Lakeway deposited the check at its Austin bank on Monday, August 20, 1976, and the check was honored and cleared the Banco National de Mexico on August 30, 1976. On August 31, 1976, the Mexican government devaluated the peso. Because of the devaluation, the exchange of pesos for U.S. dollars, yielded only $12,631.55, $8,188.45 less than the original U.S. dollar amount for the second payment. Lakeway retained both the down payment and second payment but refused to convey title to the property in question, claiming that the Bravos had not made full payment.

Appellant has predicated its appeal upon two points of error which contend that the trial court erred (1) in granting summary judgment in favor of appellees, and (2) in refusing to grant summary judgment in favor of appellant.

The contract provided that it is to be interpreted in accordance with the laws of Texas and the United States of America, and the provisions pertinent to this appeal provide that:

"1. Seller [appellant] agrees to sell and Buyers [appellees] agree to buy for a total purchase price of US$25,820.00 (MEX$322,750.00) the following described property in Lakeway Section 18, as recorded in Plat Book 3, Page 385 of Travis County clerk records, Lot Number 2060.

"2. Buyers have paid US$5,000.00 (MEX$62,500.00) as a down payment and agree to pay to the seller, at 1200 Lakeway, Austin, Texas 78746, U.S.A. the balance within * * * (15) days of the date of this contract. Seller agrees to notify Buyers in writing of the total amount due in Mexican pesos if a change in the official exchange rate occurs prior to such payment.

"3. When the total purchase price is paid, Seller agrees to convey said property to Buyers by a general warranty deed, subject to all subdivision restrictions and covenants and easements of record (including those recorded in the deed records of Travis County, Texas for the section in which this homesite is located). Also, Seller agrees to furnish Buyers with a policy of title guaranty insurance covering said property."

Appellant contends that the intention of the parties, as set forth in the contract, was for a total purchase price of $25,820.00; that how that was paid, whether in dollars or pesos, was immaterial so long as the result to seller was the required number of dollars; and that the peso figure in parenthesis was simply for the convenience of the buyer to let him know how many pesos would be required to buy the property. It urges that this intention is supported by the fact that the contract provides that "Seller agrees to notify Buyers in writing of the total amount due in Mexican pesos if a change in the official exchange rate occurs prior to such payment." We agree with these contentions.

In its conclusion, however, appellant takes the position that when the Bravos delivered the check on August 18, 1976, that Lakeway accepted the check not only on the condition that it be honored but also on the condition that it produce the required number of dollars. We disagree. As pointed out by appellees, the amount of dollars for the purchase price was absolute, but the amount of pesos could vary if seller gave written notice to buyers of a change in the official exchange rate prior to payment (pursuant to paragraph 2 of the contract). Appellees further respond that the mode of payment could be in dollars or pesos; that the down payment was in pesos with no objection from Lakeway; that on August 18, 1978, the Bravos delivered to Lakeway their check drawn upon their Mexican bank payable to Lakeway Company in the amount of 260,250 pesos; that there had been no change in the exchange rate and that such amount was the correct amount due for the final payment under the contract; that such check was received by Lakeway without objection; that when one takes a check, the check is accepted with one condition, and one condition only, that is that the check be honored for payment; and that once the check is honored and paid in due course the payment relates back and becomes absolute as of the date of the delivery of the check to payee. We agree.

In the instant case a check payable in the correct amount of pesos for final payment under the contract was delivered to Lakeway by the Bravos on August 18, 1976; such check was received by Lakeway without objection; said check was honored and cleared appellees' bank account on August 30, 1976, prior to the devaluation of the peso which occurred on August 31, 1976;

and when honored and paid in due course, the payment became absolute and related back to the date of delivery of the check on August 18, 1976; and as of said date of delivery it produced the specified value in dollars and satisfied the terms of the contract.

When a check is accepted as conditional payment and is paid in due course, it is generally held that the payment thereon becomes absolute and relates to the date of delivery of the check. Muldrow v. Texas Frozen Foods, Inc., 157 Tex. 39, 299 S.W.2d 275, 277 (1957); Texas Mutual Life Ins. Ass'n v. Tolbert, 134 Tex. 419, 136 S.W.2d 584, 590 (1940); [UCC § 3–802(1)(b)]; 70 C.J.S. Payment § 24, p. 235; 60 Am.Jur.2d, Payment, sec. 11, p. 618.

* * *

The judgment of the trial court is affirmed.

NOTE

The court apparently accepted Seller's argument that the intention of the parties was that Seller was to be paid $25,820, whether paid in dollar obligations or peso obligations. But it went on to analyze the case as one falling under UCC § 3–802(1)(b). Is the position of the court consistent? Is UCC § 3–802(1)(b) relevant? Would the issue have been different if the failure to exchange pesos into dollars prior to the devaluation date had been the result of Seller's failure to promptly present Buyer's check for payment?

PROBLEM

Buyer paid for goods bought from Seller with Buyer's check certified by Drawee Bank. Shortly after the sale Buyer decided that he did not want the goods after all and returned them to Seller. Buyer requested Drawee Bank not to pay the check. When Seller presented the check to Drawee Bank payment was refused. Does Seller have a cause of action against Buyer on the contract of sale? Does Seller have a cause of action against buyer for dishonor of the check? Is it important whether or not Seller has a cause of action against Buyer? How would your answers differ if Buyer had paid with a cashier's check issued by Drawee Bank?

(handwritten annotations) Held buyer — seller — purchaser, refused to sell; 3-802

KIRBY v. BERGFIELD

Supreme Court of Nebraska, 1970.
186 Neb. 242, 182 N.W.2d 205.

McCOWN, JUSTICE. This is an action for specific performance of a contract for the purchase and sale of real estate. The
trial court entered a decree ordering the specific performance of
the contract and the defendant sellers have appealed.

Following negotiations initiated by two representatives of the
sellers several weeks before, the parties reached an oral agreement for the purchase and sale of a 9,040-acre ranch located in
Dawes County, Nebraska. The following day, August 8, 1967,
the written contract was prepared by the sellers' attorney, and
signed by all of the parties.

The total purchase price was $352,560, "payable in manner
following: $10,000.00 down payment, receipt of which is hereby
acknowledged, and the balance of $342,560.00 by assuming and
paying promptly when due a first mortgage of the (sellers) to
the John Hancock Insurance Co. in the sum of $172,000.00;
$20,000.00 cash on or before the 1st day of November, 1967, and
the balance of $150,560.00 payable in ten years." This balance
carried interest of 5½ percent from November 1, 1967, and was
payable in semiannual installments with the balance due at the
end of 10 years. The $150,560 balance was to be represented by
a promissory note of the purchasers secured by a second mortgage on the premises.

* * *

Kirby's $10,000 check for the down payment drawn on the
First National Bank of Omaha, dated August 8, 1967, was returned for insufficient funds. A cashier's check in that sum was
deposited with the defendants' bank about August 12, 1967, and
was accepted by the defendants as the down payment. The
deed and a copy of the contract were never placed in escrow.

On November 1, 1967, the agreed closing date, the parties
met in Chadron and drove together to Crawford. Mrs. Bergfield
wanted to be positively assured that Kirbys had the money for
the $20,000 payment. The testimony is conflicting as to what
the Bergfields were told. Kirbys maintain that Bergfields were
specifically told to call Kirby's banker, Mr. Hugh Campbell, at
the Bank of Bellevue, Nebraska, if they had any doubts about
the check. Bergfields testified that Mr. Kirby told them to call
"his bank," "the Bank of Bellevue," or "his banker." The

Bergfields and their attorney all deny that the banker's name was mentioned.

The final closing was completed in the office of the defendants' attorney in the early evening of November 1, 1967. All necessary documents were executed by both parties. All of the documents except the $20,000 check were retained by the defendants' attorney until Bergfields could ascertain whether or not the check was good.

The following morning, Bergfields went to the Bank of Chadron and requested that Mr. Bare, the cashier, call the Bank of Bellevue to ascertain if there were sufficient funds in the Kirby account to cover the $20,000 check. Mr. Bare called the Bank of Bellevue and asked for the bookkeeping department. He gave the name of the account, the account number, and the amount of the check to a lady there and asked her if there were sufficient funds on hand to cover it. After a time, she returned to the telephone and indicated that there was not money in the account to cover the check. The Bergfields then continued to hold the check. It was never presented at the Bellevue Bank for payment. At the Bergfields' order, their attorney tore their signatures off the deed which was in his possession.

Sometime between November 7 and 10, 1967, Mrs. Bergfield received a call from Mr. Kirby telling her to "send the check through." She refused to do so and told him they were not going to deal with him at all. November 24, 1967, a cashier's check for $20,000 was issued by the Bank of Bellevue. On November 26, 1967, Mr. Kirby again called Mrs. Bergfield and told her he had the cashier's check available. She again refused to deal with him. On November 30, 1967, Kirby delivered the cashier's check to an attorney in Chadron and instructed him to write to the Bergfields and advise them that the money was available and he was prepared to settle the matter. His attorney did so by registered letter dated November 30, 1967. The Bergfields refused to accept delivery of the letter and it was returned unclaimed. On about December 26, 1967, Mr. Kirby's attorney delivered a copy of the contract and the $20,000 cashier's check to the Bank of Chadron, the escrow agent named in the contract. The Chadron Bank returned the cashier's check on January 2, 1968.

It was stipulated that there were insufficient funds in the Kirby account at the Bank of Bellevue from November 1, 1967, through December 31, 1967, to cover the $20,000 check. It is also undisputed that before November 1, 1967, Mr. Kirby had

made arrangements with Hugh Campbell, president of the Bank
of Bellevue, to finance the $20,000 payment. Campbell testified
that he individually made a verbal agreement with Mr. Kirby
and told him that he would arrange to take care of the check
when and if it was presented to the Bank of Bellevue for payment. Campbell alerted the people in the bookkeeping department as to the arrangement he had with Mr. Kirby.

After some unsuccessful attempts at settlement, all of which
were refused by the defendants, this action for specific performance was filed on February 29, 1968.

The appellants' position is that the telephone call to the bookkeeper of the Bellevue bank was a presentment and demand for
payment of the check, or that presentment was excused under
the terms of the Uniform Commercial Code. Both parties rely
upon interpretations based upon the technical provisions of the
Code relating to presentment. Presentment is primarily necessary to charge secondary parties, none of whom are involved in
this case. See S. 3–501, U.C.C.

Section 3–504, U.C.C., defines presentment as: "A demand
for acceptance or payment made upon the maker, acceptor,
drawee or other payor by or on behalf of the holder." That section authorizes presentment "by mail"; "through a clearing
house"; or "at the place of * * * payment specified in the
instrument"; or " * * * at the place of business * * * of
the party to * * * pay." This section does not contemplate
that the presentment of a personal check drawn on a bank may
be made by telephone. It seems obvious that payment of a personal check or refusal of payment and dishonor by the drawee
bank necessitate exhibition or delivery of the instrument under
current banking practices. The telephone call in this case constituted an inquiry as to circumstances which might indicate
whether the check would or would not be paid upon future presentment in due course. It was not a presentment and demand
for payment envisioned by section 3–504, U.C.C. The situation
here did not excuse presentment under section 3–511, U.C.C.
Neither did it constitute refusal of payment and dishonor.

The basic issue here is what effect the delivery and acceptance of the $20,000 check had upon the rights of the parties un-
der the contract. Section 3–802, U.C.C., covers this situation.
That section provides in part: "(1) Unless otherwise agreed
where an instrument is taken for an underlying obligation
* * * the obligation is suspended pro tanto until the instrument is due or if it is payable on demand until its presentment.

If the instrument is dishonored action may be maintained on either the instrument or the obligation, * * * ." The draftsmen's comment No. 3 under this section states: "It is commonly said that a check or other negotiable instrument is 'conditional payment.' By this it is normally meant that taking the instrument is a surrender of the right to sue on the obligation until the instrument is due, but if the instrument is not paid on due presentment the right to sue on the obligation is 'revived.' * * * "

Here the sellers' right to terminate the contract and impose a forfeiture upon the purchasers was suspended until the check was presented for payment and dishonored.

* * *

The trial court found that the purchasers were entitled to a decree of specific performance of the contract. The judgment of the trial court was correct and is affirmed.

D. ACCOMMODATION PARTIES

Frequently a person who is asked to take a note or check will not do so because the maker or drawer is not a good credit risk. The taker may request that a third party act as a guarantor of the obligation to pay the instrument. Sometimes this guaranty is expressly stated. UCC § 3–416 sets forth rules defining the obligation when certain common forms of guaranty language are used. But in many cases a person who intends to act as guarantor does not expressly state that intention on the instrument. Instead he simply signs the instrument as co-maker or indorser. For example, Son wants to buy from Dealer equipment for use in Son's business venture. Dealer is willing to sell to Son on credit only if Mother signs the note as co-maker along with Son. An ambiguity results. Mother as a maker of the note is clearly liable as such. UCC § 3–413(1). But she may not have directly benefitted from the transaction in the sense that she has no interest either in Son's business venture or in the equipment for which the note was given. If the three parties to the transaction understand that Mother's signature simply represents her guaranty of payment of the note Mother is said to be an "accommodation party." She is liable on the note as maker. That is precisely what Dealer bargained for. But as accommodation party she has certain rights that Son, the other maker, does not have. For example, if Son doesn't pay the note when due and Mother has to pay, it is only fair that she should be able to recover from Son the amount that she has paid. He got the benefit of the transaction and ultimately should have to bear its burdens. UCC § 3–415(5) so provides. UCC § 3–415 is the only section of the UCC specifically dealing with accommodation parties and you should study it at this point.

An accommodation party or other surety, in addition to having rights against the person whose debt is guaranteed, also has certain rights against the creditor in the transaction. If Dealer by its actions reduces the likelihood that Son will pay the debt, Mother may be released from liability on her guaranty. For example, suppose the note is a four-year installment note for $5,000 plus finance charges and the resale value of the equipment at the time of sale is $10,000. Dealer normally takes a security interest in the equipment in a case of this kind. If Son defaults, Dealer can exercise its rights under the security interest to repossess the equipment and use the value it represents to pay Son's debt. The security interest benefits Dealer but it also benefits Mother because its existence makes it less likely that she will have to pay the debt. Indeed, if Mother pays the debt on Son's default, she is entitled to have the note and the security interest transferred to her. By subrogation, she succeeds to the rights that Dealer had against Son. See Comment 5 to UCC § 3–415, UCC § 9–504(5), and Reimann v. Hybertsen, 275 Or. 235, 550 P.2d 436 (1976). But Dealer's rights to repossess the equipment can be lost to other creditors of Son if Dealer doesn't perfect the security interest by filing a financing statement. Suppose Dealer doesn't file and one of Son's creditors seizes the equipment or Son goes into bankruptcy. Mother has been hurt by Dealer's negligence. See Farmers State Bank of Oakley v. Cooper, infra, p. 89. Or, suppose Dealer allows Son to miss many installment payments without insisting on payment or resorting to the collateral. Again, this action may make ultimate default by Son more likely thereby increasing Mother's risk. Pre-Code suretyship law provided that actions of this kind that adversely affected the surety could under some circumstances result in the surety's partial or complete release from the debt. This law as applied to negotiable instruments is set forth in UCC § 3–606, which, unfortunately, is not a model of clarity. It is important to note that these rights can be, and frequently are, waived by the guarantor by the terms of the instrument. In other words the creditor may bargain for liability of all makers of the note as principal debtors. The bargain should be clearly expressed.

Often accommodation party status is acquired by indorsement of the instrument. We saw previously that an indorsement usually is made to allow a negotiation of the instrument, but liability as an indorser may be avoided by an indorsement without recourse. UCC § 3-414(1). In that case the indorsement has a negotiation function but no liability function. The accommodation indorsement is the converse. It has no function in the negotiation process. Its sole purpose is to impose indorser's liability on the signer. An indorsement which on its face is not part of the process of negotiation is referred to as an "anomalous indorsement" or an indorsement not in the chain of title. See UCC § 3-415(4) and Comment 1 to § 3-415.

FITHIAN v. JAMAR

Court of Appeals of Maryland, 1979.
286 Md. 161, 410 A.2d 569.

COLE, JUDGE. The dispute in this case involves the rights and liabilities of co-makers of a note in a suit among themselves, where none of the disputants is a holder of the note. We granted certiorari to consider two questions, which simply stated are:

1. Whether a co-maker of a note was also an accommodation maker of the note and thus not liable to the party accommodated;

2. Whether the agreement of one co-maker to assume another co-maker's obligation on a note constitutes a defense to the latter when sued for contribution by the former.

In 1967 Walter Fithian (Walter) and Richard Jamar (Richard), who were employed as printers at Baltimore Business Forms, decided to form a partnership to carry on their own printing business. They applied to the People's Bank of Chestertown, Maryland (Bank) for an $11,000 business loan to enable them to purchase some equipment. The Bank agreed to lend the money to Walter and Richard only if Walter's wife, Connie, Richard's wife, Janet, and Walter's parents, Walter William (Bill) and Mildred Fithian would co-sign the note. The Executive Vice-President of the Bank explained that the additional signatures were required to make the Bank more secure. The note, which authorized confession of judgment in the event of default, was signed on its face in the bottom right-hand corner by these six parties. The monies loaned were deposited in Walter and Richard's business checking account and were used to purchase printing equipment.

By 1969, Walter and Richard were encountering business problems. They spoke with Frank Hogans (Hogans) and Gerald Bos (Bos) (who were interested in joining the business) about forming a corporation to be called J–F Printing Co., Inc. and refinancing the note so that it (the note) could become a corporate rather than an individual obligation. The business continued to falter and on March 23, 1972 Walter, Richard, Hogans and Bos met and entered into a written agreement in their individual capacities whereby Richard was to take over management and ownership of the business in exchange for his assumption of liability for the company's outstanding obligations, one of which was the note in question in this case. The agreement also provided that should Richard default in the performance of those obligations, Walter, Hogans, and Bos would have the right to terminate the agreement and resume ownership of the business.

Pursuant to the agreement Richard assumed control of the business but was unable to make any further payments on the note. Consequently, the Executive Vice-President of the Bank requested that Bill and Mildred Fithian pay the note in full. They did and the Bank assigned the note to them for whatever disposition they might choose. Bill demanded that Richard indemnify him for the total amount Bill paid on the note.

Receiving no satisfaction from Richard, Bill and Mildred sought judicial relief. On November 10, 1976, a confessed judgment against Richard and Janet of $8,953.95, the balance on the note paid by Bill and Mildred, with interest from January 18, 1974, court costs, and attorney's fees of $472.70, was entered in the Circuit Court for Kent County. Richard and Janet filed a motion to vacate the judgment, which the circuit court granted and ordered a hearing on the merits. Prior to trial, Richard and Janet filed a third party claim against Walter and Connie averring that as co-makers of the note, Walter and Connie were liable to Richard and Janet for any judgment that Bill and Mildred might recover against Richard and Janet. Walter and Connie counterclaimed contending that the agreement barred Richard's recovery.

The matter was brought to trial on August 25, 1977 before the circuit court, sitting without a jury. The court found that the J–F Printing Company, Inc. was never a de jure corporation and that those who attempted to act under that name were merely acting in their individual capacities; that the March 23, 1972 agreement was not material to the determination of the case; that Bill and Mildred were accommodation makers for

Richard, Janet, Walter and Connnie and were entitled to collect from any one of the four.

Final judgment was entered on September 6, 1977 for Bill and Mildred against Richard and Janet in the amount of $8,953.95, the principal sum due, plus $2,288.95, representing interest from January 18, 1974 to August 25, 1977. The court denied Bill and Mildred's claim for collection fees specified in the note and also entered a judgment for Richard and Janet on Walter and Connie's counterclaim. In the third party claim of Richard and Janet against Walter and Connie, judgment was entered for Richard and Janet in the amount of $5,621.45, fifty percent of the total judgment. The costs of the case were to be divided equally between Richard and Janet and Walter and Connie.

Bill and Mildred Fithian filed a timely appeal to the Court of Special Appeals, complaining of the circuit court's adverse ruling as to the collection fees. Walter and Connie took their own appeal, challenging the lower court's findings concerning both Connie's status in relation to the note and the materiality of the March, 1972 agreement. These appeals were consolidated for oral argument in that court.

In an unreported per curiam decision filed on April 7, 1978, Fithian v. Jamar, No. 946, Sept. Term, 1977, the Court of Special Appeals affirmed the circuit court in part and reversed in part. The Court of Special Appeals reversed on the issue of collection fees, ruling that there was a "valid and enforceable contract right of Bill and Mildred to the payment of collection costs * * *."; the Court of Special Appeals affirmed the circuit court's finding that Connie Fithian was a co-maker of the note, and not an accommodation party. The Court of Special Appeals also affirmed the trial court's finding that the March, 1972 agreement was not material to the case because it was "a private agreement between only two (2) of the six (6) makers of the note."

Walter and Connie (appellants) requested review of these rulings in this Court, and we granted their petition for certiorari on June 21, 1978 to consider the two questions presented: whether Connie Fithian was an accommodation maker of the note and thus not liable to the party accommodated; and whether the March, 1972 agreement constitutes a defense to Richard and Janet's (appellees) third party claim against Walter and Connie.

Our disposition of the questioned rulings requires us to reverse and remand. The error which occurred in the court below was caused in part by a failure to fully analyze the individual rights and obligations of Connie, Walter, Janet and Richard. Therefore, in the discussion which follows, in addition to examining the two questions presented, we will clarify the resulting rights and obligations of these parties.

Richard v. Connie

Connie's purpose in signing

Since there is no dispute that Connie signed the note, the answer to the first question depends on her purpose in doing so. This is made clear by Maryland Code (1975), § 3–415(1) of the Commercial Law Article which provides that an accommodation party is "one who signs the instrument in any capacity for the purpose of lending his name to another party to it." The undisputed evidence as presented by the Executive Vice-President of the Bank was to the effect that the wives' signatures were required before the Bank would make the loan to Walter and Richard. Such practices are common among lending institutions which recognize that

> [o]ne with money to lend, goods to sell or services to render may have doubts about a prospective debtor's ability to pay. In such cases he is likely to demand more assurance than the debtor's bare promise of payment. The prospective creditor can reduce his risk by requiring some sort of security. One form of security is the Article 9 security interest in the debtor's goods. Another type of security takes the form of joining a third person on the debtor's obligation. [J. White and R. Summers, Uniform Commercial Code § 13–12, at 425 (1972)].

It is readily apparent, therefore, that Connie lent her name to facilitate the loan transaction. As such she lent her name to two parties to the instrument, Richard and Walter, to enable them to receive a *joint* loan for the purchase of equipment for their printing business, thereby giving the Bank the added assurance of having another party to the obligation. Connie signed as an accommodation party as to both Walter and Richard.

Nor is there any merit in the argument advanced by Richard that Connie must be either a co-maker or an accommodation party, that she cannot be both. The actual language of § 3–415(1) indicates that an accommodation party also signs in a particular capacity, as maker, acceptor or indorser of an instrument. The Official Comment 1 to § 3–415 explains that

> [s]ubsection (1) recognizes that an accommodation party is always a surety (which includes a guarantor), and it is his

only distinguishing feature. He differs from other sureties only in that his liability is on the instrument and he is a surety for another party to it. His obligation is therefore determined by the capacity in which he signs. An accommodation maker or acceptor is bound on the instrument without any resort to his principal, while an accommodation indorser may be liable only after presentment, notice of dishonor and protest.

Moreover, § 3–415(2) refers specifically to the liability of an accommodation party "in the capacity in which he has signed." It follows, therefore, that the fact that Connie was a co-maker of the note does not preclude her from also being an accommodation party.

Section 3–415(5) of the Commercial Law Article states that "[a]n accommodation party is not liable to the party accommodated"; thus, Connie is not liable to Richard. Our predecessors, prior to Maryland's adoption of the Uniform Commercial Code, explained the reasons for this proposition in Crothers v. National Bank, 158 Md. 587, 593, 149 A. 270, 273 (1930):

> Since the accommodating party lends his credit by request to the party accommodated upon the assumption that the latter will discharge the debt when due, it is an implied term of this agreement that the party accommodated cannot acquire any right of action against the accommodating party.

Richard contends, however, that Connie intended to accommodate only her husband, Walter. Even if there were evidence to this effect (and there is none), the subjective intent of a co-maker of a note is of little weight when objective facts and circumstances unambiguously demonstrate the capacity in which the note was signed. Seaboard Finance Co. of Connecticut, Inc. v. Dorman, 4 Conn.Cir. 154, 227 A.2d 441 (1966); Hover v. Magley, 116 App.Div. 84, 101 N.Y.S. 245 (1906). It is clear to us that the signatures of both wives were required to effect this joint business venture and thus Connie's signature was as much an accommodation to Richard as it was to Walter. We hold that Connie was an accommodation maker and that she cannot be liable to Richard, the party accommodated. The Court of Special Appeals erroneously held to the contrary.

Janet v. Connie

The preceding discussion of Connie's status demonstrates that each of the four parties, Walter, Connie, Richard, and Janet, has certain rights and obligations with respect to this note which are not affected by his or her marital status. The court below erred in not fully analyzing these separate rights and obligations. It follows that our finding that Connie has no liability to Richard in no way changes any obligation she may have to Janet. Janet, as well as Connie, is a co-accommodation maker on this note.

The question is therefore whether one co-accommodation maker who pays more than her proportionate share of the debt has a right of contribution against another co-accommodation maker. The Uniform Commercial Code contains no provision expressly dealing with the right of an accommodation party to contribution from another accommodation party. However, the Code does provide that the principles of the common law remain applicable "[u]nless displaced by the particular provisions" of the Code. Maryland Code (1975), § 1–103 of the Commercial Law Article.

That an accommodation maker has a right of contribution from a co-accommodation maker is a settled principle of the law. The Restatement of Security provides

> A surety who in the performance of his own obligation discharges more than his proportionate share of the principal's duty is entitled to contribution from a co-surety. [Restatement of Security § 149 (1941)].

* * *

Maryland has followed this rule. *Jackson v. Cupples,* 239 Md. 637, 212 A.2d 273 (1965). *Jackson* was decided after the effective date of the U.C.C. in Maryland, but the note in question had been executed prior to that date. The Court held that a co-surety who pays a debt has a right of contribution from his co-sureties.

This Court has not addressed this question in regard to a note controlled by the U.C.C. Our research revealed only one case which directly confronted the effect of the U.C.C. on the common law rule. The court stated that the U.C.C. does not change the rule of suretyship law permitting contribution by one surety from a co-surety. *McLochlin v. Miller,* 139 Ind.App. 443, 217 N.E.2d 50 (1966).

Accordingly Janet has a right of contribution against Connie. But this right to contribution is an inchoate claim which does not ripen into being unless and until Janet pays more than her proportionate share to Bill and Mildred. *Cotham and Maldonado v. Board,* 260 Md. 556, 566–67, 273 A.2d 115 (1971). Judgment can be entered on behalf of Janet against Connie, but it must be fashioned so that it may not be enforced until Janet proves she actually paid more than her proportionate share to Bill and Mildred.[1] Baltimore County v. Stitzel, 26 Md.App. 175, 184–88, 337 A.2d 721 (1975).

Richard v. Walter

[Omitted is the portion of the opinion in which the court held that Richard's agreement in 1972 to assume all liabilities of the printing business, including the note, precluded any right of contribution that Richard would otherwise have against Walter, his joint obligor on the note.]

Janet v. Walter

That the 1972 agreement serves as a defense by Walter against Richard in no way serves to insulate Walter against Janet. Janet's status as an accommodation maker is unaffected by the agreement. As an accommodation maker, Janet has a right to look to any principal, including Walter for any amounts she actually pays. Maryland Code (1975), § 3–415 of the Commercial Law Article. Janet's status as Richard's wife does not affect her status as an accommodation maker. She is entitled to judgment from either principal when she actually pays any amount of the debt.

In summary, Richard is not entitled to judgment against Walter because of the agreement. Rather, Walter is entitled to indemnification from Richard for any amount Walter is forced to pay. Richard is not entitled to judgment against Connie because an accommodation party is not liable to the party accommodated. Janet is entitled to contribution from her co-surety, Connie, the judgment being unenforceable unless and until Janet proves she actually has paid more than her proportionate share of the debt to Bill and Mildred. Similarly, Janet as a surety is entitled to judgment against Walter as a principal for any amount of the debt for which Janet proves payment.[3]

1. A surety who is called upon to pay more than his proportionate share of the debt has a right of contribution from his co-sureties in an amount not to exceed each co-surety's proportionate share of the debt. See Schindel v. Danzer, 161 Md. 384, 157 A. 283 (1931); 72 C.J.S. Principal and Surety § 369 (1951). Here the note was signed by four sureties (Bill, Mildred, Connie and Janet); Janet's proportionate share of indebtedness to her co-sureties is 25% of the debt.

3. Whether Bill and Mildred were entitled to judgment in the full amount of the debt against Janet we do not decide because Janet did not appeal from that judgment.

NOTE

In footnote 3 the court states that it does not decide whether Bill and Mildred were entitled to recover the full amount of the debt from Janet. How much were Bill and Mildred entitled to recover from Janet? 25 % ?

PROBLEM

Manny owned 50% of the capital stock of Corporation and was its President. Moe and Jack each owned 25%. Corporation needed money for working capital and borrowed it from Bank which insisted as a condition to the loan that Manny sign the note because of the precarious financial condition of Corporation. The note was signed as follows:

Corporation

By Manny, President

Manny, in his individual capacity.

The note contained the following clause. "All signers of the note are principals and not accommodation parties, guarantors or other sureties." The loan, which is unsecured, was made by crediting the entire principal amount to Corporation's account with Bank and was used entirely for corporate purposes. Corporation has defaulted on the loan. After Corporation's default on the loan to Bank, Manny paid Bank the entire unpaid balance amounting to $10,000. Is Manny an accommodation party? Is Manny entitled to reimbursement from Corporation for the $10,000 paid to Bank or are his rights limited to a claim for contribution? Would Manny's rights be any different if he owned 100% of the stock of Corporation rather than 50%?

WILMINGTON TRUST CO. v. GESULLO

Delaware Superior Court, New Castle County, 1980.
29 U.C.C.Rep. 144.

O'HARA, J. Appellant Wilmington Trust Company ("W.T.C."), plaintiff below, brought suit against appellee Leonard Gesullo ("Gesullo"), defendant below, in the Justice of the Peace Court, seeking recovery on a note signed by appellee. Following a trial on the merits judgment was entered in favor of Gesullo on June 15, 1977. W.T.C. moved for a new trial, below,

which was denied on September 7, 1977. Thereafter, this appeal
was filed in the Superior Court.

* * *

I

Around the beginning of September, 1971, Vernon Steele
(who was not made a party to the action below) desired to purchase a certain 1967 Brockway truck equipped with a diesel engine from Healthways Co., Inc. ("Healthways"). Gesullo was at
that time the chief executive officer of Healthways, a fifty percent shareholder therein, and Healthways' sales representative
in the negotiations with Steele. In order to finance this purchase Steele attempted to borrow $5,250, the purchase price,
from W.T.C. However, W.T.C. insisted as a pre-condition to approval of the loan that Steele obtain Gesullo's signature on the
note and that Steele grant to W.T.C. a security interest in the
Brockway truck. On September 24, 1971, both Steele and Gesullo signed a note with W.T.C. The proceeds of this loan, in the
amount of $5,250, were made payable by check to Steele and
Healthways. None of the loan proceeds were payable to Gesullo. Also on September 24, 1971, Steele and W.T.C. entered an
agreement, to which Gesullo was not a party, which granted
W.T.C. a security interest in the Brockway truck as collateral
for the loan. On this same date, Healthways transferred the
truck to Steele and received the $5,250 check as payment. The
security interest of W.T.C. in the truck was never entered on the
certificate of title as required by 21 Del C §§ 2331–2332, and no
other attempt to perfect, pursuant to 6 Del C § 9–302, was
made.

Installment payments were apparently made on the loan as
required until March 30, 1973. Steele contacted W.T.C. on or
about May 18, 1973 and requested that the time for making the
March 30 payment be extended to May 30, 1973. W.T.C. agreed
to the extension for which Steele paid a separate consideration
of $65. Gesullo was not contacted about this extension and did
not consent thereto either before or after W.T.C. and Steele
agreed upon the extension.

Sometime prior to September, 1974, the Brockway truck was
involved in an accident. Steele brought the damaged truck to
Healthways and requested Gesullo to have the major salvage-
able parts (i.e., engine, rear-end and transmission) removed and
installed into a Mack truck cab and frame. The rebuilt Mack
truck was then to be sold by Healthways on behalf of Steele.

On or about June 13, 1974, Gesullo contacted W.T.C. and requested a payoff figure on the 1971 loan. At first he was advised that $500 was owed thereon, and Healthways paid this amount to W.T.C. On or about June 20, 1974, a W.T.C. employee contacted Gesullo and informed him that an additional $173.54 was needed to clear the loan account. Healthways also paid this additional amount to W.T.C. On or about September 13, 1974, Healthways, on behalf of Steele, sold the Mack truck containing the Brockway parts to a third person. No lien was noted on the certificate of title to this vehicle. On or about September 16, 1975, a W.T.C. representative wrote to Gesullo claiming that an additional $1,104.56 remained to be paid in the 1971 loan and requesting Gesullo to pay this amount. Gesullo refused and this suit followed.

* * *

III

The first substantive question to be resolved is whether Gesullo was an "accommodation party" on the note. The Delaware Commercial Code, 6 Del.C. § 3–415(1), provides:

"An accommodation party is one who signs the instrument in any capacity for the purpose of lending his name to another party to it." The Delaware Study Comment to this section makes clear that an accommodation party is always a surety. This is important because a surety is entitled to certain special defenses under the Code. See 6 Del.C. § 3–606.

The most significant element in determining whether an individual is an accommodation party is the intention of the parties to the commercial transaction. 2 Anderson, Uniform Commercial Code § 3–415:9 (2d ed 1971). The most direct evidence of intention in this regard may be found where words of guarantee are expressly added to the signature of one claiming accommodation status on the face of the commercial instrument. See 6 Del.C. § 3–416(4). However, where there is no direct evidence of accommodation status on the face of the instrument, such status may nonetheless be shown by parol evidence if the rights of a holder in due course are not involved. 6 Del.C. § 3–415(3). In cases where parol evidence is admissible and necessary to a determination of the status of parties to a commercial instrument, the court will look to the facts and circumstances connected with the transaction and draw reasonable and logical inferences therefrom. MacArthur v. Cannon, Conn.App., 229 A2d 372 (1967).

Because receipt of proceeds from the instrument or other direct benefit will generally be inconsistent with accommodation status, courts have focused on this aspect of the transaction. Stockwell v. Bloomfield State Bank, Ind.App, 367 N.E.2d 42 [22 U.C.C.Rep. 726] (1977); White & Summers, Uniform Commercial Code § 13–13 at 431 (1972); 2 Anderson, supra § 3–415:9. Other important factors include the source of collateral used to secure the loan, Wilmington Trust Co. v. Sutton, Del.Super., C.A. No. 674, 1976 (unreported decision dated October 11, 1979), and the lender's motive in securing multiple signatures on the instrument. Id.; see also Stockwell v. Bloomfield State Bank, 367 N.E.2d at 44–45; and compare MacArthur v. Cannon, 229 A.2d at 377. The application of these factors in the case sub judice supports Gesullo's assertion that he was an accommodation party to Steele on the loan note.

First, the proceeds of the 1971 note were made payable to Steele and Healthways; none of the proceeds were payable to Gesullo. By turning the endorsed proceeds check over to Gesullo as Healthways' representative, Steele acquired possession of the Brockway truck. Thus, Steele received the full and direct benefit of the proceeds. By comparison, the benefit Gesullo derived from the proceeds was indirect and relatively small, i.e., as a fifty percent shareholder he had an interest in the profit (if any) which Healthways gained by sale of the truck to Steele. See Stockwell v. Bloomfield State Bank, 367 N.E.2d at 45. Secondly, only Steele provided collateral, i.e., the Brockway truck, to secure payment of the note. Gesullo was not even a party to this security agreement. Thirdly, W.T.C. initially refused to make the loan to Steele and agreed to do so only if Steele could get Gesullo to co-sign the note. This is a strong indication that W.T.C. considered Steele to be the principal obligor on the note and Gesullo only secondarily liable. Compare MacArthur v. Cannon, above, with Stockwell v. Bloomfield State Bank, above. On this point, the court takes note of a letter dated September 16, 1975 from a W.T.C. representative to Gesullo which stated:

> "On September 24, 1971, you cosigned a note * * * for Mr. Vernon P. Steele * * *

> "As comaker, you are responsible for payment of the loan in the event the original maker fails to meet his obligation with us." [See attachment to appellee's answers to appellant's first interrogatories.]

Consideration of all of these factors leads the court to conclude that Gesullo signed the 1971 note as an accommodation party for the benefit of Steele.

IV

As an accommodation party to the 1971 note, Gesullo seeks to assert special suretyship defenses under 6 Del.C. § 3–606 which provides in pertinent part:

"(1) The holder discharges any party to the instrument to the extent that without such party's consent the holder

(a) without express reservation of rights, releases, or agrees not to sue any person against whom the party has to the knowledge of the holder, a right of recourse or agrees to suspend the right to enforce against such person the instrument or collateral or otherwise discharges such person * * *; or

(b) unjustifiably impairs any collateral for the instrument given by or on behalf of the party or any person against whom he has a right of recourse."

Gesullo first argues that he is entitled to a full discharge from liability on the note because W.T.C. and Steele entered an agreement to extend the time for payment of an installment due on March 30, 1973 to May 30, 1973. The date of this agreement was May 18, 1973.

The Delaware Study Comment to § 3–606(1)(a) expressly states that "[a]n extension of time * * * [is] covered by the language 'agrees to suspend the right to enforce.'" This provision is consistent with the general rule in Delaware suretyship law that a binding agreement between the creditor and the principal debtor to extend time for payment will discharge a surety who has not consented thereto. Equitable Trust Co. v. Shaw, Del.Ch., 194 A. 24 (1937); Simpson, Handbook on the Law of Suretyship, § 73 (1950); Restatement of Security § 129 (1941).

W.T.C. does not argue that the 1973 extension agreement was not binding between itself and Steele. Also, the undisputed facts in this case clearly establish that Gesullo was, at all pertinent times, completely unaware of the 1973 extension agreement and never consented to it.[1] Moreover, there is nothing on the

---

1. It does no good to argue, as W.T.C. has done herein, that Gesullo would almost surely have agreed to the extension had he known of it.

The simple fact is that Gesullo did not consent to the extension of time.

In reaching this conclusion, the court is mindful that an accommoda-

face of the 1971 loan note, or in the circumstances of its negotiation or the negotiation of the 1973 extension agreement, to indicate that W.T.C. expressly reserved its rights against Gesullo as permitted by § 3–606(2). Compare Parnes v. Celia's, Inc., N.J. Super.App.Div., 239 A.2d 19 (1968). Therefore, Gesullo, as an accommodation party on the 1971 note, is entitled to discharge from liability thereunder pursuant to § 3–606(1)(a).

    W.T.C. has sought to avoid the discharge mandated by § 3–606(1)(a) in this case by focusing the court's attention on a provision in the 1971 security agreement executed in connection with the loan note.[2] W.T.C. claims that this provision somehow removes the 1973 extension agreement from the purview of the statute. The only possible basis for such argument is that this provision constituted either a consent by Gesullo to extensions of time or a reservation of rights by W.T.C. as against Gesullo. As to the first basis, Gesullo cannot be said to have consented to anything under a document to which he was not a party. See UCC § 3–119, Comment 2. As to the second basis, while no special form of words is required to create a reservation of rights, a creditor must clearly manifest an intention to reserve its rights against the accommodation party. 2 Anderson, supra

tion party's "consent" under the Code may be given in advance of an extension agreement between the creditor and the principal obligor, simultaneously with such agreement, or subsequent thereto. UCC § 3–606, Comment 2. Additionally, such "consent" may be expressed or may be implied from conduct of the accommodation party which shows assent to the creditor's action. White & Summers, supra § 13–15 at 436. There is simply no evidence in the record presented upon which the court could find that Gesullo had expressly or impliedly consented to the W.T.C.-Steele extension agreement either before or after its inception. To the contrary, Gesullo's unchallenged evidence indicates clearly that there was no consent clause in the 1971 note that he signed, and that he was completely unaware of the 1973 extension agreement and never discussed it with either W.T.C. or Steele at any time prior to the institution of these proceedings. Deposition of Leonard Gesullo at 20–21, 26–27. Consequently, Gesullo cannot be said to have impliedly consented to the 1973 extension agreement by making payments on the 1971 note subsequent to the agreement of which he was completely unaware.

2. The pertinent clause provides:

"Debtor further represents, warrants and agrees: (a) No delay or omission by Bank in exercising any right or remedy hereunder or with respect to any Indebtedness shall operate as a waiver thereof or of any other right or remedy, and no single or partial exercise thereof shall preclude any other or further exercise thereof or the exercise of any other right or remedy. Bank may remedy any default by Debtor hereunder or with respect to any Indebtedness in any reasonable manner without waiving the default remedied and without waiving any other prior or subsequent default by Debtor. All rights and remedies of Bank hereunder are cumulative."

Interestingly, the argument based on this clause is not discussed in the parties' briefs on the cross-motions, and was only raised by W.T.C.'s counsel at oral argument.

§ 3–606:11.   The security agreement provision relied upon by
W.T.C. provides no evidence of such intent.   The only parties
mentioned in the clause are W.T.C. ("Bank") and Steele ("Debt-
or").   There is no discussion whatsoever of rights or obligations
as between W.T.C. and Gesullo.   Therefore, on the facts presented it is impossible for the court to conclude that W.T.C. had
expressly reserved its rights against Gesullo via the security
agreement.

The only remaining issue to be resolved is the extent to
which Gesullo is entitled to be discharged from liability.   The
language of § 3–606(1)(a) indicates that an accommodation party
is entitled to discharge only "to the extent that" the creditor has
agreed to suspend its right to enforce the instrument against the
principal obligor.   On the basis of this language an argument
can be made in the instant case that Gesullo is entitled only to
pro tanto discharge limited to the amount of the March, 1973
installment ($173.54).   While reported cases discussing the appli-
cation of this pro tanto language in the context of unjustifiable
impairment of collateral under § 3–606(1)(b) are legion, counsel
for the parties have not directed the court's attention to any ex-
tension-of-time cases discussing the issue;   nor has the court's
own research disclosed any such cases decided under the Code.
Since the purpose of this statute was to "incorporate basic principles of suretyship law into the negotiable instruments law,"
Delaware Study Comment to § 3–606, the court will refer to that
body of law for assistance in determining the extent of discharge to which Gesullo is entitled on the instant note.

As stated above, the general rule in suretyship law is that a
nonconsenting surety is discharged by a binding creditor-debtor
agreement to extend time for payment.   However, in cases
where the principal debtor's obligation to pay arises in installments rather than at a single point in time, another rule comes
into play.   In such cases it has been held that where successive
payments are to be made at fixed periods, a creditor's extension
of time as to one payment will discharge the surety as to it, but
not as to subsequent payments which have not yet become due
at the time of the extension agreement.   74 Am.Jur.2d Suretyship § 50 (1974); 72 C.J.S. Principal and Surety § 170 (1951); 38
C.J.S. Guaranty § 75(a) (1943); Croydon Gas Co. v. Dickinson, 2
C.P.D. 46 (1876).   The key element which triggers operation of
this rule is a finding that the principal debtor's successive obligations to pay are divisible and severable from each other.   If
the principal's debt is not entirely divisible, then the rule of partial discharge does not apply, and an extension of time will fully

discharge the surety. 10 Williston on Contracts § 1222 (3d ed. 1967); Stearn's Law of Suretyship § 6.26 (5th ed. 1951); I Brandt, Suretyship and Guaranty § 393 (3d ed. 1905); Compare Croydon Gas Co. v. Dickinson, above, with Midland Motor Showrooms, Ltd. v. Newman, 2 K.B. 256 (1929); but see 43 Harv.L. Rev. 503 (1930).

Examples of the kinds of situations in which the rule of partial discharge has most commonly been applied include: consignment contracts where the consignee, whose performance has been guaranteed by a surety, is obligated to make periodic remittances to the consignor based upon the amount of sales during each defined period of time, e.g., I. J. Cooper Rubber Co. v. Johnson, Tenn.Supr., 182 S.W. 593 (1916); indebtedness evidenced by multiple notes which mature at different times and on which payment has been guaranteed by the same surety, e.g., Owings v. MacKenzie, Mo.Supr., 33 S.W. 802 (1896); real estate lease agreements where the rents, payment of which have been guaranteed by a surety, are to be paid in periodic installments, e.g., Sutter v. Nenninger, N.Y. Cnty., 189 N.Y.S. 662 (1921). The rationale in these cases is that the successive obligations to pay are separate and independent of each other, so that an extension of time as to one payment does not extend time for performance as to future payments. In other words, each obligation to pay is treated as though it were a separate contract.

The case at bar does not fall into any of the above-mentioned categories. There is but a single installment loan contract here, and Steele's indebtedness thereunder, for which Gesullo guaranteed payment, is evidenced by a single note. Moreover, although the note specifies that repayment was to be made in thirty-six consecutive monthly installments, there was but one debt to be satisfied, not thirty-six separate and independent debts. In such a situation it strains logic to say that the principal's debt is entirely divisible. See Midland Motor Showrooms, Ltd. v. Newman, above. On this basis alone, the court might be warranted in holding that the rule of partial discharge has no application and Gesullo should be entitled to full discharge as a result of the extension of time granted on the March, 1973 payment. However, there is another significant factor in this case which the court believes deserves consideration.

The face of the 1971 note which Gesullo signed as an accommodation party contains a rather standard acceleration clause. This clause provided in pertinent part that "if any . . . installment shall remain unpaid for a period of thirty (30) days the entire unpaid balance may be declared due and payable." At the time W.T.C. and Steele entered the binding extension agreement (May 18, 1973), the March 30 installment was already forty-nine days overdue. But for that agreement, W.T.C. could have accelerated the entire debt immediately. More importantly, Gesullo could also have accelerated Steele's repayment obligation by way of subrogation to W.T.C.'s rights and remedies had Gesullo chosen to fully satisfy the debt after Steele's default continued into May, 1973.[3] See Stearn's Law of Suretyship, supra §§ 11.1, 11.2 and 11.5; see also Restatement on Security, supra § 141. However, the extension agreement destroyed this option. In addition to extending by two months the time within which Steele could make the March payment, the agreement also necessarily suspended W.T.C.'s rights under the acceleration clause, as well as Gesullo's potential rights via subrogation, to declare the entire remaining balance immediately due and payable. Therefore, because the extent to which W.T.C. agreed "to suspend the right to enforce" the note against Steele related to the entire unpaid balance, Gesullo is entitled to be fully discharged from liability on the note pursuant to § 3–606(1)(a).

The court is aware that the decision herein is at least superficially at odds with the case of Cohn v. Spitzer, N.Y.Supr.App. Div., 129 N.Y.S. 104 (1911). Generally the facts in Cohn are not essentially dissimilar to the facts in the case at bar, and the acceleration clause in the Cohn debt instrument[4] is functionally equivalent to the instant acceleration clause. The Cohn court chose to apply the rule of partial discharge notwithstanding the presence of the acceleration clause, holding simply that the acceleration provision "was exclusively for the benefit of the obligee [i.e., the creditor] or its assigns." Id. at 106. By holding that the sureties had no rights under this provision, it appears that the court failed to give due deference to the sureties' potential rights by way of subrogation. Therefore, this Court respectfully declines to follow the Cohn rationale as to the effect

---

3. This holding is fully supported by § 3–415(5) of the Code which provides:

"An accommodation party is not liable to the party accommodated, and if he pays the instrument has a right of recourse on the instrument against such party."

4. The acceleration clause in Cohn provided that if default in the pay-

ment of any installment for principal or interest occurred and such installment remained unpaid for twenty days, the entire remaining balance "should, at the option of said obligee, its legal representatives or assigns, become and be due and payable immediately thereafter." 129 N.Y.S. at 105.

of an acceleration provision on a surety's right to full or partial discharge.

The court is confident that the rules announced herein are entirely justifiable in today's commercial marketplace and will not impose unreasonable burdens on lending institutions. While it has often been said that sureties have been ancient favorites of the law, White & Summers, supra § 13–14 at 432, their position as compared to that of creditors is rather precarious as a practical matter. Generally, the creditor owes no duty to the surety to diligently pursue the principal debtor in order to directly enforce the debtor's obligations. Stearn's Law of Suretyship, supra § 6.35. Additionally, the creditor has no duty to notify the surety of default by the principal debtor, Simpson, supra § 41, or to notify the surety that an extension of time which also expressly reserves the creditor's rights against the surety has been granted to the principal debtor. U.C.C. § 3–606, Comment 4; 72 C.J.S. Principal and Surety, supra § 153. Given these inherent disadvantages with which sureties must cope, it cannot be seriously contended that the result reached herein is overly solicitous for these "ancient favorites of the law." Moreover, the prudent lender who seeks to avoid the impact of this decision can easily do so by obtaining the surety's prior consent to an extension of time or by including an express reservation of rights in the extension agreement.

Lastly, the court notes that although most of the commentators to the Code have not addressed the impact of § 3–606 in the context of an installment loan contract which contains an acceleration provision, the one treatise which has recognized and discussed the problem appears to concur with the approach taken herein. See 2 Hart and Willier, Commercial Paper Under the U.C.C. § 13.21[3] (1976).

V

Because the court has determined that appellee is entitled to full discharge under § 3–606(1)(a), the court does not reach appellee's contention that he is also entitled to discharge under § 3–606(1)(b) allegedly because appellant unjustifiably impaired the collateral given by Steele to secure the loan. The court notes, however, that under the facts of this case Gesullo's impairment of collateral claim is not insubstantial.

VI

Based on the foregoing analysis, the court holds that summary judgment should be entered in favor of appellee Gesullo, and appellant's motion for summary judgment should be denied, and the appeal herein should be dismissed.

It is so ordered.

NOTE

In the principal case W.T.C. made the mistake of granting the extension to Steele "without express reservation of rights" against Gesullo. What should W.T.C. have done to protect itself when it granted the extension? If W.T.C. had reserved rights would Gesullo have been entitled to any notice? If W.T.C. reserved rights and Gesullo found out about it, what effect would the reservation of rights have had on Gesullo's rights? See UCC § 3–606(2).

FARMERS STATE BANK OF OAKLEY v. COOPER

Supreme Court of Kansas, 1980.
277 Kan. 547, 608 P.2d 929.

MILLER, JUSTICE:

* * *

The factual background is necessary to an understanding of the issues. In July, 1971, Dr. Michael P. Cooper, son of defendant Paul A. Cooper, Jr., moved with his wife Georgia to Oakley, Kansas. Michael, a chiropractor, intended to establish a practice in Oakley. He approached the bank for a loan in order to purchase equipment and remodel his office, rented from the bank and located on an upper floor of the bank building. The bank committed a line of credit of five thousand dollars. The president of the bank testified that when the original commitment was made, the professional equipment, household items, and automobile that were offered as security were not sufficient to completely secure the loan; therefore Paul Cooper's signature was necessary to protect the bank for the total amount.

The first promissory note in the amount of three thousand dollars was executed on August 12, 1971. It was signed by Michael P. Cooper, Georgia L. Cooper, and Paul A. Cooper, Jr. The note was secured by a security agreement of the same date, designating all equipment, instruments, and furnishings in the office and all household goods located in the Michael Cooper residence, and a 1967 Chevrolet, as security. Michael P. Cooper and Georgia Cooper, together with William B. Griffith as agent for the bank, signed the security agreement. The security agreement was never perfected.

Four additional notes for amounts under one thousand dollars, signed only by Michael P. Cooper, were made in subsequent months. The five notes were consolidated on February 12, 1972, when a note for five thousand dollars, secured by the security agreement of August 12, 1971, was executed. This note was signed by Michael, Georgia, and Paul Cooper. This note was renewed by the execution of new notes signed by all three persons on August 12, 1972, February 12, 1973, December 1, 1973, and July 1, 1974. Some payments of principal and interest were made; the face amount of the final renewal note, due January 1, 1975, was $4,550.63. The majority if not all of the payments on the notes were made by defendant Paul Cooper. The final note is on a form substantially different from the earlier notes

*   *   *

Michael's chiropractic practice did not prosper. During 1975 he moved from Oakley to the State of Washington. It then appeared that Dr. Cooper had a splendid opportunity in Washington, and the bank was hopeful that his practice would prosper there enabling him to satisfy the note. The bank gave permission to Dr. Cooper to remove the collateral to Washington. The move was not financially successful, and Dr. Cooper returned to Oakley for a short time during 1976. He then moved to Macksville, Kansas, and later returned to his home in Shawnee, Kansas. He has not practiced chiropractic medicine since his return to Kansas. Dr. Cooper disposed of some of the collateral; the only items the defendant has seen in his recent possession are a handheld vibrator, a sewing machine, and the automobile. The record does not indicate any attempt of the bank to obtain payment from Dr. Cooper or to foreclose on the remaining collateral.

On October 26, 1977, the bank filed suit against defendant Paul Cooper for the balance due on the note plus accrued interest. Paul Cooper filed an answer and counterclaim, and later filed a third-party petition against his son, Dr. Michael Cooper, and his son's wife, Georgia, for indemnity in the event a judgment is entered against Paul Cooper and in favor of the bank.

Neither Michael nor Georgia Cooper have answered or otherwise appeared in this action.

* * *

The third and determinative issue is whether the bank, by failing to perfect its security agreement and by allowing the removal of the collateral from Kansas, unjustifiably impaired the collateral, thus discharging the defendant, an accommodation party. Defendant claims discharge under [U.C.C. § 3–606(1)(b)].

The discharge provisions of that statute apply only to signers who occupy the position of sureties, such as accommodation parties.

* * *

Is defendant released from part or all of his liability because the bank failed to perfect its security agreement and Dr. Cooper has since sold a part of the collateral? Defendant contends that the failure of the bank to perfect its security agreement constituted an unjustifiable impairment of collateral. A review of the principles involved may be helpful.

An unperfected security agreement is valid and effective between the parties to the agreement according to its terms. [U.C.C. §] 9–201; and see [U.C.C. §] 9–203. Ordinarily, a financing statement must be filed to perfect it. [U.C.C. §] 9–302. Except in the circumstances encompassed by [U.C.C. §] 9–307, a secured party's interest in collateral is prior to that of a purchaser if the security interest is perfected; however, if the interest is not perfected, a buyer for value without knowledge takes free of the security interest. [U.C.C. §] 9–301(1)(c).

Defendant relies on Redlon v. Heath, 59 Kan. 255, 52 P. 862 (1898). The creditor in *Heath* recorded the mortgage in the wrong county; the error was not discovered until other mortgages, exceeding the total value of the property, had been properly filed of record. We noted in that case that the evidence showed that the mortgaged land was of sufficient value to have paid prior encumbrances as well as the amount of the improperly filed one, but that other mortgages, later filed and "sufficient in amount to absorb the entire property, took precedence and swept his security away." We held that the person who signed the note as a surety or accommodation party was released from liability because of the failure of the creditor to record the mortgage in the right county and thus protect the collateral.

The U.C.C. has codified this rule in [U.C.C. §] 3–606(1)(*b*) which provides for discharge of any party *to the extent* that without such person's consent the holder unjustifiably impairs collateral. It is clear from the statute that the release is only *pro tanto*, and the cases so hold. See Langeveld v. L. R. Z. H. Corporation, 74 N.J. 45, 376 A.2d 931, 22 U.C.C.Rep. 106 (1977), and Mikanis Trading Corp. v. Block, 59 App.Div.2d 689, 398 N.Y.S.2d 679 (1977). The failure of the holder of a security agreement to perfect it, which failure results in a loss of available collateral to an accommodation party, is an impairment of the collateral. Here, the sale of collateral was wrongful, if not criminal (see K.S.A. 21–3734), and the failure of the bank to perfect its security agreement has resulted in a loss of some of the collateral, so far as the defendant is concerned. Part of the collateral is gone, and presumably is not subject to the security agreement.

Should the defendant be released from liability? We think not. No evidence of the value of the missing collateral, or of the value of the remaining collateral, was offered. No such evidence is contained within the record.

[UCC §] 3–307(2) provides:

"When signatures are admitted or established, production of the instrument entitles a holder to recover on it unless the defendant establishes a defense."

The official U.C.C. comment to this section reads in part:

"2. Once signatures are proved or admitted, a holder makes out his case by mere production of the instrument, and is entitled to recover in the absence of any further evidence. *The defendant has the burden of establishing any and all defenses*, not only in the first instance but by a preponderance of the total evidence." (Emphasis supplied.)

The bank did not know until trial of the sale or disposal; it did not know when, to whom, or for what price or on what terms it was sold or transferred. Defendant had all this evidence available; his son, the third party defendant, had the information; defendant knew of his son's whereabouts but the bank did not; defendant could have called his son as a witness had he wished to do so.

We conclude that the burden of proof was upon defendant to establish the extent to which the collateral was impaired. See Christensen v. McAtee, 256 Or. 333, 473 P.2d 659, 8 U.C.C.Rep. 66 (1970); Langeveld v. L. R. Z. H. Corporation, 74 N.J. 45, 376 A.2d 931 (1977); and Telpner v. Hogan, 17 Ill.App.3d 152, 308

N.E.2d 7 (1974). Having failed to establish the extent of the impairment, defendant is liable for the full amount of the note.

* * *

E. LIABILITY OF TRANSFEROR

We have seen that a transfer of an instrument may or may not involve an indorsement of the instrument. If the transferor indorses the instrument he has liability as an indorser unless he indorses without recourse, UCC § 3–414(1), and if he does not indorse he has no liability at all on the instrument. UCC § 3–401(1). But a nonindorsing transferor, though not liable on the instrument, may have liability arising out of the transaction of transfer. UCC § 3–417(2) imposes certain implied warranties on nongratuitous transfers that the nonindorsing transferor makes to his transferee. In the case of an indorsing transferor the warranties are made not only to the transferee but also to subsequent holders. The indorsing transferor is subject to both the liability of UCC § 3–414(1) and that of UCC § 3–417(2). The two liabilities are distinct and different in content. An indorser's liability is to pay the instrument if dishonored. Liability under UCC § 3–417(2) is for breach of warranty. The beneficiary of the warranty must show breach of the warranty and the fact and amount of damages resulting from the breach.

HARTFORD LIFE INSURANCE CO. v. TITLE GUARANTEE CO.

United States Court of Appeals, District of Columbia Circuit, 1975.
520 F.2d 1170.

WEIGEL, DISTRICT JUDGE. This case turns upon facts which are somewhat complicated and include prior litigation before this Court. In In re Parkwood, Inc., 149 U.S.App.D.C. 67, 461 F.2d 158 (1971), we invalidated a loan entered into in violation of the District of Columbia Loan Shark Law, D.C.Code § 26–601 et seq. The effect of the decision was to render uncollectable the unpaid balance of approximately $79,000.00. The present case involves a tri-cornered dispute as to bearing the loss. The parties to that dispute are Walker & Dunlop, Inc., the original maker of that loan, Walker & Dunlop's successor-in-interest, Hartford Life Insurance Company, and two title companies, The Title Guarantee Company and The Suburban Title and Investment Corporation (hereinafter "the Title Companies"). Hartford, the plaintiff below, appeals from the District Court's order granting summary judgment in favor of defendants and denying Hartford's motion for leave to file a second amended complaint. We reverse.

In October, 1960, Walker & Dunlop, a real estate broker and mortgage banker, loaned $100,000 to Suburban Motors, Inc. The loan, evidenced by a promissory note, was to bear interest at an annual rate of 6½% and was secured by a deed of trust on real property owned by Suburban. Prior to closing the loan, Walker & Dunlop obtained a commitment from the Title Companies insuring Walker & Dunlop and its successors-in-interest against "any defect in the execution" of the deed of trust. In January, 1961, pursuant to an understanding reached before the loan was made, Walker & Dunlop transferred the note and deed of trust to Hartford, endorsing the note "without recourse."

In March, 1962, Suburban sold the property, subject to the deed of trust, to Adams Properties, Inc., a subsidiary of Parkwood, Inc. In July, 1966, these companies filed petitions for reorganization under the Bankruptcy Act. Later that year, Hartford filed a proof of claim as a secured creditor of Adams for the balance due on the note—some $79,000.00.

In May, 1968, the Trustee appointed for Adams objected to the claim on the ground that the loan had been made in violation of the Loan Shark Act, Section 601. That statute makes it unlawful to charge yearly interest on a secured loan at a higher rate than 6% unless a license has been procured to charge the higher rate.[1] Hartford asserted that Walker & Dunlop, which had no license, was exempted from the provisions of the Act because it was a "real estate broker" within the meaning of Section 610.[2] The Referee and the District Court agreed with this contention. However, in In re Parkwood, supra, this court found that Walker & Dunlop was not acting as a real estate broker when it made the loan to Suburban, that the loan was subject to the Act, and that the loan and accompanying deed of trust were void. Hartford's proof of claim was disallowed.

Hartford instituted this action in December, 1972. In its amended complaint, Hartford seeks to recover its loss from

1. D.C.Code § 26:601 provides as follows:

It shall be unlawful and illegal to engage in the District of Columbia in the business of loaning money upon which a rate of interest greater than six per centum per annum is charged on any security of

any kind * * * without procuring license * * *."

2. D.C.Code § 26:610 provides that:

(a) Nothing contained in this chapter shall be held to apply to the legitimate business of * * * real estate brokers * * *."

Walker & Dunlop on contractual theories of failure of consideration, breach of warranty, and unjust enrichment. In June, 1973,
Hartford sought leave to file a second amended complaint which,
if permitted, would add allegations of fraud and concealment.
Alternatively, Hartford seeks recovery from the Title Companies
on the basis of their undertaking in the title insurance policy.

The District Court held that the causes of action against
Walker & Dunlop in the amended complaint were barred by the
applicable statute of limitations and by the "without recourse"
endorsement on the note which Walker & Dunlop had transferred to Hartford. The Court denied Hartford's motion for
leave to file the second amended complaint on the ground that
the statute of limitations had run. As to the Title Companies,
the District Court held that to allow Hartford an insurance recovery for a loss caused by Walker & Dunlop's violation of the
Loan Shark Act would be contrary to public policy.

The District Court found that the claims alleged against
Walker & Dunlop in Hartford's amended complaint accrued in
January, 1961, when Hartford purchased the note and deed of
trust from Walker & Dunlop. Since almost twelve years elapsed
between January, 1961, and the commencement of this litigation
in December, 1972, the Court held that these claims are time-
barred by D.C.Code § 12–301(7) (1973 ed.), which sets a three-
year limitations period for actions based on contract. We disagree with the holding.

The right to sue did not accrue until the plaintiff had a cause
of action. United States v. One 1961 Red Chevrolet Impala Se-
dan, 457 F.2d 1353 (5th Cir. 1972). Hartford's cause of action
against Walker & Dunlop depended upon a prior adjudication of
the rights of the trustee in bankruptcy of Adams in In re
Parkwood. That adjudication was not finally made by this
Court until 1971. Thus, Hartford's suit against Walker &
Dunlop was commenced well within the applicable limitations period.

The borrower (first Suburban and later Adams) paid all the
installments due under the loan agreement between 1961 and
1966. Therefore, until May, 1968, Hartford had no reason to believe that its proof of claim would not be recognized. Moreover,
Hartford could not have sued Walker & Dunlop prior to May,
1968, because Hartford had not theretofore suffered any legally
cognizable damage. Hodge v. Service Machinery Co., 438 F.2d
347 (6th Cir. 1971).

A somewhat more difficult question is whether Hartford's cause of action against Walker & Dunlop accrued in May, 1968, when the Trustee in bankruptcy formally objected to Hartford's proof of claim. At that time, there was no obstruction to Hartford's filing suit against Walker & Dunlop and proceeding to judgment. However, in order to do so, Hartford would have had to abandon its substantial legal claim against the trustee. We conclude that the statute of limitations should not be invoked so as to penalize Hartford for making the wrong choice. With the benefit of hindsight, we can state that Hartford "should have been on notice" of the illegality of the loan (In re Parkwood, supra, 461 F.2d at 175–76), and that, therefore, Hartford would have been better advised to proceed immediately against Walker & Dunlop, rather than engaging in a protracted and ultimately futile legal battle with the trustee. But prior to our decision in *Parkwood*, the matter was not so clear. Both the Referee and the District Court agreed with Hartford's contention that its proof of claim was valid. Our decision on appeal was by divided vote and even the majority conceded that whether Walker & Dunlop was entitled to a Loan Shark Act exemption was "not * * * perfectly plain" from the face of the statute. 461 F.2d at 175. In these circumstances, we have concluded it would be grossly inequitable to hold that the cause of action arose prior to our decision in *Parkwood*. See Walker v. Continental Life & Accident Co., 445 F.2d 1072, 1075 (9th Cir. 1971). We find no support for such a ruling in policy or case law. We decline to make it here.

* * *

The District Court also erred in ruling that Hartford's claims against Walker & Dunlop were barred by the "without recourse" endorsement on the note transferred by Walker & Dunlop to Hartford.

The legal effect of a "without recourse" endorsement is defined by the Uniform Commercial Code. § 3–417(3), (2)(d).[4] Thus, whether or not this endorsement bars Hartford's claims against Walker & Dunlop must be determined with reference to the principles of commercial law established therein.

A "without recourse" endorsement is a qualified endorsement; it does not eliminate all obligations owed by the transfer-

---

4. Under § 3–417(2)(d), the transferor of an instrument warrants to his transferee that "[n]o defense of any party is good against him * * *." Subdivision (3) provides that "[b]y transferring 'without recourse' the transferor limits the obligation stated in subsection (2)(d) to a warranty that he has no knowledge of such a defense."

or of an instrument to his transferee. By endorsing the note "without recourse", Walker & Dunlop still warranted to Hartford that it had no knowledge of any fact which would establish the existence of a good defense against the note.[5] Walker & Dunlop breached this warranty. At all times it was fully aware of the facts relevant to our later determination that the note was unenforceable because of the illegality of the underlying loan. Walker & Dunlop's ignorance of the law is no excuse. The U.C.C. preserves the pre-Code law as to "mistake" (§ 1–103), with the consequence that a unilateral mistake of law does not ordinarily affect the liability of any indorser. 2 Anderson, Uniform Commercial Code § 3–414:7 (2d ed. 1971), p. 996.

Hartford would have destroyed its warranty protection had it not acted in "good faith". § 3–417(2); Note: "Warranties on the Transfer of a Negotiable Instrument—U.C.C. 3–417(2)," 17 Stan.L.Rev. 77, 94–96 (1964). There is no indication that it did not do so here. The U.C.C. definition of "good faith", contained in § 1–201(19), requires "honesty *in fact* in the conduct * * * concerned." (Emphasis added.) Although Hartford had full knowledge of the same facts as Walker & Dunlop and made the same "mistake" of law (see *Parkwood*, 461 F.2d at 175–76), it did not subjectively know when it accepted the note that a good defense existed against it. Therefore, it is entitled to the coverage of the warranty. See 17 Stan.L.Rev. at 95.[6]

* * *

Reversed.

---

5. The "knowledge" limitation of § 3–417(3), quoted in n. 4, supra, is not explicitly confined to knowledge of facts; however, this reading of the Section is supported by reference to Section 65 of the Uniform Negotiable Instruments Law, from which the existing Uniform Commercial Code provision is derived. That section provided that the "without recourse" indorser warranted "(4) that he has no knowledge *of any fact* which would impair the validity of the instrument or render it valueless." (Emphasis added.) See also: Armstrong v. McCluskey, 188 Ark. 406, 65 S.W.2d 558 (1933), holding that the assignor of a note "without recourse" warrants that there is no legal defense against the note arising out of the assignor's own connection with its origin, such as the defense of usury.

6. Hartford erroneously characterizes its warranty claim as based upon an express warranty of title in a 1948 agreement entered into between Hartford and Walker & Dunlop and upon the implied warranty of title specified in § 3–417(1)(a). In fact, no warranty of title claim could successfully be made in this case. It is not disputed that Walker & Dunlop had title to the instrument and that its indorsement was genuine and authorized. See 2 Anderson, supra, § 3–417:8, p. 1022.

PROBLEM

Fox is the payee of a negotiable promissory note for $1,000 signed with the name Jane Jones as maker. Fox sold the note to Fish for $900. The note was indorsed by Fox "without recourse." On the due date of the note Fish demanded payment from Jones.

Case A. Jones refused to pay because she was unable to pay. Fox knew that Jones was experiencing financial difficulties when he sold the note to Fish.

Case B. Jones refused to pay because her name on the note was a forgery.

Case C. Jones refused to pay because the note was given to Fox in partial payment for goods which were defective and not as represented to Jones by Fox. You may assume in this case that because of the defect in the goods Jones was never obligated to pay the face amount of the note to Fox, but that the defect did not constitute a valid defense to a demand for payment by Fish because of UCC § 3–305(2). HDC

In each case, after Jones refused payment, Fish promptly notified Fox of the relevant facts and demanded payment of the note by Fox. What are Fox's liabilities in each case?

F. SIGNATURES BY REPRESENTATIVES

UCC § 3–401(1) provides that "no person is liable on an instrument unless his signature appears thereon." Consider the following case: Son is at a distant college and short of funds. He has no checking account of his own but he has in his possession some blank check forms on Father's checking account. Father tells Son, "Write yourself a check for whatever you need and sign my name." If Son writes Father's name on the signature line of the check does the "signature" of Father appear on the check? Although "signature" is not defined in the UCC it is clear that by Son's hand Father has signed the check. Son is the agent of Father and Father is bound by Son's authorized act in his behalf. UCC § 3–403.

Now consider this case: Employer had a checking account that he used to pay the various obligations that he incurred in his business. He followed the practice of personally signing all checks; however, when he knew that he would be out of town for extended periods he authorized Employee to sign Employer's name to checks in payment of business bills that arrived during

Employer's absences. Bank on which the checks were drawn paid all checks whether Employer's name was written in his handwriting or that of Employee. Employer never objected to the payment by Bank of any check on which Employer's name was written by Employee. On one occasion Employer was about to leave town and instructed Employee to pay all bills arriving during his absence except that of John Doe. In violation of these orders Employee wrote a check to John Doe in payment of a bill that he submitted. Employee's act of signing Employer's name to the check was not "authorized" by Employer, in the sense that Employer never assented to it, but Employer nevertheless may be bound by the signature. The question of whether the signature is binding on Employer is determined by the law of agency. In our example, the probable result under agency law is that Employer is bound because Employee, although lacking actual authority to sign the Doe check, had apparent authority to do so. In that event, under UCC § 3–403(1) the signature would be the authorized signature of Employer.

Signatures by agents on behalf of principals occur most often with respect to the obligations of organizations such as corporations whose signatures are made by its officers or employees. Two problems arise. First, there is the question of whether the corporation is bound by the signature of the officer or employee. Second, there is the question of whether the officer or employee also becomes a party to the instrument by signing it. If it is clear that an agent is signing on behalf of a named principal, only the principal is bound. But sometimes it is not clear whether the agent's signature is in behalf of the principal or whether it is made to impose liability on the agent himself, as, for example, the case of an accommodation party. UCC § 3–403(2)(b) deals (albeit not very well) with the problem of ambiguous signatures by representatives. This provision has been the subject of much litigation and, as the following material demonstrates, has often served as a trap for the unwary.

GRIFFIN v. ELLINGER

Supreme Court of Texas, 1976.
538 S.W.2d 97.

DOUGHTY, JUSTICE. The question presented by this case is whether a corporate officer who signs a check on a corporate account without designating the capacity in which he signs is personally liable as the drawer of the check. We hold that, under the circumstances of the present case, the corporate officer is personally liable, and we therefore affirm the judgment of the Court of Civil Appeals.

Respondent O. B. Ellinger, doing business as Ellinger Paint and Drywall, sued Percy Griffin on three drafts signed by Griffin and drawn on the account of Greenway Building Company at the Northeast Bank of Houston. These drafts, totalling $3,950.00, were issued to Ellinger in payment for labor and materials furnished to Greenway for a construction project at Lakeway in Travis County. Greenway was prime contractor for the project, and Griffin was authorized to sign the drafts as president of the company. Northeast Bank had refused payment on the drafts because of insufficient funds in the Greenway account. Trial was to the court, which rendered judgment for Ellinger for $3,950.00. The Court of Civil Appeals affirmed. 530 S.W.2d 329.

Petitioner complains of the judgments below by two points of error: first, petitioner contends that the drafts show conclusively on their face that he was signing in a representative capacity only. Second, petitioner contends that extrinsic evidence establishes as a matter of law that the parties understood his signature to be in a representative capacity.

Section 3.413(b) of [Texas U.C.C.] defines the obligation of the drawer of a draft as follows:

> The drawer engages that upon dishonor of the draft and any necessary notice of dishonor or protest he will pay the amount of the draft to the holder or to any indorser who takes it up.

Griffin is liable under this section as a drawer unless his signature was only as president of Greenway. To determine whether an authorized representative is personally liable on an instrument which he signs on behalf of his principal, we must look to Section 3.403 of the Code, which provides:

(a) A signature may be made by an agent or other representative, and his authority to make it may be established as in other cases of representation. No particular form of appointment is necessary to establish such authority.

(b) An authorized representative who signs his own name to an instrument

(1) is personally obligated if the instrument neither names the person represented nor shows that the representative signed in a representative capacity;

(2) except as otherwise established between the immediate parties, is personally obligated if the instrument names the person represented but does not show that the representative signed in a representative capacity, or if the instrument does not name the person represented but does show that the representative signed in a representative capacity.

(c) Except as otherwise established the name of an organization preceded or followed by the name and office of an authorized individual is a signature made in a representative capacity.

Each of the three drafts signed by Griffin were in essentially the same form. A copy of one of the drafts is reproduced below.

The first question is whether the draft shows on its face that Griffin signed in a representative capacity only. Although the draft clearly names the person represented, it does not show that Griffin signed only in his capacity as president of Greenway. Griffin contends, however, that considering the instrument as a whole, and taking into account the normal business usage of personalized checks, it should be apparent from the instrument itself that Griffin signed only as an authorized agent of Greenway. We disagree. We recognize that it is unusual to demand the individual obligation of a corporate officer on checks drawn on the corporate account, and that the more usual way of obtaining the personal obligation of an officer on such a check would be by endorsement. Business practice and usage are proper factors to be considered in construing the particular instrument under consideration. We also recognize that an instrument may disclose on its face that a signature was executed only in a representative capacity even though the particular office or position of the signer is not disclosed thereon. Pollin v. Mindy Manufacturing Co., 211 Pa.Super. 87, 236 A.2d 542 (1967), cited by petitioner, is such a case. In *Pollin*, the plaintiff, a holder in due course of checks drawn on a corporate account, sued the signer of the checks, an agent of the corporation, asserting his personal liability as drawer. The checks, issued to pay employees of the corporation, were stamped with the name of the company and the designation "Payroll Checks"; the company name was also printed above the two signature lines in the lower right-hand corner. The defendant had signed under this printed name without designating his office or capacity. The court held, nevertheless, that the instrument considered as a whole showed that the signer was signing only in a representative capacity:

> In the present instance the checks clearly showed that they were payable from a special account set up by the corporate defendant for the purpose of paying its employees. This information disclosed by the instrument itself would refute any contention that the appellant intended to make the instrument his own order on the named bank to pay money to the payee.

236 A.2d at 545.

Unlike the checks in *Pollin*, we can find nothing on the face of the checks in the present case to show that Griffin intended to sign only in a representative capacity. Petitioner points out that each check is stamped by a "check protector," which imprinted not only the amount of the draft but also the company's name. Although the stamp clearly reveals the name of the principal, it does not aid petitioner because it gives no information as to the capacity in which *he* signed the instrument.

The fact that the name of the corporation appears on the check indicates that the account drawn upon is that of the corporation and that the funds in the account are the corporation's. While the drawer of a check is ordinarily the owner of the funds in the account drawn upon, the Code does not require that this be so. Under Section 3.413, *any person* who signs a draft engages that, upon dishonor, he will pay the amount thereof to the holder. Indeed, under Section 3.404, the signer of a draft who has no authority to draw upon the account is nevertheless liable upon his contract as drawer to any person who takes the instrument in good faith for value. Petitioner points out that, since a corporation can only act through its agents, a personal signature is always required to authorize withdrawal of funds from a corporate account. Under Section 3.403, however, one signing an instrument is personally liable thereon even though he is author-ized to and does in fact bind his principal, if he does not disclose that he is signing only in a representative capacity. In short, the burden is on the signer to relieve himself of personal liability by disclosing his agency. The fact that the instrument is an au-thorized draft drawn on a corporate account is not enough to disclose the representative character of the signature thereon. Section 3.403(c) expressly provides that the signer of an instru-ment may avoid personal liability by disclosing both the name of the organization of which he is an agent and the office he holds with the organization. Absent such a disclosure or its equiva-lent, the signer is personally liable on the instrument according to its terms, unless "otherwise established between the immedi-ate parties" under subsection (b)(2). We hold that the checks in question do not show on their face that Griffin signed only in a representative capacity. Petitioner's first point of error is there-fore overruled.

Griffin next contends that extrinsic evidence of prior dealings between the parties proves as a matter of law that he signed only as an agent of Greenway. Under Section 3.403(b), extrinsic evidence is admissible between the immediate parties to the in-strument to show that they agreed or otherwise understood that the signer would not be personally liable thereon, even though the instrument itself does not reveal the signer's representative capacity. The Code does not delineate what proof is necessary to "otherwise establish" between the parties that the signer is not personally liable on an instrument which he intended to sign only in a representative capacity. Therefore, the general princi-ples of law and equity are to be applied. Section 1.103. In Seale v. Nichols, 505 S.W.2d 251 (Tex.1974), this Court had occa-sion to construe Section 3.403(b). We there stated that, in order for an agent to avoid liability on his signature, "he must *disclose* his intent to sign as a representative to the other contracting party." 505 S.W.2d at 255. We also recognized that prior deal-ings between the parties are relevant in determining whether the parties understood the signature to be in a representative capacity.

The trial court filed findings of fact, in which it found as fol-lows: Griffin and Ellinger had "entered an agreement" that El-linger would "do certain work on the project in question." Ellin-ger was never told who owned the Lakeway project, who would pay him, or who would be responsible for the payments, nor did he inquire. Griffin never told Ellinger that the checks were signed only on behalf of the corporation; he "simply signed the checks and delivered them without comment." Ellinger "had on numerous occasions received checks drawn on Greenway Building Company, Inc. from other officers of Greenway Building Company, Inc. and had never looked to these officers for payment thereon; such other checks have been paid as presented to the paying bank."

These findings, if supported by the evidence, are sufficient to support the trial court's conclusion that Griffin was personally liable on the checks under Section 3.403. Since it was Griffin's burden to prove that he disclosed his representative capacity to Ellinger, Seale v. Nichols, supra, the judgment must stand unless the evidence shows as a matter of law that he made such disclosure.

Griffin contends that the prior dealings between the parties establish his defense as a matter of law. The evidence shows that Ellinger had received checks for work done on the project which were signed by other officers of Greenway, prior to the time that Griffin became Greenway's representative on the Lakeway construction site. Ellinger also admitted that the bills submitted for his work were billed to Greenway Building Company. These circumstances certainly do constitute evidence that Ellinger knew of Griffin's representative capacity when he received the checks signed by Griffin. There is evidence to the contrary, however. Ellinger testified that he understood that he was working for Misters Buxbaum and Wininger (officers of Greenway who signed checks prior to Griffin's arrival), and later Mr. Griffin. Ellinger further testified:

> Q. But, at the time you received these checks in payment of goods and services that you provided, you were looking to the main payer on those checks, Greenway Building Company, Inc.?
>
> A. No, I was looking for the name of Percy Griffin because he was the one giving me the checks.
>
> * * *
>
> Q. Were you aware that he was acting as an officer or in some sort of capacity for Greenway Building Company, Inc.?
>
> A. I did not. [sic]

This testimony constitutes some evidence that Ellinger was not aware of Griffin's representative capacity when he received the checks in payment for his work. The issue was therefore one for the trier of fact which the trial court resolved in favor of

Ellinger, and this Court has no authority to disturb the trial Court's findings. The judgment of the Court of Civil Appeals is affirmed.

NOTE

Griffin demonstrates two points: one can never be too careful about the form of a signature on a negotiable instrument; no case, however weak on the merits, is hopeless. Highfield v. Lang, 394 N.E.2d 204 (Ind.App.1979) involving similar facts agreed with *Griffin* on the applicability of UCC § 3–403(2)(b) but held in favor of the signing officer on the "otherwise established" point. Under *Highfield*, although the payee lost, a holder in due course taking from the payee apparently would have won. It was so held in Financial Associates v. Impact Marketing, Inc., 90 Misc.2d 545, 394 N.Y.S.2d 814 (Civ.Ct.1977). Other cases in accord with *Griffin* and *Highfield* are Seamon v. Acree, 142 Ga.App. 662, 236 S.E.2d 688 (1977) and Medley Hardwoods, Inc. v. Novy, 346 So.2d 1224 (Fla.App.1977). If any reasonable person would assume that checks such as those in *Griffin* and *Highfield* are corporate rather than personal obligations isn't UCC § 3–403(2)(b) satisfied on the ground that the check taken as a whole "shows that the representative signed in a representative capacity?"

WEATHER–RITE, INC. v. SOUTHDALE PRO–BOWL, INC.

Supreme Court of Minnesota, 1974.
301 Minn. 346, 222 N.W.2d 789.

KELLY, JUSTICE. Plaintiff, Weather-Rite, Inc., brought this action as payee on a promissory note given by Southdale Pro-Bowl, Inc., against defendant Frank Buetel, an officer of Southdale whom plaintiff alleges is an individual endorser of the note. The trial court, over plaintiff's continuing objection, admitted parol evidence concerning the execution of the note and its endorsements, and concluded that defendant had endorsed the note as an officer and agent of Southdale and not in his indiviudal capacity. Plaintiff appeals from an order denying a motion for a new trial. We affirm.

The note in question was a preprinted form. On the maker's signature line was the typewritten name of the corporate debtor, "Southdale Pro-Bowl, Inc." On the line below, one of its officers, John Dorek, signed his name and representative capacity, "President." On the third line, defendant's signature, "Frank

Buetel," appears without indication of agency status.[1] The signatures of these men also appear on the reverse side of the note: "John H. Dorek, Pres." and "Frank Buetel."

1. The significant issue raised by this appeal is whether parol evidence was properly admitted in the court below. The controlling statute, [UCC §] 3–403(2), provides:

"An authorized representative who signs his own name to an instrument

(a) is personally obligated if the instrument neither names the person represented nor shows that the representative signed in a representative capacity;

(b) except as otherwise established between the immediate parties, is personally obligated if the instrument names the person represented but does not show that the representative signed in a representative capacity, or if the instrument does not name the person represented but does show that the representative signed in a representative capacity."

Plaintiff contends that, since neither the defendant's representative capacity nor the principal on whose behalf defendant allegedly acted is shown in the endorsement, parol evidence of agency status should have been excluded. A further argument is made that the Minnesota case law is in accord with the code. This court in Giltner v. Quirk, 131 Minn. 472, 155 N.W. 760 (1915), did hold that evidence of parol contemporaneous agreement to vary the effect of an endorsement of a promissory note is inadmissible. However, in *Giltner* this court noted that there were exceptions to that rule.

Defendant argues that this situation should be an exception to the parol evidence rule applicable to the immediate parties, as provided for in [UCC §] 3–403(2)(b).

If plaintiff were a holder in due course of the note in question, we would have no difficulty in agreeing that parol evidence would be inadmissible under [UCC §] 3–403(2)(a). But where only the immediate parties are involved, the issue is less clear. There are few decisions, none of them identical to this case. One of the closest is Central Trust Co. v. J. Gottermeier Development, 65 Misc.2d 676, 677, 319 N.Y.S.2d 25, 26 (1971). The

1. Plaintiff concedes that Buetel signed the note as a maker in his ca-   pacity as an officer of Southdale Pro-Bowl, Inc.

facts and holding of that case are briefly summarized in the following excerpts from the decision:

"Plaintiff is the holder of a note * * * payable to its order * * * made by the defendant corporation and signed by John B. Gottermeier as its president. On the reverse side of the note the signature of 'John B. Gottermeier' appears under a printed guarantee agreement. * * *

"John B. Gottermeier claims that his endorsement was made in his capacity as president of the defendant corporation and not as an individual, that he is not personally obligated on the note, and that parol evidence is admissible on the trial to prove the foregoing. Neither the name of the corporation, which he claims he represented, nor the nature of the representative capacity, in which he claims he acted, appears on the portion of the instrument which bears his indorsement. Under these facts, he is personally obligated by reason of his indorsement of the note, and parol evidence is inadmissible to prove that he indorsed the note in a representative capacity."

While this may be a sound position, there is a critical distinction between the facts of that case and ours. The presence on the reverse side of the note of the signature, "John H. Dorek, Pres.," shows at least a possibility that the immediate parties understood that defendant, too, was signing in a representative capacity. Since this dispute is restricted to the immediate parties, the endorsement, ambiguous when viewed in its complete context, should be clarified by parol evidence of the circumstances surrounding its execution.[2] To this end, the trial court was correct in overruling plaintiff's objection to the admission of parol evidence.

2.   The issue of sufficiency of the evidence to support the trial court's finding that defendant endorsed the note as a corpo-

---

2. This position has the support of the Permanent Editorial Board for the Uniform Commercial Code. The board filed a brief as amicus curiae in this case, and came to the following conclusion:

"In the present case, the form of the note itself raises doubt. If the payee wanted the individual liability of the two officers of Southdale, why did it accept the indorsement: 'John H. Dorek, Pres.'? On the other hand, if Buetel thought he was signing only as an officer of Southdale, why did he not add to his signatures something to show he was vice president? Anyone looking at the present note will have at least some shadow of doubt cross his mind, and since the plaintiff is the payee, all of the parties should be allowed to tell their stories. There is a factual question which should be resolved by a jury, or a judge sitting without a jury."

rate officer rather than individually requires a brief statement of the facts. The note in question had its genesis in a contract between Weather-Rite and Southdale for installation of air-conditioning equipment at the latter's bowling alley. In payment for the completed work, a promissory note dated April 9, 1969, and payable in six installments, was executed in favor of plaintiff in the principal amount of $6,039. On April 21, 1969, a corporate officer of plaintiff met with defendant and obtained his signature below that of Dorek on both the front and back of the note. According to testimony at the trial, defendant signed twice in one continuous act after the plaintiff's officer said, "we need your signature on here as an officer of the corporation." While there was some testimony to the contrary, we cannot interfere with the trial court's findings where the evidence, taken as a whole, furnishes substantial support for them. 1B Dunnell, Dig. (3 ed.) § 411. Such is the case with the trial court's finding that defendant executed the endorsement as an officer and agent of Southdale Pro-Bowl, Inc., and not in an individual capacity.

Affirmed.

NOTES

1. Buetel was allowed to introduce parol evidence that his apparent personal indorsement was in fact a signature made in a representative capacity, i.e., an indorsement by the maker of the note. The court agreed, stating that the indorsement was ambiguous. But an indorsement by the maker of a note serves no purpose whatsoever. Is there any logical reason why the bank in this case would request officers of the corporation to indorse the note if it was not seeking the personal liability of the signers as indorsers? Either the bank officer was acting irrationally or he was seeking personal liability of the officers without making full disclosure. It may be that the court was recognizing that Buetel in signing his name to the note was unaware of the precise legal effect of his signature and that he should not be held to a liability that the bank had not openly bargained for: "defendant signed twice in one continuous act after plaintiff's officer said, 'we need your signature on here as an officer of the corporation.'" In the case of notes of organizations, is there any reason why parol evidence should not always be admissible against an immediate party to the note as regards the liability of representatives of the organization if the note does not specifically state that the representative is signing in an individual capacity or otherwise expressly indicates that the note is being

personally guaranteed? In Stage Door Restaurant, Inc. v. L. N.
Hill Co., Inc., 248 A.2d 828 (D.C.App.1969) (decided under the
NIL) a note was signed for the corporation by Kefalas as President. Kefalas and Schanker, also an officer of the corporation,
then indorsed the note by signing their names as individuals. In
spite of the fact that Schanker's indorsement was unambiguous—he signed only as an indorser—parol evidence was admitted to show that it was not the intention of the parties to the
note that Schanker have personal liability. Schanker testified
that he had never been requested to sign the note for additional
security. If a corporate officer has been induced to sign a negotiable instrument by a misrepresentation by the payee concerning the legal effect of the signature or the liability of the signing officer, the issue may not be whether the officer is liable on
the instrument but rather, whether he has a defense. In
Thompson v. First National Bank & Trust Co. in Macon, 142 Ga.
App. 174, 235 S.E.2d 582 (1977), Corporation sought a loan from
Bank which Bank could not grant because of a "legal impedi-
ment." Bank agreed to make the loan on the basis of a promissory note signed only by X, Vice President of Corporation. Proceeds of the loan were paid to Corporation. Bank's
representative assured X that he would not be held personally
liable and that Bank would look only to Corporation for payment. When Bank later sued X on the note X argued equitable
estoppel. The court held for X although it is not clear whether
the rationale was equitable estoppel or fraud. The court stated
that X could assert Bank's fraud as a defense to liability. It is
not clear, however, that Bank's assurances, although they may
have been the basis for an estoppel, were in fact fraudulently
made.

2. Not all courts agree with *Weather-Rite* and *Stage Door.*
In Lanier v. Bank of Virginia-Potomac, 39 Md.App. 589, 387 A.2d
614 (1978), a promissory note was signed with the name of the
corporation followed by the signature "By Emmet Lanier, President." On the reverse side Lanier signed his name followed by
the word "President." In an action by the payee, on a motion
for summary judgment, the court held, as a matter of law, that
Lanier was liable as an indorser. It stated "As a matter of fact,
unless he was intended to be personally responsible, the endorsement itself would have been an exercise in futility since [Lanier]
had already signed as the chief executive officer of the corporation in its capacity as maker of the note." Lanier's affidavit
stated that he intended to sign only as a representative but gave
no evidence of an agreement to that effect between him and the

payee. It is not clear what the court would have done if evidence of such an agreement had been presented. In New York Financial, Inc. v. J & W Holding Co., Inc., 30 U.C.C.Rep. 1599 (Fla.App.1981), the Court considered a promissory note executed by "J & W Holding Company, Inc. By: Richard S. Shaulis, President" which stated that it was payable "in the manner set forth on the reverse." On the reverse side of the note was a typed description of the manner of payment and a statement of the attorney's fees provided for. Shaulis signed his name after this typed statement. In a suit by the payee of the note it was held, as a matter of law, that Shaulis was personally liable as an indorser of the note. Extrinsic evidence such as the affidavit of Shaulis that he signed only as a representative was held "incompetent to vary that conclusion." Although the court thought that the signature of Shaulis was unambiguous, might it not have been made as an indication of assent by the corporation to the typed terms of the note? Are UCC § 3–402 and § 3–403(2) meant to deal with cases of this kind when only original parties are involved?

3. How does the remedy of reformation for mistake affect cases covered by UCC § 3–403(2)? American, a corporation, owed Disneyland $93,000 on open account. Disneyland insisted that the indebtedness be evidenced by ten promissory notes which it prepared. The notes did not mention American. Schwartz, the president of American, signed his name to the notes without indicating any representative capacity. Schwartz by affidavit stated that he, acting on behalf of American, and Disneyland agreed that the notes were to be obligations of American. Schwartz also swore that he mistakenly signed the notes thinking that he was carrying out this agreement. Disneyland by affidavit stated that when Schwartz executed the notes by simply signing his name to them it "elected to treat the executed Notes as a counter offer which it accepted" and to treat the notes as a guaranty by Schwartz of American's indebtedness. American paid four of the notes and then defaulted. In an action by Disneyland against Schwartz as maker of the notes it was held that under UCC § 3–403(2), as a matter of law, Schwartz was personally liable. The court dismissed Schwartz's counterclaim for reformation of the notes to substitute American for Schwartz as maker of the notes. Schwartz v. Disneyland Vista Records, 383 So.2d 1117 (Fla.App.1980). On similar facts, the Washington Supreme Court was more sympathetic to the defendant's plight and allowed reformation. St. Regis Paper Co. v. Wicklund, 93 Wn.2d 497, 610 P.2d 903 (1980). The presi-

dent of the corporation who signed the note given to evidence the corporation's open account debt testified that both he and the payee's representative agreed that the note was to be a corporate obligation only. The representative of payee testified that he understood that the note was to be a personal obligation of the president of the corporation. The court held that UCC § 3-403(2) does not apply to an action for reformation. The fact that the signature of the note was not ambiguous is not relevant. When mutual mistake is alleged parol evidence can be admitted to determine the agreement of the parties. If mutual mistake is proved by clear, cogent and convincing evidence and the rights of innocent third parties are not unfairly affected reformation can be granted. The court relied on UCC § 1-103 which incorporates into the UCC the law of mistake. It did not cite UCC § 3-401(1).

NESS v. GREATER ARIZONA REALTY, INC.

Court of Appeals of Arizona, Division 2, 1974.
21 Ariz.App. 231, 517 P.2d 1278.

HOWARD, JUDGE.

* * *

The basis for appellee's complaint was a promissory note. The pertinent allegations of the complaint are:

"II

That at all times complained of herein, Berth C. Ness was acting as the agent of and with full authority to bind the defendants and each of them in connection with all matters complained of herein and that all matters complained of herein occurred in or were to be performed in Pima County, Arizona.

III

That prior to the commencement of this action, Berth C. Ness, acting for and on behalf of the defendants and each of them, made and delivered a promissory note dated the 15th day of May, 1969, in the sum of $25,000.00 to the order of plaintiff."

[UCC § 3-401] provides:

"A. No person is liable on an instrument unless his signature appears thereon.

B.   A signature is made by use of any name, including any trade or assumed name, upon an instrument, or by any word or marker used in lieu of a written signature."

The official comment on the above mentioned statute found in Uniform Laws Annotated—Uniform Commercial Code § 3–401 provides:

"1.   No one is liable on an instrument unless and until he has signed it.   The chief application of the rule has been in cases holding that a principal whose name does not appear on an instrument signed by his agent is not liable on the instrument even though the payee knew when it was issued that it was intended to be the obligation of one who did not sign. * * * *"

Nowhere in appellee's complaint does it appear that the names of appellants appeared on the note.   Nor is it alleged that the note in any way discloses that Berth Ness signed in any capacity other than for himself individually.   A suit may not be maintained or judgment obtained on a promissory note against an undisclosed principal whose signature does not appear thereon.   Richards v. Warnekros, 14 Ariz. 488, 131 P. 154 (1913); Plains State Bank v. Ellis, 174 Kan. 653, 258 P.2d 313 (1953). See also, 11 Am.Jur.2d, Bills and Notes § 560.

The appellee could have sued appellants on the underlying obligation for which the note was given but this was not done.

* * *

NOTES

1.   Because the plaintiff-payee in *Ness* could sue defendant on the underlying obligation for which the note was given the only effect of UCC § 3–401 is to deny to plaintiff whatever procedural advantages he had in being able to sue on the note itself. See UCC § 3–307.   Any defenses of defendant against plaintiff on the underlying transaction would also have been available in a suit on the note.   UCC § 3–305(2) or § 3–306.   The most important effect of UCC § 3–401 is that it insulates defendant from any suit on the note by any subsequent holder in due course who might have taken free of any defenses that defendant might have had against the payee.   UCC § 3–305(2).

2.   Suppose in *Ness* that the note had been signed "Berth C. Ness, acting as agent."   Who is liable on the note if suit is brought by plaintiff?   Who is liable on the note if suit is brought by a holder in due course taking from plaintiff?

3.   Suppose a note is signed as follows: "John Doe, By Richard Roe, Agent." It was the intent of both Richard Roe and the payee of the note that John Doe was to be bound and that Richard Roe was not to be bound. If John Doe did not authorize Richard Roe to sign the note and is not otherwise bound by virtue of UCC § 3–403(1) or § 3–404 the signature is unauthorized and Doe is not bound on the note. UCC § 3–401(1). By general agency law an agent signing a contract on behalf of a principal warrants to the other contracting party that he is authorized to bind the principal, and is liable for any loss to the other contracting party resulting from his failure to bind the principal. Restatement, Second, Agency § 329. The rule applied to negotiable instruments is different. The unauthorized agent is liable on the instrument even though the payee did not bargain for the agent's liability. UCC § 3–404(1).

3-404(1)

Chapter 3

HOLDERS IN DUE COURSE AND
GOOD FAITH PURCHASERS

A. GOOD FAITH AND NOTICE

To qualify as a holder in due course under UCC § 3–302 a holder must, among other requirements, have taken the instrument in good faith and without notice of any defense against or claim to it on the part of any person. The meaning of good faith as applied to negotiable instruments has varied over the years. The law prior to the adoption of the NIL is traced by the Court in Howard National Bank v. Wilson, 96 Vt. 438, 120 A. 889 (1923):

Prior to the Negotiable Instruments Act, two distinct lines of cases had developed in this country. The first had its origin in Gill v. Cubitt, 3 B. & C. 466, 10 E.C.L. 215, where the rule was distinctly laid down by the court of King's Bench that the purchaser of negotiable paper must exercise reasonable prudence and caution, and that, if the circumstances were such as ought to have excited the suspicion of a prudent and careful man, and he made no inquiry, he did not stand in the legal position of a bona fide holder. The rule was adopted by the courts of this country generally and seem to have become a fixed rule in the law of negotiable paper. Later in Goodman v. Harvey, 4 A. & E. 870, 31 E.C.L. 381, the English court abandoned its former position and adopted the rule that nothing short of actual bad faith or fraud in the purchaser would deprive him of the character of a bona fide purchaser and let in defenses existing between prior parties, that no circumstances of suspicion merely, or want of proper caution in the purchaser, would have this effect, and that even gross negligence would have no effect, except as evidence tending to establish bad faith or fraud. Some of the American courts adhered to the earlier rule, while others followed the change inaugurated in Goodman v. Harvey. The question was before this court in Roth v. Colvin, 32 Vt. 125, and, on full consideration of the question, a rule was adopted

114

in harmony with that announced in Gill v. Cubitt, which has been adhered to in subsequent cases, including those cited above. Stated briefly, one line of cases including our own had adopted the test of the reasonably prudent man and the other that of actual good faith. It would seem that it was the intent of the Negotiable Instruments Act to harmonize this disagreement by adopting the latter test. That such is the view generally accepted by the courts appears from a recent review of the cases concerning what constitutes notice of defect. Brannan on Neg.Ins.Law, 187–201. To effectuate the general purpose of the act to make uniform the Negotiable Instruments Law of those states which should enact it, we are constrained to hold (contrary to the rule adopted in our former decisions) that negligence on the part of the plaintiff, or suspicious circumstances sufficient to put a prudent man on inquiry, will not of themselves prevent a recovery, but are to be considered merely as evidence bearing on the question of bad faith. 96 Vt. at 452–453, 120 A. at 894.

Gill v. Cubitt, referred to in the above quotation and decided by the Court of King's Bench in 1824, is reminiscent of Miller v. Race. It involved a stolen bill of exchange purchased by plaintiff without any inquiry about the title of the transferor. The court decided that the circumstances under which the purchase was made should have caused plaintiff to be suspicious about the transferor. Because plaintiff did not make inquiries about the title of the transferor, he was subject to the defense of theft pleaded by defendants who were the acceptors of the bill. Compare UCC § 3–306(d). In this case the purchaser of the bill was not acting in good faith because suspicious circumstances gave him notice that the bill may have been stolen. Thus, good faith and notice of the claim to the instrument were part of one package. The NIL and the UCC, however, both treat good faith and notice as two separate concepts, and this has caused some difficulties of analysis. The NIL required that for a taker to be a holder in due course he must take in "good faith" and without "notice of any infirmity or defect in the title of the person negotiating it." (Section 52.) Good faith was not defined but notice was defined in Section 56: "To constitute notice of an infirmity in the instrument or defect in the title of the person negotiating the same, the person to whom it is negotiated must have had actual knowledge of the infirmity or defect, or knowledge of such facts that his action in taking the instrument amounted to bad faith." Professor Britton agrees with the conclusion in Howard National Bank, supra, that the effect of the NIL provi-

sions, as interpreted by the courts, was to reject Gill v. Cubitt
and to adopt a test of subjective good faith. Britton, Handbook
of the Law of Bills and Notes 246 (2d ed. 1961).

The UCC, during its development, at first departed from the
NIL approach and then, in part, returned to it. UCC
§ 1–201(19), the general definition applicable to all articles of the
UCC, defines "good faith" as "honesty in fact in the conduct or
transaction concerned." This is a purely subjective standard.
The 1952 draft of the UCC in § 2–103(1)(a) applicable to sales of
goods transactions added an objective standard of conduct by
merchants. It stated that " 'Good faith' in the case of a
merchant includes observance of reasonable commercial standards." The 1952 draft also added an objective standard of conduct for purchasers of instruments. UCC § 3–302(1)(b) provided
as follows: "in good faith including observance of the reasonable commercial standards of any business in which the holder
may be engaged." The comment to this section said: "The 'reasonable commercial standards' language added here and in comparable provisions elsewhere in the Act, e.g., Section 2–103,
merely makes explicit what has long been implicit in case-law
handling of the 'good faith' concept. A business man engaging
in a commercial transaction is not entitled to claim the peculiar
advantages which the law accords the good faith purchaser—
called in this context holder in due course—on a bare showing of
'honesty in fact' when his actions fail to meet the generally accepted standards current in his business, trade or profession.
The cases so hold; this section so declares the law."

But in the later versions of the UCC the objective standard of
good faith, although retained (in modified form) in § 2–103(1)(b),
was dropped from § 3–302(1)(b). The apparent purpose of this
change in UCC § 3–302(1)(b) was to return to the subjective
standard of the NIL, the so-called "pure heart" doctrine. But
this result does not seem to have been reached. The NIL applied the good or bad faith standard to the concept of "notice."
The purchaser had notice of a defense or claim to the instrument
only if he had "knowledge of such facts that his action in taking
the instrument amounted to bad faith." The UCC has always
had an objective standard of notice. UCC § 1–201(25) states
that a person has notice of a fact when "from all the facts and
circumstances known to him at the time in question he has reason to know that it exists." Thus, through UCC § 3–302(1)(c)
and § 1–201(25) the result reached in Gill v. Cubitt, on the same
facts, could easily be reached under the UCC. Most cases probably involve situations in which the facts relevant to the issue of

good faith are the same facts giving rise to notice of a defense or claim. In those cases the issue of whether good faith is subjective or objective seems academic. See Littlefield, Good Faith Purchase of Commercial Paper: The Failure of the Subjective Test, 39 S.Cal.L.Rev. 48 (1966). There may be some cases, however, in which the good faith of the holder is affected by facts that may not constitute notice of the claim or defense to the instrument being asserted against the holder. In those cases the question of subjective good faith may have some vitality. Consider how the two concepts of good faith and notice are treated in the cases that follow.

KAW VALLEY STATE BANK & TRUST CO. v. RIDDLE

Supreme Court of Kansas, 1976.
219 Kan. 550, 549 P.2d 927.

FROMME, JUSTICE. This action was brought by The Kaw Valley State Bank and Trust Company (hereinafter referred to as Kaw Valley) to recover judgment against John H. Riddle d/b/a Riddle Contracting Company (hereafter referred to as Riddle) on two notes and to determine the priority of conflicting security agreements. The two notes were covered by separate security agreements and were given to purchase construction equipment. The Planters State Bank and Trust Company (hereinafter referred to as Planters) held a note and security interest on the same and other construction equipment acquired by Riddle. Kaw Valley had acquired the two notes and the security agreements by assignment from Co-Mac, Inc. (hereinafter referred to as Co-Mac), a dealer, from whom Riddle purchased the construction equipment.

In a trial to the court Kaw Valley was found not to be a holder in due course of one of the notes. Its claim on said note, totaling $21,904.64, was successfully defended on the grounds of failure of consideration. It was stipulated at the trial that none of the construction equipment for which the note was given had ever been delivered by Co-Mac. Kaw Valley has appealed.

* * *

Prior to the transactions in question Riddle had purchased construction equipment and machinery from the dealer, Co-Mac. A number of these purchases had been on credit and discounted to Kaw Valley by Co-Mac. Including the Riddle transactions, Kaw Valley had purchased over 250 notes and security agreements from Co-Mac during the prior ten year period. All were guaranteed by Co-Mac and by its president personally.

In May, 1971, Riddle negotiated for the purchase of a model 6–c Caterpillar tractor, a dozer and a used 944 Caterpillar wheel tractor with a two yard bucket. Riddle was advised that this machinery could be delivered but it would first be necessary for Co-Mac to have a signed note and security agreement to complete the transaction. An installment note, security agreement and acceptance of delivery of the machinery was mailed to Riddle. These were signed and returned to Co-Mac. Ten days later, the machinery not having been delivered, Riddle called Co-Mac and inquired about purchasing a D–8 Caterpillar and a #80 Caterpillar scraper in place of the first machinery ordered. Co-Mac agreed to destroy the May 11, 1971 papers and sell this larger machinery to Riddle in place of that previously ordered.

The sale of this substitute machinery was completed and the machinery was delivered after the execution of an additional note and security agreement. However, the May 11, 1971 papers were not destroyed. The note had been discounted and assigned to Kaw Valley prior to the sale of the substitute machinery. Thereafter Co-Mac, who was in financial trouble, made regular payments on the first note to Kaw Valley. The note was thus kept current by Co-Mac and Riddle had no knowledge of the continued existence of that note. The 6–c Caterpillar tractor, dozer and the used 944 Caterpillar wheel tractor were never delivered to Riddle. Riddle received no consideration for the May 11, 1971 note and no lien attached under the security agreement because the machinery never came into possession of Riddle. (See [UCC §] 9–204.) The debtor never had rights in any of the collateral.

On February 24, 1972, representatives of Riddle, Co-Mac and Kaw Valley met for the purpose of consolidiating the indebtedness of Riddle on machinery notes held by Kaw Valley and guaranteed by Co-Mac. Riddle was behind in some of his payments and wanted to consolidate the notes and reduce his monthly payments to $4,500.00. Kaw Valley disclosed eight past due machinery notes, each representing separate purchase transactions by Riddle. Riddle objected to one of these notes dated July 16, 1971, because the machinery purchased under this particular transaction had been previously returned to Co-Mac.

It was agreed by Kaw Valley that Riddle did not owe for this machinery because of the previous settlement between Co-Mac and Riddle. Kaw Valley cancelled the $5,000.00 balance shown to be due from Riddle.

Thereupon a renewal note and security agreement for $44,557.70 dated February 24, 1972, was drawn consolidating and renewing the seven remaining notes. Riddle then asked Kaw Valley if this was all that it owed the bank and he was assured that it was. The renewal note was then executed by Riddle.

It was not until March 12, 1972, that Riddle was advised by Kaw Valley that it held the note and security agreement dated May 11, 1971, which Riddle believed had been destroyed by Co-Mac. This was within a week after a receiver had been appointed to take over Co-Mac's business affairs. Riddle explained the machinery had never been delivered and Co-Mac promised to destroy the papers. No demand for payment of the May 11, 1971 note was made on Riddle until this action was filed.

Prior to the time this action was filed, Riddle executed a note and granted a security agreement in all of its machinery and equipment to Planters. This included the machinery covered in the previous consolidation transaction of February 24, 1972, with Kaw Valley and Co-Mac.

Subsequently Kaw Valley obtained possession of the machinery covered by the February 24 transaction by court order. Thereupon by agreement in writing between Kaw Valley, Planters and Riddle an immediate sale of the collateral covered in the February 24 transaction was held. By the terms of this agreement the first $22,200.00 in proceeds was to be paid to Kaw Valley in full satisfaction of the note of February 24, 1972. The money received from the sale in excess of this amount was to be paid to the Merchants National Bank to hold as escrow agent, awaiting a determination of entitlement by the court.

At the time of the trial the $22,200.00 had been received by Kaw Valley and the balance of the proceeds of the agreed sale amounting to $25,371.15 was in the hands of the escrow agent.

In the court's memorandum of decision filed November 19, 1974, the court found:

"That the proceeds remaining in plaintiff's possession from the agreed equipment sale are $25,371.15. The plaintiff claims $21,904.64 of same is due on the transaction of May 11, 1971. The parties agree that the excess of $3,466.51 should be paid to defendant Planters State Bank to apply on its August 28, 1972 claim;"

On December 20, 1974, the court entered the following payout order:

"TO THE CLERK OF THE DISTRICT COURT:

"Now on this 20th day of December 1974, you are ordered
to pay to The Planters State Bank and Trust Company the
sum of $3,466.51 now in your hands, having been paid by the
Kaw Valley State Bank and Trust Company, pursuant to the
Journal Entry of Judgment entered herein on November 19,
1974."

Although it does not appear who initiated the order, the
$3,466.51 was paid to and accepted by Planters leaving the disputed proceeds of the sale ($21,904.64) in the hands of either the
escrow agent or the court.

* * *

The primary point on appeal questions the holding of the trial
court that Kaw Valley was not a holder in due course of the note
and security agreement dated May 11, 1971.

[UCC §] 3–306 provides that unless a holder of an instrument
is a holder in due course he takes the instrument subject to the
defenses of want or failure of consideration, nonperformance of
any condition precedent, nondelivery or delivery for a special
purpose. It was undisputed in this case that Riddle received no
consideration after executing the note. The machinery was never delivered and he was assured by Co-Mac that the papers
would be destroyed. The parties so stipulated. If Kaw Valley
was not a holder in due course the proven defense was a bar to
recovery by Kaw Valley.

[UCC §] 3–302 states that a holder in due course is a holder
who takes the instrument (1) for value, (2) in good faith and (3)
without notice of any defense against it. It was not disputed
and the court found that Kaw Valley took the note for value so
the first requirement was satisfied. The other requirements
were subject to dispute. The trial court concluded:

"Kaw Valley State Bank and Trust Company is not a
holder in due course of the note and security agreement, dated May 11, 1971 for the reason that it did not establish in all
respects that it took said instruments in good faith and without notice of any defense against or claimed to it on the part
of John H. Riddle, and Kaw Valley State Bank and Trust
Company therefor took said instruments subject to the defense of failure of consideration. [Citations omitted.]"

So we are confronted with the question of what is required for a holder to take an instrument "in good faith" and "without notice of defense." We will consider the two parts of the question in the order mentioned.

"Good faith" is defined in [UCC §] 1–201(19) as "honesty in fact in the conduct or transaction concerned." The first draft of the Uniform Commercial Code (U.C.C.) as proposed required not only that the actions of a holder be honest in fact but in addition it required the actions to conform to *reasonable commercial standards*. This would have permitted the courts to inquire as to whether a particular commercial standard was in fact reasonable. (See Uniform Commercial Code, Proposed Final Draft [1950], § 1–201, 18, p. 30.) However, when the final draft was approved the test of reasonable commercial standards was excised thus indicating that a more rigid standard must be applied for determining "good faith." See White and Summers, Uniform Commercial Code [1972], § 14–6, pp. 471, 472.)

From the history of the Uniform Commercial Code it would appear that "good faith" requires no actual knowledge of or participation in any material infirmity in the original transaction.

The second part of our question concerns the requirement of the U.C.C. that a holder in due course take the instrument without notice of any defense to the instrument. [UCC §] 1–201(25) provides:

"A person has 'notice' of a fact when

"(a) he has actual knowledge of it; or

"(b) he has received a notice or notification of it; or

"(c) from all the facts and circumstances known to him at the time in question he has reason to know that it exists. A person 'knows' or has 'knowledge' of a fact when he has actual knowledge of it. 'Discover' or 'learn' or a word or phrase of similar import refers to knowledge rather than to reason to know. The time and circumstances under which a notice or notification may cease to be effective are not determined by this act."

As is apparent from reading the above statute the standard enunciated is not limited to the rigid standard of actual knowledge of the defense. Reason to know appears to be premised on the use of reasonable commercial practices. (See 2 Bender's U.C.C. Service, Hart and Willier, Commercial Paper, § 11.05[2] [1972]; Citizens Bank of Booneville v. National Bank of Commerce, 334 F.2d 257 [10th Cir. 1964]; and Universal C. I. T.

Credit Corp. v. Ingel, 347 Mass. 119, 196 N.E.2d 847.) Since "good faith" and "no notice of defense" are both required of a holder to claim the status of a holder in due course it would appear that the two standards are not in conflict even though the standards of conduct may be different.

There is little or no evidence in the present case to indicate that Kaw Valley acted dishonestly or "not in good faith" when it purchased the note of May 11, 1971. However, as to "notice of defense" the court found from all the facts and circumstances known to Kaw Valley at the time in question it had reason to know a defense existed. The court found:

> "During the period 1960 to May, 1971, plaintiff purchased from Co-Mac over 250 notes and secured transactions and held at any given time between $100,000.00 and $250,000.00 of such obligations. All of which were guaranteed by Co-Mac and personally guaranteed by D. J. Wickern, its president. Conant Wait personally handled most if not all of such transactions for plaintiff. Mr. Wait was aware that Co-Mac was making warranties and representation as to fitness to some purchasers of new and used equipment. Mr. Wait further knew that some transactions were in fact not as they would appear to be in that the money from Kaw Valley would be used by Co-Mac to buy the equipment that was the subject matter of the sale. Further, that delivery to the customer of said purchased equipment was sometimes delayed 60 to 90 days for repairing and/or overhauling of same. The plaintiff obviously on many transactions was relying on Co-Mac to insure payment of the obligations and contacted Co-Mac to collect delinquent payments. Some transactions involved delivery of coupon books to Co-Mac rather than the debtor so Co-Mac could bill service and parts charges along with the secured debt. Co-Mac collected payments directly from debtors in various transactions and paid plaintiff. Plaintiff did not concern itself with known irregularities in the transactions as it clearly was relying on Co-Mac;

> "The coupon book on the May 11, 1971 transaction was not sent to defendant Riddle; no payments on same were made by defendant Riddle; the payments were made by Co-Mac until January 25, 1972; prior to early March, 1972, defendant Riddle did not know plaintiff had the May 11, 1971 secured transaction; knowledge of said transaction came to defendant Riddle on March 12, 1972 when Mr. Wait contacted defendant Riddle's manager; that Co-Mac had shortly before

been placed in receivership; that no demand for any payment on said transaction was made by plaintiff to defendant Riddle until September 1972."

To further support its holding that Kaw Valley had reason to know that the defense existed the court found that when Kaw Valley, Co-Mac and Riddle met on February 24, 1972, to consolidate all of Riddle's past due notes Kaw Valley recognized Co-Mac's authority to act for it. Co-Mac had accepted return of the machinery on one of the eight transactions and Kaw Valley recognized its authority as their agent to do so and cancelled the $5,000.00 balance remaining due on the note held by the bank.

The cases dealing with the question of "reason to know a defense exists" seem to fall into four categories.

The first includes those cases where it is established the holder had information from the transferor or the obligor which disclosed the existence of a defense. In those cases it is clear if the holder takes an instrument having received prior or contemporaneous notice of a defense he is not a holder in due course. (Billingsley v. Mackay, 382 F.2d 290 [5th Cir. 1967].) Our present case does not fall in that category for there is no evidence that Co-Mac or Riddle informed Kaw Valley that the machinery had not been delivered when the note was negotiated.

The second group of cases are those in which the defense appears in an accompanying document delivered to the holder with the note. For example, when a security agreement is executed concurrently with a note evidencing an indebtedness incurred for machinery to be delivered in the future. In such case the instrument may under certain circumstances disclose a defense to the note, such as nondelivery of the machinery purchased. (See also Commerce Trust Company v. Denson, 437 S.W.2d 94 [Mo.App.1968], and HIMC Investment Co. v. Siciliano, 103 N.J.Super. 27, 246 A.2d 502, for other examples.) Our present case does not fall in this category because Riddle had signed a written delivery acceptance which was handed to Kaw Valley along with the note and security agreement.

A third group of cases are those in which information appears in the written instrument indicating the existence of a defense, such as when the note on its face shows that the due date has passed or the note bears visible evidence of alteration and forgery or the note is clearly incomplete. (See E. F. Corporation v. Smith, 496 F.2d 826 [10th Cir. 1974]; Srochi v. Kamensky, 118 Ga.App. 182, 162 S.E.2d 889; and Winter & Hirsch, Inc. v. Passarelli, 122 Ill.App.2d 372, 259 N.E.2d 312.) In our present case the instrument assigned bore nothing unusual on its face and appeared complete and proper in all respects.

In the fourth category of cases it has been held that the holder of a negotiable instrument may be prevented from assuming holder in due course status because of knowledge of the business practices of his transferor or when he is so closely aligned with the transferor that transferor may be considered an agent of the holder and the transferee is charged with the actions and knowledge of the transferor.

Under our former negotiable instruments law containing provisions similar to the U.C.C. this court refused to accord holder in due course status to a machinery company receiving notes from one of its dealers because of its knowledge of the business practices of the dealer and the company's participation and alignment with the dealer who transferred the note. (International Harvester Co. v. Watkins, 127 Kan. 50, Sly. ¶ 3, 272 P. 139, 61 A.L.R. 687.)

In Unico v. Owen, 50 N.J. 101, 232 A.2d 405, the New Jersey court refused to accord holder in due course status to a financing partnership which was closely connected with the transferor and had been organized to finance the commercial paper obtained by the transferor and others. The financing partnership had a voice in setting the policies and standards to be followed by the transferor. Under such circumstances the court found that the holder must be considered a participant in the transaction and subject to defenses available against the payee-transferor. In United States Finance Company v. Jones, 285 Ala. 105, 229 So.2d 495, it was held that a finance company purchasing a note from a payee for fifty percent of its face value did not establish holder in due course status and must be held subject to defenses inherent in the original transaction. Other jurisdictions have followed the rationale of Unico. See American Plan Corp. v. Woods, 16 Ohio App.2d 1, 240 N.E.2d 886, where the holder supplied forms to the payee, established financing charges and investigated the credit of the maker of the note; Calvert Credit Corporation v. Williams, 244 A.2d 494 (D.C.App. 1968), where the holder exerted total control over payee's financial affairs; and Jones v. Approved Bancredit Corp., 256 A.2d 739 (Del.1969), where ownership and management of the holder and payee were connected.

In the present case Kaw Valley had worked closely with Co-Mac in over 250 financing transactions over a period of ten years. It knew that some of these transactions were not for valuable consideration at the time the paper was delivered since the bank's money was to be used in purchasing the machinery or equipment represented in the instruments as already in possession of the maker of the note. Kaw Valley had been advised that delivery to Co-Mac's customers was sometimes delayed from 60 to 90 days. Kaw Valley continued to rely on Co-Mac to assure payment of the obligations and contacted it to collect delinquent payments. Some of these transactions, including the one in question, involved the use of coupon books to be used by the debtor in making payment on the notes. In the present case Kaw Valley did not notify Riddle that it was the holder of the note. It delivered Riddle's coupon book to Co-Mac as if it were the obligor or was authorized as its collection agent for this transaction.

Throughout the period from May 11, 1971, to February 25, 1972, Kaw Valley received and credited the monthly payments knowing that payments were being made by Co-Mac and not by Riddle. Then when Riddle's loans were consolidated, the May 11, 1971 transaction was not included by Kaw Valley, either by oversight or by intention, as an obligation of Riddle. Co-Mac occupied a close relationship with Kaw Valley and with its knowledge and consent acted as its agent in collecting payments on notes held by Kaw Valley. The working relationship existing between Kaw Valley and Co-Mac was further demonstrated on February 24, 1972, when the $5,000.00 balance due on one of Riddle's notes was cancelled when it was shown that the machinery for which the note was given had previously been returned to Co-Mac with the understanding that no further payments were due.

[UCC §] 3–307(3) provides:

"After it is shown that a defense exists a person claiming the rights of a holder in due course has the burden of establishing that he or some person under whom he claims is in all respects a holder in due course."

In the present case the court found that the appellant, Kaw Valley, had not sustained its burden of proving that it was a holder in due course. Under the evidence in this case the holder failed to advise the maker of the note of its acquisition of the note and security agreement. It placed the payment coupon book in the hands of Co-Mac and received all monthly payments from them. A close working relationship existed between the two companies and Co-Mac was clothed with authority to collect and forward all payments due on the transaction. Agency and authority was further shown to exist by authorizing return of machinery to Co-Mac and terminating balances due on purchase money paper. We cannot say under the facts and circumstances known and participated in by Kaw Valley in this transaction it did not at the time in question have reason to know that the defense existed. This was a question of fact to be determined by the trier of fact which if supported by substantial competent evidence must stand.

*   *   *

The judgment is affirmed.

PROBLEMS

1. On October 16, 1969, $8,000,000 of United States Treasury Bills in bearer form were stolen from Morgan Bank. On October 28, 1969, when the theft was discovered, Morgan Bank sent a "notice of lost securities," describing the stolen bills by serial number, to bankers and brokers throughout the country. Third Bank, upon receiving the notice placed the notice in its lost securities file. On January 30, 1970 Third Bank made loans totalling $82,000 to Bialkin. As collateral for the loans it took two treasury bills each with a face amount of $50,000. The two bills were among those stolen from Morgan Bank and were listed in the notice of lost securities. The officer of Third Bank who approved the loan to Bialkin did not check the lost securities file of Third Bank. He testified that he was not aware of its existence. Third Bank later discovered that the treasury bills had been stolen and reported it to law enforcement authorities. Morgan Bank then sued to recover the bills.

Treasury bills come within the definition of "investment securities" and are governed by Article 8 of the UCC rather than Article 3. UCC § 3–103(1). In this case Third Bank would defeat the claim of Morgan Bank if it qualified as a bona fide purchaser. UCC § 8–301. A bona fide purchaser of an investment security, defined in UCC § 8–302, is essentially the same as a holder in due course of a negotiable instrument. Did Third Bank have notice of the claim of Morgan Bank to the bills? See UCC § 1–201(25), (26) and (27). This problem is based on the facts, slightly modified, of Morgan Guaranty Trust Co. of New York v. Third National Bank of Hampden County, 529 F.2d 1141 (3d Cir. 1976).

2. In December 1957 Fazzari was induced by fraud to sign a promissory note for $400 payable to the order of Wade. After discovering the fraud, in January 1958, Fazzari notified all of

the local banks of the fraud. He personally spoke to the cashier of Odessa Bank and advised him not to purchase the note because he had been "tricked" by Wade. Three months later Odessa Bank, acting through its cashier, purchased the note. The cashier admitted that Fazzari had told him about the note in January but testified that at the time the note was purchased in April he had forgotten the incident. Did Odessa Bank take the note as a holder in due course? See UCC § 1–201(25) and the Comment to that provision. This problem is based on the facts of First National Bank of Odessa v. Fazzari, 10 N.Y.2d 394, 223 N.Y.S.2d 483, 179 N.E.2d 493 (1961).

[handwritten: Holder in due course status is denied p, overdue 3-302(1)(c)]
[handwritten: a holder who takes an instrument]

1. OVERDUE PAPER

Holder-in-due-course status is denied to a holder who takes an instrument that is overdue. UCC § 3–302(1)(c) and *[handwritten: 3-304(3)]* § 3–304(3). The late Professor Chafee discussed this principle in a famous law review article, Rights in Overdue Paper, 31 Harv. L.Rev. 1104 (1918).* He attempted to justify this thesis: A good faith purchaser for value after maturity takes subject to equities of defense but free of equities of ownership. Chafee quoted Chief Justice Shaw with regard to overdue paper: "The question instantly arises, why is it in circulation,—why is it not paid? Here is something wrong. Therefore, although it does not give the indorsee notice of any specific matter of defense, such as set-off, payment, or fraudulent acquisition, yet it puts him on inquiry." Fisher v. Leland, 58 Mass. 456, 458 (1849). Chafee *[handwritten: Inquiry]* took this to mean that a purchaser after maturity is put on inquiry as to equitable defenses, but his duty to inquire stops there. He has no duty to inquire as to equities of ownership. Chafee stated: "Equities of ownership relate to the instrument as property, but maturity, like equitable defenses, relates to liability on the contracts. It is a term of the respective promises of the parties. The possession of an overdue instrument is a clear indication that there is something the matter with the promises, whether it be a defense or only financial embarrassment or procrastination, but it does not indicate in any way that the possessor wrongfully acquired the instrument from a previous owner." Chafee, supra, at 1126. He added: "Instead of being a red flag to give warning of all hidden dangers, it [maturity] resembles more closely a printed placard calling attention to one special

peril. A person approaching a grade crossing and seeing the
sign: 'Stop, Look and Listen,' is bound to watch for trains, but
he does not assume the risk of a savage bulldog maintained on
the railroad right of way to scare off trackwalkers." Chafee,
supra, at 1122. Did this argument persuade the UCC draftsmen? See UCC § 3–306(a).

PROBLEMS

1. S agreed to sell real property to B for $58,000, of which
$6,500 was to be a down payment. At the time B made the
down payment, he insisted that S execute a promissory note to
his order for the amount of $6,500 as evidence of indebtedness
for any sums B might be called upon to expend to pay off any
claims or liens with respect to the property of which he was not
aware. In time B expended $4,244 in paying these claims. The
note, which was executed by S on March 25 and due 75 days
after date, was indorsed without recourse to Plaintiff on September 1 for a total consideration of $3,067. S refused to pay
the note and Plaintiff brought suit. How much is Plaintiff entitled to recover—$6,500, $4,244, or $3,067? See UCC §§ 3–201
and 3–306. See also Brock v. Adams, 79 N.M. 17, 439 P.2d 234
(1968).

2. Payee sold his house and as partial payment of the price
took from Maker a promissory note for $5,000 payable in month-
ly instalments over a five year period. When Payee's reserve
army unit was called to active duty he went to Banker and asked
him to collect the note during his indefinite absence. Banker
insisted that Payee indorse the note in blank and give him possession of both the note and mortgage. Later Maker fell in default on his payments and Banker, who was in financial difficulties himself, sold the note to Purchaser for value. Purchaser
knew that four payments had not been made but had no knowledge of the circumstances under which Banker had taken the
note. After Payee returned and learned of Banker's actions, he
asserted his claim of ownership against Purchaser and sued to
retake possession of the note. What result? See Justice v.
Stonecipher, 267 Ill. 448, 108 N.E. 722 (1915). See UCC
§§ 3–304(3)(a) and 3–306(a).

2. IRREGULAR PAPER

Holder-in-due-course status may also be denied to a person
who takes paper that is incomplete or irregular on its face. The

problem with respect to incomplete or irregular paper is similar to the problem regarding overdue paper discussed by Chafee. The taker of incomplete or irregular paper may be on notice that something may be wrong with the paper, but of what is he put on notice?   Under NIL § 52, to be a holder in due course the holder must have taken an instrument "complete and regular upon its face" and before it was overdue.   Thus, the two problems were treated identically.   The UCC approach is somewhat different.   UCC § 3–302, defining holder in due course, does not refer to the taking of an incomplete or irregular instrument.   Incompleteness or irregularity of the instrument is dealt with in the notice provision, UCC § 3–304(1)(a), and may or may not disqualify the taker from holder-in-due-course status.   Consider the following cases:

(Case 1)   In payment of goods, Maker signed a negotiable note in the amount of $10,000 and mailed it to Payee.   The note should have been payable in the amount of $20,000.   When Payee received the note he noticed the discrepancy and called Maker's attention to it.   Maker told Payee to change the $10,000 to $20,000.   Payee did so by erasing and typing over.   The alteration was crudely done and very obvious.   Payee then sold the note to Holder.   Holder noticed the alteration but accepted Payee's truthful explanation of the circumstances under which it was made.   When Holder demanded payment Maker refused, stating that Payee never delivered the goods for which the note was given.   Is Holder subject to the defense of Maker?   Suppose Holder, before completing the transaction, had called Maker and that Maker had verified that the $20,000 figure was correct.   How does this affect your answer?

(Case 2)   Maker signed a negotiable note payable to Corporation in the amount of $10,000.   X, President of Corporation, indorsed the note in Corporation's name and transferred it to Holder in satisfaction of a personal debt of $10,000 owed by X to Holder, who accepted X's false explanation that Corporation owed X more than $10,000 and that the transaction was an informal way of partially satisfying Corporation's debt to X.   When Holder demanded payment, Maker refused, stating that he had been fraudulently induced to sign the note and received no consideration for it.   Is Holder subject to Maker's defense?   UCC § 3–302(1)(c) and § 3–304(2).   Suppose Holder, before making that transaction, called Y, the treasurer of Corporation.   Y falsely informed Holder that X was authorized to make the transaction.   How does this affect your answer?

Is the issue in the two cases set forth above whether Holder had notice of Maker's defense or whether, in taking the note, Holder acted in good faith? If it is the latter is a subjective standard of good faith useful?

3. TRANSACTIONS WITH FIDUCIARIES

The court in *Kaw Valley* had little trouble in disposing of the subjective good faith test. Through the notice requirement it was able to impose on the bank a standard it considered to be commercially desirable. Banks and other financial institutions are the primary beneficiaries of the holder-in-due-course doctrine. When New York adopted the UCC it added an additional provision, § 3–304(7), which provides: "In any event, to constitute notice of a claim or defense, the purchaser must have knowledge of the claim or defense or knowledge of such facts that his action in taking the instrument amounts to bad faith." You will recognize this as Section 56 of the NIL in modern garb. The case that follows was decided under the New York UCC. The bank that was asserting rights as a holder in due course took the instrument from a person acting in a fiduciary capacity. Consider to what extent this element affects the good faith and notice issues.

CHEMICAL BANK OF ROCHESTER v. HASKELL

Supreme Court of New York, Appellate Division, Fourth Department, 1979.
68 A.D.2d 347, 417 N.Y.S.2d 541.

SCHNEPP, JUSTICE. Appellants, John Haskell, Paddy Chayefsky, Halsey F. Sherwood and Arthur Giliotti, together with John F. Kelly and Edward Fine (not parties to the instant actions) are limited partners in Quarry Square Associates ("Quarry"), a limited partnership organized for the purpose of developing an apartment complex in Buffalo, New York. Stanndco Developers, Inc. ("Stanndco"), a real estate development corporation which organized the partnership, is a Class A general partner of Quarry. Stanndco conducted its business by purchasing land, obtaining financing, searching out investors, forming limited partnerships and then establishing itself as general managing partner responsible for the construction and operation of the projects. David J. Quigley, Anthony J. Caldarone and Charles P. Laiosa, major shareholders in Stanndco, are Class B general partners of Quarry.

The limited partners signed the articles of partnership of Quarry in December 1972. Their individual capital contribution consisted of the payment of cash and the execution and delivery of three negotiable notes payable to Quarry which contained identical terms and were due December 1, 1973, December 1, 1974 and June 1, 1975. On February 13, 1973 Sherwood and Giliotti signed an amendment to the limited partnership agreement under which their notes were returned and payment of the balance of their capital contribution was conditioned upon the completion of certain percentages of construction of the apartment complex. At the behest of Quigley, Stanndco's Chief Executive Officer, Sherwood and Giliotti re-executed and delivered their notes to Quarry on March 26, 1973 ostensibly for its credit files. On May 25, 1973 the Chemical Bank of Rochester ("Chemical"), formerly known as the State Bank of Hilton, purchased the notes at a discount. Upon Stanndco's endorsement and delivery of the notes to Chemical, the bank then delivered to Stanndco a bank draft for the purchase price. The draft was payable to the order of Stanndco. By letters dated July 26, 1973 Chemical notified the individual makers that it had purchased the notes.

When the December 1973 notes came due Haskell defaulted while Chayefsky, Sherwood and Giliotti made payment. In January 1974 mortgage foreclosure proceedings against the project were instituted, a receiver appointed, and the mortgage eventually foreclosed. Subsequently the project was completed by the mortgagee. In February 1974 Stanndco filed a petition in bankruptcy. Haskell, Chayefsky, Sherwood and Giliotti then defaulted on the remainder of the notes held by the bank. Kelly and Fine paid their obligations on the notes.

Action No. 1 was instituted by Chemical against Haskell pursuant to CPLR 3213 to recover $63,000 with interest on his three outstanding notes and reasonable attorneys' fees. Action No. 2 was instituted by Chayefsky, as a limited partner in Quarry suing individually and on behalf of all others similarly situated, against Chemical seeking a declaration of his rights, cancellation of the notes and a judgment ordering repayment of the amount of the first note which he paid in December 1973. Sherwood and Giliotti brought a similar action requesting the same relief. In these actions Chemical interposed a counterclaim for the unpaid principal amount of the notes due December 1, 1974 and June 1, 1975 in addition to interest and legal fees. The cases were tried together and judgment was entered in favor of Chemical for the amounts stated in the notes plus interest from the date of default and attorneys' fees. The court found that Chemical was the holder in due course of all the notes in question and took free of all defenses raised by the makers.

On appeal the appellant-makers argue that Chemical is not a holder in due course and is subject to the defenses of fraud, misrepresentation and failure of consideration and that the award of attorneys' fees was improper. Sherwood and Giliotti further posit the defense of fraud in the factum. Chemical argues that appellants failed to prove a valid defense to the enforcement of the notes, that it is a holder in due course, and that the award of attorneys' fees was inadequate. In reply appellants argue that the endorsement of the notes by Stanndco to Chemical without the written consent or ratification of the limited partners violated section 98 of the Partnership Law and the Partnership Agreement, and constitutes a complete defense even if Chemical is a holder in due course.

We hold that Trial Term was correct in dismissing the defenses of fraud and misrepresentation. As appellants conceded at the conclusion of their proofs, no credible testimony supporting the defenses of misrepresentation or fraud was presented at trial.

At the same time the court allowed appellants to amend their pleadings to conform to the evidence by adding the defense of failure of consideration. Appellants argue that the abandonment of the Quarry project deprived them of the following benefits: (1) their equity interest in the apartment complex, (2) the reasonable expected appreciation of the project and profits upon eventual sale, (3) rental income from apartment units, (4) immediate tax advantages in the form of deductions during construction of interest on interim financing money and other expenses of construction, and (5) continuing tax advantages in the form of deductions of depreciation allowances and other benefits commonly arising from tax shelters. They urge that the continued construction of the project to completion was an express or implied condition precedent to payment of the notes and maintain that the abandonment of the project and the bankruptcy of Stanndco made it impossible to fulfill these conditions.

This defense has no merit as applied to appellants Chayefsky and Haskell because they received an equity interest in Quarry in consideration for the execution and delivery of their notes. Neither the bankruptcy of Stanndco nor non-completion of the project releases them from their obligations. It cannot be inferred from the proofs that continued solvency or completion of the construction was intended by the parties to operate as a condition precedent to the payment of the notes (see 10 N.Y.Jur. Contracts, § 252).

However, upon the execution of the amended articles of limited partnership by Sherwood and Giliotti, payment of their contribution was expressly conditioned upon completion of certain percentages of construction of the apartment complex. This condition precedent was not met when the specified percentages were not completed. This failure may be asserted as a valid defense by Sherwood and Giliotti against Quarry and Stanndco. The defense remains viable even though this condition was not expressed in the negotiable instruments they executed. Their defense of fraud in the factum, however, is meritless and was properly dismissed by the Trial Court. There is no proof that they were ignorant of the contents of the negotiable notes which they executed on March 26, 1973 following the execution of the amended agreement on February 13, 1973 or that they did not intend to sign them. The notes, which are clearly legible on their face, do not condition payment upon the completion of construction.

On appeal appellants further contend as a complete defense that the notes were transferred in violation of the Partnership Law. This argument was not specifically articulated by appellants before the Trial Court and generally this court will not consider questions not raised at trial. However, since the issue was litigated, the interests of justice mandate our consideration of this argument. We are not confined to a review of the particular grounds upon which the Trial Court acted (Carmody-Wait 2d, N.Y.Prac. §§ 70:302, 72:127), and if necessary we are empowered to make original findings of fact overruling those made by the Trial Court and to render judgment accordingly (Carmody-Wait 2d, N.Y.Prac. § 72:158).

The facts relating to this defense are not in dispute. In the spring of 1973 Quigley, Chairman of the Board, and Chief Executive Officer of Stanndco, sought a loan for Stanndco from Chemical. Following his initial contact, in a letter to the bank dated May 1, 1973 he described the financial structure of Quarry, the status of the project and the capital contribution of each limited partner. He outlined in detail the due dates and amounts of each note and stated, "Stanndco would like to borrow $315,000 with these notes as collateral." There was evidence that during this period of time Stanndco, which was involved in various construction projects, was experiencing financial difficulty. Chemical rejected this offer and agreed to purchase the notes, which had a face value of $315,000, at a discount. Upon receipt of the endorsed notes it delivered a bank draft in the amount of $274,390.32 payable to the order of Stanndco which was received and deposited by Stanndco in its account at the Central Trust Company. Although none of the limited partners were advised of Stanndco's disposition of the partnership notes, Stanndco, as general partner of Quarry, executed and delivered an estoppel certificate to Chemical which certified that there were no defenses or offsets against the notes.

Section 98 of the Partnership Law provides in part that a "general partner shall have all the rights and powers and be subject to all the restrictions and liabilities of a partner in a partnership without limited partners, except that without the written consent or ratification of the specific act by all the limited partners, a general partner * * * [has] no authority to * * * [p]ossess partnership property, or assign [his] rights in specific partnership property, for other than a partnership purpose" (Partnership Law, § 98, subd. 1, par. [d]).

Stanndco breached its fiduciary duty to Quarry and violated section 98 of the Partnership Law when it endorsed the notes to itself, sold them, and deposited the proceeds of the sale in its corporate account. This action by Stanndco also violated the articles of limited partnership which prohibited the disposition of a substantial part of the partnership's assets without the prior written consent of the limited partners. Moreover, Stanndco breached the articles which require that the general partner maintain bank accounts for the deposit of partnership funds. Stanndco's deposit of the proceeds of the sale in its own corporate account evidenced its intent "[to] [p]ossess partnership property * * * for other than a partnership purpose" (Partnership Law, § 98, subd. 1, par. [d]). The silence of the limited partners upon the receipt of Chemical's letter dated July 26, 1976 and their payment of the December 1973 notes did not constitute ratification by them of Stanndco's negotiation of the notes. There is nothing to show that the limited partners had any reason to suspect that Chemical held the notes other than for an indebtedness of Quarry in furtherance of its business.

The question remains as to the effect of the above violations of the Partnership Law and the original articles of limited partnership. It is clear that under the terms of section 3–306 of the Uniform Commercial Code the appellant-makers here have a valid defense to the enforcement of the notes by Chemical, if the bank is not deemed a holder in due course.

The determinative issue at this juncture is whether the weight of the evidence presented at trial supports a finding that Chemical was a holder in due course of the partnership notes.

* * *

The existence merely of suspicious circumstances does not, without more, amount to notice of an infirmity or defect (Hall v. Bank of Blasdell, 306 N.Y. 336, 340, 118 N.E.2d 464; Uniform Commercial Code, § 3–304[7]).

* * *

The mere fact that Chemical took the instruments for value does not necessarily establish its "good faith". This must be determined from all the facts and circumstances surrounding the transaction (see City of New York v. Nic Homes, 44 Misc.2d 440, 442, 253 N.Y.S.2d 926, 927, and cases cited).

The Trial Court found that Chemical's failure to investigate the progress of the construction, or the financial position of Stanndco or Quigley, brought it "perilously close" to losing its holder in due course status. Although the court found that "a prudent lender" might well have pursued an investigation, it found that the proof failed "to indicate lack of good faith". It is apparent that the court did not consider other relevant facts and circumstances disclosed by the evidence. We find that Chemical did not take the instrument in good faith and without notice of a defense or claim to it. In brief, Chemical did not sustain its burden of establishing its holder in due course status (Uniform Commercial Code, § 3–307, subd. [3]).

Stanndco's letter of inquiry dated May 1, 1973 informed Chemical that Stanndco, not Quarry, was seeking a loan. It also informed the bank that the notes, which Stanndco sought to use as collateral for the loan, constituted the contribution of the limited partners to the partnership. The letter printed on Stanndco stationery and signed by Quigley in his capacity as Chairman of the Board and Chief Executive Officer for Stanndco, in no way indicates that the notes executed by the limited partners would be used for a partnership purpose. The clear import of the letter is that Stanndco was seeking a loan for its own corporate purposes. Yet in the face of these facts, Chemical neither investigated the limited partnership nor inquired as to the scope of Stanndco's authority to negotiate the notes.

The chain of endorsements printed on the back of each note also gave the bank notice that Stanndco was negotiating the notes for its own benefit. The notes of Sherwood and Giliotti were endorsed to Stanndco from Quarry by Stanndco as general partner. Stanndco then endorsed them to Chemical. The notes of Chayefsky and Haskell, were also endorsed to Stanndco from Quarry by Stanndco, but here Stanndco did not sign in its representative capacity as general partner. These notes also were endorsed by Stanndco to Chemical.[4] The discrepancy between Stanndco's endorsements on the various notes indicates at least some irregularity. Stanndco was negotiating Quarry's notes in different capacities—agent in one case, principal in the other.

Moreover, the Chayefsky and Haskell notes reflect a previous transaction between Quarry and the Central Trust Company ("Central Trust"). These notes were first negotiated by Stanndco as general partner of Quarry to Central Trust which later endorsed them back to Quarry with recourse.[5] Central Trust's previous endorsements of the notes to Quarry evidences a recognition that the notes belong to the partnership and not to Stanndco. Yet, apparently ignoring this signal, Chemical treated the transaction as a purchase of Stanndco's property. Its bank draft was made payable to Stanndco, not the partnership.

Furthermore, the notes were purchased at a substantial discount. Although the mere fact that a note is purchased for an amount less than its face value is not of itself sufficient to charge the purchaser with notice of existing equities, it is a factor to be considered along with other factors as evidence of bad faith (Chemical Bank of Rochester v. Ashenburg, 94 Misc.2d 64, 66, 405 N.Y.S.2d 967, 970).

The circumstances here are more than just suspicious. They clearly demonstrate that Stanndco was using the partnership notes for its own corporate purposes in breach of its fiduciary duty to the limited partnership (Uniform Commercial Code, § 3-304, subd. [2]). The endorsements appearing on each note should have prompted Chemical, before consummating the sale, to make inquiries of Stanndco's authority. Any investigation would have disclosed that the general partner had not been authorized to exercise dominion over the partnership property or assign the rights of the limited partners in specific partnership

4. See Appendix # 1 and # 2 for copies of the endorsements appearing on the back of the notes.

5. See Appendix # 2.

property without their written consent or ratification.[7] Instead, Chemical blithely ignored clear warnings which signaled that the notes were being negotiated by Stanndco without proper authority and for its own use. It chose blindly to accept the notes, as several expert witnesses opined at trial, in clear violation of sound banking practices.

In view of all these facts and circumstances, we conclude that the bank did not act in good faith. It had actual knowledge or knowledge of facts sufficient to impute notice of infirmities, defects and defenses to the instrument (Uniform Commercial Code, § 3–304, subd. [7]). It had notice that Stanndco was negotiating the partnership's notes for its own corporate purpose in breach of its fiduciary duty to the limited partners (Uniform Commercial Code, § 3–304, subd. [2]). In short, the weight of the evidence supports a finding that the bank was not a holder in due course.

As a non-holder in due course, plaintiff takes subject to the defendants' claim that the notes were negotiated for the individual purpose of a general partner in breach of its fiduciary duty. Even though Quarry is not a named party in this action, the makers can assert this defense. They are not asserting "jus tertii"—but their own rights (Uniform Commercial Code, § 3–306, subd. [d]; Chemical Bank of Rochester v. Ashenburg, supra, p. 67). As limited partners, these makers are directly offended and damaged by Stanndco's breach of duty. Subdivision [d] of section 3–306 of the Uniform Commercial Code was not intended by its drafters to bar this type of defense (see Official Comment No. 5, Uniform Commercial Code, § 3–306; Chemical Bank of Rochester v. Ashenburg, supra, 94 Misc.2d pp. 67–68, 405 N.Y.S.2d p. 971). The unauthorized signature of Quarry is "wholly inoperative" and Chemical, which should have known that Quarry's endorsement was made without the consent of the limited partners, cannot recover from the signers of the instrument (Uniform Commercial Code, § 3–404).

Chemical also took the instruments subject to the defense of Sherwood and Giliotti that payment was conditioned upon completion of certain percentages of construction (Uniform Commer-

---

7. By appropriating the partnership property for its own corporate purpose, Stanndco effectively terminated the right of the limited partners to have their contribution returned. Each limited partner has a right to receive a share of the profits and to a return of his contribution after payment, among other things, of all liabilities of the partnership (Partnership Law, § 105).

cial Code, § 3–306). For this and the above-stated reasons appellants are not liable on the notes to Chemical.

* * *

Accordingly, it is held that Chemical is not a holder in due course of the notes at issue and it took possession of the notes subject to the defenses described above and the appellant-makers are not liable on the notes to Chemical. Chemical's complaint against Haskell should be dismissed. Judgment should be granted to the plaintiffs in their declaratory judgment actions limited to a finding that they are not liable to Chemical on the notes at issue. The counterclaims of Chemical should be dismissed. Similarly, the award of attorneys' fees should be vacated.

* * *

APPENDIX # 1

Copy of endorsements appearing on the notes of Sherwood and Giliotti:

Pay to the order of Stanndco Developers, Inc., with recourse, Quarry Square Associates.

Stanndco Developers, Inc., Gen'l Partner
By: D. J. Quigley, Chairman of the Board

Pay to the order of State Bank of Hilton, with recourse, Stanndco Developers, Inc.

By: T. H. Traynor, Treas.

APPENDIX # 2

Copy of endorsements appearing on the notes of Chayefsky and Haskell:

Pay to the Order of CENTRAL TRUST COMPANY ROCHESTER N.Y.
QUARRY SQUARE, ASSOCIATES
STANNDCO DEVELOPERS, GENERAL PARTNER
By
David Quigley

Pay to the order of QUARRY SQUARE, ASSOCIATES, with recourse,

CENTRAL TRUST COMPANY ROCHESTER, N. Y.
BY _____
Vice-President

Pay to the order of Stanndco Developers, Inc., with recourse,
Quarry Square Associates

Stanndco Developers, Inc.
By: D. J. Quigley, Chairman of the Board

Pay to the order of State Bank of Hilton, with recourse,
Stanndco Developers, Inc.

By: T. H. Traynor, Treas.

NOTES

1. The preceding decision was unanimously reversed by the
New York Court of Appeals, 51 N.Y.2d 85, 411 N.E.2d 1339
(1980). The court made the following statement:

The conclusion of the Appellate Division concerning
Chemical's duty to inquire raises important questions as to
the meaning of the terms "in good faith" and "without notice" as used in section 3–302. Good faith under the code is
defined as "honesty in fact in the conduct or transaction concerned" (Uniform Commercial Code, § 1–201, subd. [19]) and
it is clear that the draftsmen intended that this language set
a subjective and not objective standard. In fact, so that no
confusion would persist on this score, a proposed draft of
section 3–302 which explained good faith in terms related to
commercial reasonableness was amended to delete the of-
fending language (White and Summers, Uniform Commercial
Code [2d ed.], § 14–6, p. 563; 1954 Report of N.Y.Law Rev.
Comm., vol. 1, pp. 203–205). Thus, the inquiry is not whether
a reasonable banker in Chemical's position would have
known, or would have inquired concerning the alleged breach
by Stanndco of its partnership duties, but rather, the inquiry
is what Chemical itself actually knew. If Chemical did not
have actual knowledge of some fact which would prevent a
commercially honest individual from taking up the instruments, then its good faith was sufficiently shown (see 1955
Report of N.Y.Law Rev.Comm., vol. 2, pp. 906–907).

A similar problem is presented on the issue of whether
Chemical had notice of claims or defenses on the notes. Notice is defined for the code generally in section 1–201 (subd.

25) which states: "A person has 'notice' of a fact when (a) he has actual knowledge of it; or (b) he has received a notice or notification of it; or (c) from all the facts and circumstances known to him at the time in question he has reason to know that it exists."

Arguably, were paragraph (c) of subdivision (25) to be applied to determine whether a holder has taken an instrument "without notice * * * of any defense * * * or claim" (Uniform Commercial Code, § 3–302, subd. [1]), an objective or reasonable person standard would be appropriate. However, section 1–201 also states that its definitions are "[s]ubject to additional definitions contained in the subsequent Articles of this Act which are applicable to specific Articles or Parts thereof, and unless the context otherwise requires."

We therefore examine the explanation of notice provided in article three, which states in specific reference to notice of a claim or defense that: "the purchaser must have *knowledge* of the claim or defense or *knowledge* of such facts that his action in taking the instrument amounts to *bad faith.*" (Emphasis added.) (Uniform Commercial Code, § 3–304, subd. [7].) It is important to note that this subdivision speaks in terms of "knowledge" and not the "reason to know" language used in subdivision (3) of the same section. This is a meaningful distinction because "knowledge" under the code means "actual knowledge" (Uniform Commercial Code, § 1–201, subd. [25]). Moreover, subdivision (7) of section 3–304 was added by New York to the 1962 Official Text of the code in order to make clear that the subjective test, applicable in this State even before the enactment of the code was intended to be continued (1962 Supp. Report on the Uniform Commercial Code, N.Y.Comm. on Uniform State Laws, pp. 6–7; see Hall v. Bank of Blasdell, 306 N.Y. 336, 118 N.E.2d 464).

In applying the above principles to the facts at bar, we hold that Chemical sustained its burden of establishing itself as a holder in due course. Chemical's president, Olney, testified that he "was aware of no defense", and that as far as communication with the makers indicating the existence of defenses was concerned, there was "none whatsoever." In no way is this testimony directly controverted. On the contrary, the fact that when the makers were notified of the transfer they never communicated to Chemical the difficulties now argued, indicates that they too, were unaware of any defenses. It is unreasonable to expect in this situation that Chemical foresee improprieties in the underlying transaction which would later be disclosed. The State's interest in free flow of commercial paper does not tolerate the placing of such a burden on banks acting in good faith.

The most that can be said of the testimony offered to controvert Chemical's position is that it indicated suspicious circumstances which might well have induced a prudent banker to investigate more thoroughly than did Chemical before taking the notes. However, as has been previously indicated, this is not enough. Chemical was not bound to be " 'alert for circumstances which might possibly excite the suspicions of wary vigilance' " (Hall v. Bank of Blasdell, 306 N.Y. 336, 341, 118 N.E.2d 464, supra). There was no obligation on Chemical, as a purchaser of negotiable paper, to investigate the financial position of its transferor, or the progress of the underlying construction project. The failure of Chemical to take steps to insure that Stanndco was negotiating the instruments for partnership purposes or the fact that correspondence sent to Chemical was written on Stanndco stationery do not, in and of themselves, indicate impropriety. Nor did the fact that the notes were purchased at a discount, or that Chemical drew the check by which it purchased the drafts to the order of Stanndco and not Quarry, or the other factors incidental to the transaction, indicate in any substantial way a misuse of funds or constitute notice of misappropriation. Stanndco was a general partner vested by the limited partners with broad managing powers, and if misdealings originating in that delegation created a loss, the loss should not fall on those who dealt with Stanndco in good faith, but on those who provided the opportunity for misappropriation. There was no testimony that Chemical had any knowing part in the alleged misappropriation and, in fact, Chemical had reason to believe that Stanndco was acting for a partnership purpose at the time that it sold the notes and received the proceeds.

2. The Court of Appeals was unwilling to draw the conclusion that Chemical Bank must have known that the sale of the notes was for the benefit of Stanndco in spite of the very strong facts supporting the opposite conclusion made by the Appellate Division. If in fact the transaction was for the benefit of Quarry Associates, the prior indorsement of the notes to Stanndco is very difficult to explain. To what extent was the position of the

Court of Appeals influenced by the fact that the issue presented
was whether Chemical Bank was a holder in due course? On
this issue the legislative history of the UCC in New York strongly supports the notion that the "pure heart and empty head" theory of holder in due course is to prevail. But the issue might
have been posed in different terms. Stanndco, acting as a fiduciary, had control over the notes which were assets of its principal, Quarry Associates. Suppose Quarry had sued Chemical
Bank to recover the notes in a conversion action. Section 4 of
the Uniform Fiduciaries Act is in effect in New York and specifically deals with this kind of case.

§ 4. Transfer of Negotiable Instrument by Fiduciary

If any negotiable instrument payable or indorsed to a fiduciary as such is indorsed by the fiduciary, or if any negotiable instrument payable or indorsed to his principal is indorsed by a fiduciary empowered to indorse such instrument
on behalf of his principal, the indorsee is not bound to inquire
whether the fiduciary is committing a breach of his obligation as fiduciary in indorsing or delivering the instrument,
and is not chargeable with notice that the fiduciary is committing a breach of his obligation as fiduciary unless he takes
the instrument with actual knowledge of such breach or with
knowledge of such facts that his action in taking the instrument amounts to bad faith. If, however, such instrument is
transferred by the fiduciary in payment of or as security for
a personal debt of the fiduciary to the actual knowledge of
the creditor, or is transferred in any transaction known by
the transferee to be for the personal benefit of the fiduciary,
the creditor or other transferee is liable to the principal if the
fiduciary in fact commits a breach of his obligation as fiduciary in transferring the instrument.

Chemical Bank was aware that the notes were originally payable
to the order of Quarry and that Stanndco as a fiduciary indorsed
them over to itself and then to Chemical Bank. The Appellate
Division concluded from this that the known facts "clearly
demonstrate that Stanndco was using the partnership notes for
its own corporate purpose in breach of its fiduciary duty to the
limited partnership." But it was not necessary to go that far.
Under the last sentence of UFA § 4 actual knowledge of the
breach of fiduciary duty by Chemical Bank was not necessary.
It was enough that it knew that the transaction was for the personal benefit of Stanndco. Thus, even if Chemical Bank satisfied a subjective good faith test it might still be liable. Would a

court in a UFA § 4 action accept the statement of Chemical Bank that it didn't know for whose benefit the transaction was made when all outward indications were that the transaction was for the benefit of Stanndco?

Is it permissible to say that even if Chemical Bank took the notes in violation of UFA § 4 it might be taking in good faith for the purposes of UCC § 3–302(1)(b)? If it is, since Chemical Bank clearly did not have notice of the defense of Sherwood and Giliotti that the note was conditional on completion of the apartments, Chemical Bank can forcefully argue that the defense is cut off. Is Chemical Bank charged with notice of the claim of Quarry Associates to the notes? UCC § 3–304(2) and (4)(e). In UCC § 3–304(2) what does the phrase "in breach of duty" modify? Does UFA § 4 help you decide? See Trenton Trust Co. v. Western Surety Co., 599 S.W.2d 481 (Mo.1980), (holder not a holder in due course if it knew that a fiduciary negotiated an instrument of the beneficiary as security for the debt of the fiduciary). If Chemical Bank had notice of the claim of Quarry is Chemical Bank deprived of holder-in-due-course status by UCC § 3–302(1)(c) and thus subject to the defense of Sherwood and Giliotti? UCC § 3–306(c). Haskell and Chayefsky had no defense on the note against Quarry. Whether or not Chemical Bank was a holder in due course, to allow Haskell and Chayefsky to avoid payment is to give them a windfall. Chemical Bank's purchase of the notes was an injury only to Quarry which should be able to claim the notes from Chemical Bank and enforce them.

3. Section 6 of the Uniform Fiduciaries Act provides as follows:

§ 6. Check Drawn by and Payable to Fiduciary

If a check or other bill of exchange is drawn by a fiduciary as such or in the name of his principal by a fiduciary empowered to draw such instrument in the name of his principal, payable to the fiduciary personally, or payable to a third person and by him transferred to the fiduciary, and is thereafter transferred by the fiduciary, whether in payment of a personal debt of the fiduciary or otherwise, the transferee is not bound to inquire whether the fiduciary is committing a breach of his obligation as fiduciary in transferring the instrument, and is not chargeable with notice that the fiduciary is committing a breach of his obligation as fiduciary unless he takes the instrument with actual knowledge of such breach or with knowledge of such facts that his action in taking the instrument amounts to bad faith.

Assume that A as the managing general partner of ABC Partnership wrote a check on behalf of ABC drawn on ABC's account to the order of A and had then negotiated the check to Bank. Assume that the drawee paid the check. What liability would Bank have to ABC Partnership under § 6 of the Uniform Fiduciaries Act if a) it is assumed that the check was written in breach of fiduciary duty and b) Bank had no knowledge of the breach of duty? Is this result consistent with the result under UFA § 4? How do UCC § 3–304(2) and 4(e) affect Bank's assertion of rights as a holder in due course of the check? Assume that the drawee had refused to pay the check and Bank is suing ABC Partnership under UCC § 3–413(2). *Bank would win no Knowledge*

4. Section 5 of the Uniform Fiduciaries Act provides as follows:

§ 5. Check Drawn by Fiduciary Payable to Third Person

If a check or other bill of exchange is drawn by a fiduciary as such, or in the name of his principal by a fiduciary empowered to draw such instrument in the name of his principal, the payee is not bound to inquire whether the fiduciary is committing a breach of his obligation as fiduciary in drawing or delivering the instrument, and is not chargeable with notice that the fiduciary is committing a breach of his obligation as fiduciary unless he takes the instrument with actual knowledge of such breach or with knowledge of such facts that his action in taking the instrument amounts to bad faith. If, however, such instrument is payable to a personal creditor of the fiduciary and delivered to the creditor in payment of or as security for a personal debt of the fiduciary to the actual knowledge of the creditor, or is drawn and delivered in any transaction known by the payee to be for the personal benefit of the fiduciary, the creditor or other payee is liable to the principal if the fiduciary in fact commits a breach of his obligation as fiduciary in drawing or delivering the instrument.

Assume that A as managing general partner of ABC Partnership wrote a check on behalf of ABC drawn on ABC's account to the order of X, a personal creditor of A, in payment of A's debt to X. Assume that the drawee paid the check. What liability would X have to ABC Partnership under UFA § 5 if a) it is assumed that the check was written in breach of fiduciary duty and b) X had no knowledge of the breach of duty? Is this result consistent with the results under UFA § 4 and § 6? How do UCC § 3–304(2) and (4)(e) apply to this case?

5. Is Comment 5 to UCC § 3–304(2) helpful in interpreting UCC § 3–304(2) and (4)(e)?

4. NEGOTIABILITY IN CONSUMER TRANSACTIONS

In the typical consumer credit sale transaction the buyer signs a contract in which the buyer is obliged to pay the debt arising from the sale in installments. The contract usually provides for the granting of a security interest in the goods to secure payment of the debt. This retail installment sale contract is usually sold by the seller to a bank or other financial institution. The assignee of the retail installment sale contract may seek to take free of claims or defenses that the buyer may have had against the seller at the time of the assignment. If the buyer has given a negotiable note to evidence the debt the assignee will seek to assert rights as a holder in due course, or in the case of a nonnegotiable contract the assignee might get the benefits of negotiability by a clause in the agreement in which the buyer agrees that any claims or defenses that he might have against the seller will not be asserted against the assignee.

Professor Gilmore observes: "The most outrageous thing about article 3, a statute drafted in the 1940's, is that there is no reference in text or comment, to the then rapidly developing body of case law holding that finance companies and banks to which consumer notes were negotiated could not hold the notes free of the consumer's contract defenses because of their close connection with dealer-sellers." The Good Faith Purchase Idea and the Uniform Commercial Code: Confessions of a Repentant Draftsman, 15 Ga.L.Rev. 605, 619 (1981). Hence, the UCC is neutral on the question of whether an assignee in a consumer transaction should be entitled to the benefits of negotiability. Nothing in the UCC prevents a seller from taking a negotiable note to evidence the buyer's debt. UCC § 9–206, which deals with security interests, recognizes the validity of clauses against the assertion of claims and defenses against assignees "subject to any statute or decision which establishes a different rule for buyers or lessees of consumer goods." During the 1950's and 60's judicial hostility toward both negotiability and waiver clauses in consumer transactions grew to such an extent that in recent years assignees of consumer paper have found it extremely difficult to sustain their status as takers free of claims and defenses. As we shall see, many legislatures in the 1960's and 70's virtually abolished negotiability in consumer credit transactions. See Rohner, Holder in Due Course in Consumer Transactions: Requiem, Revival, or Reformation?, 60 Cornell L.Rev. 503 (1975).

Why has this time-honored doctrine been rejected by courts and legislatures in recent years? By subjecting credit grantors to the claims and defenses of consumer buyers, does not abolition of negotiability inevitably increase the cost of consumer credit? Judge Richard Posner, a lawyer-economist, examines the negotiability issue.[1]

Contracts are sometimes said to involve duress if the terms seem disadvantageous to purchasers and the purchasers are poor. An example is a sale on credit where the purchaser agrees that the seller may discount the purchaser's note to a finance company. The finance company, as a "holder in due course," can enforce the note free from any defense that the purchaser might have interposed in a collection suit brought by the seller. Suppose the purchaser buys a chest of drawers from a furniture store and the chest is delivered badly damaged. Meanwhile the store has discounted the purchaser's note to a finance company and the purchaser must therefore pay the full amount of the note. He has legal remedies against the furniture company if it refuses to replace the damaged chest but these may be costly to pursue.

Yet it would be incorrect to conclude that the purchaser must have been coerced into agreeing to so unfavorable a contractual provision. The holder in due course provision reduces the cost of financing installment purchases by making collection suits cheaper and more certain. In its absence this cost—which is borne at least in major part by the consumer since it is a marginal cost—would be higher. It is not obviously wiser for the consumer to decide to pay more for a product than to decide to surrender one of his legal remedies against the seller. (Of course, if the purchaser does not understand the effect of such provisions, he does not have a meaningful choice. This may be a problem but again it is one of fraud rather than of inequality of bargaining power.)

It is an attractively simple alternative to the complex bulk of statutory and case law that has grown up around the holder-in-due-course doctrine to hypothesize a "private" solution in which the finance charge rate is adjusted according to the consumer's

---

1. Posner, Economic Analysis of Law 86 (2d ed. 1977). Published by   Little, Brown & Company. Reprinted with permission.

choice of whether he wants the right to raise sales defenses against the financer as well as against the seller. But the buyer is never given this choice. And if he were, could he make an informed choice? What is the feasibility and cost of explaining to the buyer the difference between the value of the self-help remedy of refusal to make payments to an unpaid financer until settlement is reached, as against the value of the remedy of recovering his money by suit from a paid seller? Can the buyer understand and quantify the impact of making the financer subject to defenses? Will he understand that the financer can exert pressure on the dealer to encourage settlement of the buyer's claim? Surely, no paragraph in a form contract can adequately give the buyer this information.

The seller-assignor of the chattel paper is normally liable to pay the note if it is dishonored by the buyer of the goods. If the financer is independent of the seller it can be expected to rely on its rights against the assignor rather than litigate with the buyer. Whether or not the holder-in-due-course doctrine applies, recovery from the assignor would normally be a more efficient remedy than recovery against the buyer. So long as the assignor is solvent and subject to suit the assignee does not need the holder-in-due-course doctrine. The risk that the assignee takes is the insolvency or unavailability of the assignor when the defense by the buyer is asserted. This is the only time that the holder-in-due-course doctrine is needed by the financer. The issue then is whether the risk that the seller will abscond or fail should fall on the financer or the buyer.

Although abolition of negotiability in consumer transactions may raise the total cost of collecting consumer debts that cost would not be passed along to all consumers equally. Sellers with low levels of complaints from buyers should have less difficulty in collecting than sellers with dissatisfied customers. If assignees cannot take free of defenses they can be expected either to bargain for the right to reassign any contract to the seller in the event that the buyer asserts a defense or to raise their discount to provide for losses. Thus, sellers with many dissatisfied customers will have higher collection costs than sellers with few dissatisfied customers; "good" sellers are favored by abolition and "bad" sellers are disfavored. To the extent that the holder-in-due-course doctrine facilitates the collection of debts that might otherwise not be collectible it favors "bad" sellers more than "good" sellers and serves as a subsidy to the former group paid by its customers.

a.   THE JUDICIAL RESPONSE

UNICO v. OWEN

Supreme Court of New Jersey, 1967.
50 N.J. 101, 232 A.2d 405.

FRANCIS, J.   The issue to be decided here is whether plaintiff Unico, a New Jersey partnership, is a holder in due course of defendant's note.   If so, it is entitled to a judgment for the unpaid balance due thereon, for which this suit was brought.   The District Court found plaintiff was not such a holder and that it was therefore subject to the defense interposed by defendant, maker of the note, of failure of consideration on the part of the payee, which endorsed it to plaintiff.   Since it was undisputed that the payee failed to furnish the consideration for which the note was given, judgment was entered for defendant.   The Appellate Division affirmed, and we granted plaintiff's petition for certification in order to consider the problem.   47 N.J. 241, 220 A.2d 114 (1966).

The facts are important.   Defendant's wife, Jean Owen, answered an advertisement in a Newark, N.J. newspaper in which Universal Stereo Corporation of Hillside, N.J., offered for sale 140 albums of stereophonic records for $698.   This amount could be financed and paid on an installment basis.   In addition the buyer would receive "without separate charge" (as plaintiff puts it) a Motorola stereo record player.   The plain implication was that on agreement to purchase 140 albums, the record player would be given free.   A representative of Universal called at the Owens' home and discussed the matter with Mr. and Mrs. Owen.   As a result, on November 6, 1962 they signed a "retail installment contract" for the purchase of 140 albums on the time payment plan proposed by Universal.

Under the printed form of contract Universal sold and Owen bought "subject to the terms and conditions stipulated in Exhibit 'A' hereto annexed and printed on the other side hereof and made part hereof, the following goods * * *: 12 stereo albums to be delivered at inception of program and every 6 months thereafter until completion of program," a "new Motorola consolo [sic]" and "140 stereo albums of choice * * *."   The total cash price was listed as $698; a downpayment of $30 was noted; the balance of $668, plus an "official fee" of $1.40 and a time price differential of $150.32, left a time balance of

$819.72 to be paid in installments. Owen agreed to pay this balance in 36 equal monthly installments of $22.77 each beginning on December 12, 1962, "at the office of Universal Stereo Corp., 8 Hollywood Avenue, Hillside, N.J., or any other address determined by assignee." The contract provided:

> "If the Buyer executed a promissory note of even date herewith in the amount of the time balance indicated, said note is not in payment thereof, but is a negotiable instrument separate and apart from this contract even though at the time of execution it may be temporarily attached hereto by perforation or otherwise."

It was part of Universal's practice to take notes for these contracts, and obviously there was no doubt that it would be done in the Owen case. Owen did sign a printed form of note which was presented with the contract. The name of Universal Stereo Corporation was printed thereon, and the note provided for the monthly installment payments specified. On the reverse side was an elaborate printed form of endorsement which began "Pay to the order of Unico, 251 Broad St., Elizabeth, New Jersey, with full recourse;" and which contained various waivers by the endorser, and an authorization to the transferee to vary the terms of the note in its discretion in dealing with the maker.

Exhibit "A", referred to as being on the reverse side of the contract, is divided into three separate parts, the body of each part being in very fine print. The *first* section sets out in 11 fine print paragraphs the obligations of the buyer and rights of the seller. Under paragraph 1 the seller retains title to the property until the full time price is paid. Here it may be noted that Universal recorded the contract in the Union County Register's Office a few days after its execution. Paragraph 2 says that the term "Seller" as used shall refer to the party signing the contract as seller "or *if said party has assigned said contract, any holder of* said contract." (Emphasis added). It is patent that Universal contemplated assigning the contract forthwith to Unico, and it was so assigned. Of course, it was a bilateral executory contract, and since under the language just quoted "assignee" and "seller" have the same connotation, the reasonable and normal expectation by Owen would be that performance of the delivery obligation was a condition precedent to his undertaking to make installment payments. See, 3 Williston on Contracts (3d ed. Jaeger 1960) §§ 418, 418A. It has not been suggested that this assignment provision which equates "seller" with "assignee" creates such an intimate relationship between Universal and Unico as to impose Universal's delivery performance obligation on Unico as well as to transfer Universal's right to payment to Unico. Consequently the question is reserved for future consideration in an appropriate case under the Uniform Commercial Code. See § 2–210(4). In view of the comprehensive language employed, is such an assignment one for security only? Note New Jersey Study Comment 5, and Uniform Commercial Code Comment 5, to subsection 4. Universal sought under paragraph 5 to deprive Owen of his right to plead failure of consideration against its intended assignee, Unico. The paragraph provides:

"Buyer hereby acknowledges notice that the contract may be assigned and that assignees will rely upon the agreements contained in this paragraph, and agrees that the liability of the Buyer to any assignee shall be immediate and absolute and not affected by any default whatsoever of the Seller signing this contract; and in order to induce assignees to purchase this contract, the Buyer further agrees not to set up any claim against such Seller as a defense, counterclaim or offset to any action by any assignee for the unpaid balance of the purchase price or for possession of the property."

The validity and efficacy of this paragraph will be discussed hereinafter. At this point it need only be said that the design of Universal in adopting this form of contract and presenting it to buyers, not for bargaining purposes but for signature, was to get the most and give the least. Overall it includes a multitude of conditions, stipulations, reservations, exceptions and waivers skillfully devised to restrict the liability of the seller within the narrowest limits, and to leave no avenue of escape from liability on the part of the purchaser.

The *second* part of Exhibit "A" is entitled in large type, "Assignment and dealer's recommendation. This must be executed by the dealer." There follows an elaborate fine-print form of assignment of the contract and the rights thereunder to Unico, which name is part of the printed form. It is signed by Murray Feldman, President of Universal.

The *third* part of Exhibit "A" is entitled "Guaranty." It is a printed form signed by Murray Feldman, as President, and Rhea M. Feldman, as Secretary, of Universal, and also as individuals guaranteeing payment of the sums due under Owen's contract to Unico.

As Exhibit "A" appears in the appendix, the Owen note referred to above is not now attached to the contract. The record is not clear as to just how it was attached originally, i.e., by a perforated line or otherwise; indication from the agreement itself is that it was attached, and was removed after execution and after or upon endorsement to Unico. In any event it was presented to and executed by Owen with the contract, and in view of the result we have reached in the case, whether it was attached or simply presented to Owen for signature with the contract is of no particular consequence.

At this point the hyper-executory character of the performance agreed to by Universal in return for the installment payment stipulation by Owen must be noted. Owen's time balance of $819.72 was required to be paid by 36 monthly installments of $22.77 each. Universal's undertaking was to deliver 24 record albums a year until 140 albums had been delivered. Completion by the seller therefore would require 5⅓ years. Thus, although Owen would have fully paid for 140 albums at the end of three years, Universal's delivery obligation did not have to be completed until 2⅓ years thereafter. This means that 40% of the albums, although fully paid for, would still be in the hands of the seller. It means also that for 2⅓ years Universal would have the use of 40% of Owen's money on which he had been charged the high time-price differential rate. In contrast, since Universal discounted the note immediately with Unico on the strength of Owen's credit and purchase contract, the transaction, so far as the seller is concerned, can fairly be considered as one for cash. In this posture, Universal had its sale price almost contemporaneously with Owen's execution of the contract, in return for an executory performance to extend over 5⅓ years. And Unico acquired Owen's note which, on its face and considered apart from the remainder of the transaction, appeared to be an unqualifiedly negotiable instrument. On the other hand, on the face of things, by virtue of the ostensibly negotiable note and the waiver or estoppel clause quoted above which was intended to bar any defense against an assignee for the seller's default, Owen had no recourse and no protection if Universal defaulted on its obligation and was financially worthless.

Owen's installment note to Universal for the time balance of $819.72 is dated November 6, 1962. Although the endorsement on the reverse side is not dated, Unico concedes the note was received on or about the day it was made. The underlying sale contract was assigned to Unico at the same time, and it is admitted that Owen was never notified of the assignment.

Owen received from Universal the stereo record player and the original 12 albums called for by the contract. Although he continued to pay the monthly installments on the note for the 12 succeeding months, he never received another album. During that period Mrs. Owen endeavored unsuccessfully to communicate with Universal, and finally ceased making payments when the albums were not delivered. Nothing further was heard about the matter until July 1964, when the attorney for Unico, who was also one of its partners, advised Mrs. Owen that Unico held the note and that payments should be made to it. She told him the payments would be resumed if the albums were delivered. No further deliveries were made because Universal had become insolvent. Up to this Owen had paid the deposit of $30 and 12 installments of $22.77 each, for a total of $303.24. Unico brought this suit for the balance due on the note plus penalties and a 20% attorney's fee.

Owen defended on the ground that Unico was not a holder in due course of the note, that the payment of $303.24 adequately satisfied any obligation for Universal's partial performance, and that Universal's default and the consequent failure of consideration barred recovery by Unico. As we have said, the trial court found plaintiff was not a holder in due course of the note and that Universal's breach of the sales contract barred recovery.

I.

This brings us to the primary inquiry in the case. Is the plaintiff Unico a holder in due course of defendant's note?

The defendant's note was executed on November 6, 1962. The Uniform Commercial Code was adopted by the Legislature in 1961 (L.1961, c. 120), but it did not become operative until January 1, 1963. The note, therefore, is governed by the Uniform Negotiable Instruments Law. Section 52 thereof defined a holder in due course as one who (among other prerequisites) took the instrument "in good faith and for value." If plaintiff is not a holder in due course it is subject to the defense of failure of consideration on the part of Universal, both under the Negotiable Instruments Law, § 58, and the Uniform Commercial Code, § 3–306(c).

In the field of negotiable instruments, good faith is a broad concept. The basic philosophy of the holder in due course status is to encourage free negotiability of commercial paper by removing certain anxieties of one who takes the paper as an innocent purchaser knowing no reason why the paper is not as sound as its face would indicate. It would seem to follow, therefore, that the more the holder knows about the underlying transaction, and particularly the more he controls or participates or becomes involved in it, the less he fits the role of a good faith purchaser for value; the closer his relationship to the underlying agreement which is the source of the note, the less need there is for giving him the tension-free rights considered necessary in a fast-moving, credit-extending commercial world.

We are concerned here with a problem of consumer goods financing. Such goods are defined in the Uniform Commercial Code as those used or bought for use primarily for personal, family or household purposes. § 9–109(1). Although the Code as such is not applicable in this case, the definition is appropriate for our purposes. And it is fair to say also that in today's society, sale of such goods and arrangements for consumer credit financing of the sale are problems of increasing state and national concern. The consumer-credit market is essentially a process of exchange, the general nature of which is shaped by the objectives and relative bargaining power of each of the parties. In consumer goods transactions there is almost always a substantial differential in bargaining power between the seller and his financer, on the one side, and the householder on the other. That difference exists because generally there is a substantial inequality of economic resources between them, and of course, that balance in the great mass of cases favors the seller and gives him and his financer the power to shape the exchange to their advantage. Their greater economic resources permit them to obtain the advice of experts; moreover, they have more time to reflect about the specific terms of the exchange prior to the negotiations with the consumer; they know from experience how to strengthen their own position in consumer-credit arrangements; and the financer-creditor is better able to absorb the impact of a single imprudent or unfair exchange. See Curran, Legislative Controls as a Response to Consumer-Credit Problems, 8 B.C.Ind. and Com.L.Rev. 409, 435–437 (1967).

Mass marketing in consumer goods, as in many other commercial activities, has produced standardized financing contracts. Henningsen v. Bloomfield Motors, Inc., 32 N.J. 358, 389, 161 A.2d 69, 75 A.L.R.2d 1 (1960). As a result there is no real arms-length bargaining between the creditor (seller-financer) and the consumer, beyond minimal negotiating about amount of credit, terms of installment payment and description of the goods to be purchased, all of which is accomplished by filling blanks left in the jungle of finely printed, creditor-oriented provisions. In the present case the purchase contract was a typical standardized finely printed form, focused practically in its entirety upon the interests of the seller and its intended assignee. Little remained to be done but to describe the stereo record player and to fix the price and terms of installment payment by filling in the blanks. Even as to the matter inserted in the blanks, it cannot be said that there was any real bargaining; the seller fixed the price of the albums, and, as we shall see, the plaintiff Unico as the financer for Universal established the maximum length of the installment payment period under its contract with Universal. The ordinary consumer goods purchaser more often than not does not read the fine print; if he did it is unlikely that he would understand the legal jargon, and the significance of the clauses is not explained to him. This is not to say that all such contracts of adhesion are unfair or constitute imposition. But many of them are, and the judicial branch of the government within its sphere of operation in construing and applying such contracts must be responsive to equitable considerations. As the late Mr. Justice Frankfurter said in United States v. Bethlehem Steel Corp., 315 U.S. 289, 326, 62 S.Ct. 581, 599, 86 L.Ed. 855, 876 (1942):

> "But is there any principle which is more familiar or more firmly embedded in the history of Anglo-American law than the basic doctrine that the courts will not permit themselves to be used as instruments of inequity and injustice? Does any principle in our law have more universal application than the doctrine that courts will not enforce transactions in which the relative positions of the parties are such that one has unconscionably taken advantage of the necessities of the other?"

And see, Henningsen v. Bloomfield Motors, 32 N.J. at 388, 390, 161 A.2d 69; 1 Corbin on Contracts, § 128 (1963). Just as the community has an interest in insuring (usually by means of the legislative process) that credit financing contracts facilitating sales of consumer goods conform to community-imposed standards of fairness and decency, so too the courts, in the absence of controlling legislation, in applying the adjudicatory process must endeavor, whenever reasonably possible, to impose those same standards on principles of equity and public policy. An initial step in that direction of unquestioned need, and fortunately of common judicial acceptance, is the view that consumer goods contracts and their concurrent financing arrangements should be construed most strictly against the seller who imposed the contract on the buyer, and against the finance company which participated in the transaction, directly or indirectly, or was aware of the nature of the seller's consumer goods sales and installment payment operation.

The courts have recognized that the basic problem in consumer goods sales and financing is that of balancing the interest of the commercial community in unrestricted negotiability of commercial paper against the interest of installment buyers of such goods in the preservation of their normal remedy of withholding payment when, as in this case, the seller fails to deliver as agreed, and thus the consideration for his obligation fails. Many courts have solved the problem by denying to the holder of the paper the status of holder in due course where the financer maintains a close relationship with the dealer whose paper he buys; where the financer is closely connected with the dealer's business operations or with the particular credit transaction; or where the financer furnishes the form of sale contract and note for use by the dealer, the buyer signs the contract and note concurrently, and the dealer endorses the note and assigns the contract immediately thereafter or within the period prescribed by the financer. Industrial Credit Company v. Mike Bradford & Co., 177 So.2d 878 (D.C.App.Fla.1965); International Finance Corporation v. Rieger, 272 Minn. 192, 137 N.W.2d 172 (1965); Local Acceptance Company v. Kinkade, 361 S.W.2d 830 (Sup.Ct. Mo.1962); Mutual Finance Co. v. Martin, 63 So.2d 649, 44 A.L.R. 2d 1 (Sup.Ct.Fla.1953); Commercial Credit Corp. v. Orange County Mach. Wks., 34 Cal.2d 766, 214 P.2d 819 (1950); Commercial Credit Co. v. Childs, 199 Ark. 1073, 137 S.W.2d 260, 128 A.L.R. 726 (1940). Other courts have said that when the financer supplies or prescribes or approves the form of sales contract, or conditional sale agreement, or chattel mortgage as well as the installment payment note (particularly if it has the financer's name printed on the face or in the endorsement), and all the documents are executed by the buyer at one time and the contract assigned and note endorsed to the financer and delivered to the financer together (whether or not attached or part of a single instrument), the holder takes subject to the rights and obligations of the seller. The transaction is looked upon as a species of tripartite proceeding, and the tenor of the cases is that the financer should not be permitted "to isolate itself behind the fictional fence" of the Negotiable Instruments Law, and thereby achieve an unfair advantage over the buyer, State Nat. Ban of El Paso, Tex. v. Cantrell, 47 N.M. 389, 143 P.2d 592, 152 A.L.R. 1216 (1943); Buffalo Industrial Bank v. DeMarzio, 162 Misc. 742,

296 N.Y.S. 783 (City Ct.1937)[1]; and see, First & Lumbermen's Nat. Bank v. Buchholz, 220 Minn. 97, 18 N.W.2d 771 (1945); Consumer Sales Financing, 102 U.Pa.L.Rev. 782, 789–790 (1954).

Before looking at the particular circumstances of the above cases, it seems advisable to examine into the relationship between Universal and the financer Unico.

Unico is a partnership formed expressly for the purpose of financing Universal Stereo Corporation, and Universal agreed to pay all costs up to a fixed amount in connection with Unico's formation. The elaborate contract between them, dated August 24, 1962, recited that Universal was engaged in the merchandising of records and stereophonic sets, and that it desired to borrow money from time to time from Unico, "secured by the assignment of accounts receivable, promissory notes, trade acceptances, conditional sales contracts, chattel mortgages, leases, installment contracts, or other forms of agreement evidencing liens." Subject to conditions set out in the agreement, Unico agreed to lend Universal up to 35% of the total amount of the balances of customers' contracts assigned to Unico subject to a limit of $50,000, in return for which Universal submitted to a substantial degree of control of its entire business operation by the lender. As collateral security for the loans, Universal agreed to negotiate "to the lender" all customers' notes listed in a monthly schedule of new sales contracts, and to assign all conditional sale contracts connected with the notes, as well as the right to any monies due from customers.

Specific credit qualifications for Universal's record album customers were imposed by Unico; requirements for the making of the notes and their endorsement were established, and the sale contracts had to be recorded in the county recording office. All such contracts were required to meet the standards of the agreement between lender and borrower, among them being that the customer's installment payment term would not exceed 36 months and "every term" of the Unico-Universal agreement was to "be deemed incorporated into all assignments" of record sales contracts delivered as security for the loans. It was further agreed that Unico should have all the rights of Universal under the contracts as if it were the seller, including the right to enforce them in its name, and Unico was given an irrevocable power to enforce such rights.

1. On appeal to the Supreme Court, this case was reversed on the sole ground that the defendant-appel- lee failed to appear. 6 N.Y.S.2d 568 (1937).

In the event of Universal's default on payment of its loans, Unico was authorized to deal directly with the record buyers with respect to payment of their notes and to settle with and discharge such customers. Unico was empowered to place its representatives on Universal's premises with full authority to take possession of the books and records; or otherwise, it could inspect the records at any time; and it was given a "special property interest" in such records. Financial statements were required to be submitted by Universal "at least semiannually"; and two partners of Unico were to be paid one-quarter of one per cent interest on the loans as a management service charge, in addition to the interest to be paid Unico. Significant also in connection with the right to oversee Universal's business is a warranty included in the contract. It warrants that Universal owns free and clear "all merchandise referred to and described in [the sales] contracts, * * * at the time of making the sale creating such contracts." Obviously this was not the fact, otherwise Universal would not have discontinued shipping records to its customers, such as Owen. If Universal did not have such a store of records, as warranted, Unico might well have had reason to suspect its borrower's financial stability.

This general outline of the Universal-Unico financing agreement serves as evidence that Unico not only had a thorough knowledge of the nature and method of operation of Universal's business, but also exercised extensive control over it. Moreover, obviously it had a large, if not decisive, hand in the fashioning and supplying of the form of contract and note used by Universal, and particularly in setting the terms of the record album sales agreement, which were designed to put the buyer-consumer in an unfair and burdensome legal strait jacket and to bar any escape no matter what the default of the seller, while permitting the note-holder, contract-assignee to force payment from him by enveloping itself in the formal status of holder in due course. To say the relationship between Unico and the business operations of Universal was close, and that Unico was involved therein, is to put it mildly. There is no case in New Jersey dealing with the contention that the holder of a consumer goods buyer's note in purchasing it did not meet the test of good faith negotiation because the connection between the seller and the financer was as intimate as in this case. Compare, James Talcott, Inc. v. Shulman, 82 N.J.Super. 438, 198 A.2d 98 (App.Div.1964); Westfield Investment Co. v. Fellers, 74 N.J.Super. 575, 181 A.2d 809 (Law Div.1962).

There is a conflict of authority in other jurisdictions (Annotation, 44 A.L.R.2d 8 (1955)), but we are impelled for reasons of equity and justice to join those courts which deny holder in due course status in consumer goods sales cases to those financers whose involvement with the seller's business is as close, and whose knowledge of the extrinsic factors—i.e., the terms of the underlying sale agreement—is as pervasive, as it is in the present case. Their reasoning is particularly persuasive in this case because of the unusual executory character of the seller's obligation to furnish the consideration for the buyer's undertaking.

In Commercial Credit Corp. v. Orange County Mach. Wks., 34 Cal.2d 776, 214 P.2d 819 (1950), Machine Works was in the market for a press. Ermac Company knew of one which could be purchased from General American Precooling Corporation for $5000, and offered to sell it to Machine Works for $5500. Commercial Credit was consulted by Ermac, and agreed to finance the transaction by taking an assignment of the contract of sale between Ermac and Machine Works. For a substantial period before this time, Ermac had obtained similar financing from Commercial Credit and had some blank forms supplied to it by the latter. By a contract written on one of these forms, which was entitled "Industrial Conditional Sales Contract," Ermac agreed to sell and Machine Works bound itself to purchase the press.

The terms of the contract were very much like those in the case now before us. The purchase price was to be paid in 12 equal monthly installments, "evidenced by my note of even date to your order." As to the note, the contract said:

"Said note is a negotiable instrument, separate and apart from this contract, even though at the time of execution it may be temporarily attached hereto by perforation or otherwise."

It provided also, as in our case:

"This contract may be assigned and/or said note may be negotiated without notice to me and when assigned and/or negotiated shall be free from any defense, counterclaim or cross complaint by me."

The note originally was the latter part of the printed form of contract, but could be detached from it at a dotted or perforated line.

Machine Works made the required down payment to Ermac, which in turn under its contract with Commercial assigned the contract and endorsed the note to the latter. Commercial then gave its check to Ermac for $4261. Ermac sent its check to Precooling Corporation, which refused to deliver the press to Machine Works when the check was dishonored. Commercial sued Machine Works as a holder in due course of its note to Ermac. Machine Works contended Commercial was not entitled to the status of such a holder because the sales contract and attached note should be construed as constituting a single document. Machine Works contended also that the finance company was a party to the original transaction rather than a subsequent purchaser, that it took subject to all equities and defenses existing in its favor against Ermac, and that the claimed negotiability of the note was destroyed when it and the conditional sales agreement were transferred together as one instrument.

The Supreme Court of California said the fact that the contract and note were physically attached at the time of transfer to Commercial would not alone defeat negotiability. But the court pointed out that Commercial advanced money to Ermac (with which it had dealt previously and whose "credit had been checked and financial integrity demonstrated"), with the understanding that the agreement and note would be assigned and endorsed to it immediately; and that "[i]n a very real sense, the finance company was a moving force in the transaction from its very inception, and acted as a party to it." In deciding against Commercial, the court said:

> "When a finance company actively participates in a transaction of this type from its inception, counseling and aiding the future vendor-payee, it cannot be regarded as a holder in due course of the note given in the transaction and the defense of failure of consideration may properly be maintained. Machine Works never obtained the press for which it bargained and, as against Commercial, there is no more obligation upon it to pay the note than there is to pay the installments specified in the contract."

In the case before us Unico was brought into existence to finance all Universal's sales contracts, and it was a major factor in establishing the terms upon which the financing and installment payment of the resulting notes and installment delivery of the record albums were to be engaged in. As in the case just cited, it too was "in a very real sense" a party not only to the Owen contract, but to all others similarly procured by Universal.

* * *

The *Martin* case, decided by the Supreme Court of Florida, is frequently cited by the courts of other states. Martin purchased a deep freezer and meat saw from an appliance dealer on an installment payment conditional sale agreement. He executed the agreement and a note (attached thereto by perforations) for payment of the balance due in monthly installments. On the following day the sale agreement and note were assigned and endorsed respectively to the plaintiff-finance company. The freezer turned out to be an outmoded model and otherwise totally unfit for Martin's purposes, and when neither the dealer nor the financer remedied the defects he declined to make further payments on the note.

The finance company prepared and furnished to the dealer the printed forms of conditional sale agreement and promissory note employed in the transaction. The forms designated the financer as the specific assignee of the contract and note; its office was designated as the place of payment of the note installments; it investigated and approved Martin's credit, agreed to purchase his contract and note, and by written assignment took the contract and note contemporaneously from the dealer.

In deciding that the finance company was not a holder in due course, the court declared it saw no reason why the concurrent execution of such a contract along with a promissory note, whether the note is a separate piece of paper or is attached to the contract by perforations, of itself should in any way affect "any of the characteristics of the note which give it commercial value." But, referring to the conflicting decisions in various states, it said that in situations such as the one before it, the better rule is that the note and the contract should be considered as one instrument. It approved the language of the Arkansas Supreme Court in Commercial Credit Co. v. Childs, supra, to the effect that the financer was so closely connected with the entire transaction that it could not be heard to say that it, in good faith, was an innocent purchaser for value; rather, to all intents and purposes it was a party to the agreement and instrument from the beginning.

The finance company in *Martin*, as in this case, contended that to deny it holder in due course status would seriously affect the mode of transacting business in Florida. In answer, the Court said:

> "It may be that our holding here will require some changes in business methods and will impose a greater burden on the finance companies. We think the buyer—Mr. & Mrs. Gener-

al Public—should have some protection somewhere along the line. We believe the finance company is better able to bear the risk of the dealer's insolvency than the buyer and in a far better position to protect his interests against unscrupulous and insolvent dealers." 63 So.2d at p. 653.

In our judgment the views expressed in the cited cases provide the sound solution for the problem under consideration. Under the facts of our case the relationship between Unico and Universal, and the nature of Unico's participation in Universal's contractual arrangements with its customers, if anything are closer and more active than in any of those cases, and in justice Unico should not be deemed a holder in due course of the Owen note. Adoption of such a rule is consistent in theory with the Court of Errors and Appeals' holding in General Contracts etc. Corp. v. Moon Carrier Corp., 129 N.J.L. 431, 435, 29 A.2d 843 (E. & A.1943), where it was said that where a note refers to or is accompanied by a collateral contemporaneous agreement, or the purchaser has actual knowledge of the collateral agreement, he takes subject to its contents and conditions. Moreover, although as we have already noted, the Uniform Commercial Code is not applicable because its effective date was subsequent to Owen's note, the principle we now espouse is consistent with § 3–119 thereof. That section provides that:

> "As between the obligor and his immediate obligee or any transferee the terms of an instrument may be modified or affected by any other written agreement executed as a part of the same transaction, except that a holder in due course is not affected by any limitation of his rights arising out of the separate written agreement if he had no notice of the limitation when he took the instrument."

For purposes of consumer goods transactions, we hold that where the seller's performance is executory in character and when it appears from the totality of the arrangements between dealer and financer that the financer has had a substantial voice in setting standards for the underlying transaction, or has approved the standards established by the dealer, and has agreed to take all or a predetermined or substantial quantity of the negotiable paper which is backed by such standards, the financer should be considered a participant in the original transaction and therefore not entitled to holder in due course status. We reserve specifically the question whether, when the buyer's claim is breach of warranty as distinguished from failure of consideration, the seller's default as to the former may be raised as a

defense against the financer.   Cf. Eastern Acceptance Corp. v.
Kavlick, 10 N.J.Super. 253, 77 A.2d 49 (App.Div.1950).

II.

Plaintiff argues that even if it cannot be considered a holder
in due course of Owen's note, it is entitled to recover regardless
of the failure of consideration on the part of Universal, because
of the so-called waiver of defenses or estoppel clause contained
in the sale contract.   The clause says:

> "Buyer hereby acknowledges notice that this contract may
> be assigned and that assignees will rely upon the agreements
> contained in this paragraph, and agrees that the liability of
> the Buyer to any assignee shall be immediate and absolute
> and not affected by any default whatsoever of the Seller
> signing this contract; and in order to induce assignees to
> purchase this contract, the Buyer further agrees not to set
> up any claim against such Seller as a defense, counterclaim
> or offset to any action by any assignee for the unpaid bal-
> ance of the purchase price or for possession of the property."

This provision is the fifth of 11 fine print paragraphs on the
reverse side of the sale contract.   The type is the same as in the
other clauses; there is no emphasis put on it in the context, and
there is no evidence that it was in any way brought to Owen's
attention or its significance explained to him.   But regardless,
we consider that the clause is an unfair imposition on a consumer goods purchaser and is contrary to public policy.

The plain attempt and purpose of the waiver is to invest the
sale agreement with the type of negotiability which under the
Negotiable Instruments Law would have made the holder of a
negotiable promissory note a holder in due course and entitled to
recover regardless of the seller-payee's default.

In our judgment such a clause in consumer goods conditional
sale contracts, chattel mortgages, and other instruments of like
character is void as against public policy for three reasons: (1) it
is opposed to the policy of the Negotiable Instruments Law
which had established the controlling prerequisites for negotiability, and provided also that the rights of one not a holder in
due course were subject to all legal defenses which the maker of
the instrument had against the transferor.   § 58; (2) it is opposed to the spirit of N.J.S. 2A:25–1, N.J.S.A., which provides
that an obligor sued by an assignee "shall be allowed * * *
all * * * defenses he had against the assignor or his representatives before notice of such assignment was given to him."

(It is conceded here that plaintiff gave no notice of the assignment to defendant); and (3) the policy of our state is to protect conditional vendees against imposition by conditional vendors and installment sellers. See, N.J.S.A. 17:16C–1 et seq.; and see, Dearborn Motors Credit Corporation v. Neel, 184 Kan. 437, 337 P.2d 992 (1959); Quality Finance Company v. Hurley, 337 Mass. 150, 148 N.E.2d 385 (1958); American Nat. Bank v. A. G. Sommerville, Inc., 191 Cal. 364, 216 P. 376 (1923); San Francisco Securities Corporation v. Phoenix Motor Co., 25 Ariz. 531, 220 P. 229 (1923); Annotation, 44 A.L.R.2d 8, 167 (1955); Helstad, Consumer Credit Legislation: Limitations on Contractual Terms, 8 B.C.Ind. and Comm.L.Rev. 519, 531 (1967); Felsenfeld, Some Ruminations About Remedies in Consumer-Credit Transactions, Id. at pp. 535, 549 (1967).

Section 9–206(1) of the Uniform Commercial Code (Secured Transactions) deals with this problem. It provides:

"Subject to any statute or decision which establishes a different rule for buyers of *consumer goods,* an agreement by a buyer that he will not assert against an assignee any claim or defense which he may have against the seller is enforceable by an assignee who takes his assignment for value, in good faith and without notice of a claim or defense, except as to defenses of a type which may be asserted against a holder in due course of a negotiable instrument under the Chapter on Commercial Paper (Chapter 3). A buyer who as part of one transaction signs both a negotiable instrument and a security agreement makes such an agreement." (Emphasis ours).

In this section of the Code, the Legislature recognized the possibility of need for special treatment of waiver clauses in consumer goods contracts. Such contracts, particularly those of the type involved in this case, are so fraught with opportunities for misuse that the purchasers must be protected against oppressive and unconscionable clauses. And section 9–206 in the area of consumer goods sales must as a matter of policy be deemed closely linked with section 2–302 which authorizes a court to refuse to enforce any clause in a contract of sale which it finds is unconscionable. We see in the enactment of these two sections of the Code an intention to leave in the hands of the courts the continued application of common law principles in deciding in consumer goods cases whether such waiver clauses as the one imposed on Owen in this case are so one-sided as to be contrary to public policy. Cf. Williams v. Walker-Thomas Furniture Co., 121 U.S.App.D.C. 315, 350 F.2d 445, 448–449 (1965).

For reasons already expressed, we hold that they are so opposed to such policy as to require condemnation. As the New Jersey Study Comment to section 2–302 indicates, the practice of denying relief because of unconscionable circumstances has long been the rule in this state. See, Henningsen v. Bloomfield Motors, supra, 32 N.J. at 386, 161 A.2d 69 *passim;* Kuzmiak v. Brookchester, Inc., 33 N.J.Super. 575, 111 A.2d 425 (App.Div. 1955); Reinhardt v. Passaic-Clifton Nat. Bank, 16 N.J.Super. 430, 84 A.2d 741 (App.Div.1951), affirmed 9 N.J. 607, 89 A.2d 242 (1952); Hemhauser v. Hemhauser, 110 N.J.Eq. 77, 158 A. 762 (Ch.1932); N.J.S. 12A:2–302, N.J.S.A., New Jersey Study Comment 1. Elzey v. Ajax Heating Company, 10 N.J.Misc. 281, 158 A. 851 (Cir.Ct.1932), has been cited as contrary to the result we have reached on this point. To the extent that it is in conflict, it is overruled.

For the reasons stated, we hold the waiver clause unenforceable and invalid against Owen.

III.

We agree with the result reached in the tribunals below. Plaintiff offered no proof in the trial court to show that the value of the 12 albums Owen received before breach of the contract by Universal, together with that of the record player at the time of the breach (assuming its value was material in view of the seller's representation that there was to be no charge for it), was in excess of the $303.24 paid by Owen under the contract. Moreover, there has been no suggestion throughout this proceeding that plaintiff is entitled to a partial recovery on the note in its capacity as an assignee thereof. Accordingly, the judgment for the defendant is affirmed.

For affirmance: CHIEF JUSTICE WEINTRAUB and JUSTICES JACOBS, FRANCIS, PROCTOR, HALL and HANEMAN—6.

For reversal: None.

b. THE LEGISLATIVE RESPONSE

Consumer Credit Sales

Consumer credit sales are regulated in most states by statute. Most states have taken the position that the holder in due course doctrine should be abrogated with respect to notes given by buyers to sellers of consumer goods or services. The approach taken is to prohibit the taking of a negotiable note from the buyer and to invalidate waiver of defenses clauses in the installment sale contract. The Uniform Consumer Credit Code, in effect in 11 jurisdictions, is an example of this kind of legislation. The 1974 Official Text provides as follows:

Section 3.307   [Certain Negotiable Instruments Prohibited]

With respect to a consumer credit sale or consumer lease, [except a sale or lease primarily for an agricultural purpose,] the creditor may not take a negotiable instrument other than a check dated not later than ten days after its issuance as evidence of the obligation of the consumer.

Section 3.404   [Assignee Subject to Claims and Defenses]

(1) With respect to a consumer credit sale or consumer lease [, except one primarily for an agricultural purpose], an assignee of the rights of the seller or lessor is subject to all claims and defenses of the consumer against the seller or lessor arising from the sale or lease of property or services, notwithstanding that the assignee is a holder in due course of a negotiable instrument issued in violation of the provisions prohibiting certain negotiable instruments (Section 3.307).

(2) A claim or defense of a consumer specified in subsection (1) may be asserted against the assignee under this section only if the consumer has made a good faith attempt to obtain satisfaction from the seller or lessor with respect to the claim or defense and then only to the extent of the amount owing to the assignee with respect to the sale or lease of the property or services as to which the claim or defense arose at the time the assignee has notice of the claim or defense. Notice of the claim or defense may be given before the attempt specified in this subsection. Oral notice is effective unless the assignee requests written confirmation when or promptly after oral notice is given and the consumer fails to give the assignee written confirmation within the period of time, not less than 14 days, stated to the consumer when written confirmation is requested.

*   *   *

(4) An agreement may not limit or waive the claims or defenses of a consumer under this section.

The Federal Trade Commission in 1975 promulgated rules (16 C.F.R. Part 433—Preservation of Consumers' Claims and Defenses) designed to prevent the use of waiver of defenses clauses in consumer credit sales and leases. Any consumer credit contract (including a promissory note) arising out of a consumer credit sale or lease must contain a bold-faced legend stating in effect that any holder of the contract is subject to all claims and defenses that the debtor has against the seller of the goods or services. The effect of the legend is to cause any assignee of the note or sales contract to take subject to the buyer's claims and defenses against the seller. If the seller violates the FTC rule and fails to include the legend he is subject to a civil suit by the FTC in which the court may "grant such relief as the court finds necessary to redress injury to consumers *   *   * resulting from the rule violation *   *   *. Such relief may include, but shall not be limited to, rescission or reformation of contracts, the refund of money or return of property, the payment of damages, and public notification respecting the rule violation *   *   *; except that nothing in this subsection is intended to authorize the imposition of any exemplary or punitive damages." 15 U.S.C. § 57b(a)(1) and (b). Nothing in the FTC rule suggests that an assignee could not acquire holder in due course status with respect to a negotiable note not containing the legend. The brunt of the rule falls on the seller, and its effectiveness apparently depends solely on the enforcement, or threat of enforcement, by the FTC.

Purchase Money Loans

Under traditional law, a financer who loans money directly to a debtor for the purpose of buying goods or services is not subject to claims or defenses the buyer may have against the seller. However, the purchase money loan transaction bears a close functional resemblance to the assigned paper transaction discussed above. In both cases the seller desires to get cash for his product as soon as possible; the buyer has no cash to pay; and the financer is willing to provide the money. In the purchase money loan, the financer makes a direct loan to the buyer; in the assigned paper case, the financer buys the buyer's credit contract from the seller. Customs differ among the states: in some consumer goods financing is done by purchase money loans, but in most the assigned-paper transaction predominates.

If financers are subject to consumer defenses in assigned-paper transactions, incentive is present to convert to purchase money loans or credit card transactions to free financers of consumer defenses. By the latter part of the 1960's consumer representatives began to advocate subjecting purchase money lenders to consumer claims and defenses in situations in which there was a sufficiently close relationship between the seller and the lender to warrant doing so. But how close must this relation be? The task of defining the requisite relationship has been difficult.

Under the FTC rule referred to above the seller is guilty of an unfair or deceptive act if it accepts the proceeds of a purchase money loan (§ 433.2(b)) unless the loan agreement between the debtor and the purchase money lender contains the requisite notice. Presumably if the loan agreement does contain the notice, the lender thereby subjects itself to defenses arising out of the sale. Section 433.1(d) defines purchase money loan to include two cases: (1) the seller refers consumers to the lender, or (2) the seller is affiliated with the lender by common control, contract or business arrangement (defined as "any understanding, procedure, course of dealing, or arrangement, formal or informal, between a creditor and a seller, in connection with the sale of goods or services to consumers on the financing thereof"). It is not at all clear what constitutes affiliation by business arrangement. In the very common case of the secured loan the loan is made for a particular purpose and the lender will be aware that a particular seller is involved in the transaction, but, without more, this should not mean that the lender's right to repayment is subject to any defenses that the borrower has against the seller. There is no problem in the case in which the seller steers the buyer to the lender or the case in which the lender will make loans only if the proceeds are used to purchase from the particular seller. Suppose the buyer of an automobile from a dealer shows that the lender has made loans to borrowers who used the proceeds to purchase automobiles from the same dealer. Have the lender and the dealer become affiliated by an informal course of dealing? Must the seller in each case inquire about the buyer's source of funds to determine whether the required legend was required and was in fact made? Suppose the seller insists that the lender include the legend on the note of the borrower. What incentive does the lender have to comply with the request? See White & Summers, Uniform Commercial Code, 1137–1145 (2d ed. 1980).

Compare the following provision of the Uniform Consumer Credit Code (1974 Official Text) dealing with the same problem.

Section 3.405 [Lender Subject to Claims and Defenses Arising from Sales and Leases]

(1) A lender, except the issuer of a lender credit card, who, with respect to a particular transaction, makes a consumer loan to enable a consumer to buy or lease from a par-

ticular seller or lessor property or services [, except primarily for an agricultural purpose,] is subject to all claims and defenses of the consumer against the seller or lessor arising from that sale or lease of the property or services if:

(a) the lender knows that the seller or lessor arranged for the extension of credit by the lender for a commission, brokerage, or referral fee;

(b) the lender is a person related to the seller or lessor, unless the relationship is remote or is not a factor in the transaction;

(c) the seller or lessor guarantees the loan or otherwise assumes the risk of loss by the lender upon the loan;

(d) the lender directly supplies the seller or lessor with the contract document used by the consumer to evidence the loan, and the seller or lessor has knowledge of the credit terms and participates in preparation of the document;

(e) the loan is conditioned upon the consumer's purchase or lease of the property or services from the particular seller or lessor, but the lender's payment of proceeds of the loan to the seller or lessor does not in itself establish that the loan was so conditioned; or

(f) the lender, before he makes the consumer loan, has knowledge or, from his course of dealing with the particular seller or lessor or his records, notice of substantial complaints by other buyers or lessees of the particular seller's or lessor's failure or refusal to perform his contracts with them and of the particular seller's or lessor's failure to remedy his defaults within a reasonable time after notice to him of the complaints.

* * *

Credit Cards

Use of the credit card to finance the purchase of goods or services is an increasingly popular alternative to the assigned paper and purchase money loan transactions. We again have a seller desiring the equivalent of cash, a buyer (cardholder) needing credit, and a financer (card issuer) willing to grant the credit. If the financer should take subject to consumer defenses in the assigned paper and purchase money loan cases, why not in the functionally similar tripartite credit card case?

This issue was hotly debated at the state level in the late 1960's. Card issuers maintained that in view of the fact they had only the most tenuous relationship with retailers honoring their cards, they should not be subjected to claims and defenses arising out of sales made pursuant to their cards. The card issuer, it was contended, should be no more involved in the sale transaction financed by a credit card than should a drawee bank in a sale paid for by a check drawn on the bank. Moreover, would not subjecting card issuers to sales defenses ultimately restrict the acceptability of credit cards by retailers who would fear that the card issuer would exercise its right to charge back against the retailer debts as to which the cardholder raised claims or defenses? Would a retailer in Maine feel secure in honoring a credit card presented by a cardholder who lives in California when he knows that if the cardholder claims the goods are defective the retailer may end up with an unsecured claim against the debtor three thousand miles away?

In 1971 California enacted a provision, Civil Code § 1747.90, that served as the model for § 1666i of the Fair Credit Billing Act, 15 U.S.C. § 1666 et seq., enacted by Congress in 1974, which is set out below. What is the reason for the limitations in § 1666i(a)(2) and (3)? See Brandel & Leonard, Bank Charge Cards: New Cash or New Credit? 69 Mich.L.Rev. 1033 (1971).

§ 1666i. Rights of Credit Card Customers

(a) Subject to the limitation contained in subsection (b), a card issuer who has issued a credit card to a cardholder pursuant to an open end consumer credit plan shall be subject to all claims (other than tort claims) and defenses arising out of any transaction in which the credit card is used as a method of payment or extension of credit if (1) the obligor has made a good faith attempt to obtain satisfactory resolution of a disagreement or problem relative to the transaction from the person honoring the credit card; (2) the amount of the initial transaction exceeds $50; and (3) the place where the initial transaction occurred was in the same State as the mailing address previously provided by the cardholder or was within 100 miles from such address, except that the limitations set forth in clauses (2) and (3) with respect to an obligor's right to assert claims and defenses against a card issuer shall not be applicable to any transaction in which the person honoring the credit card (A) is the same person as the card issuer, (B) is controlled by the card issuer, (C) is under direct or indirect common control with the card issuer, (D) is a franchised dealer in the card issuer's products or services, or (E) has obtained the order for such transaction through a mail solicitation made by or participated in by the card issuer in which the cardholder is solicited to enter into such transaction by using the credit card issued by the card issuer.

(b) The amount of claims or defenses asserted by the cardholder may not exceed the amount of credit outstanding with respect to such transaction at the time the cardholder first notifies the card issuer or the person honoring the credit card of such claim or defense. For the purpose of determining the amount of credit outstanding in the preceding sentence, payments and credits to the cardholder's account are deemed to have been applied, in the order indicated, to the payment of; (1) late charges in the order of their entry to the account; (2) finance charges in order of their entry to the account; and (3) debits to the account other than those set forth above, in the order in which each debit entry to the account was made.

B. VALUE

1. INTRODUCTORY NOTE

If Thief steals a negotiable instrument from Owner and sells it to unsuspecting Holder it may make sense to give Holder rights in the instrument at the expense of Owner. One or the other must bear a loss. As we saw in Chapter 1, although each is equally innocent the negotiability doctrine tips the scales in favor of Holder in order to carry out a policy objective of encouraging free commerce in instruments. But if Holder has paid nothing for the instrument, denying him the right to defeat Owner's title results in no loss to Holder except the loss of a windfall. Thus, if Thief makes a gift of the instrument to Holder it seems unfair to allow Holder to profit at the expense of Owner. Since, in this case, an unfair result is not necessary in order to carry out the objective of encouraging free commerce in instruments Holder loses. UCC § 3–302(1)(a) provides that only a holder who took the instrument for value is a holder in due course. Taking for value is defined in UCC § 3–303. Although the taking for value requirement can be explained in part by distinguishing between loss and windfall, this distinction is not always clearly apparent in the cases covered by UCC § 3–303. The problems that follow illustrate the cases covered by that section. In each problem, and the cases that follow, you might ask yourself the question whether the holder-in-due-course doctrine is necessary in order to protect some interest of the holder or whether the doctrine simply confers on the holder a windfall. If there is a windfall, is the result justified by commercial necessity? You might also ask the question whether, if the doctrine did not exist, the taking of the instrument in the particular transaction would have been discouraged.

PROBLEMS

In each of the following problems make these assumptions: Maker gave to Payee a negotiable note in the amount of $1,000 payable on a stated date. Maker's issuance of the note was induced by Payee's fraudulent promise to deliver goods which were never delivered. In each case, Payee, prior to the due date, negotiated the note to Holder who had no notice of the fraud. On the due date Holder demanded payment of Maker who refused and asserted the defenses of fraud in the inducement and failure of consideration.

1. Payee negotiates the note to Holder in consideration of Holder's agreement to perform services for Payee. Before Holder is obligated to begin performance of the promised services the note falls due. Was there consideration for the transfer of the note from Payee to Holder? Was the note taken for value by Holder? If Holder cannot enforce the note against Maker what rights does he have against Payee?

2. Payee sells the note to Holder who pays $900 cash for the note. Is Maker's defense good against Holder? If Maker is liable, how much can Holder recover? Suppose Holder paid $600 cash for the note and promised to pay an additional $300 cash in 60 days. At the time Holder demanded payment the 60 days had not yet expired. How much can Holder recover? See O. P. Ganjo, Inc. v. Tri-Urban Realty Co., Inc., 108 N.J.Super. 517, 261 A.2d 722 (1969).

3. Payee was indebted to Holder on a loan made several years before and past due. Holder demanded payment but Payee was unable to pay. In order to forestall legal action by Holder, Payee negotiated Maker's note to Holder as collateral for payment of Payee's loan. When the note became due Payee was still unable to repay the loan. Holder thereupon demanded payment of the note by Maker. Is Maker's defense good against Holder? If Holder had taken the note in partial payment of the loan would the result have been different? In that case, when

Maker refused to pay the note, what rights did Holder have against Payee?

2. ANTECEDENT CLAIMS AND SECURITY INTERESTS IN INSTRUMENTS

Checks are usually deposited by the payee in a bank. The bank accepting the deposit normally credits the account of the depositor in the amount of the check and forwards the check to the drawee for payment. The bank is considered to be acting as agent for the depositor in obtaining payment of the check. UCC § 4–201. As we saw previously, the credit given is normally provisional in nature. When the check is paid by the drawee the provisional credit becomes final, i.e., the credit represents a debt owed by the bank to the depositor. UCC § 4–213(3). If the check is not paid by the drawee the depositary bank has a right to charge back the provisional credit. UCC § 4–212(1). Frequently, the depositary bank will also be a creditor of the depositor because of a past transaction such as a loan. If a debt owing to the depositary bank is past due the depositary bank may exercise a common-law right to set off against the debt any amounts which the bank owes the depositor. For example, if the depositor owes the depositary bank $1,000 on a past-due loan and the depositor has an $800 final credit balance in his checking account, the depositary bank may simply wipe out the $800 balance by applying it to reduce the $1,000 loan balance.[1] In addition to this right of set off a depositary bank has a closely-related common-law right known as a banker's lien.[2] For example, if

---

1. The bank's right of set off may be limited by statute. See, for example, Calif. Financial Code § 864 which limits set offs with respect to certain consumer-type installment debt owed to the bank.

2. Restatement, Security § 62 provides as follows: "General possessory liens exist in favor of * * * (c) a banker, as security for the general balance due him from a customer, upon commercial paper and other instruments which can be used as the basis of credit and which are deposited with him in the regular course of business." California recognizes the lien by statute. "A banker, or a savings and loan association, has a general lien, dependent on possession, upon all property in his hands belonging to a customer, for the balance due to the

banker or savings and loan association from such customer in the course of the business." Civil Code § 3054(a). The lien may be important to the bank in the event of the depositor's insolvency. In Goggin v. Bank of America, 183 F.2d 322 (9th Cir. 1950), the depositor owed the bank $600,000 on a loan. At the time of the depositor's bankruptcy the bank held commercial paper delivered by the depositor for collection and credit to its general deposit account. After bankruptcy and after written notice by the depositor attempting to terminate the authority of the bank to act as agent for collection, the bank collected the commercial paper. In an action by the receiver of the depositor's estate in bankruptcy to recover the proceeds for the estate, it was held (a) that the

the depositor owes the depositary bank $1,000 on a past-due loan and deposits a check to his account in the regular course of business, the depositary bank has a lien in the check as security for the $1,000 debt. Although the bank when it forwards the check to the drawee for payment acts as agent for the depositor, it also has a property interest in the check represented by the lien. Thus, the bank can collect the check and apply the proceeds to the debt owed by the depositor. Since the taking of an instrument for an antecedent debt is value the depositary bank could attain the rights of a holder in due course. These two related but separate common-law rights—set off and banker's lien—are preserved under UCC § 1–103. See Comment 1 to UCC § 4–208. The two common-law rights are frequently confused. It is not uncommon for a court to refer to the banker's lien as a right of set off or to refer to the right of set off as a lien. When the

---

bank had a banker's lien on the commercial paper at the date of bankruptcy, (b) that the authority of the bank to collect the paper was not affected by either bankruptcy or the attempt of the depositor to revoke the bank's authority, and (c) that the bank was entitled to apply the proceeds to reduction of the loan balance. If the bank had collected the paper prior to bankruptcy it would have been entitled after bankruptcy to set off the mutual debts existing at the time of bankruptcy. In the actual case decided the set off after bankruptcy was based on the bank's lien existing at the time of bankruptcy. The right of set off in bankruptcy is subject to certain limitations. See Bankruptcy Code, 11 U.S.C. § 553. The banker's lien may also be the basis for cutting off claims of third parties to the paper deposited by the depositor. In Wyman v. Colorado National Bank, 5 Colo. 30 (1879), plaintiff drew a draft on a drawee in London payable to the order of First Bank with which plaintiff had an account. Plaintiff's intent was to have First Bank collect the draft and deposit the proceeds to plaintiff's account. First Bank indorsed the draft and sent it to Second Bank with orders to collect it. At that time First Bank was indebted to Second Bank on an overdraft. Second Bank sent the draft to London for collection. After the draft was paid but before Second Bank was paid the proceeds Second Bank was notified that the draft was the property of plaintiff and that First Bank had failed. The court held that Second Bank got a lien on the draft immediately upon receipt of the draft and became a holder for value without notice of plaintiff's claim, thereby cutting off the claim. In effect Second Bank took the draft as security for the antecedent debt represented by the overdraft. Compare UCC § 3–303(a) and (b). The issue in cases like *Wyman* is whether the deposited paper "belongs" to the customer making the deposit. For example, if Second Bank had been aware that First Bank was acting solely as collecting agent with respect to the draft the lien would not have attached. But in cases of undisclosed agency there is no notice of the claim of the owner of the item and the apparent ownership of the paper by the depositor has been recognized by some courts as sufficient to allow the lien to attach. A rationale for the banker's lien is stated in Gibbons v. Hecox, 105 Mich. 509, 513, 63 N.W. 519, 520 (1895). "The reason for allowing the lien is that any credit which a bank gives by discounting notes or allowing an overdraft to be made is given on the faith that money or securities sufficient to pay the debt will come into the possession of the bank in the due course of future transactions."

Setoff if mutual debts

lien

bank is asserting a right in an uncollected check it is relying on a lien. A set off can occur only if there are mutual debts. There can be no present right of set off with respect to an uncollected check because until collected the check does not represent a debt of the bank.

Depositary banks may acquire rights as holders in due course under other provisions of the UCC. Suppose there is no debt owing by the depositor when the check is deposited. Whether the depositary bank has given value for the check is determined under UCC § 4–209 which states that the bank has given value to the extent that it has a security interest in the check. UCC § 4–208 states rules for determining when a security interest arises. This security interest is in addition to the bank's common-law banker's lien. See Comment 1 to UCC § 4–208. By virtue of UCC § 4–208 the depositary bank has a security interest under subsection (a) if the check is deposited and the resulting credit is withdrawn, under subsection (b) if the check is deposited and the depositor is given the right to withdraw the credit, and under (c) if the bank makes a loan or cash payment based on the check. In these cases the bank is in effect treated as a lender to the depositor taking as security a security interest in the check. In the case in which the depositor is not allowed to withdraw the funds the bank does not have a security interest and is not a holder in due course. It has committed no funds and is fully protected by its ability to charge back the depositor's account in the event of non-payment.

Bank's Security interest

In most cases the depositor has an existing credit balance in his account when he makes a deposit and there may be a series of deposits and withdrawals from the account. In those cases, whether credit for a particular check has been withdrawn cannot be determined except by applying some mechanical tracing rule. Such a rule is provided by the last sentence of UCC § 4–208(2) which states that "credits first given are first withdrawn." This rule is usually referred to as the first-in-first-out or FIFO rule.

PROBLEM

Depositor makes deposits and withdrawals to his checking account in Depositary Bank as follows:

			Balance
November 1	Existing Balance		400
" 2	Deposit – check	500	900
" 3	Withdrawal – check	400	500

no value · FIFO · 4–208(2)

Balance

November 4	Deposit – cash	600	1100
" 5	Withdrawal – check	500	600
" 7	" "	600	–0–
" 7	Charge-back	500	(500)

value

The check deposited on November 2 was not paid by Drawee Bank because the drawer had stopped payment. Depositary Bank received notice of dishonor on November 6. Depositary Bank has brought action against the drawer of the November 2 check. Drawer defends by alleging lack of consideration for the check. Did Depositary Bank give value for the check? Comment 3 to UCC § 3–303 states: "An executory promise to give value is not itself value, except as provided in paragraph (c). The underlying reason of policy is that when the purchaser learns of a defense against the instrument or of a defect in the title he is not required to enforce the instrument, but is free to rescind the transaction for breach of the transferor's warranty (Section 3–417). There is thus not the same necessity for giving him the status of a holder in due course, cutting off claims and defenses, as where he has actually paid value. A common illustration is the bank credit not drawn upon, which can be and is revoked when a claim or defense appears." Is this comment relevant to this problem? Is the last sentence of UCC § 4–208(2) consistent with this comment?

UCC § 4–208(1)(a) refers not only to cases in which a credit has been withdrawn, but also to cases in which the credit has been "applied." The latter term refers to cases in which the credit has been used by the bank to pay an obligation to itself or to make a payment to a third party. This provision is considered in the cases that follow.

LAUREL BANK & TRUST CO. v. CITY NATIONAL BANK OF CONNECTICUT

Superior Court of Connecticut, Appellate Session, 1976.
33 Conn.Sup. 641, 365 A.2d 1222.

SPONZO, JUDGE. In this action the facts may be summarized as follows: The plaintiff and the defendant were at all times pertinent to this case commercial banks duly authorized to conduct business in this state and had checking account facilities available for their respective customers. On March 27, 1973, and for some time prior thereto, one A. S. Maisto maintained two checking accounts with the plaintiff. One account was No. O–41190–6 and was conducted under the name of "Tony's Sunoco," and the other account, No. O–41233–3, was maintained under the name of "B & D Automotive." On the same date A. S. Maisto had an account with the defendant at its office in the town of Cheshire.

Between the hours of 1 p. m. and 2 p. m. on March 27, 1973, Maisto purchased from the defendant an official check, or cashier's check, in the amount of $3446. That cashier's check was paid for with two checks plus cash. One of the checks was in the amount of $2585.50 and was drawn by Maisto on the account No. O–41190–6 that was maintained with the plaintiff. In order to draw an official check, the defendant's teller had to obtain the approval of an officer. As a result of that requirement, an officer of the defendant bank telephoned the plaintiff bank and was assured by an unknown person in the bookkeeping department that "Maisto's check for an amount over $2500 was good at this time." The defendant then issued its official check to Maisto.

On March 27, 1973, at about 4:15 p. m., that cashier's check together with other items, all of which totaled $9501, were deposited by Maisto with the plaintiff in account No. O–41233–3, which at the time of deposit was overdrawn to the extent of $21,079.43. That transaction was entered as a check deposit in the plaintiff's bookkeeping record for March 28, 1973, since all banking transactions occurring after 3 p. m. are recorded as received on the next day. The deposit of $9501 was provisionally credited by the plaintiff to the B & D Automotive account, No. O–41233–3, subject to later withdrawal or reversal of credit, and the overdrawn balance was reduced by that amount.

On March 28, 1973, the plaintiff returned the check in the amount of $2585.50 to the defendant because of insufficient funds. The plaintiff presented the official or cashier's check in the amount of $3446 to the defendant through normal bank collection procedures and the defendant dishonored the check in that it stopped payment thereon. The check was returned to the plaintiff unpaid, remains unpaid to date, and is the subject matter of this action. The signature of the drawer on the cashier's check has been admitted.

The trial court concluded that the plaintiff was a mere holder of the cashier's check because it did not establish that it took the check for value. It also concluded that the defendant established a defense of want of consideration because the $2585.50 check which was one of the items used to purchase the cashier's check was subsequently dishonored. Accordingly, the court rendered judgment for the plaintiff in the amount of $860.50, the difference between the $3446 cashier's check and the $2585.50 check. The plaintiff has appealed from that judgment.

* * *

Since the signature on the cashier's check has been admitted, the mere production of the instrument would entitle the plaintiff to recover, even if it were a mere holder, unless the defendant sustained its burden of establishing a want or failure of consideration. [UCC §] 3–306(c) and [UCC §] 3–307(2). Once a defendant meets his burden of proving that a defense exists, in order to prevail the person claiming the rights of a holder in due course has the burden of establishing that he, or the person under whom he claims, is in all respects a holder in due course. [UCC §] 3–307(3).

A cashier's check is a bill of exchange drawn by a bank as drawer upon itself as drawee and made to the order of a payee who, as in this case, may also be the purchaser of the check. Under [UCC §] 3–410, such a check is considered accepted when issued to the payee. See Ross v. Peck Iron & Metal Co., 264 F.2d 262, 269 (4th Cir.). The fact that a cashier's check is said to be "accepted when issued" does not mean, as the plaintiff contends, that the defendant is obligated to pay regardless of any defenses and regardless of whether the plaintiff is a mere holder or a holder in due course. See Bank of Niles v. American State Bank, 14 Ill.App.3d 729, 732, 303 N.E.2d 186. With respect to the issuing bank's ability to stop payment on a cashier's check, analogies to a customer's right to stop payment on an ordinary check are inapposite and confusing. TPO Incorporated v. Federal Deposit Insurance Corporation, 487 F.2d 131, 136 (3d Cir.). The proper approach is to view the issuing bank, acting in its dual role as drawer and drawee, as the equivalent of a maker of a negotiable promissory note payable on demand. [UCC §§] 3–104, 3–118(a).

It is clear that the defendant bank did establish the failure of consideration for issuance of the cashier's check, because the check drawn on the plaintiff which Maisto transferred in payment for the cashier's check was returned for insufficient funds. That defense of want of consideration would be effective against a party who was not a holder in due course. [UCC §] 3–306. If the plaintiff was a mere holder, the trial court was correct in concluding that the defendant had sustained its burden of proving that there was a partial want of a consideration to the extent of $2585.50 and in awarding a judgment in favor of the plaintiff in the amount of $860.50 after deducting the sum of $2585.50 from the cashier's check in the amount of $3446.

Since the plaintiff alleged in its reply that it was a holder in due course, it assumed the burden of establishing that it was in all respects a holder in due course. [UCC §] 3–307(3). To be a holder in due course, the plaintiff must have taken the cashier's check for value, in good faith, and without notice that it was overdue or dishonored or that there was any defense against it or claim to it on the part of any person. [UCC §] 3–302(1).

The plaintiff contends that the deposit of $9501 made on March 28, 1973, was a cash deposit. That contention has no merit because the unchallenged finding of the court is that it was a check deposit. The principal issue in this case is whether the provisional credit made by the plaintiff against the B & D Automotive account, which was overdrawn in the amount of $21,079.43, constituted value under [UCC §] 3–302(1). The credit entered was subject to a later withdrawal or reversal of the credit by the plaintiff. The trial court concluded that no value was given because the credit was not extended irrevocably. That conclusion was erroneous.

[UCC §] 3–303(b) provides that a holder takes for value "when he takes the instrument in payment of or as security for an antecedent claim against any person whether or not the claim is due * * *." [UCC §] 4–208(1)(a) elaborates on that concept and provides that "[a] bank has a security interest in an item and any accompanying documents or the proceeds of either * * * in case of an item deposited in an account to the extent to which credit given for the item has been withdrawn or applied * * *." [UCC §] 4–209 completes that thought, stating that "[f]or purposes of determining its status as a holder in due course, the bank has given value to the extent that it has a security interest in an item provided that the bank otherwise complies with the requirements of section 3–302 on what constitutes a holder in due course."

In order to comprehend how the plaintiff became a holder for value under the provisions of the statutes referred to, it is necessary to state the parameters of the security interest with relation to the value concept. It is clear that if a depositor's account is not overdrawn and he deposits a check which is credited to his account but not drawn on, then no value is given. See Universal C. I. T. Credit Corporation v. Guaranty Bank & Trust Co., 161 F.Supp. 790, 792 (D.Mass.). It is clear under [UCC §] 4–208(1)

(a) that a bank has given value and is a holder in due course to the extent that a depositor actually draws against a check given for collection, even if the check is later dishonored. It is immaterial that the bank takes the check for collection only and can charge back against the depositor's account the amount of the uncollected item. Citizens Bank of Booneville v. National Bank of Commerce, 334 F.2d 257, 261 (10th Cir.); Citizens National Bank of Englewood v. Fort Lee Savings & Loan Assn., 89 N.J. Super. 43, 47, 213 A.2d 315.

The reason for that rule is to prevent the hindrance to commercial transactions which would result if depository banks refused to permit withdrawal prior to clearance of checks. By giving the bank a security interest in the amount credited prior to notice of a stop payment order or other notice of dishonor, [UCC §§] 4–208 and 4–209 allow continuation of that common practice while protecting the bank as a holder in due course. Citizens National Bank of Englewood v. Fort Lee Savings & Loan Assn., supra.

While Maisto did not draw upon the deposit of $9501, the deposit was applied to his overdraft or antecedent debt on a provisional basis. Under the circumstances it appears that where the plaintiff applied the deposit, even provisionally, to Maisto's overdrawn account, it gave value and thus cut off the defense of want of consideration. In a leading case, Bath National Bank v. Sonnenstrahl, Inc., 249 N.Y. 391, 394, 164 N.E. 327, 328, it was stated: "Though title to a draft left by a depositor with the bank for collection does not pass absolutely to the bank where the full amount of the draft was credited to the depositor, 'for convenience and in anticipation of its payment,' and 'the bank could have cancelled the credit, as it clearly accepted no risk on the paper,' yet if the depositor 'had overdrawn, and this draft had been credited to cover the overdraft, or if the company had drawn against the draft, the bank could hold the paper until the account was squared.' It would then be a holder for value. St. Louis & San Francisco Ry. Co. v. Johnston, 133 U.S. 566, 10 S.Ct. 390, 33 L.Ed. 683."

[UCC §] 4–201(1) provides, in part, that "[u]nless a contrary intent clearly appears and prior to the time that a settlement given by a collecting bank for an item is or becomes final as provided in subsection (3) of section 4–211 and sections 4–212 and 4–213 the bank is an agent or subagent of the owner of the item and any settlement given for the item is provisional. * * * [A]ny rights of the owner to proceeds of the item are subject to rights of a collecting bank such as those resulting from outstanding advances on the item and valid rights of setoff." That provision, which makes the bank an agent of its customer, is to be construed harmoniously with [UCC §] 4–208(1) which does not derogate from the banker's general common-law lien or right of setoff against indebtedness owing in deposit accounts.

In the present case, the plaintiff's action in provisionally crediting a $9501 deposit to the antecedent debt of the depositor was an exercise of its common-law right of setoff, [UCC §] 4–208(1) and also gave the plaintiff a security interest sufficient to constitute value. In Sandler v. United Industrial Bank, 23 A.D.2d 567, 256 N.Y.S.2d 442, a check was deposited in an account which was overdrawn and the bank credited the deposit in part to repay the overdrawn account and applied the balance to a new item presented for payment. The maker of the check died that evening and his bank returned his check unpaid. The court held that the collecting bank became a holder for value prior to the maker's death. See Bowling Green, Inc. N. H. v. State Street Bank & Trust Co. of Boston, 307 F.Supp. 648, 654–55 (D.Mass.).

To make a collecting bank a holder for value where it applies a deposit to an overdrawn account is a result consistent with logic and good banking practice. If an account is overdrawn, it is highly doubtful that a bank would pass over an opportunity to erase or reduce the overdraft. That opportunity arises when the customer makes a deposit. The bank credits or sets off the overdraft and waits for final settlement as a holder for value. If the check is dishonored, the bank may then reverse the provisional granting of credit to the overdraft and proceed not only against its customer but also against the drawee bank. If it can proceed against the drawee bank, the latter can then recover from its customer.

The trial court erred in concluding that the plaintiff was not a holder for value when it applied Maisto's deposit, which included the cashier's check in the amount of $3446, to an overdraft in his account, subject to reversal upon dishonor.

There is error, the judgment is set aside and the matter is remanded for a trial limited to the issue of whether the plaintiff took the cashier's check in good faith and without notice that it was overdue, dishonored or that there was any defect or defense.

NOTE

Laurel Bank represents an orthodox analysis of UCC § 4–208(1)(a). A contrary analysis of that provision was made by the New York Court of Appeals in Marine Midland Bank-New York v. Graybar Electric Co., Inc., 41 N.Y.2d 703, 395 N.Y.S.2d 403, 363 N.E.2d 1139 (1977). Dynamics was indebted to the bank on a loan. A check of Graybar payable to Dynamics was deposited in Dynamics account with the bank which forwarded it for collection. On the day of the deposit the credit given for the check was "set off" against Dynamics' loan debt to the bank. The check was not paid because Graybar had stopped payment. The bank then brought an action against Graybar as drawer of the check. Under the court's analysis of the case the bank's rights to recover the amount of the check depended upon whether it was a holder in due course and this in turn depended upon whether the bank took the check for value. The court analyzed this issue as follows:

> As to value, the bank contends that it took the July 25 check for value because under the Uniform Commercial Code "A holder takes the instrument for value (a) to the extent that * * * he acquires a *security interest in or a lien on the instrument* * * * or (b) when he takes the instrument in *payment of or as security for an antecedent claim* against any person whether or not the claim is due" (Uniform Commercial Code, § 3–303; emphasis added). Further, the bank notes that the Uniform Commercial Code accords to it a "security interest" in a check "to the extent to which credit given for the item is withdrawn or *applied*" (§ 4–208, subd. [1], par. [a]; emphasis added). Thus, the bank's position is that, by its setoff, it took the check in payment of its antecedent loan, and also that by applying the credit for the check to the loan, the bank acquired a security interest therein. For these reasons, the bank argues that it has given value under the Uniform Commercial Code (see, also, § 4–209).

> Dynamics argues that a bank and its depositor must "bilaterally" agree, either expressly or impliedly, to the creation of a security interest in an item. Examples of an implied agreement are said to be participating in the withdrawal of funds, or applying the credit which the bank has given for the item prior to collection. Furthermore, Dynamics argues, the bank must give value unconditionally and irrevocably by actually extinguishing the depositor's debt upon receipt of the check, even though not yet collected. Dynamics is thus

arguing that under the circumstances presented here the
bank has not given value.

A bank, of course, gives value to the extent that a credit
given for an item is withdrawn by the party whose account
was credited.(Uniform Commercial Code, § 4–208, subd. [1],
par. [a]; see, e.g., Long Is. Nat. Bank v. Zawada, 34 A.D.2d
1016, 312 N.Y.S.2d 947, supra). Value is also given by a
holder when it takes a check in payment of, or as security
for, an antecedent debt (§ 3–303, subd. [b]; see e.g., Kelso &
Co. v. Ellis, 224 N.Y. 528, 536–537, 121 N.E. 364, 366; American Exch. Nat. Bank v. New York Belting & Packing Co., 148
N.Y. 698, 703, 43 N.E. 168, 169). Long before the enactment
of the Uniform Commercial Code, however, the entry of a
credit on a bank's books was held not to be parting with
value under circumstances manifesting that the pre-existing
debt or a part thereof was not, in fact, extinguished in consideration for the item for which the credit was given (see
Sixth Nat. Bank of City of N. Y. v. Lorillard Brick Works
Co., Sup., 18 N.Y.S. 861, affd., 136 N.Y.S. 667, 33 N.E. 335).
The basis for that decision was that the bookkeeping entry of
the credit was not a parting with value (see, also, Citizens'
State Bank v. Cowles, 180 N.Y. 346, 349, 73 N.E. 33, 34; see,
generally Holders In Due Course—Bank, Ann., 59 A.L.R.2d
1178, § 8, at pp. 1195–1197).

These events present somewhat of a hybrid situation in
that the bank first gave Dynamics a credit for the Graybar
check and then applied this credit, by way of setoff, to Dynamics' indebtedness to it. A literal reading of the Uniform
Commercial Code suggests that under section 4–208 (subd.
[1], par. [a]) and subdivision (b) of section 3–303 the net result of the credit followed by the setoff is that the bank had
taken the check for value. The difficulty with this analysis
is, however, that the credit given to Dynamics' account was
provisional because the bank could and did reverse the credit
after notice of the stop payment order, thereby reinstating
that portion of the loan against which the credit was set off.

Considering first the credit given to Dynamics' account
for the Graybar check, it is established that the giving of a
provisional credit is not a parting with value under the Uniform Commercial Code. In discussing the notion that it is
not necessary to give holder in due course status to one who
has not actually paid value, the Official Commentary to the
Uniform Commercial Code cites as an illustration "the bank

credit not drawn upon, which can be and is revoked when a claim or defense appears" (Official Comment 3, Uniform Commercial Code, § 3–303; see Bankers Trust Co. v. Nagler, 16 A.D.2d 477, 229 N.Y.S.2d 142; see, also, Brady, Bank Checks [4th ed.], § 4.6, p. 77).

* * *

Turning then to the argument that by applying the credit by way of setoff to Dynamics' indebtedness the bank gave value, the following is relevant. The clearest instance of giving value in this sort of case is where a bank actually extinguishes a debt by, for example, parting with a note in exchange for a check and then seeking to collect on the check (see Citizens Bank of Booneville v. National Bank of Commerce, 10 Cir., 334 F.2d 257). With respect to subdivision (1) of section 4–208, however, one text has suggested that its purpose was to give "the bank protection in any case in which it is not clear that the bank purchased the item outright, but in which it is clear that the bank has done something, of advantage to the depositor, more than giving the depositor a mere credit on the bank's books" (Clarke, Bailey & Young, Bank Deposits and Collections [1963], p. 56). Here, the bank argues that by applying the credit to Dynamics' indebtedness it was giving value as contemplated under section 4–208.

This argument should be rejected. To say that the bank was doing something of advantage to Dynamics by applying the credit to that depositor's indebtedness is to ignore what actually occurred. The bank was merely seeking to protect itself and not giving value, in any traditional sense, or under the Uniform Commercial Code. Since the credit given to the Dynamics account was not, as noted, available to Dynamics, there is no reason for allowing the bank to benefit from this credit, particularly since the bank reinstated that portion of the debt against which the credit was applied upon learning that payment was not to be forthcoming on the check. Under this analysis the bank is in no worse position than any other creditor, and the bank's unilateral agreement to take the credit for the indebtedness, conditioned on payment of the check for which the credit was given, is recognized for what it was—an attempt to recoup its losses.

This is not to diminish the bank's right of setoff of mutual debts in a bankruptcy situation (see Studley v. Boylston Bank, 229 U.S. 523, 33 S.Ct. 806, 57 L.Ed. 1313; New York

County Bank v. Massey, 192 U.S. 138, 24 S.Ct. 199, 48 L.Ed. 380). Nor is this holding intended to suggest that the setoff was impermissible simply because the check was uncollected at the time of the setoff (see Bath Nat. Bank v. Sonnenstrahl, 249 N.Y. 391, 164 N.E. 327). Rather, this determination is based on the conclusion that what the bank did was merely give a provisional credit for the Graybar check. That the bank unilaterally agreed to apply this provisional credit to Dynamics' indebtedness should not elevate the transaction to the level of those instances where value is considered to be given under the Uniform Commercial Code. Therefore, since the bank did not give value, it is not a holder in due course and cannot recover on the check.

The Court of Appeals suggests that an antecedent debt can constitute value only in cases in which the debt was "extinguished" in consideration of the instrument for which the credit was given. Taking a personal check for an underlying obligation does not normally "extinguish" the obligation. UCC § 3–802(1)(b) states that the underlying obligation is suspended until the check is presented; if the check is dishonored the obligation revives. It is a rare case indeed in which a personal check is accepted in absolute payment of an obligation. Thus, in the normal case, the check is taken as provisional payment. This is similar to the provisional credit given by the depositary bank for an uncollected check. In both cases the credit given for the check is reversed if the check is not paid. But, under UCC § 3–802(1)(b), the person taking the check may sue on it and there is no indication in the UCC that the fact that the debt was not extinguished affects the taking-for-value question. One of the arguments against recognizing an antecedent debt as value is that the creditor taking the instrument is often given a windfall. He may not have made any detrimental reliance and if the instrument is not enforceable he is in no worse position than he was before taking the instrument. This argument was rejected by the drafters of the NIL and the UCC. Before New York adopted the NIL, the common-law rule in that state did not recognize an antecedent debt as value for holder-in-due-course purposes. See Kelso & Co. v. Ellis, 224 N.Y. 528, 121 N.E. 364 (1918). *Marine Midland* appears to be a step backward in the direction of the old New York doctrine.

BOWLING GREEN, INC. v. STATE STREET BANK AND TRUST CO.

United States Court of Appeals, First Circuit, 1970.
425 F.2d 81.

COFFIN, CIRCUIT JUDGE. On September 26, 1966, plaintiff Bowling Green, Inc., the operator of a bowling alley, negotiated a United States government check for $15,306 to Bowl-Mor, Inc., a manufacturer of bowling alley equipment. The check, which plaintiff had acquired through a Small Business Administration loan, represented the first installment on a conditional sales contract for the purchase of candlepin setting machines. On the following day, September 27, a representative of Bowl-Mor deposited the check in defendant State Street Bank and Trust Co. The Bank immediately credited $5,024.85 of the check against an overdraft in Bowl-Mor's account. Later that day, when the Bank learned that Bowl-Mor had filed a petition for reorganization under Chapter X of the Bankruptcy Act, it transferred $233.61 of Bowl-Mor's funds to another account and applied the remaining $10,047.54 against debts which Bowl-Mor owed the Bank. Shortly thereafter Bowl-Mor's petition for reorganization was dismissed and the firm was adjudicated a bankrupt. Plaintiff has never received the pin-setting machines for which it contracted. Its part payment remains in the hands of defendant Bank.

Plaintiff brought this diversity action to recover its payment from defendant Bank on the grounds that the Bank is constructive trustee of the funds deposited by Bowl-Mor. In the court below, plaintiff argued that Bowl-Mor knew it could not perform at the time it accepted payment, that the Bank was aware of this fraudulent conduct, and that the Bank therefore received Bowl-Mor's deposit impressed with a constructive trust in plaintiff's favor. The district court rejected plaintiff's view of the evidence, concluding instead that the Bank was a holder in due course within the meaning of [UCC] §§ 4–209 and 3–302, and was therefore entitled to take the item in question free of all personal defenses. Bowling Green, Inc., etc. v. State Street Bank and Trust Co., 307 F.Supp. 648 (D.Mass.1969).

Plaintiff's appeal challenges the conclusion of the district court in three respects. First, plaintiff maintains that the Bank has not met its burden of establishing that it was a "holder" of the item within the meaning of [UCC] § 1–201(20), and thus cannot be a "holder in due course" within the meaning of § 4–209 and § 3–302. Second, plaintiff argues that the Bank's close working relation with Bowl-Mor prevented it from becoming a holder in good faith. Finally, plaintiff denies that defendant gave value within the meaning of § 4–209 for the $10,047.54 which it set off against Bowl-Mor's loan account.

Plaintiff's first objection arises from a technical failure of proof. The district court found that plaintiff had endorsed the item in question to Bowl-Mor, but there was no evidence that Bowl-Mor supplied its own endorsement before depositing the item in the Bank. Thus we cannot tell whether the Bank is a holder within the meaning of § 1–201(20), which defines holder as one who takes an instrument endorsed to him, or to bearer, or in blank. But, argues plaintiff, once it is shown that a defense to an instrument exists, the Bank has the burden of showing that it is in all respects a holder in due course. This failure of proof, in plaintiff's eyes, is fatal to the Bank's case.

We readily agree with plaintiff that the Bank has the burden of establishing its status in all respects. [UCC] § 3–307(3), on which plaintiff relies to establish the defendant's burden, seems addressed primarily to cases in which a holder seeks to enforce an instrument, but Massachusetts courts have indicated that the policy of § 3–307(3) applies whenever a party invokes the rights of a holder in due course either offensively or defensively. Cf. Elbar Realty Inc. v. City Bank & Trust Co., 342 Mass. 262, 267–268, 173 N.E.2d 256 (1961). The issue, however, is not whether the Bank bears the burden of proof, but whether it must establish that it took the item in question by endorsement in order to meet its burden. We think not. The evidence in this case indicates that the Bank's transferor, Bowl-Mor, was a holder. Under [UCC] § 3–201(a), transfer of an instrument vests in the transferee all the rights of the transferor. As the Official Comment to § 3–201 indicates, one who is not a holder must first establish the transaction by which he acquired the instrument before enforcing it, but the Bank has met this burden here.

We doubt, moreover, whether the concept of "holder" as defined in § 1–201(20) applies with full force to Article 4. Article 4 establishes a comprehensive scheme for simplifying and expediting bank collections. Its provisions govern the more general rules of Article 3 wherever inconsistent. [UCC] § 4–102(1). As part of this expediting process, Article 4 recognizes the common bank practice of accepting unendorsed checks for deposit. See Funk, Banks and the U.C.C. 133 (1964). § 4–201(1) provides that the lack of an endorsement shall not affect the bank's status as agent for collection, and § 4–205(1) authorizes the collecting bank to supply the missing endorsements as a matter of course. In practice, banks comply with § 4–205 by stamping the item "deposited to the account of the named payee" or some similar formula. Funk, supra at 133. We doubt whether the bank's status should turn on proof of whether a clerk employed the appropriate stamp, and we hesitate to penalize a bank which accepted unendorsed checks for deposit in reliance on the Code, at least when, as here, the customer himself clearly satisfies the definition of "holder". Section 4–209 does provide that a bank must comply "with the requirements of section 3–302 on what constitutes a holder in due course," but we think this language refers to the enumerated requirements of good faith and lack of notice rather than to the status of holder, a status which § 3–302 assumes rather than requires. We therefore hold that a bank which takes an item for collection from a customer who was himself a holder need not establish that it took the item by negotiation in order to satisfy § 4–209.

[Omitted is the portion of the opinion in which the court rejected the plaintiff's second ground for reversal.]

This brings us to plaintiff's final argument, that the Bank gave value only to the extent of the $5,024.85 overdraft, and thus cannot be a holder in due course with respect to the remaining $10,047.54 which the Bank credited against Bowl-Mor's loan account. Our consideration of this argument is confined by the narrow scope of the district court's findings. The Bank may well have given value under § 4–208(1)(a) when it credited the balance of Bowl-Mor's checking account against its outstanding indebtedness. See Banco Espanol de Credito v. State Street Bank & Trust Co., 409 F.2d 711 (1st Cir. 1969). But by that time the Bank knew of Bowl-Mor's petition for reorganization, additional information which the district court did not consider in finding that the Bank acted in good faith and without notice at the time it received the item. We must therefore decide whether the Bank gave value for the additional $10,047.54 at the time the item was deposited.[5]

5. Defendant suggests that we can avoid the analytical problems of § 4–209 by simply holding that the Bank's inchoate right to set off Bowl-Mor's outstanding indebtedness against deposits, as they were made constituted a giving of value. See Wood v. Boylston National Bank, 129 Mass. 358 (1880). There are, however, some pitfalls in this theory. First, under prior law a secured creditor could not exercise its right of set-off without first showing that its security was inadequate. Forastiere v. Springfield Institution for Savings, 303 Mass. 101, 104, 20 N.E.2d 950 (1939). Second, although the Uniform Commercial Code forswears any intent to

Resolution of this issue depends on the proper interpretation of § 4–209, which provides that a collecting bank has given value to the extent that it has acquired a "security interest" in an item. In plaintiff's view, a collecting bank can satisfy § 4–209 only by extending credit against an item in compliance with § 4–208(1). The district court, on the other hand, adopted the view that a security interest is a security interest, however acquired. The court then found that defendant and Bowl-Mor had entered a security agreement which gave defendant a floating lien on Bowl-Mor's chattel paper. Since the item in question was part of the proceeds of a Bowl-Mor contract, the court concluded that defendant had given value for the full $15,306.00 at the time it received the deposit.[a]

With this conclusion we agree. Section 1–201(37) defines "security interest" as an interest in personal property which secures payment or performance of an obligation. There is no indication in § 4–209 that the term is used in a more narrow or specialized sense. Moreover, as the official comment to § 4–209 observes, this provision is in accord with prior law and with § 3–303, both of which provide that a holder gives value when he accepts an instrument as security for an antecedent debt. Reynolds v. Park Trust Co., 245 Mass. 440, 444–445, 139 N.E. 785 (1923). Finally, we note that if one of the Bank's prior loans to Bowl-Mor had been made in the expectation that this particular instrument would be deposited, the terms of § 4–208(1)(c) would have been literally satisfied. We do not think the case is significantly different when the Bank advances credit on the strength of a continuing flow of items of this kind. We therefore conclude that the Bank gave value for the full $15,306.00 at the time it accepted the deposit.

change a banker's right of set-off, § 4–201 does change the presumption that a bank owns items deposited with it. This presumption played a role under prior law in assessing the bank's rights against uncollected commercial paper. Compare Wood v. Boylston National Bank, supra, with Boston-Continental National Bank v. Hub Fruit Co., 285 Mass. 187, 190, 189 N.E. 89 (1934) and American Barrel Co. v. Commissioner of Banks, 290 Mass. 174, 179-181, 195 N.E. 335 (1935).

   a. [Eds.] The bank secured its loan to Bowl-Mor by a security inter-

est in Bowl-Mor's installment sale contracts (defined as chattel paper by UCC § 9–105(1)(b)). Its security interest applied not only to the chattel paper but also to any proceeds of the chattel paper. UCC § 9–306. Bowling Green's check to Bowl-Mor, since it was in payment of the first installment of its sales contract, was proceeds. Under UCC § 9–306 and § 9–203 the bank automatically obtained a security interest in this check as soon as Bowl-Mor obtained "rights" in the check, which in this case was when Bowl-Mor received the check.

We see no discrepancy between this result and the realities of commercial life. Each party, of course, chose to do business with an eventually irresponsible third party. The Bank, though perhaps unwise in prolonging its hopes for a prospering customer, nevertheless protected itself through security arrangements as far as possible without hobbling each deposit and withdrawal. Plaintiff, on the other hand, not only placed its initial faith in Bowl-Mor, but later became aware that Bowl-Mor was having difficulties in meeting its payroll. It seems not too unjust that this vestige of caveat emptor survives.

Affirmed.

NOTES

1. For comments on *Bowling Green,* see Hawkland, "Depository Banks as Holders in Due Course," 76 Comm'l L.J. 124 (1971); Note, *"Bowling Green:* The Bank as a Holder in Due Course," 71 Colum.L.Rev. 302 (1971); Note, "Commercial Banking—How Can a Bank Become a Holder and Give Value in Order to Attain Holder in Due Course Status?" 12 B.C.L.Rev. 282 (1970).

2. On the indorsement issue *Bowling Green* has been followed in Nida v. Michael, 34 Mich.App. 290, 191 N.W.2d 151 (1971), and rejected in United Overseas Bank v. Veneers, Inc., 375 F.Supp. 596 (D.Md.1974). In the latter case the court took the position that a depositary bank must actually supply a missing indorsement if it seeks to be a holder. "Although both § 3–201(3) and § 4–205(1) provide an absolute right to a transferee and to a depository bank, respectively, to have an endorsement, neither can be read as making the right to an endorsement the equivalent of the endorsement." 375 F.Supp. at 605.

3. In footnote 5 the court's reference to "the Bank's inchoate right to set off" is apparently meant to apply to the banker's lien. It is clear that a banker's lien is not a security interest under UCC § 4–208, but Comment 1 to that section states that "Subsection (1) does not derogate from the banker's common-law lien or right of set-off against indebtedness owing in deposit accounts." The Comment to UCC § 4–209 states that that section is in accord with the prior law (NIL § 27) and with UCC § 3–303. NIL § 27 states: "Where the holder has a lien on the instrument, arising either from contract or by implication of law, he is deemed a holder for value to the extent of his lien." UCC § 3–303(a) states that a holder takes for value "to the extent that * * * he acquires a security interest in or a lien on the

instrument otherwise than by legal process." Assuming that the Bowl-Mor loan was due at the time the check was deposited, there is abundant authority, including Wood v. Boylston National Bank, 129 Mass. 358 (1880), cited by the court, which supports the defendant's argument that it acquired a lien in the check when it was deposited. But the Massachusetts courts seem to severely restrict the banker's lien by their reading of the special deposit rule, which is a qualification on a bank's ability to obtain a lien. This qualification states that the banker's lien does not apply to items deposited for a special purpose. See Jones on Liens § 251 (3d ed. 1914). Two examples illustrate the doctrine. In Bank of the United States v. Macalester, 9 Pa. 475 (1849), the obligor on interest coupons payable to bearer deposited funds with Bank, which as its agent was to use the funds to pay holders of the coupons who presented them for payment. At the time of the deposit the obligor on the coupons was indebted to Bank. Instead of paying the coupons Bank asserted a lien on the deposited funds to pay the debt owing to it. The court held that because the funds were deposited for a special purpose Bank could not assert a lien against them. In Rockland Trust Co. v. South Shore National Bank, 366 Mass. 74, 314 N.E.2d 438 (1974), the court stated that "it seems at least doubtful" that a depositary bank could assert a lien against a certified check deposited to the account of its customer for the purpose of having the funds represented by the check wired to a third party to whom its customer was indebted. But the Massachusetts courts have also applied the special deposit rule to checks deposited for collection stating in effect that the depositary bank acting as agent of its customer to collect the check cannot claim any beneficial interest in the check. Under the Massachusetts reading of the rule the qualification apparently destroys the banker's lien in most of the cases to which it has historically been applied, and the bank is limited to a right of set off after the check is paid. See Boston-Continental National Bank v. Hub Fruit Co., 285 Mass. 187, 189 N.E. 89 (1934).

4. Under UCC § 3–303(a) the acquisition of a lien constitutes taking for value. The existence of the lien does not depend upon the bank's making any accounting entries to "apply" the check to the outstanding debt. See Maryland Casualty Co. v. National Bank of Germantown & Trust Co., 320 Pa. 129, 182 A. 362 (1936). By contrast UCC § 4–208(1)(a) states that the bank gets a security interest in the deposited check at the time that credit given for it was "applied." The court indicates that this refers to the time when Bowl-Mor's deposit account, which

had been credited with the amount of the check, was charged $10,047.54 in reduction of the loan. Suppose a check payable to Customer was indorsed by Customer to Depositary Bank and delivered to one of its officers in reply to a demand by Depositary Bank to immediately cover an overdraft. Thereafter, but before the check was deposited to Customer's account the drawer of the check told the officer handling the transaction that the check was issued without consideration. At what time was "credit given for the item * * * applied"? UCC § 4–208(1)(a). At what time did Depositary Bank "take the instrument in payment of or as security for an antecedent claim"? UCC § 3–303(b). At what time did Depositary Bank "acquire * * * a lien on the instrument otherwise than by legal process"? UCC § 3–303(a). See Peoria Savings & Loan Association v. Jefferson Trust & Savings Bank of Peoria, 81 Ill.2d 461, 43 Ill.Dec. 712, 410 N.E.2d 845 (1980).

3. ANTECEDENT CLAIMS AND SECURITY INTERESTS IN GOODS

The depositary bank in *Bowling Green* was able to assert rights in the deposited check as a holder in due course because its Article 9 security interest in the check securing an antecedent debt satisfied the taking-for-value requirement. Thus, without giving any new value and without showing any detrimental reliance, it was able to profit from its customer's fraud against Bowling Green. An analogous problem is raised in the case of goods. Negotiability is provided by UCC § 2–403(1) and value is provided, as in *Bowling Green*, by an antecedent debt and an Article 9 security interest. An example is the next case, Matter of Samuels & Co., Inc. This case presented a number of complex issues under the Bankruptcy Act and under the UCC. It has been severely edited so that only the discussion pertaining to UCC § 2–403(1) is presented. The dissenting opinion of Judge Godbold represents the law. His view was finally adopted by the entire Fifth Circuit en banc, and other cases are in accord. Judge Ingraham's opinion reflects the great reluctance of the Fifth Circuit panel to accept the fact that the UCC allowed the finance company to simply appropriate, without payment, the cattle of the hapless farmers. The final chapter in the drama is revealed in the note following the case.

MATTER OF SAMUELS & CO., INC.

United States Court of Appeals, Fifth Circuit, 1975.
510 F.2d 139.

INGRAHAM, CIRCUIT JUDGE.

* * *

To briefly reiterate, the relevant facts are as follows. Samuels & Co., Inc., is a Texas meatpacking firm that purchases, processes and packages meat and sells the meat within and without the State of Texas. Since 1963 Samuels' operations, including its cattle purchases, have been financed on a weekly basis by C.I.T. Corporation. To secure its financing, C.I.T. has properly perfected a lien on Samuels' assets, inventory and all after-acquired property, including livestock that is from time to time purchased for slaughter and processing.

From May 12 through May 23, 1969, the appellants, fifteen cattle farmers, delivered their cattle to Samuels. Although the sellers did not receive payment for the sale simultaneously with delivery of the cattle, checks were subsequently issued to the sellers. On May 23, 1969, before these checks had been paid, C.I.T., believing itself to be insecure, refused to advance any more funds to Samuels for the operation of the packing plant. On that same day Samuels filed a petition in bankruptcy. Since C.I.T. refused to advance more funds, although apparently aware that there were unpaid checks outstanding, the appellants' checks issued in payment for cattle were dishonored by the drawee bank.

Because of the fungible nature of the cattle, the beef has long since been butchered and processed and sold through the normal course of business. The proceeds from the cattle sales have been deposited with the trustee in bankruptcy pending the outcome of this litigation. The issues in this case concern the priority of interest in these proceeds between a creditor of the debtor, which holds a perfected security interest in the debtor's after-acquired property, and a seller of goods to the debtor. Since the sellers have not been paid, they claim a superior right to the deposited proceeds and argue that they are now entitled to payment out of these proceeds. The finance corporation, on the other hand, contends that the sellers are merely unsecured creditors of the bankrupt and are not entitled to a prior claim to the funds, and alternatively that the finance corporation qualified as a good faith purchaser of the cattle and is therefore im-

mune to the sellers' claims of non-payment. For the reasons
that follow, we conclude that the sellers should prevail.

I.

In order to determine which provisions of the Texas Business
& Commerce Code govern the relationships among the parties,
the first question that must be resolved is whether this commercial venture was a cash or credit transaction. The significance
of classifying a sale as a cash or credit transaction relates back
to the common law and the historical passing of title concept.
Under the common law, a sale for cash, as opposed to a sale on
credit, meant that the seller of goods implicitly reserved the incidents of ownership or title to the goods until payment was made
in full. If the buyer failed to make payment, the seller could
regain possession of the goods by instituting an action in replevin. Additionally, since the buyer of goods for cash did not obtain title to the goods until the seller was paid, the defaulting
buyer was incapable of passing title to a third party. Based on
the cash sale doctrine, an unpaid seller could even reclaim goods
sold by an intermediary to one who otherwise qualified as a
bona fide purchaser.

When the owner of goods sold them on credit, however, all
the incidents of ownerhsip, including title, passed to the buyer.
If the buyer subsequently failed to make payment, the seller's
rights were only those of a creditor for the purchase price, and
he had no right against the merchandise. Since in a sale on
credit the buyer obtained all the incidents of ownership in the
goods, including title, he was able to convey his interest in the
goods, absolute ownership, to a third party without recourse on
behalf of the seller. Corman, Cash Sales, Worthless Checks and
the Bona Fide Purchaser, 10 Vanderbilt Law Review 55 (1956);
Gilmore, The Commercial Doctrine of Good Faith Purchaser, 63
Yale L.J. 1057, 1060 & n. 10 (1954).

Underlying the different characteristics and consequences of
cash and credit sales are the expectations and intentions of the
three parties concerned. When goods are sold for cash, the seller is assuming virtually no risk of loss because he believes that
he has full payment for the goods in his hands. When the sale
is for credit, however, the seller assumes a far more substantial
risk and voluntarily relinquishes the incidents of ownership to
the buyer. The buyer, possessed of these incidents of ownership, is capable of conveying title to a bona fide purchaser, completely terminating the rights of the seller in the goods. The

credit seller recognizes that he will receive full payment for his merchandise only if the business of the buyer progresses normally and sales are made to third parties in the normal course of business. Note, The Owner's Intent and the Negotiability of Chattels: A Critique of Section 2–403 of the Uniform Commercial Code, 72 Yale L.J. 1205, 1220 (1963). Although commercial transactions and the law governing such relationships has developed significantly since the conception of these doctrines, this reasoning with respect to the different risks assumed by the different sellers underlie and differentiate the two concepts and is as valid a distinction today as it was when the doctrines were originally conceived.

The Uniform Commercial Code as adopted by the State of Texas has to some extent modified the common law doctrines of cash and credit sales. It is clear that the historical concept of passing title to goods is not emphasized in the Code, and the location of title generally is not regarded as being determinative of the rights of adverse parties. Helstad, Deemphasis of Title Under the Uniform Commercial Code, 1964, Wisconsin L.R. 362. Instead of implementing the fictional concept of title, the countervailing interests of the parties are sometimes defined in terms of various rights, privileges, powers and immunities. But even though the title concept is so reduced in significance, the Code recognizes and adopts the fundamental distinctions of the common law between cash and credit sales, at least with respect to the rights of the unpaid seller against the defaulting buyer. The Code deals with a sale on credit in provisions separate from those dealing with cash sales. Section 2–702 specifically sets forth the credit seller's remedy and provides that when "the seller discovers that the buyer has received goods on credit while insolvent, he may reclaim the goods upon demand made within ten days after receipt * * *." UCC § 2–702(2). This provision goes on to define the seller's priority rights against other specific parties, providing that "[t]he seller's right to reclaim under Subsection (2) is subject to the rights of a buyer in the ordinary course or other good faith purchaser or lien creditor under this chapter (Section 2–403)." Id. § 2–702(3). Although this section authorizes a limited right against the goods, it generally recognizes that when the sale is on a credit basis, all the incidents of ownership pass to the buyer who may then convey this interest to certain third parties. The seller stands merely as a general creditor for the purchase price.

With respect to cash sales, however, § 2–507 of the Code explicitly recognizes that "unless otherwise agreed," "[w]here payment is due and demanded on the delivery to the buyer of goods * * *, [the buyer's] right as against the seller to retain or dispose of them is conditional upon his making payment due." Like the cash sale doctrine at common law, § 2–507 provides that when the buyer is to pay cash for the goods, the validity of the transaction is dependent upon his making payment, and when the buyer fails to pay, he does not even have the right to possess the goods. Absolute ownership does not pass to the buyer until payment is complete.

The limited interest conveyed to the buyer prior to payment under § 2–507(2) is reemphasized in § 2–511(3), which deals specifically with the situation where payment for goods is made by check that is later dishonored. Section 2–511(3) provides that payment by check "is conditional and is defeated as between the parties by dishonor of the check on due presentment." Underlying this provision is the principle that, in order to encourage and facilitate commercial sales and economic growth generally, the recipient of a check in payment for goods "is not to be penalized in any way" for accepting this commercially acceptable mode of payment. Id. Comment 4.

Even though the Code deemphasizes the title concept of the common law, these two provisions strongly suggest that the underlying philosophy of the common law cash sale doctrine has been embodied here. Like the traditional cash sale doctrine, the existence of a valid contractual relationship between the buyer and seller is dependent upon the buyer's completing his part of the bargain and paying for the merchandise. When the buyer fails to pay, he no longer has even the right to possess the goods.

Mindful of these principles we turn to the facts of the instant case to determine whether the sale of the cattle to the packing house was on a cash or credit basis. This sale of goods must be regarded as a cash transaction rather than a credit transaction because of the established course of dealing between the buyer and sellers. A course of dealing, as defined by the Texas Commercial Code, is a "sequence of previous conduct between the parties to a particular transaction which is fairly to be regarded as establishing a common basis of understanding for interpreting their expressions and other conduct." UCC § 1–205(1). As suggested by the Supreme Court in *Stowers*, supra, the Packers and Stockyards Act and the regulations issued thereunder so outline the course of conduct to be followed as between the cattle seller and the purchasing meat packer.

According to the Act and regulations, when a cattle grower sells his livestock on what is termed a "grade and yield" basis, the contract price to be paid is left open because it has yet to be determined. Before the purchase price can be determined, the cattle must be slaughtered and the carcasses chilled for twenty-four hours. After the meat is chilled, the Department of Agriculture grades it and determines the yield, and at that time the contract price can be set. When the price is set, a point sometime after delivery, a check is issued to the seller. 9 CFR §§ 201.43(b),—.99.

While a lapse of time occurring between delivery of the cattle and payment, even if only a day, might be considered an extension of credit, the course of dealing between the parties establishes that this was a sale for cash. The delay between delivery and payment was not credit, but rather was the result of a procedure mandated by the Act and regulations that governed the relationship between the buyer and seller when cattle are sold on a grade and yield basis. This procedure apparently had been followed since the inception of the regulations requiring such conduct. Moreover, not only do the Act and regulations prescribe such a course of conduct, all the cattle sellers regarded this commercial venture as a cash transaction, and there is nothing in the record to suggest that the buyer regarded the delay in issuing the check as credit. The course of conduct prescribed by the Act and regulations, coupled with the undisputed intent of the cattle sellers, compels the conclusion that this was a cash and not a credit affair. Engstrom v. Wiley, 191 F.2d 684 (9th Cir., 1951); In re Helms Veneer Corp., 287 F.Supp. 840 (W.D.Va., 1968).

* * *

Nor does the seller's ultimate reclamation of the cattle, or rather proceeds from sale of the cattle, prejudice the rights of any creditors. When a sale is made on credit, the purchased merchandise belongs to the estate of the bankrupt and all the seller has is a security interest in the property. If the seller failed to perfect his interest, he stands as a general creditor with the rest of the unsecured creditors and is entitled only to his proportionate share of the bankrupt's estate. To allow him to recover his loss in full from the estate would prejudice the rights of the other creditors. In re Colacci's of America, Inc., Bar Control of Colorado v. Gifford, 13 U.C.C.Rep. 1023 (10th Cir., 1973); Engstrom v. Wiley, supra, 191 F.2d at 689; Engelkes v. Farmers Co-op Co., 194 F.Supp. 319 (N.D.Iowa, 1961).

But when the sale is for cash, the merchandise belongs to the bankrupt's estate only if the buyer pays for the goods. If payment is not made, the seller is not a mere creditor and therefore is not compelled to share proportionately with the general creditors of the estate. The general creditors are not entitled to any portion of these assets because the goods do not belong to the bankrupt estate. The seller's reclamation of the goods does not remove any assets of the bankrupt in which general creditors would share and thus does not prejudice the rights of the seller on credit. Since the seller for cash is not a creditor and is not required to share with the general creditors in the estate as a creditor, he is entitled to his merchandise.

*   *   *

III.

The third question is whether C.I.T. qualifies as a good faith purchaser. Under § 2–403 of the Code, the buyer of goods from a seller is vested with a limited interest that it can convey to a good faith purchaser and thus create in the purchaser a greater right to the goods than the buyer itself had. This is possible even when the buyer obtains the goods as a result of giving a check that is later dishonored or when the purchase was made for cash. But in order to attain this status, the proponent must be a *purchaser* that gives *value* and acts in *good faith*. While C.I.T. gave value for the goods within the meaning of the Code, it failed to meet the test of a purchaser or one acting in good faith.

With regard to C.I.T.'s status as a purchaser, the Code broadly defines this term as one who take "by sale, discount, negotiation, mortgage, pledge, lien, issue or reissue, gift or any other voluntary transaction creating an interest in property." UCC § 1–201(32); see id. § 1–201(33). As noted earlier, C.I.T. does not have an interest in the cattle because its rights in the collateral are derivative of its debtor's rights in it. When Samuels failed to pay for the cattle, its rights in the cattle terminated and thus so did C.I.T.'s. C.I.T.'s status as a good faith purchaser is also defeated with regard to its acting in good faith. The Code defines good faith as "honesty in fact in the conduct or transaction concerned." UCC § 1–201(19). Implicit in the term "good faith" is the requirement that C.I.T. take its interest in the cattle without notice of the outstanding claims of others. See Greater Louisville Auto Auction v. Ogle Buick, Inc., supra,

387 S.W.2d at 21. See also Fidelity and Casualty Co. v. Key Biscayne Bank, 501 F.2d 1322, 1326 (5th Cir. 1974)

It is true that the evidence does not reveal any breach of an express obligation on C.I.T.'s behalf to continue financing the packing house after Samuels filed a petition in bankruptcy. Nor does the good faith element require the creditor to continue to finance the operation of a business when it is apparent that the business is unprofitable and is going bankrupt. But because of the integral relationship between C.I.T. and Samuels, we do not see how C.I.T. could have kept from knowing of the outstanding claims of others. C.I.T. maintained close scrutiny over the financial affairs of Samuels' operations. C.I.T. had been financing Samuels' packing house operations for at least six years, and the financing involved the flow of millions of dollars. The amount of cash advances made to Samuels was not predetermined or determined arbitrarily, but was calculated only after C.I.T. examined weekly the outstanding accounts and the current inventory of the business. From such a continuous and prolonged study of the business to determine the amount of each weekly advance, C.I.T. must have been intricately aware of the operations and financial status of the business.

Since C.I.T. was so intimately involved in Samuels' financial affairs, it must have known that when it refused to advance additional funds, unpaid checks issued to cattle sellers by Samuels would be dishonored. Samuels' operations were totally dependent on the financing of C.I.T. and both parties knew it. From its enduring involvement in the weekly financing, C.I.T. apparently knew that Samuels was purchasing and processing cattle up until the very time of filing the petition. Knowing that cattle had been purchased and processed immediately preceding its refusal to advance more money, C.I.T. must have known as a result of this refusal that some cattle sellers who had recently delivered their cattle to Samuels would not be paid. Because C.I.T. and Samuels were so intertwined in the management of the financial affairs of the business, we do not think that C.I.T. can plausibly claim, in complete honesty, that it was unaware of the claims of the unpaid cattle sellers. Since C.I.T. was aware of these outstanding claims, it does not qualify as a good faith purchaser.

* * *

V.

We believe it inequitable to deny the claims of the stock farmers who produced and delivered the cattle, in favor of the

mortgagee who refused to advance the money before bankruptcy.

*　*　*

It is our firm belief that the approach to the Code outlined
above is eminently reasonable and conforms with the Code's express provisions and underlying policies. We do not believe that
the drafters of the Code intended for the unpaid sellers to walk
away from this transaction with nothing, neither their goods nor
the purchase price, while the mortgagee enjoys a preferred lien
on that for which it refused to advance payment. Based on our
understanding of the Code, such a result is insupportable.

We again reverse the judgment of the district court.

GODBOLD, CIRCUIT JUDGE (dissenting): *the current law*

I dissent.

This case raises one primary question: under the Uniform
Commercial Code as adopted in Texas, is the interest of an un- *issue*
paid cash seller in goods already delivered to a buyer superior or
subordinate to the interest of a holder of a perfected security
interest in those same goods? In my opinion, under Article
Nine, the perfected security interest is unquestionably superior
to the interest of the seller. Moreover, the perfected lender is
protected from the seller's claims by two independent and theo-
retically distinct Article Two provisions. My result is not the
product of revealed truth, but rather of a meticulous and dispassionate reading of Articles Two and Nine and an understanding
that the Code is an integrated statute whose Articles and Sections overlap and flow into one another in an effort to encourage
specific types of commercial behavior. The Code's overall plan,
which typically favors good faith purchasers, and which encour-
ages notice filing of nonpossessory security interests in person-
alty through the imposition of stringent penalties for nonfiling,
compels a finding that the perfected secured party here should
prevail.

My brothers have not concealed that their orientation in the
case before us is to somehow reach a result in favor of the sellers of cattle, assumed by them to be "little fellows," and against
a large corporate lender, because it seems the "fair" thing to do.
We do not sit as federal chancellors confecting ways to escape
the state law of commercial transactions when that law produces
a result not to our tastes. Doing what seems fair is heady stuff.
But the next seller may be a tremendous corporate conglomer-
ate engaged in the cattle feeding business, and the next lender a

'small town Texas bank. Today's heady draught may give the majority a euphoric feeling, but it can produce tomorrow's hang over.

I. Rights under § 2–403

My analysis begins with an examination of the relative rights of seller and secured party under § 2–403(1).

Section 2–403 gives certain transferors power to pass greater title than they can themselves claim. Section 2–403(1) gives good faith purchasers of even fraudulent buyers-transferors greater rights than the defrauded seller can assert. This harsh rule is designed to promote the greatest range of freedom possible to commercial vendors and purchasers.

The provision anticipates a situation where (1) a cash seller has delivered goods to a buyer who has paid by a check which is subsequently dishonored, § 2–403(1)(b), (c), and where (2) the defaulting buyer transfers title to a Code-defined "good faith purchaser." The interest of the good faith purchaser is protected *pro tanto* against the claims of the aggrieved seller. §§ 2–403(1); 2–403, Comment 1. The Code expressly recognizes the power of the defaulting buyer to transfer good title to such a purchaser even though the transfer is wrongful as against the seller. The buyer is granted the *power* to transfer good title despite the fact that under § 2–507 he lacks the *right* to do so.

The Code definition of "purchaser" is broad, and includes not only one taking by sale but also covers persons taking by gift or by voluntary mortgage, pledge or lien. § 1–201(32), (33). It is therefore broad enough to include an Article Nine secured party. §§ 1–201(37); 9–101, Comment; 9–102(1), (2). Thus, if C.I.T. holds a valid Article Nine security interest, it is by virtue of that status also a purchaser under § 2–403(1). See First Citizens Bank and Trust Co. v. Academic Archives, Inc., 10 N.C.App. 619, 179 S.E.2d 850 (1971); Stumbo v. Paul B. Hult Lumber Co., 251 Or. 20, 444 P.2d 564 (1968); In re Hayward Woolen Co., 3 U.C.C. Rep. 1107 (D.Mass.1967).

While I shall discuss in detail infra, the implications of C.I.T.'s security interest under Article Nine and under other Article Two provisions, I here note that C.I.T. is the holder of a perfected Article Nine interest which extends to the goods claimed by the seller Stowers.

Attachment of an Article Nine interest takes place when (1) there is agreement that the interest attach to the collateral; (2)

the secured party has given value; and (3) the debtor has rights in the collateral sufficient to permit attachment. [1962 UCC] § 9–204(1).

(1) *The agreement:* In 1963, Samuels initially authorized C.I.T.'s lien in its after-acquired inventory. The agreement between these parties remained in effect throughout the period of delivery of Stowers' cattle to Samuels.

(2) *Value:* At the time of Stowers' delivery, Samuels' indebtedness to C.I.T. exceeded $1.8 million. This pre-existing indebtedness to the lender constituted "value" under the Code. § 1–201(44).

(3) *Rights in the collateral:* Finally, upon delivery, Samuels acquired rights in the cattle sufficient to allow attachment of C.I.T.'s lien. The fact that the holder of a voluntary lien—including an Article Nine interest—is a "purchaser" under the Code is of great significance to a proper understanding and resolution of this case under Article Two and Article Nine. The Code establishes that purchasers can take from a defaulting cash buyer, § 2–403(1). Lien creditors are included in the definition of purchasers, § 1–201(32), (33). A lien *is* an Article Nine interest, §§ 9–101, Comment; 9–102(2); 9–102, Comment. The existence of an Article Nine interest presupposes the debtor's having rights in the collateral sufficient to permit attachment, [1962 UCC] § 9–204(1). Therefore, since a defaulting cash buyer has the power to transfer a security interest to a lien creditor, including an Article Nine secured party, the buyer's rights in the property, however marginal, must be sufficient to allow attachment of a lien. And this is true even if, *arguendo,* I were to agree that the cash seller is granted reclamation rights under Article Two. See First National Bank of Elkhart Cty. v. Smoker, 11 U.C.C. Rept.Serv. 10, 19 (Ind.Ct.App., 1972); Evans Products Co. v. Jorgensen, 245 Or. 362, 421 P.2d 978 (1966).

If the Article Nine secured party acted in good faith, it is prior under § 2–403(1) to an aggrieved seller. Under the facts before us, I think that C.I.T. acted in good faith.

* * *

MATTER OF SAMUELS & CO., INC.

United States Court of Appeals, Fifth Circuit, 1976.
526 F.2d 1238.

Before BROWN,* CHIEF JUDGE, WISDOM, GEWIN, BELL, THORNBERRY, COLEMAN, GOLDBERG, AINSWORTH, GODBOLD, DYER, MORGAN, CLARK, INGRAHAM, RONEY and GEE, CIRCUIT JUDGES.

PER CURIAM. The action of the panel [1] is reversed and the judgment of the District Court is affirmed.

The court en banc adopts as its opinion the dissenting opinion of Judge Godbold with the additional comments which we set out in the margin.[3]

The judgment of the District Court is affirmed.

GEE, CIRCUIT JUDGE (specially concurring):

Troubled by the seeming harshness of the result, I nevertheless concur, despite its effect to force a cash seller to act like a credit seller to protect his interest. It asks much of these small cattle dealers, selling their cattle for cash, that they wrangle with the complicated provisions of art. 9 to protect themselves against an insufficient funds check, but this seems to be the clear demand of the Texas Code. In the normal course of dealing, such a check will give a seller an action on the instrument as well as for breach of the contract of sale, all in addition to the remedy of reclamation read into the Code by some courts. This protection is adequate except in cases such as this, where the buyer writes a bad check and subsequently declares bankruptcy.

---

* Chief Judge Brown did not participate in the decision of this case.

1. 510 F.2d 139 (C.A.5, 1975).

3. In remanding the case to this court the Supreme Court left open for our determination the question of whether "a course of conduct mandated by the Act or regulations might not, just as any other course of conduct, be relevant or even dispositive under state law." Mahon v. Stowers, 416 U.S. 100, 113–114, 94 S.Ct. 1626, 1633, 40 L.Ed.2d 79, 89 (1974). The evidence of course of dealings, see Texas Business and Commercial Code, § 1.205(a), shows that the plaintiffs and Samuels had a history of dealing in the manner mandated by the Act

and the regulations. That course of dealing is the basis for the view, shared by the majority members and the dissenting member of the panel, that the sales of livestock to Samuels by plaintiffs were cash sales.

Also we note a matter not mentioned in the dissenting opinion of Judge Godbold. The District Court, which accepted the Referee's findings of fact but rejected his conclusions of law, held that C.I.T. and the trustee in Bankruptcy were good faith purchasers for value, and the Supreme Court in its opinion referred to them as such. 416 U.S. at 104, 94 S.Ct. at 1628, 40 L.Ed.2d at 84.

All sellers who accept checks run the same risk—some take out
insurance against such a loss by the simple procedure of drawing up and filing a security agreement giving them rights in the
goods sold to secure the purchase price.

Such an agreement can be filed in advance, so there is no
need to wait until one receives a check to fill out a security
agreement and race to file it before the bank dishonors the
check. The very nature of this transaction recommended taking
this simple additional precaution of filing a purchase money security interest—the cows were immediately slaughtered, making
it impossible to recover the "goods" if the deal fell through, and,
too, the delayed pricing arrangement transformed the "cash
sale" into a credit transaction for all commercial purposes regardless of how the two parties characterized it. Comment 6 to
art. 2–511 says acceptance of a check postdated by even one day
"insofar as *third parties* are concerned, amounts to a delivery
on credit and the [seller's] remedies are set forth in the section
on buyer's insolvency (§ 2–702)." As Judge Hughes pointed out
in the district court opinion, Stowers' delivery of livestock to the
bankrupt without perfecting a security interest therein placed
the bankrupt in such a position that it could transfer good title
to a good faith purchaser for value, which is precisely what Samuels did.

NOTE

The Packers and Stockyards Act was amended in 1976 to protect unpaid cash sellers from the result reached in *Samuels.*
See 7 U.S.C. § 196.

4. IRREVOCABLE COMMITMENT TO THIRD PARTY

In the following case, Crest Finance Co., Inc. v. First State
Bank of Westmont, the Supreme Court of Illinois based its decision on the last clause of UCC § 3–303(c). That provision can be
illustrated by the following example: Contractor agreed to construct a building for Owner under a contract requiring Owner to
obtain a letter of credit from Bank guaranteeing payment of
drafts by Contractor on Bank for the account of Owner for
amounts due under the contract. Bank issued a letter of credit
for the benefit of Contractor which under UCC § 5–106(2) was
irrevocable without Contractor's consent. To induce Bank to issue the letter of credit Owner negotiated to Bank a negotiable
note of Maker payable to Owner. The due date of Maker's note
is prior to the date on which Bank is required to honor the first

draft of Contractor under the letter of credit. Assume Maker
refused to pay the note when it fell due and that Maker had a
complete defense on the note against Owner. Bank apparently
has not given value under UCC § 3–303(a) although the language is ambiguous as applied to this case. Bank has issued the
letter of credit but has not yet started its performance under it.
But this case is different from Problem 1, supra p. 171. There,
Holder had not yet performed and nonpayment of the note excused performance. Here, nonpayment of the note does not excuse Bank's performance to Contractor. The letter of credit
cannot be revoked because of failure of consideration. Under
UCC § 3–303(c) this commitment to Contractor which Bank cannot avoid constitutes value and Bank can enforce the note as a
holder in due course. To the extent that a commitment is irrevocable it is treated as tantamount to performance. Consider
whether UCC § 3–303(c) was properly applied in *Crest Finance*.

CREST FINANCE CO., INC. v. FIRST STATE BANK OF WESTMONT

Supreme Court of Illinois, 1967.
37 Ill.2d 243, 226 N.E.2d 369.

HOUSE, JUSTICE. Plaintiff, Crest Finance Company, Inc.,
filed a declaratory judgment action against the original defendant, First State Bank of Westmont, seeking a declaration that it
was entitled to possession of certain commercial paper, asking
that the bank be enjoined from disposing of or encumbering the
paper and praying its return. About two weeks thereafter Joseph E. Knight, Director of the Department of Financial Institutions, took possession of the bank and appointed the Federal Deposit Insurance Corporation receiver. Upon petition, the
receiver was granted leave to intervene and to make Leo
Niederberger a third-party defendant. The circuit court of Cook
County entered a decree finding the paper to be Westmont's
property, ordered recovery by the receiver of $605,882.46 from
plaintiff and Niederberger, representing collections on the paper
to October 23, 1963, and enjoining plaintiff from making further
collections.

The Appellate Court, First District, held that insofar as possible, the pre-agreement status of the parties be restored, that
Niederberger refund the sale price of Crest's stock in the sum of
$600,000 to Westmont, and that the paper belonged to Crest.

(66 Ill.App.2d 364, 214 N.E.2d 526.) We granted Niederberger's petition for leave to appeal.

This controversy arose out of an agreement by Niederberger to sell to Lester A. Brock all of the 750 outstanding shares of Crest, evidenced by certificates issued in the name of Niederberger and his wife jointly. Crest is an Illinois corporation engaged in the business of installment loans to relatively small business enterprises. Its loans were secured by notes, assignments of accounts receivable and liens on other collateral. Crest's receivables on February 28, 1963, approximately a month prior to the agreement, were $1,334,279.51, after deducting for deferred income and allowance for losses.

Brock was introduced to Niederberger by a broker and offered to buy Crest's stock for $600,000. In the negotiations leading up to an agreement Brock stated that he was acting not for himself but for a principal, the identity of whom he did not then disclose. He later testified that his principal was Lawrence A. Stickell.

Brock was closely associated with Stickell and Norman H. Weaver. They had gained control of First State Bank of Westmont in February, 1963. The bank's deposits were approximately $6,000,000 and its capital and surplus were about $350,000. These men proceeded to loot the bank in the manner hereinafter explained. (All three of them have been convicted in Federal court, and Stickell, a member of the bar, has had his name removed from the roll of attorneys.)

A meeting held at the office of Crest on April 2, 1963, was attended by Niederberger and his attorney, Brock, Otto Stephani (the latter a broker who brought Brock and Niederberger together and to whom Niederberger paid a fee of $30,000), Wayne E. Willard, executive vice-president and cashier of Westmont, and two other persons, Urban, an employee of Westmont, and Ash, an employee of Crest.

The agreement was in the form of a letter offer by Brock to Niederberger dated March 30, 1963, and accepted by the latter at the meeting on April 2, 1963. The letter agreement provided that Brock was to pay $600,000 for the stock, that Niederberger's guarantees of some of Crest's indebtedness were to be eliminated by substitution of Brock's guarantee or payment, and Niederberger was to co-operate with Brock in the operation of Crest for three months at $1,000 per month, with Brock retaining an option for an additional three months at compensation to be agreed upon.

Willard attended the meeting under instructions from Stickell and Weaver. He was told he was to pick up paper (notes and other evidence of debt) for Westmont. He took four cashier's checks of Westmont to the meeting, one of which was signed by an assistant cashier. The others were unsigned and all were in blank as to payee and amount. At the meeting, three of the cashier's checks were completed. The one signed by the assistant cashier was drawn on Continental Illinois National Bank and Trust Company of Chicago and was made payable to Niederberger for $300,000. Two others drawn on the Mercantile National Bank of Chicago, for $150,000 each, were signed by Willard and made payable to Niederberger. The checks were delivered to Niederberger during the meeting.

At the time the cashier's checks were delivered, Crest bank loans which had been guaranteed by Niederberger, totaled approximately $900,000. Apparently Niederberger was unwilling to deliver the stock certificates representing his shares in Crest until relieved of his guarantees of its loans. Whereupon the parties agreed that the certificates would be placed in escrow with Niederberger's counsel. The latter executed a brief escrow statement acknowledging receipt of the certificates, agreeing to hold the stock as escrowee pending written advice from his client (which of course, could not be withheld arbitrarily) that he had been released from all personal liability as guarantor of Crest, and agreeing to deliver the stock to Brock upon receipt of notice from Niederberger that his guarantees had been released.

After delivery of the checks, Brock and Willard were given access to Crest's files. During the late afternoon of April 2 and throughout the days of April 3 and April 4 Willard photostated installment notes and other paper held by Crest evidencing loans made by it (as well as the collateral relating to such loans), endorsed a receipt on each photostat and placed them in Crest's files. At the close of each day he removed the original material to Westmont's files. He gave a receipt to Helen Ware, a Crest employee, for the paper removed each day and then sealed Crest's vault where the remaining securities were kept for the night. The notes removed by Willard were payable to Crest and were unendorsed. Willard apparently was uninstructed as to the face amount of paper to be removed. He made no tabulation as he removed the paper, but he estimated that at the close of the day on April 4, he had removed about $900,000 in face amount. Willard's banking experience was limited. He was dominated in his activities for Westmont by Stickell, Weaver and Brock and the record does not indicate he was a party to the fraudulent conduct of the three. He read none of the documents presented at the April 2 meeting and none were read to him. He was unaware that the cashier's checks of Westmont were delivered to pay Brock's purchase price for stock of Crest rather than for purchase of Crest installment paper by Westmont.

After Willard completed removing Crest paper, he charged, by a "debit ticket" dated April 3, 1963, Westmont's accounts receivable ledger with $600,000 to offset the $600,000 in cashier's checks payable to Niederberger, thus indicating on Westmont's records a purchase by it of accounts receivable for $600,000. Apparently Brock, Weaver, and Stickell believed Westmont had or would have $957,000 in Crest installment notes as the result of Willard's transfers. (The Director of Financial Institutions checked this paper and located $868,158 in face amount, later found by the receiver to total $900,976 in face amount.) To account for the $357,000 excess, Willard prepared another "debit ticket" charging accounts receivable of Westmont with this additional amount. As an offset $357,000 was credited to a checking account which Brock, purporting to act for Crest, had opened with Westmont.

On the evening of April 4, although the escrow condition was unperformed and although the certificates were still held by the escrowee unendorsed, Brock proceeded to hold a stockholders meeting of Crest, at which he elected himself, Jack E. Sohn and Landra K. Ryan as directors. These directors then held a meeting. They elected Brock president and Sohn vice-president. To support Crest's purported sale of installment paper to Westmont they authorized Crest's sale of accounts receivable to Westmont in an amount not exceeding $1,000,000. They authorized Crest to "loan" practically the whole of the $357,000 bank balance to Stickell and Weaver and companies owned by them.

To complete the picture, the directors of Westmont met on April 4, authorized the purchase by Westmont of $957,000 of notes from Crest. In the minutes of this meeting the amount to be purchased was initially left blank, $957,000 later being inserted at the direction of Weaver and Stickell. Following these authorizations Brock, acting for Crest, purported to assign the installment notes and other paper to Westmont; funds of the bank were disbursed for the "loans" to Stickell and Weaver and their companies, and the amounts disbursed for these loans were charged to the Westmont checking account of Crest. At this point nearly $957,000 in funds of Westmont had been diverted to the personal uses of Brock, Stickell and Weaver.

Examiners for the Director of Financial Institutions began an examination of Westmont in April of 1963. On April 18 the Director found that the managers of Westmont were violating the Banking Act, and on May 16, he took possession of Westmont. On May 24 the Director appointed the Federal Deposit Insurance Corporation as Westmont's receiver.

Niederberger stands on the proposition that the sale was consummated since the placing of the stock in escrow was an irrevocable commitment, that he was the holder in due course of cashier's checks totaling $600,000, and the appellate court erroneously directed him to pay the proceeds of the checks to the receiver. The receiver counters with the assertion that Niederberger does not qualify as a holder in due course because he did not give "value" within the meaning of the Uniform Commercial Code, in that the sale of Crest stock was not consummated and the certificates evidencing ownership had not been transferred to Brock.

The effect of article 3 of the Code (Ill.Rev.Stat.1965, chap. 26, par. 3–101 et seq.) must be considered. Section 3–302(1) reads: "A holder in due course is a holder who takes the instrument (a) for value; and (b) in good faith; and (c) without notice that it is overdue or has been dishonored or of any defense against or claim to it on the part of any person." Section 3–302(2) states: "A payee may be a holder in due course." Section 3–303 provides: "A holder takes the instrument for value (a) to the extent that the agreed consideration has been performed or that he acquires a security interest in or a lien on the instrument otherwise than by legal process; or (b) when he takes the instrument in payment of or as security for an antecedent claim against any person whether or not the claim is due; or (c) when he gives a negotiable instrument for it or makes an irrevocable commitment to a third person."

The cashier's checks delivered to Niederberger, one signed by an assistant cashier and the other two signed by Willard, the cashier of Westmont, were negotiable instruments. If Niederberger became a holder in due course, the drawer bank (Westmont) could not recover from the paying banks nor from Niederberger. There is no evidence to substantiate lack of good faith on Niederberger's part or that he had any notice of any infirmities in the drawing or delivery of the checks at the time of delivery, so that provisions (b) and (c) of section 3–302(1) were complied with. (Subsequent knowledge does not impair holder-in-due-course status; sec. 3–304(6); see comment 12, sec. 3–304 of the Code; cf. Drumm Construction Co. v. Forbes, 305 Ill. 303, 137 N.E. 225, 26 A.L.R. 764.) This leaves only the question of whether Niederberger gave "value" for the three checks to determine his holder-in-due-course status.

The receiver asserts that placing the stock in escrow was an executory contract and that the agreed consideration (delivery of the stock) had not been performed in accordance with section 3–303(a) of the Code so that Niederberger had not parted with "value" for the checks. This ignores the "irrevocable commitment" language in section 3–303(c) which, according to comment 6 is new but recognizes an exception to the rule that an executory promise is not value. "Irrevocable commitment" in section 3–303(c) cannot be read to mean complete performance, otherwise it would be surplusage because the situation would have been covered by section 3–303(a). Here, Niederberger made an actual, physical delivery of the certificates evidencing ownership of the stock to the escrow agent without anything further to be done on his part except notify the escrowee when he had been relieved of his bank guarantees. Thus the transfer was irrevocable. The only remaining act to complete delivery was solely within the power of the buyer; that is, to either substitute his name on the guaranteed paper or pay the obligations. The failure to endorse was unimportant since assignment was legally enforcible under the terms of the agreement. In our opinion, delivery to the escrow agent and the agreement to execute all documents necessary to consummate the sale constituted an "irrevocable commitment" within the meaning of section 3–303(c), comparable to an unrestricted letter of credit used as an illustration in comment 6 heretofore referred to.

The fact that Brock (or his principal) was a beneficiary of the escrow agreement does not, in our view, affect the irrevocable character of the escrow commitment made by Niederberger, nor render it a commitment of a type not covered by section 3–303(c). For example, had the Crest stock increased in value, the receiver, upon fulfilment of the escrow condition, might by appropriate proceedings, obtain Brock's interest in the Crest shares, demand delivery of the certificate by the escrowee, and demand completion of the transfer by the escrowee. Niederberger and the escrowee would have had no defense to this demand.

Since Niederberger had parted with "value," he met all the statutory standards to be a holder in due course of the cashier's checks and was entitled to retain their $600,000 proceeds.

* .* *

The judgment of the Appellate Court, First District, is *affirmed* in part and reversed in part, and the cause is remanded to the circuit court of Cook County for further proceedings, not inconsistent with this opinion.

Affirmed in part and reversed in part and remanded, with directions.

KLUCZYNSKI, J., took no part in the consideration or decision of this case.

SCHAEFER, JUSTICE (dissenting). The opinion holds that Niederberger is entitled to retain the $600,000 of Bank funds which he received because he was a holder in due course of the Bank's checks in that amount. As the opinion notes, a holder in due course must, in addition to other requirements, have given "value" for the instrument. (Ill.Rev.Stat.1963, chap. 26, par. 3–302.) The majority holds that Niederberger gave value when he placed the Crest stock in escrow with directions not to release it to Brock until Brock relieved him of his obligations as a guarantor. By placing the stock in escrow, in the view of the majority, Niederberger made an "irrevocable commitment to a third person" which constitutes giving of value as defined in section 3–303(c). That section states: "A holder takes the instrument for value * * * (c) when he gives a negotiable instrument for it or makes an irrevocable commitment to a third person."

I am unable to agree that an "irrevocable commitment" was made, or that the purchaser of the stock was a "third person", within the meaning of section 3–303(c).

The comments to section 3–303 state that "an executory promise to give value is not itself value, except as provided in paragraph (c)." To fall within paragraph (c) and thus constitute value, an executory promise must be irrevocable. The comment explains that the Code refuses to treat other promises as value because a person who has taken a defective instrument but has given only a promise in return does not need the protection against claims and defenses afforded the holder in due course. He can protect himself from loss by refusing to carry out his part of the bargain and treating it as rescinded. The comment states: "The underlying reason of policy is that when the purchaser learns of a defense against the instrument or of a defect in the title he is not required to enforce the instrument, but is free to rescind the transaction for breach of the transferor's warranty (Section 3–417)." The person who has made an irrevocable commitment, however, cannot rescind.

The Code adopts a principle applied in equity, stated by Judge Story, in Wormley v. Wormley, 8 Wheat. 421, 449, 5 L.Ed. 651, "It is a settled rule in equity that a purchaser without notice, to be entitled to protection, must not only be so at the time of the contract or conveyance, but at the time of the payment of the purchase money."

The principle is recognized in cases holding that when a bank has received a negotiable instrument and credited it to the transferor's bank account, the bank has not given value and is not a holder in due course. Instead, it has merely made an executory promise to the depositor to pay him a sum on demand. See First State Bank and Trust Co. v. First Nat. Bank of Canton, 314 Ill. 269, 273, 145 N.E. 382 (1924); Brannan, Negotiable Instruments Law 520 (Beutel ed., 1948).

As applied to the present case this principle indicates that Niederberger was not a holder in due course. At no time had he given value as defined in section 3–303(c). His undertaking was contingent upon the elimination of his personal liability as a guarantor. When Niederberger learned that the checks had been fraudulently obtained, he was in a position to rescind his agreement with Brock, as the comment to section 3–303 suggests, on the ground that when Brock negotiated the checks he had breached his transferor's warranty that "(a) he has a good title to the instrument * * * and the transfer is otherwise rightful; and * * * (d) no defense of any party is good against him; * * *." (Ill.Rev.Stat.1963, chap. 26, par. 3–417(2)). These warranties had been breached since the instruments were obtained from the bank by fraud and without consideration.

Section 3–303 of the Commercial Code expresses a policy of withholding "holder in due course" status from the transferee of a negotiable instrument when the transferee can effectively protect himself against infirmities in the instrument. Whether the transferee can protect himself depends, under section 3–303, upon whether his commitment is "irrevocable" and to a "third person." In the present case Niederberger's commitment was conditional, and the condition was not fulfilled. And in my opinion it is inappropriate to treat Brock as "third person" within the meaning of section 3–303. He was the transferor of the instrument involved.

C. DEFENSES TO WHICH HOLDER IN DUE COURSE IS SUBJECT

1. THE REAL DEFENSES

Although a holder in due course takes free of all claims to the instrument he does not take free of all defenses. The so-called "real defenses" are those to which even a holder in due course is subject and they are listed in UCC § 3–305(2)(a), (b), (c), and (d).

BURCHETT v. ALLIED CONCORD FINANCIAL CORP.

Supreme Court of New Mexico, 1964.
74 N.M. 575, 396 P.2d 186.

CARMODY, JUSTICE. Plaintiffs-appellees filed separate complaints to have certain notes and mortgages held by defendant-appellant cancelled and declared void. The cases were consolidated below and on this appeal, which is from the judgments voiding the instruments.

The facts, except for one small detail, are the same. It seems that a man named Kelly represented himself as selling Kaiser aluminum siding for a firm named Consolidated Products of Roswell. None of the parties knew Kelly, nor had they seen him before. In each case, Kelly talked to the husband and wife (appellees) at their homes, offering to install aluminum siding on each of their houses for a certain price in exchange for the appellees' allowing their houses to be used for advertising purposes as a "show house," in order to further other sales of aluminum siding. Kelly told both of the families that they would receive a $100 credit on each aluminum siding contract sold in a specified area in Clovis, and that this credit would be applied toward the contract debt, being the cost of the installation of the siding on the appellees' houses. The appellees were assured, or at least understood, that by this method they would receive the improvements for nothing.

Following the explanation by Kelly, both families agreed to the offer and were given a form of a printed contract to read. While they were reading the contract, Kelly was filling out

blanks in other forms. After the appellees had read the form of
the contract submitted to them, they signed, *without reading*,
the form or forms filled out by Kelly, assuming them to be the
same as that which they had read and further assuming that
what they signed provided for the credits which Kelly assured
them they would receive. Needless to say, what appellees
signed were notes and mortgages on the properties to cover the
cost of the aluminum siding, and contracts containing no mention of credits for advertising or other sales.

One additional fact occurred in the case of the appellees
Beevers. A few days after the original signing, Kelly again approached Mr. Beevers at his home and told him that the televi-
sion and newspaper authorization that he had previously executed had been destroyed and he needed another one. Mr. Beevers,
again without reading what was submitted, signed the additional
form. Kelly then went to Mrs. Beevers' place of employment
and she also signed the same without any examination, in view
of Kelly's representations and her observation that her husband
had already signed the form. The instrument was the promissory note.

Within a matter of days after the contracts were signed, the
aluminum siding was installed, although in neither case was the
job completed to the satisfaction of appellees. Sometime later,
the appellees received letters from appellant, informing them
that appellant had purchased the notes and mortgages which
had been issued in favor of Consolidated Products and that appellees were delinquent in their first payment. Upon the receipt
of these notices, appellees discovered that mortgages had been
recorded against their property and they immediately instituted
these proceedings.

Suit was actually brought not only against the appellant but
also against James T. Pirtle, doing business under the name of
Consolidated Products, Shirley McVay, a notary public in Roswell, and Kelly. No service was obtained upon Kelly, and the
other parties to the proceedings below did not appeal because
the judgment merely voided the notes and mortgages.

In both cases, the trial court found that the notes and mortgages, although signed by the appellees, were fraudulently procured. The court also found that the appellant paid a valuable
consideration for the notes and mortgages, although at a discount, and concluded as a matter of law that the appellant was a
holder in due course. The findings in both of the cases are substantially the same, with the exception that the court found in

appellant held to
was *be an HDC —*

the Burchett case that the Burchetts were not guilty of negligence in failing to discover the true character of the instruments signed by them. There is no comparable finding in the Beevers case.

It is of passing interest to note that there was a definite conflict in the testimony, particularly with reference to the Burchetts, as to what, if any, of the instruments were actually signed by the Burchetts. However, at the appellees' request, the documents were submitted to an expert who determined that the signatures of all the parties were genuine, and the trial court accepted the expert's determination.

The trial court's decisions are grounded upon two propositions, (1) that the acknowledgments on the mortgages were nullities and therefore that the mortgages were not subject to record, and (2) that fraud in their inception rendered the notes and mortgages void for all purposes.

The theory relating to the first of the above reasons would seem to be that inasmuch as the acknowledgments were invalid the instruments were not entitled to be recorded and therefore appellant, which would not have purchased the unrecorded mortgages, is in no better position than the original mortgagee. However, these conclusions by the trial court are really of no consequence, in view of its conclusion that the appellant was a holder in due course. Actually, because of the trial court's determination that appellant was a holder in due course, it makes no difference whether the instruments were entitled to record or not; thus we do not deem it necessary for decision to consider the effect of the void acknowledgments. The only real question in the case is whether, under these facts, appellees, by substantial evidence, satisfied the provisions of the statute relating to their claimed defense as against a holder in due course.

In 1961 our legislature adopted, with some variations, the Uniform Commercial Code. The provision of the code applicable to this case is § 3–305(2)(c), which, so far as material, is as follows:

"To the extent that a holder is a holder in due course he takes the instrument free from

"* * *

"(2) all defenses of any party to the instrument with whom the holder has not dealt except

"* * *

"(c) such misrepresentation as has induced the party to sign the instrument with neither knowledge nor reasonable opportunity to obtain knowledge of its character or its essential terms; and

" *   *   * ."

Although fully realizing that the official comments appearing as part of the Uniform Commercial Code are not direct authority for the construction to be placed upon a section of the code, nevertheless they are persuasive and represent the opinion of the National Conference of Commissioners on Uniform State Laws and the American Law Institute. The purpose of the comments is to explain the provisions of the code itself, in an effort to promote uniformity of interpretation. We believe that the official comments following § 3–305(2)(c), Comment No. 7, provide an excellent guideline for the disposition of the case before us. We quote the same in full:

"7. Paragraph (c) of subsection (2) is new. It follows the great majority of the decisions under the original Act in recognizing the defense of 'real' or 'essential' fraud, sometimes called fraud in the essence or fraud in the factum, as effective against a holder in due course. The common illustration is that of the maker who is tricked into signing a note in the belief that it is merely a receipt or some other document. The theory of the defense is that his signature on the instrument is ineffective because he did not intend to sign such an instrument at all. Under this provision the defense extends to an instrument signed with knowledge that it is a negotiable instrument but without knowledge of its essential terms.

"The test of the defense here stated is that of excusable ignorance of the contents of the writing signed. The party must not only have been in ignorance, but must also have had no reasonable opportunity to obtain knowledge. In determining what is a reasonable opportunity all relevant factors are to be taken into account, including the age and sex of the party, his intelligence, education and business experience; his ability to read or to understand English, the representations made to him and his reason to rely on them or to have confidence in the person making them; the presence or absence of any third person who might read or explain the instrument to him, or any other possibility of obtaining independent information; and the apparent necessity, or lack of it, for acting without delay.

"Unless the misrepresentation meets this test, the defense is cut off by a holder in due course."

We observe that the inclusion of subsection (2)(c) in § 3–305 of the Uniform Commercial Code was an attempt to codify or make definite the rulings of many jurisdictions on the question as to the liability to a holder in due course of a party who either had knowledge, or a reasonable opportunity to obtain the knowledge, of the essential terms of the instrument, before signing. Many courts were in the past called upon to determine this question under the Uniform Negotiable Instruments Law. Almost all of the courts that were called upon to rule on this question required a showing of freedom from negligence, in order to constitute a good defense against a bona fide holder of negotiable paper.

One of the clearest statements of the rule under the Negotiable Instruments Law, which has received widespread approval, appears in United States v. Castillo (D.N.M.1954), 120 F.Supp. 522, as follows:

"Although a holder in due course holds an instrument such as the instant one free from any defect of title, and free from defenses available to prior parties among themselves insofar as a voidable instrument is concerned, where fraud in the inception is present, such as here, such fraud makes the instrument an absolute nullity and not merely voidable. However, to completely invalidate the enforceability of a negotiable promissory note the fraud perpetrated must be such as to induce the maker of the note to execute the same under the mistaken belief that the instrument being signed is something other than a promissory note and must come about as a direct result of misrepresentation on the part of the payee or his agent. Naturally, the maker cannot be guilty of negligence in signing a written instrument and then defend upon the ground of lack of knowledge where in the exercise of reasonable prudence the attempted fraud could be discovered; and, generally it is no defense to the enforcement of an obligation like the instant one to insist that a fraud has been wrought where the maker does not take the care to read the instrument being signed, inasmuch as such an omission generally constitutes negligence. If such were not the general rule, where a person is of average intelligence and is qualified to read, then every negotiable instrument would be clouded with the possible defense that the maker did not read the instrument prior to signing it. However, the failure to read an instrument is not negligence per se but must be considered in light of all surrounding facts and circumstances with particular emphasis on the maker's intelligence and literacy."

* * *

We believe that the test set out in Comment No. 7 above quoted is a proper one and should be adhered to by us. (By giving approval to this Comment, we do not in any sense mean to imply that we thereby are expressing general approval of all the Comments to the various sections of the Uniform Commercial Code.) Thus the only question is whether, under the facts of this case, the misrepresentations were such as to be a defense as against a holder in due course.

The facts and circumstances surrounding each particular case, both under the Negotiable Instruments Law and the Uniform Commercial Code, require an independent determination. See United States v. Castillo, supra; United States v. Tholen (N.D.Iowa 1960), 186 F.Supp. 346; First National Bank of Philadelphia v. Anderson, supra; Equitable Discount Corp. v. Fischer, supra.

Applying the elements of the test to the case before us, Mrs. Burchett was 47 years old and had a ninth grade education, and Mr. Burchett was approximately the same age, but his education does not appear. Mr. Burchett was foreman of the sanitation department of the city of Clovis and testified that he was familiar with some legal documents. Both the Burchetts understood English and there was no showing that they lacked ability to read. Both were able to understand the original form of contract which was submitted to them. As to the Beevers, Mrs. Beevers was 38 years old and had been through the ninth grade. Mr. Beevers had approximately the same education, but his age does not appear. However, he had been working for the same firm for about nine years and knew a little something about mortgages, at least to the extent of having one upon his property. Mrs. Beevers was employed in a supermarket, and it does not appear that either of the Beevers had any difficulty with the English language and they made no claim that they were unable to understand it. Neither the Beevers nor the Burchetts had ever had any prior association with Kelly and the papers were signed upon the very day that they first met him. There was no showing of any reason why they should rely upon Kelly or have confidence in him. The occurrences took place in the homes of appellees, but other than what appears to be Kelly's "chicanery," no reason was given which would warrant a reasonable person in acting as hurriedly as was done in this case. None of the appellees attempted to obtain any independent information either with respect to Kelly or Consolidated Products, nor did they seek out any other person to read or explain the instruments to them. As a matter of fact, they apparently didn't believe this was necessary because, like most people, they wanted to take advantage of "getting something for nothing." There is no dispute but that the appellees did not have actual knowledge of the nature of the instruments which they signed, at the time they signed them. Appellant urges that appellees had a reasonable opportunity to obtain such knowledge but failed to do so, were therefore negligent, and that their defense was precluded.

We recognize that the reasonable opportunity to obtain knowledge may be excused if the maker places reasonable reliance on the representations. The difficulty in the instant case is that the reliance upon the representations of a complete stranger (Kelly) was not reasonable, and all of the parties were of sufficient age, intelligence, education, and business experience to know better. In this connection, it is noted that the contracts clearly stated, on the same page which bore the signatures of the various appellees, the following:

> "No one is authorized on behalf of this company to represent this job to be 'A SAMPLE HOME OR A FREE JOB.'"

The conduct of the Beevers in signing the additional form some weeks after the initial transaction, without reading it, is a graphic showing of negligence. This, however, is merely an added element and it is obvious that all of the parties were negligent in signing the instruments without first reading them under the surrounding circumstances. See First National Bank of Philadelphia v. Anderson, supra, which held that the mere failure to read a contract was not sufficient to allow the maker a defense under § 3–305 of the Uniform Commercial Code. In our opinion, the appellees here are barred for the reasons hereinabove stated.

Although we have sympathy with the appellees, we cannot allow it to influence our decision. They were certainly victimized, but because of their failure to exercise ordinary care for their own protection, an innocent party cannot be made to suffer.

* * *

The finding of the trial court that Burchetts were not guilty of negligence is not supported by substantial evidence and must fall. We determine under these facts as a matter of law that both the Burchetts and the Beevers had a reasonable opportunity to obtain knowledge of the character or the essential terms of the instruments which they signed, and therefore appellant as a holder in due course took the instruments free from the defenses claimed by the appellees.

* * *

Other points are raised, but, in view of our determination, need not be answered.

The judments will be reversed and the cause is remanded to the district court with directions to dismiss appellees' complaints. It is so ordered.

NOTES

1. Like *Burchett*, many of the cases decided under UCC § 3–305(2)(c) involve buyers of consumer goods victimized by fraudulent or high pressure sales tactics, but some courts have imposed a less exacting standard of care on the consumer. See, for example, American Plan Corp. v. Woods, 16 Ohio App.2d 1, 240 N.E.2d 886 (1968). The importance of these cases has been greatly reduced because the holder of the consumer note is denied holder-in-due-course status under consumer-protection legislation and judicial precedent discussed earlier.

2. The defense of duress is similar to that of fraud in the factum in that it is based on the lack of consent by the maker of the instrument to assume the obligation represented by the instrument. It is not often seen in the reported cases. In Day v. Roy E. Friedman & Co., 29 U.C.C.Rep. 929 (Ala.1980), Day worked for Friedman as a licensed commodities broker. Under the employment agreement Day was obliged to guarantee payment to Friedman of any deficiencies in the accounts of customers procured by Day which resulted from losses from trading on margin. When Day left Friedman's employ he signed a note for amounts owing under the guaranty agreement. Day set up as a defense the fact that the note was signed under duress because under existing commodities exchange rules Day could not work for another employer as a broker until he had first settled his debts with Friedman. On motion for summary judgment, the court held that Day was entitled to a trial on this issue. "Since duress is a matter of degree, it is clearly a matter for the finder of fact. It is evident from the record * * * that there was at least a scintilla of evidence on the issue of duress." In this case, however, the plaintiff was the original payee not a subse-

quent holder in due course. In contrast, consider Deputy v. Stapleford & Willis, 19 Cal. 302 (1861), the product of an earlier and more heroic age. One Deputy was coerced into signing a deed to real estate. "The circumstances attending this coercion were of the most aggravating character. Deputy had been imprisoned, chained to the floor by the leg, manacled, hung two or three times, whipped with a raw hide in the intervals between the hangings, and threatened with death by hanging, unless he executed the deed, but without receiving any consideration therefor." 19 Cal. at 302. Baldwin, J., stated: "It is to be regretted, for the sake of public justice, that the alleged outrage, in which the claim of the plaintiff to the relief he seeks in his bill had its origin, cannot be redressed by a restoration of the property of which he was lawlessly deprived. The deed to Stapleford, though procured by fraud and duress, was only voidable, and the vendee of Stapleford, purchasing in ignorance of the facts can hold the property. This seems to be the rule supported by the general current of decisions." 19 Cal. at 305. Compare Comment 6 to UCC § 3-305.

3. The rights of a holder in due course against a surety on a note on which the obligor has a real defense are discussed in Wladis, Article 3 Suretyship and the Holder in Due Course: Requiem for the Good Samaritan, 70 Geo.L.J. 975 (1982).

SANDLER v. EIGHTH JUDICIAL DISTRICT COURT

Supreme Court of Nevada, 1980.
96 Nev. 622, 614 P.2d 10.

BATJER, JUSTICE. Nevada National Bank filed suit against Jerrold Sandler to recover the proceeds from several checks written by Sandler. Sandler wrote the checks on a Maryland bank account to John Hutchings and others for gambling and to cover gambling losses incurred by Sandler, and by Hutchings in Sandler's behalf, during private "freeze out" games of "21". The checks were all negotiated to Nevada National Bank. The district judge denied Sandler's motion for summary judgment. Sandler petitions this court for a writ of mandamus to compel the district judge to grant summary judgment in his favor.

A writ of mandamus will issue to compel entry of a summary judgment when there is no genuine issue as to any material fact and the movant is entitled to judgment as a matter of law. Manufacturers & Traders Trust v. District Court, 94 Nev. 551, 583 P.2d 444 (1978); Hoffman v. District Court, 90 Nev. 267, 523

P.2d 848 (1974); Holloway v. Barrett, 87 Nev. 385, 487 P.2d 501 (1971); Dzack v. Marshall, 80 Nev. 345, 393 P.2d 610 (1964); *see* NRCP 56(c); NRAP 3A(b)(5). In this case it is undisputed that the checks were drawn by Sandler to engage in gambling or delivered to John Hutchings for the express purpose of engaging in gambling ventures. As a matter of law, checks drawn for the purpose of gambling are void and unenforceable in this state. Sea Air Support, Inc. v. Herrmann, 96 Nev. 574, 613 P.2d 413 (1980); Corbin v. O'Keefe, 87 Nev. 189, 484 P.2d 565 (1971); Wolpert v. Knight, 74 Nev. 322, 330 P.2d 1023 (1958).

Nevada National Bank seeks to avoid the defense that the checks are void and unenforceable (Statute of 9 Anne, C. 14, § 1) by claiming to be a holder in due course immune to that defense. NRS 104.3305 provides that a holder in due course takes an instrument free from: "2. All defenses of any party to the instrument with whom the holder has not dealt except: * * * (b) Such other incapacity, or duress, or illegality of the transaction, as renders the obligation of the party a nullity[.]" A holder in due course is not immune to real defenses; that is, those defenses which render the check, and the underlying obligation created thereby, entirely void. Bankers Trust Co. v. Litton Systems, 599 F.2d 488 (2d Cir. 1979); Middle Georgia Livestock Sales v. Commercial Bank & Trust Co., 123 Ga.App. 733, 182 S.E.2d 533 (1971); White & Summers, Uniform Commercial Code, § 1410 at 487–488. Because the Statute of Anne renders the checks herein void *ab initio*, the defense may be asserted against Nevada National Bank. Pacific National Bank v. Hernreich, 240 Ark. 114, 398 S.W.2d 221 (1966). Therefore, summary judgment in favor of Sandler must be granted.

Accordingly, a writ of mandamus shall issue directing the district judge to grant Sandler's motion for summary judgment.

Writ granted.

NOTES

1. Gambling, if licensed, is legal in Nevada. The check involved in *Sandler* was given in a private game which apparently was unlicensed. But in a companion case, Sea Air Support, Inc. v. Herrmann, 96 Nev. 574, 613 P.2d 413 (1980), the Nevada Supreme Court held that a check given to buy gambling chips from a hotel-casino that apparently was licensed was also unenforceable for the same reasons stated in *Sandler*. These decisions were based on the Statute of 9 Anne, Chapter 14, § 1 (1710) which provided " * * * for the furthur preventing of all ex-

cessive and deceitful gaming, be it enacted * * * that all notes, bills, bonds, judgments, mortgages or other securities or conveyances whatsoever, given, granted, drawn, or entered into, or executed by any person or persons whatsoever, where the whole or any part of the consideration of such conveyance or securities shall be for any money or other valuable thing whatsoever, won by gaming * * * or for the reimbursing or repaying any money knowingly lent or advanced at the time and place of such play, to any person * * * so gaming shall be utterly void, frustrate and of none effect * * *." This statute is interpreted in Nevada to prevent the collection at law of all gambling debts. West Indies, Inc. v. First National Bank of Nevada, 67 Nev. 13, 214 P.2d 144 (1950). Although well-advised gambling casinos will not accept checks in payment of gambling chips, hotels which operate gambling casinos apparently will readily pay cash for checks of customers with good credit. Are those checks enforceable if the customer uses the cash to buy chips? The Nevada Supreme Court even-handedly denies justice not only to the casino but also to the customer. In Weisbrod v. Fremont Hotel, 74 Nev. 227, 326 P.2d 1104 (1958), the casino refused to pay $12,500 which the plaintiff claimed as holder of a winning $3.50 ticket on a keno game. He brought suit but was denied relief. The court made the following statement: "This is not to say that the state provides no adequate protection to the gambling patron. It must be recognized that the state has an interest in seeing that its licensees honestly and honorably respect their gambling obligations. Repudiation of such obligations would most certainly be regarded as reflecting upon the suitability of one to hold a state license. * * * No licensee is likely to place his license in jeopardy through refusal to pay a gambling debt found to be properly due." Is this statement consistent with the public policy represented by the Statute of Anne?

2. Other cases of illegality are not common. Some usury statutes declare contracts for a rate of interest in excess of that allowed to be void as to principal and interest. Under statutes of that kind a holder in due course takes subject to the illegality defense. See, for example, Hare v. General Contract Purchase Corp., 220 Ark. 601, 249 S.W.2d 973 (1953).

PROBLEM

Welch lost all of his cash while gambling at the Carefree Casino in Las Vegas. He tried to buy additional gambling chips

with a personal check payable to Carefree but Carefree refused
to accept it. Welch had in his possession his monthly paycheck
from Bigg Corporation which he had received the day before.
Welch indorsed it over to Carefree which accepted it in payment
of gambling chips. Welch then lost all of the chips on one big
roll of the dice. Welch returned home to Los Angeles and, con-
trite and without funds, successfully appealed to his employer
for help. Bigg gave a stop payment order to the drawee of the
check. The check was subsequently dishonored and Carefree
has demanded payment from Bigg. Is Carefree a holder of the
check? Is Carefree a holder in due course? May Bigg safely
pay the check? Must Bigg pay the check? What should Welch
do to protect himself? See UCC § 3-207, § 3-306 and § 3-603.
If the check had been cashed by Carefree at Nevada Bank and
Nevada Bank was seeking payment what would be the rights
and obligations of Welch, Bigg and Nevada Bank?

2. DEFENSES AGAINST A HOLDER IN DUE COURSE WHO DEALT WITH THE OBLIGOR AND DEFENSES AGAINST A HOLDER NOT IN DUE COURSE

UCC § 3-302(2) provides that a payee of an instrument may
be a holder in due course. Whether the payee is a holder in due
course is important on the question of whether the payee takes
free of claims to the instrument by another person under UCC
§ 3-305(1) or of defenses of a party liable on the instrument by
virtue of UCC § 3-305(2). The latter question is discussed in
Bucci v. Paulick that follows. Holder-in-due-course status may
also be important in determining rights under UCC § 3-418
against a person who pays or accepts an instrument. That question will be discussed in Chapter 9. UCC § 3-306 deals with the
rights of a holder not in due course. The *Olsen-Frankman* case
discusses the meaning of UCC § 3-306(b).

BUCCI v. PAULICK

Superior Court of Pennsylvania, 1980.
277 Pa.Super. 492, 419 A.2d 1255.

HESTER, JUDGE. Presently before the court is Appellant's
appeal from the entry of a money judgment entered upon a directed verdict for Appellees. Following the denial of Appellant's Motion for New Trial, this timely appeal followed.

We reverse and remand for a new trial.

The facts may be briefly summarized as follows: Appellant-maker entered into a written contract with Appellees-payees whereby appellees were to install asphalt paving at Appellant's apartment building parking lot. The paving job was completed in May, 1975, and appellant was to have paid the price in full upon completion.

Payment in full upon completion was not made however, and on September 10, 1975, Appellant made payment to Appellees, by tendering to them a check for $6,500.00 and a promissory note of even date in the face amount of $7,593.00 and bearing interest at 10% per annum. The note was due six (6) months from its date. Appellees agreed to this payment schedule.

Payment was not made by Appellant-maker when the note became due, and subsequently, appellees-payees sued on the promissory note.

Appellant filed an Answer and New Matter to Appellees' Complaint in Assumpsit wherein Appellant alleges

"8. Subsequent to September 10, 1975, it became apparent to Defendant that the work and materials provided by the Plaintiff to the Defendant and the installation of asphalt made by the Plaintiffs was improperly done, defective and deficient. Thereby resulting in a failure of consideration in that the binder and top course of the pavement was insufficient and un-uniform thickness and improperly installed and furthermore, in that the base of slag was not properly installed compacted and was not of a uniform thickness throughout the installation."

"9. As a direct and approximate result of Plaintiff's deficient and improper installation of materials thereby constituting a breach of his obligations to the defendant. The defendant's pavement has become cracked and has lifted up and split in major portions of the paved area and will in large measure be necessary to replace at the great cost and effort of the Defendant, and such costs of replacement far exceeds the value of the note given on September 10, 1975. Thereby constituting a full and complete failure of consideration and a total defense to this action."

Thereafter Appellees filed a Reply to New Matter wherein they denied that the materials and installation were improper, defective and deficient; rather, Appellees claimed that the materials and paving work was done in a proper and workmanlike manner.

Succinctly stated, Appellees brought suit on the note; Appellant attempted to defend on the underlying asphalt contract.

The case was tried before Judge John P. Flaherty and a jury on September 14, 1977. Appellee John Sciarretti testified for the Appellees. In response to objections by appellees, appellant Paulick's testimony was strictly limited to the circumstances surrounding the execution of the note. Specifically the lower court precluded appellant and his available expert witness(es) from giving testimony concerning the alleged defective material and poor workmanship involved in the asphalt job. The lower court reasoned:

> " * * * We have an action brought on an instrument. The question is if the payee in this case is a holder in due course, then at least and in this action the failure of consideration would not be material (T48).
>
> * * * But if in fact legally (Appellee) is a holder in due course, then the defense of want of consideration is foreclosed (T.55)."

Accordingly, at the close of Appellant's court-limited testimony, the court granted Appellee's motion for a directed verdict. Appellant filed a Motion for New Trial which was denied on April 11, 1978, by a court *en banc.* Judgment was thereafter entered upon payment of the verdict fee on April 28, 1978, in the amount of $9197.57. It is from the entry of this money judgment that this appeal has been taken.

It is agreed by the parties and this Court, that the instant case is subject to and governed by the provisions of the Uniform Commercial Code, hereinafter "UCC" (Act of 1953, Apr. 6, P.L. 3, 12A P.S. § 1–101.)

A review of the record convinces us that the lower court was correct in classifying appellees/payees of the note as "holders in due course". U.C.C. § 3–302 provides in relevant part:

(1) A holder in due course is a holder who takes the instrument

    (a) for value; and

    (b) in good faith; and

    (c) without notice that it is overdue or has been dishonored or of any defense against or claim to it on the part of any person.

(2) A payee may be a holder in due course.

We disagree however with the lower court's conclusion that as "holders in due course", the appellees/payees are not subject to the defense of failure of consideration. We believe that in the instant case, they are.

UCC § 3–305 provides in relevant part:

To the extent that a holder is a holder in due course he takes the instrument free from

(1) all claims to it on the part of any person; and

(2) all defenses of any party to the instrument *with whom the holder has not dealt.* (emphasis added)

The record is clear that appellees/payees dealt *directly* with appellant/maker.

On cross-examination:

Q. What was that contract? What was the underlying thing that was to be accomplished?

A. The work performed at Lou Paulick's apartment building.

Q. Who was to actually accomplish the work? Was the Company to accomplish the work or were you to sublet it or what?

A. My company was to perform the work. (R.14a–15a)

Q. So we can agree that perhaps a couple of months after September 1975, Mr. Paulick brought to your attention what he felt or what he announced to you were in his opinion problems with the job?

A. Yes. (R.25a)

Appellant generally concurred with Appellees' above recollection:

* * * And up until that point, the paving was in generally good repair. It wasn't until after I gave the note that the paving started to break up. (R.63a)

And critically,

Q. Can we agree, sir, that the note was taken by you and given by Mr. Paulick for certain asphalt paving work that was done by you?

A. Yes. (R.28a–29a)

There appears to exist an inherent definitional inconsistency between § 3–302(2) and § 3–305(2). As in the case at Bar, appellees/payees are "holders in due course" (§ 3–302(2)) and at the same time have dealt *directly* with the appellant/maker (§ 3–305(2)); *quaere,* do the holders in due course take the in-

strument (note) free from the defense of failure of consideration?

We believe that they do not. We conclude that appellees, as
parties to the underlying transaction out of which the *execution*
of the note arose and, *at the same time, payees* on the note upon which the instant lawsuit was brought, even as holders in due
course, are not free from a defense of any party (here the appellant-maker) with whom they *have dealt*. We therefore, conclude
that the defense of failure of consideration, should have been
available at trial [2] to appellant/maker.

Held

Therefore, we reverse and remand for a New Trial consistent
with this Opinion.

PRICE, J., files a dissenting statement.

PRICE, JUDGE, dissenting:

The majority has presented the basic facts underlying the
controversy presented in this appeal. It is my opinion, however,
that the trial court should be affirmed since I believe the defense of failure of consideration is not available to appellant under the facts here presented.

Section 3–408 of the Uniform Commercial Code provides: *3 - 408*

"Want or failure of consideration is a defense as against
any person not having the rights of a holder in due course,
except that no consideration is necessary for an instrument
or obligation thereon given in payment of or as security for
an antecedent obligation of any kind." (Emphasis supplied)

In my opinion, the above-cited section applies directly to the
promissory note in this case and to the circumstances of the
note. If no consideration is necessary, as I believe, then appellant may not utilize the defense of failure of consideration.

I would affirm the order of April 28, 1978, denying the grant
of a new trial.

---

2. The lower court indicated that
had Appellant raised its defense of
failure of consideration on the underlying contract via a counterclaim rather than by Answer and New Matter,
evidence supporting said defense
would have been admissible:

(" * * * but it would seem to me
that all could have been avoided by
the filing of a counterclaim." T.54);

and in its Opinion: "(Appellant)
failed to file a counterclaim on the
underlying contract, and merely alleged in "New Matter" that the underlying contract had been
breached."

We believe that the aforementioned
purely technical distinction is neither
critical nor dispositive of the instant
controversy.

NOTE

The dissenting judge treats the note as having been given for an antecedent debt, i.e., the note was given on September 10 for a debt due and payable the previous May. The majority treats the note as having been given for the work performed by the payees. Is this distinction relevant if the maker's defense is that nothing was owing to the payees because of the deficiency of the work performed? Payees had a cause of action against the maker on either the note or the underlying sales contract. It is clear that the maker could use the payees' deficient performance as a defense to an action on the sales contract. Is there any reason why this defense should not be available if the suit is based on the note which represents payees' right to payment for the work performed? The status of payees as holders in due course depended upon whether they had notice of the deficiency in the work performed at the time they took the note. Should this question bear on the issue of whether they are entitled to be paid if in fact they did not substantially perform the contract? If maker's defense of total failure of consideration is upheld did the payees take the note for value? Is the reference in UCC § 3–408 to a holder in due course meant to apply only to a holder in due course who takes free of defenses under UCC § 3–305(2)?

Since in most cases the payee of an instrument has dealt with the obligor, whether he is a holder in due course will not have any importance with respect to rights under UCC § 3–305. The payee will be subject to the defenses of the obligor as though he were not a holder in due course. There are some cases in which the payee has not dealt with the obligor and in those cases holder-in-due-course status does cut off defenses. Examples are given in Comment 2 to UCC § 3–302.

OLSEN–FRANKMAN LIVESTOCK MARKETING SERVICE, INC. v. CITIZENS NATIONAL BANK OF MADELIA

United States Court of Appeals, Eighth Circuit, 1979.
605 F.2d 1082.

BRIGHT, CIRCUIT JUDGE. Appellant Olsen-Frankman Livestock Marketing Service, Inc. (Olsen-Frankman), a livestock commission company operating in Sioux Falls, South Dakota, appeals from a judgment dismissing its action for damages for fraud against Citizens National Bank of Madelia, Minnesota (Bank). We reverse and remand for further proceedings.

At trial, Olsen-Frankman asserted that the Bank made false representations concerning the solvency of a cattle feeder operating under the name of John T. Keim & Sons (Keim), and that as a result Olsen-Frankman was unable to stop payment on two checks totalling over $56,000, which it had issued to Keim to pay for cattle. At the time of the Bank's representations, Keim owed Olsen-Frankman over $100,000 for cattle purchased through it. Having made these representations, the Bank, as holder (not in due course) of the two checks, arranged for their payment by the drawee bank before Olsen-Frankman learned that Keim was insolvent.

Olsen-Frankman sought damages equal to the amount of those checks, plus interest. Notwithstanding that the jury answered special verdicts generally in favor of Olsen-Frankman, the trial court dismissed the action, holding that no damages arose from the fraud because Olsen-Frankman could not have asserted Keim's collateral indebtedness to offset its obligations on the two checks held by the Bank. We examine this ruling in light of the jury's resolution of certain disputed factual issues.

The district court in its unpublished opinion aptly summarized those facts and the history of the litigation as follows:

> This controversy arose out of the financial chaos occasioned by the bankruptcy of John Keim. During the early months of 1975, Keim operated a cattle feedlot business [near Madelia, Minnesota] variously under the names of John T. Keim & Sons and G. M. Grain Co., Inc. In August of 1975, an involuntary petition in bankruptcy was filed against Keim and his businesses. Each was adjudicated bankrupt in November, 1975. Shortly thereafter the several of Keim's creditors filed actions against one another attempting to recover the full amount of their respective losses.

> This case involves the claim of plaintiff [Olsen-Frankman] with regard to a transaction occurring in July, 1975. Plaintiff issued two checks, each for a little more than $23,000, one to John T. Keim [& Sons] and the other to G. M. Grain Co., in payment for cattle sold to plaintiff. These checks were negotiated by Keim to defendant bank [at Madelia, Minnesota]. Defendant had previously done business with Keim, and its officers had become aware that Keim's credit was severely overextended. Because of the bank's concern over Keim's financial situation, one of the bank's vice presidents,

Clarence Goodburn, telephoned one of plaintiff's officers, David Frankman, to inquire whether the checks would be honored. Frankman replied that they would be honored and inquired whether there was any problems [sic] with Keim's financial condition. Goodburn answered in the negative.

Plaintiff's position at trial was that this response was a false representation and that if the truth about Keim's credit conditions had been told, plaintiff would have stopped payment on the checks and, through set-off of a previous debt of Keim's could have avoided liability on the instruments.

The jury's special verdict found that the bank did make a fraudulent misrepresentation, the bank was a holder of the two checks, the bank was not a holder in due course, plaintiff was damaged in the amount of $56,692.25 and G. M. Grain Co., Inc., was owner of the cattle sold to plaintiff for which the checks were issued.

* * *

Both in their pleadings and in arguing their respective rights before the trial court, the parties approached the issue of whether damages resulted from the Bank's representations by assuming that Olsen-Frankman had stopped payment on the two checks and, thereafter, the Bank sought to collect on them. Thus, the issue became whether Olsen-Frankman could defend against the Bank's claim by asserting a setoff arising out of an indebtedness of over $100,000 owed Olsen-Frankman by Keim.

The applicable Uniform Commercial Code (U.C.C.) section [is] U.C.C. § 3–306.

* * *

Focusing on subsection (b) of this U.C.C. provision, the appellee Bank asserts that the phrase "all defenses of any party which would be available in an action on a simple contract" does not contemplate a defense by way of setoff arising from an independent transaction extrinsic to the instrument. To the contrary, appellant urges that specific provisions of * * * Minnesota * * * law authorize a drawer of a check to set off against a mere holder the obligations owed to the drawer by the payee. The Minnesota statute which appellant cites reads as follows:

If a thing in action be assigned, an action thereon by the assignee shall be without prejudice to any set-off or defense existing at the time or before notice of the assignment; but this section does not apply to negotiable paper, transferred in good faith and upon good consideration before due. [Minn. Stat. § 540.03 (1974).]

We turn now to these conflicting contentions.

* * *

II. *Setoff in Minnesota Under U.C.C. § 3–306.*

The crux of the dispute between the parties centers on whether under [UCC §] 3–306 a mere holder (the Bank) who sues on a negotiable instrument is liable by way of setoff for a collateral indebtedness owed by the payee-transferor (Keim) to the drawer of the instrument (Olsen-Frankman).   An examination of the Minnesota setoff statute, the U.C.C. commentary and pertinent provisions of the predecessor negotiable instruments law, i.e., section 58 of the Negotiable Instrument Law (N.I.L.), demonstrates that in Minnesota, contrary to the rule in some other states, a drawer may offset extrinsic debts owed to him by the payee against his obligations on an instrument to a holder not in due course.

We begin our examination of the right to setoff in Minnesota under U.C.C. § 3–306 by reviewing the history of Minnesota's setoff statute and the prior negotiable instruments law.[5] The provisions of the Minnesota setoff statute originated in the territorial days and have continued as part of the general statutes and revised laws of that state. See Minn.Stat. § 540.03 (1974) (corresponds to Rev.Stat. (Terr.), ch. 70, § 28). In 1913, Minnesota enacted provisions of the N.I.L. (Minn.Stat. §§ 335.01–335.80 (1961) (repealed 1965) (originally enacted as 1913 Minn.Laws ch. 272, §§ 1–196)). Minnesota adopted the U.C.C. in 1965; it became effective July 1, 1966. Minn.Stat. § 336.10–105 (1974).

In Gould v. Svendsgaard, 141 Minn. 437, 170 N.W. 595 (1919), the Minnesota Supreme Court, citing Minnesota's version of section 58 of the N.I.L. and the setoff statute, held that the maker of a promissory note could assert a setoff claim against a post-maturity transferee where the maker held the claim against the payee at the time the transferee took the note. The N.I.L. sec-

---

5. Official Comment 3 to U.C.C. § 3–306 makes an historical review particularly relevant. It notes that "[p]aragraph (b) restates the first sentence of the original Section 58 [of the Negotiable Instruments Law]." Minn.Stat.Ann. § 336.3–306, Official Code Comment 3 (West 1966).

tion cited in Gould v. Svendsgaard, supra, and referred to in Official Comment 3 to U.C.C. § 3–306, provided in relevant part:

> In the hands of any holder other than a holder in due course, a negotiable instrument is subject to the same defenses as if it were non-negotiable. [Minn.Stat. § 335.221 (1961) (repealed 1965) (corresponds to N.I.L. § 58).]

Commenting on Stegal v. Union Bank & Federal Trust Co., 163 Va. 417, 176 S.E. 438, 95 A.L.R. 582 (1934), a leading case discussing the right of setoff under N.I.L. section 58, the court in United Overseas Bank v. Veneers, Inc., 375 F.Supp. 596, 607–08 (D.Md.1974), observed:

> The court [in *Stegal,* supra] further held that section 58 would have no effect at all on the prior law of the state with regard to set-off; in other words, section 58 would not change prior statutes or decisions which stated that prior party set-off was available in a suit on a negotiable instrument by a transferee not a holder in due course. Ample support for these conclusions may be found in Note (a) to section 58 of the N.I.L., which states:
>
>> It is not deemed expedient to make provisions as to what equities the transferee will be subject to; for the matter may be affected by the statutes of the various states relating to set-off and counter-claim. On the question whether only such equities may be asserted as attach to the bill, or whether equities arising out of collateral matters may also be asserted, the decisions are conflicting. In an act designed to be uniform in the various states, no more can be done than fix the rights of holders in due course.

The *United Overseas Bank* opinion held that under U.C.C. § 3–306(b) the right of a drawer to assert a setoff against a transferee (not a holder in due course) rested upon the drawer's rights according to state law existing before the enactment of the N.I.L. As already noted, U.C.C. § 3–306(b) intended no substantive change in N.I.L. section 58, and Minnesota allowed setoffs both prior and subsequent to its adoption of the N.I.L.

* * *

In their hornbook on the Uniform Commercial Code, Professors White and Summers comment that section 3–306 "does little more than summarize basic rules of contract law." J. White and R. Summers, Handbook of the Law Under the Uniform Commercial Code 490 (1972). The authors note that under contract principles set forth in section 167(1) of the Restatement of Contracts, all defenses to a contract claim may be asserted against an assignee of a contract except for those defenses based on facts arising after the obligor has notice of the assignment.[13] The language of the Minnesota setoff statute clearly adopts this contract principle with regard to setoffs. See Minn.Stat. § 540.03 (1974).

In summary, the history of the Minnesota setoff statute and negotiable instrument law, the U.C.C. Comment and the views of legal scholars indicate that the obligor on a negotiable instrument may set off against a holder not in due course an existing obligation owed by the obligee on the instrument. Under the setoff statute, the transfer of a negotiable instrument to one not a holder in due course occurs " * * * without prejudice to any set-off or defense existing at the time or before notice of the assignment[.]" Minn.Stat. § 540.03 (1974). Thus, in the present case the Bank took these checks subject to any existing setoff rights of Olsen-Frankman.

The Bank's argument to the contrary relies upon language in *Bank of Wyandotte v. Woodrow*, 394 F.Supp. 550 (W.D.Mo. 1975), which rejected any right of setoff against a holder not in due course arising from collateral transactions between the parties to the instrument. Judge Oliver in *Wyandotte* construed the Code term "defenses" (*see* U.C.C. § 3–306(b)) to mean technical defenses to the instrument, not setoffs arising from separate transactions with the check payee. He observed that under the applicable state law of Missouri one not a holder in due course is

> * * * subject only to such infirmities and defenses as are connected with the (instrument) itself and not such as grow out of separate and distinct transactions between the original parties. [394 F.Supp. at 556, quoting Glaus v. Gosche, 118 S.W.2d 42, 45 (Mo.App.1938).]

That conclusion, although quite appropriate, does not constitute persuasive authority here because Minnesota, unlike Missouri, statutorily allows a setoff. See Minn.Stat. § 540.03 (1974).

---

13. Restatement of Contracts § 167(1) (1932) provides:

An assignee's right against the obligor is subject to all limitations of the obligee's right, to all absolute and temporary defenses thereto, and to all *set-offs* and counterclaims of the obligor which would have been available against the obligee had there been no assignment, provided that such defenses and *set-offs* are based on facts existing at the time of the assignment, or are based on facts arising thereafter prior to knowledge of the assignment by the obligor. (Emphasis added.)

We conclude that the Uniform Commercial Code does not bar the assertion of a statutory setoff claim against a transferee of an instrument who does not qualify for the protections afforded a holder in due course. Accordingly, contrary to the district court, we hold that under Minnesota law appellant Olsen-Frankman might have asserted a right of setoff in a suit on these checks by appellee Bank, and to the extent that Olsen-Frankman can sustain such a setoff, it is entitled to damages against the Bank attributable to the latter's fraudulent misrepresentation.

III. *The Validity of the Setoff Claim.*

As an affirmative defense, the Bank asserted in its pleadings that Olsen-Frankman's right of setoff, if any, applied only to the check for $28,346.12 issued to John T. Keim & Sons because Olsen-Frankman's records showed no indebtedness owed by G. M. Grain Co., the payee of the second check.

This argument may be well taken. The right of setoff exists only as to "mutual" debts. See Henderson v. Northwest Airlines, Inc., 231 Minn. 503, 43 N.W.2d 786 (1950). Here the record shows mutual debts only between Olsen-Frankman on the one hand, and John T. Keim & Sons on the other.

On appeal, Olsen-Frankman does not dispute this mutuality requirement; rather, it contends that the evidence establishes that G. M. Grain company and John Keim & Sons constituted a single entity. According to this theory, the $100,000 indebtedness constitutes a debt of Keim and/or G. M. Grain Company as one entity, and therefore mutuality exists in fact with respect to both payees.

Appellant's theory that John T. Keim & Sons and G. M. Grain Company were one and the same seems to have first surfaced in its reply brief. At trial, Olsen-Frankman did not advance this theory but rather contended that Keim owned the cattle. Olsen-Frankman presented evidence that in payment for livestock purchased on July 17, 1975, it contemplated the issuing one check to Keim for the cattle. However, at the request of Gary Keim, a son of John Keim who brought in the loads of cattle, it issued two checks and split the proceeds between Keim and G. M. Grain Company.[14] Appellee Bank introduced evidence at trial indicat-

---

14. Appellant's theory that Keim owned all the cattle circumvents the mutuality problem regarding G. M. Grain Company. As a gratuitous assignee of one-half of Keim's interest in the cattle sale proceeds, G. M. Grain Company would have taken the check subject to Olsen-Frankman's claim against Keim. See Minn.Stat. § 540.03 (1974).

ing that, on the contrary, G. M. Grain owned the cattle. The jury by answer in the special verdict determined that on July 17, 1975, G. M. Grain Company owned the cattle in question.

Whether under the pleadings and trial record the appellant should now be permitted to advance the theory that Keim and G. M. Grain constituted a single entity, thereby establishing complete mutuality of indebtedness between Olsen-Frankman and both payees on the two checks in question, is a matter that we do not address. This question, as well as the substance of the claim if allowed, should be considered in the first instance by the district court.

On the record before us, appellant has demonstrated a right of setoff, hence a claim of damages for fraud, only with respect to the check made out to John T. Keim & Sons, for $28,346.12. This right remains subject to certain other defenses asserted by the Bank.

* * *

Accordingly, we reverse the holding of the district court, vacate its judgment of dismissal, and remand for further proceedings consistent with this opinion. Appellant is entitled to costs on this appeal.

NOTE

The law is not uniform regarding the question of what kind of defenses can be asserted against a holder not in due course. Some of the common defenses that can be asserted are specifically listed in UCC § 3–306(c). Other defenses on the instrument itself, such as discharge, incapacity and fraud or duress in the execution of the instrument can also be asserted. With respect to counterclaims and set-offs, whether arising out of the transaction giving rise to the instrument or an independent transaction, the UCC leaves the matter to be decided by general law. A claim in recoupment against the payee based on the transaction out of which the instrument arose is allowed as a defense to liability in that it reduces the liability on the underlying transaction represented by the instrument. The primary problem is with respect to claims of set-off or counterclaims against the original payee of the instrument arising out of a transaction independent of that giving rise to the instrument. These claims are in no way a defense to liability on the instrument, rather they are simply used to reduce the amount of recovery by the holder. The extent to which these claims can be asserted against a subsequent holder of the instrument is commonly governed by statutes specifically dealing with such claims. As is indicated in *Olsen-Frankman* these statutes vary from state to state. Compare United Overseas Bank v. Veneers, Inc., 375 F.Supp. 596, 606–610 (D.Md.1974) (denying the right of set-off) with Community Bank v. Ell, 278 Or. 417, 564 P.2d 685 (1977) (allowing the right of set-off). See Morris, The Use of Set-Off, Counterclaim and Recoupment: Availability Against Commercial Paper, 62 W.Va.L.Rev. 141 (1962). An analogous problem is presented under UCC § 3–305(2) with respect to a holder in due course who has dealt with the party sued on the instrument. The holder is subject to all defenses on the instrument of the defendant and is subject to whatever counterclaims or rights of set-off the general law provides.

Chapter 4

PROCEDURAL ASPECTS OF ENFORCING INSTRUMENTS

A. ENFORCEMENT BY NONHOLDERS

UCC § 3–301 states an important right of the holder of an instrument. The holder, whether or not he is the owner, may enforce payment in his own name. The corollary to this rule is that if there is a holder of the instrument only the holder may enforce the instrument. But sometimes there is no holder. That can occur if the person to whom the instrument is payable is not the person in possession of the instrument. There are two principal categories to consider: (1) those in which a person claiming ownership of the instrument is not in possession of the instrument; and (2) those in which the person in possession claims ownership but the instrument is payable to somebody else. The second category covers cases in which the instrument was transferred but not negotiated, i.e., the transfer did not result in the transferee becoming a holder because a necessary indorsement was not made. The two cases that follow illustrate the two categories.

INVESTMENT SERVICE CO. v. MARTIN BROTHERS CONTAINER & TIMBER PRODUCTS CORP.

Supreme Court of Oregon, 1970.
255 Or. 192, 465 P.2d 868.

DENECKE, JUSTICE. The plaintiff, the assignee of the depositary bank, brought this action against the drawer of a dishonored check. The payee of a check made by the defendant drawer deposited the check in the depositary bank, which, in turn paid checks drawn by payee on its account against the balance created by the deposit of drawer's check. The drawer sent a timely stop-payment order to the payor bank who, therefore, refused to honor the check when the depositary bank sent the check to the payor bank for collection. This action is for the sum of $2,042.21, the amount the depositary bank paid out of the payee's account against the credit for drawer's check before that check was returned dishonored. The trial court held for the defendant and plaintiff appeals.

On May 22 the defendant, Martin Bros., drew a check on its account in a Tennessee bank, payable to the order of Quinco, Inc. The next day Quinco deposited the check in its checking account in U.S. National Bank of Oregon (US). US sent the check through the Federal Reserve Bank system to the Tennessee drawee bank for collection. After deposit of the check and before its collection, US paid checks drawn by Quinco on its US checking account. Before presentment of the check to the Tennessee Bank, Martin Bros. ordered the Tennessee bank to stop payment of the check. The Tennessee bank did so and returned the check dishonored to US. US charged the amount of this check back against Quinco's account, which resulted in the account being overdrawn.

On June 8, in response to a request from Quinco, US sent the check to Quinco's attorney. The attorney requested the check so that he could commence an action for Quinco against the drawer, Martin Bros., on the check. There was no direct evidence of any agreement accompanying the delivery of the check to Quinco's attorney.

Quinco commmenced an action on June 15 for the entire face amount of the check, $2,937. The complaint alleged that Quinco "now holds said check." Sometime thereafter Quinco became bankrupt and a trustee was appointed. Quinco's lawsuit was dismissed for lack of prosecution about six months after the judgment in the present case.

Shortly after Quinco filed its lawsuit, it executed and delivered to US a document entitled "Assignment." This was done entirely on the initiative of Quinco's attorney.

On September 20 Investment Service Co. commenced this litigation as assignee of US's interest in the check. Since US's rights in the check are determinative here, we shall refer to US as plaintiff instead of Investment Service Co. Prior to the April trial of this litigation, US asked Quinco's attorney for the check. US received the check in March, and it was received in evidence in this litigation.

The principal issue in the case is whether the plaintiff bank can recover as a holder in an action on the check after it unconditionally returned physical possession of the check to the payee, with whom the check reposed at the time the bank commenced this action, and charged the check back to the payee's account.

When US initially received the check from Quinco, US became a "holder" of the check within the meaning of Oregon's Uniform Commercial Code (UCC) § 1–201(20). * * * US was in possession of the check and the check was properly indorsed. The payee, Quinco, did not indorse the check; however, [UCC § 4–205] provides that the bank may make the indorsement for the customer. The bank did make such indorsement in this case.

US initially proceeded upon the ground that it was a holder in due course and the defendant contested this status. On appeal, however, whether or not plaintiff is a holder in due course is immaterial because defendant challenges only US's status as a holder and does not assert any defense which would relieve it of an obligation to pay an ordinary holder.

If US had retained possession of the check from the time the check was returned dishonored, US would have been able to recover from the defendant drawer. The difficulty is created because US delivered the check to Quinco. The issue is whether US retained sufficient rights in the check to maintain this action.

Under §§ 51 and 191 of the Negotiable Instruments Law (NIL) (OCLA 69–401, 69–1101), the general law was that one could not maintain an action on a bill or note unless the plaintiff had possession of the bill or note.

* * *

"The owner of an instrument who is not in possession cannot sue thereon for he is not the holder under section 51 nor a transferee under section 49." Britton, Bills and Notes, 184 (2d ed. 1961).

Gilmore emphasizes the need for possession by the following illustration:

" * * * Take first the case of a negotiable instrument: if A wishes to make a transfer of the instrument to B, the only effective method is a delivery of the instrument to B. So long as B holds the instrument in pledge (assuming the transfer to have been for security), no one can acquire superior rights to the instrument or against the obligor through anything A may do. If, however, A, retaining possession of the instrument, delivers to B a written declaration that he has transferred the instrument to B and holds it as B's property, B's possession of the written declaration may given him rights against A but will not protect him against subsequent good faith purchasers of the instrument from A or against A's creditors and will not even give him the right to collect the instrument from the obligor. * * *" 1 Gilmore, Security Interests in Personal Property, § 1.2, 11 (1965).

* * *

Lost instruments were treated under the NIL as an exception to the rule that possession is a prerequisite to recovery:

> " * * * While a person out of possession normally cannot sue on the instrument, an exception exists in favor of the holder or owner who lost the instrument or from whom it was stolen. The holder of a lost instrument may sue thereon." Britton, supra, at 184.

* * *

The UCC is probably more exacting on the requirement of possession as a prerequisite than was the NIL. As stated, the NIL provides that to begin an action under usual circumstances one must be a holder and to be a holder one must be in possession. Although no exceptions to this principle were expressed in the NIL, the courts made exceptions such as in the case of a lost or pledged instrument. The UCC does contain an express exception to the requirement that one must have possession of an instrument to maintain an action thereon. That exception is [UCC § 3–804], providing that an owner of a lost instrument can maintain an action upon the instrument if he can prove the instrument is lost. Under the usual rules of statutory construction the specification of one exception to the requirement of possession leads to a construction of the entire statute that no other exceptions to the requirement of possession are intended. This construction is fortified by the official comment to [UCC § 3–804].

* * *

That part of the comment that is particularly significant is that the owner of a lost instrument is not a "holder" because he is not in possession. Also, if one is not in possession for some cause other than because the instrument is lost he cannot be a "holder." Except for [UCC § 3–804], just referred to, and other provisions not here material, one cannot maintain an action upon the instrument if he is not a "holder." Thus possession of the instrument is a prerequisite to maintaining an action on it with the sole exception here material of [UCC § 3–804]. This exception is clearly of no avail to plaintiff.

Two reasons are the probable basis for the requirement of possession. The most important is the danger of exposing the drawer to double liability if the drawer is required to pay one who does not have physical possession of the note.

* * *

In the instance of an instrument claimed lost, the comment to [UCC § 3–804], concerning lost instruments, states: "If the claimant testifies falsely, or if the instrument subsequently turns up in the hands of a holder in due course, the obligor may be subjected to double liability."

In the instant case payment by the defendant to US at the time US instituted this action could have resulted in double liability for Martin Bros. Payment to US would not have been a bar to Quinco's recovery on the check based upon Quinco's then existing rights as a holder. Since Quinco was the payee, it could, upon reacquisition of the check, strike all the endorsements. [UCC § 3–208]. In that event, US would no longer be a holder, not only because US no longer had possession, but also because the check was no longer endorsed to US. To be a holder, the instrument must be "issued or indorsed to him [the person claiming to be a holder] or to his order or to bearer or in blank." [UCC § 1–201(20)]. Payment to US would not be payment to a holder pursuant to [UCC § 3–601 or § 3–603] and, therefore, payment to US would not discharge the drawer.

* * *

In addition, one in the position of Quinco at the outset of this litigation could negotiate the note to a holder in due course. In that event, the holder in due course could have enforced the check against the drawer [UCC § 3–305] and the fact that the drawer had already paid US would not have prevented recovery by the holder in due course. [UCC § 3–601, § 3–602].

The other reason for the requirement of possession as a prerequisite to recovery on a negotiable instrument is the necessity for simplicity and clarity in the law of commercial paper in order to facilitate commercial dealings. The basic principle of commercial dealings in negotiable instruments is that one who presents an instrument which on its front and back establishes the right of payment is entitled to be paid and one who cannot make such a showing is not entitled to be paid. Exceptions to this should be rare; the UCC expresses only one, [UCC § 3–804], concerning lost instruments.

* * *

We hold that under the UCC, as well as the NIL, the plaintiff must prove the instrument is in its possession if it is not shown to be lost.

* * *

Lastly, US contends that at the time of the trial it was a holder having physical possession of the check and that the time of trial, rather than the time of the commencement of the action is the relevant time. US did have possession at the time of trial; however, we conclude that the relevant time was the commencement of the action.

Dolin v. Darnall, supra (115 N.J.L. 508, 181 A. 201, 102 A.L.R. 454), expressly held that possession of the negotiable instrument at the commencement of the action was essential and it was not sufficient that the plaintiff subsequently obtained possession by the time of trial. Johnson v. United Securities Corporation, 194 A.2d 132 (D.C.Mun.App.1963), followed Dolin v. Darnall, supra (115 N.J.L. 508, 181 A. 201):

> "Without proof that appellee was in possession of the note at the time it commenced the action, it could not maintain the action as a holder of the note. Regaining possession of the note after commencing the action would not cure the defect. * * *." 194 A.2d at 133.

On the other hand, Professor Britton states: "It is probably sufficient if the plaintiff is the holder at the time of trial."

* * *

Our decisions are to the effect that a cause of action or suit must exist at the commencement of the litigation and litigation is premature if a necessary element of the cause of action does not occur until after the commencement of the action. We have not found an articulation of the reasons for such policy but presume that it is to discourage speculative litigation.

* * *

Affirmed.

O'CONNELL, JUSTICE (dissenting). The record shows that plaintiff introduced the check into evidence at the time of the trial. It is clear, then, that the bank was the holder of the check at that time. And I understand that the majority of the court would concede that the bank could have brought the action if the check had come into its possession prior to the commencement of the action. So the decision in this case is made to rest solely upon the extremely technical ground that the elements of a cause of action must exist at the commencement of the action and the defect is not cured by evidence at the trial which supplies the missing element in the cause of action.

Whatever may be said in defense of this rule, I do not think that it should be applied when it is asserted by the defendant for the first time on appeal. If defendant had set up this defense at the time of trial, plaintiff would simply have refiled his action and the cause of action would have then been good. As it is, plaintiff is denied relief on appeal on technical grounds which plaintiff can readily circumvent by filing a new action and, as I understand the majority opinion, plaintiff will be entitled to recover as a holder of the check.

PERRY, C.J., joints in this dissent.

NOTES

1. The court in the principal case referred to UCC § 3–208, which covers cases in which a prior holder reacquires the instrument either by negotiation from the present holder or by a transfer other than negotiation. Although the language of the section is ambiguous, the right of the prior holder to further negotiate the instrument should arise only if the reacquisition results from a transfer giving him ownership. If he reacquires by negotiation he is a holder. If he reacquires other than by negotiation he can obtain holder status by striking his indorsement and any subsequent indorsements. The latter case is a modification to the rule of UCC § 3–204 that "any instrument specially indorsed becomes payable to the order of the special indorsee and may be further negotiated only by his indorsement." Reacquisition without indorsement of the transferor to whose order the instrument was payable can be illustrated by two examples: (1) a former holder, A, repurchases the instrument from the present holder, B; and (2) a holder, A, negotiates the instrument to B as part of an underlying transaction and then reacquires the instrument when the underlying transaction is rescinded. In each case A is the owner of the instrument after reacquisition, but his paper title is clouded and B's signature may not be easily obtainable. UCC § 3–208 is a rule of convenience which relieves A of the burden of obtaining an indorsement where no substantive purpose is served. Compare the rights of other transferees of unindorsed instruments in UCC § 3–201(3), § 4–201(1) and § 4–205(1).

2.   Payment of an instrument under UCC § 3–804 alleged to be lost, destroyed or stolen involves the same risk to the payor as that noted in the principal case.   If a person in possession of the instrument is able to negotiate the instrument to a holder in due course the payor will have to pay again because the first payment does not discharge him.   UCC § 3–603.   The payor is protected by the last sentence of UCC § 3–804 which states: "The court may require security indemnifying the defendant against loss by reason of further claims on the instrument." Some states have varied this language.   In California the sentence reads: "The court shall require a sufficient indemnity bond indemnifying the defendant against loss by reason of further claims on the instrument."   In New York the sentence reads: "The court shall require security, in an amount fixed by the court, not less than twice the amount allegedly unpaid on the instrument, indemnifying the defendant   *   *   *   against loss, including costs and expenses, by reason of further claims on the instrument   *   *   *."   Which version is preferable?   The New York version has caused difficulties.   In 487 Clinton Avenue Corp. v. Chase Manhattan Bank, 63 Misc.2d 715, 313 N.Y.S.2d 445 (1970), the payee of certified checks for $20,000 was forced to give the unindorsed checks to an armed robber.   The drawee, Chase, demanded a surety bond of $40,000 as a condition to paying the check.   The plaintiff offered as security to deposit the $20,000 plus an additional $2,500 to cover Chase's expenses in an interest-bearing account with Chase.   Under the plaintiff's proposal Chase would have control of the account but plaintiff would get the interest.   Chase refused.   The court held that under the New York statute the posting of security was discretionary.   It then held that the offer of plaintiff gave Chase adequate security and it was bound to accept it.   The case was decided two years after the checks were stolen.   In Chase Manhattan Bank v. Concord Utilities Corp., 7 U.C.C.Rep. 52 (N.Y.Civ.Ct., N.Y.Co.1969), Chase, this time a plaintiff, was suing the drawer of a check that Chase had lost.   Held: Chase was required to post security, but because it was a bank a letter of indemnity was sufficient security.   In Diaz v. Manufacturers Hanover Trust Co., 92 Misc.2d 802, 401 N.Y.S.2d 952 (1977), the Court refused to follow *487 Clinton* and held that the posting of security in twice the amount of the instrument was mandatory.   That case involved certified checks for $37,000 lost by the plaintiff. Plaintiff was required to post an indemnity bond of $74,000 notwithstanding the statement of the court that "the petitioner is being deprived of her life savings."   If a court finds that it is

very unlikely that the payor would have to pay twice, could it comply with the New York statute by simply requiring a letter of indemnity of the plaintiff as was done in *Chase Manhattan*, or is payor entitled to the equivalent of an indemnity bond regardless of the degree of risk?   Compare Comment to UCC § 3–804.   When does the security requirement terminate?

SMATHERS v. SMATHERS

Court of Appeals of North Carolina, 1977.
34 N.C.App. 724, 239 S.E.2d 637.

In separate actions plaintiff seeks to recover on two promissory notes, each of which was signed by defendants and made payable to the order of John H. Smathers. Although the notes were not indorsed, plaintiff alleged she is presently the owner and holder of the notes by assignment. Defendants answered and admitted that they executed the notes to John H. Smathers, who was the father of the male defendant, but alleged that it was the understanding of the parties that defendants would not have to pay the notes and that they were only for record in the later settlement of the John H. Smathers Estate. Defendants also denied that plaintiff is the owner of the notes. The two actions were consolidated for trial and were tried by the court without a jury.

At trial, plaintiff introduced the notes in evidence and stipulated that they had never been indorsed by the payee. Plaintiff testified that the notes had been given to her husband by his father, John H. Smathers, the payee, and that they came to her as result of her husband's death three years ago. There was also evidence that John H. Smathers had died and that First Union National Bank was executor of his estate.

At conclusion of the evidence, the court entered judgment finding "as a matter of law that the plaintiff is the owner and holder of the two promissory notes being sued on and pursuant to Section 25–3–301 on General Statutes of North Carolina is entitled to enforce payment in her own name." From judgment for plaintiff for the amount of the notes plus interest, defendants appeal.

PARKER, JUDGE. [UCC §] 1–201(20) defines a "holder" as "a person who is in possession of a document of title or an instrument or an investment security drawn, issued or indorsed to him or to his order or to bearer or in blank." The notes upon which plaintiff sues were not drawn, issued or indorsed to her or to her order or to bearer or in blank. Therefore, plaintiff is not the holder of the notes within the meaning of the Uniform Commercial Code, G.S. Ch. 25, and the trial court erred in according her the rights of a holder under [UCC §] 3–301.

* * *

[UCC §] 3–201(1) provides in part that "[t]ransfer of an instrument vests in the transferee such rights as the transferor has therein * * *." However, subsection (3) of that section provides that until the instrument is indorsed "there is no presumption that the transferee is the owner." Referring to this clause of subsection (3), Official Comment No. 8 to Section 3–201 of the U.C.C. states:

> The final clause of subsection (3), which is new, is intended to make it clear that the transferee without indorsement of an order instrument is not a holder and so is not aided by the presumption that he is entitled to recover on the instrument provided in Section 3–307(2). The terms of the obligation do not run to him, and he must account for his possession of the unindorsed paper by proving the transaction through which he acquired it.

In the present case, the plaintiff testified to some of the circumstances under which she obtained possession of the notes, but the trial court made no findings of fact with respect thereto. Indeed, the trial court, which heard this case without a jury, made no findings of fact whatsoever as it was required to do by G.S. 1A–1, Rule 52(a)(1). Instead, it based its judgment for the plaintiff entirely upon its finding "as a matter of law that the plaintiff is the owner and holder" of the notes. Since we have found that legal conclusion was in error, defendants are entitled to a new trial. Upon a new trial, plaintiff may be able to establish that she is the transferee of the notes and thus under [UCC §] 3–201(1) has such rights as her transferor had therein. This may include the right to maintain an action to enforce payment of the notes, subject, however, to any defenses which defendants could have asserted against her transferor.

New Trial.

NOTE

Smathers demonstrates that the difference between the rights of a holder and the rights of a nonholder asserting the rights of a holder under UCC § 3–201(1) is procedural in nature. Under UCC § 3–307 the holder is entitled to recover on the instrument simply by producing it in court. The burden is on the defendant to prove a defense. Since the plaintiff in *Smathers* was not a party to the instrument, her rights were purely derivative. Once the plaintiff has proved her rights on the instrument as a transferee she has the same rights and burdens as her transferor. The defendant has the burden of proving a defense. If a defense is proved that is not good against a holder in due course the plaintiff to take free would have to prove that her transferor was a holder in due course.

PROBLEM

Maker issued to X a promissory note payable to the order of X. At maturity the note, unindorsed, was presented for payment to Maker by Y. Y stated that he purchased the note from X, that X neglected to indorse it, and that Y was unable to obtain the indorsement of X because his whereabouts were unknown. When Maker refused to pay, Y brought an action on the note. Y introduced the testimony of several witnesses to the effect that Y had purchased the note from X. The court found that Y was entitled to enforce the note under UCC § 3–201(1) and gave judgment for Y. Maker paid the judgment after obtaining possession of and cancelling the note. A month later X demanded payment of the note from Maker stating that the note had been stolen from him by an unknown person. Maker refused to pay. X then brought an action on the note under UCC § 3–804. If X can prove that the note was stolen from him is he entitled to enforce it? Does the policy expressed by *Investment Service* and the last sentence of UCC § 3–804 apply to actions by nonholders relying on UCC § 3–201(1)?

B. PROOF OF SIGNATURES

The burden is normally on the plaintiff to prove all elements that make up his cause of action against the defendant. As applied to a suit on an instrument it means that the plaintiff has the burden of proving that the instrument is genuine and that he has title to the instrument or is otherwise entitled to enforce it. The holder of an instrument may be a stranger to the original transaction that gave rise to the instrument and there may have been negotiations of the instrument prior to that under which he took. The holder thus might have difficulty in proving that the instrument was in fact the act of the maker or drawer and that the indorsements under which he is asserting his rights were genuine. Under the UCC the holder has this burden; however, the burden is greatly diminished by certain presumptions set forth in UCC § 3–307(1).

BATES & SPRINGER, INC. v. STALLWORTH

Court of Appeals of Ohio, 1978.
56 Ohio App.2d 223, 382 N.E.2d 1179.

KRENZLER, PRESIDING JUDGE.

* * *

The appellant in its complaint sought judgment upon a promissory note incorporated into a lease agreement and allegedly signed by the appellee. [UCC § 3–307(1)] sets forth the applicable law:

"Unless specifically denied in the pleadings, each signature on an instrument is admitted. When the effectiveness of a signature is put in issue:

"(1) the burden of establishing it is on the party claiming under the signature; but

"(2) the signature is presumed to be genuine or authorized except where the action is to enforce the obligation of a purported signer who has died or become incompetent before proof is required."

The statute provides that when the effectiveness of a signature becomes an issue in a case the burden of establishing it is on the party claiming under the signature. The signature is presumed valid, but this presumption is rebuttable and may be overcome by evidence to the contrary. If the party denying the signature introduces sufficient evidence to overcome the rebuttable presumption, then the case is decided upon all of the evidence introduced at trial with the party claiming under the signature having the burden of establishing the effectiveness of the signature by a preponderance of the evidence as in other civil cases. Naturally, it is for the trier of the facts to determine whether the person relying on the effectiveness of the signature has satisfied his burden of proof by a preponderance of the evidence.

In the case before us, the appellee in his answer denied execution of the instrument and thus put the effectiveness of the signature at issue. The appellant, as the party claiming under the signature, therefore bore the burden of establishing the signature's effectiveness at trial, although under the statute the appellant had the benefit of a rebuttable presumption that the signature was genuine or authorized. Consequently, until evidence was introduced to rebut the presumption, the appellant was not required to prove the authenticity of the signature.

The appellant introduced in evidence the instrument under which it sought recovery and thus established a *prima facie* case. See Petty v. First National Bank (1976), 50 Ohio App.2d 365, 363 N.E.2d 599; Bentz v. Mullins (1970), 24 Ohio App.2d 137, 265 N.E.2d 317; Leedy v. Ellsworth Construction Co. (1966), 9 Ohio App.2d 1, 222 N.E.2d 653. At this point it became the appellee's obligation as the one denying the signature to introduce evidence to show the forged or unauthorized character of the signature.

Ohio courts interpreting the application of [UCC § 3–307(1)] have not heretofore addressed the question of the strength of the evidentiary showing required of the party denying the effectiveness of a signature. In search of the proper standard we note that the Committee Comment to the statute states:

"The presumption rests upon the fact that in ordinary experience forged or unauthorized signatures are very uncommon, and normally any evidence is within the control of the defendant or more accessible to him. He is therefore required to make some sufficient showing of the grounds for his denial before the plaintiff is put to his proof. His evidence need not be sufficient to require a directed verdict in his favor, but it must be enough to support his denial by permitting a finding in his favor. Until he introduces such evidence the presumption requires a finding for the plaintiff. Once such evidence is introduced the burden of establishing the signature by a preponderance of the total evidence is on the plaintiff."

Under the evidentiary standard suggested by the Comment, more than merely some evidence must be introduced to rebut the presumption. The evidence introduced by the party denying the signature must be sufficient to permit, yet not require, a finding in his favor. This is a fair and reasonable interpretation of the statutory language.

We conclude [UCC § 3–307(1)] requires that in order to rebut the presumption of the signature's authenticity the party denying the signature must introduce evidence to support his denial which if believed would be sufficient to permit the trier of fact to make a finding in his favor. This is not to say that to overcome the presumption such party must introduce evidence sufficient to entitle him to a directed verdict. The interpretation we place on the statute does not produce an evidentiary standard markedly different from existing Ohio law generally on the quantum of evidence necessary to overcome a rebuttable presumption. See In re Estate of Walker (1954), 161 Ohio St. 564, 120 N.E.2d 432; Brunny v. Prudential Ins. Co. (1949), 151 Ohio St. 86, 84 N.E.2d 504; Ginn v. Dolan (1909), 81 Ohio St. 121, 90 N.E. 141; cf. Snyder v. Stanford (1968), 15 Ohio St.2d 31, 238 N.E.2d 563.

To illustrate, if the party seeking to recover on an instrument places it in evidence and the adverse party introduces no evidence to rebut the presumption of validity of the signature thereto, then the party claiming under the signature will prevail. If the adverse party merely makes a general denial at trial as to the signature's validity but fails to introduce any other evidence to rebut the presumption of authenticity which attaches to the signature, then the party claiming under the signature will still prevail. However, if the party denying the signature's validity introduces evidence sufficient to overcome the rebuttable presumption of validity, then the case will be decided upon all of the evidence introduced at trial with the burden of proof being upon the party claiming under the signature to establish its effectiveness by a preponderance of the evidence.

The trial court's findings of fact disclose that appellee introduced some evidence to support his denial. Without a transcript or statement of the relevant evidence, we must presume regularity to the proceedings below and assume sufficient competent evidence was introduced to rebut the presumption of the signature's authenticity.

With the presumption of the signature's authenticity thus laid aside, the burden of establishing the signature's effectiveness by a preponderance of the evidence rested with the appellant. The trial court noted in its findings that the appellant presented no evidence—beyond introduction of the instrument—to refute the appellee's evidence. The trial court concluded that the appellee did not sign the instrument and entered judgment against the appellant on the promissory note.

In this case the effect of the trial court's judgment is that the appellant did not meet its burden of proof on the issue of the effectiveness of the signature which appeared on the instrument. Without a transcript of the actual evidence adduced at trial by the parties, this court cannot determine that the trial court's conclusion was in error, and we therefore must affirm the judgment entered below.

NOTES

1. UCC § 3–307(1) is directed to the question of unauthorized signatures. In the case of the unauthorized signature of the maker or drawer the person whose purported signature is in issue has a defense to liability. UCC § 3–401(1). In the case of an unauthorized indorsement the plaintiff is denied the status of holder. § 3–202(1). An analogous problem is raised by cases in which there is an irregular indorsement but the issue is not forgery or lack of authority. Suppose that a promissory note is payable to the order of Mary Smith. The instrument contains one indorsement "Pay to the order of John Doe" followed by the signature "Mary Jones." At maturity Doe demands payment of the maker who refuses. Is Doe entitled to enforce the note? If so, what must he prove? If Mary Jones and Mary Smith are the same person it is clear that Doe is a holder notwithstanding the irregularity of the indorsement. The payee may indorse using any name or no name at all. UCC § 3–401(2). In our case Mary may have had the surname Smith when single and the surname Jones after she married. Or, she may simply have adopted the surname Jones without legal cause. The problem is one of proof. Who has the burden of proving that Mary Smith and Mary Jones are or are not the same person? Though cases of major or minor discrepancies between the name of a payee and the name used in the indorsement are very common the UCC does not clearly deal with the problem. Since, as a practical matter, most instruments are collected by banks the payor will usually pay despite an irregularity in an indorsement because the instrument will usually bear the stamp of the collecting bank "Prior indorsements guaranteed." UCC § 3–203 deals with one aspect and one example of this problem but it does not cover all cases. Does UCC § 3–307(1) apply?

In Watertown Federal Savings & Loan Association v. Spanks, 346 Mass. 398, 193 N.E.2d 333 (1963), a promissory note was payable to "Greenlaw & Sons Roofing & Siding Co." It was indorsed "Greenlaw & Sons." The maker challenged the indorsement. No evidence with respect to the indorsement was introduced. The court held that the case was governed by UCC § 3–307(1). "There was no evidence whatsoever to counter the presumption of the indorsement's regularity existing under § 3–307(1)(b). Thus the signature of Greenlaw was established under § 3–307(2), and the bank, as the holder of the note * * * is entitled to recover." Would the court have made the same analysis if the indorsement had been "United States Steel

Corporation?" UCC § 3–307(1)(b) deals with the issue of whether a signature is "genuine or authorized." Does it apply at all to an indorsement which on its face does not purport to be the signature of the payee? In Young v. Hembree, 181 Okl. 202, 73 P.2d 393 (1937), decided under the NIL, a check was payable to "Horn & Faulkner Oil Trust" and indorsed to the plaintiff by the signature "Horn & Faulkner." The court held that plaintiff was not a holder. He was entitled as a transferee of the check to assert only the rights of his transferor. " * * * on its face, the indorsement is not that of the payee, and there is no evidence in the record to show that they are one and the same firm or legal entity."

2. The cases are not clear on the question of the quantum of evidence by the defendant necessary to rebut the presumption of validity of signatures. In Jax v. Jax, 73 Wis.2d 572, 243 N.W.2d 831 (1976), defendant made a "positive denial" that she executed and delivered the note in question. The court held that the defendant "must do more than simply deny that the signature is [hers]. * * * Here the defendant introduced no evidence to support a finding that the signature on the note was forged or unauthorized. The presumption of validity, therefore was not rebutted." It is not clear from the facts whether defendant testified that she did not sign the note or whether the denial was based on the pleadings. Specimens of her signature were introduced by the plaintiff. In Esposito v. Fascione, 111 R.I. 91, 229 A.2d 165 (1973), Father as part of a loan transaction signed a promissory note payable to the plaintiff in the plaintiff's presence. The plaintiff insisted that Father also obtain the signatures of Mother and Daughter. Father later delivered the note bearing the purported signatures of Mother and Daughter to the plaintiff. In an action on the note Daughter testified that she never signed the note. Father and Mother also testified that Daughter had not signed. "The denial of all defendants that the signature on the note was that of [Daughter], along with her assertion that she was without knowledge of the transaction, and the sample of her signature as defendants' Exhibit B, constitute evidence sufficient to rebut the presumption that the signature was genuine or authorized." See also Metropolitan Mortgage Fund, Inc. v. Basiliko, 44 Md.App. 158, 407 A.2d 773 (1979).

3. There is a special problem of proof in cases in which the obligor has died or has become incompetent after signing. UCC § 3–307(1)(b) provides no presumption in those cases. Under so-called "Dead Man's Statutes" in the enforcement of a contract allegedly made by a person dead at the time of trial the contract

must be proved by evidence other than the testimony of the adverse party. In re Estate of Carr, 436 Pa. 47, 258 A.2d 628 (1969), involved these facts. Joseph Carr died leaving a small estate; Stanley Heinricher notified the executor that he had a judgment note, signed by decedent in his favor. A portion of the opinion follows:

> Heinricher himself took the stand to prove his note. Katusin's counsel objected on the ground that the testimony was inadmissible by virtue of the Dead Man's Statute, Act of May 23, 1887, P.L. 158, § 5, 28 P.S. § 322. The court properly ruled it inadmissible. Counsel for Heinricher then offered a recording receipt from the Prothonotary's Office of Allegheny County, showing a judgment on a note in favor of Heinricher and against a Joseph Carr. Katusin's counsel objected on the ground that the burden was on Heinricher to prove the signature was genuine and that the judgment debtor was the decedent. Although Heinricher did not produce any such proof, the court ruled it admissible and held the claim valid. We disagree.
>
> The Uniform Commercial Code, 12A P.S. § 3–307, provides: "When the effectiveness of a signature is put in issue (a) the burden of establishing it is on the party claiming under the signature; but (b) the signature is presumed to be genuine * * * except where the action is to enforce the obligation of a purported signer who has died * * * before proof is required, * * *" Since the purported signer has died, Heinricher, the party claiming under the signature, has the burden of establishing it as genuine. This he has not done. There is no proof at all that the "Joseph Carr" on the note is the deceased "Joseph Carr," and the name is hardly an uncommon one. Hence, we must disallow Heinricher's claim.

Chapter 5

UNAUTHORIZED PAYMENT AND DISHONOR

A. BANK COLLECTION

---

1. THE EXISTING PAYMENTS SYSTEM

This chapter is about the process of paying debts. In the cases and problems that follow something has gone wrong—the check is forged or the bank is negligent—and the courts are faced with allocating the loss. Before reading these materials you should know something about the payments system in this country.

Checks. Before 1960 payment was usually either by cash or by checks drawn on accounts in commercial banks. As a payment mechanism the check has shortcomings. Banks find checks costly to process, and we will see later how they have attempted to reduce the expense of the check-clearing process. From the drawer's standpoint, the check amounts to a delayed cash transaction. When the check is presented to the drawee bank, payment must be made immediately; if the drawer's account is inadequate to cover the check, dishonor results. With respect to payees and subsequent holders, the check payment mechanism has a number of defects. First, several days may ensue before the payee or holder obtains the use of the drawer's money; the interim is referred to as the "float" period. Second, the drawer may have no money in his account or may stop payment on the check; in both instances the payee or holder must proceed against the drawer for he has no rights against the drawee bank on which the check was written. Thus the seller of goods or services who accepts a check in payment must determine at his peril the likelihood of payment. The absence of any guarantee that a check will eventuate in payment inhibits acceptance of checks in locations other than those close to the buyer's home.

254

Credit cards. Some of the disadvantages of checks have been reduced by the emergence of credit cards. At first the only credit cards in circulation were the so-called Travel and Entertainment (T & E) cards (like those issued by American Express, Diners Club, and Carte Blanche), cards issued by retailers for use only at their outlets, and those issued by oil companies for use at service stations. In the 1960's both the BankAmericard (now Visa) and the Master Charge (now Master Card) programs spanned the nation with the now ubiquitous bank credit card. Both sellers and buyers found benefits in the credit card system that grew to supplement the check payment mechanism. Sellers could rely on the credit card, so long as certain authorization procedures were observed, as a guarantee by the card issuer of the cardholder's creditworthiness. The buyer could delay payment for a so-called "free period" after making a purchase by use of the card without incurring a finance charge or could pay in instalments and pay a finance charge on the balances remaining each month. National acceptance of credit cards has eventuated, allowing consumers to make purchases in distant places without the necessity of carrying cash. Formerly in bank card cases the sales slips cleared through the banking system like checks. Now the transaction is "truncated" and the slips stay with the merchant bank.

Financial institutions. In the 1970s and 80s major steps were taken to make thrift institutions (savings and loans, credit unions, and mutual savings banks) more competitive with commercial banks. These institutions were given the right to allow their depositors to have checking accounts. The thrifts also began to issue credit cards. By the same token commercial banks were, for the first time, permitted to pay interest on demand deposits. Now commercial banks and thrift institutions compete on a much more equal basis.

Electronic fund transfers. The cost of our paper-based payments system has been estimated at between $10 and $20 billion annually.[1] Cash and checks must be produced, distributed, guarded, insured, protected against forgery and fraud, and, most expensive of all, physically transferred from bank to bank through the complex check clearing system. Because of this cost the financial industry has shown considerable interest in utilizing electronic fund transfer (EFT) systems in the payment process.

1. Final Report of National Commission on Electronic Fund Transfers p. 142 (1977).

In 1974 Congress established the National Commission on Electronic Fund Transfers to study the area preparatory to federal regulation. Their Final Report was submitted in 1977. The Electronic Fund Transfer Act, 15 U.S.C. § 1963 et seq., was enacted in November 1978; most of its provisions went into effect eighteen months after enactment. The most helpful reference on the subject is Penney & Baker, The Law of Electronic Fund Transfer Systems (1980). Examples of EFT systems are:

1. Point-of-Sale (POS) systems. The buyer pays for goods or services by using a plastic coded card, called an access or debit card, inserted in a terminal in the merchant's establishment. The card contains the necessary account information in machine-readable form to allow the buyer's account to be instantly debited. When the buyer's account is debited, the merchant's account is automatically credited with the amount of the sale. For various reasons, these POS systems have not become popular. The customer has no float period or right to stop payment as he would have in a check transaction. Moreover, start-up costs for merchants and banks are high.

2. Automated teller machine (ATM). The most popular form of EFT is the rapidly growing ATM system. Here terminals are located in places convenient to customers and are available for use most of the hours of the day. The customer can use an access card and a personal identification number (PIN) to make deposits to and withdrawals from his deposit account in a bank or thrift institution. The attractiveness of these terminals to financial institutions is shown by the estimate that the cost of a human teller-handled deposit is $1.35, while an ATM deposit costs only 98¢; a withdrawal handled by a human teller costs $1.70 compared to 72¢ for one from an ATM.[2]

3. Automated clearing house (ACH). This sytem allows depositors to authorize their employers to make payroll deposits by use of magnetic tapes. The employer's bank delivers a magnetic tape coded with the payroll information to an automated clearing house facility where a computer sorts out the deposits and delivers completed tapes to the employees' banks. Depositors may also use this system for automatic deduction of recurring bills like mortgage payments or insurance premiums.

---

2. Los Angeles Times, Part IV, p. 1, Feb. 21, 1982: "For Bank Customers the Free Ride is Over."

4. Telephone bill payment. The customer may call his bank or thrift institution, identify himself, and direct that institution to pay designated creditors.

The emergence of EFT in the 1970s provoked discussion on whether the UCC should be expanded to cover other payment mechanisms like EFT and credit cards as well as checks. Since 1977 the UCC Permanent Editorial Board has been at work drafting a New Payments Code (NPC) designed to cover both paper and electronically based payment systems, including credit cards but excluding cash and promissory notes. "The basic rationale of the NPC is that the legal rights defined for parties to payment transactions ought to be as similar for each payment system as is possible. That is, any dissimilar principles should be based on a clear technological or other necessity, and not on historical accident or the ability of special interests to wrest concessions. The goal is to have economics, not legal rules, dictate the choice of payment systems; to create an environment in which the underlying efficiencies and costs will determine the choice by institutions and consumers of the best payment system." [3]

2. BANK COLLECTION UNDER ARTICLE 4

More than any other article of the UCC, Article 4 was drafted to give legal recognition and support to a structure of existing business procedures and practices—the process of check collection as it was carried out in the 1950's. The following article explains in simple language that check collection process and what Article 4 was intended to do.

———

Malcolm, How Bank Collection Works—Article 4 of the Uniform Commercial Code, 11 How.L.J. 71 (1965).*

The Article of the Code that I shall discuss is "Bank Deposits and Collections." This Article and the subject matter involved are rather technical and specialized. To give a general understanding of the Article it would be helpful first to outline two

3. Brandel & Geary, Electronic Fund Transfers and the New Payments Code, 37 Business Lawyer 1065, 1074 (1982). Copyright 1982 by American Bar Association. All rights reserved. Reprinted with permission.

* Reprinted by permission of the Howard Law Journal. Some of author's footnotes omitted.

hypothetical but illustrative cases and then relate a number of the rules of Article 4 to these two cases.

The first case is probably the most simple type of bank collection case. John Jones and William Smith are both residents of Washington and each carries a commercial banking account with the Riggs National Bank. Jones owes Smith $10 and decides to pay this bill by check. He draws a check for $10 on Riggs and delivers it to Smith. Smith deposits the $10 check in his account at Riggs at about 9:30 a.m. on Monday. Riggs processes that check through a series of processes and on Tuesday credits Smith's account with $10 and debits Jones' account with $10. After these credits and debits have been completed the $10 check is filed with other checks drawn by Jones and paid by Riggs and at the end of the month is returned to Jones. Here we have probably the most simple type of a bank collection case, but a number of quite interesting legal problems may arise even in this simple case.

In the second hypothetical case let us suppose that an orange grower has his orange grove somewhere in the southwest portion of California. The orange grower succeeds in making a sale of a carload of oranges to a grocery concern located in Bangor, Maine. The sale is one on credit with thirty-day terms, and before the end of the thirty days the grocery concern decides to pay for the carload of oranges by drawing its check for $5,000 on the Bangor Trust Company in favor of the orange grower. The grocery concern then mails the check to the orange grower in southwest California so that when it is received, the check has to be collected. The steps required to effect this collection constitute the second hypothetical case.

Let us suppose that the orange grower lives in a small town in California by the name of Morina and carries his bank account with the Morina Trust Company. Having received the $5,000 check the orange grower deposits that check with the Morina Trust Company. The Morina Trust Company does a certain amount of processing of the check and either on the day of deposit or on the next business day enters a provisional credit to the account of the orange grower and (because in bank bookkeeping there must always be a debit to offset a credit) at approximately the same time the Morina Trust Company enters a provisional debit in the account which that bank carries with its correspondent city bank, the San Diego National Bank. On the same day that these two entries are made the Morina Trust Company forwards the check for $5,000 together with another group of checks drawn on points outside of Morina to the San Diego National Bank with a request to the San Diego bank to collect the check and credit the account of the Morina Trust Company.

On the following day the San Diego National Bank receives the group of checks from the Morina Trust Company, including the $5,000 check payable to the orange grower. The San Diego bank then proceeds to sort this group of checks on the basis of the bank on which each check is drawn and after this sorting process is completed it accumulates another group of checks, including the $5,000 check payable to the orange grower, and forwards this group of checks to the Federal Reserve Bank of Los Angeles. In all probability at about the time this group of checks is forwarded the San Diego bank enters a provisional credit for all or some of the checks it has received from the Morina Trust Company, in the account of the Morina Trust Company with the San Diego bank, and also probably enters a provisional debit in its account with the Federal Reserve Bank of Los Angeles for the group of checks which are forwarded to the Reserve Bank. Since the $5,000 item is included in the larger sum credited to the Morina Trust Company and also in the larger sum debited to the Federal Reserve Bank of Los Angeles, the books of the San Diego bank are still in balance as far as that $5,000 item is concerned.

Probably on the next business day following this action of the San Diego bank the Federal Reserve Bank of Los Angeles receives the group of checks from the San Diego Bank together with similar groups of checks from substantially all other banks in the southern California area. The Los Angeles Reserve Bank credits the account of the San Diego Bank with the Reserve Bank for the total amount of all of the items received from the San Diego Bank in that particular cash letter. The Los Angeles Reserve Bank puts all the many incoming checks received by it from other banks through a sorting process which sorting process is again based upon the bank or banks upon which the various items are drawn. Since the $5,000 check payable to the orange grower is drawn on the Bangor Trust Company of Bangor, Maine, this check with other checks drawn on banks in the New England area are sorted and grouped together and forwarded by the Federal Reserve Bank of Los Angeles to the Federal Reserve Bank of Boston. On the same day that this group of checks is forwarded the Los Angeles Reserve Bank debits the account of the Federal Reserve Bank of Boston on its books with the total amount of the checks forwarded to the Boston bank.

In Boston the Federal Reserve Bank of that city goes through a process substantially the same as that of the Los Angeles Reserve Bank. It enters provisional debits and credits and sorts in one group all the checks that it has received from all sources all over the United States which are drawn upon the Bangor Trust Company. When this sorting and other processing has been completed it forwards a group of checks directly to the Bangor Trust Company for presentation and payment. Included in this group is the $5,000 check to the orange grower.

We shall assume that this group of checks is received by the Bangor Trust Company in its mail on Monday morning. That bank starts processing the group of checks received from the Federal Reserve Bank of Boston, together with all other checks drawn and presented on it. One of the most important parts of this processing is to again sort all of the checks so received on the basis of the account on which they are drawn. In the case of the $5,000 check, it is sorted against the account or name of the grocery concern that drew it. At some time on Tuesday morning that check has been processed far enough so that it reaches the bookkeeper who handles the account of the grocery concern to ascertain whether there are sufficient funds to cover the check and then decides whether to pay it or dishonor it. If it turns out that there are insufficient funds in the grocery company's account to cover the check and the decision is made to dishonor it, then the check has to be returned through the various banks in the chain out to the Morina Trust Company. As it moves back to California all of the provisional debits and credits entered in this series of banks have to be reversed, or offsetting entries of $5,000 have to be made. On the other hand if the decision of the bookkeeper in the Bangor Trust Company is to pay the $5,000 check and the necessary steps are taken to complete this payment then it is necessary to finalize this payment through all of the banks through which the $5,000 check passed, which finalization process can take place in various ways.

The case of the orange grower's $5,000 check drawn by the grocery concern in Bangor, Maine, is illustrative of one of the more complicated types of bank collection cases. To visualize the volume and complexity of the bank collection process as a whole it is necessary to think of about fifty million variations of these two cases taking place every business day. In such a mental picture there would be checks moving from Seattle,

Washington to Miami, Florida; from Duluth, Minnesota to New Orleans, Louisiana; from Casper, Wyoming to Washington, D.C.; and of course the many thousands of checks deposited in one bank in Washington and drawn on another bank in Washington or in one bank in Washington on another bank in Baltimore and so on ad infinitum. Estimates indicate that not less than fifty million items are handled as a part of the bank collection process by all the banks in the United States, every single business day. In terms of single banks the size of this bank collection process may further be illustrated. The Federal Reserve Bank of Boston handles and processes in excess of one million checks or items every business day. The larger banks in Washington, D.C. probably handle and process in excess of two hundred thousand checks per day. Smaller banks, of course, handle fewer checks but even the smaller banks handle and process several thousand checks and other items every business day.

Reflection upon the bank collection process indicates that here we have a vast, machine-like, volume operation with literally tremendous numbers of items and dollars and which might well be likened to the bloodstream of our economy. We have a steady flow of items and dollars that perform a vital and essential function. So long as the flow continues we are almost completely unaware that it is taking place, just as we are substantially unaware of the flow of blood through our bodies. But produce a stoppage of this flow for a week or even for a day as, for example, during the bank holiday in 1933 and conditions approaching chaos would strike our economy almost instantly; or produce a minor stoppage or obstruction at some stage in this operation and the confusion and irritation which would result would be amazing.

Another interesting commentary on bank collections is that automation is progressing in this field very rapidly. Much of this process which has been described has been mechanized for many years. Sorting machines, tabulating machines, recording machines, and stamping machines have long been used in small as well as large banks. And now another great step forward in automation is far advanced. Magnetic ink symbols appearing on most checks are designed to sort checks to banks and accounts and to permit bookkeeping and record making by electronic computers with an absolute minimum of human handling. It is almost approaching the stage that when the $5,000 check is first deposited by the orange grower in the California bank and is "encoded" by that bank, from there until it is returned to the grocery concern in Maine, every step in the process by every bank is under automation with only the most limited handling by human hands.

Here then is the subject matter of Article 4 of the Uniform Commercial Code. The drafting problem for the Article was one of stating in modern terms and concepts the legal rules affecting this flow operation. Of course they had to be fair but, equally, the rules had to recognize the tremendous, machine-like, flow nature of the bank collection process and facilitate the smooth functioning of this process rather than throw irritants or blockages in its path.

* * *

Terminology

In drafting Article 4, as in all other articles of the Code, great care was used in selecting, defining and using precise terms. It would have been impossible to state rules accurately unless this were done. It is important to consider some of these defined terms so as to be familiar with and to use the same terminology.

In our orange grower case the Morina Trust Company in southwestern California is the "depositary bank." The San Diego National Bank, the Federal Reserve Bank of Los Angeles, the Federal Reserve Bank of Boston are all "intermediary banks." The Bangor Trust Company is the "payor bank." The Morina Trust Company and all three of the intermediary banks are also "collecting banks." The Federal Reserve Bank of Boston, inasmuch as it presents the $5,000 check on the Bangor Trust Company, is a "presenting bank."

In thinking about the bank collection process as a whole, however, it must be kept in mind that every bank will probably be functioning in every one of these capacities at different times and with respect to different items. For example, in the simple Jones-Smith case the Riggs Bank is a "depositary bank" for Smith and a "payor bank" for Jones, and it serves in both capacities at the same time. Further, on every business day the Riggs Bank and probably every other bank will be a "depositary bank" as to a substantial number of items deposited with it, an "intermediary bank" as to a substantial number of items that are working through its transit department and a "payor bank" as to a further substantial number of items that are drawn upon that bank. These definitions of banks appear in Section 4–105 of the Code.

In the orange grower case the orange grower is a "customer" of the Morina Trust Company. The grocery concern is a "customer" of the Bangor Trust Company. Both Smith and Jones are "customers" of the Riggs Bank. But also under the definition of "customer" in Section 4–104, the Morina Trust Company is a "customer" of the San Diego National Bank.

Because in the bank collection process notes, drafts and other instruments are collected as well as checks, the single generic term "item" as used in Article 4 to refer to any one of these instruments that banks may be collecting.

"Midnight deadline" is an important term used in Article 4. The significance of this term may be illustrated in the case of the Morina Trust Company. If the $5,000 check were deposited with that trust company on Wednesday, the midnight deadline of the Morina Trust Company which would be the latest time during which it would be proper for it to forward this item to the San Diego bank would be midnight on Thursday.

The term "settle" is an important term in Article 4. In Section 4–104, "settle" is defined as meaning to pay in cash, by clearing house settlement, in a charge or credit, or by remittance or otherwise as instructed. The definition further states that a settlement may be either provisional or final. Here again it was considered desirable to select a broad generic term that could cover every type of debit or credit, remittance, payment in cash or otherwise made with respect to an item without its being important, as that term is used, whether the settlement is provisional or final.

Forwarding of the Item for Collection

In the past one of the most fertile sources of litigation in the bank collection process has been whether a bank handling an item for collection has purchased the item or simply acts as an agent in its collection. Many cases have been litigated on this question because under pre-Code law the rights of a customer or a bank could well be different depending upon which status was adopted. In this welter of cases the resulting law was in almost hopeless confusion. Consequently one of the first potential benefits of Article 4 of the Code is to eliminate this problem entirely and (it is hoped) the litigation that has gone with it. In the last sentence of Section 4–201, subsection (1), it is provided that when an item is handled by banks for purposes of presentment, payment and collection the relevant provisions of the article apply regardless of whether the status is purchaser or that of agent. The remaining provisions of Section 4–201(1) produce the result that in the great preponderance of situations, the status of the bank will be that of an agent or subagent for collection, which agency will continue until a prescribed time when by virtue of the completion of the collection process the relationship shifts automatically into one of debtor and creditor. Thus, in the orange grower case when the $5,000 check is deposited in the Morina Trust Company that Trust Company becomes an agent of the orange grower for the collection of the item and so also do the San Diego National Bank, Federal Reserve Bank of Los Angeles, and the Federal Reserve Bank of Boston, and these agencies continue until the item is sufficiently processed either by the Bangor Trust Company or by one of the banks in the return process so that the relationship shifts to one of debtor and creditor between one bank and another in the chain and between the Morina Trust Company and the orange grower. Section 4–201 is one of the important sections of Article 4 and should provide answers to questions of this type and should eliminate many old problems that have been the source of much litigation.

Section 4–202 lays down the general responsibility of banks in undertaking the collection of items. It is to use ordinary care in the normal steps in the collection process. The section specifies the areas where ordinary care is required and certain other areas where banks do not have responsibility.

Section 4–203 adopts the chain of command theory. For example, the Federal Reserve Bank of Los Angeles will take its orders solely from the San Diego National Bank with respect to the $5,000 check. That does not mean that the San Diego National Bank does not itself have to give the proper orders, but if the Federal Reserve Bank of Los Angeles acts in the manner directed by the San Diego bank it need not concern itself with any actual or possible instructions that it might receive either from the Morina Trust Company or the orange grower.

Section 4–204 states in rather general terms certain principles controlling how items should be sent forward. More specifically it approves in certain instances (already existing in practice) when items may be forwarded directly to payors. For example, the Section specifically approves the Federal Reserve Bank of Boston forwarding the $5,000 check directly to the Bangor Trust Company in Maine.

At the present time under the N.I.L. the warranties of the N.I.L. produce the result that in each of the transfers of the

$5,000 check from the orange grower to the Morina Trust Company, from the Morina Trust Company to the San Diego Bank, from the San Diego Bank to the Los Angeles Reserve Bank and from the Los Angeles Reserve Bank to the Federal Reserve Bank of Boston, each transferor makes very definite and important warranties to each transferee. However, under the N.I.L., when the Federal Reserve Bank of Boston forwards the item and presents it on the Bangor Trust Company it makes no warranties whatsoever. To correct that situation it became the practice for many years that each bank in this chain of banks would put a rubber stamp indorsement on the back of the $5,000 check saying in effect "All Prior Indorsements Guaranteed." The purpose of each of these rubber stamp indorsements was to confer upon the Bangor Trust Company a guarantee or warranty with respect to the genuineness of the indorsements. However, as a practical matter, there is just as much reason to state as a matter of law that certain warranties run from the Federal Reserve Bank of Boston to the Bangor Trust Company as there is to have warranties run in each of the other transfers in the chain. Consequently, Section 4-207 prescribes a series of presentment warranties made whenever an item is presented on a payor bank, at the same time preserving and clarifying the warranties made between transferors and transferees. Of course, also, these warranties appearing in Section 4-207 are almost identically the same as similar warranties prescribed in Section 3-417 of Article 3 on Commercial Paper.

Final Payment of Item by Payor Bank

As previously indicated under pre-Code law there were no less than ten different rules under court decisions in the several states as to when an item was finally paid by the payor bank. Using the Jones-Smith and the orange grower $5,000 check cases as illustrative, some of these rules will be considered.

In the case where Jones gave Smith a check for $10 on the Riggs Bank and Smith deposited this check at 9:30 a.m. on Monday in that Bank, a number of cases have held that the $10 check was paid at 9:30 a.m. on Monday morning when Smith deposited it. Decisions in Arizona, California, Minnesota, Nebraska, Ohio, Texas and Wisconsin have so held.

Under deferred posting practices in effect in almost all of the 50 states of the United States, Jones' check for $10 and the $5,000 check of the grocery concern in Bangor, Maine would not reach the bookkeepers either of the Riggs Bank of Washington or of the Bangor Trust Company in Bangor until sometime on Tuesday morning. At that time the respective bookkeepers in each payor bank would make a determination to pay or dishonor the $10 check or the $5,000 check. If we assume this decision is made at about 11:00 a.m. on Tuesday, under Nineteenth Ward Bank v. First National Bank,[5] each of the items would be paid at 11:00 a.m. on Tuesday.

In the case of the $5,000 check payable to the orange grower let us assume that the Bangor Trust Company accounts for that check to the Federal Reserve Bank of Boston by drawing a remittance draft on The First National Bank of Boston payable to the Federal Reserve Bank of Boston. A decision in Minnesota in 1951 in the case of Bohlig v. First National Bank,[6] held that even though the Bangor Trust Company had deposited the remittance draft in the mail addressed to the Federal Reserve Bank of Boston, so long as it was possible for the Bangor Bank to withdraw that letter from the mails the item was not finally paid. This rule has come to be known as the "fishback" rule, because there is no final payment so long as the payor bank can "fishback" its remittance out of the mails.

Other cases have held that there would be no final payment of the $5,000 check payable to the orange grower until the remittance draft was mailed by the Bangor Trust Company to the Federal Reserve Bank, was received by the Federal Reserve Bank in Boston and was in turn paid in the Boston Clearing House. This might well be as late as Thursday or Friday in our hypothetical case.

These variations in the rules of the several states as to when an item is finally paid by the payor bank are not only unfortunate and confusing themselves in producing uncertainty in the law, but they are doubly unfortunate in view of the fact that the time when an item was paid under existing law was important as affecting a number of other related problems. For example, who bears the loss in the event of failure of a bank? When is a stop payment order effective? When is a notice of bankruptcy effective? Consequently it is not surprising that this variation in rules produced a substantial amount of litigation.

Section 4–213 of Article 4 resolves that problem by stating in subsection (1) when an item is finally paid by the payor bank. These rules are necessarily technical. It is accurate to say that one of the great potential benefits of Article 4 with respect to

5. 184 Mass. 49, 67 N.E. 670 (1903).   6. 233 Minn. 523, 48 N.W.2d 445 (1951).

the law of bank collections is to resolve this difficult issue of when an item is finally paid by the payor bank.

Final Settlement for Paid Item Through Collecting Banks and to Original Customer

Let us assume in our orange grower $5,000 check case that the bookkeeper for the account of the Bangor grocery concern decided that the $5,000 check should be paid at 11:00 a.m. on Tuesday and further that at 12:00 noon she had completed posting this $5,000 item as a debit to the account of the grocery concern. Assuming other necessary conditions have been met, under subsection (1) of Section 4-213 the $5,000 check was finally paid at 12:00 noon on Tuesday in Bangor, Maine. However, to complete the full bank collection process it is still necessary to see how this $5,000 final payment at 12:00 noon on Tuesday gets back to the orange grower in southwestern California. There can be almost an infinite number of variations of facts which would affect this result in different ways, but three alternative possibilities will suffice to illustrate the effect.

In our $5,000 check case let us assume that as the check moved eastward from California to Maine the facts were as outlined in the hypothetical case. In each bank in the chain, provisional debits and credits were entered which provisional settlements were not to become final unless and until the items were finally paid and final settlement was received for it. Consequently on these facts in each of the Morina Trust Company, the San Diego National Bank, the Federal Reserve Bank of Los Angeles and the Federal Reserve Bank of Boston both the $5,000 debit and the $5,000 credit went through the books of each bank so that all the bookkeeping steps required with respect to this item were made and completed as the item moved eastward, all in the hope that it would ultimately be paid in Bangor, Maine. On these assumptions subsection 2 of Section 4-213 provides that automatically upon the item being finally paid at 12:00 noon on Tuesday in Bangor, Maine, every one of the other provisional settlements (the provisional debits and credits in each bank) automatically become final at identically the same second and the collection process on that item was finally completed. This clause has been referred to as the "Zinger" clause because when the item is finally paid at 12:00 noon on Tuesday in Bangor, Maine—Zing—settlement for it automatically becomes final through the entire chain of banks all the way back to California at identically the same time. Interestingly enough, as a matter of bookkeeping and accounting this has been taking place for the last fifteen or twenty years in bank collections, but prior to the work on Article 4 on the Code no one had appreciated or analyzed what was taking place and certainly no rule of law, either by statute or decision, in any way enunciated this important and interesting result.

The fact that these settlements all become final automatically at 12:00 noon on Tuesday does not mean, however, that one minute later the Morina Trust Company in California is obligated to pay out those funds to the orange grower. Subsection 4(a) of Section 4–213 recognizes that in cases of this type the Morina Trust Company is entitled to have a reasonable time to know that this item has been finally paid and not until such reasonable time has elapsed does the orange grower have the right to withdraw the $5,000 resulting from the collection of this item.

Let us suppose next that instead of the Federal Reserve Bank of Boston having handled this particular item by a provisional debit to the account of the Bangor Trust Company it merely forwarded the item with a request to pay and remit. Under this arrangement, when the item was paid at 12:00 noon on Tuesday the Bangor Trust Company accounted for the $5,000 by mailing a remittance draft drawn on The First National Bank of Boston payable to the Federal Reserve Bank. On these facts the Federal Reserve Bank of Boston would not receive final settlement for the item until the remittance draft was presented and paid.

Similarly, if in forwarding the $5,000 check the Morina Trust Company never entered any provisional debits or credits whatsoever, but simply forwarded the item for collection and remittance, or in other words, for collection and return of the proceeds after final payment, then the collection process would not be completed nor would there be any final settlement until, by a series of steps, the $5,000 resulting from the final payment at noon at Tuesday worked its way back from Bangor, Maine to Morina, California.

If it turned out to be the case that there were insufficient funds in the account of the grocery concern to pay the $5,000 check or for some other reason it was dishonored by the Bangor Trust Company then, insofar as provisional debits or credits had been entered as the item moved eastward from California to Maine, it would be necessary to reverse these entries or put through offsetting entries of $5,000 each as the unpaid check is returned through the chain of banks from Maine to California.

Provision for these chargebacks and refunds are made in Section 4–212.

Miscellaneous Provisions

Referring briefly now to various other miscellaneous provisions, Section 4–214 prescribes the rights of the parties in the event that insolvency of a bank occurs at some time while the collection process is going on.

Within the last 15 years the practice of so-called "deferred posting" has been adopted by substantially all banks in the country and has been authorized by statutes in more than forty states. Deferred posting rules consistent with those in effect in substantially all states are set forth in Sections 4–301 and 4–302.

One of the difficult problems that has repeatedly faced banks in connection with the collection, presentation and payment of items is when the item should have priority over notices of bankruptcy and like notices, stop orders, legal attachments or process or setoffs, or conversely when these four types of legal events should be given priority over items being processed as a part of the collection process. Specific rules with respect to these problems appear in Section 4–303.

* * *

Flexibility

As has been stated earlier the bank collection process is a tremendous, machine-like, flow, volume operation. Article 4 recognizes this fact and sets forth a series of what might well be called traffic rules designed to keep this flow moving smoothly. Some of these rules are general but a substantial number of them are quite precise and definite. However, the sponsors and draftsmen have recognized at all times that in any volume operation as large as that of bank collections, there are bound to be at all times some variations from the norm and there is certain to be in the period of time in which Article 4 is likely to be controlling law, changes in practices and procedures that almost certainly will make one or more rules of the Article inappropriate under new and changing conditions. It would be a very bad thing if by virtue of changes in practices in the next five or ten year period, it turned out to be the case that one of the quite specific rules of Article 4 was completely inappropriate to the new practices and conditions.

To guard against this type of risk and possibility Section 4–103 provides for a very wide potential of variation by agreement. Subsection (1) of that Section provides that no agreement can disclaim a bank's responsibility for its own lack of good faith or failure to exercise ordinary care or can limit the measure of damages for such lack or failure. But beyond these two single restrictions subsection (1) of 4–103 provides that the effect of anything in the Article may be varied by agreement. Consequently, in the event of an unusual or abnormal case or in the event of changing conditions and circumstances over the years the possibility exists that by agreement of the parties any rule of Article 4 proving to be unworkable can be waived or modified and some alternative rule selected.

Conclusion

Article 4 is the result of a long struggle with complexity, a compromise of various points of view. It is not contended that the Article is a miracle of perfection. It does, however, contain workable, practical rules that are fair and equitable in foreseeable cases. The Article is sufficient flexibility to enable the parties to work out, with greater certainty of result than heretofore, any needed special treatment by "agreement otherwise" or by the traditional methods by which the collection system has developed. In the same manner approval can be secured for any innovations. It is also gratifying to observe that now that the Article has been in effect in Pennsylvania since July 1, 1954, in Massachusetts since October 1, 1958 and in approximately twenty additional states for shorter periods, there has been an absolute minimum of litigation under it.

WEST SIDE BANK v. MARINE NATIONAL EXCHANGE BANK

Supreme Court of Wisconsin, 1968.
37 Wis.2d 661, 155 N.W.2d 587.

The plaintiff (appellant herein), West Side Bank (hereinafter referred to as West Side), claims that Marine National Exchange Bank (hereinafter Marine) had made "final payment" on a check that West Side had presented to Marine and that, hence, it could no longer honor its customer's (the maker's) stop-payment order, but was accountable to West Side for the amount of the check. West Side has appealed from an order denying its motion for summary judgment.

The facts giving rise to this action are these: On Thursday, August 11, 1966, the stock brokerage firm of Paine, Webber, Jackson & Curtis (hereinafter Paine, Webber) issued a check in the amount of $262,600 drawn on Marine to one Byron Swidler. That same day Swidler deposited this check to his account at West Side. On Friday morning, West Side, through the Milwaukee clearing house, presented the check to Marine for payment. On Friday evening, Marine commenced the process of posting by sending the check (with others) through sorting and encoding machines and through the electronic computer.

As a part of the computer process, the account of the customer was charged with the item and a "paid" stamp affixed to the check. Had the conditions of the customer's account at the time of the computer run warranted it, the computer would have prepared and printed an unposted or no-account report, an overdraft report, an uncollected-funds report, or a large-item report.

The item, being for more than $500, appeared on the large-item report, but since the Paine, Webber account was not deficient in any respect, the result of the computer run was to charge the item to the customer and to stamp it "paid." On the morning of Monday, August 15, 1966, the report of the computer was submitted to the bookkeeper; and since the computer run revealed no deficiencies, and was not rejected by the computer, the item was photographed, cancelled and filed in the Paine, Webber account. West Side contends that at this point Marine completed the "process of posting" and made "final payment," shifting responsibility for the item from the maker to the payor bank. Thereafter, at about 4:00 p.m. on Monday, August 15, Marine discovered and informed Paine, Webber that a check drawn by Swidler in the amount of $270,000 payable to Paine, Webber had been dishonored as an NSF check. Thereupon, Paine, Webber stopped payment of the check for $262,600 payable to Swidler. Upon the receipt of the stop-payment order, Marine withdrew the item from the Paine, Webber file and notified West Side that the check was being returned because of the stop-payment order. The check entries were reversed in the computer run Monday night by crediting Paine, Webber and stamping the check "payment stopped" and "cancelled in error." The check was returned to West Side at the morning exchange of the clearing house on Tuesday, August 16, 1966.

West Side's suit is brought upon the theory that the Uniform Commercial Code, which became effective in Wisconsin on July 1, 1965, provides that an item is finally paid by a payor bank and the bank is accountable therefor when it has "completed the process of posting the item to the indicated account of the drawer, maker or other person to be charged therewith." [UCC § 4–213(1)(c)] The trial judge concluded that final payment had not been made and denied the motion of West Side for summary judgment.

HEFFERNAN, JUSTICE.

Were West Side's affidavits in support of summary judgment defective for lack of personal knowledge

Marine alleges on this appeal that West Side's affidavits are on their face defective for they purport to state the internal procedures of Marine that would only be known to an officer or employee of Marine. This court has uniformly held that affidavits made by persons who do not have personal knowledge are insufficient and will be disregarded and that affidavits made only on the basis of the affiant's information and belief fail to establish evidentiary facts, and mere assertions of ultimate facts are equally ineffectual. While these propositions of law urged by the respondent are without doubt correct, yet it appears that this defense, the procedural inadequacy of the affidavits, is raised for the first time on appeal. Had the question been raised in the trial court and West Side's affidavits were then found insufficient, the appellant would have been entitled to renew its motion upon the submission of affidavits in compliance with the summary-judgment statute.

It is thus apparent that it would be unjust to allow the respondent to prevail upon an argument raised for the first time in this court. In essence, the factual controversy that Marine asserts arises out of the fact that Marine claims to have an additional and crucial step in its "process of posting" a final exercise of judgment for the purpose of determining whether for any reason whatsoever the entries theretofore made are to be reversed or errors corrected. Marine asserts that it is not until this point that there is determination of "final payment." While the affidavit of West Side disputes this assertion, it is essentially its position that, as a matter of law, the provision for the reversal of entries applies only to errors of a mechanical or clerical nature and is not relevant to the judgment factors that enter into final payment and that final payment is determined at an earlier stage of the proceedings when the "process of posting" is completed.

Marine, by failure to object to West Side's affidavits in the trial court, has waived the right to do so now, and West Side has chosen not to base its argument on the factual dispute but upon the proposition that, although the facts are as asserted by Marine, they are irrelevant as a matter of law and ineffective to defer the time of "final payment" as defined in the Uniform Commercial Code. We therefore conclude that it is proper for this Court to consider the legal issues insofar as they are relevant to sustaining or reversing the order denying the plaintiff's motion for summary judgment.

Did Marine become accountable to West Side for the amount of the check by "final payment" of the item

The Uniform Commercial Code provides that, upon final payment, the payor bank shall become accountable for the amount of the item [UCC § 4–213(1)(a)]. Insofar as [UCC § 4–213] is relevant to this case it provides that an item is finally paid when the bank has "completed the process of posting the item to the indicated account of the drawer, maker or other person to be charged therewith" [UCC § 4–213(1)(c)].

The "process of posting" is defined in [UCC § 4–109].

* * *

It is upon this statute [UCC § 4–109] that the appellant primarily relies. It contends that the "process of posting" was completed when Marine decided to pay the item as was evinced by verification of the signature, ascertainment that there were sufficient funds to the credit of the drawer's account, charging of the account, stamping the check "paid" or "cancelled," and filing the check with the customer's file as a voucher to be returned to him. It is clear that all of these steps were carried out by Marine and that they constituted the performance of at least the first four of the steps required in the process of posting.

Marine, however, contends that until the fifth step, "correcting or reversing an entry or erroneous action with respect to the item," is considered and determined, either affirmatively or negatively, the process of posting is not completed. Marine contends that it may defer this decision until the last possible time that will allow it to make a return of the item; and only (in the absence of some other unequivocal conduct) upon its decision not to reverse the entries or upon its failure to make a timely return of the item is there final payment.

West Side contends that Marine's interpretation would minimize the effect of [UCC § 4–213(1)], and would almost completely negate the possibility of using completion of the "process of posting" as the benchmark for determining final payment. Marine's argument in essence is that, so long as time remains in which entries can be reversed (until the clearinghouse deadline), a check is not finally paid under the Code. Marine contends, and the trial court agreed, that subsec. (5) of [UCC § 4–109] permitting the payor bank to reverse any entry, whether the original entry was correct or erroneous. West Side contends that this subsection permits only the correction of an error or the reversal of erroneous action.

It would appear whatever rationale may be offered to the contrary, and they are numerous, reason must yield to the plain meaning of the statute. No limitation is set forth in the legislation. The phrase the legislature used was "reversing an entry." Only by the most strained interpretation is it possible to glean from the face of the statute the inference that the entry must have been made in error. While the legislative intent may have been otherwise, and there is evidence that some authors prominent in the preparation of the Code concluded that only erroneous entries were intended, yet it is not within the province of this Court to seek secondary sources of legislative intent where the meaning of the statute is plain and unambiguous.

Persuasive argument for West Side's position is found in 38 Ind.L.J. (1962–1963) 696, 717, wherein the interpretation urged by Marine is discussed:

> "Subsections (a), (b), and (c) set out points of time which are somewhat earlier than what has normally been considered the 'process of posting,' whereas subsection (d) is the action which has normally been held to constitute the vital determining factor. Without the detailed definition of section 4–109, subsection (d) would stand as the relevant activity of the payor for accountability under section 4–213(1)(c), however, subsection (e) of 4–109 broadens the definition of the 'process of posting' to make it almost meaningless. A payor bank, it appears, is now able to reverse an entry which was previously considered final. In other words, the payor bank can perform one of the vital steps in (a), (b), (c) or (d) and it would not be accountable since, by the plain meaning of subsection (e), it can correct or reverse an entry as it sees fit.

> "Why such extreme latitude is permitted after the Code has gone to great lengths to set out a precise point of time

for payor accountability is difficult to comprehend. Perhaps, in the desire to be consistent, this subsection should be read narrowly to apply *only* to erroneous entries. If it can be limited to mechanical errors of the entry, then the preciseness of section 4–213(1) will not be lost. If it is not narrowed to this point, however, the payor bank would be able to charge the account of the drawer and later reverse this charge, contending that the initial entry was erroneous, since it did not realize that the drawer had insufficient funds.

"It is thus seen that the plain meaning of section 4–109 would destroy the effect of section 4–213(1)(c) and negate the effect of the Code for consistency in each section where final payment is a consideration. Perhaps, if litigation should arise under any of the final payment sections, the narrow construction would appeal to the court, but until such a time a result of such litigation is unpredictable. If limitation and clarification is not possible, the only alternative would seem to be repeal of subsection (e)."

We can only echo the sentiments expressed in the commentator's last sentence. If the interpretation that is urged by Marine, which we accept, fails to comport with the intent of the framers of the Code, there must be a resort to legislative clarification. We cannot, however reasonable West Side's argument might be, conclude that the interpretation of the trial court constitutes a deviation from the intent of the framers of the Code.

Fairfax Leary, Jr., formerly the reporter for Article 4 of the Code, writing in 49 Marquette L.Rev. (1965–1966) 331, pointed out that the "process of posting" is a combination of two diverse elements—one is the element of judgment in determining whether or not payment should be made and the other is the mechanical element of recording the item. The oral arguments of both parties to this appeal and the affidavits in support and in opposition to the motion make it clear that the computer merely records the information fed into it and only after the computerized facts are sorted and recorded do the officers and employees of the bank apply the judgment factors that culminate in the decision to pay.

The Leary article, considering the prejudgment recording by the computer, stresses the need for the maximum time for the correction of entries and argues that this procedure is an integral part of the "process of posting." He states at page 360:

"And so one of the included steps in the process of posting includes the correction of errors and the reversal of entries. It would seem to follow, then, that the subdivision of Section 4–213(1) based on 'completion of the process of posting' would not be satisfied, until the time within which entries could be reversed had expired. So long as time remains in which entries could be reversed, it would, in view of the enumeration of 'reversal of entries' as one of the steps included in the 'process of posting', be difficult for a court to say that the 'process of posting' had been completed. Normally, in the non-clearings-cash-letter-for-credit-in-an-account situation this means that the process of posting is not completed until the expiration of the midnight deadline where the bank is working three shifts in its processing of checks, otherwise at the close of operations next preceding the midnight deadline."

We conclude, rejecting the constricted meaning of [UCC § 4–109(5)] urged by the appellant, that the plain meaning of the statute permits the reversal of entries for any reason whatsoever (subject to the good-faith provisions of the Code) if made within the time limited for return of items to the clearing house.

Do clearing house rules allowing return of unacceptable items on second business day following presentment supersede the process of posting rule under the Code?

Marine argues that, even if it were held accountable under the Code, it is exonerated from liability by reason of the clearinghouse agreement to which both Marine and West Side are signatories. By-law IV, sec. 3, of the clearing-house agreement expressly provides that unacceptable items are returnable through the exchanges on the second business day following the date they are presented at the exchange. Marine returned the Swidler check to West Side within the time limit. [UCC § 4–103(1)] specifically provides that the effect of the Code may be varied by agreement, and [UCC § 4–103(2)] provides that clearing-house rules have the effect of such agreements.

Fletcher R. Andrews, Dean of the School of Law at Western Reserve University, in his article, The City Clearing House: Payment, Returns, and Reimbursement, recognized before the adoption of the Code that clearing-house rules are strong evidence of the intention of banks regarding the time in which a decision to pay a check may be made. Dean Andrews states:

"Consequently, the only problem causing any difficulty arises when the drawee bank debits the drawer's account, and later wishes to cancel the entry, treat the check as dishonored, and return it to the presenting bank within the time stipulated by the clearing house rule. In debiting the drawer's account, the bank has performed an act which ordinarily is considered payment. But the banks, by rule, have agreed that items may be returned before a certain hour. Since payment is a matter of intent, and the parties have set down their intent in the rules of the clearing house, the solution of the problem becomes merely a matter of interpretation of the rule. * * *

"It may conceivably be argued that a [returned] * * * item means only an item which never has been charged against the drawer's account, by reason of the discovery of a shortage of funds, forgery, or the like. The argument gains in plausibility when it is recalled that checks are inspected for irregularities, omissions, forgeries, and other defects before being entered in the general ledger, and that the bookkeeper examines the state of the drawer's account before making his entry. As a consequence, the item might be regarded as 'good' or 'paid' when, after successfully completing the several tests, it is finally charged against the drawer. Yet this interpretation seems to overlook the fundamental purpose of the rule, which is to permit the banks to wait until a certain time before finally deciding whether to honor or dishonor the items presented. Had the banks wished to make the debiting of the drawer's account the last 'rite,' they could easily have said so in their rule. In the absence of a provision to that effect, the rule should be interpreted to mean that the check is not paid until the expiration of the return period."

In view of the express approval of the statutes that the Code may be waived or altered by agreement, we are compelled to hold that the clearing-house agreement supersedes any inconsistent portions of the Code, and in this instance additionally serves to expand the time in which entries may be reversed. Moreover, such modifications are within the stated purpose of [UCC § 1–102(2)(b)] "to permit the continued expansion of commercial practices through custom, usage and agreement of the parties."

Related to the desirability of recognizing local agreements in derogation of specific provisions of the Code is the statute's express standard that final payment is dependent not upon some objective universal standard, but upon the subjective test of "the usual procedure followed by the payor bank." [UCC § 4–109] The affidavits of Marine tend to show that no decision in respect to payment was made until a judgment was reached regarding the reversal or nonreversal of entries and that the process of posting was not completed until the time for reversal expires. The recent case of Gibbs v. Gerberich (1964), 1 Ohio App.2d 93, 98, 203 N.E.2d 851, stressed the subjective test to be applied:

> "The key point in a bank's completion of the 'process of posting' is the completion of all of the steps followed in a *particular* bank's payment procedure." (Emphasis supplied.)

While a motion for summary judgment does not constitute a trial by affidavit, it is apparent that the affidavits of Marine, if believed at trial, would lead to the conclusion that the exercise of judgment following the computerized phase of the posting process to determine whether or not entries should be reversed constituted an essential part of Marine's process of posting and making "final payment."

The rules of the Milwaukee County Clearing House Association, upon which Marine relies, reflect the practical problems involved in handling quantities of bank checks by mechanical or electronic devices. The use of such devices rests upon the assumption that there will be sufficient time after the mechanical processes are completed for the human factor of judgment to be exercised and upon the statistically derived conclusion that only a very small proportion of the checks in circulation will present problems that require individual treatment. It has been estimated that in 1963 the Federal Reserve System handled 4,700,000,000 items for collection and the Federal Reserve Bank of Chicago alone handled 700,000,000. The annual check volume countrywide is believed to exceed 50,000,000 a day and 13,000,000,000 a year. Fairfax Leary, Jr., in 49 Marquette Law Review 331, 333, 334, points out that two principles have guided the selection of rules governing the law of check collections:

> "One is that the rules must be suitable for a bulk processing of large numbers of checks at little cost. The second, which is a corollary of the first, is that rules to ensure a proper allocation of losses incurred in the area of the one eighth of one percent of bad items should not be so restrictive as to clog the free flow and smooth handling of the almost unanimous number of *good checks, collections in bulk, and deferred posting.*"

It would appear that the rules of the Milwaukee County Clearing House Association urged by Marine comport with these principles. Because of the tremendous volume of checks being handled, the rule recognizes that the payor bank needs a grace period following the computer phase to make the determination to pay or not to pay. Recognition of the viability of such a rule effectuates the purpose of the Code as expressed in comment to the 1962 Official Text of Art. 4, Bank Deposits and Collections, Uniform Commercial Code, at page 361, where it was stated that one of the goals of the Code was to provide "for flexibility to meet the needs of the large volume handled and the changing needs and conditions that are bound to come with the years."

We conclude that the order of the trial court denying the appellant's motion for summary judgment must be affirmed.

Order affirmed.

NOTES

1. UCC § 4–213 determines when a bank is "accountable" for an item; UCC § 4–303 determines when an item is subject to one of four types of legal events (usually described as the "four legals"): notice (of death or insolvency), a stop order, attachment or other legal process, and set-off. Why did the court decide *West Side*, which concerned one of the four legals, with no reference to UCC § 4–303?

2. Does *West Side* mean that Marine Bank had a period between the time when the item was cancelled and filed on Monday morning (that is when the normal process of posting was completed) and the hour beyond which the entry could not be reversed, during which Marine could at its absolute discretion choose whether or not to honor stop orders and attachments, to invoke set-off, or to observe notice? If this is so, would it not usually be to the interest of the payor bank to reverse the entry in cases in which a stop order was received or a set-off was asserted during this interim period, but against its interest to do so in cases in which an attachment or notice of insolvency was received? Is this sound policy? See Malcolm, Reflections on *West Side Bank:* A Draftsman's View, 18 Cath.U.L.Rev. 23, 30 (1968); Rohner, Posting of Checks: Final Payment and the Four Legals, 23 Bus.Law 1075, 1086–88 (1968). See also Leary and Tarlow, Reflections on Articles 3 and 4 For a Review Committee, 48 Temple L.Q. 919 (1975).

3. When Article 4 was studied by bank counsel in California in 1961, they challenged the process-of-posting test for final payment. The multibranch California banks had centralized, computerized bookkeeping systems which processed items before they were sent out to the proper branches for verification of sig-

natures. Counsel feared that under the process-of-posting test an item might be considered paid before it had been verified in the branch office. In response to this opposition and to complaints emanating from New York UCC § 4–109 was added in the 1962 official text. However, California's distrust of a posting test for payment persisted, and upon enactment in 1963 the California version of Article 4 deleted the process-of-posting provision (paragraph (d)) from UCC § 4–303(1) and substituted the following: "(d) The cutoff hour (Section 4107) or the close of the banking day if no cutoff hour is fixed of the day on which the bank received the item;". The process-of-posting provision (paragraph (c)) was deleted from UCC § 4–213(1) and UCC § 4–109 was dropped entirely.

SUN RIVER CATTLE CO. v. MINERS BANK OF MONTANA

Supreme Court of Montana, 1974.
164 Mont. 237, 521 P.2d 679.

PER CURIAM. This appeal was originally heard on November 27, 1973; an opinion issued January 14, 1974; a rehearing was granted and argued. This opinion replaces that appearing in 31 St.Rep. 44.

This is a case involving three separate plaintiffs and six separate checks. The plaintiffs are cattle raisers and brought this action to recover $74,868.02, plus interest which represents the total of the six checks drawn by Schumacher's New Butte Butchering, hereinafter referred to as New Butte, on its account at Miners Bank of Montana, hereinafter referred to as Miners. One check was payable to Bruce Beck & Son, two to Louis Skaar & Sons, and three to Sun River Cattle Co., who will be referred to hereinafter, respectively, as Beck, Skaar and Sun River individually and as plaintiffs collectively. Each of the checks was accepted by the plaintiff payees in payment for cattle sold and delivered to New Butte. A summary of the history of all six checks is as follows:

The Beck check dated April 28, 1970, was for the amount of $12,478.63. This check was sent by Beck's bank to Miners, stamped "Paid," run through New Butte's checking account and deducted from the balance on May 11, 1970, (a Monday). The check was reversed and added to the balance on May 13, 1970, and returned to Beck's bank for insufficient funds. The check was sent back to Miners, stamped "Paid", run through New

Butte's checking account, deducted from the balance on May 20, 1970, reversed on May 21, 1970, and returned to Beck's bank for insufficient funds. It was then returned to Miners "for collection" June 4, 1970, received by Miners on June 8, 1970, and retained by Miners until July 7, 1970, when it was returned to Beck's bank.

The first Skaar check, dated April 14, 1970, was for the amount of $11,514.74. This check was sent by Skaar's bank to Miners, stamped "Paid", run through New Butte's checking account, deducted from the balance on April 27, 1970, reversed April 28, 1970, and added to the balance and returned to Skaar's bank for insufficient funds on April 28, 1970. The check was sent back to Miners, run through New Butte's checking account and deducted from the balance on May 11, 1970, reversed and added to balance May 13, 1970, and returned to Skaar's bank for insufficient funds. It was returned by Skaar's bank "for collection" on May 15, 1970, received by Miners on May 18, 1970, and retained by Miners until July 27, 1970, when it was returned to Skaar's bank.

The second Skaar check, dated May 4, 1970, was for the amount of $12,434.26. This check was sent by Skaar's bank to Miners, stamped "Paid", run through New Butte's checking account, deducted from the balance on May 12, 1970, reversed on May 13, 1970, and added to the balance and returned to Skaar's bank for insufficient funds. The check was returned by Skaar's bank to Miners "for collection", received by Miners on May 20, 1970, and retained by Miners until July 27, 1970, when it was returned to Skaar's bank.

The first Sun River check, dated April 27, 1970, was for the amount of $12,882.57. This check was deposited in the First National Bank of Great Falls on April 28, 1970, and sent to Miners. It was stamped "Paid May 1, 1970", run through New Butte's checking account and deducted May 1, 1970, (a Friday). The check was reversed and added to the balance on May 4, 1970, (a Monday) and returned to First National Bank of Great Falls. The check was sent back to Miners "for collection" on May 8, 1970, received by Miners on May 11, 1970, and has never been returned.

The second Sun River check, dated May 4, 1970, in the amount of $13,114.23, and the third Sun River check, dated April 1, 1970, (although the invoice for this load of cattle is dated April 28, 1970) in the amount of $12,443.59, were both sent to Miners directly "for collection". The second check was sent on May 6,

1970, and received by Miners on May 7, 1970, and the third was sent on May 12, 1970, and received by Miners May 13, 1970. These checks have never been returned. None of the checks have been paid.

In 1962 the original transaction between Miners and New Butte took place when Miners loaned New Butte some $289,500. In 1968 refinancing of New Butte became necessary in an amount in excess of Miners' lending capacity.

Refinancing was carried out with two separate loans. One was for $200,000 with Miners having a 30% participation and the remaining 70% spread among seven sister banks. The other was for $100,000, 90% of which was guaranteed by the Small Business Administration (hereinafter referred to as SBA). The loans were made to provide working capital, and to comply with federal regulations as to slaughterhouses.

Miners filed financing statements with the county clerk of Silver Bow County and the secretary of state. A list of equipment was attached to the statement filed with the secretary of state; no such list was attached to the one filed with the county clerk and recorder. No amounts being secured are shown on the statements but Mr. Pitts, Miners' president at the time, stated that they were designed to cover both loans. Witness Pitts testified that the lien of the $200,000 loan was first as to all equipment but that the $100,000 loan was first as to the accounts receivable and inventory.

Miners also took mortgages securing the $200,000 loan as follows: mortgage on New Butte's plant and a mortgage from Harold F. Schumacher and Loretta Schumacher covering their home and personal property. Securing the $100,000 loan Miners took a mortgage from New Butte to Miners covering the plant and equipment and a mortgage from the Schumachers covering their home and personal property.

In each instance the mortgage securing the $200,000 loan was filed first. None of these mortgages has been foreclosed.

Miners also filed a security agreement with the registrar of motor vehicles securing the $200,000 loan and also took an assignment on Schumacher's life insurance as security for the $200,000 loan. The policies were cashed for the cash value.

In December of 1969, New Butte closed down its operation for financial reasons. Operations were resumed in January 1970. At this time a financing firm, Douglas Guardian, with its program of warehousing receipts and accounts receivable financing became involved in cooperation with Miners and New Butte. Advances by Miners under the warehouse receipts plan approximated $390,000. The amounts advanced by Miners under the accounts receivable financing exceeded $400,000. The warehouse receipts program started January 15, 1970, and ended May 22, 1970; the accounts receivable financing covered a period from January 30, 1970, to May 11, 1970.

During the first seven months of 1970, the New Butte checking account was overdrawn in amounts ranging from nominal to as much as $55,000 for all but 87 of those days.

As of May 18, 1970, the $100,000 loan was current in payments. All payments on the $200,000 were made currently through May 28, 1970. On June 2, 1970, the SBA took over the assets of the business. Neither loan was in default at that time. On May 29, and June 1, 1970, Miners' president, Pitts, debited the New Butte account for $12,000 and $9,000 and credited those amounts to the $100,000 SBA loan.

Pitts admitted that he was looking carefully to the account on May 29, 1970, so that he could put in the withdrawal slip for $12,000 and be sure that Miners got ahead of anybody else. He stated that he personally handled the withdrawal.

As to the $9,000 withdrawal, Pitts testified that he kept strict watch of the account and when there was enough deposited, he personally put in a withdrawal slip. On June 18, 1970, Miners credited the $200,000 loan with $4,602, which represented 30% of the total of $15,342 as the result of a sale of equipment by New Butte. The proceeds were not deposited in New Butte's account but were applied directly to the $200,000 loan and that credit was enough to discharge in advance the principal and interest for six months. There was no foreclosure of the security interests nor were the proceeds of the sales placed into New Butte's account.

The bank in this instance knew of the condition of the account of New Butte, it had intimate knowledge of the transactions, it was the "on the ground" representative of the sister banks who shared in the loan and it had more than the usual normal interest in the activities of New Butte.

Plaintiffs brought this action against New Butte and Miners to recover the amounts of the checks plus interest and damages. After a trial without a jury in the second judicial district, Judge James D. Freebourn presiding, found for the plaintiffs against New Butte and found against the plaintiffs and for defendant

Miners. Plaintiffs appeal that part of the judgment which exculpated Miners.

Plaintiffs present five issues for review, which are summarized as follows: (1) Whether Miners is liable for holding the Beck check and the first Skaar check past the midnight deadline provided for in [UCC § 4–302], and (2) whether Miners is liable for holding all six of the checks past the midnight deadline as provided for in the statute. Plaintiffs' remaining issues involve the question of good faith, which the district court specifically found was exercised by Miners in its dealings with plaintiffs. The question of good faith will be considered in connection with plaintiffs' first two issues.

* * * The issues presented by plaintiffs are of first impression to this Court, and there are few cases in other jurisdictions which have construed the effect of the sections of the Uniform Commercial Code which are determinative of the issues presented for review.

Plaintiffs' first and second issues raise questions concerning Article 4 of the Uniform Commercial Code. (Hereafter, references to the Uniform Commercial Code will be made by the section number only; the title number will be omitted). Generally plaintiffs argue that Miners is liable for the face amount of the checks for not complying with what is commonly referred to as the "midnight deadline" rule. Defendant argues that with respect to the first issue section 4–108 is an exception to section 4–302 and with respect to the second issue section 4–103 is an exception to section 4–302 and under these sections Miners is not liable. Initially, we will generally discuss the construction of section 4–302, which provides:

"In the absence of a valid defense such as breach of a presentment warranty (subsection (1) of section 4–207), settlement effected or the like, if an item is presented on and received by a payor bank the bank is accountable for the amount of

"(a) a demand item other than a documentary draft whether properly payable or not if the bank, in any case where it is not also the depositary bank, retains the item beyond midnight of the banking day of receipt without settling for it or, regardless of whether it is also the depositary bank, does not pay or return the item or send notice of dishonor until after its midnight deadline; or * * * *."

The "midnight deadline" is midnight of the banking day following the day of the receipt of the item by the payor bank.

Section 4–104(1)(h). A payor bank is a bank by which an item is payable as drawn or accepted. Section 4–105(b). There is no question but that Miners is the payor bank. The checks involved herein are demand items. Section 4–104(1)(g) and section 3–104(1) and (2).

Section 4–302 was construed in the case of Rock Island Auction Sales v. Empire Packing Co., 32 Ill.2d 269, 204 N.E.2d 721, 18 A.L.R.3d 1368, where the Illinois court held that the word "accountable" in the statute is synonymous with "liable." We agree.

Essentially, section 4–302 says that in the absence of a valid defense, a demand item, retained beyond the "midnight deadline" by the payor bank without either paying, returning, or giving notice of dishonor renders the payor bank liable to the payee for the face amount of the item.

In addition, there is a fundamental requirement of good faith under the specific provision of section 1–201(19), which reads as follows:

" 'Good faith' means honesty in fact in the conduct or transaction concerned."

Furthermore, 1–203 provides:

"Every contract or duty within this act imposes an obligation of good faith in its performance or enforcement."

Plaintiffs' first issue concerns the Beck check dated April 28, 1970, and the first Skaar check dated April 14, 1970. These checks were submitted as cash items to Miners on May 11, 1970, and were not returned until May 13, 1970. Plaintiffs contend that because of the delay that Miners violated the "midnight deadline" rule. Facts not heretofore set forth relevant to this issue and undisputed are as follows:

The Computer Corporation of Montana, a data processing company, is a wholly owned subsidiary of Bancorporation of Montana which processed checks for eleven banks in the Bancorporation chain, including Miners. Items to be processed for Miners are sent to Computer Corporation in Great Falls by armored car between 5:00 p.m. and 6:00 p.m. of the day of receipt and are usually back at Miners by 8:00 a.m. the following morning. The checks normally reach Great Falls about 10:30 p.m. On May 11, 1970, the day on which Miners received the checks under discussion, the armored car broke down and did not reach Computer Corporation until 1:30 a.m. the morning of May 12, 1970. Ordinarily the work on Miners' checks would have been processed by

11:30 p.m.; the checks would have started back to Butte by armored car at 4:00 a.m. and have reached Miners at 7:00 a.m.

On the morning of May 12, 1970, the computer malfunctioned, and the checks which would have normally been returned to Miners on the morning of May 12, 1970, did not arrive until 2:30 p.m. that afternoon.

Ken Mahle, vice-president of Miners at the time of the trial, outlined the procedures which were followed each day after the receipt of the checks from the Computer Center. He could not, however, testify as to what occurred on May 12, 1970. There was no testimony as to what actually happened on the day after the checks were received by Miners.

Miners contend that it is this type of situation which section 4–108(2) was intended to cover. Section 4–108(2) provides:

"Delay by a collecting bank or payor bank beyond time limits prescribed or permitted by this act or by instructions is excused if caused by interruption of communication facilities, suspension of payments by another bank, war, emergency conditions or other circumstances beyond the control of the bank provided it exercises such diligence as the circumstances require."

The Official Code Comment on this point states:

"4.   Subsection (2) is another escape clause from time limits. This clause operates not only with respect to time limits imposed by the article itself but also time limits imposed by special instructions, by agreement or by Federal Reserve regulations or operating letters, clearing house rules or the like. The latter time limits are 'permitted' by the Code. This clause operates, however, only in the types of situation specified. Examples of these situations include blizzards, floods, or hurricanes, and other 'Act of God' events or conditions, and wrecks or disasters, interfering with mails; suspension of payments by another bank; abnormal operating conditions such as substantial increased volume or substantial shortage of personnel during war or emergency situations. *When delay is sought to be excused under this subsection the bank must 'exercise such diligence as the circumstances require' and it has the burden of proof.*" (Emphasis supplied.)   3 Anderson, Uniform Commercial Code 191.

The effect of section 4–108(2) is to excuse a payor bank from the standard of strict accountability of section 4–302 and to hold it to a standard of "diligence as the circumstances require."

Under section 4–108(2) there must be a showing that the circumstances were beyond the control of the bank and that the bank exercised such diligence as the circumstances require. As the Official Code Comment states, the burden is on the bank.

The district court found that Miners' failure to pay or return the checks or to give notice of dishonor within the prescribed time was due to circumstances beyond its control. The district court also found that Miners exercised the required diligence and that no evidence was introduced showing that Miners failed to exercise due care.

The evidence as to the events in question is undisputed. This Court in In re Wadsworth's Estate, 92 Mont. 135, 150, 11 P.2d 788, 792 stated:

> " * * * But where, as here, there is no dispute as to the facts, this court is in as favorable a position in applying the law as the district court, and in such instances will not hesitate to do so. (Citing authority.) And a judgment or order unsupported by the evidence will be reversed on appeal to this court. (Citing authority.)"

The only evidence produced by Miners was what the ordinary operating procedures were.

As we have heretofore stated, Miners had more than the usual normal interest in the activities of New Butte. It necessarily follows that under the circumstances of this case that the degree of diligence required under 4–108(2) is greater than under normal circumstances.

Miners argues that the testimony of Mahle as to normal operating procedures constitutes a showing of due diligence. While there may be instances where a showing as to what occurs on a normal operating day may constitute a showing of diligence under circumstances where the delay is similar as to the one in the instant case, this case is not one of those instances. Miners' interest in New Butte was more than usual, and a showing of diligence by Miners required more than testimony as to what the normal operating procedures were. Miners' burden under the circumstances of this case is greater for the reason that its relationship and interest in New Butte was significantly more than ordinary. Miners did not meet its burden as imposed by section 4–108(2).

Under the exception of section 4–108(2) the bank must show: (1) A cause for the delay; (2) that the cause was beyond the control of the bank; and (3) that under the circumstances the bank exercised such diligence as required. In the absence of any one of these showings, the excuse for the delay will not apply, and the bank will be held liable under the provisions of section 4–302. Since Miners did not meet its burden, it is therefore liable for the face amount of the Beck check and the first Skaar check under the strict accountability rule of section 4–302.

Having illustrated that Miners had more than a normal interest in the activities of New Butte and that the exception of 4–108(2) is not applicable herein, we now consider plaintiff's second issue which concerns all six checks. For the reason that we have found in considering plaintiff's issue No. 1 that liability attached as to the Beck check and the first Skaar check as of May 13, 1970, under section 4–302, our consideration of the second issue will be with reference to the remaining four checks. The second Skaar check and the first Sun River check were ultimately sent to Miners "for collection". The second and third Sun River checks were sent directly to Miners for collection. The second Skaar check was received by Miners on May 20, 1970, and retained until July 27, 1970, a period of more than two months. The three Sun River checks were never returned by Miners.

Plaintiffs contend that Miners, the payor bank, may not become a collecting bank and therefore, cannot take a check for collection and hold the same beyond the regular midnight deadline. Plaintiffs rely upon the following cases:

In *Rock Island* the seller of cattle received the buyer's $14,706.90 check on the same day. On that day the seller deposited the check in seller's bank and it was received by the payor bank on Thursday, three days later. The buyer's account in the payor bank was inadequate to pay the check, and the payor bank, relying on the buyer's assurances that additional funds would be deposited, held the check until the following Tuesday, when it marked the check "not sufficient funds", placed it in the mail to a Federal Reserve Bank and sent notice of dishonor by telegram to the Federal Reserve Bank. The court held the payor bank liable for the amount of the item under section 4–302.

Section 4–302 was also involved in the case of Farmers Coop. Livestock Mkt. v. Second Nat. Bank, 427 S.W.2d 247 (Ky.1968). The buyer's alleged agent signed a draft in the amount of $7,687.01 payable to the seller. The instrument was drawn on the defendant bank and contained the notation " 'To (be) charged to Acct. of Robert Martin' ". It was deposited with Northwestern Bank and sent by Northwestern direct to defendant bank on

October 1, with an accompanying letter. The letter, among other things, stated:

"'We enclose for collection   *   *   *'

"'Wire non-payment of items $1,000.00 or over.'

"'Please send us your draft.'

"'Please wire if unpaid upon arrival, but hold for payment with advice to us.   *   *   *'"

The instrument was received by defendant bank on October 4, and although there were sufficient funds in Martin's account to pay the check, defendant bank had not been authorized by Martin to make payment, so no charge was made to his account. No wire was sent to Northwestern as Northwestern had requested. On October 6, Northwestern called the defendant bank and "'was told that Martin had not come into the bank to authorize payment of the instrument in question.'" It was undisputed that the defendant bank had failed to take action before the "midnight deadline."

There was a dispute as to whether the instrument was a "check" or a "draft." The Court said that this was an immaterial distinction and that the important question was whether the instrument was a demand item referred to in section 4–302(a). The Court quoted the definition of an "item", and said a demand item would obviously be one on demand, and held the instrument in this case was a demand item. The Court also held that the defendant bank was clearly the "payor" bank and clearly liable for the amount of the item.

The defendant bank contended that it was a collecting bank because the letter accompanying the draft contained the words, "'We enclose for collection   *   *   *'", and the defendant bank treated the item as a collection item. In this regard, the Court on page 250 said:

"*   *   * The use of the term 'collection' in the letter certainly cannot be said to have destroyed the statutory scheme governing the collection process. The letter also said 'Please wire if unpaid upon arrival.' This draft was presented for *payment.* (Had appellee wired as instructed, it would have discharged its duty as the payor bank and subsequent action to settle this account would have been governed by other considerations.) With respect to how appellee treated this item, we can only say that it took the risk of loss by failure to comply with the law.   *   *   *"

Miners asserts several reasons why it is not liable under section 4–302. The first of these is that section 3–511(4) excuses notice of dishonor where a check has been presented to the bank and payment refused at least once before. Miners argues that the "midnight deadline" rule does not apply and relies on Leaderbrand v. Central State Bank of Wichita, 202 Kan. 450, 450 P.2d 1. Section 3–511(4) provides:

"Where a draft has been dishonored by nonacceptance a later presentment for payment and any notice of dishonor and protest for nonpayment are excused unless in the meantime the instrument has been accepted."

The Kansas court in *Leaderbrand* held that under section 3–511, once notice of dishonor had been given, an additional notice of dishonor was not required. In Wiley v. Peoples Bank and Trust Company, 5 Cir., 438 F.2d 513, the court rejected *Leaderbrand* and held section 3–511(4) inapplicable for the reason that "acceptance applies only to time items. It has nothing to do with demand items." Likewise, we hold that section 3–511(4) is inapplicable to the checks under consideration herein, for section 3–511(4) does not apply to demand items.

Another reason contended by Miners takes into consideration the practice of submitting checks "for collection". It is Miners' position that any obligation it may have had to observe the midnight deadline rule was negated under section 4–103 by specific agreement between the parties and by a general custom and practice within the banking industry for the handling of checks sent for collection. Section 4–103 provides in part:

"*Variation by agreement—measure of damages—certain action constituting ordinary care.* (1) The effect of the provisions of this chapter may be varied by agreement except that no agreement can disclaim a bank's responsibility for its own lack of good faith or failure to exercise ordinary care or can limit the measure of damages for such lack or failure; but the parties may by agreement determine the standards by which such responsibility is to be measured if such standards are not manifestly unreasonable.

"(2) Federal Reserve regulations and operating letters, clearinghouse rules, and the like, have the effect of agreements under subsection (1), whether or not specifically assented to by all parties interested in items handled.

"(3) Action or nonaction approved by this chapter or pursuant to Federal Reserve regulations or operating letters constitute the exercise of ordinary care and, in the absence of special instructions, action or nonaction consistent with clearinghouse rules and the like or with a general banking usage not disapproved by this chapter, prima facie constitutes the exercise of ordinary care."

It is plaintiffs' position that since the checks here are demand items any agreement to vary the terms of section 4–302 is directly contrary to the express terms of the instruments. While section 4–302 holds a payor bank strictly liable, section 4–103 is clearly designed to make an exception to section 4–302 by agreement between the parties.

As the Official Code Comment states:

" *   *   *   Section 4–103 states the specific rules for variation of Article 4 by agreement and also certain standards of ordinary care. In view of the technical complexity of the field of bank collections, the enormous number of items handled by banks, the certainty that there will be variations from the normal in each day's work in each bank, the certainty of changing conditions and the possibility of developing improved methods of collection to speed the process, it would be unwise to freeze present methods of operation by mandatory statutory rules. This section, therefore, permits within wide limits variation of provisions of the Article by agreement." 3 Anderson, Uniform Commercial Code 165.

The question then becomes whether under the circumstances of the instant case there was an agreement between the parties excepting Miners from the strict liability rule of 4–302.

The district court found that a prior course of dealing between plaintiffs and Miners shows the existence of an agreement. The definition of an agreement as used herein is found in section 1–201(3) where it states:

" 'Agreement' means the bargain of the parties in fact as found in their language or by implication from other circumstances *including course of dealing* or usage of trade or course of performance as provided in this act (sections 87A–1–205 and 87A–2–208). Whether an agreement has legal consequences is determined by the provisions of this act, if applicable; otherwise by the law of contracts (section 87A–1–103)." (Emphasis supplied.)

Section 1–205(1) provides as to course of dealing:

> "A course of dealing is a sequence of previous conduct between the parties to a particular transaction which is fairly to be regarded as establishing a common basis of understanding for interpreting their expressions and other conduct."

Miners has attempted to establish a course of dealing as to plaintiff Sun River and plaintiff Skaar because each had one check sent for collection paid from the New Butte account after being held past the "midnight deadline." The holding and paying of one check is not sufficient to form "a sequence of previous conduct" which is necessary to establish a course of dealing.

In addition, the Uniform Commercial Code does not contemplate that the course of dealing may constitute the entire agreement, but merely gives meaning to or supplements the express terms of an existing agreement. See 1 Anderson, Uniform Commercial Code 175, 176. Miners could show but one previous transaction—clearly insufficient to establish a course of dealing.

Miners also claims that Sun River used its banker, Malcolm Adams of the First National Bank of Great Falls, as its agent and that because Adams understood that the check would be held by Miners that this constituted an agreement. This asserted agreement between Miners and Sun River is ineffective in view of the fact of Miners' obvious lack of fairness and the standard imposed upon it by its own more than normal relationship with New Butte. Contrary to the district court's finding of good faith, it is this Court's view that Miners did not act in compliance with fair dealings contemplated by the Uniform Commercial Code.

We present this question: How effective or reliable may an agreement be, assuming there is one, when the bank's president, himself, is looking closely to the account and withdraws money therefrom for purposes of applying the money to a loan which is not in default? It is true that a bank may have the right of setoff or may pay checks in any order that it chooses (section 4–303) or a secured party may upon default take possession of collateral without judicial process and dispose of it in any commercially reasonable fashion (sections 9–503 and 9–504). Under the facts here, however, Miners' unique position with relation to New Butte establishes a standard of care greater than under normal situations, and for any agreement to come within the exception in this case requires more than what Adams may have understood. In addition, Miners cannot shield itself by asserting that the alleged agreement is an exception in light of its own lack of fairness.

While Miners stood in an advantageous position with respect to its own interests, these plaintiffs stood with no recourse whatsoever after having provided essential inventory, namely cattle, for the operations of New Butte.

In its argument Miners also claims that oral notice of dishonor was given to plaintiff Skaar with respect to the check under consideration. Whereas, under sections 4–104(3) and 3–508, oral notice of dishonor may be sufficient to meet the requirements of section 4–302, the circumstances here required more than oral notice. In one conversation that Skaar had with Pitts on May 11, 1970, Pitts indicated that the checks would clear because things were looking better. Pitts did indicate, however, that it was going to take time. In view of what subsequently happened, any notice given to Skaar or purported agreement between Miners and Skaar under the facts here are not sufficient to release Miners from the strict liability rule of 4–302.

Defendant's final contention is that strict compliance with section 4–302 is also varied by custom and practice. The district court found that the established custom and practice followed by the banking industry in Montana in handling checks "for collection" in the absence of special instructions and writing is to hold the check for an arbitrary length of time.

We have heretofore established that there was no agreement between the parties which varied the provisions of section 4–302. In the absence of an agreement the strict liability rule of section 4–302 applies. Custom and practice is relevant under section 4–103(3), if at all, only with respect to the establishment of what standard constitutes ordinary care. The standard of care imposed upon Miners in the instant case was more than ordinary, and therefore, custom and practice are not relevant.

Clearly, the four checks under consideration herein are subject to the rule of section 4–302. Miners cannot now claim that the statute is varied either by agreement as provided in 4–103 or by custom and practice, particularly where Miners has assumed a position in relation to its customer, New Butte, which imposes a greater standard of care and responsibility than under normal situations. Miners cannot prevail in its argument when it has demonstrated a disregard for good faith dealings contemplated by the Uniform Commercial Code.

For the foregoing reasons, the judgment of the district court is reversed.

NOTES

1.   In Port City State Bank v. American National Bank, 486 F.2d 196 (10th Cir.1973), American National decided to phase out its manual bookkeeping system and to replace it with a computerized operation.   With prudence worthy of a banker, it "paralleled" its manual system with the computer system for two weeks.   Finally the manual bookkeeping equipment was removed, and on December 1 (Monday) the computer took over. At approximately 10:00 a.m. on December 1, the computer developed a "memory error."   Despite assurances from the manufacturer that repairs would not take "too long," they were not completed until early morning on Tuesday.   In the belief that the computer would soon be repaired, the bank did nothing about processing Monday's business until late that night when bank personnel took the items to a back-up computer installation 2½ hours away.   They worked through the night until told their own computer was operational again, whereupon they returned to the bank and the computer promptly had another memory failure.   Work on Monday's business was finally completed on Tuesday night on the back-up system, and the midnight deadline was missed.   The court held that the bank had used sufficient diligence under UCC § 4–108(2) to be excused.   What else could the bank have done in the *Sun River* case?

2.   Under UCC § 4–302(a) a bank is not accountable for the amount of a "documentary draft" (UCC § 4–105) by retention beyond its midnight deadline.   For a discussion of the meaning of "documentary draft" with respect to UCC § 4–302, see Wiley v. Peoples Bank & Trust Co., 438 F.2d 513 (5th Cir.1971).

NEVADA STATE BANK v. FISCHER

Supreme Court of Nevada, 1977.
565 P.2d 332.

THOMPSON, JUSTICE.   The Nevada State Bank charged Lucile Fischer's account $2,000 when it received notice that a check in that amount, endorsed by her, had been dishonored.   Therefore, she commenced this action against the Bank for wrongfully so debiting her account.

The district court ruled that her liability as endorser was discharged since notice of dishonor was not timely given her. Judgment was entered in her favor together with interest, costs, and attorney fees. The Bank appeals from that judgment. We affirm.

The facts are not disputed. On May 1, 1970, Mrs. Fischer endorsed a $2,000 check payable to the drawer and drawn on the Clayton Bank of Clayton, Missouri. She did this as an accommodation to the payee-drawer. The Nevada State Bank cashed the check for the payee-drawer and initiated collection through Valley Bank of Nevada that same day.

On July 28, 1970, the Valley Bank of Nevada notified Nevada State Bank that the check had been dishonored stating "original lost in transit—account closed." On July 29, 1970, the Nevada State Bank debited Mrs. Fischer's account for $2,000 and notified her in writing of the payor bank's dishonor of the check.

The record does not disclose which of the several banks involved in the collection process either lost the check or delayed action with regard to it. It is clear, however, that Nevada State Bank acted promptly upon receiving notice of dishonor. Whether it was permissible in these circumstances for that bank to charge its innocent depositor rather than to look to one of the other banks involved is the issue for our decision.

1. Lucile Fischer endorsed the check as an accommodation party and is liable in the capacity in which she signed. [UCC § 3–415]. By endorsing the check she engaged that upon dishonor and any necessary notice of dishonor and protest, she would pay the instrument according to the tenor at the time of her endorsement. [UCC § 3–414(1)].

An endorser is a secondary party, [UCC § 3–102(1)(d)], whose liability is subject to the preconditions of presentment, [UCC § 3–501(2)(b)], and proper notice of dishonor, [UCC § 3–501(2)(a)]. Where, without excuse, any necessary presentment or notice of dishonor is delayed beyond the time it is due, an endorser is discharged. Such is the command of [UCC § 3–502(1)].

It is the contention of Nevada State Bank that since it initiated collection within one day of the endorsement and notified the endorser of dishonor within one day of receipt of such notice by it, "delay" does not exist and Mrs. Fischer, as endorser, is not discharged from liability.

An uncertified check must be presented for payment, or collection initiated thereon, within a reasonable time, which in this case is presumed to be seven days. [UCC § 3–503(2)(b).] Although the record does not advise us when presentment was made to the proper party, [UCC § 3–504], we do know that Nevada State Bank initiated collection within one day after cashing the check. Consequently, bank collection was timely initiated.

In our view, however, the second precondition to liability of the endorser, that is, timely notice of dishonor, was not met. Although the Nevada State Bank notified Mrs. Fischer within its midnight deadline, [UCC § 4–104(1)(h)], after receipt of notice of dishonor from Valley Bank of Nevada, this fact, alone, does not resolve the timeliness issue.

The record does not disclose at what point in time the check first was dishonored. We know only that almost ninety days elapsed between Mrs. Fischer's endorsement of the check and her receipt of notice of its dishonor. It is apparent that one of the several banks involved in the collection process violated its midnight deadline in giving notice of dishonor. Had such bank given timely notice, Mrs. Fischer would have learned within a reasonable time that the check had been dishonored.

Prompt action by all parties to the transaction is contemplated before an endorser may be held liable. As stated in the official comment to sec. 3–503 of Uniform Commercial Code:

> "The endorser who has normally merely received the check and passed it on and does not expect to have to pay it, is entitled to know more promptly whether it is to be dishonored, in order that he may have recourse against the person with whom he has dealt."

As already expressed, at sometime in the chain of collection a midnight deadline was violated. Notwithstanding such violation, we are asked to conclude that notice of dishonor given ninety days after initiation of bank collection was timely. We decline to so conclude. Mrs. Fischer's liability as an endorser was discharged when the violation of the midnight deadline by a bank, identity unknown, resulted in unreasonable delay in notice of dishonor. The Nevada State Bank may look to the violator for its recovery. Cf. Fromer Distributor's Inc. v. Bankers Trust Company, 36 A.D.2d 840, 321 N.Y.S.2d 428 (1971). Its customer-endorser should not be held responsible for a violation of law committed by another bank involved in the chain of collection.

Affirmed.

NOTE

The court assumed that "at sometime in the chain of collections a midnight deadline was violated." This may or may not have been the case. What is the effect on the rights of Depositary Bank and Customer in each of the following assumptions that could have explained the delay: (1) Payor Bank delayed in dishonoring the check. UCC § 4–213(1)(d). (2) Payor Bank dishonored promptly but a collecting bank delayed in reversing a provisional credit and returning the item. UCC § 4–212(1). (3) Payor Bank dishonored promptly and all banks acted promptly after dishonor, but, after collection was initiated, one of the collecting banks delayed in sending the item on for collection. UCC § 3–503(2); § 4–202(1)(a) and (2); and § 4–103(5). (4) All banks acted promptly in forwarding the item for collection and in returning the item; the delay was caused by a delay in delivery of the mails.

B. CHECKS WITH FORGED OR UNAUTHORIZED SIGNATURE OF DRAWER AND STOP PAYMENT ORDERS

1. RIGHTS OF DRAWER AND DRAWEE

K & K MANUFACTURING, INC. v. UNION BANK

Court of Appeals of Arizona, Division 2, 1981.
129 Ariz. 7, 628 P.2d 44.

HATHAWAY, CHIEF JUDGE. In this case we must apply articles three and four of the Uniform Commercial Code to determine who should bear the risk of loss when a dishonest employee forges her employer's name as drawer on a number of checks on his business and personal checking accounts, then appropriates the proceeds for her personal use.

Appellant Bill J. Knight is the president and majority stockholder of both K & K Manufacturing, Inc. and Knight Foundry & Manufacturing, Inc. Knight Foundry employed about 80 people at the time of trial, while K & K Manufacturing, which was formed to accomplish the contracting, buying and selling for the foundry business, employed only two persons when the events which form the basis of this action occurred. These two employ-

ees were Knight and a bookkeeper, Eleanor Garza. The bookkeeper's duties at K & K Manufacturing were very broad, including picking up the company mail and Knight's personal mail
from a common post office box, preparing checks for Knight's
signature to pay both company and personal bills, and making
entries in a cash disbursement journal reflecting the expenses
for which the checks were written. Most importantly, it was her
responsibility to reconcile the monthly statements prepared and
sent by appellee Union Bank, where Knight kept both his business and personal checking and savings accounts. No one
shared these duties with Miss Garza.

Between March 1977 and January 1978, Miss Garza forged
Knight's signature on some 66 separate checks drawn on his
personal or business accounts at Union Bank. The majority of
these checks were made payable to her. The total amount of
the forgeries on the K & K Manufacturing account was
$49,859.31. The total on Knight's personal account was $11,350.
The bank paid each such check and Miss Garza received or was
credited with the proceeds.

We need not concentrate on the details of the fraud, except
to comment that it proved to be effective for nearly one year.
Miss Garza assured that the disbursement journal balanced by
overstating legitimate expenditures, forging checks to herself
for the difference, and later showing the forged check as "void."
Upon receipt of appellee's monthly statement and cancelled
checks, she removed and concealed the bad checks. The proceeds from most of the forgeries were deposited directly into her
personal account rather than taken in cash. She usually presented the bad checks to the bank tellers with numerous authorized checks, and spread her banking transactions among several
tellers so that no one teller knew the extent of her business.

Eventually, an in-house audit showed the discrepancies in the
1977 disbursements. Appellants brought this action against appellee for breach of contract, seeking repayment of the funds
the bank paid out on checks with unauthorized signatures. After a court trial, judgment was entered in favor of appellant
Knight for $5,500, representing the amount paid out of his per-
sonal account on forged checks from March 28 to May 20, 1977.
This figure included eight forged checks paid by the bank prior
to the mailing of its monthly statement containing a record of
the payments and the checks themselves to Knight on May 6,
plus a 14-day period. Since no forged checks on the K & K Manufacturing account were paid prior to May 20, judgment was en-

tered for appellee against it.   In addition, the trial court made
findings of fact and conclusions of law.   Both Knight and K & K
Manufacturing have appealed.

Appellants contend that findings 13, 14 and 15 are not supported by the evidence.   They argue the record shows their actions were not negligent and that the bank's practices and procedures were negligent as a matter of law.   The disputed findings
are as follows:

"13. Defendant bank [appellee] paid all the checks in good
faith and in accordance with reasonable commercial standards.

14. Defendant bank did not fail to exercise ordinary care in
paying the checks.

15. The plaintiffs [appellants] did not exercise reasonable
care and promptness to examine the bank statements and
cancelled checks in order to discover the forgeries."

Our duty begins and ends with the inquiry of whether the
trial court had before it evidence which reasonably supports its
actions, viewed in a light most favorable to sustaining its findings.   United Bank v. Mesa N.O. Nelson Co., 121 Ariz. 438, 590
P.2d 1384 (1979).   We will not weigh conflicting evidence or set
aside the trial court's findings unless they are clearly erroneous.
Id.   The determination of which actions are commercially reasonable and what constitutes ordinary care on the part of the
bank, as well as reasonable care and promptness on the part of
the depositor, are questions of fact for the trier of fact.   See
West Penn Administration, Inc. v. Union National Bank, 233 Pa.
Super. 311, 335 A.2d 725 (1975).

The concept of which party bears the loss in a forgery situation such as the one presented here is addressed in articles three
and four of the Uniform Commercial Code, covering commercial
paper and bank deposits and collections.

* * *

[The Court quotes UCC § 4–406.]

These provisions impose a duty on the depositor to check his
monthly statement for unauthorized signatures or alterations on
checks.   If the depositor fails to do so, after the first forged
check and statement relating thereto is sent to him, plus a reasonable period not exceeding 14 days, he is precluded from asserting the unauthorized signature or alteration against the
bank.   U.C.C. Sec. 4–406, comment 3.   The burden of proof of
depositor's negligence is on the bank.   Even if the bank suc-

ceeds in establishing the depositor's negligence, if the customer establishes that the bank failed to exercise ordinary care in paying the bad checks, the preclusion rule of [UCC § 4–406(2)] does not apply. U.C.C. Sec. 4–406, comment 4.

We first address the issue of whether appellee met its burden of proof of showing that appellants failed to exercise * * * "reasonable care and promptness" in examining the monthly statements. The record shows that appellants trusted Miss Garza completely with both writing checks and reconciling the monthly statements. No spot checks were made by Knight or the controller at Knight Foundry, both of whom had access to the banking records. Knight was informed by a bank officer that his personal account was overdrawn on 12 occasions in 1977, yet did nothing to discover the reasons therefor. Knight testified he was aware Miss Garza's work was often inaccurate as well as tardy in 1977 and 1978.

Appellants argue they were not negligent in relying on a previously honest employee, citing Jackson v. First National Bank, 55 Tenn.App. 545, 403 S.W.2d 109 (1966). We decline to follow *Jackson*, which held, contrary to the bulk of authority that since a defalcating financial secretary had been a longtime faithful and trusted member of the church he cheated, the church could not be found negligent. Misplaced confidence in an employee will not excuse a depositor from the duty of notifying the bank of alterations on items paid from the depositor's account. Bank of Thomas County v. Dekle, 119 Ga.App. 753, 168 S.E.2d 834 (1969); Westport Bank and Trust Co. v. Lodge, 164 Conn. 604, 325 A.2d 222 (1973); Rainbow Inn, Inc. v. Clayton National Bank, 86 N.J.Super. 13, 205 A.2d 753 (1964); Kiernan v. Union Bank, 55 Cal.App.3d 111, 127 Cal.Rptr. 441 (1976). We adopt the majority view that the depositor is chargeable with the knowledge of all facts a reasonable and prudent examination of his bank statement would have disclosed if made by an honest employee. Pine Bluff National Bank v. Kesterson, 257 Ark. 813, 520 S.W.2d 253 (1975); Exchange Bank & Trust Co. v. Kidwell Construction Co., 463 S.W.2d 465 (Tex.Civ.App.1971); Faber v. Edgewater National Bank, 101 N.J.Super. 354, 244 A.2d 339 (1968); J. White & R. Summers, Uniform Commercial Code, 630 (2nd ed. 1980). The trial court's finding number 15 is amply supported by the evidence.

Secondly, we turn to the question of whether appellants met their burden of proof of demonstrating appellee did not exercise ordinary care in paying the bad checks, and did not act in good faith and in accordance with reasonable commercial standards. There appears to be no dispute regarding the good faith of appellee in paying the forgeries. The issue is whether its method of ascertaining unauthorized signatures on its depositor's checks met the standard of care under the circumstances.

Implied in the debtor/creditor relationship between a bank and its checking account depositor is the contractual undertaking on the part of the bank that it will only discharge its obligations to the depositor upon his authorized signature. Hennesy Equipment Sales Co. v. Valley National Bank, 25 Ariz.App. 285, 543 P.2d 123 (1975). The mere fact that the bank has paid a forged check does not mean the bank has breached its duty of ordinary care, however. See Comment, 12 Ariz.L.Rev. 417, 425 (1970).

At trial, an operations officer for appellee testified as to the methods employed during the period the forgeries occurred to discover unauthorized signatures on depositor's checks. She testified that checks were organized so that a bundle from the same account could be compared with the authorized signature on the bank's signature card. A staff of five filing clerks handled an average of approximately 1,000 checks each per hour in this manner. She testified it was common for a file clerk to become familiar with the drawer's signature in large accounts such as appellants'. An official of a large Arizona bank testified that tellers and file clerks are not trained to be handwriting experts. He testified that in his opinion, because most large banks have completely abandoned physical comparison of checks with the signature card, the system employed by appellee was better than the norm of the banking community in Southern Arizona.

In view of this and other evidence, we conclude that there was sufficient evidence to support findings 13 and 14 and the judgment entered below. Similar methods of comparing drawer's signatures have been upheld as constituting ordinary care and being within reasonable commercial standards across the country. See Nu-Way Services Inc. v. Mercantile Trust Co. National Association, 530 S.W.2d 743 (Mo.App.1975); Huber Glass Co. v. First National Bank, 29 Wis.2d 106, 138 N.W.2d 157 (1965); Terry v. Puget Sound National Bank, 80 Wash.2d 157, 492 P.2d 534 (1972); Parsons Travel, Inc. v. Hoag, 18 Wash.App. 588, 570 P.2d 445 (1977). Appellant Knight and his controller admitted the forgeries were quite good. Appellants also argue that because the bank tellers recognized Miss Garza was cashing large checks made to herself and her boyfriend and that she was driving an expensive sports car, they had a further duty to check the validity of the drawer's signature. This evidence was balanced by testimony that Miss Garza thoroughly explained the reasons for the large checks as increased salary, bonuses, and payment of Knight's expenses while he was out of town. Knight and Miss Garza were in the bank together on a regular basis and the tellers knew Miss Garza was authorized to handle large amounts of Knight's money. See Cooper v. Union Bank, 9 Cal.3d 123, 371, 507 P.2d 609, 107 Cal.Rptr. 1 (1973).

* * *

Affirmed.

NOTES

1. UCC § 4–401 states that a bank may charge its customer's account the amount of any item that is "properly payable." The corollary is that the customer's account may not be charged for items not properly payable. A check is simply an order by the customer to the bank to pay. If the signature on the check is a forgery or is not authorized by the drawer no order to pay by the drawer has been made and the check is not properly payable. Compare UCC § 3–401 and the material on signatures by representatives in Chapter 2.

2. The court allowed the customer to recover for forged checks on Knight's personal account paid prior to May 20, the 14th day after the bank statement was mailed to Knight. No recovery was allowed for any forged checks on the K and K account since no forged checks on that account were paid prior to May 20. Is this result supported by the language of UCC § 4–406?

3. As the court indicates there is some disagreement in the courts on the question of what constitutes "reasonable care and promptness" by the customer in discovering the unauthorized signature and in notifying the bank when the wrongdoer is the person designated by the customer to check the monthly statement. Under UCC § 1–201(27) the customer would seem to be bound by the information supplied by the bank when that information reaches the customer's employee who is authorized to receive it and act on it. Under the law of agency, if that employee fails to notify the bank of the forgery the customer should be bound by the employee's conduct regardless of whether the employee's failure to notify is due to negligence or is the deliberate act of the employee to cover up his own wrongdoing. The issue should not be whether the customer was negligent in the proce-

dure chosen for reviewing the bank statements if the employee
receiving and acting on the statements was the designated agent
of the customer for that purpose. See Seavey, Notice Through
An Agent, 65 U. of Pa.L.Rev. 1, 7–8 (1916).

4. UCC § 3–406 recognizes a duty on the part of the drawee
bank to act according to reasonable commercial standards. UCC
§ 4–406 recognizes a duty of the drawee to use ordinary care in
paying the item. Under either section the bank's failure to meet
the standard precludes it from asserting the conduct of the customer as a defense to its wrongful payment. Why is this duty
imposed on the bank? Suppose Drawee paid a series of checks
bearing the forged signature of Employer. All of the checks
were payable to Employee, who was the forger, and were deposited in another bank in which Employee had an account. An employee of the bank examined each check but did not detect the
forgery. Case # 1. The forgery was crudely made and did not
resemble Drawer's specimen signature. Case # 2. The forgery
was skillfully done and was very difficult to detect. In each
case assume that the checks in issue were paid more than two
weeks after the bank made available to Employer a monthly
statement enclosing similarly-forged checks that it had paid, and
before Employer notified the bank of any forgery. What should
be the liability of the bank in each case? It is indicated in the
principal case that "most large banks have completely abandoned physical comparison of checks with the signature card."
This practice is apparently followed because the cost of checking
signatures exceeds the dollar amount of forged checks which
are an insignificant percentage of all checks processed. Suppose in our two hypothetical cases that the bank was among
those that did not check signatures of checks. Would this fact
change your answers? What is the effect of UCC § 4–103(3)?
If the cost of checking signatures exceeds losses on forged
checks what is the effect of imposing a duty of care on the
bank? How should that duty of care be defined?

5. In Pine Bluff National Bank v. Kesterson, 257 Ark. 813,
520 S.W.2d 253 (1975), the bank paid checks of a trust bearing
the signatures of two trustees. There were three trustees of
the trust and the agreement with the bank required the signatures of all three on checks. The court held that the authorized
signature of the trust was comprised of the signature of all
three trustees; therefore, the bank paid checks bearing an unauthorized signature of the trust and UCC § 4–406 applied. Wolfe
v. University National Bank, 270 Md. 70, 310 A.2d 558 (1973),
represents a contrary view. In that case the customer, a part-

nership, agreed with its bank that all checks drawn on the partnership account had to be signed by two of the three partners.
The bank paid out on 37 checks signed by only one partner.
Customer brought suit nearly two years after the last check in
issue was written, and the bank claimed the one-year limitation
in UCC § 4–406(4) barred the action. The court disagreed stating: "UCC § 4–406 is inapplicable here because it is only concerned with unauthorized signatures and alterations. An 'unauthorized signature' 'means one made without actual, implied or
apparent authority and includes a forgery,' UCC § 1–201(43)
* * * The signatures of the * * * [the partners who
signed] were not forged, not made without authority, nor did
they constitute an alteration of any kind."   310 A.2d at 560.
The court saw the infirmity not as the presence of an unauthorized signature but the absence of a second authorized signature. In deciding whether the bank is entitled to the protection
of UCC § 4–406 is there any rational basis for distinguishing between a forged signature and a signature, though not a forgery,
which does not authorize the bank to make the payment? In
Madison Park Bank v. Field, 64 Ill.App.3d 838, 21 Ill.Dec. 583,
381 N.E.2d 1030 (1978), the court suggests the following: "Had
this statute been intended to include protection to a bank where
there is an absence of a signature such could have been written
into the law. That such a provision is not in the law is readily
understandable since an unauthorized, altered or forged signature would be more readily discoverable by a depositor; however, discovering a missing signature places no undue onus on a
bank. All that would be necessary on the part of the bank to
check the correct number of signatures on a check would be a
quick perusal of the signature card in the bank's possession."
Is this observation valid considering the trend of banks to dis-
continue entirely the uneconomic procedure of comparing checks
to the signature card?

PROBLEM

Company required two signatures on its checks, those of its
president and treasurer. The latter forged the president's signature and signed his own name, on five checks payable to his
own order which he deposited in his depositary bank. You may
assume that the checks were paid by the payor bank on January
5, February 5, March 5, April 5, and May 5. Each check was
returned in groups of other cancelled checks to the company
some 10 days after it was paid by the payor. The treasurer was
the only employee of the company who saw the returned can-

celled checks. The forgery of the president's name on the third
check was not up to the treasurer's usual high artistic standards; in fact, it was an obvious forgery. The other forgeries
were quite good. The treasurer's wrong-doing was finally discovered in June when he withdrew his large account from the
depositary bank and left town for parts unknown. For which
checks should the payor bank be liable to the company? See
UCC § 4–406.

2. CHECK PROCESSING

We have remarked that the existing check processing system
in which checks are physically moved through the banking system from the depositary bank to the drawee bank and then back
to the drawer is very expensive. The first major improvement
in the check processing system was the development of "magnetic ink character recognition" (MICR) in the 1950s. Under
this system magnetically-encoded, machine-readable information
was placed on checks that allowed the checks to be handled by
reader sorter machines. Look at your canceled checks and note
the numbers in the special type font at the bottom of the check.

Financial institutions are now experimenting with check truncation systems designed to reduce or abolish the physical delivery of checks through the banking system.[1] The technology
now exists (called "imaging") for the depositary bank to send
electronically to the drawee bank information including the two
banks' identification numbers, the dollar amount and number of
the checks, the date of the check, the payee's name, and an im-
age of the drawer's signature. The drawee can make its decision to pay the check based on this electronic data. The depositary bank then microfilms the check and destroys the original.
The drawer receives a periodic statement with the check number, dollar amount, and, perhaps, the payee's name.

The ultimate truncation system described above is not yet in
effect for it would require an elaborate electronic link-up system
between banks that is not now in existence. But more simple
systems are growing more common in which the drawee bank
receives the checks from the depositary bank but retains them
and sends the customer only a periodic statement containing information about those checks paid from his account.

---

1. This discussion is based on Penney & Baker, The Law of Electronic
Fund Transfer Systems pp. 2–1 to
2–12 (1980).

The question arises how check truncation affects the duty of the customer under UCC § 4–406 to examine his bank statement to discover unauthorized signatures and alterations. See Comment 2 to UCC § 4–406. Under the simple truncation system, the drawee retains the checks; under the complex system the depositary bank retains them. Under the simple system the drawee bank may be said to be holding the "items pursuant to a request or instructions of the customer." Under the complex system it is difficult to say that the drawee bank has activated the customer's duty to examine his statement for forgeries under UCC § 4–406 unless a court were willing to read "item" to include the electronic information about the check in drawee's possession. Presumably, unless the drawee sends the items to the customer or holds them for the customer, the customer has no duty to look for forgeries under UCC § 4–406 and notify the bank of them.

3. RIGHTS OF DRAWEE AND HOLDER: FINALITY OF PAYMENT

a. UNAUTHORIZED SIGNATURE OF DRAWER

We have seen that if the name of the ostensible drawer of a check is forged the drawer is not liable on the check and the drawee to whom the check is directed is not authorized to debit the account of the ostensible drawer. UCC § 3–401 and § 4–401. If the drawee, thinking that the check was drawn by the ostensible drawer, pays the check to a holder who presents it for payment, it has made payment under a mistake of fact. The case is similar to that of a shopkeeper who receives a $10 bill from a customer who owes him $8. Thinking that the money received was a $20 bill the shopkeeper gives the customer $12 change. The shopkeeper is entitled to get back the $10 paid by mistake. Does a similar rule apply to the drawee who pays a forged check? Price v. Neal, 3 Burr. 1354, 97 Eng.Rep. 871 (1762), dealt with that question. Two bills of exchange were drawn on Price and were indorsed to Neal, a bona fide purchaser for value. Price paid Neal on the first bill and then accepted the second bill which was subsequently purchased by Neal. After Price paid the second bill he learned that the signature of the drawer of the bills had been forged. Price sued Neal to get his

money back. Lord Mansfield, in deciding in favor of the defendant, stated:

It is an action upon the case, for money had and received
to the plaintiff's use. In which action, the plaintiff can not
recover the money, unless it be against conscience in the defendant, to retain it: and great liberality is always allowed,
in this sort of action.

But it can never be thought unconscientious in the defendant, to retain this money, when he has once received it upon a
bill of exchange indorsed to him for a fair and valuable consideration, which he had bona fide paid, without the least priority or suspicion of any forgery.

Here was no fraud: no wrong. It was incumbent upon
the plaintiff, to be satisfied "that the bill drawn upon him
was the drawer's hand," before he accepted or paid it: but it
was not incumbent upon the defendant, to inquire into it.
Here was notice given by the defendant to the plaintiff of a
bill drawn upon him; and he sends his servant to pay it and
take it up. The other bill he actually accepts; after which
acceptance, the defendant innocently and bona fide discounts
it. The plaintiff lies by, for a considerable time after he has
paid these bills; and then found out "that they were forged:"
and the forger comes to be hanged. He made no objection to
them, at the time of paying them. Whatever neglect there
was, was on his side. The defendant had actual encourage-
ment from the plaintiff himself, for negotiating the second
bill, from the plaintiff's having without any scruple or hesita-
tion paid the first: and he paid the whole value, bona fide. It
is a misfortune which has happened without the defendant's
fault or neglect. If there was no neglect in the plaintiff, yet
there is no reason to throw off the loss from one innocent
man upon another innocent man: but, in this case, if there
was any fault or negligence in any one, it certainly was in the
plaintiff, and not in the defendant.

The rule of Price v. Neal is incorporated into the UCC in
§ 3–418 read in conjunction with UCC § 3–417(1) and § 4–207(1).
The latter two sections are parallel provisions. The first applies
generally to warranties made to payors and acceptors of instruments. The second applies specifically to warranties made in
the bank-collection process to payors and acceptors of instruments.

FIRST NATIONAL CITY BANK v. ALTMAN

New York Supreme Court, New York County, Special Term, 1966.
3 U.C.C.Rep. 815.

Aff'd w/o opinion, 277 N.Y.S.2d 813 (App.Div. 1st Dept. 1967).

TIERNEY, J. This is a motion by defendant Altman for summary judgment and a cross-motion by defendant Trade Bank and Trust Company for leave to pay the sum of $23,900.75 into court, and for related relief.

The facts are as follows:

This action was brought to recover the proceeds of two checks, in the respective sums of $22,300.80 and $23,900.75, drawn on the account of J. W. Mays, Inc., a depositor in plaintiff bank, deposited in Altman's account in the Trade Bank and Trust Company, collected by said bank, and credited to Altman's account, on the ground that the signature of the drawer had been forged and the checks were not issued or drawn by J. W. Mays, Inc., nor with its authority or consent; and that payment was made by mistake, in good faith, in reliance on the endorsements of both defendants, without notice or knowledge of any defect in the instruments or in defendants' title thereto, and in the belief that the instruments had been drawn by the depositor, J. W. Mays, Inc.

Defendant Altman interposed an answer consisting of a general denial, an affirmative defense and counterclaim that plaintiff was negligent in failing to discover the forgery before making payment and that its negligence caused him to part with merchandise of the value of the checks, and an additional affirmative defense of estoppel as a result of such negligence. The answer of the Trade Bank and Trust Company consists of a general denial.

Defendant Altman is a wholesale diamond dealer. A Mr. Nieman presented himself at Altman's place of business and introduced himself as a buyer for J. W. Mays, Inc. Nieman selected a number of unset diamonds which Altman placed inside an envelope and sealed. Altman kept the diamonds. A few days later, Nieman sent a letter, on his own stationery, confirming the sale. He also enclosed a check drawn on plaintiff bank against the account of J. W. Mays, Inc., in the sum of $22,300.80, as full payment for the diamonds. Altman deposited the check in his account. Nieman then revisited Altman's place of business and selected more diamonds. The same procedure was followed, and Nieman's letter confirming the sale arrived with a check for $23,900.75, in full payment of the second group of diamonds. Altman, immediately upon receipt, deposited each check into his account at the Trade Bank. When Nieman requested delivery of the first envelope of diamonds, Altman communicated with the Trade Bank and determined that the first check had been paid defendant bank by the drawee, prior to turning over the diamonds. He turned over the second selection of diamonds several days later, but did not first ascertain that the second check had been paid, although in fact plaintiff had made payment; that same afternoon the Trade Bank notified him that plaintiff bank had given notice that both checks had been forged and that payment had been made by mistake.

Payment or acceptance of any instrument is final in favor of "a person who has in good faith changed his position in reliance on the payment" (UCC § 3–418). This legal principle was long ago enunciated in Price v. Neal, 3 Burr. 1354 (1762) where it was held that a drawee who pays an instrument on which the signature of the drawer is forged is bound on his acceptance and cannot recover back his payment from a holder in due course, or a person who has in good faith changed his position in reliance on the payment.

In moving for dismissal of the complaint defendant Altman contends that the doctrine of Price v. Neal is a bar to a recovery by plaintiff on either of the two forged checks herein.

The facts are clear that with respect to the first packet of diamonds, defendant Altman did not make delivery thereof until he had first ascertained that the check by which payment therefor had been made had been paid by plaintiff. Accordingly, defendant Altman, the payee of the check, does qualify as a person who changed his position in reliance on the drawee's payment. However, in all of the circumstances, the court is of the view that the issue of his good faith presents a triable issue of fact which precludes summary dismissal of the action based on the first check (see Banca C.I. Trust Co. v. Clarkson, 274 N.Y. 69, 8 N.E.2d 281). It has been held that the negligence of the purchaser, at the time he acquired title to the instrument, in not making inquiries which, if made, might reveal the fact of forgery, releases the drawee from the rule of Price v. Neal, and enables the drawee to recover from the purchaser the amount paid to him on the instrument (Whitney, The Law of Modern Commercial Practices, 2d ed., section 338, p. 504 [1965]).

Inasmuch as defendant Altman did not determine that the second check had been paid by plaintiff prior to delivery of the second packet of diamonds, said defendant is not in a position to claim the status of "a person who has * * * changed his position in reliance on the payment." Therefore, the proscription against the drawee stated in the rule of Price v. Neal loses its impact and all the issues relative to plaintiff's right to recover the proceeds of the second check remain in issue.

Accordingly, the motion for summary judgment dismissing the complaint is denied.

There is no real opposition to the cross-motion by defendant Trade Bank and Trust Company to deposit the proceeds of the second check into court. Therefore, the cross-motion is granted to the extent of directing said defendant to turn over the sum of $23,900.75 to the proper authorities. Otherwise the cross-motion is denied. Any taxable costs or disbursements shall be chargeable to the unsuccessful party at the conclusion of this litigation.

NOTES

1. At the time the first check was paid by the drawee bank was payment made to Altman as a holder in due course? Had he given value at that point? With respect to that check was Altman "a person who has in good faith changed his position in reliance on the payment?" At the time the second check was paid by the drawee bank was payment made to Altman as a holder in due course? Should the rights of Altman depend upon whether he released the second packet of diamonds before or after the check was paid? Must the change of position required by UCC § 3–418 relate to payment of the check which has already been made or is it sufficient that Altman changed his position in contemplation of payment which in fact was made? Holders in due course who are protected under UCC § 3–418 by definition have given value. If the drawee bank is able to recover the amount paid on the check the holder in due course will suffer an out-of-pocket loss. A person who is not a holder in due course because he has not given value does not suffer this kind of loss if the drawee bank recovers. See Comment 3. But a change of position in reliance on the payment may result in an out-of-pocket loss for such a person if the drawee bank recovers. To this extent the change of position substitutes for the missing giving of value for the check. Altman did in fact give value in good faith for both checks. If he had turned over both packets of diamonds immediately upon receipt of the checks would he

have been a holder in due course entitled to the protection of UCC § 3–418? Should his position be different if he turned over the diamonds after payment by the drawee bank?

2. The court suggests that Altman may have been negligent in taking the checks. What is the relevance of negligence? See Comment 4 to UCC § 3–418.

3. Payee drew a check for $500 payable to himself and forged customer's name as drawer. Payee offered the check to Dealer as the down payment for a used car but Dealer refused to take the check until it was certified. Payee obtained certification from Bank on which the check was drawn. Payee then indorsed the check to Dealer who took the check as the down payment and delivered the car to Payee. The next day, before presenting the check for payment, Dealer learned from his credit reporting agency that Payee had a criminal record that included arrests for forgery. Dealer immediately presented the check to Bank for payment without disclosing the information about Payee's criminal record. Bank paid Dealer in cash the amount of the check. Ten days later Bank discovered the forgery and demanded repayment from Dealer who refused. Is Bank entitled to recover from Dealer? See UCC § 3–418 and § 3–417(1) (b)(iii). Suppose Dealer, when he presented the check for payment, told Bank about Payee's criminal record. Bank called its customer and when it determined that the check was a forgery refused to pay Dealer. What rights does Dealer have against Bank? See UCC § 3–413(1), the Official Comment to that section, and Comment 4 to UCC § 3–417.

4. The first clause of UCC § 3–418 apparently refers to UCC § 4–301 which allows a payor bank to revoke a provisional settlement that was given when the check was received if it decides not to pay the check. Thus UCC § 3–418 does not cut off the drawee's right to recover for payment by mistake until settlement has become final. But Comment 5 also refers to UCC § 4–213 which states that an item is "finally paid" by a payor bank when the bank has taken certain acts in regard to the item including payment in cash and posting of the item to the drawer's account. If "finally paid" in that section is the same as "finality of payment" in § 3–418, the limitations of § 3–418 on payments to holders in due course and persons relying on the payment do not apply if, as is normally the case, the payment is made by a payor bank. Thus, UCC § 3–418 as applied to payments would apply to very few cases. UCC § 4–213 is not limited to payments to holders in due course or to persons changing

position in reliance on the payment, and it takes precedence over UCC § 3–418 in bank-collection cases. UCC § 4–102(1). This apparent conflict between UCC § 3–418 and § 4–213 is presented in the case that follows these Notes. See also a thorough discussion of the problem in White & Summers, Uniform Commercial Code 613–618 (2d ed. 1980).

b. STOP-PAYMENT ORDERS: CHECKS

NORTHWESTERN NATIONAL INSURANCE CO. OF MILWAUKEE v. MIDLAND NATIONAL BANK

Supreme Court of Wisconsin, 1980.
96 Wis.2d 155, 292 N.W.2d 591.

DAY, JUSTICE. Northwestern National Insurance Company (Northwestern) instituted this action to recover the value of two checks totaling $49,978.20 from Midland National Bank (Midland), the payor bank. It was alleged that Midland failed to revoke a provisional settlement for the items within its midnight deadline under [UCC § 4–301(1)] and by failing to meet this deadline Midland became accountable for the value of the checks under [UCC § 4–302].

* * *

I.

The basis facts underlying this controversy are not disputed. Towne Realty (Towne), the drawer of the disputed checks, was engaged in a joint venture with two other principals as a prime contractor for a construction project at the Hill Air Force Base in Utah. Larry T. Smith, Inc. (Smith, Inc.), a construction company, was a subcontractor hired to perform concrete and utility work on the Hill Air Force Base project.

Smith, Inc. had been having financial difficulty before and during the undertaking of this contract. Northwestern was acting as a surety on a number of Smith, Inc.'s contracts. In December, 1974, Smith, Inc. notified Northwestern that it would require financial assistance in order to complete its several construction contracts. On December 17, 1974, Northwestern, Smith, Inc., Larry T. Smith, and Geraldine Smith entered into an agreement whereby Smith, Inc. agreed to deposit the funds it earned from construction contracts into an account in the Bank of Fountain Valley, Security, Colorado. The account was called

"W. Robert Ward Trustee" account. W. Robert Ward was an attorney retained by Northwestern.

Although Northwestern was not a surety for Smith, Inc.'s Hill Air Force Base contract, the funds generated from that contract were to be deposited in the W. Robert Ward Trustee account. The contract was considered a profitable one which would generate funds to enable the completion of contracts upon which Northwestern acted as a surety.

After funds were deposited in the trustee account, they were to be disbursed upon the approval of George Mueller or W. Robert Ward to the account of Smith, Inc., which was held in the same bank and to be used for such things as payroll and general operating expenses of Smith, Inc. Mr. Mueller was the claims manager of Northwestern's Denver office. Mr. Mueller and Mr. Ward acted on behalf of Northwestern and the trustee account was a vehicle to protect Northwestern's advances and status as surety for Smith, Inc.

Sometime in August of 1975, Smith, Inc., submitted a bill in excess of $100,000. to Towne Realty for work done on the Utah project. Payment was not immediately forthcoming and Larry T. Smith, the principal officer of Smith, Inc., went to Milwaukee to meet with representatives of the joint venture to urge them to pay Smith, Inc., the moneys which were claimed to be due.

On August 14, 1975, the day before Mr. Smith was to meet with representatives of the joint venture, he met with a vice president of Northwestern. Northwestern was informed by Smith that Towne Realty was losing money on the Hill Air Force Base job. A decision was made to withdraw the crews from the construction site. Mr. Mueller and Mr. Ward were advised of this decision. A memorandum was prepared of the meeting between Mr. Smith and the vice president of Northwestern. The memorandum stated in part:

> " * * * [T]he decision was not whether or not we should pull off the job in Salt Lake but only a matter of timing as to when. Larry had been promised another $38,000 on complete estimate No. 13 to Towne Realty (on which he had already gotten the $50,000 partial payment) by August 20, 1975. Also a consideration is when to pull the equipment off the job since it would be nice to do this on a weekend to avoid possible attempts at attachment by Towne or Woerfel. * * * [W]e decided that we would wait and try to get as much money as we could the following weekend. Also, we decided to make one last effort to see if we couldn't force

more money out of Towne Realty this week   As a consequence, Larry Smith is going to call on * * * the number
two man at Towne, this afternoon and give him a pitch for
the $106,000 which is currently due and owing. * * * We
took into consideration the fact that Towne has been in violation of their contract—behind schedule on payment—for
months and that Larry does have a valid reason for walking
off the job."

Mr. Smith then met with representatives of the joint venture
on August 15, 1975. As a result of this meeting, Towne Realty,
Inc., issued two checks on its Hill Air Force Base account at the
Midland bank. Each check was made payable to Larry T. Smith
and Northwestern National Insurance Company. Check number
2375 was in the amount of $21,000. and check number 2376 was
in the amount of $28,978.20.

The two checks were issued on August 15th and sent to Mr.
Mueller in Colorado, who received them on August 20, 1975. On
that day, Mr. Mueller endorsed the checks and delivered them to
Mr. Smith, who also endorsed them. Mr. Smith then presented
the checks at the Bank of Fountain Valley on the same day.
The president of the Colorado bank was questioned as to the
fastest way to collect on the checks and was told by Mr. Smith
of his intention to pull the crews off the Utah job. The president of the Colorado bank then called Midland to determine
whether there were sufficient funds in Towne's account to cover
the checks. Midland informed him that there were sufficient
funds. It was then decided that rather than submitting the
checks for collection through the federal reserve system, it
would be faster to airmail them directly to Midland for collection. The Colorado bank did that on August 20, 1975.

On the same day, Smith pulled all his crews off the air force
project. When Towne was informed of this action, its attorney
called Midland on August 20th and issued a stop payment order
on both checks. This stop payment order was subsequently confirmed in writing. Towne also sent a mailgram to Mr. Smith
demanding that he continue performance on the contract at the
air force base.

The stop payment order on the two checks was apparently
entered into the bank's computer on the day the order was received, August 20, 1975.

On Friday, August 22, 1975, Midland received the two checks
which had been airmailed by the Colorado bank. Rather than
rejecting these checks, Midland held them and did not reject pay-

ment on them until Wednesday, August 27, 1975. Midland returned the checks to the Colorado bank on August 28, 1975.

A succession of errors committed by employees of Midland, described by its operations officer as "neglect" resulted in the failure to promptly implement the stop order.

W. Robert Ward, as Trustee, assigned all of his interest in the checks and any claims he might have against Midland to Northwestern. The W. Robert Ward Trustee account no longer exists.

The trial court entered the finding that the stop payment order issued to the bank was the direct result of the termination of performance by Smith, Inc., of his contract at Hill Air Force Base. The trial court also found that on August 20, 1975, Smith, Inc., and Northwestern were aware that the two checks probably would not be paid, and that Smith, Inc. and Northwestern should have reasonably expected that the "normal defensive reaction of the joint venture would be to stop payment on the two checks when it found that Smith, Inc., had pulled its crews off the job." At all times relevant to this action, the Towne Realty account contained sufficient funds to cover the checks.

II.

The check collection procedure to be followed by banks in this state is controlled by Article 4 of the Uniform Commercial Code. * * * When a check is presented for payment to a bank, a process begins whereby the check is transferred from the depositary bank, the first bank to which an item is transferred for collection, to any intermediary or collecting banks, until the check is presented to the bank upon which it is payable as drawn. This bank is known as the payor bank, which in this case is Midland. * * * The payor bank is required to give the "presenting" bank a provisional credit by midnight of the banking day of receipt of the check. The requirement that a provisional credit be given within a specified time period is not the same as the time within which the payor bank may revoke a provisional credit. This process is known as settling for the check. R.C. Higgins and D.B. Phemister, "Article 4 Bank Deposits and Collections." Uniform Commercial Code Handbook ABA Sec. Of Corporate Banking And Business Law 135 (1964).

Final payment by a payor bank may occur in a number of ways set forth in [UCC § 4-213]. When a payor bank makes a provisional settlement and fails to revoke that settlement in a timely manner, payment on the check will be deemed final. [UCC § 4–213]

Revocation of a provisional settlement is governed by [UCC § 4–301(1)]. This section allows revocation and the recovery of any payment if, before payment becomes final under [UCC § 4–213(1)] and before the "midnight deadline" is reached, the bank returns the item or "[s]ends written notice of dishonor or nonpayment if the item is held for protest or is otherwise unavailable for return." The payor bank, Midland, readily concedes that it missed the midnight deadline.

In most cases the proper method of revoking a provisional settlement for a check presented for payment is to return the item.

* * *

The consequences attending the late return of a check are found in [UCC § 4–302]. This section provides that in the absence of a valid defense, a payor bank is accountable for the amount of a demand item "if the bank * * * retains the item beyond midnight of the banking day of receipt without settling for it or * * * does not pay or return the item or send notice of dishonor until after its midnight deadline * * *." Although the term accountable is not defined in the statute, it has been construed to impose liability for the full amount of the demand item regardless of the actual damages sustained.

* * *

III.

Midland also asserts that Northwestern was not a holder in due course and did not in good faith change its position in reliance on payment of these checks. Under [UCC § 3–418] it is argued that Northwestern therefore is not entitled to recover. * * * Official Comment 5 by the drafters of this provision states in part:

> "This section is * * * also limited by the bank collection provision (Section 4–301) permitting a payor bank to recover a payment improperly paid if it returns the item or sends notice of dishonor within the limited time provided in that section. But notice that the latter right is sharply limited in time, and terminates in any case when the bank has made final payment, as defined in Section 4–213."

This comment, when read in conjunction with sec. 3–418 demonstrates an intent on the part of the drafters of the Code to exclude the payor bank's liability provision under sec. 4–302 from the operation of sec. 3–418. "Pre-Code law, discussions of the draftsmen and others at the time of Code adoption, and post Code cases all suggest that a party does not have to be either a holder in due course or one who changes his position in order to claim the protection of 4–213 and 4–302." J. White and R. Summers, Uniform Commercial Code, § 16–2, 526 (1972).

A final argument under the Code is made by Midland. It is asserted that Northwestern did not act in good faith and therefore recovery should be denied. Every contract or duty within the scope of the Uniform Commercial Code imposes an obligation of good faith in its performance or enforcement. [UCC § 1–203]. Good faith means honesty in fact in the conduct or transaction concerned. [UCC § 1–201(19)] We need not address this question, because we do not perceive the indicia of fraud which Midland so strenuously asserts. The trial court made no specific finding of the lack of good faith on the part of the payee Northwestern. It is admitted that both the payees on the disputed checks knew that the contract was not going to be completed before they obtained the checks from Towne Realty. However, it has been asserted, and not sufficiently contradicted, that the checks were for work already completed by Larry Smith, Inc. We do not believe that Midland has demonstrated bad faith on the part of Northwestern or Smith, Inc. There may be a contractual dispute as to the damages sustained by Towne Realty, or whether the work was completed to satisfaction, or whether there were set off rights. But those are contract disputes and they do not concern us here. We, therefore, do not express any opinion as to the applicability of the reasoning of the Virginia Supreme Court in Bartlett v. Bank of Carroll, 218 Va. 240, 237 S.E.2d 115 (1977) cited to us by Midland.

* * *

We conclude therefore that Northwestern was entitled to recover the value of two checks in the amount of $49,978.20 from Midland.

Judgment reversed and cause remanded with directions to enter judgment pursuant to the opinion.

NOTE

What can Midland do after this decision? It has paid the debt of its customer but it has not complied with its customer's stop-payment order. The customer had the right under UCC § 4–403 to order the drawer to stop payment and the drawer was bound to honor the stop-payment order so long as it is received in time to allow the drawee to act on it. See UCC § 4–303. Midland therefore improperly paid the check. UCC § 4–401. If Midland is required, without qualification, to reverse the debit to its customer's account resulting from the improper payment its customer gets a windfall. Midland cannot recover the amount paid on the check because under the holding of the principal case that payment was final under UCC § 4–213 and § 4–302. Thus, Midland would bear the loss. There are two related provisions designed to avoid this result and, at the same time, to protect the interests of the customer whose stop-payment order was not honored. They are UCC § 4–403(3) and § 4–407 and they are considered in the case that follows this Note.

SIEGEL v. NEW ENGLAND MERCHANTS NATIONAL BANK

Supreme Judicial Court of Massachusetts, 1982.
386 Mass. 672, 437 N.E.2d 218.

HENNESSEY, CHIEF JUSTICE. We are called upon to define the respective rights of a bank and its depositor when the bank has paid a post-dated check before maturity and deducted the amount of the check from the depositor's account. Applying the Uniform Commercial Code, G.L. c. 106, we conclude that the bank must recredit the depositor's account, but may then assert against the depositor any rights acquired by prior holders on either the instrument or the transaction from which it arose. In the course of this opinion, we shall describe the parties' responsibilities of proof with respect to the bank's subrogation claim. We remand for a further hearing on the question of subrogation.

The plaintiff's decedent, David Siegel, maintained a checking account with the defendant, New England Merchants National Bank. On September 14, 1973, Siegel drew and delivered a $20,000 check to Peter Peters, post-dated November 14, 1973. Peters immediately deposited the check in his own bank, which forwarded it for collection. The defendant bank overlooked the date on the check, and, on September 17, paid the item and charged it against Siegel's account. Siegel discovered the error in late September when another of his checks was returned for insufficient funds. He informed the bank that the check to Peters was post-dated November 14, and asked the bank to stop

payment of the check.   Later, he requested that the bank return
the $20,000 to him.

When the bank refused to restore the $20,000, Siegel brought
this action for wrongful debit of his account.   The bank denied
liability, raised defenses of waiver, estoppel and ratification, and
filed counterclaims asserting rights on the instrument and rights
of subrogation.   Two banks in the collecting chain became parties, one permitted to intervene as a party defendant and the
other impleaded by the bank.   The bank also impleaded Peters,
the payee, who filed a suggestion of bankruptcy.   The case was
later dismissed as against the two collecting banks.

After a trial, jury-waived, the judge found that the check was
post-dated by agreement between Peters and Siegel, without
fraudulent purpose, and that Siegel had acted with reasonable
speed to inform the bank of the error.   He also found that Peters had paid no money to Siegel since receiving the check.   The
judge ruled that (1) the check was a negotiable instrument;   (2)
the check was not payable until November 14;   (3) the bank was
negligent in paying it before that date;   (4) the bank had no right
to debit Siegel's account;   (5) Siegel had not waived his rights or
ratified the bank's action and was not estopped from demanding
the $20,000;   and (6) the wrongful debit caused Siegel a loss of
$20,000.   He also rejected the bank's counterclaims as having no
merit.   He then entered judgments for Siegel against the bank
in the amount of $20,000, for Siegel on the bank's counterclaims;
and for the bank against Peters for $20,000.   The bank ap-
pealed, and we transferred the case to this court on our own
motion.   We vacate the judgment and remand the case for further consideration of the bank's subrogation claims.

1.   *Wrongful Debit and Subrogation.*

The parties agree that the bank should not have paid the
check when Peters presented it on September 14, and had no
right at that time to charge it against Siegel's account.   [UCC]
§§ 3–114, 4–401(1).   See Smith v. Gentiolotti, 371 Mass. 839, 840,
359 N.E.2d 953 (1977).   Their differences center instead on
whether the bank's wrongful action caused Siegel any loss, so as
to entitle him to damages.   Siegel contends, and the judge ruled,
that his loss must be $20,000 because that amount was debited
from his account.   The bank contends that there was no loss,
because Siegel drew the check with the intention that it eventually be paid, and the bank could rightfully have charged it
against his account on November 14.   We believe that the draft-

ers of the code anticipated disputes such as this, and provided a logical system for their resolution.

We begin with [UCC] § 4–401(1), which governs bookkeeping between depositor and bank. A bank may charge any "properly payable" item against its depositor's account. Implicitly, the bank may not charge items, such as post-dated checks, that are not properly payable. If the charge is unauthorized, it follows that the depositor has a valid claim to the amount of the charge by virtue of the account itself. Cf. Stone & Webster Eng'r Corp. v. First Nat'l Bank & Trust Co., 345 Mass. 1, 5, 184 N.E.2d 358 (1962) (relationship of bank and depositor as debtor and creditor).

As the bank points out, the depositor's realization of this claim may produce unjust enrichment. Even when an item is not properly payable, due to prematurity or a stop payment order, the bank's payment may discharge a legal obligation of the depositor, or create a right in the depositor's favor against the payee. See [UCC] §§ 3–601(1)(a), 3–603(1), 3–802(1)(b); J. White & R. Summers, Uniform Commercial Code 542 (2d ed. 1980). If the depositor were permitted to retain such benefits, and recover the amount of the check as well, he would profit at the bank's expense. Therefore, § 4–407 provides that upon payment, the bank is "subrogated" to any rights prior holders may have had against the drawer-depositor, on either the check or the initial underlying transaction, and to any rights the drawer may have against the payee or other holders.[5] * * *

Thus, the code fixes the rights of the bank and the depositor by a two part adjustment. The depositor has a claim against the bank for the amount improperly debited from its account, and the bank has a claim against the depositor based on subrogation to the rights of the payee and other holders. The bank may assert its subrogation rights defensively when its depositor brings an action for wrongful debit. See Universal C.I.T. Credit Corp. v. Guaranty Bank & Trust Co., supra at 794–795.

Here, the bank asserted a subrogation claim based on the rights of Peters, the payee.[6] Neither party, however, introduced evidence concerning Peters's rights against Siegel.[7] A question

---

5. * * *

At the time a bank asserts subrogation rights, the check will of course have been paid, and prior holders will have no rights against the drawer. See [UCC] §§ 3–601(1)(a), 3–603(1), 3–802(1)(b). Therefore, we under-

stand § 4–407 to refer to rights existing prior to the payment.

6. The bank waived all claims based on the rights of the collecting banks.

7. The trial judge did find that the transaction between Peters and Siegel

then arises as to what matters each party was obligated to prove in order to prevail.

Section 4–403(3) of the code provides that when the problem is one of improper payment over a stop order, the "burden of establishing the fact and amount of loss * * * is on the customer." G.L. c. 106, § 4–403(3). Here, of course, the bank's liability is for premature payment rather than for payment over a stop order. Nevertheless, these two forms of improper payment have in common the problem of unjust enrichment, and we believe that § 4–403(3) is a source of useful analogy.

The rule of § 4–403(3), that a depositor must prove his loss, may at first seem at odds with our earlier conclusion that § 4–401(1) provides the depositor with a claim against the bank in the amount of the check, leaving the bank with recourse through subrogation under § 4–407. See Mitchell v. Republic Bank & Trust Co., 35 N.C.App. 101, 104, 239 S.E.2d 867 (1978); Thomas v. Marine Midland Tinkers Nat'l Bank, 86 Misc.2d 284, 288–289, 381 N.Y.S.2d 797 (N.Y.Sup.Ct.1976); J. White & R. Summers, supra at 684–691. We believe, however, that § 4–403(3) was intended to operate within the process of credit and subrogation established by §§ 4–401(1) and 4–407. See § 4–403, comment 8. When a bank pays an item improperly, the depositor loses his ability to exercise any right he had to withhold payment of the check. His "loss," in other words, is equivalent to his rights and defenses against the parties to whose rights the bank is subrogated—the other party to the initial

arose out of Siegel's sale of a shopping mall to Peters, and Peters's subsequent default on payments due Siegel on notes, and that Siegel and Peters had agreed to the post-dating of the check. He also found that Peters had "made no payment to [Siegel] since he received the check, either as payment on the notes or as a repayment of the $20,000 extended by the check." The bank objects to these findings on the ground that there is no evidence in the record to support them. The bank appears to be correct on this point. In any event, the judge's findings, while they tend to suggest that the transaction was a loan, do not clearly establish either that Peters was entitled to receive the money on November 14, or that Siegel had a right to cancel the transaction before the check became due. It should be noted that the mere circumstance that the transaction was a loan, and that the loan had since proved uncollectible, would not necessarily mean that the bank's premature payment had caused the depositor a loss. If the payee was unconditionally entitled to receive the loan, the risk that he would not repay it was a risk the depositor assumed in making the loan, and was not increased by the bank's action. Section 4–407, by extending the bank's subrogation to rights on the instrument as well as to rights on the transaction, makes clear that the depositor could not recover in this situation. Thus, to defeat the bank's subrogation rights the depositor must establish a condition on the right to cash the check, an element of fraud, or some other defense good against the payee as a holder of the instrument.

transaction and other holders of the instrument. Section 4–403(3) simply protects the bank against the need to prove events familiar to the depositor, and far removed from the bank, before it can realize its subrogation rights. The depositor, who participated in the initial transaction, knows whether the payee was entitled to eventual payment and whether any defenses arose. Therefore, § 4–403(3) requires that he, rather than the bank, prove these matters. Cf. Knowles v. Gilchrist Co., 362 Mass. 642, 651–652, 289 N.E.2d 879 (1972) (when goods are damaged in the hands of a bailee, bailee, who is best informed, must establish due care).

This view of the three relevant sections of the code suggests a fair allocation of the burden of proof. The bank, which has departed from authorized bookkeeping, must acknowledge a credit to the depositor's account. It must then assert its subrogation rights, and in doing so must identify the status of the parties in whose place it claims. If the bank's subrogation claims are based on the check, this would entail proof that the third party subrogor was a holder, or perhaps a holder in due course. This responsibility falls reasonably upon the bank, because it has received the check from the most recent holder and is in at least as good a position as the depositor to trace its history.

The depositor must then prove any facts that might demonstrate a loss. He must establish defenses good against a holder or holder in due course, as the case may be. See [UCC] §§ 3–305, 3–306. If the initial transaction is at issue, he must prove either that he did not incur a liability to the other party, or that he has a defense to liability. Thus the bank, if it asserts rights based on the transaction, need not make out a claim on the part of its subrogor against the depositor. Responsibility in this area rests entirely with the depositor, who participated in the transaction and is aware of its details. Further, the depositor must establish any consequential loss.[8]

---

8. Several courts have harmonized § 4–403(3) with §§ 4–404(1) and 4–407 in terms of shifting burdens of production and persuasion. "Simply because a bank pays a check over a stop payment order does not entitle the customer to recover damages against the bank, but it does establish a *prima facie* case for the customer. The bank must present evidence to show absence of loss, or the right of the payee of the check to receive pay- ment. Then the customer must sustain the ultimate burden to show why there was a defense to payment of the item." Southeast First Nat'l Bank v. Atlantic Telec, Inc., 389 So.2d 1032, 1033 (Fla.Dist.Ct.App.1980). Mitchell v. Republic Bank & Trust Co., 35 N.C. App. 101, 104, 289 S.E.2d 867 (1978). Thomas v. Marine Midland Tinkers Nat'l Bank, 86 Misc.2d 284, 290–291, 381 N.Y.S.2d 797 (N.Y.Sup.Ct.1976). Although our analysis will often have

A further hearing is necessary to determine the question of subrogation in the present case. The judge ruled that the check was a negotiable instrument, see § 3–114(1), and the evidence at trial fairly indicated that Peters was a holder. See § 1–201(20). Thus the burden, under the rules we have set out, was upon Siegel to prove a defense good against a holder of the instrument. However, the trial record makes clear that neither the parties nor the judge was proceeding with these rules in mind. Indeed, the judge excluded, at the bank's strenuous request, evidence offered by Siegel concerning the transaction between Siegel and Peters. We believe, therefore, that Siegel's executrix should have an opportunity to present evidence that Siegel suffered a loss.

* * *

In sum, Siegel had a valid claim against the bank for premature payment in the amount of the item paid, but the bank was entitled to assert the rights of prior holders on the check and on the transaction from which it arose. We vacate the judgment and remand for a further hearing to determine those rights. At the hearing, the bank must establish the status of its subrogor. Siegel's executrix must establish any defenses to liability on the instrument as well as the absence of rights or presence of defenses on the underlying transaction.

PROBLEMS

Consider the effect of UCC § 3–418 and § 4–213 on the following problems:

1. C, a creditor of D, demanded that D pay his debt. D drew a check on Bank to the order of C in payment of the debt which C accepted even though he believed that the check was probably not good. C then called Bank to inquire whether the check was good and was informed that D did not have sufficient funds in his account to cover the check. C nonetheless went to Bank and presented the check for payment over the counter. Bank's teller, who knew C, paid the check in cash without checking the status of D's account. Three days later Bank notified C that it dishonored D's check for insufficient funds and demanded repayment from C. C refused. Is Bank entitled to recover from C?

the same result as that of the cited cases, it may in some cases give greater force to § 4–403(3).

2.   Drawer drew a check on Bank for $5,000 to the order of Payee, Drawer's daughter, and delivered it to her as a wedding gift.   Payee deposited the check in her account with Bank which debited Drawer's account and credited Payee's account for $5,000.   Drawer's account was overdrawn at the time but the clerk handling the transaction overlooked it.   Three days later Bank discovered the error and reversed the credit to Payee's account notifying her that Bank had dishonored the check for insufficient funds.   Payee then sued Bank for $5,000, the amount of the check.   Is Payee entitled to recover?

NOTES

1.   Suppose Bank induces its checking-account customer to sign a stop-payment form containing the following clause: "In requesting you to stop payment of this or any other item, the undersigned agrees to hold you harmless for all expenses and costs incurred by you on account of refusing payment of said item, and further agrees not to hold you liable on account of payment contrary to this request if same occurs through inadvertence, accident or oversight, or if by reason of such payment other items drawn by the undersigned are returned insufficient."   Is this clause, or any part of it, enforceable?   See UCC § 4–103(1) and § 4–403:   Opinion of Attorney General of Connecticut, 25 U.C.C.Rep. 238 (1978).

2.   In view of the fact that the customer has an absolute right to stop payment by complying with UCC § 4–403, is the drawee bank entitled to impose a charge for processing a stop-payment order?   See Opinion of Attorney General of Michigan, 30 U.C.C.Rep. 1626 (1981).   A typical charge for a stop order is $6.   Could a bank legally impose a $60 charge for a stop order?

c.   STOP-PAYMENT ORDERS: CREDIT CARDS AND ELECTRONIC FUND TRANSFERS

If a buyer pays for goods by check he may stop payment of the check.   But in an increasing number of cases buyers pay for goods and services by use of credit cards.   A credit cardholder has no right to stop the card issuer from paying the merchant who honored the card.   The cardholder's only remedy is to assert against the card issuer claims or defenses that the cardholder may have against the merchant.   See the discussion of the Fair Credit Billing Act, supra, pp. 169–170.

Consider the case of electronic fund transfers. Suppose a customer pays for goods or services by using his EFT access card in a merchant's point-of-sale (POS) terminal, thereby instantly debiting his deposit account and crediting merchant's account for the amount of the sale. If the customer discovers that the goods are defective, does he have a right akin to a bank customer's right to stop payment on a check? This issue was addressed by the National Commission on Electronic Fund Transfers in its Final Report, submitted in 1977, at pp. 50–52:

> The ability to stop payment on a check gives consumers a degree of protection for a short period of time against merchants who would sell defective goods or others whose goods or services are less than the consumer feels he was promised in the bargain. Although the right to stop payment has been exercised infrequently in relation to the total number of checks written,[17] it is likely that the potential to stop payment on checks has an inhibiting effect on some who might otherwise take unfair advantage of consumers. On the other hand, the ability of consumers capriciously to stop payment no doubt causes many vendors of goods or services to refuse to accept checks.
>
> A consumer who uses credit cards for his retail purchases also obtains some protection against defective merchandise and unsatisfactory service. If, for example, a local purchase exceeds $50, the card issuer may often be subject to the claims of the purchaser against the person who honored the credit card.

*   *   *

> Cash—the most widely accepted payment medium—provides no protection of the type afforded by stop payment. A consumer who pays with cash takes the risk that his purchase will be defective or the service delivered, unsatisfactory. His payment is final at the time of purchase, and his only protection is to deal with reputable parties.
>
> With EFT, stop payment could be provided in at least two ways for POS transactions. First, a procedure called "value dating" could be used. Under that system the debiting of the consumer's account and crediting of the merchant's account are delayed for a short time—such as two days—al-

---

17. In 1973, stop payment orders where entered for approximately .029 percent of all checks written. Bank Administration Institute, The Impact of Exception Items on the Check Collection System (Park Ridge, Ill.: 1974).

though all the necessary information is captured at the time of the transaction. A consumer could be permitted to "stop payment" before the value date.

With on-line POS systems, however, the payment between consumer and merchant is typically made instantaneously. It is literally not possible to stop a payment before it has been effected. Therefore, the second method of stopping payment is more accurately a reversal of payment. The purpose of reversibility is to give the consumer a two- or three-day period within which he could reverse his payment merely by instructing his depository institution to do so. As with checks, the consumer could stop payment for any reason or for no reason at all.

Some people believe that stop payment or reversibility should be mandated for all EFT systems in order to protect consumers. Others believe that consumers may not accept EFT without reversibility. For example:

If payments are to be "final" in the EFTS context in a shorter time than in the current "paper world," it may be necessary to make some provision to permit customers to reverse charges to their accounts in a way similar to stop payment even after "final payments." This may be required in order to satisfy consumer advocates and to gain wider acceptance in marketing the system to the public.

The Commission concluded that reversibility for EFT payments at the point of sale should not be required by legislation. Conflicting market interests and differing operational characteristics of EFT systems are likely to allow for reversibility in some cases but not in others. Many merchants consider POS services advantageous only if they eliminate the risks involved in check acceptance. With mandatory reversibility, ultimate payment could not be assured. Even if the return of merchandise was required—as some have suggested—sellers of consumable goods, such as restaurants, would not be protected against fraud. Moreover, the merchants most likely to accept EFT services are the large retailers who generally allow customers to return merchandise within a reasonable period of time if it is accompanied by the sales receipt. Disreputable merchants are unlikely to accept EFT with required reversibility.

One of the primary advantages of POS debit transactions to consumers is acceptability of the debit card without need for any type of credit or background check at the point of sale. If an EFT system indicates that there are funds available (either directly or through the cardholder's overdraft line), a merchant needs no other information regarding the consumer. If reversibility of all transactions were mandated, many merchants would probably refuse to accept EFT at all, and those who did would probably seek some way to evaluate the risk that a potential EFT user might reverse a transaction without returning the merchandise. On the other hand, EFT providers may prefer reversibility on the theory that it will improve consumer acceptance of EFT, and many reputable merchants may be willing to accept EFT even with reversibility because it eliminates check handling and many of its attendant risks, such as insufficient funds.

Some consumer advocates seem to endorse the concept of mandatory reversibility of EFT transactions because they fear that eventually EFT will be the only method of payment available. It is clear, however, that all consumers will not use EFT systems just as all consumers do not use checks, and it is unlikely that any consumer will use EFT services exclusively. EFT is likely to expand the range of payment alternatives rather than replace existing methods. Thus, a consumer who wishes to retain the leverage afforded by the "stop payment" tool and whose EFT system does not offer this feature would be able to use a check or credit card. In addition, EFT systems can offer features such as value dating, which is a deferred payment that could make a stop payment privilege possible.

The Commission concluded that the proper arena for resolving these different views on the reversibility of consumer-initiated EFT transactions is the marketplace, where competing interests will vie for market acceptability. *Therefore, the Commission recommends that no legislation be passed at this time that specifies rights or procedures for stop payment or reversibility in customer-initiated EFT transactions.*

Congress followed the Commission's recommendation. The only stop payment countenanced by the Electronic Fund Transfer Act, 15 U.S.C. § 1693 et seq., is with respect to preauthorized transfers from a customer's account. Thus if a customer authorizes its bank to pay periodic insurance premiums from his account, the bank must honor the customer's stop-payment order if given at least three days in advance of the date of the payment or face liability to the customer for damages under 15 U.S.C. § 1693(e)(a) and § 1693h(3).

C. FORGED AND UNAUTHORIZED INDORSEMENTS

---

1. RIGHTS OF DRAWEE

PROBLEM

Drawer drew a check to the order of Payee. The check was stolen from Payee by Thief who forged Payee's blank indorsement. Thief then delivered the check to Harold, a good faith purchaser for value. Harold deposited the check in his account with Depositary Bank which presented the check and received payment from Drawee. Depositary Bank gave credit to Harold and the credit was withdrawn. Payee then notified Drawer of the theft. Drawer notified Drawee but was informed that the check had already been paid. Is Drawee entitled to charge the account of Drawer for the amount of the check? UCC § 4–401. Is Drawee entitled to recover the amount of the check from Depositary Bank or Harold? UCC § 3–418, § 3–417(1), § 4–213 and § 4–207. Is the result in this case consistent with the opinion of Lord Mansfield in Price v. Neal?

The preceding Problem is discussed by Judge Goldberg in Perini Corp. v. First National Bank of Habersham County, 553 F.2d 398, 403–406 (5th Cir. 1977):

A. The Code Framework

Perpetuating a distinction introduced into the legal annals by Lord Mansfield in the eighteenth century, the Code accords separate treatment to forged drawer signatures (hereinafter "forged checks") and forged indorsements. In general, the drawee bank is strictly liable to its customer drawer for payment of either a forged check or a check containing a forged indorsement. In the case of a forged indorsement, the drawee generally may pass liability back through the collection chain to the party who took from the forger and, of course, to the forger himself if available. In the case of a forged check, however, liability generally rests with the drawee. The patchwork of provisions from which this general allocation of liability emerges merits more detailed description.

1. Forged Indorsements

A check bearing a forged indorsement, included in the § 1–201(43) definition of unauthorized signatures,[6] is not "properly payable." J. White and R. Summers, Uniform Commercial Code 559 (1972).[7] Regardless of the care exercised, a drawee bank is with few exceptions liable to its drawer customer for payment of such a check. See § 4–401.

Upon recrediting the drawer's account after payment over a forged indorsement, the drawee will seek redress against prior parties in the collection chain through an action for breach of the statutory warranty of good title. Each person who obtains payment of a check from the drawee and each prior transferor warrants to the party who in good faith pays the check that he has good title to the instrument. §§ 3–417(1)(a), 4–207(1)(a). A forged indorsement is ineffective to pass title; see § 3–417, Comment 3. The drawee may therefore bring a breach of warranty action against a person who presented a check bearing a forged indorsement. These warranty actions will continue up the collection chain to the party who took from the forger or to the forger himself.

Additionally, payment of a check bearing a forged indorsement constitutes conversion under § 3–419(1)(c). This conversion action at least provides the check's "true owner,"

---

6. Section 1–201(43) provides:

"Unauthorized" signature or indorsement means one made without actual, implied or apparent authority and includes a forgery.

7. A check drawn to the order of the payee, i.e., an order instrument, may not be negotiated without the payee's indorsement. See § 3–202(1). The unauthorized indorsement by the forger does not operate as the true payee's signature. See § 3–404(1), which provides that "any unauthorized signature is wholly inoperative as that of the person whose name is signed unless he ratifies it or is precluded from denying it." A forged indorsement check therefore lacks the payee's indorsement and, without that necessary indorsement, may not be negotiated. See § 3–202(1). Negotiation is necessary to confer holder status on a check's transferee. Id. Accordingly, the transferee of a forged indorsement check does not become a holder. Only a holder or the holder's agent may properly present the check for payment. See § 3–504(1). Thus the UCC reaffirms the general pre-Code rule that a drawee may not charge its drawer customer's accounts for payment of an order instrument bearing a forged indorsement. See White and Summers, supra, at 559.

It may be assumed for purposes of this introductory sketch that the analysis described for forged indorsement checks equally applies to checks drawn to a principal and indorsed by an ostensible agent with no showing of representative capacity. Considerations unique to the representative capacity problem are developed more fully in Part III infra.

the payee or indorsee from whom it was stolen and whose name was falsely indorsed, direct relief from the drawee. See White and Summers, supra, 500. Without the conversion action the true owner would have to seek payment from the drawer, who might be overcautious and unaware of his right to force the drawee to recredit his account for any payment over a forged indorsement.

The danger created by forged indorsements is that the party designated by the instrument as entitled to its proceeds will appear with a claim to those proceeds after payment has been made to the malefactor. The statutory actions for improper payment, conversion, and breach of warranty of good title combine, however, inartfully, to safeguard the drawer against double liability and to assure the payee of payment. The loss falls on the party who took the check from the forger, or on the forger himself.

2. Forged Checks

As opposed to diverting an intended payment to someone other than the intended recipient, forged checks present the problem of depleting the ostensible drawer's funds when he had intended no payment. The Code's treatment of forged checks, however, begins in the same place as its treatment of forged indorsements. The forgery does not operate as the ostensible drawer's signature. See § 3–404(1). Payment consequently is not to the ostensible drawer's order and violates the drawee bank's strict duty to charge its customer's account only for properly payable items. See § 4–401(1).

The Code's analysis of forged check liability not only begins with the drawee, however; it also generally ends there. The drawee's payment of a forged check is final in favor of a holder in due course or one who has relied on the payment in good faith. § 3–418. This final payment rule codifies and attempts to clarify the rule of Price v. Neal, 3 Burr. 1354 (K.B.1762), "under which a drawee who accepts or pays an instrument on which the signature of the drawer is forged is bound on his acceptance and cannot recover back his payment." § 3–418, Comment 1. Prior parties in the collection chain who meet the prerequisites set out in § 3–418 will be immunized by its final payment rule from any liability for negligence in dealing with the forged check.

The above scheme allocating forgery losses among the various parties to the check collection process operates without regard to fault. The drawee's duty to charge its customer's

account only for "properly payable" items and the warranty
of title given by prior parties in the chain of transfer impose
standards of strict liability.

Fault does occupy a secondary role in the UCC treatment
of forgery losses. One whose negligence substantially contributes to the making of an unauthorized signature cannot
assert the invalidity of that signature against a holder in due
course or a drawee who without negligence pays the check.
§ 3–406. Thus the drawee can pass the loss back to a drawer or forward to a prior party in the collection chain whose
negligence substantially contributed to a forgery. The complaining party's negligence will not, however, bar otherwise
available recovery against a party, including a drawee, who
is also negligent. Id. Additionally, while nothing in the
Code precludes a bank and its customer from modifying the
forgery loss rules by contract, the bank cannot enforce an
agreement permitting it to act in violation of reasonable commercial standards. § 4–103(1).

B. The Code Policy: Incompletely Greasing the Commercial
   Wheels

In sum, the Code, while allowing for some modification on
the basis of fault or agreement, sets up a system of strict
liability rules allocating loss according to the type of forgery.
The system uneasily rests on two policy bases. First, it incorporates an at least partially outmoded notion of the relative positions of drawee banks and prior parties in the collection chain with respect to detecting different types of
forgeries. Second, it incompletely serves the notion that
commerce will be facilitated by bringing to the swiftest practicable conclusion the processing of a check transaction.

As mentioned, the separate treatment given forged
checks and forged indorsements harkens back to the eighteenth century decision of the King's Bench in Price v. Neal.
That decision left forged check liability on the drawee on the
view that, as against other parties in the line of transfer, the
drawee stood in the best position to recognize the signature
of the drawer, its customer. The corollary principle for
forged indorsements is that the person who takes the check
from the forger—frequently, as here, the depositary bank—
is in the best position to detect the bogus indorsement.

Reaffirming Price v. Neal in the final payment rule of
§ 3–418, the Code drafters recognized that the case's apprais-
al of relative opportunity to scrutinize drawer signatures was

somewhat unrealistic in a nation where banks may handle
some 60 million checks daily [9] The contemporary pace of
commerce has eroded the five senses used by bankers in the
face-to-face era of Price versus Neal; little remains save the
sensory activity of punching keys. While the drafters thus
concluded that Price v. Neal had been drained of all its per-
sonality, they nevertheless insisted that its conclusion survives. The drafters noted that modern groundwork for the
final payment rule could be found in the

> less fictional rationalization * * * that it is highly de-
> sirable to end the transaction on an instrument when it is
> paid rather than reopen and upset a series of commercial
> transactions at a later date when the forgery is discov-
> ered.

§ 3–418, Comment 1. In recognition of the frenetic commerce of our time, the thrust of the UCC here and elsewhere
is for speed and facility at some expense to exact checks and
balances.

Leaving forged check liability on the drawee may serve
well this finality policy. That policy, however, does not itself
justify separate treatment for forged checks and indorsements. The concern that commercial transactions be swiftly
brought to rest applies with equal force to both varieties of
wrongdoing. See White and Summers, supra, at 522–23;
Comment, Allocation of Losses From Check Forgeries Under
the Law of Negotiable Instruments and the Uniform Commercial Code, 62 Yale L.J. 417, 459–60 (1953).

While finality viewed alone calls for equal treatment of
forged checks and forged indorsements, one might still maintain that forged indorsements merit separate rules. The

9. For a discussion of the volume of checks processed and the resultant interplay between the law of forgery losses and bankers' perceptions of the forgery problem, see Murray, Price v. Neal in the Electronic Age: An Empirical Survey, 87 Banking L.J. 686 (1970). We note the commentator's interesting observation that many banks do not record separately losses from forged checks and forged in- dorsements, contrary to the implicit assumption in the final payment rule that the two types of losses represent security breakdowns in different func- tions of a bank—accepting checks for deposit to its customers accounts and paying checks drawn by its custom- ers—which might call for different protective measures.

On the other hand, the author does suggest specific measures for protect- ing banks against forged check losses. The possibility remains that the sepa- rate allocation of strict liability for forged check and forged indorsement losses may act as some incentive for the development of those precautiona- ry measures that consistent with the press of business will most effectively reduce the risk of loss from either type of forgery.

modern demands of commerce have as the drafters recognized, deprived drawees of any superior opportunity to detect forged drawer's signatures. Only a concern for finality therefore justifies placing forged check losses on drawee banks.

Such simple expedients as requiring identification, however, may still permit transferees of checks to provide a significant protection against forged indorsements that drawees cannot. To insure such protective measures are taken, it may be sensible to override the finality policy and to place forged indorsement losses on the depositary bank or other party who takes from the forger.   *   *   *

2. RIGHTS OF OWNER

Suppose Drawer drew a check to the order of Payee and delivered it to him in payment of an obligation. The check was then stolen from Payee by Thief who deposited the check in Depositary Bank after forging Payee's indorsement. The check was paid by Drawee Bank and the resulting credit was withdrawn by Thief. What are the remedies of Payee? Under UCC § 3–802 the obligation for which the check was given was suspended and it does not revive until dishonor of the check which has not yet occurred in this case. If Drawer is willing to give Payee another check Payee's problem is solved. Drawer can insist that Drawee Bank recredit Drawer's account and Drawee Bank has a cause of action against Depositary Bank under UCC § 4–207(1) for breach of warranty of title. The ultimate loss lies with Depositary Bank whose only claim is against Thief. But Payee has no right to this cooperation from Drawer who may be unwilling to bear the risk of enforcing his rights against Drawee Bank. If Drawer refuses to give Payee a new check Payee must assert his rights as owner of the stolen check. There are three possible defendants, Drawer, Drawee Bank and Depositary Bank. Payee could enforce his right to payment of the stolen check against Drawer under UCC § 3–804 and § 3–413(2). Presentment to Drawee Bank in this case should be excused. UCC § 3–511(2)(c). But in most cases Payee sues either Depositary Bank or Drawee Bank. The following case discusses those causes of action.

COOPER v. UNION BANK

Supreme Court of California, 1973.
9 Cal.3d 371, 107 Cal.Rptr. 1, 507 P.2d 609.

Mosk, Justice. We here consider the rights of the true owner of a negotiable instrument which has been collected and paid on a forged indorsement. The question has not previously arisen in this state under the Uniform Commercial Code, and has seldom been addressed in other jurisdictions.[1]

The record recounts a typical tale of forgery. Plaintiff Joseph Stell, an attorney, employed one Bernice Ruff as a secretary and bookkeeper. During a period of approximately a year and one-half Ruff purloined some 29 checks intended for Stell and forged the necessary indorsements thereon.[2] She cashed

1. The only case directly on point with respect to the liability of a collecting bank to the true owner appears to be Ervin v. Dauphin Deposit Trust Company (Pa.Ct. of Com.Pls., 1965), 38 Pa.Dist. & Co.R.2d 473 [3 U.C.C.Rep. 311]. This case has received considerable attention from commentators; see, e.g., Advanced ALI–ABA Course of Study on Banking and Secured Transactions under the Uniform Commercial Code (ALI 1968) pages 54–57 (dialogue between Prof. E. Allan Farnsworth and Fairfax Leary, Jr.); Bailey, The Law of Bank Checks (4th ed. 1969) § 15.14, pages 496–501; Clark & Squillante, The Law of Bank Deposits, Collections and Credit Cards (1970) pages 141–147. The Ervin case appears to reach the same conclusion expressed herein. In Harry H. White, Lbr. Co. v. Crocker Citizens Nat. Bank (1967), 253 Cal.App.2d 368, 376, 61 Cal.Rptr. 381, the court held that the true owner of an instrument has a cause of action against the collecting bank under the code, but did not deal with the bank's possible defenses. The court stated, however, that the code appeared not to change pre-existing California law with respect to the liability of collecting banks. See also Salsman v. National Community Bank (Super. Ct.N.J.1968), 102 N.J.Super. 482, 246 A.2d 162, which held a collecting bank liable on the ground it had violated reasonable commercial standards.

Federal Deposit Ins. Corp. v. Marine Nat. Bank of Jacksonville (5th Cir. 1970), 431 F.2d 341 and Belmar Trucking Corp. v. American Trust Co. (N.Y. Civ.Ct.1970), 8 U.C.C.Rep. 73, were decided on the same basis. Except for the Ervin case, these decisions do not discuss the issue of whether the collecting bank retains the proceeds of the instrument. See also Stone & Webster Engineering Corp. v. First Nat. Bank and Trust Co. (1962), 345 Mass. 1, 184 N.E.2d 358 (action by drawer against collecting bank denied). There appear to be no cases discussing in detail the right of the true owner to recover from the payor bank under the Uniform Commercial Code; in the Ervin case, however, such an action was upheld on demurrer. (See Annot: Construction and Effect of U.C.C. Art. 3, Dealing With Commercial Paper, 23 A.L.R.3d 932, 1002–1004.)

2. Twenty-one of the checks were made out to Stell. Of these, one was intended for Stell personally, fourteen were intended for a joint venture of which Stell and the other plaintiffs were members, and six were intended for a receivership of which Stell was receiver. The remaining eight instruments were made out in the name of and intended for one Rebecca Smithson, one of Stell's clients. Stell has been assigned the rights of the receivership and of Rebecca Smithson.

some of these checks at defendants Union Bank and Crocker Citizens National Bank and deposited the remainder (except one that was cashed elsewhere) to her personal account at the latter bank. The entire amount of such deposits was subsequently withdrawn by Ruff prior to discovery of the forgeries. Certain of the checks were forwarded to and paid by defendants Crocker Citizens National Bank, Security First National Bank, and First Western Bank and Trust Company; the remainder were drawn on payors who are not parties to this action.

Stell and his partners bring this action in conversion against both the collecting and the payor banks to recover the amounts of the instruments handled by them on the forged indorsements. The critical California Commercial Code provision [3] is section 3419 which establishes that "(1) An instrument is converted when * * * (c) It is paid on a forged indorsement." Notwithstanding this language, the superior court denied recovery on the basis of section 3419, subdivision 3, which provides: "(3) Subject to the provisions of this code concerning restrictive indorsements a representative, including a depositary or collecting bank, who has in good faith and in accordance with reasonable commercial standards applicable to the business of such representative dealt with an instrument or its proceeds on behalf of one who was not the true owner is not liable in conversion or otherwise to the true owner beyond the amount of any proceeds remaining in his hands."

The court concluded that all defendants in the case, including payor as well as collecting banks, qualified as representatives, had acted in good faith and in accordance with reasonable commercial standards, and had no proceeds remaining in their hands. Thus defendants were held immune from liability. The court also found that plaintiffs had been negligent in failing to discover Ruff's defalcations by April 1, 1966, approximately six months following their commencement, and that such negligence substantially contributed to the making of the subsequent forged indorsements. On this additional basis it held plaintiffs were "precluded from asserting such forgeries or lack of authorized signatures against any of the respective Defendants herein on checks presented after April 1, 1966."

We hold that the trial court relied on an erroneous interpretation of section 3419 and that therefore the judgment must be

3. All code references are to the California Commercial Code unless otherwise indicated.

reversed in part. Inasmuch as collecting banks and payor banks raise distinctive issues under section 3419, the application of this section to the two categories of banks will be discussed separately.

Collecting Banks

It is clear, excluding for the moment the issue of plaintiffs' negligence, that defendant collecting banks are liable for conversion unless they can establish a defense under section 3419, subdivision (3). A careful study of this provision, however, reveals no possible defense in this case after it becomes evident that the court below erroneously held defendant collecting banks had parted with the proceeds of the fraudulently indorsed instruments. The code, unfortunately, fails to define the word "proceeds" in the context of bank collection. Therefore, to fully comprehend the code section we must examine the concept of proceeds as it was understood prior to enactment of the code and to general theory of bank collection found elsewhere in the code and in other parts of the law.[4]

Whether defendant depositary banks have any proceeds of the fraudulently indorsed checks remaining in their hands is resolved through a bifurcated inquiry: first, did they receive any proceeds and second, have they parted with any proceeds they may have received? Each of these queries is more complex than superficially appears. A collecting bank obviously does not receive any proceeds of an instrument unless such proceeds are forwarded to it from a payor bank. Under the dominant theory of bank collection that preexisted the code and which the code has left unchanged, however, the amounts a payor bank remits on a forged indorsement are not considered the proceeds of the instrument. The explanation for this result lies in the relationship between a payor bank and its customer, the depositor-drawer. The relationship is one of debtor and creditor: the bank is indebted to the customer and promises to debit his account only at his direction. If the bank pays, on an instrument drawn by its customer, any person other than the designated payee or a person to whom the instrument is negotiated, the bank's indebtedness to the customer is not diminished. If the bank does debit the customer's account, the customer can compel the bank to recredit the sum. Inasmuch as the full amount of the instru-

---

4. For an extensive discussion of the history of legal treatment of forged indorsements and the environment from which the Uniform Commercial Code provisions grew, see Kessler, Forged Indorsements (1938) 47 Yale L.J. 863.

ment remains in the account of the drawer when the bank pays
on a forged indorsement, the bank manifestly does not part with
the proceeds of the instrument but merely remits other funds
from its own account.[5]

Ratification by Collecting Bank

General bank collection theory also instructs us that the true
owner, in bringing an action against a collecting bank for conversion of a check collected on a forged indorsement, is deemed
to have ratified the collection of the proceeds from the payor
bank. This ratification transmutes the remittance of funds by
the payor bank into an authorized act for which it may debit its
customer's account.[6] In the case at bar, it appears that plaintiffs' action against defendant collecting banks constitutes such
a ratification, and these banks, therefore, must be considered to
have received the proceeds of the instruments.

Ratification of collection, however, does not constitute a ratification of the collecting banks' delivery of the proceeds to the
wrong person. The dominant pre-code law established, on the
contrary, that the proceeds were held, after collection by the collecting bank, for the benefit of the true owner.[7] Again resort-

5. "The general rule must be conceded that the undertaking of a bank
is to pay out the depositor's money only on the order of the depositor and in
accordance with that order. If it pays
out money on a check drawn to order,
* * * upon a forged indorsement
of the payee's name, it has not paid in
accordance with the depositor's order,
and in the absence of anything further, has no right to charge such payment against the depositor's account."
(Los Angeles Inv. Co. v. Home Sav.
Bank (1919), 180 Cal. 601, 604, 182 P.
293, 294; see Britton, Bills and Notes
(2d ed. 1961) § 142, pp. 406–407;
§ 147, p. 422; 10 Am.Jur.2d, Banks,
§§ 622, 623, pp. 586–589; Johnson &
Parachini, Forged Indorsements and
Conflict of Laws (1965) 82 Banking
L.J. 95; see also cases cited in Beutel,
Brannan's Negotiable Instruments
Law (7th ed. 1948) § 23, pp. 445–447.)
It appears that nothing in the Uniform Commercial Code changes this
relationship between a bank and its
depositor. It is consequently preserved by section 1103, which provides: "Unless displaced by the particular provisions of this code, the
principles of law and equity, including
the law merchant and the law relative

to capacity to contract, principal and
agent, estoppel, fraud, misrepresentation, duress, coercion, mistake, bankruptcy, or other validating or invali-
dating cause shall supplement its
provisions."

6. Although courts have employed
various theories in holding collecting
banks liable, the theory of ratification
appears to have dominated. (See
Mackey-Woodward, Inc. v. Citizens
State Bank (1966), 197 Kan. 536, 419
P.2d 847, 853–854; United States
Portland Cement Co. v. United States
Nat. Bank of Denver (1916), 61 Colo.
334, 157 P. 202; Independent Oil
Men's Assn. v. Fort Dearborn Nat.
Bank (1924), 311 Ill. 278, 142 N.E. 458,
459; Britton, Bills and Notes (1961)
supra, § 147, pp. 422–424.) The ratifi-
cation doctrine has been firmly estab-
lished in the law of California; see
Morgan v. Morgan (1963), 220 Cal.
App.2d 665, 678, 34 Cal.Rptr. 82;
Jones v. Bank of America (1942), 49
Cal.App.2d 115, 121–122, 121 P.2d 94;
George v. Security Trust and Savings
Bank (1928), 91 Cal.App. 708, 267 P.
560.

7. See authorities cited in footnote
6, supra.

ing to general banking theory, we find that the amounts a collecting bank remits to a person who transfers to the bank a check bearing a forged indorsement do not constitute the proceeds of the instrument. This result is quite clear in the case of an instrument cashed over the counter. At the time the bank takes such an instrument it has obviously not made any prior collection and, thus, has nothing that could be considered proceeds. The money paid over the counter is, consequently, the bank's own money. Upon collection of the instrument, the proceeds become merged with the bank's general funds and are therefore retained by the bank. (See Advanced ALI–ABA Course of Study on Banking and Secured Transactions under the Uniform Commercial Code (ALI 1968) supra, p. 56.)

A bank that accepts an instrument for deposit likewise ultimately retains the proceeds of that instrument. Such a bank is initially considered to be an agent of the person who delivers the instrument to it for collection. When, however, the bank receives a final settlement for an item it has forwarded for collection, the agency status typically ends, and the bank becomes a mere debtor of its customer. As a mere debtor, it becomes entitled to use the proceeds as its own.[8]

The foregoing view was expressed by Justice Cardozo for the United States Supreme Court in the following terms: "Whether a fiduciary relation continues even afterwards [when the collecting bank has completed the business of collection] upon the theory that the proceeds of the collection until remitted to the forwarder are subject to a trust, depends upon the circumstances. In the absence of tokens of a contrary intention, the better doctrine is, where the common law prevails, that the agency of the collecting bank is brought to an end by the collection of the paper, the bank, from then on being in the position of a debtor, with the liberty, like debtors generally, to use the proceeds as its own." (Jennings v. United States Fidelity & Guaranty Co. (1935), 294 U.S. 216, 219, 55 S.Ct. 394, 395, 79 L.Ed. 869.)[9]

It is significant that the Commercial Code does not make a collecting bank accountable to its customer for the *proceeds* of an instrument but only for "the *amount* of the item." (§ 4213, subd. (3); italics added.) Justice Cardozo's conception of the

---

8. See 5 Scott on Trusts (3d ed. 1967) section 534, pages 3712–3718.

9. We disagree, however, with any implication that might be read into *Jennings* that the collecting bank does not receive the proceeds of the instrument for the purpose of section 3419 when the instrument is collected through a clearing house and the proceeds are used to offset liabilities of the collecting bank.

post-collection status of collecting banks is clearly preserved: "[I]f a collecting bank receives a settlement for an item which is or becomes final the bank is accountable to its customer for the amount of the item. One means of accounting is to remit to its customer the amount it has received on the item. If previously it gave to its customer a provisional credit for the item in an account its receipt of final settlement for the item 'firms up' this provisional credit and makes it final. When this credit given by it so becomes final, in the usual case *its agency status terminates and it becomes a debtor to its customer for the amount of the item.*" (§ 4213, U.Com.Code, com. 9; italics added.)

As suggested by Justice Cardozo, the parties can by mutual agreement extend the agency relationship until the amount of an instrument is received by the customer. Under such an agreement the proceeds would be maintained as a separate fund until paid over to the customer.[10] The ordinary banking transaction, however, contains no such agreement, and it is apparent that there was none in the present case. Defendant collecting banks, on the contrary, became debtors, and the proceeds of the instruments were completely merged with the banks' own funds. The effect of this commingling is that the banks retain the proceeds of the instruments even though amounts set forth in the instruments, in the banks' own money, were remitted to Ruff. This conclusion is derived by reference to the law of constructive trusts. The cases in that area establish that money received by a bank and mingled with the bank's funds is traceable by a proper claimant into those funds. This result is unaffected by withdrawals so long as the amount of the cash on hand is not diminished below the amount of the claimant's money that has been mingled with the fund.[11] Since it is obvious that no such severe diminution of funds occurred in the present case, defendant collecting banks must be deemed to retain the proceeds of the in-

---

10. Restatement Second of Agency, section 398; Seavey, The Law of Agency (1964) section 153, page 250.

11. Scott on Trusts, supra, section 540, page 3734, states: "Where the bank has mingled cash of the claimant with its own cash, it is perfectly well settled that the right of the claimant to follow his money is not lost. The mere fact that the cash of the claimant is indistinguishably mingled with the cash of the bank does not cut off the claimant's interest, but he ac-quires an equitable lien upon the whole of the mingled cash in the bank. This is in accordance with the general rule as to the effect of mingling funds. It is immaterial that withdrawals have been made from the cash and additions of the bank's own money have been made, so long as the amount of cash on hand is not diminished below the amount of the claimant's money which has been mingled in the fund."

struments transferred by Ruff, regardless of whether those instruments were cashed or accepted for deposit.[12]

Our conclusion that defendant collecting banks did not part with the proceeds of the instruments in making the various payments to Ruff is reinforced by several additional factors. To begin with, had the draftsmen of the Commercial Code intended to absolve collecting banks from liability by virtue of such payments, it seems probable they would have employed language more explicit than that of retaining or parting with proceeds. Instead, the words "for value" could have been employed. The collecting banks in this case are in a situation comparable to that of a holder in due course under the Commercial Code or a bona fide purchaser under the law of constructive trusts inasmuch as they took property and in return gave consideration to the transferor. With respect to a holder in due course or a bona fide purchaser, however, this consideration is termed "value." (§ 3302; 5 Scott on Trusts, supra, §§ 474–475, pp. 3454–3456.) The fact that different terminology is contained in section 3419, subdivision (3), suggests that the ambiguous language of this provision was not intended to refer to the giving of such consideration. If the draftsmen and the Legislature had intended to protect collecting banks that had merely given value for an instrument, it may be assumed they would have clearly said so.

Secondly, an examination of the law existing prior to the enactment of the Uniform Commercial Code reveals a nearly unanimous agreement among the jurisdictions that the true owner of an instrument collected on a forged indorsement could recover in a direct suit against a collecting bank even though the bank had acted in good faith and with the highest degree of care and even

---

12. Ervin v. Dauphin Deposit Trust Co. (1965), supra, 38 Pa.Dist. & Co.R.2d 473 [3 U.C.C.Rep. 311, 319], arrives at this same conclusion. The court states: "When [the collecting bank] purchased or cashed the forged checks drawn on other banks it did so with its own money and then, in putting them through for collection it obtained from the drawee banks money which belongs to the plaintiff." Commentators have suggested that the *Ervin* case may stand for the rule that the collecting bank parts with the proceeds if it accepts an instrument for deposit in an account and later pays out the money in the account but does not part with the proceeds if it cashes the instrument. (Advanced ALI–ABA Course of Study on Banking and Secured Transactions under The Uniform Commercial Code (ALI 1968) supra, pp. 54–57 (dialogue between Professor E. Allan Farnsworth and Fairfax Leary, Jr.); Clark & Squillante, The Law of Bank Deposits, Collections and Credit Cards (1970) pp. 143–144.) There appears to be no practical rationale for this arbitrary solution, and the *Ervin* decision clearly appears to negate it: "As far as the problem in the instant case is concerned we can find no distinction between the *cashing* of a forged check and the *accepting* of such check for deposit." (3 U.C.C.Rep. at p. 315.)

though it had remitted the amount of the instrument to a prior party.[13] Since the rule had apparently operated satisfactorily, there is no reason to believe the code draftsmen or the Legislature would have wished to modify it to make direct suits extremely difficult. As discussed below, the payor bank is in effect strictly liable to the true owner if it pays an instrument on a forged indorsement. The collecting banks that handled the instrument for collection are, in turn, strictly liable to the payor bank for breach of warranty of good title. (§ 4207.) [14] Because

13. "The vast majority of cases in this country hold, in the absence of negligence, laches or estoppel, that a collecting bank which cashes a check on a forged or unauthorized indorsement of the payee, and procures the proceeds thereof from the drawee, is liable to the payee who is the true owner of the check." (Mackey-Woodward, Inc. v. Citizens State Bank (1966), supra, 197 Kan. 536, 419 P.2d 847, 852.) See, e.g., Morgan v. Morgan (1963), supra, 220 Cal.App.2d 665, 677, 34 Cal.Rptr. 82; Jones v. Bank of America (1942), supra, 49 Cal.App.2d 115, 122, 121 P.2d 94; George v. Security Trust and Savings Bank (1928), supra, 91 Cal.App. 708, 267 P. 560; Henderson v. Lincoln Rochester Trust Co. (1951) 303 N.Y. 27, 100 N.E.2d 117, 119–120; Independent Oil Men's Assn. v. Fort Dearborn Nat. Bank (1924), supra, 311 Ill. 278, 142 N.E. 458, 459; Gresham State Bank v. O & K Construction Co. (1962), 231 Or. 106, 370 P.2d 726, 729; United States Portland Cement Co. v. United States Nat. Bank of Denver (1916), supra, 61 Colo. 334, 157 P. 202. See Annot: Right of check owner to recover against one cashing it on forged or unauthorized indorsement and procuring payment by drawee, 100 A.L.R.2d 670; 10 Am.Jur.2d, Banks, section 632, pages 599–600. The leading case reaching a result that opposed the general rule (Tibby Bros. Glass Co. v. Farmers' and Mechanics' Bank (1908), 220 Pa. 1, 69 A. 280) was expressly overruled in a subsequent decision (Lindsley v. First Nat. Bank (1937), 325 Pa. 393, 190 A. 876).

14. "§ 4207. [Warranties of Customer and Collecting Bank on Transfer or Presentment of Items; Time for Claims] (1) Each customer or collecting bank who obtains payment or acceptance of an item and each prior customer and collecting bank warrants to the payor bank or other payor who in good faith pays or accepts the item that (a) He has a good title to the item or is authorized to obtain payment or acceptance on behalf of one who has good title. * * * "
(§ 3417 provides for a parallel remedy against non-bank transferors of instruments.) The remedies of direct action by the true owner and of circuitous action through the payor bank are not strictly coincident inasmuch as the payor's warranty action may be barred by his failure to act in a timely fashion. Section 4207, subdivision (4), provides: "Unless a claim for breach of warranty under this section is made within a reasonable time after the person claiming learns of the breach, the person liable is discharged to the extent of any loss caused by the delay in making claim." This proviso is of small significance with respect to forged indorsements since the forgery is rarely, if ever, discovered soon enough to prevent loss. The fact that the direct action and the circuitous action might result in different allocation of liability in one improbable situation appears insufficient to justify the diseconomy and injustice created by circuitous action. Moreover, assuming the payor bank failed to make a timely claim to the collecting bank, which failure proximately resulted in the collecting bank's payment of the amount of an instrument on a forged indorsement, and that the true owner recovered from the collecting bank in a direct action, it would appear that the collecting bank should be able to recover its loss from the payor bank, if not under the code, in

liability ultimately rests with the first collecting bank, it is unlikely that such a bank was intended to have a ready defense in a direct suit by the true owner. Requiring cumbersome and uneconomical circuity of action to achieve an identical result would obviously run contra the code's explicit underlying purposes "to simplify, clarify and modernize the law governing commercial transactions." (§ 1102, subd. (2)(a).)

Such a modification would also create a significant potential for injustice. In cases involving forged indorsements collecting banks are generally the most feasible defendants. A forger typically transfers instruments bearing forged indorsements to only one or two banks for collection. Often the banks are located near the true owner. Thus it would be practical for him to bring a suit against such banks. The payors, by contrast, may be situated in many and distant states or in foreign countries, and the drawers may be equally geographically diverse. Even though the collecting banks would be ultimately liable after initial suits were brought in all the various fora, the expense and difficulty of bringing such suits would have the actual effect of freeing the collecting banks from any responsibility. The true owner would be required to shoulder the loss that should have been that of the banks; thus the banks would receive a windfall. That section 3419, subdivision (3), was intended to produce this unjust result is highly doubtful.

Had such substantial and controversial deviation from prior law been intended, moreover, it could be expected that the official commentary to section 3419 would have so stated and would have included extensive explanation of the reasons for the change. Neither the California nor the uniform comment to this section, however, contains any such discussion. The comments, on the contrary, are brief and state that section 3419, subdivision (3), is merely a codification of prior decisions (U.Com.Code com. 5) and is entirely consistent with prior California law (Cal. com. 5).

The prior decisions to which the Uniform Commercial Code comment makes reference are presumably a line of cases primarily involving defendants that had acted as investment brokers and had marketed negotiable securities, remitting the consideration received to their customers.[15] The relationships between

an action for common law negligence or in a suit in equity to prevent unjust impoverishment.

15. E.g., Pratt v. Higginson (1918), 230 Mass. 256, 119 N.E. 661; Gruntal v. National Surety Co. (1930), 254 N.Y. 468, 173 N.E. 682; First Nat. Bank of Blairstown v. Goldberg (1941), 340 Pa. 337, 17 A.2d 377.

the representatives and their customers in those cases appear to have been true agency relationships that did not merge into debtor-creditor relationships upon collection of the proceeds. Unlike the ordinary bank collection transaction, in which the collecting bank and its customer have tacitly agreed a debtor-creditor relationship will emerge upon collection, the ordinary agency transaction gives rise to no such debt when the agent receives funds intended for the principal. Such funds, instead of being mingled, must be kept separate from the agent's own funds and identified as the property of the principal.[16] Thus, when the true agent remits the amount of an instrument to his customer, the agent actually does part with the proceeds. It is to this kind of situation, rather than to the typical bank collection transaction, that section 3419, subdivision (3), appears to be addressed.

Defendant collecting banks are, therefore, liable to plaintiffs for the amounts of those instruments received by them as of April 1, 1966. Plaintiffs' negligence, however, bars them from recovering for conversion of instruments received after that date. Plaintiffs do not dispute the trial court's finding that their negligence substantially contributed to the conversion of these instruments, and it appears, viewing the evidence in the light most favorable to the judgment, substantial evidence existed to justify such a finding. Stell had been retained by Ruff in 1963 because of her insolvency and because of litigation instituted against her by several creditors. She had informed Stell at that time that her financial difficulties were primarily due to considerable gambling losses she had sustained. A short time thereafter he hired her as a secretary and bookkeeper. He exercised practically no supervision over her, never reviewed the books, and never checked the bank reconciliation of deposits on the accounts she handled. Only during an annual examination made for tax return purposes by one of Stell's partners were Ruff's records reviewed, and even then, despite the suspicious absence of an entry, her accounts were accepted without checking for accuracy or veracity.

Section 3404 provides: "Any unauthorized signature is wholly inoperative as that of the person whose name is signed unless he ratifies it *or is precluded from denying it.* * * *" (Italics added.) The Uniform Commercial Code comment to this section adds the following explanation: "The words 'or is precluded from denying it' are retained in subsection (1) to recognize the

---

16. Restatement Second of Agency, section 398; Seavey, The Law of Agency (1964) section 153, page 250.

possibility of an estoppel against the person whose name is signed, as where he expressly or tacitly represents to an innocent purchaser that the signature is genuine; *and to recognize the negligence which precludes a denial of the signature."* (§ 3404, U.Com.Code com. 4; italics added.) The preclusion language of section 3404 is essentially the same as that of section 23 of the Negotiable Instruments Law (former § 3104 of the Civ.Code). This language has been interpreted to provide for equitable estoppel in order to avoid an unconscionable result.[17] We conclude that the doctrine must be invoked in the present case. Plaintiffs' negligent failure to discover Ruff's patent defalcations was directly responsible for defendant depositary banks' detrimental change of position in paying Ruff the amount of the instruments. Defendants acted entirely in good faith, and, though their conduct with respect to certain of the instruments may have fallen somewhat below reasonable commercial standards, it was not sufficiently egregious to shift the balance of the scales in plaintiffs' favor.

For the purposes of this case, therefore, plaintiffs are precluded from denying the forged signatures are operative indorsements. Ruff is then deemed to be a "holder," which the code defines as "a person who is in possession of a document of title or an instrument or an investment security drawn, issued or indorsed to him or to his order or to bearer or in blank." (§ 1201, subd. (20).) Good faith payment or satisfaction to the holder of an instrument discharges a party to the extent of his payment or satisfaction, even though the holder may have acquired the instrument by theft. (§ 3603, subd. (1).) Defendant collecting banks are thus discharged on the instruments received by them after April 1, 1966.

Payor Banks

All but three of the instruments paid by defendant payor banks had been transferred for collection by collecting banks that are also parties to this suit. As indicated above, plaintiffs ratified the collection of these instruments by bringing this action against the collecting banks. This ratification retroactively validates the payor banks' remission of proceeds and provides a

17. See Beutel, Brannan's Negotiable Instruments Law (7th ed. 1948) section 23, pages 455–464; Britton, Bills and Notes (2d ed. 1961) section 128, pages 343–344. See also Annot: Payee's prior negligence facilitating forging of indorsement as precluding recovery from bank paying check, 87 A.L.R.2d 638; Annot: When depositor-drawer of check is "precluded," under Negotiable Instruments Law, § 23, from setting up forgery of indorsement or want of authority against drawee bank, 39 A.L.R.2d 641.

defense to an action for conversion. With respect to these instruments, therefore, no liability exists as to any payor bank. Two of the instruments on which this action is based, however, were presented by Ruff directly to the payor, Crocker Bank. The one remaining instrument was collected through banks that are not parties to this action and was also paid by Crocker. With respect to these three instruments no ratification occurred, and we must therefore consider whether Crocker is liable for their conversion.

The conclusion of the court below that section 3419, subdivision (3), shields defendant payor banks from liability is erroneous.[18] Even if we assume arguendo that section 3419, subdivision (3), was intended to apply to payor banks, the provision would afford them no protection in cases such as this. As we stated above, the amounts a payor bank transfers to a collecting bank on a forged indorsement do not constitute the proceeds of the instrument, unless the true owner ratifies the collection. It follows that, absent such ratification, the proceeds remain in the hands of the payor bank. The payor bank is, consequently, liable for the full amount of the instrument notwithstanding section 3419, subdivision (3).

It is not now necessary for us to undertake an extensive analysis of the applicability of section 3419, subdivision (3), to payor banks. Inasmuch as the three instruments that concern us were all transferred by Ruff after April 1, 1966, plaintiffs'

---

18. It appears clear that section 3419, subdivision (3), was not intended to apply to nondepositary payor banks. The fact that the provision expressly includes depositary and collecting banks but does not mention payor banks creates a strong negative inference in this regard. The applicability of the term "representative" to nondepositary payor banks is also doubtful. It is significant that the extensive commentary on section 3419 by numerous experts in the law of commercial paper apparently does not contain a single suggestion that the defense of section 3419, subdivision (3), is available to nondepositary payor banks. Some commentators have declared outright that the defense is not available. (E.g., 6C Willier & Hart, U.C.C. Reporter-Digest, § 3–419, A2; Allocation of Losses from Check Forgeries Under the Law of Negotiable Instruments and The Uniform Commercial Code (1953) 62 Yale L.J. 417, 471.) Others arrive at the same conclusion by implication in discussing the defense only in the context of depositary and collecting banks. (E.g., Advanced ALI–ABA Course of Study on Banking and Secured Transactions Under the Uniform Commercial Code (ALI 1968) p. 54; Bailey, The Law of Bank Checks (4th ed. 1969) § 15.14, pp. 496–501; Clark & Squillante, The Law of Bank Deposits, Collections and Credit Cards (1970) pp. 141–147; Cosway, Negotiable Instruments—Comparison of Washington Law and the Uniform Commercial Code (1968) 43 Wash.L.Rev. 499, 543; 2 New York Law Revision Commission Study of the Uniform Commercial Code (1955) p. 1079; O'Malley, Common Check Frauds and the Uniform Commercial Code (1969) 23 Rutgers L.Rev. 189, 231.)

negligence stands as a bar to recovery. Section 3406 states that "Any person who by his negligence substantially contributes to a material alteration of the instrument or to the making of an unauthorized signature is precluded from asserting the alteration or lack of authority against a holder in due course or against a drawee or other payor who pays the instrument in good faith and in accordance with the reasonable commercial standards of the drawee's or payor's business."

The record contains substantial evidence to support the trial court's finding that Crocker acted in good faith and in accordance with reasonable commercial standards in handling the three instruments. Ruff held an account with Crocker, and at the time the account was opened, she had been introduced to the bank by one of its established customers. Nothing on the face of the instruments would have led the bank to suspect they were irregular in any way. A single branch of a large bank, as the testimony indicated, may handle several thousand instruments bearing third party indorsements in a single day. Considering this burden, it would be commercially unreasonable to expect payor banks to undertake foolproof efforts to verify ostensibly valid indorsements. Crocker's diligence with respect to the check received through bank collection channels is, of course, particularly evident, inasmuch as Crocker apparently received the instrument with all prior indorsements guaranteed by the collecting banks. Having acted in good faith and in accordance with reasonable commercial standards, Crocker is therefore entitled to invoke the defense of section 3406.[19]

Conclusion

We conclude that defendant collecting banks are liable for the amount of any instrument received by them prior to April 1, 1966. The record reveals that only 7 of the 29 misappropriated checks were received by that date, and each of them was taken for collection by defendant Union Bank. The total amount of these seven checks is $2,791.11. The judgment is therefore reversed with directions to enter judgment against Union for

---

19. We find no merit to plaintiffs' additional contention that the findings of the trial court were insufficiently specific to support the judgment in that the court failed to state precisely what procedures constitute reasonable commercial practices. After outlining the procedures defendant banks had followed, the court concluded that they had acted in accordance with reasonable commercial standards. These findings are sufficient under Code of Civil Procedure section 634 to assure adequate review of the trial court decision. (Whitney Inv. Co. v. Westview Dev. Co. (1969), 273 Cal.App.2d 594, 604, 78 Cal.Rptr. 302.)

$2,791.11 plus the appropriate interest due on the amounts of
each of the seven checks. With respect to the other defendants
the judgment is affirmed. The parties shall bear their own costs
on appeal.

NOTES

1. In *Cooper* the court held that liability of the collecting
banks was governed by UCC § 3–419(1)(c) in that they "paid"
the checks on forged indorsements. Although that provision is
ambiguous it apparently was not meant to apply to non-payor
banks. "Payment" of an instrument is contrasted with "purchase" and it refers to the transaction in which the instrument is
taken up by the person designated in the instrument as the pay-
or or by someone who is obligated under the instrument to make
payment. A check is normally paid by the drawee or "payor
bank" (UCC § 4–105(b)) or, in the case of dishonor, by a secondary party such as the drawer (UCC § 3–413(2)) or indorser
(UCC § 3–414(1)). Such payment results in the discharge of the
person paying. UCC § 3–603. A depositary bank other than
the payor bank which takes the check from its customer for
value purchases the check but does not pay it. A depositary
bank which does not purchase the check but which acts solely as
an agent for collection does not pay the check when it gives its
customer final credit for it. The check is paid by the payor bank
and the depositary bank merely acts as a conduit of this payment. Thus, the reference in UCC § 3–419(1)(c) would appear to
be to the act of the payor bank and not the depositary bank.
Stone & Webster Engineering Corp. v. First National Bank &
Trust Co., 345 Mass. 1, 184 N.E.2d 358 (1962), infra p. 367. The
pre-Code cases were not in agreement concerning the liability of
a drawee who paid on a forged indorsement. Since the drawee
of an uncertified check has no liability on the check some courts
held that payment on a forged indorsement could result in no
liability. Other courts disagreed, holding that the drawee was
liable to the owner of the check on either a conversion theory or
an inexplicable theory of "constructive acceptance." UCC
§ 3–419(1)(c) was apparently designed to resolve this disagreement by adopting the conversion theory. See Comment 3 to
UCC § 3–419. UCC § 3–419(1), however, is not all-inclusive.
Conversion actions recognized by general law are not negated
because not specifically recognized in the section. For example,
a depositary bank that takes a check payable jointly to two payees but indorsed by only one is liable in conversion to the nonindorsing payee if it collects the check and allows the indorsing

payee to withdraw the proceeds. Berkheimer's, Inc. v. Citizens
Valley Bank, 270 Or. 807, 529 P.2d 903 (1974). The liability is
based on UCC § 1–103 not § 3–419(1). Most of the pre-Code
cases held that a collecting bank that collected a check with a
forged indorsement was liable to the owner of the check on a
conversion theory. The theory of these cases is expounded in
Cooper. Thus, the conclusion of *Cooper* that collecting banks
are liable in conversion is correct even if UCC § 3–419(1)(c) does
not literally apply.

2. UCC § 3–419(3) specifically applies to depositary and collecting banks and its apparent meaning is that the depositary
bank is liable only to the extent that it has not paid out to its
customer the proceeds collected. *Cooper* by its construction of
the word "proceeds" effectively reads the section out of the statute insofar as depositary or collecting banks are concerned.
Most cases have followed *Cooper* on this point although there is
contrary authority. In *Berkheimer's,* cited in Note 1, the depositary bank relied on UCC § 3–419(3) as a defense. The court
assumed that that section applied but found for plaintiff on the
ground that defendant did not meet the burden of showing that
it acted in accordance with reasonable commercial standards.
Unlike many cases of forged or unauthorized indorsements
which cannot be easily detected, the defect in the indorsement in
that case could be readily detected by examining the instrument.
See also Beyer v. First National Bank of Dillon, 612 P.2d 1285
(Mont.1980). In Jackson Vitrified China Co. v. People's American Bank of North Miami, 388 So.2d 1059 (Fla.App.1980), the
court specifically rejected the *Cooper* reading of UCC
§ 3–419(3). It said:

> Faced with the reasonably clear intention of the drafters
> of the Code, our sole remaining task is the choice between
> following what appears to be bad law, or 'adapting' that law
> to what we perceive to be commercial reality, as some other
> states' courts have done.

> Our role commands adherence to lawful legislative de-
> cree. A judicial assay into lawmaking is inappropriate;
> moreover, the false assumption of power to do so diminishes
> public respect for our lawful authority, which is essential to a
> government of laws.

> We believe that the laws of commerce would benefit by
> the absence of * * * UCC § 3–419(3) * * *.

It is the law, nonetheless, and we are bound by its terms.
* * *

3. The court in *Cooper* states that by bringing action against the depositary banks the plaintiffs ratified collection of the checks by these banks and that this ratification retroactively validated the payments by the payor banks. Why should the payee lose his cause of action against the payor banks just because he brought an action against the depositary banks? In this case there were three converters: the forger, the depositary bank and the payor bank. In other than bank-collection cases, the normal rule regarding multiple converters is that the plaintiff is entitled to sue all but is entitled to only one satisfaction. Since the depositary bank must, and can, bear the risk of loss the rule stated by *Cooper* which releases the payor bank may not cause difficulty in the case decided. But the plaintiffs in *Cooper* originally brought action against Ruff as well as the collecting and payor banks; the action against Ruff was dismissed in the course of the proceedings in the trial court. See Cooper v. Union Bank, 27 Cal.App.3d 85, 103 Cal.Rptr. 610 (1972). Why doesn't this mean that the plaintiffs ratified the payment by depositary bank to Ruff? Does the court's discussion of ratification demonstrate the danger of "thinking like a lawyer"? In an earlier case decided by the California Supreme Court, Pacific Coast Cheese, Inc. v. Security First National Bank, 45 Cal.2d 75, 286 P.2d 353 (1955), Employee altered checks drawn by Employer to the order of Employee by raising the amount payable. These checks were paid by Drawee Bank. When Employer discovered the fraud it filed a criminal complaint against Employee as well as a civil action in which it recovered judgment for the amount that the checks were raised. The judgment was not satisfied. Employer then sued Drawee Bank for the same amount. Drawee Bank defended on the theory that Employer's suit was barred under the doctrine of election of remedies by reason of the judgment against Employee. The court held that the doctrine is based on estoppel and operates only if the party asserting it has been injured; Drawee Bank was in no way injured or prejudiced by the action against Employee. Is this case distinguishable from *Cooper?* It was not cited in *Cooper.*

NOTE: NEGLIGENCE AND OTHER CONDUCT AS BASIS OF ESTOPPEL TO DENY VALIDITY OF SIGNATURES

In *Cooper* the plaintiffs were found by the trial court to have been negligent "at least by April 1, 1966" in not discovering the defalcations of Ruff. See Cooper v. Union Bank, 27 Cal.App.3d 85, 103 Cal.Rptr. 610 (1972). The Supreme Court of California held that this negligence could be used by the collecting banks as the basis for an estoppel against the plaintiffs under UCC § 3–404(1). The court stated that this negligence was "directly responsible for defendant depositary banks' detrimental change of position in paying Ruff the amount of the instruments." NIL § 23, on which the UCC provision is based, provided as follows: "When a signature is forged or made without the authority of the person whose signature it purports to be, it is wholly inoperative, and no right to retain the instrument, or to give a discharge therefore, or to enforce payment thereof, against any party thereto, can be acquired through or under such signature, unless the party, against whom it is sought to enforce such right, is precluded from setting up the forgery or want of authority." The NIL contained no section comparable to UCC § 3–406. Many of the cases that interpreted NIL § 23 in the common situation exemplified by *Cooper* held that negligence in choosing the employee or negligence in supervising the employee and discovering the fraud could not be used as the basis for an estoppel. See, for example, R. Mars, The Contract Co. v. Massamutten Bank of Strasburg, 285 F.2d 158 (4th Cir. 1960). Under these decisions the bank asserting the estoppel would have to show that it relied to its detriment on conduct of the owner of the check that induced it to accept the forged indorsement as valid. In a *Cooper* situation the negligence of the owner of the check may have facilitated or contributed to the fraud by Ruff but it may not have induced the defendant banks to pay Ruff the proceeds of the forged-indorsement checks. The rationale of these cases would appear to be changed by UCC § 3–406 which also provides an estoppel but which adopts a less stringent standard. See Thompson Maple Products, Inc. v. Citizens National Bank of Corry, 211 Pa.Super. 42, 234 A.2d 32 (1967). That section states that "any person who by his negligence substantially contributes to * * * the making of an authorized signature is precluded * * *." But that section can be used, by its express terms, only by holders in due course or payors of the instrument and it is subject to the qualification that the person asserting the estoppel be a person who acted in accordance with reasonable commercial standards. Consider this case. Drawer drew a check payable to Plunkett, intending that it be sent to a Plunkett who lived in Alabama. Drawer's check was mistakenly sent to a person with the same name who lived in Illinois. The Illinois Plunkett, knowing that the check was not meant for him, cashed it at Depositary Bank which forwarded it for collection. It was returned by the drawee bank because Drawer had stopped payment. Depositary Bank sued Drawer

under UCC § 3–413(2). Could Drawer defend on the basis that
Depositary Bank took the check under a forged indorsement, or
was it precluded by UCC § 3–406? See Park State Bank v. Arena Auto Auction, Inc., 59 Ill.App.2d 235, 207 N.E.2d 158 (1965).
If Depositary Bank cannot rely on UCC § 3–406 because it is not
a holder, it takes the loss notwithstanding the fact that Drawer
was negligent and Depositary Bank was not. Suppose the check
had been paid and Drawer objected to the payment. Payor
Bank would have had a defense under UCC § 3–406 and if it had
asserted the defense the loss would have fallen on Drawer. If
Payor Bank had failed to assert the defense and attempted to
recover against Depositary Bank for breach of warranty under
UCC § 4–207(1)(a) would Depositary Bank have had a good defense based on Payor Bank's refusal to assert valid defenses
(compare UCC § 4–406(5)) or based on Payor Bank's failure to
prove that the breach of warranty caused it any damages? See
Stone & Webster, infra p. 367.

The court in *Cooper* apparently assumed without discussion
that the estoppel referred to in UCC § 3–404(1) could be invoked
by a finding of negligence by the plaintiffs without reference to
UCC § 3–406. It is significant that in this case the defendants
did not technically fall within the language of UCC § 3–406.
They were not payors. They could qualify as holders in due
course only if the indorsements were valid—the question at issue. Furthermore, because their conduct in the words of the
court "may have fallen somewhat below reasonable commercial
standards," they did not meet the conduct standards of that section.

The court did apply § 3–406 when it considered the liability
of the payor banks. Of course in that case the qualifications of
UCC § 3–406 were met by the defendants. A literal reading of
UCC § 3–406 would deny any protection to depositary banks in
all cases of forged indorsements because they could not qualify
either as holders or payors. Was that result intended? Is it
significant that the Official Comments to UCC § 3–406 refer to
holders in due course and banks taking the instrument only with
respect to altered instruments? Is there any reason to protect a
payor bank but not a depositary bank in the case of a forged
indorsement, or to protect a depositary bank in the case of alteration or a forged check but not in the case of a forged indorsement? Was it the intention of the drafters of the UCC that the
effect of negligence on unauthorized signatures be governed by
either of the two sections so that the qualifications of UCC
§ 3–406 could be avoided by simply resorting to UCC § 3–404(1)

which is unqualified? For a discussion of UCC § 3–406 see Whaley, Negligence and Negotiable Instruments, 53 N.C.L.Rev. 1 (1974).

The estoppel referred to in UCC § 3–404(1) may arise in cases of unauthorized signatures of agents or purported agents signing in behalf of a principal. A signature not actually authorized by the principal may nonetheless be binding on the principal if the agent has apparent authority. Apparent authority is based on a principle that resembles estoppel in that it depends on manifestations by the principal to the third party as to the authority of the ostensible agent on which the third party relies. In fact, in most, but not all, cases of apparent authority the principal would also be bound on an estoppel theory. A signature binding on the principal because of apparent authority is treated as authorized under UCC § 3–403(1). See Comment 1. Orthodox agency doctrine treats the act of the ostensible agent to which the estoppel applies as unauthorized even though the principal is estopped to deny the lack of authority. This fine distinction states in effect that the principal is bound if the third party wants to enforce the obligation but that the principal does not get the benefit of the contract if the third party repudiates. There are some cases in which the agent has neither actual nor apparent authority to act for the principal but in which the conduct of the principal will estop him from asserting the lack of authority. For example, A is in possession of an instrument payable to P and A purports to indorse the instrument in P's name and to sell it on P's behalf to T. A has no actual or apparent authority to indorse or sell the instrument. If P is aware that the transaction is about to occur and does not notify T of the true facts, although he could easily do so, he will be estopped to deny A's lack of authority and is not entitled to recover from T. This result would follow whether P's failure to notify T is deliberate or is the result of negligence. See Restatement, Second, Agency § 8B. The Restatement rule is not limited by a requirement that the belief by T be the result of nonnegligent behavior on his part. UCC § 3–406 does not cover this case but it can be dealt with under UCC § 3–404(1). With respect to cases of negligence that contribute to the making of a forged indorsement when the rights of the depositary bank are involved it seems reasonable to apply the standards of UCC § 3–406 but the section does not literally apply. One could either apply UCC § 3–406 in spite of its language (see *Gresham State Bank* set forth following this Note) or one might use UCC § 3–404(1). The court in *Cooper* apparently followed the latter

course but it did not borrow the standards of UCC § 3–406.
Rather, it protected the depositary banks because their conduct,
though below reasonable commercial standards, was not "sufficiently egregious." Would the court in *Cooper* have applied
that standard to the payor bank?

GRESHAM STATE BANK v. O AND K CONSTRUCTION CO.

Supreme Court of Oregon, 1962.
231 Or. 106, 370 P.2d 726.

O'CONNELL, JUSTICE. This suit was instituted by the Gresham State Bank, interpleading O and K Construction Company
and Ada Zimmerman, dba Zimmerman's Twelve Mile Store, to
determine the rights of the defendants to $5,622.98 which was
tendered into court by plaintiff bank, This sum represented the
amount of money credited to defendant Zimmerman's account in
the plaintiff bank upon Zimmerman's deposit of various checks
made payable to defendant O and K Construction Company.
Zimmerman's Store had cashed the checks upon presentment by
F. C. McKenna, a bookkeeper employed by the defendant construction company. McKenna was not authorized to endorse or
receive the proceeds of the checks. O and K Construction Company filed a cross-complaint alleging that the checks in question
did not bear a valid endorsement of the construction company
and sought recovery for conversion of the checks.

The trial court entered an order discharging plaintiff of all
liability upon the condition that plaintiff pay into court the sum
of $5,622.98, which condition plaintiff met. The court also de-
creed that plaintiff should receive $500 attorneys fees and its
costs incurred in the suit, the amount to be paid out of the money tendered into court.

The court then proceeded to determine the claims of the defendant O and K Construction Company and the defendant Zimmerman to the fund deposited in court by plaintiff. The court
entered a judgment for defendant Zimmerman. The judgment
also provided that plaintiff and defendant Zimmerman recover
their costs and disbursements from defendant O and K Construction Company. Defendant Zimmerman filed a statement of
disbursements including $549 previously paid to plaintiff out of
the interpleaded funds. Upon objection made by defendant O
and K Construction Company the court disallowed the claim for

$549. From the order disallowing the claim defendant Zimmerman cross-appeals.

On or about December 15, 1956, the O and K Construction Company employed Francis McKenna to work in its office located at Twelve Mile Corner near Gresham, Oregon. McKenna's principal duties were to keep the books of the company and to perform other office duties in connection with the business, including answering the telephone, opening the mail, receiving payments made to the company by check or in cash and to give receipts for such payments, and various other duties which we shall describe in more detail below. Although McKenna was required to be at the office of the company during the regular working hours from Monday to Saturday, he was permitted to carry on his own private bookkeeping service for others. Osburn and Kniefel, the officers of the company, were seldom present at the office, their work requiring them to be elsewhere in connection with the operation of the contracting business; consequently they exercised very little supervision over the details of McKenna's work for the company.

From time to time McKenna, in the course of his employment, received checks made payable to the construction company. He was authorized to deposit these checks in the First National Bank of Gresham, which was located about a mile from the company's office. To facilitate the making of these deposits McKenna was furnished a rubber stamp bearing the inscription "For deposit only at the First National Bank." The office supplies also included another rubber stamp with the inscription "O & K Construction Co., Route 1, Gresham, Oregon," which was intended to be used in marking statements, invoices, sales books and other similar items.

During the years 1957, 1958 and 1959 McKenna endorsed 30 checks which had been made payable to the company and cashed them at Zimmerman's Twelve Mile Store, which was also located at Twelve Mile Corner about one half block from the office of the O and K Construction Company. The unauthorized endorsement was made by using the stamp "O & K Construction Co., Route 1, Gresham, Oregon" under which McKenna signed his name, followed by the designation "Office Manager" in some instances and "Bkpr" in others. These checks were cashed at Zimmerman's Store. The store maintained a special check cashing counter at which was maintained a "Regis-Scope" machine by which the check and the person cashing it could be photographed. No inquiry concerning McKenna's right to endorse and cash the checks was made of the officers of the O and K Construction Company. After the checks were cashed, the Zimmerman Store endorsed them and deposited them to its account at the plaintiff bank. The checks were sent through the regular banking channels and paid by the drawee banks. In May, 1959, McKenna's defalcations were discovered, whereupon the O and K Construction Company obtained the cancelled checks from the various makers and made a formal demand upon the drawee banks for the face amount of the checks. The drawee banks in turn made demand upon the plaintiff bank. As these demands were made upon the plaintiff bank, it withdrew from the account of Zimmerman's Store an amount equal to the check and placed it in a suspense account. After the last check had been presented the bank filed this suit in interpleader.

The defendant O and K Construction Company relies upon the rule that one who makes payment upon an unauthorized endorsement of the payee's name is liable to the payee for conversion.

Defendant Zimmerman contends that the loss falls upon the defendant construction company on the basis of any one of the following grounds: (1) that McKenna had implied or apparent authority to endorse the checks and to present them to Zimmerman's for payment on behalf of the construction company; (2) the construction company is precluded from recovery by its negligence; (3) where one of two innocent parties must suffer the loss should fall upon the one whose acts made the loss possible.

The third contention adds nothing to the first two. There is no legal principle which places the loss upon one of two innocent parties merely because one acted and the other did not. The law makes the choice upon the basis of fault or some other consideration warranting the preference. In the present case we must decide upon some such rational ground which of the two defendants should be favored.

We begin with the well established rule that one who obtains possession of a check through the unauthorized endorsement of the payee's name acquires no title to it and is liable to the payee for the amount of the check unless the payee is precluded from setting up the want of authority.

The evidence is clear that McKenna had neither the express nor implied authority to endorse the checks other than for deposit. Defendant Zimmerman contends that if there was not an implied authority the facts disclose that McKenna was clothed with apparent authority. To support this contention Zimmerman points to various instances where, it is alleged, the conduct of Osburn and Kniefel constituted indicia of authority in McKenna to make the endorsements.

It is argued that in supplying McKenna with a rubber stamp bearing the name and address of the construction company, he was provided with the means of endorsing paper and thus representing that he had authority to do so. This does not constitute the creation of an appearance of authority. Whatever appearance of authority arose from the use of the stamp was not created by the O and K Construction Company; it was created by McKenna himself. Certainly the mere furnishing of a name and address stamp by the company for use in its office did not create an ostensible authority to endorse checks and receive payment for them. Stamps of this character are used in most offices; the supplying of them signals nothing with respect to the authority of those employed to use them. Where there are other facts from which third persons might reasonably infer that authority was granted the principal may be held liable.[3]

Other facts are relied upon by Zimmerman as a basis for the alleged appearance of authority. It is pointed out that McKenna had authority to receive checks and cash in payment of accounts owing to the construction company; that he was in charge of the office without supervision approximately 85% of the time; that he dealt with people who came to the office; that he used the company's charge account at Zimmerman's Store; that he was permitted to use money out of the petty cash fund; that Osburn and Kniefel were frequently in Zimmerman's Store with McKenna; that Zimmerman's employees who cashed the checks in question relied upon the fact that McKenna was the office manager of the construction company. We fail to see how these and the other facts recited by Zimmerman create an appearance of authority to endorse checks and to receive the cash for them.

---

3. Glens Falls Indemnity Co. v. Palmetto Bank, 104 F.2d 671 (4th Cir. 1939) (stamp used by assistant treasurer who had express authority to sign checks and conduct business); Kenney v. North Capitol Sav. Bank, 61 App.D.C. 258, 61 F.2d 521 (1932) (the evidence showed that the principal knew and approved of his agent's use of an unqualified endorsement stamp to deposit money in the principal's account); Edgecombe Bonded Warehouse Co. v. Security Nat. Bank, 216 N.C. 246, 4 S.E.2d 863 (1939) (checks were endorsed by the secretary-treasurer who had implied authority to endorse the corporation's checks; apparently the use of the stamp was thought insignificant); Hartford Accident & Indemnity Co. v. Bear Butte Valley Bk., 63 S.D. 262, 257 N.W. 642 (1934) (the company had on previous occasions allowed its employee to stamp checks with a blank endorsement and receive cash for the company; when the employee later kept the proceeds the company was estopped to deny authority).

The mere fact that an employee has charge of a company's office does not entitle third persons dealing with the employee to assume that he has the authority to execute or endorse the company's negotiable paper. We find no evidence to support a finding that McKenna was clothed with apparent authority.

The contention that defendant O and K Construction Company was precluded from recovery because of its negligence presents a more difficult legal problem. There was evidence to support a finding that Osburn and Kniefel were negligent in failing to scrutinize the records of the company over the three-year period during which the defalcation occurred. They made little individual effort to examine their books during that period and no audit was made. Neither of them knew much about bookkeeping and, largely because of that fact, McKenna was able to maneuver the records in such a way as to conceal the misappropriation of the company's funds. Osburn and Kniefel could have discovered the diversion of these funds by checking the bank statements against the company's records showing receipt of payment from various customers. But this was not done and the falsification by McKenna of office records and accounts served to deceive Osburn and Kniefel on the few occasions when they superficially checked the records. During the period in question the company's account was overdrawn on several occasions which, it is argued, should have alerted the officers of the company to the possibility of a misappropriation of their funds. However, apparently it was not uncommon for the company to have overdrafts even when all of its funds found their way to the bank.

It is our conclusion that, although under the circumstances it does not appear that Osburn and Kniefel were seriously at fault in not discovering McKenna's deception, their conduct can be regarded as constituting negligence. To so conclude does not, however, solve the problem in this case. The conduct of both defendant Zimmerman and defendant O and K Construction Company contributed to the successful forgery—Zimmerman in failing to make inquiry as to McKenna's authority to endorse the checks in question, and O and K Construction Company in failing to examine its records. The question is: Who should bear the loss under these circumstances?

In a considerable number of cases it has been held that the negligence of an employer in detecting the dishonest conduct of his employee does not preclude recovery against the payor of an instrument forged by the employee. In some cases this conclusion is reached on the theory that the employer's negligence is not the proximate cause of the loss; the payor's failure to inform himself as to the employee's authority being regarded as the sole cause of the loss.[4]

On the other hand, a substantial number of cases recognize that the payor's duty to ascertain the authority of the employee-endorser is not absolute and that the employer's negligence may bar his recovery against the payor.[5]

It seems evident that the O and K Construction Company's negligence was a causal factor contributing to the forgery.

4. R. Mars, The Contract Co. v. Massanutten Bank of Strasburg, 285 F.2d 158 (4th Cir. 1960); Universal Carloading & Distributing Co. v. South Side Bank, 224 Mo.App. 876, 27 S.W.2d 768 (1930); Britt Co. v. Barefoot & Tatum Drugs, Inc., 240 N.C. 755, 83 S.E.2d 883 (1954). Cf., Washington Loan and Trust Co. v. United States, 77 U.S.App.D.C. 284, 134 F.2d 59 (1943) (drawer v. payor bank which had paid on endorsement forged by drawer's employee); B. F. Saul Co. v. Rich Wine and Liquor Co., 120 A.2d 208 (D.C.Mun.App.1956) (payor on forged endorsement v. negligent drawer); Home Indemnity Co. of New York v. State Bank, 233 Iowa 103, 8 N.W.2d 757 (1943) (assignee of drawer v. bank which had paid on forged endorsement of payee); Greenville Nat. Exch. Bank v. Nussbaum, Tex.Civ. App., 154 S.W.2d 672 (1941) (drawer v. payor bank which had paid on endorsement forged by drawer's employee).

The rule is the same in cases where the drawer of the check sues the drawee bank for charging to the drawer's account money paid on a check bearing the forged endorsement of the payee. Hensley-Johnson Motors v. Citizens Nat. Bank, 122 Cal. App.2d 22, 264 P.2d 973 (1954); Los Angeles Inv. Co. v. Home Sav. Bank, 180 Cal. 601, 182 P. 293, 5 A.L.R. 1193 (1919); Jordan Marsh Co. v. Nat. Shawmut Bank, 201 Mass. 397, 87 N.E. 740, 22 L.R.A.,N.S., 250 (1909); Provident Sav. Bank & Trust Co. v. Western & Southern Life Ins. Co., 41 Ohio App. 261, 179 N.E. 815 (1931); Coffin v. Fidelity-Philadelphia Trust Co., 374 Pa. 378, 97 A.2d 857, 39

A.L.R.2d 625 (1953); Annotation, 39 A.L.R.2d 641, 647 (1955).

5. Kenney v. North Capitol Sav. Bank, 61 App.D.C. 258, 61 F.2d 521 (1932) (payee's negligence in knowingly allowing his employee to use a rubber stamp to endorse checks in blank estopped him from denying the employee's authority to receive cash for checks); Fidelity & Casualty Co. of New York v. First Nat. Bank & Trust Co., 71 N.D. 415, 1 N.W.2d 401 (1941) (principal's failure to inform bank after he knew of agent's defalcations prevented him from asserting lack of authority); Hartford Accident & Indemnity Co. v. Bear Butte Valley Bk., 63 S.D. 262, 257 N.W. 642 (1934) (payee's actions in permitting employee to use a stamp containing an unqualified endorsement and in permitting him to collect accounts in cash or by check was a failure to exercise ordinary care and created an apparent authority in the employee). Cf., Kansas City, Memphis & Birmingham R. R. Co. v. Ivy Leaf Coal Co., 97 Ala. 705, 12 So. 395 (1892) (suit by payee v. drawer to recover amount of check which payee's employee had diverted for his own purposes. Payee's practice of allowing its employee to cash such checks prevented it from asserting want of authority); Morris v. Hofferberth, 81 App.Div. 512, 81 N.Y.S. 403 (1st Dept.), affirmed, 180 N.Y. 545, 73 N.E. 1127 (1903) (suit by payee to charge drawer for money due on account. The account had been paid to payee's employee by check, the proceeds of which were appropriated by the employee. Held: Because payee's employee had managerial powers, an apparent authority was created).

Each of the parties had a duty to exercise due care in connection with the checks in question. Each failed to perform its duty. The question is how to allocate the loss under such circumstances. The conduct of each could be described in terms of negligence. Applying the accepted rule in other negligence cases, the defendant construction company would be barred from recovery because of its contributory negligence. But, it is not necessary or desirable to extend the doctrine of contributory negligence beyond its present scope and there are special reasons why we should not do so in the law of commercial paper.

The pattern for decision in cases such as the one before us is found in § 3–406 of the Uniform Commercial Code which was adopted by the enactment of Oregon Laws 1961, Ch. 726, § 73.4060, to be effective on September 1, 1963. That section (Or.Laws 1961, Ch. 726, § 73.4060; UCC § 3–406) provides as follows:

> "Any person who by his negligence substantially contributes to a material alteration of the instrument or to the making of an unauthorized signature is precluded from asserting the alteration or lack of authority against a holder in due course or against a drawee or other payor who pays the instrument in good faith and in accordance with the reasonable commercial standards of the drawee's or payor's business."

Although this section is not operative until September 1, 1963, it expresses the legislative view as of the time of its enactment. There is no existing Oregon statute or adjudicated case which announces a contrary principle. As we have already indicated the cases in other jurisdictions are in conflict. We are, therefore, free to adopt the principle which, in our opinion, will comport with the needs of the business community in dealing with commercial paper under circumstances such as we have here. We believe that Section 3–406 of the Uniform Commercial Code expresses the appropriate principle. We therefore adopt it. We believe that it is particularly appropriate to do so because it conforms to the view taken, at least tentatively, by the 1961 Legislative Assembly in adopting Oregon Laws 1961, Ch. 726 with a postponed effective date.

It is apparent that this section requires a weighing process in choosing between the owner of the forged instrument and the payor in allocating the loss. Translating the section in terms of the factual situation before us, the O and K Construction Company is not precluded from asserting McKenna's lack of authority unless two conditions exist: (1) that O and K Construction

Company's negligence "substantially contributes" to the making of the unauthorized signature [7] and, (2) that Zimmerman made payment on the instrument in good faith "and in accordance with the reasonable commercial standards of the * * * payor's business." [8]

The requirement that the negligence "substantially contributes" to the making of the unauthorized signature is necessary to satisfy the test of factual causation; it is the equivalent of the "substantial factor" test applied in the law of negligence generally. See Restatement, Torts § 433, p. 733 (Supp.1948); Prosser on Torts, § 44, pp. 218–223 (2d ed. 1955).

There was sufficient evidence to establish the negligence of the O and K Construction Company in failing to check its records and that this negligence substantially contributed to the making of the unauthorized signatures (at least with respect to those checks which were cashed after there was sufficient time for the company to examine its records and discover the depletion of its funds).[9]

This leaves for our consideration the conduct of Zimmerman in cashing the checks. Defendant O and K Construction Company is not precluded from recovery unless Zimmerman's conduct was "in accordance with the reasonable commercial standards" of its business.

Ordinarily the customary practices of a business must be established by evidence. However, it has been judicially recog-

7. The Official Code Comment, § 3–406:1 states: "It should be noted that the rule as stated in the section requires that negligence 'substantially' contribute to the alteration," [or lack of authority]. The comment further notes that "no attempt is made to specify what is negligence, and the question is one for the court or the jury on the facts of the particular case."

8. The Official Code Comment, § 3–406:1 states: "The section protects parties who act not only in good faith (Section 1–201) but also in observance of the reasonable standards of their business. Thus any bank which takes or pays an altered check which ordinary banking standards would require it to refuse cannot take advantage of the estoppel."

9. Cf., Detroit Piston Ring Co. v. Wayne County & Home Sav. Bank,

252 Mich. 163, 233 N.W. 185, 75 A.L.R. 1273 (1930) (depositor's failure to exercise ordinary care in examining returned checks will relieve drawee bank of liability for all payments made after fraud reasonably should have been discovered); Scott v. First Nat. Bank, 343 Mo. 77, 119 S.W.2d 929 (1938) (drawer v. drawee bank to recover money paid from drawer's account on forged endorsement of payee; drawer recovered on first 15 checks but was precluded by negligence on last 25). See generally, Allocation of Losses from Check Forgeries Under the Law of Negotiable Instruments and the Uniform Commercial Code, 62 Yale L.J. 417 (1953); Kessler, Forged Indorsements, 47 Yale L.J. 863 (1938).

nized in many adjudicated cases that one who cashes a check endorsed by an agent has the duty to inquire as to the agent's authority to make the endorsement.[10] We can, therefore, take judicial notice of this duty to make inquiry as a part of the "reasonable commercial standards" of a business. As we have already indicated, the duty to inquire is not absolute; the payor may rely upon the apparent authority of the agent or may assert an estoppel against the principal upon some other ground. We have already stated that there was not sufficient evidence to establish apparent authority. Zimmerman attempts to establish such authority by evidence that McKenna frequently was in the company of Osburn or Kniefel in Zimmerman's Store; that McKenna had authority to purchase for the construction company items in the store which were charged to the construction company's account; that he had authority to disperse funds from the petty cash account; that he was in charge of the office approximately 85% of the time, and that he had authority to receive payments on debts owed to the company, as well as to deal generally with people who called at the office. This conduct would not entitle a reasonable man to assume that McKenna had the authority to endorse the construction company's commercial paper. It seems quite evident that Zimmerman's employees cashed these checks not because they relied upon any appearance of McKenna's authority but because they lulled themselves into a false inference, i.e., they apparently assumed that, because McKenna was entrusted with some authority to handle the construction company's business, he had the authority to endorse checks. The cases establish that this is not a reasonable inference.

In testing Zimmerman's conduct by the standard of ordinary commercial practice, it is to be noted that the checks were not cashed by McKenna in connection with any purchase of items in the store on behalf of the construction company. McKenna received the whole amount of the check. Moreover, the amounts paid to him were substantial, including several checks for $300 or more.

---

10. "Power to indorse and negotiate commercial papers is not implied from an express authority to transact other business for the principal, unless such power be necessary to execute the express authority." Embden State Bank v. Schulze, 49 N.D. 777, 193 N.W. 481 (1923); Anderson, Uniform Commercial Code § 3–404:2, p. 629 (1961), "A third person dealing with a purported agent should communicate with the principal to verify the agent's authority to sign."

See cases cited at note 4, supra, holding that because of a payor's duty to verify a purported agency the principal's negligence was not a proximate cause of the loss.

Ordinarily, it is the usual practice for a company to deposit checks received by it and to pay for its expenditures by checks drawn on its own account. There was nothing about the character of the O and K Construction Company to warrant an assumption by Zimmerman or his employees that these large amounts of cash were needed to carry on the construction company's business. Had Zimmerman exercised the degree of prudence customary in their business McKenna's unusual practice of calling for cash would have indicated to Zimmerman that something may have been wrong in McKenna's management of the company's financial affairs.

It is argued that, since no complaint was made by the construction company after the checks were cashed, Zimmerman was led to believe that McKenna's practice was authorized. Under the circumstances, it would have been more reasonable to infer that McKenna had devised a scheme to cover his defalcations.

We hold that, as a matter of law, Zimmerman did not make payment of the checks in accordance with the reasonable commercial standards of his business.

We have accepted the statement in [UCC § 3–406] as the guiding principle in disposing of this issue in the case. However, ample support for the position we take may be found in cases which reach a similar conclusion without benefit of an expression of legislative policy. Where the payor's negligence consists of his failure to ascertain the authority of the agent who forges the endorsement of his principal, the great weight of authority holds that the principal's negligence does not bar him from recovery. The leading case on the subject, California Stucco Co. of Washington v. Marine Nat. Bank, 148 Wash. 341, 268 P. 891, 67 A.L.R. 1531 (1928), holds that, in the absence of actual or apparent authority, the negligence of the principal in failing to supervise his employees, resulting in the forgery, is not a defense to an action against the payor. The court, quoting from Standard Steam Specialty Co. v. Corn Exchange Bank, 220 N.Y. 478, 116 N.E. 386, L.R.A.1918B, 575 (1917), said that " '[t]he stringent rules of agency and the arbitrary rules of the law of negotiable paper alike protect the principal from such unauthorized acts.' " [12] More frequently the rationale is in terms of proximate cause; the principal's negligence in supervising his dishonest employee is not regarded as the proximate cause of a loss

---

12. California Stucco Co. of Washington v. Marine Nat. Bank, 148 Wash. 341 at 345, 268 P. 891, 892, 67 A.L.R. 1531, 1534 (1928).

arising out of the payor's failure to ascertain the agent's authority.

In some of the cases it is explained that the negligence of the principal, to be a causative factor, must relate to the creation of an appearance of authority in the agent.[14] It would seem more accurate to say that, although the principal's negligence is a causal factor contributing to the loss (reasonable care in supervising his dishonest employee would have prevented it), the payor's negligence outweighs that of the principal in the usual case and he should, therefore, be required to bear the loss.[15] This analysis, recognizing the negligence of both parties as causative factors, would bar the principal in an action against the payor, if the doctrine of contributory negligence were applied.[16] We have indicated above that we would not extend the contributory negligence doctrine to this type of case. It is apparent that [UCC § 3–406] is based upon the same assumption because it permits a negligent principal to recover against a payor who fails to make payment of the instrument in accordance with the reasonable commercial standards of the payor's business.

---

14. R. Mars, The Contract Co. v. Massanutten Bank of Strasburg, 285 F.2d 158 (4th Cir. 1960); Hensley-Johnson Motors v. Citizens Nat. Bank, 122 Cal.App.2d 22, 264 P.2d 973 (1954); Jordan Marsh Co. v. Nat. Shawmut Bank, 201 Mass, 397, 87 N.E. 740, 22 L.R.A.,N.S., 250 (1909); Greenville Nat. Exch. Bank v. Nussbaum, Tex.Civ.App., 154 S.W.2d 672 (1941).

15. It appears that, in some of the cases, the exclusion of the principal's negligence is simply another way of saying that the payor's duty to ascertain the agent's authority is absolute in the absence of ostensible authority created in the agent by the principal.

16. It is probable that courts which treat the payor's negligence as the sole proximate cause do so in order to escape the doctrine of contributory negligence in this class of cases. Compare, Home Indemnity Co. of New York v. State Bank, 233 Iowa 103, 146, 8 N.W.2d 757, 782 (1943) ("It is not a question of comparative negligence. The appellee cannot relieve itself by showing its good faith, or its exercise of care") and American Sash & Door Co. v. Commerce Trust Co., 332 Mo. 98, 110, 56 S.W.2d 1034, 1038 (1932) ("It is not simply a question of using due care and of offsetting negligence against contributory negligence") with Union Tool Co. v. Farmers', etc. Nat. Bk., 192 Cal. 40, 47, 218 P. 424, 427, 28 A.L.R. 1417 (1923) ("Assuming that the plaintiff was negligent * * * the depositing bank may not escape liability for the payment of amounts paid on forged checks unless it has itself been free from negligence.")

See also, Shepard & Morse Lumber Co. v. Eldridge, 171 Mass. 516, 527–528, 51 N.E. 9, 14, 41 L.R.A. 617, 68 Am.St.Rep. 446 (1898) ("The doctrine of contributory negligence as a defense to actions of tort is now of most frequent application; but we have been referred to no instance in which it has been held applicable to actions upon commercial paper. * * * Nothing could more completely unsettle commercial dealings than to extend that doctrine to suits brought by holders of negotiable paper against other parties thereto.").

In the ordinary case it seems proper that the negligent payor, rather than the negligent principal, should bear the loss caused by an agent's unauthorized endorsement of his principal's check. An important factor supporting this conclusion is the relative ease with which the payor, having knowledge of the agency, can ascertain the agent's authority, as compared with the difficulty with which an employee's dishonesty may be detected by his employer. The employer must overcome the obstacles which the employee devises for the very purpose of making it difficult to detect the defalcations.[17] Certainly under the circumstances of the present case, it was more reasonable for the officers of the O and K Construction Company to assume that their employee was honest than it was for Zimmerman to assume that he had the authority to endorse checks and receive payment in cash for no ostensible corporate purpose.[18]

We hold that, because of defendant Zimmerman's negligent failure to act in accordance with the reasonable commercial standards of its business, the defendant O and K Construction Company, although negligent, is not precluded from recovering upon the forged checks. [UCC § 3–406] indicates that the payor's failure to act in accordance with reasonable commercial standards might bar him from setting up the owner's negligence no matter how gross it might be. It is not necessary for us to decide whether the statute will be so interpreted. In the present case the negligence of the O and K Construction Company was clearly outweighed by that of Zimmerman.

We hold that, under these circumstances, Zimmerman cannot rely upon the construction company's negligence to bar the latter's recovery. We reach this conclusion upon a de novo examination of the record, this being a proceeding in equity. The same conclusion would be permissible had this been an action at

---

17. See Corker, Risk of Loss from Forged Indorsements, 4 Stan.L.Rev. 24, 30 (1951) ("The party with the best opportunity to avoid the loss should bear it").

18. Shepard & Morse Lumber Co. v. Eldridge, 171 Mass. 516, 528, 51 N.E. 9, 14, 41 L.R.A. 617, 68 Am.St. Rep. 446 (1898) (employer "has the right to assume that his clerk will not commit a crime * * *"); Detroit Piston Ring Co. v. Wayne County & Home Sav. Bank, 252 Mich. 163, 178, 233 N.W. 185, 190, 75 A.L.R. 1273 (1930) (relying "implicitly upon the honesty and faithfulness of a clerk, whom they had no reason to suspect of dishonesty * * * we do not think * * * should operate as an estoppel of the plaintiff"); Shipman v. Bank of State of New York, 126 N.Y. 318, 329, 27 N.E. 371, 373, 12 L.R.A. 791 (1891) (reposing confidence in an employee who is in fact dishonest does not estop plaintiff from asserting his employee's lack of authority); Welsh v. German American Bank, 73 N.Y. 424, 430 (1878) ("the fact that plaintiff entrusted the checks to his clerk * * * made him no more responsible than if he had entrusted them to an expressman").

law because, as we have indicated, Zimmerman's failure to act in accordance with reasonable commercial standards can be declared as a matter of law.

* * *   *for Δ O + K*

Reversed and remanded.

NOTES

1. The court treated the case as a claim by O and K against Zimmerman based on Zimmerman's negligence. It then considered the question of whether O and K's contributory negligence was a bar to recovery. Since the court had already found that McKenna had no actual or apparent authority to indorse the checks Zimmerman was, without more, guilty of conversion when he took the checks and paid McKenna. Zimmerman's liability is not based on negligence. Rather, Zimmerman was asserting negligence by O and K as the basis of an estoppel against O and K. The issue then was whether Zimmerman could use O and K's negligence as a defense when Zimmerman himself was negligent. Is UCC § 3–406 applicable?

2. McKenna had authority to indorse checks received in the course of his employment, but only for deposit to O and K's bank account. If McKenna indorsed and cashed the checks should the issue be forged indorsement or whether Zimmerman had notice of McKenna's breach of fiduciary duty? See UCC § 3–304(2) and (4)(e) and Transactions With Fiduciaries, supra p. 130.

3. In Hutzler v. Hertz Corp., 39 N.Y.2d 209, 383 N.Y.S.2d 266, 347 N.E.2d 627 (1976), the defendant in a personal injury action, Hertz, settled the case by drawing a check payable jointly to the plaintiff and her attorney after receiving plaintiff's general release. Plaintiff's attorney indorsed the check and forged plaintiff's indorsement. He obtained payment of the check and absconded. When plaintiff discovered the facts she got a new lawyer and sued Hertz for negligence in not comparing the forged signature and her valid signature on the release. She also sued the drawee bank for conversion. The lower court granted summary judgment against Hertz for the amount of the check and in favor of the drawee bank. Hertz appealed but plaintiff didn't. The court gave judgment for Hertz. It held that plaintiff was bound by the acts of her dishonest agent who was authorized to settle the case and receive payment. If Hertz had paid by a check payable to the attorney it would have been discharged notwithstanding the attorney's failure to pay plain-

tiff. Hertz should not be put in a worse position if it gave a check payable to both plaintiff and the attorney. In both cases the settlement payment (the proceeds of the check) was received by the attorney authorized by the client to receive payment. Restatement Second, Agency § 178(2) supports this holding. The court also relied on UCC § 3–404(1), stating " * * * we would hold that a person whose name is forged on an instrument by his agent is, by his unwise selection of this agent, estopped or 'precluded from denying' the unauthorized signature." Do you agree? How does this rationale apply to *Gresham?* The court expressed compassion for the hapless Mrs. Hutzler but noted that she had had a good cause of action against the drawee bank. Unfortunately her lawyer neglected to appeal the erroneous holding of the lower court to the contrary. Could the drawee bank have defended on the basis of the court's reading of UCC § 3–404(1)?

3. RIGHTS OF DRAWER

In most cases of forged indorsements the check is stolen from the payee and the thief obtains payment after forging the indorsement. In a large percentage of the cases the thief is an employee of the payee. Since the check, in the typical case, was received by the payee in payment of an obligation which becomes suspended under UCC § 3–802 the burden is on the payee, as owner of the check, to assert his rights on the instrument against either the depositary bank or the payor bank. But in some cases the check is stolen before it reaches the payee. In this case UCC § 3–802 does not apply. If the stolen check has been paid the drawer must pay the payee with a new check since the underlying obligation remains unsatisfied. The drawer, of course, should not suffer any loss, at least if he is not at fault in contributing to the theft and forgery. The payment by the payor bank was wrongful and drawer is entitled to have his account credited for the amount of the payment. This remedy of the drawer is clear and convenient since the drawer in most cases will have his account in a local bank. Nevertheless, there have been a number of cases in which the drawer, instead of suing the payor bank, sued the depositary bank. Such a suit might be brought in the uncommon case in which the depositary bank is a local bank and the payor bank is out of state, or in cases in which a suit against the payor bank is subject to some defense or is otherwise barred. By suing the depositary bank the drawer may be seeking to avoid this defense or bar to his suit.

STONE & WEBSTER ENGINEERING CORP. v. FIRST NATIONAL BANK & TRUST CO.

Supreme Judicial Court of Massachusetts, 1962.
345 Mass. 1, 184 N.E.2d 358.

WILKINS, CHIEF JUSTICE. In this action of contract or tort in four counts for the same cause of action a demurrer to the declaration was sustained, and the plaintiff, described in the writ as having a usual place of business in Boston, appealed. G.L. (Ter. Ed.) c. 231, § 96. The questions argued concern the rights of the drawer against a collecting bank which "cashed" checks for an individual who had forged the payee's indorsement on the checks, which were never delivered to the payee.

In the first count, which is in contract, the plaintiff alleges that between January 1, 1960, and May 15, 1960, it was indebted at various times to Westinghouse Electric Corporation (Westinghouse) for goods and services furnished to it by Westinghouse; that in order to pay the indebtedness the plaintiff drew three checks within that period on its checking account in The First National Bank of Boston (First National) payable to Westinghouse in the total amount of $64,755.44; that before delivery of the checks to Westinghouse an employee of the plaintiff in possession of the checks forged the indorsement of Westinghouse and presented the checks to the defendant; that the defendant "cashed" the checks and delivered the proceeds to the plaintiff's employee who devoted the proceeds to his own use; that the defendant forwarded the checks to First National and received from First National the full amounts thereof; and that First National charged the account of the plaintiff with the full amounts of the checks and has refused to recredit the plaintiff's checking account; wherefore the defendant owes the plaintiff $64,755.44 with interest.

Count 2, also in contract, is on an account annexed for money owed, namely $64,755.44, the proceeds of checks of the plaintiff "cashed" by the defendant on forged indorsements between January 1, 1960, and May 15, 1960.

Counts 3 and 4 in tort are respectively for conversion of the checks and for negligence in "cashing" the checks with forged indorsements.

By order, copies of the three checks were filed in court. The checks are respectively dated at Rowe in this Commonwealth on January 5, March 8, and May 9, 1960. Their respective amounts are $36,982.86, $10,416.58 and $17,355. They are payable to the order of "Westinghouse Electric Corporation, 10 High Street, Boston." The first two checks are indorsed in typewriting, "For Deposit Only: Westinghouse Electric Corporation By: Mr. O. D. Costine, Treasury Representative" followed by an ink signature "O. D. Costine." The Third check is indorsed in typewriting, "Westinghouse Electric Corporation By: [Sgd.] O. D. Costine Treasury Representative." All three checks also bear the indorsement by rubber stamp, "Pay to the order of any bank, banker or trust co. prior indorsements guaranteed   *   *   * [date] [1] The First National Bank & Trust Co. Greenfield, Mass."

The demurrer, in so far as it has been argued, is to each count for failure to state a cause of action.

*   *   *

1. Count 1, the plaintiff contends, is for money had and received. We shall so regard it. "An action for money had and received lies to recover money which should not in justice be retained by the defendant, and which in equity and good conscience should be paid to the plaintiff." Cobb v. Library Bureau, 268 Mass. 311, 316, 167 N.E. 765, 767; Adams v. First Nat. Bank, 321 Mass. 693, 694, 75 N.E.2d 502; Trafton v. Custeau, 338 Mass. 305, 308, 155 N.E.2d 159.

The defendant has no money in its hands which belongs to the plaintiff. The latter had no right in the proceeds of its own check payable to Westinghouse. Not being a holder or an agent for a holder, it could not have presented the check to the drawee for payment. Uniform Commercial Code §§ 3–504(1), 1–201(20). See Am.Law Inst.Uniform Commercial Code, 1958 Official Text with comments, § 3–419, comment 2: "A negotiable instrument is the property of the holder." See also Restatement 2d: Torts, Tent. draft no. 3, 1958, § 241A. The plaintiff contends that "First National paid or credited the proceeds of the checks to the defendant and charged the account of the plaintiff, and consequently, the plaintiff was deprived of a credit, and the defendant received funds or a credit which 'in equity and good conscience' belonged to the plaintiff."

In our opinion this argument is a non sequitur. The plaintiff as a depositor in First National was merely in a contractual relationship of creditor and debtor. Forastiere v. Springfield Ins.

---

1. The respective dates are January 13, March 9, and May 11, 1960. Each check bears the stamped indorsement of the Federal Reserve Bank of Boston and on its face the paid stamp of The First National Bank of Boston.

for Sav., 303 Mass. 101, 103, 20 N.E.2d 950; Krinsky v. Pilgrim Trust Co., 337 Mass. 401, 405, 149 N.E.2d 665. The amounts the defendant received from First National to cover the checks "cashed" were the bank's funds and not the plaintiff's. The Uniform Commercial Code does not purport to change the relationship. See §§ 1–103, 4–401 to 4–407. Section 3–409(1) provides: "A check or other draft does not of itself operate as an assignment of any funds in the hands of the drawee available for its payment, and the drawee is not liable on the instrument until he accepts it." This is the same as our prior law, which the Code repealed. See, formerly, G.L. c. 107, §§ 150, 212. Whether the plaintiff was rightfully deprived of a credit is a matter between it and the drawee, First National.

If we treat the first count as seeking to base a cause of action for money had and received upon a waiver of the tort of conversion—a matter which it is not clear is argued—the result will be the same. In this aspect the question presented is whether a drawer has a right of action for conversion against a collecting bank which handles its checks in the bank collection process. Unless there be such a right, there is no tort which can be waived.

The plaintiff relies upon the Uniform Commercial Code § 3–419, which provides, "(1) An instrument is converted when * * * (c) it is paid on a forged indorsement." This, however, could not apply to the defendant, which is not a "payor bank," defined in the Code, § 4–105(b), as "a bank by which an item is payable as drawn or accepted." See Am.Law Inst.Uniform Commercial Code, 1958 Official Text with comments, § 4–105, comments 1–3; G.L. c. 106, §§ 4–401, 4–213, 3–102(b).

A conversion provision of the Uniform Commercial Code which might have some bearing on this case is § 3–419(3).[3] This section implicitly recognizes that, subject to defences, including the one stated in it, a collecting bank, defined in the Code, § 4–105(d), may be liable in conversion. In the case at bar the forged indorsements were "wholly inoperative" as the signatures of the payee, Code §§ 3–404(1), 1–201(43), and equally so both as to the restrictive indorsements for deposits, see § 3–205

3. "Subject to the provisions of this chapter concerning restrictive indorsements a representative, including a depositary or collecting bank, who has in good faith and in accordance with the reasonable commercial standards applicable to the business of such representative dealt with an instrument or its proceeds on behalf of one who was not the true owner is not liable in conversion or otherwise to the true owner beyond the amount of any proceeds remaining in his hands." See Code §§ 1–201(35); 4–201(1).

(c), and as to the indorsement in blank, see § 3–204(2). When the forger transferred the checks to the collecting bank, no negotiation under § 3–202(1) occurred, because there was lacking the necessary indorsement of the payee. For the same reason, the collecting bank could not become a "holder" as defined in § 1–201(20), and so could not become a holder in due course under § 3–302(1). Accordingly, we assume that the collecting bank may be liable in conversion to a proper party, subject to defences, including that in § 3–419(3). See A. Blum Jr.'s Sons v. Whipple, 194 Mass. 253, 255, 80 N.E. 501, 13 L.R.A.,N.S., 211. But there is no explicit provision in the Code purporting to determine to whom the collecting bank may be liable, and consequently, the drawer's right to enforce such a liability must be found elsewhere. Therefore, we conclude that the case must be decided on our own law, which, on the issue we are discussing, has been left untouched by the Uniform Commercial Code in any specific section.

In this Commonwealth there are two cases (decided in 1913 and 1914) the results in which embrace a ruling that there was a conversion, but in neither was the question discussed and, for aught that appears, in each the ruling seems to have been assumed without conscious appreciation of the issue here considered. Franklin Sav. Bank v. International Trust Co., 215 Mass. 231, 102 N.E. 363; Quincy Mut. Fire Ins. Co. v. International Trust Co., 217 Mass. 370, 140 N.E. 845, L.R.A.1915B, 725. See Newburyport v. Spear, 204 Mass. 146, 148, 149, 90 N.E. 522; Brown v. First Nat. Bank, 216 Mass. 298, 103 N.E. 780; Phelan v. Atlantic Nat. Bank, 301 Mass. 463, 468, 17 N.E.2d 697; John T. D. Blackburn, Inc. v. Livermore, 317 Mass. 20, 56 N.E.2d 593; Kendall v. Fidelity Trust Co., 230 Mass. 238, 119 N.E. 861. Compare Childs, Jeffries & Co. Inc. v. Bright, 283 Mass. 283, 186 N.E. 571. The Franklin Sav. Bank case cannot be distinguished on the ground of the limited powers of a city treasurer. That issue was important as charging the bank with notice of the treasurer's lack of authority to indorse but, that fact established there was this further question as to whether there was a remedy in tort for conversion.

The authorities are hopelessly divided. We think that the preferable view is that there is no right of action. Jurisdictions denying such right are California Mill Supply Corp. v. Bank of America Nat. Trust & Sav. Ass'n, 36 Cal.2d 334, 340–341, 223 P.2d 849; First Nat. Bank v. North Jersey Trust Co., 14 A.2d 765, 18 N.J.Misc. 449, 451–452; Trojan Pub. Corp. v. Manufacturers Trust Co., 298 N.Y. 771, 83 N.E.2d 465, affirming 273

App.Div. (N.Y.) 843, 76 N.Y.S.2d 845; Virginia-Carolina Joint Stock Land Bank v. First & Citizens Nat. Bank, 197 N.C. 526, 150 S.E. 34; Lavanier v. Cosmopolitan Bank & Trust Co., 36 Ohio App. 285, 173 N.E.2d 216; Land Title & Trust Co. v. Northwestern Nat. Bank, 196 Pa. 230, 46 A. 420, 50 L.R.A. 75; United States v. Bank of Coney Island, 36 F.2d 829, 830 (D.C.E.D.N.Y.). See Britton, Bills and Notes, § 144; 36 Harv.L.Rev. 879. Expressing a contrary view, but not all on the ground of conversion, are Washington Mechanics' Sav. Bank v. District Title Ins. Co., 62 App.D.C. 194, 65 F.2d 827, 828 (D.C.); Gustin-Bacon Mfg. Co. v. First Nat. Bank, 306 Ill. 179, 137 N.E. 793; Home Indem. Co. v. State Bank, 233 Iowa 103, 8 N.W.2d 757; Sidles Co. v. Pioneer Valley Sav. Bank, 233 Iowa, 1057, 1063, 8 N.W.2d 794; Railroad Bldg. Loan & Sav. Ass'n v. Bankers' Mortgage Co., 142 Kan. 564, 51 P.2d 61, 102 A.L.R. 140; Levin v. Union Nat. Bank, 224 Md. 603, 168 A.2d 889; Life Ins. Co. v. Edisto Nat. Bank, 166 S.C. 505, 165 S.E. 178; National Surety Corp. v. City Bank & Trust Co., 248 Wis. 32, 20 N.W.2d 559.

We state what appears to us to be the proper analysis. Had the checks been delivered to the payee Westinghouse, the defendant might have been liable for conversion to the payee. The checks, if delivered, in the hands of the payee would have been valuable property which could have been transferred for value or presented for payment; and, had a check been dishonored, the payee would have had a right of recourse against the drawer on the instrument under § 3–413(2). Here the plaintiff drawer of the checks, which were never delivered to the payee (see Gallup v. Barton, 313 Mass. 379, 381, 47 N.E.2d 921), had no valuable rights in them. Since, as we have seen, it did not have the right of a payee or subsequent holder to present them to the drawee for payment, the value of its rights was limited to the physical paper on which they were written, and was not measured by their payable amounts. Trojan Pub. Corp. v. Manufacturers Trust Co., 298 N.Y. 771, 773, 83 N.E.2d 465. See Judkins v. Tuller, 277 Mass. 247, 250, 178 N.E. 540; Massachusetts Lubricant Corp. v. Socony-Vacuum Oil Co. Inc., 305 Mass 269, 271, 25 N.E.2d 719.

The enactment of the Uniform Commercial Code opens the road for the adoption of what seems the preferable view. An action by the drawer against the collecting bank might have some theoretical appeal as avoiding circuity of action. See Home Indem. Co. v. State Bank, 233 Iowa 103, 135–140, 8 N.W.2d 757. Compare 36 Harv.L.Rev. 879. It would have been in the interest of speedy and complete justice had the case been tried with the action by the drawer against the drawee and with an action by the drawee against the collecting bank. See Nichols v. Somerville Sav. Bank, 333 Mass. 488, 490, 132 N.E.2d 158. So one might ask: If the drawee is liable to the drawer and the collecting bank is liable to the drawee, why not let the drawer sue the collecting bank direct? We believe that the answer lies in the applicable defences set up in the Code.[4]

The drawer can insist that the drawee recredit his account with the amount of any unauthorized payment. Such was our common law. Murphy v. Metropolitan Nat. Bank, 191 Mass. 159, 163, 77 N.E. 693; Jordan Marsh Co. v. National Shawmut Bank, 201 Mass. 397, 405, 87 N.E. 740, 22 L.R.A.,N.S., 250; Barmby v. Merrimack Coöp. Bank, 285 Mass. 37, 40, 188 N.E. 378; Santa Maria v. Industrial City Bank & Banking Co., 326 Mass. 440, 442, 95 N.E.2d 176. This is, in effect, retained by the Code §§ 4–401(1),[5] 4–406(4). But the drawee has defences based upon the drawer's substantial negligence, if "contributing," or upon his duty to discover and report unauthorized signatures and alterations. §§ 3–406, 4–406. As to unauthorized indorsements, see § 4–406(4).[6] Then, if the drawee has a valid defence which it waives or fails upon request to assert, the drawee may not assert against the collecting bank or other prior party presenting or transferring the check a claim which is based on the forged indorsement. § 4–406(5).[7] See Am.Law Inst.Uniform Commercial Code, Official Text with comments, § 4–406, comment 6, which shows that there was no intent to change the prior law as to negligence of a customer. See Jordan Marsh Co. v. National Shawmut Bank, 201 Mass. 397, 407–411, 87 N.E. 740; Blacker & Shepard Co. v. Granite Trust Co., 284 Mass. 9, 13–14, 187 N.E. 53. If the drawee recredits the drawer's account and is

---

4. Cases where a payee has acquired rights in an instrument may stand on a different footing.

5. "As against its customer, a bank may charge against his account any item which is otherwise properly payable from that account * * * ."

6. "Without regard to care or lack of care of either the customer or the bank a customer who does not within one year from the time the statement and items are made available to the customer (subsection [1]) discover and report his unauthorized signature or any alteration on the face or back of the item or does not within three years from that time discover and report any unauthorized indorsement is precluded from asserting against the bank such unauthorized signature or such alteration."

7. "If under this section a payor bank has a valid defense against a claim of a customer upon or resulting from payment of an item and waives or fails upon request to assert the defense the [drawee] may not assert against * * * [a] collecting bank or other prior party presenting or transferring the item a claim based upon the unauthorized signature or alteration giving rise to the customer's claim."

not precluded by § 4–406(5), it may claim against the presenting bank on the relevant warranties in §§ 3–417 and 4–207, and each transferee has rights against his transferor under those sections.

If the drawer's rights are limited to requiring the drawee to recredit his account, the drawee will have the defences noted above and perhaps others; and the collecting bank or banks will have the defences in § 4–207(4) [8] and § 4–406(5), and perhaps others. If the drawer is allowed in the present case to sue the collecting bank, the assertion of the defences, for all practical purposes, would be difficult. The possibilities of such a result would tend to compel resort to litigation in every case involving a forgery of commercial paper. It is a result to be avoided.

[The court sustained demurrers to all plaintiff's counts.]

NOTE

The court in *Stone & Webster* states that in the case of a check paid on a forged indorsement the proper remedy of the drawer is to assert his rights under UCC § 4–401 to require the drawee to recredit the account; but that the drawer's action under UCC § 4–401 is subject to the defenses given to the drawee under UCC § 3–406 and § 4–406. It goes on to say that "if the drawee has a valid defence which it waives or fails upon request to assert, the drawee may not assert against the collecting bank or other prior party presenting or transferring the check a claim which is based on the forged indorsement." The court cites UCC § 4–406(5), but that subsection applies only to defenses "under this section." Thus a defense based on UCC § 3–406 is not specifically covered. But the action of the drawee bank is based on breach of warranty. If the drawee bank can validly debit the account of its customer because of UCC § 3–406 has it suffered any damages as a result of the breach of warranty? Can it, in effect, forgive the negligence of its customer and shift the loss to the collecting bank? Mellon National Bank & Trust Co. v. Merchants Bank of New York, 15 U.C.C.Rep. 691 (U.S. Dist.Ct.S.D.N.Y.1972), involving altered checks, holds that the failure of the drawee to assert defenses against the drawer under UCC § 3–406 does not prevent the drawee from recovering against the collecting bank for breach of warranty under UCC

8. "Unless a claim for breach of warranty under this section is made within a reasonable time after the person claiming learns of the breach, the person liable is discharged to the extent of any loss caused by the delay in making claim."

§ 4–207. The remedy of the collecting bank, if any, would be an action on the instrument against the drawer (see Comment 2 to UCC § 3–406) but in *Mellon* the court found that the collecting bank which acted solely as an agent for collection was not a holder in due course and therefore had no rights under UCC § 3–406. In the case of a forged indorsement collecting or depositary banks would not literally qualify under UCC § 3–406 because they are neither holders nor payors. In Sun 'N Sand, Inc. v. United California Bank, 21 Cal.3d 671, 148 Cal.Rptr. 329, 582 P.2d 920 (1978), Justice Mosk, writing for the court, also addressed these questions. Contrary to *Stone & Webster* Justice Mosk states that the drawer of a check paid on a forged indorsement may proceed directly against a collecting bank on the theory that its warranties under UCC § 4–207, including the warranty of good title, were made not only to the payor bank but also to an "other payor who in good faith pays" the item. He declined to read the term "payor" as a "term of art used in a narrow, technical sense" and stated that it is the drawer who ultimately pays when his account is charged in the amount of the check. He justified his conclusion by stating a policy of avoiding cumbersome and uneconomical circuity of action. Justice Mosk also stated that the collecting bank would have the benefit of defenses against the drawer under UCC § 3–406 (he again uses "payor" in a non-technical sense) and any defenses of the drawee against the drawer under UCC § 4–406 by virtue of subsection (5). According to Justice Mosk that subsection "implies that [UCC § 4–406] defenses, available to a drawee bank against claims of its depositors, are also available to a collecting bank in a direct action by the depositor." Under this analysis it would appear that the collecting bank would be entitled to defenses under UCC § 3–406 if it is a defendant in an action by the payor bank for breach of warranty under UCC § 4–207.

4. FICTITIOUS PAYEES, PAYROLL PADDING AND OTHER EMPLOYEE FRAUD

KRAFTSMAN CONTAINER CORP. v. UNITED COUNTIES TRUST CO.

Superior Court of New Jersey, 1979.
169 N.J.Super. 488, 404 A.2d 1288.

DREIER, J. S. C. Plaintiff Kraftsman Container Corporation (customer) brought this breach of contract action against United

Counties Trust Company (bank), alleging that the bank was negligent in cashing checks drawn on the customer's checking account at the bank. Defendant bank has moved for summary judgment based upon provisions of the Uniform Commercial Code (U.C.C.). The pivotal issue is one of first impression in New Jersey.

The facts are uncontroverted. Plaintiff maintained a checking account with defendant bank. The customer's treasurer, who also acted as bookkeeper, was authorized to draw and sign checks on behalf of the customer. Over a four-year period ending in December 1975 the treasurer drew and signed over 100 checks payable both to fictitious parties and to actual creditors of the customer. He retained the checks and then cashed them at the bank, converting the funds to his own use. The checks ranged in amounts from $200 to $3,000, with the sum of the embezzled funds totaling $46,714.28. In most instances the treasurer indorsed the checks, usually illegibly, although the bank's tellers cashed some of the checks without any indorsement. It was the normal procedure of the bank to require that any party cashing a check indorse it, but the tellers did not obtain the treasurer's personal indorsement, nor did they make any inquiry regarding any of the illegible or missing payee indorsements. The customer had employed accountants throughout the four-year period to review its cancelled checks and the customer's monthly bank statements, but the scheme remained undetected for four years.

The bank claims by way of the present motion that it is shielded from liability by the terms of [UCC § 3–405(1)(b).] Plaintiff responds that the bank's failure to exercise reasonable care in guarding against improper payment of the checks renders the bank liable for the amount embezzled. The application of a "reasonable care" negligence standard to a bank in a fictitious-payee indorsement case is the novel proposition urged upon this court.

Articles 3 and 4 of the U.C.C. * * * set forth the duties, rights and liabilities of banks and their customers concerning commercial paper. Under § 4–401(1) a bank may charge a customer's account only for checks which were properly payable by the bank. Wrongful payment by the bank renders it liable to the customer, who must be reimbursed. This broadly defined duty of the bank is modified by other provisions which define the obligations of the customer. Section 3–406 precludes a customer from claiming wrongful payment when its own negligence has substantially contributed to the making of a material alteration or an unauthorized signature. The customer is required by § 4–406(1) to (3) to be reasonably careful and prompt in examining the periodic bank statements and cancelled checks to discover and report alterations or the unauthorized use of its signature. Failure of the customer to discharge these duties may relieve the bank from liability under § 4–406(2) and (3).

The customer acknowledges that its treasurer was authorized to draw and sign its checks. Therefore none of the drawer's signatures were unauthorized, and plaintiff cannot have been negligent in failing to discover an unauthorized signature. Section 3–406 is thus inapplicable, as are the provisions of § 4–406(1) to (3) which impose upon the customer the duty of discovering its own unauthorized signatures or alterations. The dispute here is over the relative duties of the parties regarding indorsements. The only reference to indorsements in § 4–406 is found in subsection (4), where the time limitation for "asserting against the bank such unauthorized signature or indorsement" is set at three years from the availability to the customer of the relevant bank statement and checks, "Without regard to care or lack of care of either the customer or the bank." [2]

Liability for payment on a forged indorsement is treated by the U.C.C. as a separate concept. The basic rule is that a bank which pays a check on a forged indorsement is liable, since a forged indorsement is wholly inoperative as the signature of the actual payee (§ 3–404), and is thus not properly payable under § 4–401. A check validly issued but wrongfully paid by the bank on a forged indorsement entitles the customer to a credit. The commitment of the U.C.C. to finality, Perini Corp. v. First Nat'l Bank of Habersham Cty., Ga., 553 F.2d 398, 21 U.C.C.Rep. 929 (5 Cir. 1977), reh. den. 557 F.2d 823 (5 Cir. 1977), is manifested by allocating the forgery loss to the bank.

2. Plaintiff customer concedes that 12 of the checks which are the subject of its claim, as well as the bank statements covering those checks, were received by plaintiff more than three years before it reported the unauthorized indorsements. Plaintiff is precluded by § 4–406(4) from asserting any unauthorized indorsement on these items. See Bd. of Higher Ed. of the City of N. Y. v. Bankers Trust Co., 86 Misc.2d 560, 383 N.Y.S.2d 508, 19 U.C.C.Rep. 599 (Sup.Ct.1976). However, plaintiff's claim here is technically not an assertion of either the lack of indorsement or an unauthorized indorsement, since the indorsements were effective under § 3–405. Rather, plaintiff asserts breach of contract based upon the bank's failure to act reasonably to protect its customers' interests. Therefore the claims on these older checks are not barred by § 4–406(4), but are subject to the six-year statute of limitation, N.J.S.A. 2A:14–1. Summary judgment on those checks must therefore be denied, and these items included in the total claim, subject to the standards set forth infra.

The risk of loss may shift. Section 3–405 deems effective an indorsement by anyone in the name of a fictitious payee.[3] The treasurer in the instant case, drawing and signing checks on behalf of the customer, plainly had the requisite intent under the statute. Twellman v. Lindell Trust Co. v. Continental Bank & Trust Co., 534 S.W.2d 83, 19 U.C.C.Rep. 604 (Mo.Ct.App.1976).

There is no qualifying language in § 3–405 setting forth a standard of care to be applied to either the bank or its customer. This is in contrast to § 3–406, which would specifically penalize the customer for negligence substantially contributing to a material alteration or an unauthorized signature. In that situation a bank is required to pay the item "in good faith and in accordance with the reasonable commercial standards of the drawee's or payor's business" under § 3–406, but the preclusion of a customer from asserting the unauthorized signature or material alteration under § 4–406(2) is inapplicable if the customer establishes the bank's "lack of ordinary care" under § 4–406(3). The conspicuous absence in § 3–405 of either an "ordinary care" or "good faith" standard signals that a test for a bank's liability for payment on improper indorsements must be found elsewhere. Prudential Ins. Co. of America v. Marine Nat'l Exchange Bank of Milwaukee, 371 F.Supp. 1002, 14 U.C.C.Rep. 462 (E.D.Wis.1974); Hicks-Costarino Co., Inc. v. Pinto, N.Y.L.J., Feb. 23, 1978, 23 U.C.C.Rep. 680 (Sup.Ct.1978). Plaintiff urges that a standard of simple negligence applies. Defendant asserts that it is shielded from liability by § 3–405. There are no New Jersey cases construing the standard to be applied.

Read independently of other U.C.C. provisions, § 3–405 apparently shifts the fictitious-payee indorsement loss to the customer without regard to any lack of care on the part of the bank. Wright v. Bank of California, Nat'l Ass'n, 276 Cal.App.2d 485, 81 Cal.Rptr. 11, 6 U.C.C.Rep. 1165 (D.Ct.App.1969). Yet the bank may not pay over such an indorsement with impunity. Section 1–203 of the U.C.C. imposes on every contract subject to its provisions an obligation of good faith which, under § 1–102(3), may not be disclaimed by agreement. Although § 4–103(1) specifies that a bank may not disclaim responsibility for its own lack of good faith or failure to exercise ordinary care, § 4–401(2) allows the bank to charge its customer's ac-

---

3. This provision expands the common law fictitious-payee rule to apply also to imposters and real parties who are intended by the maker or one acting on the maker's behalf to have no interest in the item. References in this opinion to the "fictitious-payee" rule are intended to cite these broader § 3–405 principles.

count only when payment has been in good faith. "Good faith" itself is defined in § 1–201(19) as "honesty in fact in the conduct or transaction concerned."

While the good faith requirement is invariable throughout the U.C.C. by way of § 1–102(3), the more rigorous and objective negligence standard of ordinary care does not have such general applicability. Simple negligence on the part of a bank should not, and has been found not to affect the operation of § 3–405; only bad faith should bar the bank from invoking § 3–405 to defeat the customer's claim. See e.g., Bd. of Higher Ed. of the City of N. Y. v. Bankers Trust Co., N.Y.L.J. May 13, 1976, 19 U.C.C.Rep. 599 (Sup.Ct.1976) (bank's summary judgment motion in a similar case denied because of bona fide factual issues regarding bank's bad faith); McConnico v. Third Nat'l Bank of Nashville, 499 S.W.2d 874, 13 U.C.C.Rep. 641 (Tenn.Supp.Ct. 1973) (§ 3–302 "holder in due course" standards of good faith and notice applied where bank deviated from accepted banking practices and checks contained irregularities); Hicks-Costarino Co., Inc. v. Pinto, supra (court looked for gross negligence or wilful ignorance as evidence of bad faith but found none); Prudential Ins. Co. of America v. Marine Nat'l Exchange Bank of Milwaukee, supra (ordinary care argument rejected.)

These authorities are in accord with U.C.C.Comment No. 6 to § 4–406:

Nothing in this section is intended to affect any decision holding that a customer who has notice of something wrong with an indorsement must exercise reasonable care to investigate and to notify the bank. *It should be noted that under the rules relating to impostors and signatures in the name of the payee (Section 3–405) certain forged indorsements on which the bank has paid the item in good faith may be treated as effective notwithstanding such discovery and notice.* If the alteration or forgery results [from] the drawer's negligence the drawee who pays in good faith is also protected. Section 3–406. [Emphasis supplied]

The bank must fulfill at least a threshold requirement to invoke the protection of § 3–405. The provision requires "[a]n indorsement by any person in the name of a named payee." The checks before the court in Wright v. Bank of California, Nat'l Ass'n, supra, had no indorsements. The court acknowledged that § 3–405 is generally meant to shift the loss on a fictitious

payee indorsement from the drawee bank to the employer of a
dishonest malefactor, but it also noted that

> * * * the statute explicitly requires *some* indorsement in
> order to exempt the drawee bank from liability on a check
> payable to a fictitious payee * * *. We conclude that
> section 3[–]405 does not insulate respondent for [sic] liability
> for negligence. [81 Cal.Rptr. at 14, 6 U.C.C.Rep. at 1170]

The suggested precautions set out in § 3–405, such as a bank
requirement that a presenting party provide reasonable identification and authority to cash a check, are cited by the court. Id.
at 81 Cal.Rptr. 11, 6 U.C.C.Rep. at 1170.

In Travco Corp. v. Citizens Federal S. & L. Ass'n, 42 Mich.
App. 291, 201 N.W.2d 675, 11 U.C.C.Rep. 799 (Ct.App.1972), the
court was even more specific in requiring indorsements in the
name of the named payee. There the customer's treasurer drew
and signed checks payable to fictitious payees. The indorsements did not match the payees' names. The court rejected application of § 3–405 because the checks were not indorsed in the
name of a payee, and judgment was entered against the bank
because it had paid over an inadequate indorsement. A similar
finding was made in Twellman v. Lindell Trust Co. v. Continental Bank & Trust Co., supra, where reliance on § 3–405(1)(c) was
rejected because the forged indorsement did not precisely match
the name of the payee.

Defendant bank seeks here to invoke § 3–405(1)(b) to defeat
plaintiff customer's claim. The bank must have at the very
least required indorsements in the name of the named payee.
§ 3–405; Travco Corp. v. Citizens Federal S. & L. Ass'n;
Twellman v. Lindell Trust Co. v. Continental Bank & Trust Co.,
and Wright v. Bank of California, Nat'l Ass'n, all supra. This
court construes § 3–405 as requiring an indorsement substantially identical to the name of the named payee.

Those checks cashed by defendant bank without any indorsement must be excluded from § 3–405 protection. Summary
judgment is therefore denied the bank regarding the unindorsed
checks. Summary judgment is also denied as to those checks
exhibiting illegible indorsements; the illegibility of the indorsements raises a question of fact as to whether payment by the
bank constituted a lack of "good faith" on the part of the bank.
§ 3–405; Travco Corp. v. Citizens Federal S. & L. Ass'n, supra;
Twellman v. Lindell Trust Co. v. Continental Bank & Trust Co.,
supra; R. 4:46–2; Judson v. Peoples Bank & Trust Co., 17 N.J.
67, 110 A.2d 24 (1954).

Finally, plaintiff has raised a material question of fact as to the propriety of the bank's conduct over the entire four-year period. The transactions are to be viewed as a whole, since bad faith may be evidenced by a consistent failure by the bank to monitor and investigate a series of irregular transactions. Bd. of Higher Ed. of the City of N. Y. v. Bankers Trust Co., supra. Effective indorsements do not relieve the bank from liability if there is proof of a course of dealing so irregular in nature that the bank is shown to have violated its own policies and to have failed to act according to the standard of honesty-in-fact. § 1–203; § 1–201(19); McConnico v. Third Nat'l Bank of Nashville, supra. Although there is no evidence that any bank employees were acting as confederates, not once was the treasurer asked to indorse the checks himself; nor was he ever questioned regarding the illegible or missing payee indorsements.

Viewing all of the evidence in the light most favorable to the customer, this court cannot say that as a matter of law defendant bank acted in good faith. R. 4:46–2; Judson v. Peoples Bank & Trust Co., supra.[5] This matter, therefore, is also reserved for trial.

PROBLEM

Customer has a checking account at Bank A. X is employed by Customer as an officer authorized to write checks for Customer. Y is employed by Bank A as an officer authorized to approve payment of checks drawn on Bank A. X and Y agree to a money-making scheme carried out as follows: X opens an account in Bank B in the name of Doe Corporation; X writes a check on Customer's account at Bank A payable to Doe Corporation in the amount of $1,000,000; X then indorses the check in the name Doe Corporation and deposits it in the Doe account at Bank B; Bank B presents it for payment to Bank A; Y approves the check for payment; payment is made to Bank B and the account of Customer is debited in the amount of $1,000,000; X

---

5. The court is in no way overlooking the evidence that plaintiff itself may have been negligent. The customer is not excused from its own duties by entrusting performance of those duties to a dishonest agent. Faber v. Edgewater Nat'l Bank of Edgewater, 101 N.J.Super. 354, 244 A.2d 339 (Law Div.1968).

Although the issue was not raised by the parties here, it must be left to the trial court to determine whether the bank may be estopped from alleging the customer's negligence if the bank is found to have violated the higher U.C.C. good faith requirement, or whether to compare the fault of the parties if the conduct of the customer is also determined to have fallen to the level of "bad faith." Cf. Draney v. Bachman, 138 N.J.Super. 503, 351 A.2d 409 (Law Div.1976).

transfers the $1,000,000 to a bank in Brazil; X and Y also depart for Brazil. Have X and Y stolen the money of Customer or of Bank A or of Bank B? Does UCC § 3–405 help you decide this question? Does UCC § 1–203?

NOTES

1. Cases to which UCC § 3–405(1)(b) and (c) apply involve fraud by an employee of the drawer of the check. UCC § 3–406 and UCC § 4–406, which we have already examined, also typically are applied to cases of employee fraud. Under the former section the wrongdoer is usually an employee of the payee of the check while under the latter section fraud by the drawer's employee is typical. In all of the cases the policy question is that of determining whether the loss shall be borne by the employer of the wrongdoer or by the bank which takes or pays the forged check or the check bearing the forged indorsement. Under UCC § 3–406 and § 4–406 the statutory technique is to assign the loss according to negligence standards. The drawer or payee of the check, as the case may be, has a duty of care to the bank in preventing the forgery and the bank in turn has a duty of care to the drawer or payee in taking or paying the check to discover the forgery. Under these sections the loss is assigned to the bank unless it can show that the drawer or payee was negligent and even then it can avoid liability only if it shows that its own conduct was not negligent. Although cases arising under UCC § 3–405(1)(b) and (c) involve similar policy considerations the statutory technique is quite different. Because these provisions validate the indorsement at issue the effect is to throw the loss on the drawer-employer of the wrongdoer. The theory seems to be that the drawer is in the best position to prevent the fraud by choosing and supervising employees and that any loss should be a cost of the drawer's enterprise rather than a cost to be imposed on the bank and eventually on all of the bank's customers. See Comment 4 to UCC § 3–405. Under this view the bank is not charged with any policing duty; there is no requirement that the bank exercise due care or follow reasonable commercial standards. Is there any policy basis for applying different standards to cases covered by UCC § 3–405 and cases covered by UCC § 3–406 and § 4–406?

2. The court in *Kraftsman*, by inserting UCC § 1–203 into the equation, puts a gloss on UCC § 3–405(1)(b) and (c) that brings them closer to UCC § 3–406 and § 4–406. If the limitation of UCC § 1–203 is restricted to cases of dishonesty by the

bank's employees, as UCC § 1–201(19) suggests, the bank will be protected in all cases except those that resemble the Problem that precedes these Notes. But the court's requirement of good faith encompasses a standard more severe than honesty in fact. How does this standard, and the standard adopted by other courts in the cases cited in *Kraftsman*, compare with the standard imposed by UCC § 3–406—"in good faith and in accordance with the reasonable commercial standards of the drawee's or payor's business"?

3.   In United States v. Bank of America National Trust & Saving Association, 438 F.2d 1213 (9th Cir. 1971), the court held that UCC § 3–405(1)(c) cannot protect a bank cashing a Treasury check with a forged indorsement against suit by the Government until the United States Supreme Court alters its views expressed in National Metropolitan Bank v. United States, 323 U.S. 454, 65 S.Ct. 354, 89 L.Ed. 383 (1945), to the effect that the negligence of the Government in failing to discover the fraud does not provide a defense to a bank cashing a Treasury check with a forged indorsement. Black, J., believed this view was "unanimously accepted by state and federal courts" and should be "accepted as the general federal rule." (323 U.S. at 457) United States v. City National Bank & Trust Co., 491 F.2d 851 (8th Cir. 1974), is in accord.

4.   In Fidelity and Deposit Co. of Maryland v. Chemical Bank New York Trust Co., 62 Misc.2d 509, 309 N.Y.S.2d 266, rev'd 65 Misc.2d 619, 318 N.Y.S.2d 957 (1970), the court, in considering the meaning of UCC § 3–405(1)(a), discussed pre-UCC New York law:

> In September, 1964, the common law stood as follows: The relation existing between a bank and a depositor being that of debtor and creditor the bank can justify a payment on the depositor's account only upon the actual direction of the depositor (Critten v. Chemical National Bank, 171 N.Y. 219, 63 N.E. 969; Seaboard Nat. Bank v. Bank of America, 193 N.Y. 26, 85 N.E. 829). The drawee of a bill or a check or the person purchasing it takes the paper relying solely on the reputed responsibility of their transferors and its apparent genuineness and they therefore deal at their peril (Crawford v. West Side Bank, 100 N.Y. 50, 2 N.E. 881; American Surety v. Empire Trust Co., 262 N.Y. 181, 186 N.E. 436).

> "The impostor rule" originally developed as an exception in face-to-face dealings, and later was extended to mail swindles having the same general characteristics. Inherent in

this rule is the concept that as between the impostor and the rest of the world an impostor-payee acquires title to commercial paper issued by the drawer-maker whose only recourse is then to the impostor, subsequent endorsements notwithstanding (United States v. Bank of America, 274 F.2d 366).

More specifically, New York's application of the common law revolved about the "dominant intent" of the drawer. Where the drawer dealt with "A" and delivered a check to his order as "X," nice distinctions had to be drawn to determine whether the wrong was forgery or something else (cf. Strang v. Westchester, 235 N.Y. 68, 138 N.E. 739). In determining whether there was a forgery, the true test was whether or not the endorsement of the name of the payee was made by the person who was intended by the drawer to be the payee (Halsey v. Bank of New York and Trust Co., 270 N.Y. 134, 200 N.E. 671).

Thus, if the drawer intended to pay the impostor physically present and identified by prior dealings the "impostor defense" held (Mohr v. Lawyers Trust Co., 282 N.Y. 770, 27 N.E.2d 48). But if the drawer clearly intended to pay the payee named and in his true identified capacity, then all unauthorized endorsements were forgeries whether the impostor was physically present at the inception or not (Cohen v. Lincoln Savings Bank, 275 N.Y. 399, 10 N.E.2d 457). Note that the two cases last cited concerned independent dupes caught in the same net.

Finally, where the impostor misrepresented himself as the agent of the proposed payee, as between the drawer who delivered a check or draft to an impostor representing himself as the agent of the payee and the drawee who pays it or a holder who purchases it, the courts have held that the endorsement is a forgery and ensuing loss falls on the one who pays or purchases (Strang v. Westchester, 235 N.Y. 68, 138 N.E. 739; cf. 81 A.L.R.2d 1365, 1398; N.Y.Jurisprudence, vol. 41, sec. 263 and footnote).

309 N.Y.S.2d at 271-272.

What change does UCC § 3-405(1)(a) make in New York law? What is the reason for the distinction between misrepresentation as to identity and as to agency? See Comment 2 to UCC § 3-405. See Thieme v. Seattle-First National Bank, 7 Wn. App. 845, 502 P.2d 1240 (1972). Does UCC § 2-403(1)(a) make this distinction? Consider the Problems that follow.

PROBLEMS

1. Impostor falsely represented to Drawer that he was Smith to whom Drawer owed money. Thinking that Impostor was Smith Drawer drew a check to the order of Smith and delivered it to Impostor. Impostor indorsed the name of Smith to the check and cashed it at Drawee Bank. Drawee Bank debited Drawer's account in the amount of the check. When Drawer discovered the fraud he demanded that Drawee Bank recredit the account. Who wins under UCC § 3–405(1)(a)? If Drawer intended the payee of the check to be Smith did Drawer "issue" the check to Impostor? See UCC § 3–102(1)(a).

2. Impostor falsely represented to Drawer that he was the president of Smith Corporation to which Drawer owed money. In reliance on Impostor's representation Drawer drew a check to the order of Smith Corporation and delivered it to Impostor. Impostor indorsed the name of Smith Corporation to the check and cashed it at Drawee Bank. Drawee Bank debited Drawer's account in the amount of the check. When Drawer discovered the fraud he demanded that Drawee Bank recredit the account. Who wins? Was the check "issued" to Impostor?

D. INCOMPLETE INSTRUMENTS AND ALTERED INSTRUMENTS

1. INSTRUMENTS OTHER THAN CERTIFIED CHECKS

In the forged check and forged indorsement cases we have examined the question of allocating the risk of loss between a drawer who is asserting that the check cannot be enforced against him contrary to his order as stated in the check, and a person who has paid the check or taken it for value in good faith thinking that the drawer's order was being carried out. We have seen that the drawer wins unless some conduct by him or his employees that contributed to the loss can be used as the basis for an estoppel. UCC § 3–404(1), § 3–405(1), § 3–406 and § 4–406. A similar problem, and a similar resolution of the problem, is presented in the case of incomplete or altered instruments.

Assume that A is indebted to B but is not sure of the precise amount of the debt. In payment of the debt A sends to B his check payable to B, leaving the amount of the check blank. A instructs B to complete the check by filling in the amount of the debt. If the amount of the debt is $10 and B fills in the check for that amount there is no difficulty in enforcing the check against A. B has acted as A's authorized agent to complete the check and A is liable just as though he had completed the check himself. UCC § 3–115(1) states this result. But suppose B exceeds his authority and fills in $10,000 rather than $10. UCC § 3–115(2) covers this case and treats it as a case of material alteration, i.e., a case in which A's original order stated in the check was changed by B against the wishes of A. An example is a check originally made out in the amount of $10 that was then altered by B to read $10,000. UCC § 3–407 states rules for allocating loss between the drawer, on the one hand, and on the other hand, holders in due course and all other persons. UCC § 3–406 also applies to alteration as does UCC § 4–401(2) and § 4–406.

How is our example of unauthorized completion resolved by UCC § 3–407? Can B enforce the check for any amount against A? What would be the rights of a holder in due course to whom B negotiated the check? What are the rights of the drawee who paid the check? Compare the case of a check raised from $10 to $10,000. How do the rights of the various parties differ? What relationship is there between UCC § 3–406 on the one hand and, on the other hand, the last clause of UCC § 3–407(3), and UCC § 4–401(2)(b)?

PROBLEM

Drawer drew and delivered a typewritten check for $10 payable to the order of Payee. Without Drawer's consent Payee raised the amount of the check to $10,000 by adding three zeroes after the figure "10" and adding the word "thousand" after the word "ten." Payee then deposited the check in his account with Depositary Bank which obtained payment from Drawee. Drawee debited Drawer's account $10,000. Payee withdrew the $10,000 from his account with Depositary Bank and absconded. When Drawer received the cancelled check he notified Drawee of the alteration. Drawee advises you of these facts and states that an examination of the check indicates that Drawer when he wrote the check left blank spaces in the amount lines that allowed the additions to be made by Payee without evidence of alteration. Drawee wants to avoid any unnecessary litigation expense but is unwilling to accept the loss represented by the alteration. What advice do you give Drawee? See UCC § 3–406, § 4–207(1)(c) and § 4–401(2).

2. CERTIFIED CHECKS

The liability of a bank that certifies an altered check has long troubled the courts. The common law view that a bank which certified an altered check was liable on the check only as originally drawn was justified in Marine National Bank v. National City Bank, 59 N.Y. 67, 17 Am.Rep. 305 (1874):

> That an acceptor of a bill of exchange by acceptance only admits the genuineness of the signature of the drawer, and does not admit the genuineness of the indorsements, whether of the drawee of the same bill, or of any other person whose name appears upon it, or any other part of the bill, is elementary and sustained by an unbroken current of authority. (Story on Bills, §§ 262, 263, and cases cited in notes.) Judge Story says the reason usually assigned is, that when the bill is presented for acceptance the acceptor looks to the handwriting of the drawer with which he is presumed to be acquainted, and he affirms its genuineness by giving credit to the bill, by his acceptance in favor of the legal holder thereof. But the acceptor cannot be presumed to have any such knowledge of the other facts upon which the rights of the holder may depend. In analogy to this, courts have held that the certificate only holds the bank for the truth of the facts presumed to be within its own knowledge, viz., the genuineness of the signature of the drawer and the state of his account. Moneys paid upon checks and drafts which have been forgeries, either in the body of the instrument or in the indorsements, or in any respect, except the name of the drawer, have uniformly been held recoverable as for money paid by mistake, and expressly upon the ground that payment, as an admission of the genuineness of the instrument, was the same as an acceptance, and only operated as an admission of the signature of the drawer. 59 N.Y. at 76–77.

However, two leading cases, National City Bank v. National Bank of the Republic, 300 Ill. 103, 132 N.E. 832 (1921), and Wells Fargo Bank & Union Trust Co. v. Bank of Italy, 214 Cal. 156, 4 P.2d 781 (1931), interpreted the NIL as changing the common law rule and as binding a certifying bank to the tenor of the instrument at the time of certification. What result is reached under the UCC? See UCC § 3–413(1).

After the California and Illinois decisions banks adopted the practice of qualifying their certifications: "payable as originally drawn." What is the effect of qualified certifications under the UCC? See UCC § 3–417(1)(c)(iii) and § 4–207(1)(c)(iii).

PROBLEMS

The following problems are designed to test your understanding of UCC § 3–413(1), § 3–417(1)(c) and § 4–207(1)(c).

1. Payee of a check for $10 fraudulently raises the check to $10,000 and negotiates it to Holder who takes it as a holder in due course.

    a. Holder presents the check for payment and is paid $10,000. What are the rights of Drawee Bank against Holder?

    b. Holder obtains certification of the check by Drawee and later presents the certified check for payment and is paid $10,000. What are the rights of Drawee Bank against Holder?

2. Payee of a check for $10 fraudulently raises the check to $10,000 and has the check certified by Drawee Bank. Payee then negotiates the check to Holder who takes as a holder in due course.

    a. Holder presents the check for payment and is paid $10,000. What are the rights of Drawee Bank against Holder?

    b. Holder presents the check for payment but payment is refused because Drawee Bank has discovered the alteration. What are the rights of Holder against Drawee Bank?

3. Drawer draws a check payable to Payee for $10 and has it certified by Drawee Bank. Drawer then raises the check from $10 to $10,000 and delivers it to Payee who takes as a holder in due course.

    a. Payee presents the check to Drawee Bank for payment but Drawee Bank refuses because of the alteration. What are the rights of Payee against Drawee Bank?

    b. Payee presents the check to Drawee Bank for payment and Drawee Bank pays Payee $10,000. What are the rights of Drawee Bank against Payee?

BROWER v. FRANKLIN NATIONAL BANK

United States District Court, S.D. New York, 1970.
311 F.Supp. 675.

WYATT, DISTRICT JUDGE. This is a motion by defendant Franklin National Bank, a successor in interest to the Federation Bank & Trust Company (the Bank) for summary judgment in its favor (Fed.R.Civ.P. 56(b)). For reasons to be given, the motion must be denied.

*   *   *

The complaint, filed May 27, 1968, avers that in July 1967 one Anthony Ricci maintained a checking account at the Bank's branch on Williamsbridge Road in the Bronx; that on July 12, 1967 Anthony drew two checks on the Bank in the amounts of $8 and $10 payable to the plaintiff Frederick J. Brower (Frederick) and procured the Bank's certification of those checks; that Anthony subsequently raised the checks from $8 to $28,600 and from $10 to $10,000 and delivered them to Frederick in payment for real property in New Jersey; that the Bank refused to honor the checks because they had been "raised"; that the Bank was negligent in certifying the checks, among other things, because when certified they contained blank spaces and could easily be raised. Frederick claims damages of $75,000.

It may be noted that the complaint purports to plead a claim based on negligence of the Bank in certifying the checks under circumstances which made it easy to raise them thereafter and thus to cause them to be passed off to plaintiff in their altered form. The claim ought to be treated, however, as in legal theory based on the Bank's certifications but governed by New York Uniform Commercial Code § 3–406: "Any person who by his negligence substantially contributes to a material alteration of the instrument * * * is precluded from asserting the alteration * * * against a holder in due course * * *." It may be noted that plaintiff does not sue simply for the amounts of the two checks as raised, $38,600, but rather for $75,000 averring other damages, such as dishonor of his own checks, impairment of "credit standing", etc.

Defendant, in its answer, raised two defenses: lack of diversity jurisdiction (no evidence in support has been offered and the point is not pressed) and failure to state a claim upon which relief can be granted.

Discovery has been concluded and a note of issue was filed September 15, 1969. No demand for jury trial has been made by either side.

Apart from damages, there is no dispute as to any material fact. The facts are as follows:

On July 12, 1967, Anthony presented two checks, numbered 139 and 140, to the Bank for certification. "Every item" (apparently the date, payee's name, drawer's name and the amount) in both checks was filled out. Number 139 was in the amount of $10; number 140 in the amount of $8. Both were payable to "Mr. F. Brower." The checks were certified by the Assistant Manager of the Bank. The certification stamp does not show the amount for which the checks were certified.

Check number 139 was raised after certification apparently by Anthony from $10 to $10,000 and deposited by Frederick in the Plainfield Trust State National Bank, Plainfield, New Jersey. Check number 140 was likewise raised after certification from $8 to $28,600 and deposited in the National Bank of New Jersey, bearing the endorsements of "Mr. F. Brower" and "Edward A. Ryan." Both checks were presented to the Bank on July 19, 1967 and were returned unpaid, because the checks had been altered as to amount. Neither check has been paid and this action was commenced to secure payment.

Before adoption of the Uniform Commercial Code (U.C.C.) effective in 1964, the law of New York appears to have been clear that a bank certifying a check was not liable on its certification for an altered amount of the check, whether alteration took place after or before certification. Continental Nat. Bank v. Tradesmen's Bank, 173 N.Y. 272, 278, 65 N.E. 1108 (1903); Clews v. Bank of New York etc., 89 N.Y. 418, 422 (1882); National Reserve Bank v. Corn Exchange Bank, 171 App.Div. 195, 157 N.Y.S. 316 (1st Dept. 1916).

Under the U.C.C. this rule is changed and the certifying bank is liable on its certification where the alteration was *before* certification. The engagement in certifying is now to pay the check "according to its tenor at the time of his engagement". U.C.C. § 3–413(1). If alteration (raising) occurs *after* certification, the certifying bank is not bound by its certification to pay the instrument as raised.

As to *negligence*, at common law it was believed, on the authority of Young v. Grote, 4 Bing. 253 (1827), that a *drawer* who negligently drew a check in such a way as to make it easy to raise the check was responsible to a drawee who paid the raised check in good faith.

It was sought in a leading English case to extend this rule to the acceptor. Just as here, a check was drawn for 500£ with spaces left so that it could be raised to 3,500£. As originally drawn, it was presented and certified (accepted); thereafter it was raised to 3,500£ as planned and negotiated to a holder in due course. It was said as against the acceptor that the acceptance was negligent because the check was in such form that alteration (raising) was made easy and was a likely result. The House of Lords refused to sanction an action against an acceptor for negligence because there is no duty on an acceptor to take precautions against a possible alteration. Scholfield v. Earl of Londesborough, (1896) A.C. 514.

The plain words of the Uniform Commercial Code § 3–406 seem clearly to change the old rule and to authorize this action. "Any person who by his negligence substantially contributes to a material alteration of the instrument * * * is precluded from asserting the alteration * * * against a holder in due course * * *." U.C.C. § 3–406.

The certifying bank would certainly seem to be included in the words "any person." Under the averments of the complaint, plaintiff should be given an opportunity to show at trial that he is "a holder in due course."

Plaintiff therefore is entitled to a trial of the issues (a) whether or not he is "a holder in due course", and if he is such a holder, (b) whether defendant was or was not guilty of negligence when it certified these checks and if it was negligent (c) whether or not such negligence substantially contributed to the raising of the checks.

There are lower court decisions in New York which reach a contrary result. Sam Goody, Inc. v. Franklin Nat. Bank, 57 Misc.2d 193, 291 N.Y.S.2d 429 (Sup.Ct.Nassau Cty.1968); Wallach Sons, Inc. v. Bankers Trust Co., 307 N.Y.S.2d 297 (Civ.Ct. New York Cty.1970). After carefully reading the opinions in these two cases and with great deference to the two distinguished judges who wrote them, I cannot accept their result and feel that the Court of Appeals of New York would not reach their result.

It is, of course, true that the plaintiff is here in form suing in tort whereas his claim is more properly on the certification. The effect of negligence and its substantial contribution to the raising, if proved, is not to give rise to a tort claim but to preclude the Bank "from asserting the alteration." The Bank would not appear to be liable in any event for more than the amount of the checks as altered. See Official Comment 5, McKinney's U.C.C. § 3–406, page 263. However, the form of pleading adopted by plaintiff would not justify dismissing his action.

The motion is denied.

So ordered.

PROBLEMS

1. Thief stole a check payable to Payee and had it certified. He then wrote Payee's name on the back as an indorsement and transferred the check to Depositary Bank that paid value in good faith without notice of the forged indorsement. Depositary Bank obtained payment of the check from Drawee Bank. Drawee Bank then discovered the forged indorsement. What are the rights of Drawee Bank against Depositary Bank?

2. Thief stole a check payable to Payee and altered the check by erasing Payee's name and inserting Thief's name. Thief then obtained certification of the check and indorsed it to Depositary Bank that paid value in good faith without notice of the alteration. Depositary Bank obtained payment of the check from Drawee Bank. Drawee Bank then discovered the alteration. What are the rights of Drawee Bank against Depositary Bank?

E. CUSTOMER'S DEATH, INCAPACITY OR BANKRUPTCY

The bank's authority to pay a check of a customer may be revoked by the express direction of the customer, as in the case of a stop-payment order, but it may also be revoked by operation of law as in the case of the death, adjudication of incompetency or bankruptcy of the customer. The risk to the bank in making unauthorized payment in these cases is similar to that involved in the case of stop-payment orders. UCC § 4–405(1) deals specifically with the bank's authority in the case of death or incapacity and UCC § 4–405(2) gives to the bank additional authority in the case of death. On the latter point see Comments 3 and 4 to UCC § 4–405.

The authority of the bank to act in the case of the bankruptcy of the customer is not dealt with by the UCC because the question is governed by federal rather than state law. Under Bankruptcy Code § 541(a) the property of the bankrupt (including his bank accounts) passes to the estate in bankruptcy when the bankruptcy case is commenced, but under Bankruptcy Code § 542(c) a bank, until it has actual notice or actual knowledge of the bankruptcy of its customer, may continue to pay checks of the customer. The latter provision codifies the result of Bank of Marin v. England, 385 U.S. 99, 87 S.Ct. 274, 17 L.Ed.2d 197 (1966), which recognized the same right of the bank under the previous statute, the Bankruptcy Act of 1898.

F. WRONGFUL DISHONOR

---

1. CHECKS

LOUCKS v. ALBUQUERQUE NATIONAL BANK

Supreme Court of New Mexico, 1966.
76 N.M. 735, 418 P.2d 191.

La Fel E. Oman, Judge, Court of Appeals.

The plaintiffs-appellants, Richard A. Loucks and Del Martinez, hereinafter referred to as plaintiffs, Mr. Loucks and Mr. Martinez, respectively, were partners engaged in a business at Albuquerque, New Mexico, under the partnership name of L & M Paint and Body Shop.

By their complaint they sought both compensatory and punitive damages on behalf of the partnership, on behalf of Mr. Loucks, and on behalf of Mr. Martinez against the defendants-appellees, Albuquerque National Bank and W. J. Kopp, hereinafter referred to as defendants, the bank, and Mr. Kopp, respectively.

Prior to March 15, 1962 Mr. Martinez had operated a business at Albuquerque, New Mexico, under the name of Del's Paint and Body Shop. He did his banking with defendant bank and he dealt with Mr. Kopp, a vice-president of the bank.

On February 8, 1962 Mr. Martinez borrowed $500 from the bank, which he deposited with the bank in the account of Del's Paint and Body Shop. He executed an installment note payable to the bank evidencing this indebtedness.

On March 15, 1962 the plaintiffs formed a partnership in the name of L & M Paint and Body Shop. On that date they opened a checking account with the bank in the name of L & M Paint

and Body Shop and deposited $620 therein.   The signatures of
both Mr. Loucks and Mr. Martinez were required to draw money
from this account.   The balance in the account of Del's Paint
and Body Shop as of this time was $2.67. This was drawn from
this account by a cashier's check and deposited in the account of
L & M Paint & Body Shop on April 18, 1962.

Two payments of $50.00 each were made on Mr. Martinez'
note of February 8, 1962, or on notes given as a renewal thereof.
These payments were made by checks drawn by plaintiffs on the
account of L & M Paint and Body Shop.   The checks were payable to the order of the bank and were dated June 29, 1962 and
August 28, 1962.   A subsequent installment note was executed
by Mr. Martinez on October 17, 1962 in the principal amount of
$462 payable to the order of the bank.   This was given as a re-
placement or renewal of the prior notes which started with the
note of February 8, 1962.

Mr. Martinez became delinquent in his payments on this note
of October 17, 1962 and the bank sued him in a Justice of the
Peace court to recover the delinquency.

As of March 14, 1963 Mr. Martinez was still indebted to the
bank on this note in the amount of $402, and on that date, Mr.
Kopp, on behalf of the bank, wrote L & M Paint and Body Shop
advising that its account had been charged with $402 represent-
ing the balance due "on Del Martinez installment note," and the
indebtedness was referred to in the letter as the "indebtedness
of Mr. Del Martinez."

The charge of $402 against the account of L & M Paint and
Body Shop was actually made on March 15, 1963, which was a
Friday.

Although Mr. Martinez at one time testified he telephoned
Mr. Kopp on either Friday or the following Monday about this
charge, when he was questioned more closely he admitted he discussed the matter with Mr. Kopp by telephone on Friday.   Mr.
Loucks testified that as he recalled, it was on Monday.   Both
plaintiffs went to the bank on Monday, March 18, and talked
with Mr. Kopp.   They both told Mr. Kopp that the indebtedness
represented by the note was the personal indebtedness of Mr.
Martinez and was not a partnership obligation.   Mr. Loucks explained that they had some outstanding checks against the partnership account.   Mr. Kopp refused to return the money to the
partnership account.   There was evidence of some unpleasant-
ness in the conversation.   The partnership account, in which

there was then a balance of only $3.66, was thereupon closed by the plaintiffs.

The bank refused to honor nine, and possibly ten, checks drawn on the account and dated between the dates of March 8 and 16, inclusive.

The checks dated prior to March 15 total $89.14, and those dated March 15 and 16 total $121.68. These figures do not include the tenth check to which some reference was made, but which was not offered into evidence and the amount of which does not appear in the record.

The case came on for trial before the court and a jury. The court submitted the case to the jury upon the question of whether or not the defendants wrongfully made the charge in the amount of $402 against the account of L & M Paint and Body Shop. The allegations of the complaint concerning punitive damages and compensatory damages, other than the amount of $402 allegedly wrongfully charged by the defendants against the partnership account, were dismissed by the court before the case was submitted to the jury. The jury returned a verdict for the plaintiffs in the amount of $402.

The plaintiffs have appealed and assert error on the part of the trial court in taking from the jury the questions of (1) punitive damages, (2) damages to business reputation and credit, (3) damages for personal injuries allegedly sustained by Mr. Loucks, and (4) in disallowing certain costs claimed by plaintiffs.

*   *   *

The plaintiffs, as partners, sought recovery on behalf of the partnership of $402 allegedly wrongfully charged against the partnership account. This question was submitted to the jury, was decided in favor of the partnership, and against the defendants, and no appeal has been taken from the judgment entered on the verdict. They also sought recovery on behalf of the partnership of $5,000 for alleged damages to its credit, good reputation, and business standing in the community, $1,800 for its alleged loss of income, and $14,404 as punitive damages.

Each partner also sought recovery of $5,000 for alleged damages to his personal credit, good reputation and business standing. Mr. Martinez sought punitive damages individually in the amount of $10,000, and Mr. Loucks sought punitive damages individually in the amount of $60,000. Mr. Loucks also sought $25,000 by way of damages he allegedly sustained by reason of an ulcer which resulted from the wrongful acts of the defendants.

The parties have argued the case in their respective briefs and in their oral arguments upon the theory that the questions here involved, except for Point IV, which deals with the disallowance by the trial court of some claimed costs, are questions of the damages which can properly be claimed as a result of a wrongful dishonor by a bank of checks drawn by a customer or depositor on the bank, and of the sufficiency of the evidence offered by plaintiffs to support their claims for damages.

Both sides quote [UCC § 4–402]. * * *

It would appear that the first question to be resolved is that of the person, or persons, to whom a bank must respond in damages for a wrongful dishonor. Here, the account was a partnership account, and if there was in fact a wrongful dishonor of any checks, such were partnership checks.

We have adopted the Uniform Commercial Code in New Mexico. In [UCC § 4–402] it is clearly stated that a bank "is liable to its customer." In [UCC § 4–104(1)(e)], entitled "Definitions and index of definitions" it is stated that:

"(1) In this article unless the context otherwise requires

"(e) 'Customer' means any person having an account with a bank or for whom a bank has agreed to collect items and includes a bank carrying an account with another bank;
* * * "

This requires us to determine who is a "person" within the contemplation of this definition. Under part II, article I of the Uniform Commercial Code, entitled "General Definitions and Principles of Interpretation," we find the term "person" defined in [§ 1–201(30)] as follows: " 'Person' includes an individual or an organization * * * ."

Subsection (28) of the same section expressly includes a "partnership" as one of the legal or commercial entities embraced by the term "organization."

It would seem that logically the "customer" in this case to whom the bank was required to respond in damages for any wrongful dishonor was the partnership. The Uniform Commercial Code expressly regards a partnership as a legal entity. This is consistent with the ordinary mercantile conception of a partnership. * * *

The Uniform Partnership Act, which has been adopted in New Mexico and appears as chapter 66, article I, N.M.S.A.1953, recognizes that a partnership has a separate legal entity for at least some purposes. See Attaway v. Stanolind Oil & Gas Company, 232 F.2d 790 (10th Cir. 1956); I. Rowley, Partnership, § 1.3F at 22 (2d Ed.1960); Jensen, Is a Partnership Under the Uniform Partnership Act an Aggregate or an Entity, 16 Vand.L. Rev. 377 (1963).

Suits may be brought in New Mexico by or against the partnership as such. Sections 21–6–5 and 21–1–1(4)(*o*), N.M.S.A. 1953. A partnership is a distinct legal entity to the extent that it may sue or be sued in the partnership name. National Surety Co. v. George E. Breece Lumber Co., 60 F.2d 847 (10th Cir. 1932).

* * *

The relationship, in connection with which the wrongful conduct of the bank arose, was the relationship between the bank and the partnership. The partnership was the customer, and any damages arising from the dishonor belonged to the partnership and not to the partners individually.

The damages claimed by Mr. Loucks as a result of the ulcer, which allegedly resulted from the wrongful acts of the defendants, are not consequential damages proximately caused by the wrongful dishonor as contemplated by § 50A–4–402, N.M.S.A. 1953. In support of his right to recover for such claimed damages he relies upon the cases of Jones v. Citizens Bank of Clovis, 58 N.M. 48, 265 P.2d 366 and Weaver v. Bank of America Nat. Trust & Sav. Ass'n., 59 Cal.2d 428, 30 Cal.Rptr. 4, 380 P.2d 644. The California and New Mexico courts construed identical statutes in these cases. The New Mexico statute appeared as § 48–10–5, N.M.S.A.1953. This statute was repealed when the Uniform Commercial Code was adopted in 1961.

Assuming we were to hold that the decisions in those cases have not been affected by the repeal of the particular statutory provisions involved and the adoption of the Uniform Commercial Code, we are still compelled by our reasoning to reach the same result, because the plaintiffs in those cases were the depositor in the California case and the administratrix of the estate of the deceased depositor in the New Mexico case. In the present case, Mr. Loucks was not a depositor, as provided in the prior statute, nor a customer, as provided in our present statute. No duty was owed to him personally by reason of the debtor-creditor relationship between the bank and the partnership.

It is fundamental that compensatory damages are not recoverable unless they proximately result from some violation of a legally-recognized right of the person seeking the damages, whether such be a right in contract or tort. Hedrick v. Perry, 102 F.2d 802 (10th Cir. 1939); 72 Am.Jur.2d, Damages, §§ 1, 2, and 11; 25 C.J.S. Damages §§ 18 and 19.

Insofar as the damage questions are concerned, we must still consider the claims for damages to the partnership. As above stated, the claim on behalf of the partnership for the recovery of the $402 was concluded by judgment for plaintiffs in this amount. This leaves (1) the claim of $5,000 for alleged damage to credit, reputation and business standing, (2) the claim of $1,800 for alleged loss of income, and (3) the claim of $14,404 as punitive damages.

The question with which we are first confronted is that of whether or not the customer, whose checks are wrongfully dishonored, may recover damages merely because of the wrongful dishonor. We understand the provisions of [UCC § 4–402] to limit the damages to those proximately caused by the wrongful dishonor, and such includes any consequential damages so proximately caused. If the dishonor occurs through mistake, the damages are limited to actual damages proved.

It is pointed out in the comments to this section of the Uniform Commercial Code that:

" *   *   *

"This section rejects decisions which have held that where the dishonored item has been drawn by a merchant, trader or fiduciary he is defamed in his business, trade or profession by a reflection on his credit and hence that substantial damages may be awarded on the basis of defamation 'per se' without proof that damage has occurred. *   *   * "   Uniform Commercial Code, § 4–402, Comment 3.

If we can say as a matter of law that the dishonor here occurred through mistake, then the damages would be limited to the "actual damages proved." Even if we are able to agree, as contended by defendants in their answer brief, that the defendants acted under a mistake of fact in " *   *   *   that Mr. Kopp acting on behalf of the bank thought that the money was invested in the partnership and could be traced directly from Mr. Martinez to the L & M Paint and Body Shop," still defendants cannot rely on such mistake after both Mr. Martinez and Mr. Loucks informed them on March 15 and 18 that this was a personal obligation of Mr. Martinez and that the partnership had outstanding checks. At least it then became a question for the

jury to decide whether or not defendants had wrongfully dishonored the checks through mistake.

The problem then resolves itself into whether or not the evidence offered and received, together with any evidence properly
offered and improperly excluded, was sufficient to establish a
question as to whether the partnership credit and reputation
were proximately damaged by the wrongful dishonors. There
was evidence that ten checks were dishonored, that one parts
dealer thereafter refused to accept a partnership check and Mr.
Loucks was required to go to the bank, cash the check, and then
take the cash to the parts dealer in order to get the parts; that
some persons who had previously accepted the partership checks
now refused to accept them; that other places of business denied the partnership credit after the dishonors; and that a sales-
man, who had sold the partnership a map and for which he was
paid by one of the dishonored checks, came to the partnership's
place of business, and ripped the map off the wall because he
had been given "a bad check for it."

This evidence was sufficient to raise a question of fact to be
determined by the jury as to whether or not the partnership's
credit had been damaged as a proximate result of the dishonors.
This question should have been submitted to the jury.

Damages recoverable for injuries to credit as a result of a
wrongful dishonor are more than mere nominal damages and
are referred to as " * * * compensatory, general, substantial, moderate, or temperate, damages as would be fair and reasonable compensation for the injury which he [the depositor]
must have sustained, but not harsh or inordinate damages.
* * * " 5A Michie, Banks and Banking, § 243 at 576.

What are reasonable and temperate damages varies according to the circumstances of each case and the general extent to
which it may be presumed the credit of the depositor would be
injured. Valley National Bank v. Witter, 58 Ariz. 491, 121 P.2d
414. The amount of such damages is to be determined by the
sound discretion and dispassionate judgment of the jury.
Meinhart v. Farmers' State Bank, 124 Kan. 333, 259 P. 698, 701.

The next item of damages claimed on behalf of the partnership, which was taken from the jury, was the claim for loss of
income in the amount of $1,800 allegedly sustained by the part-
nership as a result of the illness and disability of Mr. Loucks by
reason of his ulcer. We are of the opinion that the trial court
properly dismissed this claim for the announced reason that no
substantial evidence was offered to support the claim, and for

the further reason that the partnership had no legally-enforceable right to recover for personal injuries inflicted upon a partner.

Even if we were to assume that a tortious act had been committed by defendants which proximately resulted in the ulcer and the consequent personal injuries and disabilities of Mr. Loucks, the right to recover for such would be in him. An action for damages resulting from a tort can only be sustained by the person directly injured thereby, and not by one claiming to have suffered collateral or resulting injuries. Ware v. Brown, 29 Fed.Cas. 220 (No. 17,170) (S.D.Ohio 1869); Commercial Credit Company v. Standard Baking Co., 45 Ohio App. 403, 187 N.E. 251; General Home Improvement Co. v. American Ladder Co., 26 N.J.Misc. 24, 56 A.2d 116.

As was stated by Mr. Justice Holmes in Robins Dry Dock & Repair Co. v. Flint, 275 U.S. 303, 48 S.Ct. 134, 72 L.Ed. 290:

" * * * no authority need be cited to show that, as a general rule, at least, a tort to the person or property of one man does not make the tort-feasor liable to another merely because the injured person was under a contract with that other, unknown to the doer of the wrong. * * * The law does not spread its protection so far."

The last question of damages concerns the claim for punitive damages. The trial court dismissed this claim for the reason that he was convinced there was no evidence of willful or wanton conduct on the part of defendants. Punitive or exemplary damages may be awarded only when the conduct of the wrong-doer may be said to be maliciously intentional, fraudulent, oppressive, or committed recklessly or with a wanton disregard of the plaintiffs' rights. Stewart v. Potter, 44 N.M. 460, 104 P.2d 736; Gray v. Esslinger, 46 N.M. 421, 130 P.2d 24; Jones v. Citizens Bank of Clovis, supra; Whitehead v. Allen, 63 N.M. 63, 313 P.2d 335.

Malice as a basis for punitive damages means the intentional doing of a wrongful act without just cause or excuse. This means that the defendant not only intended to do the act which is ascertained to be wrongful, but that he knew it was wrong when he did it. Jones v. Citizens Bank of Clovis, supra; Hussey v. Ellerman, 215 S.W.2d 38 (Mo.App.1948).

Although, as expressed above, we are of the opinion that there was a jury question as to whether defendants acted under a mistake of fact in dishonoring the checks, we do not feel that the unpleasant or intemperate remark or two claimed to have been made by Mr. Kopp, and his conduct, described by Mr. Martinez as having "run us out of the bank more or less," are sufficient upon which an award of punitive damages could properly have been made. Thus, the trial court was correct in taking this claim from the jury.

* * *

It follows from what has been said that this cause must be reversed and remanded for a new trial solely upon the questions of whether or not the partnership credit was damaged as a proximate result of the dishonors, and, if so, the amount of such damages.

It is so ordered.

NOTES

1. In Kendall Yacht Corp. v. United California Bank, 50 Cal. App.3d 949, 123 Cal.Rptr. 848 (1975), Corporation was the depositor and Laurence and Linda Kendall were officers and prospective shareholders who personally guaranteed Corporation's debts to Bank. Corporation never issued stock and "it was, in effect, nothing but a transparent shell, having no viability as a separate and distinct legal entity." 123 Cal.Rptr. at 853. The court held that the Kendalls were "customers" within the meaning of UCC § 4–402. "Thus it was entirely foreseeable that the dishonoring of the Corporation's check would reflect directly on the personal credit and reputation of the Kendalls and that they would suffer the adverse personal consequences which resulted when the Bank reneged on its commitments." 123 Cal.Rptr. at 853. The court allowed recovery by the Kendalls of damages for emotional distress under UCC § 4–402. Cf. Farmers Bank of the State of Delaware v. Sinwellan Corp., 367 A.2d 180 (Del. 1976).

2. The common law rule was stated in 2 Morse, Banks and Banking 1007–1008 (6th ed., Voorhees, 1928): "[T]he better authority seems to be, that, even if * * * actual loss or injury is not shown, yet more than nominal damages shall be given. It can hardly be possible that a customer's check can be wrongfully refused payment without some impeachment of his credit, which must in fact be an actual injury, though he cannot from the nature of the case furnish independent distinct proof thereof. It is as in cases of libel and slander, which description of suit, indeed, it closely resembles, inasmuch as it is a practical slur upon the plaintiff's credit and repute in the business world. Special damage may be shown, if the plaintiff be able; but, if he

be not able, the jury may nevertheless give such temporary (*sic*) damages as they conceive to be a reasonable compensation for that indefinite mischief which such an act must be assumed to have inflicted, according to the ordinary course of human events." (Editor's note: the word "temperate" appeared in prior editions instead of "temporary.") At the behest of the American Bankers Association a number of states enacted a version of the following: "No bank shall be liable to a depositor because of the nonpayment through mistake or error, and without malice, of a check which should have been paid unless the depositor shall allege and prove actual damage by reason of such nonpayment and in such event the liability shall not exceed the amount of damage so proved." Cal.Civ.Code § 3320 (repealed). This is the kind of statute referred to in Comment 1 to UCC § 4–402.

2.   CREDIT CARDS AND ELECTRONIC FUND TRANSFERS

PROBLEMS

1.   Cardholder was issued a MasterCard with a $300 credit limit. She went to Typewriter City, which honors MasterCard cards, with the intention of buying a typewriter for her son as a birthday present. MasterCard's agreement with Typewriter City set a "floor limit" of $50; that is if a transaction involved more than this amount, "telephonic authorization" from Master-Card's local office was required. After Cardholder had selected the typewriter she wanted, at a price of $120, the sales clerk requested telephonic authorization for the sale. Owing to a computer mix-up, MasterCard's telephone clerk erroneously told Typewriter City that Cardholder had already exceeded the $300 limit on her card. Cardholder, an emotional person by nature, was outraged; she needed the machine immediately because her son's birthday was the next day. A heated argument ensued between Cardholder and the manager of Typewriter City; other customers stared; Cardholder finally stamped out in tears. It was some weeks before the mistake was corrected and customer could use her card again. Cardholder was not placated by the letter of apology she received from MasterCard and insists that she suffered extreme emotional distress because of the mix-up. Would you advise her that she has a cause of action against MasterCard?

2.   Typewriter City has an electronic point-of-sale (POS) terminal that allows customers to pay for goods or services by use

of a plastic access card and the customer's personal identification number (PIN). Suppose that instead of using the Master-Card as in Problem 1, Cardholder used her access card for the $120 sale. The funds transfer was not made because the computer mistakenly indicated that Cardholder had overdrawn her bank account. As in Problem 1 Cardholder became greatly upset and sued the institution issuing the access card. What are Cardholder's rights under the following provision of the Electronic Fund Transfers Act, 15 U.S.C. § 1693 et seq.?

§ 1693h. Liability of financial institutions

Action or failure to act proximately causing damages

(a) Subject to subsections (b) and (c) of this section, a financial institution shall be liable to a consumer for all damages proximately caused by—

(1) the financial institution's failure to make an electronic fund transfer, in accordance with the terms and conditions of an account, in the correct amount or in a timely manner when properly instructed to do so by the consumer, except where—

(A) the consumer's account has insufficient funds;

(B) the funds are subject to legal process or other encumbrance restricting such transfer;

(C) such transfer would exceed an established credit limit;

(D) an electronic terminal has insufficient cash to complete the transaction; or

(E) as otherwise provided in regulations of the Board;

(2) the financial institution's failure to make an electronic fund transfer due to insufficient funds when the financial institution failed to credit, in accordance with the terms and conditions of an account, a deposit of funds to the consumer's account which would have provided sufficient funds to make the transfer, and

(3) the financial institution's failure to stop payment of a preauthorized transfer from a consumer's account when instructed to do so in accordance with the terms and conditions of the account.

Acts of God and technical malfunctions

(b) A financial institution shall not be liable under subsection (a)(1) or (2) of this section if the financial institution shows by a preponderance of the evidence that its action or failure to act resulted from—

(1) an act of God or other circumstance beyond its control, that it exercised reasonable care to prevent such an occurrence, and that it exercised such diligence as the circumstances required; or

(2) a technical malfunction which was known to the consumer at the time he attempted to initiate an electronic fund transfer or, in the case of a preauthorized transfer, at the time such transfer should have occurred.

Intent

(c) In the case of a failure described in subsection (a) of this section which was not intentional and which resulted from a bona fide error, notwithstanding the maintenance of procedures reasonably adapted to avoid any such error, the financial institution shall be liable for actual damages proved.

For a discussion of § 1693h, see Penney & Baker, The Law of Electronic Fund Transfer Systems pp. 13–12 through 13–15 (1980).

Chapter 6

DOCUMENTS OF TITLE AND LETTERS OF CREDIT

A. DOCUMENTARY SALES

The UCC sets a pattern of inspection-acceptance-payment for a typical sale of goods. Buyer when he accepts the goods is obligated to pay the price (UCC § 2–607) but acceptance normally presupposes an opportunity by Buyer to inspect the goods (UCC § 2–606). Thus, unless Seller agrees to give Buyer credit, delivery and acceptance of the goods and payment for the goods take place contemporaneously. In a face-to-face transaction Buyer is protected by his ability to reject the goods if his inspection discloses that they are not as warranted, and Seller, because he still has possession of the rejected goods, is in a position to adequately protect his interests in disposing of the goods. However, where Buyer and Seller are physically remote from each other, different considerations apply. Buyer's power to reject the goods, whether exercised rightfully or wrongfully, while serving to protect his interests can be damaging to the interests of Seller. Seller may find himself having to dispose of rejected goods in a distant market where he is not adequately represented. We have seen that UCC § 2–603 deals with this problem by placing on Buyer certain duties with respect to rejected goods, but Seller has no assurances that these duties will be carried out. It may be small solace to unpaid Seller that he has a cause of action against Buyer for breach of contract or for Buyer's failure to perform duties imposed by the UCC. Seller, if he knows and trusts Buyer, may be willing to give him credit and simply ship the goods. In many cases, however, particularly those involving international sales, Seller may not be willing to take the risk that the goods will be rejected and not paid for when delivered. If Seller has sufficient bargaining power he can demand payment prior to shipment, but in that case, Buyer is left to the mercy of Seller. Since Buyer has no assurance that he will ever get the goods he may be unwilling to accept these terms. A method of protecting the interests of both Buyer and Seller in this kind of case is provided by the documentary sale.

The documentary sale involves the use of a bill of lading and a sight draft, and often a third document, a letter of credit. We saw previously that a bill of lading can be either nonnegotiable (a "straight bill") or negotiable (an "order bill"). A straight bill acknowledges instructions from the shipper or consignor to deliver the goods to a named consignee at a specified destination. The shipper under a straight bill, however, has control of the goods in that he can change the destination or the consignee at any time before delivery; the carrier will normally follow those instructions regardless of who has possession of the bill of lading. See UCC § 7–303. The order bill in this respect is different. Under an order bill the goods are to be delivered only to the holder of the bill of lading and only upon its surrender. UCC § 7–403. Thus, the shipper while he retains possession of the order bill has maximum control of the goods, and when he delivers the order bill to Buyer loses all control of the goods. See UCC § 7–303. The order bill of lading thus represents the right to receive the goods. Because the goods are represented by the order bill, it can be used as a device for giving a security interest in the goods. Possession of the order bill by the holder is for these purposes tantamount to possession of the goods. If Seller ships the goods to Buyer but has a bill of lading issued to himself or his order, the goods represented by the bill of lading in effect become collateral for the obligation of Buyer under the sales contract. A shipment made in this manner is known as a shipment under reservation. See UCC § 2–505.

The second document used in a documentary sale is the sight draft. A sight draft is simply an order by the drawer of the draft to the drawee of the draft to pay, on presentation of the draft to the drawee ("on sight") a stated sum of money to a named payee or to his order. In the case of a documentary sale the drawer is Seller, the drawee is Buyer or Buyer's bank, and the payee is usually Seller, or a bank or other financial institution that either is acting as Seller's collecting agent or is acting in its own behalf as purchaser of the draft from Seller.

The object of a documentary sale is to assure Seller that he will receive payment for the goods prior to the time that they arrive at their destination, and to assure Buyer that at the time he pays for the goods he will have effective control of the goods. To carry out these objectives, an order bill of lading is used. Although details of the transaction may vary, the basic pattern of a documentary sale is as follows: Seller ships the goods to Buyer and takes from the carrier an order bill of lading. Seller takes the order bill of lading, to which is attached a sight draft for the amount owed by Buyer for the goods, to Seller's bank. The bank is directed to present the draft to Buyer for payment, and upon payment to simultaneously deliver the order bill of lading. Since Buyer is in a distant place the presentation of the draft and the exchange of the bill of lading for the amount of the draft is made by a correspondent bank in Buyer's city that acts as agent of Seller's bank. Or in some cases, Seller may send the documents directly to his agent in Buyer's city. The proceeds of the draft are remitted through the chain of agents to Seller. Sometimes Seller's bank purchases or "discounts" the draft at the outset and takes the order bill of lading as security for payment of the draft. In that event Seller is paid immediately for the goods and the proceeds of the draft when paid by Buyer are paid to Seller's bank.

Although Buyer, by getting possession of the order bill of lading is assured of control of the goods, this type of exchange denies to Buyer the right to inspect the goods prior to payment of the price. At the time the exchange is made the goods normally will not have arrived at their destination. Buyer can look only to the description of the goods in the bill of lading to assure himself that he will be receiving the goods bargained for.

Although this type of exchange assures Seller that he will be paid for the goods prior to giving up control of them, it does not guarantee that Buyer in fact will pay the draft when presented. Buyer may not pay either because financially unable to pay, or because he is repudiating his contract obligations. If Buyer doesn't pay, Seller will have to find some other destination for the goods that are at that point in transit to Buyer. A third document, the irrevocable letter of credit, can be used to eliminate this risk. The irrevocable letter of credit, used in a variety of commercial transactions, is frequently used in documentary sales involving overseas shipments where the consequences to Seller of nonpayment by Buyer are particularly onerous. The irrevocable letter of credit, in this context, is simply a document usually issued by a bank ("the issuer") at the request of Buyer ("the customer") in which the issuer undertakes to honor drafts of Seller ("the beneficiary") when those drafts are presented in accordance with conditions stated in the letter of credit, including the presentation of described bills of lading. See UCC § 5–103(1)(a). Because the irrevocable letter of credit is for the benefit of the beneficiary, once it has been delivered to the beneficiary or he has been advised of its issuance it can't be revoked without his consent. See UCC § 5–106. The letter of credit represents an obligation of the issuer independent of the underlying transaction between the beneficiary and the customer, and if the draft is presented in accordance with the terms of the credit with all supporting documents the issuer must honor it. See UCC § 5–114(1). In that case Buyer cannot prevent payment by the issuer even if Seller is in breach of the underlying contract. If the documents appear on their face to comply with the credit the only remedy of Buyer is to enjoin the issuer from paying, but the injunction can be granted only in case of fraud in the transaction, forged documents, or other defect not apparent on the face of the documents. See UCC § 5–114(2)(b).

B. DOCUMENTS OF TITLE

---

1. BILLS OF LADING

Bills of lading are regulated by many federal and state statutes. State law is found primarily in Article 7 of the UCC but that article has limited application. UCC § 7–103 makes Article 7 subject to "any [applicable] treaty or statute of the United States, regulatory statute of this State or tariff, classification or regulation filed or issued pursuant thereto." Federal law plays a dominant role in the regulation of bills of lading. The Federal Bills of Lading Act, 49 U.S.C. §§ 81–124, applies to carriages of goods by a common carrier from any state to a foreign country or to another state, or from any state that passes through a foreign country or another state. Coverage of Article 7 is thus limited to carriages of goods in which the goods never leave the state of origin and to shipments of goods from a foreign country to any state. In the latter case, however, if an ocean bill of lading is involved the Carriage of Goods by Sea Act, 46 U.S.C. §§ 1300–15, and the Harter Act, 46 U.S.C. §§ 190–195, apply. With respect to the liability of the carrier for loss or damage to the goods the Carmack Amendment to the Interstate Commerce Act, 49 U.S.C. § 20, applies to interstate shipments. There are numerous other federal and state statutes, as well as regulations of the Interstate Commerce Commission, that may apply to a particular case involving rights under a bill of lading.

Thus, the rights and obligations of parties to a bill of lading are in the majority of cases decided by federal law, principally the Bills of Lading Act. That Act is almost identical to the Uniform Bills of Lading Act which was the applicable state law in a majority of the states prior to adoption of Article 7 of the UCC.

KORESKA v. UNITED CARGO CORP.

Supreme Court of New York, Appellate Division, First Dept., 1965.
23 A.D.2d 37, 258 N.Y.S.2d 432.

PER CURIAM.   Plaintiff, an Austrian manufacturer and seller of thermographic copying paper, appeals from an order denying his motion for summary judgment for the value of paper allegedly converted by defendant United Cargo Corporation.   United, a carrier, having issued a negotiable order bill of lading for the goods, consisting of four large packages, delivered them to the New York purchaser without requiring or taking up the bill of lading, and before plaintiff had received his purchase price.

The substantial question presented is whether United has raised a triable issue of fact in contending that it was excused from its duty of requiring surrender of the bill of lading before delivering the goods.   United urges that it was so excused by an oral waiver made by plaintiff's agent and also by a binding trade custom or course of dealing.

It is concluded that United has failed to raise any triable issue as to the alleged oral waiver, and that the order denying plaintiff's motion for summary judgment should be reversed, and his motion granted.

The material facts are as follows.   Defendant United is the operator of a container delivery service between the United States and Europe.   Plaintiff Koreska had either sold or had contracted to sell the goods in issue to a New York buyer, third-party defendant Parker Whitney, Ltd.   Thereafter a forwarding agency, Allgemeine Land und Seetransportgesellschaft Hermann Ludwig,* procured from United the negotiable bill of lading, naming Koreska's collecting agent, a New York bank, as consignee.   The document required that the arrival notice be sent to the New York buyer, Parker Whitney.   On arrival of the goods in New York, in November, 1963, United delivered them to the buyer, Parker Whitney, without requiring the bill of lading.

* * *

It is claimed that there are contested factual issues whether the seller, Koreska, waived the requirement that United, the issuer of the negotiable document of title, take it up before deliv-

---

* There is inconclusive but uncontradicted evidence in the record that Allgemeine functioned as an agent for United in Germany in receiving merchandise shipped through United.

ering the goods. United's New York import manager states that in accordance with a regular course of dealing between the parties Allgemeine's New York representative, on behalf of Koreska, orally authorized United to make delivery to Parker Whitney without awaiting presentment of the bill of lading. Allgemeine's New York representative, on the other hand, denies having given such permission, denies that Allgemeine was acting as Koreska's agent, and denies knowledge of such a course of dealing or trade custom.

Although there may be factual issues with respect to the making of the oral waiver and the existence of the course of dealing, United has failed to give any evidentiary facts showing that Allgemeine was Koreska's agent for purposes of modifying the terms of the bill of lading. The evidentiary facts are to the contrary. Another bill of lading, covering a prior sale from Koreska to Parker Whitney expressly refers to Allgemeine as "agent of UCC", meaning agent of defendant United. Moreover, both this prior bill of lading and the one covering the goods in issue show the New York bank as consignee and require that the goods be delivered to its order. Thus the New York bank was known to United to be the appropriate New York representative of Koreska on all matters relating to delivery of the goods.

It is hornbook law that an agent may be one party's agent for one purpose and another party's agent for another (2 N.Y. Jur., Agency, § 205). Thus, Allgemeine may have had powers, not shown in this record, to bind United with respect to the issuance of a bill of lading and perhaps to bind Koreska with respect to receipt thereof and payment therefor. Even if such be the case, the agent's powers are limited to the particular purpose for which the agency is, or appears to be, created (id. § 143; Northern Assurance Co., Limited, of London v. B. A. W. Trucking Co., 252 App.Div. 323, 299 N.Y.S. 308; Doubleday v. Kress, 50 N.Y. 410). In the *Northern Assurance* case, Mr. Justice Callahan, on behalf of this Court held:

> "While an agent appointed to ship goods has implied authority to accept customary bills of lading, and make reasonable terms concerning affreightment, this rule does not permit the agent to modify the terms of the contract of shipment on which the principals have already agreed. [Citing authorities]." (252 App.Div. p. 324, 299 N.Y.S. p. 310)

The language and the rule as stated are precisely applicable to the situation in this case. Thus, United's conclusory statement that Allgemeine is Koreska's agent is doubly defective. It is not an evidentiary fact, as is required to avoid summary judgment (CPLR 3212[b]); and it is not even probative of Allgemeine's power to bind Koreska in the manner claimed.

Even if a factual issue had been raised with respect to Allgemeine's agency, Koreska would be entitled to summary judgment. In the case of an order, or negotiable bill of lading, as opposed to a straight, or non-negotiable bill, it is ordinarily the consignee or other holder of the negotiable bill, who alone is entitled to authorize a diversion or modification of the delivery term (former Personal Property Law, § 197, cf. § 198; cf. U.C.C. §§ 7–303[1][a], 7–403 eff. Sept. 27, 1964). Even if Allgemeine obtained possession of the bill after authorizing a waiver, as claimed by United, it was never a holder with power to divert, in the absence of an actual indorsement of the bill to it (former Pers.Prop.Law §§ 197[b], 198[c]; cf. U.C.C. § 1–201[20]). Moreover the seller-shipper, Koreska, never became a consignee or holder, and therefore did not, under these rules, have the power to divert the goods without the cooperation of its collecting agent-consignee, the New York bank. It follows that its alleged agent, Allgemeine, similarly had no such power.

A further reason why United may not avail itself of the alleged waiver, is that the waiver was oral only, and would modify the express term of the bill that delivery was to be made at the order of the New York bank consignee. One of the conditions printed on the back of the bill provides:

"None of the terms of this bill of lading shall be deemed to have been waived by any person unless by express waiver signed by such person, or his duly authorized agent."

Ordinary prudence, moreover, would dictate that the carrier require that such instructions be noted on the bill itself (cf. U.C.C. § 7–303[2]).

For similar reasons evidence of the course of dealing or trade custom is also without significance. The express term, requiring delivery in accordance with the consignee's order, is controlling, whenever the course of dealing or trade custom is inconsistent with it (see Gravenhorst v. Zimmerman, 236 N.Y. 22, 32–34, 27 A.L.R. 1465; Rothstein Corp. v. Kerr S.S. Co., 21 A.D.2d 463, 251 N.Y.S.2d 81, aff'd 15 N.Y.2d 897, 258 N.Y.S.2d 426, 206 N.E.2d 360; cf. U.C.C. § 1–205[4]).

In the absence of a triable issue of fact, summary judgment must be granted. Summary relief is, moreover, particularly appropriate in commercial cases, such as this, where the injured party is far away and has relied on documentary rights and evidence. If a trade custom or the oral waiver by an unknown purported agent, contrary to the plain terms of trade documents, were given the effect contended for by United, the ability of such a distant person to engage in foreign trade in reliance on negotiable documents of title would be severely and unduly handicapped. Allowance of such a practice is certainly destructive of the integrity of documents used in international trade throughout the world.

Accordingly, the order denying plaintiff Koreska's motion for summary judgment should be reversed on the law, and summary judgment for $13,939.72, the invoice price, in favor of plaintiff, granted, with costs and disbursements to plaintiff-appellant against defendant-respondent.

Order, entered on October 19, 1964, reversed on the law with $30 costs and disbursements to appellant and the motion for summary judgment for $13,939.72, the invoice price, in favor of plaintiff is granted. The order of this Court entered on April 1, 1965 is vacated.

All concur except BOTEIN, P. J., and STEVENS, J., who dissent in a dissenting opinion by STEVENS, J.

[The dissenting opinion is omitted.]

CLOCK v. MISSOURI–KANSAS–TEXAS RAILROAD CO.

United States District Court, E.D.Missouri, 1976.
407 F.Supp. 448.

NANGLE, DISTRICT JUDGE. Plaintiff Gerald Clock brought this action to recover the cost of goods which were allegedly converted by defendant Missouri-Kansas-Texas Railroad Company. By amended complaint, plaintiff added Stanley L. Crawford as defendant. Plaintiff also alleges that defendant Railroad breached its obligation to deliver the goods. Prior to the filing of plaintiff's amended complaint, defendant Railroad filed a third-party complaint against Crawford, alleging that if the Railroad should be liable to plaintiff, third-party defendant would be liable to the Railroad to the extent of the liability to plaintiff. Crawford now being a defendant in this action, defendant Railroad's complaint is in fact a cross-claim and will be treated as such.

This case was tried before the Court without a jury. The Court having considered the pleadings, the testimony of the witnesses, the documents in evidence, and being otherwise fully advised in the premises, hereby makes the following findings of fact and conclusions of law as required by Rule 52, Federal Rules of Civil Procedure:

FINDINGS OF FACT

1. Plaintiff, Gerald Clock, is, and was at all times relevant herein, a citizen of the State of Indiana. Defendant, Missouri-Kansas-Texas Railroad Company ("Railroad") is a corporation incorporated under the laws of the State of Delaware, having its principal place of business in Texas. Defendant Stanley L. Crawford, is, and was at all times relevant herein, a citizen of the State of Oklahoma.

2. On January 14, 1975, Crawford sold two carloads of bulk ammonium nitrate fertilizer to Buford Cunningham and received two checks in payment therefor. On the same date, the goods were placed in the care and custody of defendant Railroad for shipment from Oklahoma to Eaton Agricultural Center in Indiana. Defendant Railroad issued bills of lading to cover the goods. The bills of lading were signed by Crawford. Both bills of lading specify on the top of each that they are

UNIFORM STRAIGHT BILL OF LADING ORIGINAL— NOT NEGOTIABLE

3. At the time of sale, Crawford knew that Cunningham was going to sell the goods to a third party. Soon after the sale to Cunningham, Cunningham did sell the goods to plaintiff for $30,195.12. At the time of this sale, plaintiff had no knowledge of any infirmities in title, or right to possession, by Cunningham.

4. On January 23, 1975, the bank notified Crawford that there were insufficient funds in Cunningham's account to cover the checks. Accordingly, they were returned to Crawford.

5. The goods were still in transit at this point. Crawford instructed the Railroad to hold the railroad cars containing the goods until further instructions from him. Defendant Railroad complied.

6. On February 3, 1975, Crawford certified to defendant Railroad that he was the true owner of the goods and he issued a reconsignment order on the goods, instructing that they be

sent to Farmers Union Coop, instead of Eaton Agricultural Center. Defendant Railroad complied with these instructions.

7. Plaintiff furnished replacement goods to Eaton Agricultural Center of a like quantity and value, and acquired the right, title and interest of Eaton Agricultural Center to the goods, by reason of an assignment by Eaton Agricultural Center executed on February 10, 1975.

CONCLUSIONS OF LAW

This Court has jurisdiction over the subject matter and of the parties. 28 U.S.C.A. § 1332.

The bills of lading involved herein are straight bills of lading. 49 U.S.C.A. §§ 82, 86. It is clear that "[a] straight bill can not be negotiated free from existing equities * * *". 49 U.S. C.A. § 109. While not negotiable, straight bills are transferable. The transferee stands in the shoes of the transferor, acquiring no additional rights over those held by the transferor. See Arizona Feed v. Southern Pacific Transportation Co., 21 Ariz.App. 346, 519 P.2d 199 (1974); Southern Pacific Co. v. Agencia Joffroy, S.A., 65 Ariz. 65, 174 P.2d 278 (1946); Quality Shingle Co. v. Old Oregon Lumber & Shingle Co., 110 Wash. 60, 187 P. 705 (1920); [UCC §] 7–104.

A carrier may deliver goods to "[a] person lawfully entitled to the possession of the goods" or to the consignee. 49 U.S.C.A. § 89. The question for determination therefore is whether Crawford was lawfully entitled to possession of the goods. While it is true that title passes to a buyer when the seller completes his performance under the contract, [UCC §] 2–401, it is equally true that

> where the buyer * * * fails to make a payment due * * * the aggrieved seller may
>
> (a) withholding delivery of such goods;
>
> (b) stop delivery by any bailee * * *;
>
> * * *
>
> (d) resell and recover damages * * *;
>
> * * *
>
> (f) cancel. [UCC §] 2–703.

It is the Court's conclusion, therefore, that upon the failure of the checks presented by Cunningham to Crawford, Crawford was "lawfully entitled to the possession of the goods." Plaintiff, as transferee of a straight bill of lading, can not have any greater rights than did Cunningham, and can not have the status of a bona fide purchaser for value. Since Crawford was entitled to possession of the goods, defendant Railroad can not be liable for delivering the goods in accordance with Crawford's instructions. 49 U.S.C.A. § 89. Turner Lumber & Investment Co. v. Chicago, R. I. & P. Ry. Co., 223 Mo.App. 564, 16 S.W.2d 705 (1929).

The applicable provisions of the Commercial Code provide that

(1) Unless the bill of lading otherwise provides, the carrier may deliver the goods to a person or destination other than that stated in the bill or may otherwise dispose of the goods on instructions from

(b) the consignor on a nonnegotiable bill notwithstanding contrary instructions from the consignee * * *. [UCC §] 7–303.

Under the facts established herein, Crawford was the consignor, as Crawford was "the person from whom the goods have been received for shipment." [UCC §] 7–102(c). Since the bills of lading were nonnegotiable, and defendant Railroad delivered the goods pursuant to the instructions of the consignor, there can be no liability. See Comments, [UCC §§] 7–303 and 7–504(3).

Under 49 U.S.C.A. § 112, the authority of the shipper to stop shipment in transit and redirect it is well established. See Weyerhaeuser Timber Co. v. First National Bank of Portland, 150 Or. 172, 38 P.2d 48 (1934); Cashmere Fruit Growers' Union v. Great Northern Railway Co., 149 Wash. 319, 270 P. 1038 (1928), cert. denied, 279 U.S. 851, 49 S.Ct. 347, 73 L.Ed. 994; Quality Shingle Co. v. Old Oregon Lumber & Shingle Co., supra. The same right is recognized in the Commercial Code. See [UCC §§] 2–703 and 2–705. Accordingly there can be no recovery by plaintiff against Crawford.

Plaintiff has claimed that both the Railroad and Crawford converted the shipments in question to their own use. Conversion has been defined as " * * * an *unauthorized* assumption and exercise of the right of ownership over the personal property of another to the exclusion of the owners' right". Carson Union May Stern Co. v. Pennsylvania Railroad Co., 421 S.W.2d 540 (Mo.App.1967) [emphasis in the original]. Having concluded that Crawford was lawfully entitled to possession of the goods, it is clear that recovery for conversion will not lie.

The cases cited by plaintiff are inapposite as they involve a bona fide purchaser for value. Under the authority of 49 U.S. C.A. § 81 et seq., there can not be such status where one is a transferee under a straight bill of lading. North American Van Lines, Inc. v. Heller, 371 F.2d 629 (5th Cir. 1967) is equally unavailing since the Court concludes that Crawford was lawfully entitled to possession.

Accordingly, judgment will be for defendants Railroad and Crawford. Since plaintiff will not recover any damages from defendant Railroad, judgment will be for defendant Crawford on the Railroad's cross-claim.

NOTES

1. In *Clock*, when Crawford gave his reconsignment order to Railroad he certified that he was "the true owner of the goods." If we assume that the contract of sale was a shipment contract, who had title to the goods at the time of the reconsignment order? See UCC § 2–401(2). Did the right of Crawford to reconsign the goods depend on who had title to the goods at that time? Did the right of Crawford to reconsign the goods depend on who had possession of the bill of lading? See UCC § 2–703 and § 2–705. Suppose Crawford wrongfully reconsigned the goods, i.e., assume that the checks of Cunningham had not been returned for insufficient funds. Would Railroad have been liable to Clock, who was the transferee of the bill of lading from Cunningham? See UCC § 7–303(1). Would Crawford have been liable to Clock? See UCC § 7–504(1). Would Farmers Union Coop, which received the goods on reconsignment, have been liable to Clock? See UCC § 7–504(3).

2. What would your answers to the questions asked in the preceding note have been if the bill of lading had been an order bill to the order of Cunningham which had been delivered to Cunningham at the time of receipt by Crawford of Cunningham's checks?

2. WAREHOUSE RECEIPTS

**Dolan, Good Faith Purchase and Warehouse Receipts:
Thoughts on the Interplay of Articles 2, 7, and 9 of the UCC**

30 Hast.L.J. 1, 2–3 (1978).[*]

Functions of the Warehouse Receipt

Historically, documents of title such as warehouse receipts facilitated the practice of storing and transporting commodities. More recently, the receipt has taken on significant marketing and financing features.

The Marketing Function

For some purchasers, delivery is not an essential part of the purchase transaction. Grain dealers, for example, frequently purchase from producers and sell to industry consumers without moving the grain from the elevators to which the producers delivered it for drying and storing after harvest. Customarily these buyers and sellers effect such transfers by negotiable warehouse receipts. The producer obtains the receipt, which describes the grain according to industry standards; the grain dealer then purchases the receipt and transfers it, perhaps through a series of buyers, to a buyer who desires to ship or otherwise take possession of the grain. This last purchaser then surrenders the receipt to the elevator and takes delivery. The result is that the parties have achieved the marketing of the grain without incurring unnecessary transportation expenses.

Similarly, in the cotton industry a producer will deliver cotton to a gin for processing and storing. The gin will issue a negotiable receipt for the cotton with a sample attached. Brokers then display the samples to buyers who may be located in markets distant from the gin. Upon receipt of a satisfactory offer, the broker forwards the receipt with a draft through banking channels. When the purchaser honors the draft the bank delivers the receipt; the purchaser, unless he desires to resell the cotton without taking possesssion, will surrender the receipt to the gin and take delivery of the goods. Again, the receipt simplifies the marketing process and saves transportation costs.

[*] Reprinted with the permission of the author and the Hastings Law Journal. The author's footnotes are omitted.

The Financing Function

In transactions similar to the foregoing illustrations, market conditions or production schedules may force a buyer to hold a commodity. During that interval the buyer owns a valuable asset but cannot utilize it and, therefore, may seek to borrow against it. Lenders will grant credit on the security of the stored commodity by taking the negotiable warehouse receipt. When the borrower finds a buyer for the commodity or is prepared to use it in its own production process, the borrower will pay off the loan, obtain the receipt from the creditor and surrender the receipt to the warehouse against delivery of the goods.

Some borrowers use nonnegotiable receipts in connection with inventory financing. This form of inventory loan satisfies a lender's policing requirements in situations in which the lender fears his collateral may disappear quickly. The borrower delivers the inventory to a "field warehouse," usually a part of the borrower's premises controlled by an independent, field-warehouse company. The warehouse then issues nonnegotiable receipts to the lender. When the borrower needs inventory to fill customer orders, he will satisfy a portion of the loan; the lender in turn will issue delivery orders to the field warehouse, which will then release part of the inventory to the borrower.

These models illustrate typical patterns through which business people employ warehouse receipts to save transaction costs and to achieve liquidity. The models also forecast the potential conflicts in these commodity paper transactions. With respect to each purchase, for example, there is the classic tension between the purchaser, on the one hand, and the seller's secured lender, on the other. Conflicts between purchasers and lenders claiming an interest in the same goods may also arise because some sellers will enter into a contract of sale with more than one buyer or grant a security interest to more than one lender.

I.C.C. METALS, INC. v. MUNICIPAL WAREHOUSE CO.

Court of Appeals of New York, 1980.
50 N.Y.2d 657, 431 N.Y.S.2d 372, 409 N.E.2d 849.

OPINION OF THE COURT

GABRIELLI, JUDGE. At issue on this appeal is whether a warehouse which provides no adequate explanation for its failure to return stored property upon a proper demand is entitled to the benefit of a contractual limitation upon its liability. For the reasons discussed below, we conclude that proof of delivery of the stored property to the warehouse and its failure to return that property upon proper demand suffices to establish a prima facie case of conversion and thereby renders inapplicable the liability-limiting provision, unless the warehouse comes forward with evidence sufficient to prove that its failure to return the property is not the result of its conversion of that property to its own use. If the warehouse does proffer such evidence and is able to persuade the trier of facts of the truth of its explanation, then the limitation of liability will be given effect and the bailor will be required to prove the warehouse to be at fault if it is to recover even those limited damages allowed by the provision.

The facts relevant to this appeal are undisputed and may be simply stated. In the autumn of 1974, plaintiff, an international metals trader, delivered three separate lots of an industrial metal called indium to defendant commercial warehouse for safekeeping. The parties have stipulated that the three lots of indium, which had an aggregate weight of some 845 pounds, were worth $100,000. When the metal was delivered to defendant, it supplied plaintiff with warehouse receipts for each lot. Printed on the back of each receipt were the terms and conditions of the bailment, as proposed by defendant. Section 11 of those terms and conditions provided as follows: "Limitation of Liability— Sec. 11. The Liability of the warehouseman as to all articles and items listed on the face of this warehouse receipt is limited to the actual value of each article and item, but the total liability of the warehouseman shall not exceed in any event for damage to any or all the items or articles listed on this warehouse receipt the sum of fifty ($50.00) dollars; provided, however, that such liability may, on written request of the bailor at the time of signing this warehouse receipt or within twenty (20) days after receipt of this warehouse receipt, be increased on part or all of the articles and items hereunder, in which event, increased rates shall be charged based upon such increased valuation, but the warehouseman's maximum liability shall in no event exceed the actual value of any or all of the articles and items in question. In no case shall the liability be extended to include any loss of profit".[1] Plaintiff did not request any increase in defendant's contractual liability, nor did it inform defendant of the value of the metal.

---

1. In light of our disposition of the main issue presented by this case we need not and accordingly do not determine whether this limitation applies to loss of bailed property as well as damage to that property.

For almost two years, defendant billed plaintiff for storage of each of the three lots by means of monthly invoices that specifically identified the stored metal, and plaintiff duly paid each invoice. Finally, in May of 1976, plaintiff requested the return of one of the three lots of indium. At that point defendant for the first time informed plaintiff that it was unable to locate any of the indium. Plaintiff then commenced this action in conversion, seeking to recover the full value of the indium. In response, defendant contended that the metal had been stolen through no fault of defendant's and that, at any rate, section 11 of the terms printed on each warehouse receipt limited plaintiff's potential recovery to a maximum of $50 per lot of indium.

Special Term granted summary judgment to plaintiff for the full value of the indium. The court found that plaintiff had made out a prima facie case of conversion by proffering undisputed proof that the indium had been delivered to defendant and that defendant had failed to return it upon a proper demand. As to defendant's contention that the metal had been stolen, the court concluded that this allegation was completely speculative and that defendant had failed to raise any question of fact sufficient to warrant a trial on the issue. Finally, Special Term held that the contractual limitation upon defendant's liability was inapplicable to an action in conversion. The Appellate Division, 67 A.D.2d 640, 412 N.Y.S.2d 531, affirmed the judgment in favor of plaintiff and we granted defendant leave to appeal to this court. We now affirm the order appealed from.

Absent an agreement to the contrary, a warehouse is not an insurer of goods and may not be held liable for any injury to or loss of stored property not due to some fault upon its part (Uniform Commercial Code, § 7–204, subd. [1]). As a bailee, however, a warehouse is required both to exercise reasonable care so as to prevent loss of or damage to the property (Buffalo Grain Co. v. Sowerby, 195 N.Y. 355, 88 N.E. 569) and, a fortiori, to refrain from itself converting materials left in its care (see Prosser, Torts [4th ed.], § 15). If a warehouse does not convert the goods to its own use and does exercise reasonable care, it may not be held liable for any loss of or damage to the property unless it specifically agrees to accept a higher burden. If, however, the property is lost or damaged as a result of negligence upon the part of the warehouse, it will be liable in negligence. Similarly, should a warehouse actually convert stored property to its own use, it will be liable in conversion. Hence, a warehouse which fails to redeliver goods to the person entitled to their return upon a proper demand, may be liable for either negligence or conversion, depending upon the circumstances (see, generally, White & Summers, Uniform Commercial Code [2d ed.], § 20–3).

A warehouse unable to return bailed property either because it has lost the property as a result of its negligence or because it has converted the property will be liable for the full value of the goods at the time of the loss or conversion (Procter & Gamble Distr. Co. v. Lawrence Amer. Field Warehousing Corp., 16 N.Y.2d 344, 266 N.Y.S.2d 785, 213 N.E.2d 873; 1 Harper and James, Torts, § 2.36), unless the parties have agreed to limit the warehouse's potential liability. It has long been the law in this State that a warehouse, like a common carrier, may limit its liability for loss of or damage to stored goods even if the injury or loss is the result of the warehouse's negligence, so long as it provides the bailor with an opportunity to increase that potential liability by payment of a higher storage fee (compare Klar v. H. & M. Parcel Room, 270 App.Div. 538, 541, 61 N.Y.S.2d 285, affd. without opn. 296 N.Y. 1044, 73 N.E.2d 912, with Rapp v. Washington Stor. Warehouse & Van Co., 75 Misc. 16, 134 N.Y.S. 855; see Uniform Commercial Code, § 7–204, N.Y.Anns.; see, also Magnin v. Dinsmore, 56 N.Y. 168; Reichman v. Compagnie Generale, Transatlantique, 290 N.Y. 344, 49 N.E.2d 474). If the warehouse converts the goods, however, strong policy considerations bar enforcement of any such limitation upon its liability (see Magnin v. Dinsmore, 70 N.Y 410, 416; Reichman v. Compagnie Generale Transatlantique, supra, 290 N.Y. at p. 352, 49 N.E.2d 474). This rule, which has now been codified in subdivision (2) of section 7–204 of the Uniform Commercial Code, is premised on the distinction between an intentional and an unintentional tort. Although public policy will in many situations countenance voluntary prior limitations upon that liability which the law would otherwise impose upon one who acts carelessly (compare Ciofalo v. Vic Tanney Gyms, 10 N.Y.2d 294, 220 N.Y.S.2d 962, 177 N.E.2d 925, with Gross v. Sweet, 49 N.Y.2d 102, 424 N.Y.S.2d 365, 400 N.E.2d 306; but see General Obligations Law, §§ 5–321, 5–322, 5–323, 5–325, 5–326), such prior limitations may not properly be applied so as to diminish one's liability for injuries resulting from an affirmative and intentional act of misconduct (see, generally, Restatement, Torts 2d, § 500; Restatement, Contracts 2d, Tent Draft No. 12, § 337), such as a conversion. Any other rule would encourage wrongdoing by allowing the converter to retain the difference between the value of the converted property and the limited amount of liability provided in the agreement of storage. That result would be absurd. To avoid such an anomaly, the law provides that when a warehouse converts bailed property, it thereby ceases to function as a warehouse and thus loses its entitlement to the protections afforded by the agreement of storage (see Magnin v. Dinsmore, 70 N.Y. 410, 417–418, supra). In short, although the merely careless bailee remains a bailee and is entitled to whatever limitations of liability the bailor has agreed to, the converter forsakes his status as bailee completely and accordingly forfeits the protections of such limitations. Hence, in the instant case, whether defendant is entitled to the benefit of the liability-limiting provision of the warehouse receipt turns upon whether plaintiff has proven conversion or merely negligence.

Plaintiff has proffered uncontroverted proof of delivery of the indium to defendant, of a proper demand for its return, and of defendant's failure to honor that demand. Defendant has failed to make a sufficient showing in support of its suggested explanation of the loss to defeat plaintiff's motion for summary judgment. Its unsupported claim that the metal was stolen does not suffice to raise any issue of fact on this point.[3] Upon this record, it is beyond cavil that plaintiff would be entitled to judgment had it elected to sue defendant in negligence (see Golden v.

---

3. The explanation proffered by the warehouse in such a case must be supported by sufficient evidence and cannot be merely the product of speculation and conjecture. "The explanation must show with reasonable certainty how the loss occurred, as, by theft or fire * * * It is not enough to show that defendant-bailee used reasonable care in its system of custody if mysterious disappearance is the only 'explanation' given" (PJI 4:93, at pp. 1090–1091; see Dalton v. Hamilton Hotel Operating Co., 242 N.Y. 481, 488–489, 152 N.E. 268). In the instant case, defendant offered proof of the following facts in support of its claim that the indium had been stolen: "(1) the storage of the indium in three different locations in two different buildings, and the absence of any indication in [defendant] Municipal's records that the indium was moved, negate the possibility of misdelivery; (2) the storage of the indium without special precautions, because [plaintiff] ICC failed to advise Municipal of its true value, supports the likelihood of theft; (3) the form of the indium (small bars) would have facilitated removal without detection; (4) a recently discharged employee was experienced in 'weighing and sampling' and thus presumably was aware of the value of indium; (5) there was a series of alarms, any one of which could have been caused by a theft; (6) Municipal promptly reported the loss to the police; and (7) ICC reported the loss to its insurers as a theft and continued to employ Municipal's services, thus negating any suspicion that Municipal had misappropriated the indium or had been grossly negligent in its care." Viewed most favorably to defendant, this evidence would indicate at most that theft by a third party was one possible explanation for the defendant's failure to redeliver the indium to plaintiff. This is simply insufficient, since the warehouse is required to show not merely what might conceivably have happened to the goods, but rather what actually happened to the goods. Defendant proved only that theft was possible, and presented no proof of an actual theft. Hence, the proffered explanation was inadequate as a matter of law.

Romer, 20 Hun. 438; Dalton v. Hamilton Hotel Operating Co., 242 N.Y. 481, 488–489, 152 N.E. 268; Stewart v. Stone, 127 N.Y. 500, 506, 28 N.E. 595; PJI 4:93, at p. 1090; 1 Harper and James, Torts, § 2.27, at p. 172; McCormick, Evidence [2d ed.], § 343, at pp. 808–809). We now hold that such a record also suffices to sustain plaintiff's action in conversion, thereby rendering inapplicable the contractual limitation upon defendant's liability.[4]

The rule requiring a warehouse to come forward with an explanation for its failure to return bailed goods or be cast in damages in negligence is based upon practical necessity. As is noted above, a warehouse may only be held liable for loss of or damage to bailed goods if the loss or damage is due to the negligence of the warehouse or if the warehouse has converted the property. Hence, in order to recover damages for lost or damaged goods, a bailor must prove either that the warehouse was negligent or that it converted the goods. Since bailed property is in the possession of and under the sole control of the warehouse at the time of injury or loss, however, it is the warehouse which is in the best, if not the only, position to explain the loss of or damage to the property. Indeed, such information normally will be exclusively in the possession of the warehouse and will not be readily accessible to the bailor. Because of this, the law properly refuses to allow a warehouse, which has undertaken for a fee to securely store goods belonging to another, to avoid liability by simply pleading ignorance of the fate of the stored merchandise. To allow the warehouse to so easily escape its responsibilities would be to place the bailor in an untenable position and would serve to encourage both dishonesty and carelessness. Clearly, the temptation to convert stored property would be significantly increased could the warehouse then avoid all civil liability by simply denying all knowledge of the circumstances of the loss and placing upon the bailor the well nigh impossible burden of determining and proving what happened to his property while it was hidden from sight in the depths of the defendant's warehouse. Similarly, such a rule would reward those

4. We emphasize at this point that we do not suggest by our holding in this case that proof of negligence will support a recovery in conversion. Rather, our holding is limited to those situations in which the warehouse fails to provide an adequate explanation for its failure to return stored goods. If the warehouse comes forward with an explanation supported by evidentiary proof in admissible form, the plaintiff will then be required to prove that the loss was due to either negligence or conversion, depending on the circumstances. For plaintiff to recover in conversion after the warehouse has established a prima facie explanation for its failure to deliver, the trier of facts must find all the traditional elements of conversion.

warehouses with the least efficient inventory control procedures, since they would be most able to honestly plead ignorance of the fate of goods entrusted to their care.

To prevent such absurd results, the law has long placed upon the warehouse the burden of advancing an adequate explanation of the reasons for its failure to properly return stored property (see PJI 4:93, at p. 1090; Richardson, Evidence [10th ed.], § 109). This does not mean that the warehouse is required to prove that it acted properly, nor does this doctrine shift the burden of proof to the warehouse. Rather, the warehouse must come forward and explain the circumstances of the loss of or damage to the bailed goods upon pain of being held liable for negligence. If the warehouse does provide an explanation for the loss or damage, the plaintiff then must prove that the warehouse was at fault if he is to recover (see Textile Overseas Corp. v. Riveredge Warehouse Corp., 275 App.Div. 236, 88 N.Y.S.2d 429). A few illustrations of this principle may be of some assistance. Where the warehouse simply refuses to return bailed property upon a legitimate demand and does not advance any explanation for that refusal, the plaintiff will be entitled to recover without more. Similarly, where the warehouse does suggest an explanation for the loss but is unable to proffer sufficient evidentiary support for that explanation to create a question of fact, as in this case, the plaintiff will be entitled to recover without more. Where, however, the warehouse proffers sufficient evidence supporting its explanation to create a question of fact, the jury must be instructed that if it believes that explanation, the plaintiff must be denied any recovery unless he has proven that the warehouse was at fault (Uniform Commercial Code, § 7–403, subd. [1], par. [b]). In other words, if the jury is persuaded that the goods were accidentally mislaid or destroyed in a fire or accident or stolen by a third party, the plaintiff cannot recover unless he has proven that the loss or the fire or the accident or the theft were the proximate result of either a purposive act or a negligent commission or omission by the warehouse.

Although it has long been settled that this is the rule in an action in negligence, there has been considerable inconsistency and uncertainty as to the application of this principle to an action in conversion. Thus, although we have on occasion declared that a bailor establishes a prima facie case of conversion by simply proving delivery to the bailee and an unexplained failure to return the stored goods upon demand (Procter & Gamble Distr. Co. v. Lawrence Amer. Field Warehousing Corp., 16 N.Y.2d 344, 266 N.Y.S.2d 785, supra; see Claflin v. Meyer, 75 N.Y. 260, 263;

Bank of Oswego v. Doyle, 91 N.Y. 32, 41; accord 1 Harper and
James, Torts, § 2.27), we have at other times indicated that
something more is needed to maintain an action in conversion
and that a plaintiff will be required to provide positive evidence
of an intentional act by the warehouse inconsistent with the
plaintiff's interest in the property (Reichman v. Compagnie
Generale Transatlantique, 290 N.Y. 344, 352, 50 N.E.2d 251, supra; see, also, Wamsley v. Atlas S. S. Co., 168 N.Y. 533, 61 N.E.
896; Central School Dist. No. 3 of Towns of Amherst, Cheektowaga & Clarence v. Insurance Co. of North Amer., 43 N.Y.2d
878, 403 N.Y.S.2d 496, 374 N.E.2d 393). We deem it unnecessary to engage in an extended discussion of each of the precedents
in this area, for they appear essentially irreconcilable. Rather,
we have decided to take this opportunity to re-examine the matter and to determine the most appropriate resolution of this controversy.

We now conclude that there exists no sound reason to apply
a different rule to the two types of action where, as here, the
bailee comes forward with insufficient proof of its explanation
for the loss of the bailed goods. The same policy considerations
which prevent a warehouse from avoiding liability in negligence
by a declaration of ignorance appear equally applicable to an action in conversion. Indeed, as a practical matter, a bailor will be
even less able to prove conversion by a warehouse than he
would negligence, since a warehouseman who actually converts
stored property will generally strive mightily to prevent knowledge of his malfeasance from coming to light. The possibility of
fraud is obvious, for a dishonest warehouseman might well be
encouraged to convert bailed property if he could then obtain the
benefit of a contractual limitation of liability by the simple expe-
dient of professing ignorance as to the fate of the goods. The
rule requiring a warehouse to explain the loss of or damage to
the goods lest it be held liable would be severely undermined
could a warehouse avoid the bulk of potential liability in such a
case by means of a contractual provision.

We note, moreover, that the requirement that a warehouse
provide an explanation for loss of property entrusted to it is certainly not overly harsh, nor does it impose a heavy burden upon
the warehouse. The warehouse must only offer proof of what
actually happened to the goods and need not show that it was
free from fault, for once the warehouse makes the initial required showing, the burden of proving the warehouse to be at
fault will fall squarely upon the plaintiff. No greater duty of
care is created by this rule, nor does it establish any sort of

strict liability. Certainly a warehouse may reasonably be required to keep track of goods entrusted to it and to supply an accurate explanation of any loss to the bailor.

Finally, where a warehouse does not explain the cause of the loss, it would appear as reasonable to assume that this profession of ignorance is due to the fact that the warehouse has converted the goods as to presume that it is due to the fact that the warehouse has been negligent. Indeed, one who commits an intentional wrong is more likely to attempt to cover his tracks than one who has been at most negligent, especially in light of the disparity in potential liability created by the insertion of a limitation of liability clause. For all these reasons, we conclude that plaintiff was entitled to summary judgment in its action in conversion. Quite simply, plaintiff proved delivery of the indium to defendant warehouse and defendant's subsequent failure to return the metal, whereas defendant has not come forward with adequate evidentiary proof in admissible form to support its suggested explanation of that failure. That being so, the limitation on liability was inapplicable, and plaintiff was entitled to recover the actual value of the missing indium.

Accordingly, the order appealed from should be affirmed, with costs.

JASEN, JUDGE (dissenting). My disagreement with the majority stems from their conclusion that plaintiff is entitled to summary judgment on the theory of conversion absent any proof whatsoever that defendant converted the indium metal to its own use or the use of another. The plaintiff bailor having failed to demonstrate in an evidentiary manner an intentional act by the defendant bailee which worked to deprive the plaintiff of its property, the defendant should not be held liable for the conversion of the stored property.

* * *

Conversion is viewed as requiring "an intentional exercise of dominion or control over a chattel which so seriously interferes with the right of another to control it that the actor may justly be required to pay the other the full value of the chattel." (Restatement, Torts 2d, § 222A; see, generally, Prosser, Torts [4th ed.], § 15.) Thus, one who does not intentionally exercise dominion or control over property is not liable for conversion, even though his act or omission may be said to constitute negligence. As was stated in Magnin v. Dinsmore, 70 N.Y. 410, 417: "A conversion implies a wrongful act, a mis-delivery, a wrongful disposition, or withholding of the property. A mere nondelivery will not constitute a conversion, nor will a refusal to deliver, on demand, if the goods have been lost through negligence, or have been stolen." (See, also, Restatement, Torts 2d, § 224, Comment *b*.)

While proof of delivery to a bailee, of a demand for the property's return, and of a failure of the bailee to return the goods establishes a prima facie case of negligence, these items of proof do not, in my opinion, constitute a prima facie case of conversion. The majority, obviously recognizing this fact, resorts to a newly created presumption of conversion in order to sustain the judgment rendered plaintiff below. Such legal reasoning is unwarranted.

First, I would consider the law in this commercial area well settled and in accordance with the basic principle that a cause of action sounding in conversion will not be maintainable absent proof of intentional wrongdoing by the bailee. (See, e.g., Central School Dist. No. 3 of Towns of Amherst, Cheektowaga & Clarence v. Insurance Co. of North Amer., 43 N.Y.2d 878, 403 N.Y.S.2d 496, 374 N.E.2d 393, affg. 55 A.D.2d 1021, 391 N.Y.S.2d 492; Reichman v. Compagnie Generale Transatlantique, 290 N.Y. 344, 352, 50 N.E.2d 251; Wamsley v. Atlas S. S. Co., 168 N.Y. 533, 536–538, 61 N.E. 896; Magnin v. Dinsmore, 70 N.Y. 410, 417–419, supra; see, generally, 5 N.Y.Jur., Bailment, § 45.) [3] Here, plaintiff has presented no proof whatsoever of an intentional wrongdoing by defendant, and the majority's conclusion that this "record * * * suffices to sustain plaintiff's action in conversion" flies in the face of this established rule that an action for conversion requires an evidentiary showing that defendant bailee *intentionally* acted in a manner so as to deprive plaintiff of its property.

Second, I take issue with the policy reasons cited by the majority to support their obliteration of the distinction between negligence and conversion—that the bailee is in the better position to explain what happened to the goods and, thus, should be required to come forth with such explanation; and that instances of fraud would proliferate if a bailee could merely pro-

---

3. Although this court did affirm a grant of summary judgment to plaintiff on a theory of conversion when the bailee failed to explain satisfactorily the loss of the goods in Procter & Gamble Distr. Co. v. Lawrence Amer. Field Warehousing Corp., 16 N.Y.2d 344, 266 N.Y.S.2d 785, 213 N.E.2d 873, it has been conjectured that we "may have held the warehouseman absolutely liable without realizing it." (White & Summers, Uniform Commercial Code [1972], p. 674.)

fess ignorance as to the goods' disappearance and, then, claim as a sanctuary the contractual limitation of liability. While I would agree that a bailee should keep track of goods entrusted to it and that a bailee is in a better position than the bailor to explain what happened to the goods, it does not follow that its failure to produce the stored goods upon demand should serve as the vehicle to thrust upon the bailee the burden traditionally placed upon a plaintiff bailor when suing in conversion to demonstrate an intentional act by the defendant bailee which worked to deprive that plaintiff of its property. As a matter of public policy, I believe the burden of proving a wrongful act such as conversion should remain upon the party claiming it, rather than the one accused of the wrongdoing.

There is simply no rational reason, under the guise of policy considerations, to shift the burden of coming forward with evidence of what "actually happened" [4] to the goods when a cause of action is framed in conversion. If the bailor is seeking to circumvent the contractual limitation on damages, agreed upon by the parties as a condition of the bailment, the bailor should be put to the task of demonstrating that the bailee converted the goods to its own use or the use of another. To hold otherwise is to permit the bailor to have its cake and eat it too. This is so because the bailor, as in this case, need not declare the full value of the goods and, as a result, is required to pay only a *de minimus* bailment fee, rather than a fee based on actual value; yet, upon loss of the goods, it may seek compensation for their full value even though it was never disclosed to the bailee.

This, it seems to me, is fundamentally unfair, especially when one considers that plaintiff voluntarily signed as a condition of bailment a contractual limitation of liability ($50) as to each article and item stored, although the true value of the three lots of indium was $100,000. The limitation of liability and the actual value of the stored property were known to plaintiff, and yet it

---

4. The majority stesses that their holding is limited to only requiring a warehouseman to establish, in the first instance, "a prima facie explanation for its failure to deliver" the goods (p. 655, n. 4, 431 N.Y.S.2d p. 377, n. 4, 409 N.E.2d p. 854, n. 4). However, I derive little solace from this qualification, inasmuch as a bailee "is required to show not merely what might conceivably have happened to the goods, but rather what *actually* happened to the goods" (p. 644, n. 3, 431 N.Y.S.2d p. 377, n. 3, 409 N.E.2d p. 853, n. 3 [emphasis added]). Since we are concerned with cases involving unexplained losses, the majority opinion sanctions, for all practical purposes, the imposition of full liability for the value of the goods stored whenever the bailee is unable to deliver the stored goods or explain "what actually happened to the goods." This, I suggest, is an onerous burden upon the warehouseman.

chose not to avail itself of the opportunity to declare the full value of the goods to insure that it would be made whole in case of loss. Plaintiff had only to be candid about the true value of the goods entrusted to defendant and pay a storage rate commensurate with the risk in order to protect itself from any and all loss, whether such loss be precipitated by fraud, conversion, negligence, or otherwise. Having not exercised this option and, thus, having paid a much lower storage fee than what would have been charged had the bailee known the true value of the goods and been responsible for the same, the bailor should be held to the terms of the bailment absent an affirmative evidentiary showing of intentional wrongdoing by the bailee. In this commercial setting, dealing as we are with sophisticated businessmen, we should not reach out and relieve the plaintiff of its failure to protect itself contractually. I can only read the majority's opinion as doing violence to the law, without rhyme or reason.

For the above-stated reasons, I would reverse the order of the Appellate Division and grant summary judgment to defendant.

COOKE, C.J., and JONES, WACHTLER, FUCHSBERG and MEYER, JJ., concur with GABRIELLI, J.

JASEN, J., dissents and votes to reverse in a separate opinion.

Order affirmed.

BRANCH BANKING & TRUST CO. v. GILL

Supreme Court of North Carolina, 1977.
293 N.C. 164, 237 S.E.2d 21.

[Woodcock was the manager of Farmers Grain Elevator at Warsaw ("Elevator"), a public warehouse, and was also Secretary-Treasurer of Southeastern Farmers Grain Association, Inc. ("Southeastern"), which was engaged in the business of buying and selling grain. All warehouse receipts issued by Elevator bore Woodcock's signature. The plaintiff, Branch Banking & Trust Co. ("Bank") loaned money to Southeastern under an agreement which provided that warehouse receipts representing stored grain would be pledged as security for the loans. Bank was aware that Woodcock was employed by both Elevator and Southeastern. Southeastern pledged to Bank 13 negotiable warehouse receipts (numbered 974–986) issued by Elevator as collateral for loans totalling $314,354.38. The 13 warehouse receipts were fraudulently issued by Woodcock. They did not represent any grain deposited by Southeastern with Elevator.]

SHARP, CHIEF JUSTICE. In our earlier opinion in this case we held: (1) that the Bank did not take the 13 fraudulent warehouse receipts (Nos. 974–986) by "due negotiation" and thus did not acquire the rights specified in [UCC §] 7–502; (2) that "nothing else appearing" the Bank was merely a transferee of the negotiable warehouse receipts and thus acquired no greater rights or title than its transferor, Southeastern;   *   *   *

Our prior holding that the Bank did not take the 13 receipts through "due negotiation" is clearly correct.

*   *   *

By their terms, the grain the 13 warehouse receipts purportedly represented was to be delivered to Southeastern or to its order. These receipts, therefore, were negotiable documents of title. [UCC §] 1–201(15), [UCC §] 7–102(1)(e), [UCC §] 7–104(1)(a). These receipts, however, were not indorsed by Southeastern at the time they were delivered to the Bank. Neither Woodcock, the secretary-treasurer, nor any other officer of Southeastern ever signed the receipts. Upon Bank's request for its indorsement, Southeastern's bookkeeper, Mrs. Carlton, stamped the name "Southeastern Farmers Grain Association, Inc." on the reverse side of the receipts.

As we said in our former opinion, "[T]he affixing of the payee's (or subsequent holder's) name upon the reverse side of a negotiable document of title by rubber stamp is a valid indorsement, if done by a person authorized to indorse for the payee and with intent thereby to indorse. Mayers v. McRimmon, 140 N.C. 640, 53 S.E. 447. However, the Superior Court found that Mrs. Carlton, who stamped the name of Southeastern upon the reverse side of these receipts, had neither the authority nor the intent thereby to indorse them in the name of Southeastern. The evidence supports these findings and would support no contrary finding." Trust Co. v. Gill, State Treasurer, 286 N.C. 342, 358, 211 S.E.2d 327, 338 (1975). Since the receipts were not properly indorsed to the Bank, they were not negotiated to it. The Bank, therefore, not having acquired the receipts through "due negotiation," did not acquire the rights provided in [UCC §] 7–502.

Under [UCC §] 7–506 the Bank could compel Southeastern to supply the lacking indorsement to the 13 receipts. However, the transfer "becomes a negotiation only as of the time the indorsement is supplied." Since the Bank was specifically informed of the fraud surrounding the issuance of the receipts on the evening of 7 May 1970 any subsequent indorsement by Southeastern would be ineffective to make the Bank "a holder to whom a negotiable document of title [was] duly negotiated." [UCC §] 7-501(4).

Thus, because of the lack of proper negotiation, the Bank became a mere transferee of the 13 warehouse receipts. The status of such a transferee is fixed by [UCC §] 7-504(1) which provides: "A transferee of a document, whether negotiable or nonnegotiable, to whom the document has been delivered but not duly negotiated, acquires the title and rights which his transferor had or had actual authority to convey." Here Southeastern, the Bank's transferor, had no title by way of the fraudulent receipts to any grain held by Elevator, and it had no rights against Elevator. Woodcock, acting for and on behalf of Southeastern, had fraudulently procured the issuance of these receipts to Southeastern without the deposit of any grain. Then, as Southeastern's manager, he had pledged them to Bank in substitution of 16 previously issued receipts purportedly representing corn deposited in Elevator. However, at least six of these represented no grain at the time they were issued, and between the warehouse examiner's inspections of 10 February 1970 and May 1970,—without requiring the surrender of any receipts—Elevator had delivered to or for the account of Southeastern nearly 113,000 bushels of grain more than Southeastern allegedly had in storage there. Thus, Elevator had no obligation to deliver any grain to Southeastern, and it did not become obligated to Bank merely because Southeastern transferred the receipts.

The foregoing discussion analyzes the Bank's rights and Elevator's liabilities under [UCC §] 7-502 and [UCC §] 7-504. The primary purpose of these two sections is to determine the priority of competing claims to valid documents and goods *actually* stored in a warehouse and to determine the issuer's liability for a misdelivery of goods *actually received* by it. Generally, a holder of negotiable warehouse receipts acquired through "due negotiation" will receive paramount title not only to the documents but also to the goods represented by them, the purpose of U.C.C., Art. 7, Part 5, being to facilitate the negotiability and integrity of negotiable receipts.

In situations where there are actual goods, and there are conflicting claims either to them or to the documents, [UCC §] 7-502, [UCC §] 7-503, and [UCC §] 7-504 determine the priority of these claims. In the present case, since the 13 receipts represented no grain in storage at the time of their issuance and no grain was subsequently acquired by the warehouseman, no question of who has paramount title to goods arises. The sole question is under what circumstances and to whom is an *issuer* liable for the issuance of warehouse receipts when it has not received the goods which the receipts purportedly cover? [UCC §] 7–203 covers this situation.

*   *   *

The purpose of [UCC §] 7–203 is to protect specified parties to or purchasers of warehouse receipts by imposing liability upon the warehouseman when either he or his agent fraudulently or mistakenly issues receipts (negotiable or nonnegotiable) for misdescribed or nonexistent goods. This section, coupled with the definition of issuer (UCC § 7–102(1)(g)), clearly places upon the warehouseman the risk that his agent may fraudulently or mistakenly issue improper receipts. The theory of the law is that the warehouseman, being in the best position to prevent the issuance of mistaken or fraudulent receipts, should be obligated to do so; that such receipts are a risk and cost of the business enterprise which the issuer is best able to absorb. See J. White and R. Summers, Uniform Commercial Code 690 (1972).

In the Comment to [UCC §] 7–203 it is said: "The issuer is liable on documents issued by an agent, contrary to instructions of his principal, without receiving goods. No disclaimer of the latter liability is permitted." *Issuer* is defined by [UCC §] 7–102 as "a bailee who issues a document. * * * Issuer includes any person for whom an agent or employee purports to act in issuing a document if the agent or employee has real or apparent authority to issue documents, notwithstanding that the issuer received no goods or that the goods were misdescribed or that in any other respect the agent or employee violated his instructions." Under these provisions Elevator would clearly be liable to the Bank on the 13 fraudulent receipts issued by its agent Woodcock *provided* the Bank could carry its burden of affirmatively proving that it came within the protection of [UCC §] 7–203.

*   *   *

We now consider whether the Bank qualifies for this protection. At the outset of our discussion we note that [UCC §] 7–203 contains no requirement that the purchaser take negotiable documents through "due negotiation" before he can recover from the issuer. (Compare this section with the analogous U.C.C. provision covering bills of lading, which provides protection to "a consignee of a nonnegotiable bill who has given value in good faith or a holder to whom a negotiable bill has been duly negotiated relying in either case upon the description * * *." [UCC §] 7–301(1).) Of course, had the Bank met all the requirements of due negotiation it also would have met the requirements of [UCC §] 7–203.

To be entitled to recover under [UCC §] 7–203 a claimant has the burden of proving that he (1) is a party to or *purchaser of a document of title* other than a bill of lading; (2) *gave value* for the document; (3) took the document in *good faith;* (4) *relied* to his detriment upon the description of the goods in the document; and (5) took *without notice* that the goods were misdescribed or were never received by the issuer. Many of these terms are defined in Article 1 of the U.C.C., and those definitions are also made applicable to Article 7.

Under [UCC §] 1–201(33) and [UCC §] 1–201(32) Bank acquired the 13 negotiable warehouse receipts by purchase. Further, when Bank surrendered to Southeastern its old notes and the 16 receipts securing them, taking in return the new notes secured by the 13 receipts, it gave "value." Under [UCC §] 1–201(44) a person, *inter alia*, gives "value" for rights if he acquires them "(b) as security for or in total or partial satisfaction of a pre-existing claim; or (d) generally, in return for any consideration sufficient to support a simple contract." It now remains to determine whether Bank, at the time it relinquished the 16 old receipts in return for the 13 receipts, was acting (1) without notice that no goods had been received by the issuer for the 13 receipts, (2) in good faith, and (3) in reliance upon the descriptions in the receipts.

The trial court, after making detailed findings as to facts known to Bank at the time it accepted the 13 receipts, found and concluded the ultimate fact that "the plaintiff Bank did not receive warehouse receipts numbered 974 through 986 in good faith without notice of claims and defenses." This finding, although stated in the negative in order to use the precise language of [UCC §] 7–501(4), is equivalent to a positive finding that Bank took the 13 receipts with notice that they were spurious. On the same findings the judge also concluded that plaintiff did not come into court with "clean hands." This finding likewise is equivalent in import and meaning to a finding that Bank did not take the 13 receipts in good faith. Trust Co. v. Gill, State Treasurer, 286 N.C. 342, 364, 211 S.E.2d 327, 342; 27 Am.Jur.2d, Equity § 137 (1966); 30 C.J.S. Equity § 93 (1965).

Upon these findings he held that plaintiff had no cause of action either at law or in equity based on the 13 receipts against either the State Warehouse Superintendent or against the State Treasurer as custodian of the State Indemnity and Guaranty Fund. We must, therefore, determine whether these findings are supported by competent evidence.

Upon our reconsideration of this case we have concluded (1) that the record evidence fully supports the trial judge's findings that Bank did not take the receipts in good faith and without notice that they had been fraudulently issued and (2) that his findings compel his conclusions of law.

[The court's review of the evidence on the issue of good faith is omitted.]

The Code was not designed to permit those dealing in the commercial world to obtain rights by an absence of inquiry under circumstances amounting to an intentional closing of the eyes and mind to defects in or defenses to the transaction. See General Investment Corp. v. Angelini, 58 N.J. 396, 278 A.2d 193 (1971). Nor did the General Assembly, when, by G.S. 106–435, it created the State Indemnifying and Guaranty Fund to safeguard the State Warehouse System and to make its receipts acceptable as collateral, intend that it should encourage individuals or financial institutions to engage in transactions from which they would otherwise have recoiled. On the contrary, the fund was created to protect those parties to or purchasers of warehouse receipts who, acting in good faith and without reason to know that the goods described thereon are misdescribed or nonexistent, suffer loss through their acceptance or purchase of the receipt. Lacy v. Indemnity Co., 189 N.C. 24, 126 S.E. 316 (1925).

The case comes down to this: Plaintiff Bank based its right to recover on the 13 fraudulent warehouse receipts numbered 974–986 for which Elevator received no grain. Its action, if any, was under [UCC §] 7–203. Therefore, if plaintiff could prove it acquired the receipts in good faith and without notice of the fraud, it was entitled to recover; otherwise, not. The trier of facts, upon sufficient evidence, found that plaintiff did not acquire the receipts in good faith and without notice.

The judgment of the trial court is therefore affirmed as to all defendants and our former decision as reported in 286 N.C. 342, 211 S.E.2d 327 (1975) is withdrawn.

Affirmed.

PROBLEM

Smith is manager of Grain Elevator, a public warehouse which also engages in the business of buying and selling grain. Grain Elevator stores in one common mass both the grain which it owns and the grain deposited by farmers for which it issues warehouse receipts. Smith is authorized to issue warehouse receipts on behalf of Grain Elevator. Smith is also President of Grain Corporation which is engaged in the business of buying and selling grain.

During a six-month period the following transactions occurred: 100 farmers each deposited with Grain Elevator 1,000 units of grain for which Grain Elevator issued warehouse receipts; Grain Elevator stored in its elevator 10,000 units which it owned; and Grain Elevator sold 40,000 units to various buyers in ordinary course of business. No other withdrawals of grain were made during the period. At the end of the period there were 70,000 units of grain in the elevator and there were outstanding warehouse receipts covering 100,000 units of grain. At that time Smith, acting on behalf of Grain Elevator, fraudulently issued a warehouse receipt to Grain Corporation for 20,000 units of grain. No grain was deposited by Grain Corporation. Grain Corporation then delivered this warehouse receipt to Bank as collateral for a loan made contemporaneously. Bank acted in good faith and had no knowledge of the circumstances surrounding the issuance of the warehouse receipt. It believed that the warehouse receipt represented grain deposited with Grain Elevator by Grain Corporation.

Both Grain Elevator and Grain Corporation are now insolvent. Grain Elevator has in storage the same 70,000 units of grain on hand at the end of the six-month period. There are outstanding warehouse receipts covering 100,000 units of grain deposited by the 100 farmers and 20,000 units covered by the warehouse receipt held by Bank. Bank's loan to Grain Corporation remains unpaid.

Assume that in the insolvency proceedings any person who can prove ownership of the grain in the possession of Grain Elevator is entitled to take delivery free of the claims of the creditors of Grain Elevator.

1. What rights do the 100 farmers have against the customers of Grain Elevator who purchased the 40,000 units of grain during the six-month period? UCC § 7–205. Does UCC § 2–403(2) also apply to this case?

2. What rights do the 100 farmers and Bank have to the grain held by Grain Elevator? Do these rights depend upon whether the warehouse receipt involved is negotiable or non-negotiable? UCC §§ 7–207, 7–402 and 7–403. Is UCC § 7–502 relevant to this case?

C. LETTERS OF CREDIT

Baird, Standby Letters of Credit in Bankruptcy

49 U. of Chi.L.Rev. 130, 133–135 (1982).*

I. THE LETTER-OF-CREDIT TRANSACTION

A. Background

As recently as twenty years ago, letters of credit were used principally in international sales. No seller willingly sends its goods across national borders unless it is confident it will be paid, because no seller welcomes the prospect of having its goods in the care of unknown parties in a foreign port, where finding a new buyer may be impossible and bringing a legal action extremely difficult. The letter of credit as we now know it arose in the middle of the nineteenth century in response to this problem.

Although letter-of-credit transactions vary, their basic structure can be stated briefly. In a typical letter-of-credit transaction, a seller specifies that payment be made with a letter of credit in its favor. The buyer (known as the "customer" in the letter-of-credit transaction) contracts with the bank to issue the letter. The bank, knowing the creditworthiness of its customer, is willing to issue the letter for a small fee, typically some fraction of one per cent of the price of the goods. The bank sends the letter to the seller, promising to pay the full price of the goods when the seller presents it with a draft and the documents specified in the letter. These documents typically include a negotiable bill of lading.

This arrangement benefits all parties to the transaction. The seller can manufacture goods to the buyer's order, confident it will be paid regardless of what befalls the buyer, because it can rely on the bank's commitment. The buyer that secures the letter of credit is better off than if it had advanced cash to the

* Reprinted with the permission of the author and the University of Chi- cago Law Review. Some of the au-thor's footnotes are omitted.

seller, because it does not become liable for the price until a trustworthy party (the bank) has possession of a negotiable document of title. The bank, in turn, earns a fee for issuing the letter and exposes itself to only a small risk, because it can readily assess the creditworthiness of its customer and, as the holder of a negotiable bill of lading, it has a perfected security interest in the goods involved in the transaction.

The linchpin of the letter-of-credit transaction is the unique legal relationship between the bank and the beneficiary.[16] Unlike a guarantor, the bank is primarily liable whenever the beneficiary presents a draft and documents that conform to the letter. Unlike its counterpart in a third-party beneficiary contract, the bank may not invoke the defenses its customer might have on the underlying contract. Moreover, the status of a beneficiary of a letter of credit is radically different from that of a payee of a check, who has no right to compel payment from the drawee bank. In the letter-of-credit transaction, the beneficiary does have the right to compel payment, and once the letter of credit is issued, the customer is powerless to stop payment in the absence of fraud. This difference exists because a letter of credit, unlike a negotiable instrument such as a check, is a binding and irrevocable obligation of the bank itself, not of the customer who procured it. The legal relationship between bank and beneficiary is governed by special principles which, like the law merchant in an earlier era, are nearly uniform throughout the world.

B. The Standby Letter of Credit

The archetypal letter-of-credit transaction described above is the means by which the parties pay one another if the underlying transaction takes place as planned. Standby letters of credit, in contrast, are never drawn upon if the transaction runs smoothly. For example, a builder might require a developer to have a bank issue a letter of credit in its behalf to ensure payment if the developer defaults. Such a letter of credit might require that the bank honor the builder's draft when accompa-

---

16. In their discussion of the legal relationship created by the letter of credit, Professors White and Summers note that a letter of credit is not like other devices creating legal obligations, but rather that

a letter of credit is a letter of credit. As Bishop Butler once said, "Everything is what it is and not another thing." Thus, when a beneficiary

sues an issuer for refusal to honor drafts drawn pursuant to a letter of credit, his theory is not that of breach of contract, nor does he sue "on a negotiable instrument." Rather, he sues "on a letter of credit."

J. White & R. Summers, supra note 15, § 18–2, at 715 (footnotes omitted).

nied by an architect's certificate that the building was finished and a statement by the builder that it had not been paid. In this kind of transaction, the bank usually will issue the letter only if the developer gives it a security interest in some property to which the bank will have recourse if the letter is drawn upon. If all goes well, the builder never presents its draft because it has been paid on schedule by the developer. If the developer defaults, however, the builder is still assured payment under the letter of credit. The bank then must seek reimbursement from the developer or enforce its security interest.

The parties to this transaction might employ a standby letter of credit in a different way. The developer might want to ensure that any money it advances to the builder is used to build the building. The developer could require the builder to have its bank issue a letter of credit in the developer's favor. Such a letter might provide that the developer's draft, accompanied by its statement that the builder had defaulted on its obligations, would be honored by the bank. Unlike the negotiable document of title specified in the usual commercial letter-of-credit transaction, the documents in the standby letter-of-credit transaction have no intrinsic value. For this reason, the bank is likely to insist that the builder give it a security interest as a condition of the letter's issuance.

Standby letters of credit also are used in transactions involving sales of goods. A supplier of raw materials, for example, might prefer to have a letter of credit in its favor from the buyer's bank rather than a security interest in the goods. Alternatively, a buyer of manufactured goods might want to protect itself when it advances money to finance its seller's purchase of raw materials. Such a buyer risks more in the event of default than one who sells on credit, because the buyer cannot easily acquire a purchase money security interest in the raw materials its seller uses. As the beneficiary of a standby letter of credit issued by the seller's bank, however, the buyer obtains equivalent protection.

A business that wishes to raise money may issue commercial paper backed by a standby letter of credit. This type of transaction involves larger dollar amounts than other uses of letters of credit. The business's bank may be more willing to accept the risk of its customer's insolvency than will the buyers of commercial paper. The buyers, however may be willing to extend cash to the business if they can rely on the bank to ensure repayment. The letter of credit makes it easy for all of the parties to allocate among themselves the risk of the business's failure. The business acquires the cash it needs, the bank lends its credit to the business without having to supply cash, and the buyers of commercial paper enjoy a relatively safe investment. As in the other letter-of-credit transactions, all parties directly involved benefit.

DATA GENERAL CORP., INC. v. CITIZENS NATIONAL BANK OF FAIRFIELD

United States District Court, D. Connecticut, 1980.
502 F.Supp. 776.

ELLEN B. BURNS, DISTRICT JUDGE. Plaintiff, a Delaware corporation with its principal place of business in Westboro, Massachusetts, designs and produces computer hardware and software. Plaintiff entered into a contract, dated November 13, 1976, with B.B.S. Systems, Inc. (hereinafter B.B.S.), located in Fairfield, Connecticut, to sell certain computer equipment to B.B.S., which equipment was to be used by the Town of North Haven. Some time thereafter, defendant, Citizens National Bank of Fairfield, a national banking corporation located in Fairfield, Connecticut, was contacted to serve as the issuing bank in a letter of credit in which plaintiff would be the beneficiary. A letter was written on April 4, 1977, by defendant's president, Mr. Raymond T. Bogert, to plaintiff, Bogert Affidavit, Exh. 1 (filed June 14, 1979), and a Mailgram was returned on April 13, 1977. On April 22, 1977, Bogert mailed two letters to plaintiff, with copies sent to B.B.S. One letter [Exhibit 2] read in full:

> Based on Assignment of funds to us by the subject and originating from the Town of North Haven, this Bank hereby commits to honor your draft in an amount not to exceed $83,000 relative to the Data General–B.B.S. OEM contract of November 13, 1975, provided:
>
> 1) Said draft is in bankable form, and
>
> 2) Said draft is accompanied by a certification that the items called for in Town of North Haven purchase order No. 12991, dated 3/2/77, have been delivered and have successfully completed the Data General standard diagnostic test.
>
> We have endeavored to cover all the essential elements in your Mailgram of April 13, but if there are any questions, please contact the undersigned.

* * * The other letter [Exhibit 3] read in full:

Based on Assignment of funds to us by the subject and originating from the Town of North Haven, this Bank hereby commits to honor your draft in an amount not to exceed $83,000, relative to the Data General–B.B.S. OEM contract of November 13, 1975, provided:

1) Said draft is in bankable form, and

2) Said draft is accompanied by a certification provided by Data General Corp. that all the equipment supplied by Data General Corp. as called for in B.B.S. Systems purchase order #TNH–01 dated 12–12–76, will have completed the running of the Data General Standard Diagnostic Test.

3) This amount will be paid directly to Data General Corp., Route 9, Westboro, Mass. 01591, no later than 30 days after receipt by Citizens National Bank of Fairfield, unless Data General Corp. has recieved [sic] payment in full from B.B.S. Systems Inc. Any partial payment from B.B.S. Systems, Inc. against referenced purchase order number will reduce the amount to be covered under this document.

* * *

On October 21, 1977, plaintiff mailed a letter to Mr. Robert Winstanley, of the defendant bank, certifying that the computer equipment had passed the required tests and also enclosing a draft, dated October 20, 1977, for payment in the amount of $82,070.50. * * * On February 16, 1978, Winstanley wrote a letter to plaintiff in which he denied the bank's obligation to make payment against the October 20, 1977 draft. * * * In this suit, based upon diversity jurisdiction, plaintiff claims it is entitled to payment of $82,070.50 plus attorneys fees and costs.

Defendant opposes plaintiff's motion for summary judgment on the grounds that there are genuine issues of material facts to be resolved, including questions whether there had been a valid contract between plaintiff and defendant, whether plaintiff had made its acceptance of the contract known to defendant, whether acceptance was a condition precedent to the letter of credit, whether the April 22, 1977, letter constituted the letter of credit, whether the assignment of funds from B.B.S. to defendant was a condition of the letter of credit, and whether all other conditions were met. The court disagrees, for suits concerning letters of credit are especially appropriate for determination by motions for summary judgment, whether on cross-motions by both parties, * * * motions for summary judgment by the defendant bank, * * * or motions for summary judgment by the plaintiff beneficiary * * *.

Letters of credit are governed by Article 5 of the Uniform Commercial Code [hereinafter U.C.C.] * * *. Letters of credit commonly are used to facilitate commercial transactions between reluctant sellers and buyers, both of whom hesitate to initiate the exchange of money for goods. In a letter of credit, one or more banks function as intermediaries to avoid such an impasse. * * * A letter of credit is designed to provide an assurance to the selling party of prompt payment upon presentation of documents, thereby substituting the credit of the bank for that of the buyer. * * * The particular letter of credit in this case falls within the ambit of U.C.C. § 5–102(1)(a) as a "credit issued by a bank if the credit requires a documentary draft or a documentary demand for payment." A letter of credit is defined as "an engagement by a bank or other person made at the request of a customer and of a kind within the scope of U.C.C. § 5–102 that the issuer will honor drafts or other demands for payment upon compliance with the conditions specified in the credit." U.C.C. § 5–103(1)(a). The defendant here is the issuer, i.e., the bank or other person issuing a credit. U.C.C. § 5–103(1)(c). The plaintiff, the seller of the computer equipment, is the beneficiary, for it is the "person who is entitled under its terms to draw or demand payment." U.C.C. § 5–103(1)(d). B.B.S., the buyer of the equipment, is the customer, as that company was the "buyer or other person who causes an issuer to issue a credit." U.C.C. § 5–103(1)(g). The U.C.C. provides that no particular form of phrasing be required for a letter of credit. The only requisites are that the letter of credit be in writing and signed by the issuer. U.C.C. § 5–104(1).

In a letter of credit situation, there are ordinarily three separate and distinct contracts involved: (1) the contract between a bank and its customer (usually the buyer) whereby the bank agrees to issue the letter of credit to the beneficiary (usually the seller); (2) the contract of sale between the buyer and the seller whereby, among other things, the seller agrees to obtain payment under the letter of credit by drawing drafts thereunder and presenting them to the bank accompanied by documents specified by the buyer; and (3) the letter of credit itself, which is a contract between the bank and the beneficiary (usually the seller) whereby the bank agrees to pay the drafts drawn under the letter of credit and presented to it by the beneficiary if they are accompanied by the requisite documents. * * * A letter of credit is entirely independent of the underlying contract of sale between the customer and beneficiary; as long as the documents of the beneficiary are in order, the issuing bank must honor the demand for payment, regardless of whether the goods conform to the contract of sale.   U.C.C. § 5–114, comment 1; U.C.C. § 5–109(1)(a) and comment 1. * * * This independence is even true in cases in which the letter of credit specifically incorporated the underlying contract of sale, * * * or when an inadvertent error in the price was made. * * * The sole interest of the issuing bank in a letter of credit transaction is in the documents to be presented, unless the parties agree otherwise; those documents must be exactly as stated in the letter of credit and the bank is obligated to pay only if the beneficiary has strictly complied with the terms of the letter.[5] * * * The bank's function is "basically ministerial," * * * for the bank is deprived of any discretion not granted within the letter of credit itself. * * *

Defendant argues that the letter of credit was not binding upon it because plaintiff failed to "accept" the terms of the agreement.   Such an acceptance was explicitly required in the letter of credit agreement in Okay Industries, Inc. v. Continental Bank of Harvey, Civil No. H78–342 (D.Conn. June 18, 1979), reprinted in 5 Conn.L.T., No. 34, at 9, col. 1 (Aug. 20, 1979), in which the defendant issuing bank requested the plaintiff beneficiary to indicate satisfaction with the letter of credit's provisions by signing acceptance on a copy of the letter and returning it to the defendant.   Id. at 9 col. 2 and n. 1.   No such explicit instructions were made here.

Defendant suggests that it cannot ascertain which letter of credit, if any, was accepted by plaintiff.   It is clear that the April 4, 1977, letter was rejected as plaintiff asked for major revisions in its telex of April 13, 1977.   A more difficult question would be to determine which of the letters of April 22, 1977, is the operable letter of credit.   Plaintiff has proceeded on the assumption that the more detailed letter [Exhibit 3] is the applica-

---

5.   Two different standards have developed: if the beneficiary sues an issuing bank for dishonoring a draft drawn pursuant to a letter of credit, "strict compliance" with the terms of the credit is required; however, if a customer sues an issuing bank for dishonor, [Ed.: The court may have used the word "dishonor" inadvertent-

ly. It probably meant "wrongful payment."] all that needs to be proven is "substantial compliance."   Far Eastern Textile, Ltd. v. City National Bank & Trust, 430 F.Supp. 193, 196 (S.D. Ohio 1977); Marine Midland Grace Trust Co. v. Banco del Paris, S.A., 261 F.Supp. 884, 889 (S.D.N.Y.1966).

ble letter. The court is not troubled by this selection as [Exhibit 3] is more comprehensive and rigorous than [Exhibit 2]. The only material differences are that paragraph 2 of [Exhibit 3] specifies that the certification is to be supplied by the plaintiff and paragraph 3 specifies the manner of payment, a term which was lacking in [Exhibit 2]. Paragraph 3 of [Exhibit 3] is less favorable to plaintiff as it allows defendant to offset against the funds due plaintiff any partial or full payment from B.B.S. to plaintiff. As long as plaintiff voluntarily has chosen to abide by [Exhibit 3], a letter of credit which imposes upon plaintiff more rigorous and less favorable terms than those found in [Exhibit 2], the court has no problem finding that [Exhibit 3] constitutes the appropriate letter of credit.

There are a number of theories under which summary judgment for the plaintiff may be granted. The first theory requires the determination of whether the April 22, 1977, letter of credit was revocable or irrevocable. U.C.C. § 5–103(1)(a) states that a letter of credit "may be either revocable or irrevocable." No indication is given how to construe a letter of credit which fails to indicate its revocability or irrevocability. However, comment 1 states:

> Neither the definition nor any other section of this Article deals with the issue of when a credit, not clearly labelled as either revocable or irrevocable falls within the one or other category although the Code settles this issue with respect to the sales contract (Section 2–325). This issue so far as it effects [sic] an issuer under the Article is intentionally left to the courts for decision in the light of the facts and general law (Section 1–103) with due regard to the general provisions of the Code in Article 1 particularly Section 1–205 on course of dealing and usage of trade.

Certain legal consequences flow from categorizing a letter of credit as revocable or irrevocable. U.C.C. § 5–106(1)(b) provides that, unless otherwise agreed, a letter of credit is "established" as regards a beneficiary "when he receives a letter of credit or an authorized written advice of its issuance." Receipt by the beneficiary, not acceptance, is the pivotal action. Once an irrevocable letter of credit is "established," unless otherwise agreed, as regards a beneficiary, it "can be modified or revoked only with his consent." U.C.C. § 5–106(2). Conversely, after a revocable letter of credit is "established," unless otherwise agreed, it "may be modified or revoked by the issuer without notice to or consent from the * * * beneficiary." U.C.C. § 5–106(3).

Therefore, if the April 22 letter of credit were revocable, defendant had statutory authority to revoke and hence dishonor it; however, if the letter were irrevocable, defendant lacked such authority.

As the district court commented in Beathard v. Chicago Football Club, Inc., 419 F.Supp. 1133, at 1137, "(t)here is a dearth of case law on the question of what constitutes an irrevocable letter of credit." Some states have resolved this problem by appropriate legislation. For example, Fla.Stat. § 675.103 (1977) (U.C.C. § 5–103) requires a letter of credit to state whether it is revocable or irrevocable. Furthermore, the statute provides, "[I]n the absence of such statement [it] shall be presumed to be irrevocable." * * * Other states allow for reference to the Uniform Customs and Practices for Documentary Credits (hereinafter U.C.P.). New York, for example, is one of three states which added a subsection (4) to section 5–102, which reads:

> Unless otherwise agreed, this Article 5 does not apply to a letter of credit or a credit if by its terms or by agreement, course of dealing or usage of trade such letter of credit or credit is subject in whole or in part to the Uniform Customs and Practice for Commercial Documentary Credits fixed by the Thirteenth or by any subsequent Congress of the International Chamber of Commerce.

N.Y. Uniform Com.Law § 5–102(4) (McKinney). Therefore, if the parties provide that a letter of credit is subject to the U.C.P., the U.C.C. does not apply. J. White & R. Summers, supra, § 18–3, at 612. Article One of the U.C.P. provides that "all credits, therefore, should clearly indicate whether they are revocable or irrevocable. In the absence of such indication, the credit shall be deemed to be revocable even though an expiry date is stipulated." Prior to the adoption of the U.C.C., New York case law provided that an ambiguous letter of credit was to be construed as irrevocable, thus protecting the beneficiary. Laudisi v. American Exchange National Bank, 239 N.Y. 234, 146 N.E. 347 (1924). There is an interesting question concerning the extent to which the U.C.C. has replaced this prior law; White and Summers believes it has. "Now by virtue of the New York amendment to Article Five, it appears that the U.C.P. governs in New York and that the New York case law which would otherwise have dictated a different result has been superseded." J. White and R. Summers, supra, § 18–3, at 613. This could be true, however, only if the particular letter of credit specifies that only the U.C.P. applies, or both the U.C.C. and U.C.P., for the U.C.C. allows for reference to prior law if a situation or rule is not covered by the U.C.C., U.C.C. § 5–102(3) and comment 2. In Beathard v. Chicago Football Club, Inc., supra, the parties themselves stated that their letter of credit was "subject" to the U.C.P. In *Beathard*, plaintiffs were players for a new football team, the Chicago Winds, which arranged for payment of plaintiffs' salaries by a letter of credit with the Mid-City National Bank. The issuing bank failed to honor plaintiffs' drafts, stating that the credit had been revoked. The court ruled for the bank because, by incorporating the U.C.P. by reference, the players allowed the letter of credit to be construed as revocable, in the absence of any indication to the contrary. 419 F.Supp. at 1138.

The letter of credit here does not make any reference to the U.C.P., nor does the Connecticut version of the U.C.C. provide any guidance. White and Summers advise that the best way to ensure that a letter of credit will be construed as irrevocable is to state so explicitly,

> Article Five does not state that letters of credit are presumed to be irrevocable, yet it is a rare beneficiary who will look with delight upon a revocable credit. If the letter of credit is silent, the answer to whether it is irrevocable depends on case law. Thus, for practical purposes, it would appear that a further formal requirement for the issuance of an irrevocable letter of credit is that it expressly state that it is irrevocable.

J. White and R. Summers, supra, § 18–4, at 616.

A situation similar to the instant case arose in West Virginia Housing Development Fund v. Sroka, 415 F.Supp. 1107 (W.D.Pa. 1976), in which the customer, a developer and mortgagor, arranged for a letter of credit from the defendant issuing bank for the benefit of the plaintiff beneficiary, a mortgagor. The defendant dishonored the letter of credit, arguing that the letter was revocable and had been revoked properly. The court granted summary judgment for the plaintiff, finding that a revocable letter of credit is "in reality, an illusory contract" because of the issuing bank's ability to revoke it without the beneficiary's knowledge or consent. 415 F.Supp. at 1111. Construing an ambiguous letter of credit as revocable would impede the "purpose and function" of such letters. Id. at 1112.

This court finds the reasoning of the *West Virginia* case persuasive. The bank's role in a letter of credit is to facilitate commercial transactions between its customer and the beneficiary by creating an arrangement whereby the beneficiary seller can deal freely with the buyer without fear that payment will be withheld. A revocable letter of credit provides the beneficiary seller with little protection. Therefore, unless otherwise provided in the letter of credit itself, there should be a presumption in favor of irrevocability. The court finds the April 22, 1977, letter to be an irrevocable letter of credit. The credit was established upon its receipt, by plaintiff, U.C.C. § 5–106(1)(b), obviating the need for acceptance. Once an irrevocable letter of credit is established, the issuing bank cannot revoke or modify the letter without the beneficiary's consent, U.C.C. § 5–106(2). Therefore, the letter of credit here was still in effect when plaintiff presented its draft to the defendant bank. The bank having dishonored the draft at that time, plaintiff's motion for summary judgment is granted.

Summary judgment for plaintiff is also appropriate under a theory that letters of credit are not formal contracts which mandate the standard contractual requirements of offer, acceptance, and consideration. Indeed, the definitional section, section 5–103(1)(a), defines a letter of credit as an "engagement" to honor drafts, not a "contract." Similarly, section 5–105 provides that no consideration is necessary to establish a letter of credit. White and Summers agree:

> The obligations, particularly those of an issuer to a beneficiary, that arise under a letter of credit are not exclusively contractual in nature, and it is unfortunate that some of the Code comments suggest as much. It is true that the issuer's customer and the beneficiary will ordinarily have a contract, for instance, for the purchase and sale of goods, for the construction of a ship, or the like, and it is also true that the issuer and the customer will ordinarily have a contract between them whereby the customer pays a fee and the issuer issues the letter of credit. But the resulting letter of credit is not itself a contract, and the issuer's obligation to honor drafts drawn by the beneficiary is not, strictly speaking, contractual. The beneficiary does not enter into any agreement with the issuer.

J. White and R. Summers, supra, § 18–2, at 607. Therefore, under such an analysis, no acceptance is necessary, and hence defendant's argument fails.

* * *

NOTES

1. One of the problems that has arisen with respect to standby letters of credit is whether the use of a letter of credit as a general guaranty device conflicts with federal and state laws forbidding banks from guaranteeing the obligations of others. For example, in New Jersey Bank v. Palladino, 77 N.J. 33, 389 A.2d 454 (1978), Palladino sought a loan from New Jersey Bank which was willing to make the loan only if the borrower produced "some sort of collateral or support for the note." Palladino obtained a letter from First State Bank addressed to New Jersey Bank which stated that First State Bank would "assume the obligation" arising from a note signed by Palladino in the amount of $50,000, and that First State Bank would honor the commitment upon notice that the loan had not been paid. The New Jersey statute denied power to First State Bank to "guarantee the obligations of others" subject to an exception which allowed it "to issue letters of credit authorizing holders thereof to draw drafts upon it." The court noted that Article 5 of the UCC applies "to a credit issued by a bank if the credit requires a documentary draft or a documentary demand for payment." UCC § 5–102(1)(a). "Documentary demand for payment" is defined as a demand "honor of which is conditioned upon the presentation of a document or documents" and "document" is defined as "any paper including * * * notice of default and the like." UCC § 5–103(1)(b). The court held that the letter of First State Bank was a letter of credit within these definitions, stating that the notice of default was intended by the parties to be a written notice and therefore was a "document." The court noted that this "standby letter of credit" was "akin to a guaranty, for the bank's sole function is to act as surety for its customer's failure to pay," but it followed cases decided in other jurisdictions holding that standby letters of credit fall within the exception to the prohibition against banks acting as sureties. A dissenting opinion stated that the standby letter of credit was in substance identical to a guaranty and that to allow its use was to erode the statutory policy against bank guaranties. It also stated: "The difference between conventional letters of credit and the standby variety in terms of bank solvency is clear. In the former, typically used to finance sales of goods, the issuing bank's obligation arises only on the delivery of shipping documents evidencing title to the goods. The bank is therefore secure. In the standby letter of credit situation, by the time the bank is called upon to meet the demand of the benefici-

ary there has typically been a default of the bank customer to the beneficiary and there is no practicable recourse by the bank because of the insolvency of the customer." For a discussion of "standby" or "guaranty" letters of credit see, in addition to the Baird article cited above, Verkuil, Bank Solvency and Guaranty Letters of Credit, 25 Stan.L.Rev. 716 (1973).

2. UCC § 5–115 sets forth the remedies that are available to "the person entitled to honor" for breach of the issuer's obligation. Subsection (1) covers damages for wrongful dishonor while subsection (2) covers anticipatory repudiation. This section was drafted with the traditional sales transaction in mind. If the seller, as beneficiary of the letter of credit, presents a draft for payment and it is wrongfully dishonored he is entitled to the face amount of the draft plus the incidental damages specified in UCC § 2–710 less any amount that the seller realizes upon disposition of the goods in the underlying sales transaction. In the case of anticipatory repudiation the seller has the same rights against the issuer that he would have against the buyer under UCC § 2–610. In effect the seller is made whole by being able to recover from the issuer as guarantor of the obligation of the buyer. How does this section apply to transactions not involving sales of goods in which a letter of credit is used? This question was presented in In re F & T Contractors, Inc., 17 B.R. 966 (Bkrtcy.Mich.1982), which involved the anticipatory repudiation of a standby letter of credit guaranteeing certain obligations in connection with a real estate construction project. The plaintiff was not the beneficiary of the letter of credit but the contractor which the court held was a customer under the letter of credit. The plaintiff claimed consequential damages for loss of profits and increased costs as a result of delays in completing the project which were caused by the breach. The court stated:

> It is the opinion of this court that a letter of credit transaction which is authorized by Article 5 of the Uniform Commercial Code is not restricted to the damage provisions provided in Article 2 of the Uniform Commercial Code. If the underlying transaction concerns a sale of goods and the letter of credit is issued to insure payment to the seller upon breach by the buyer, then § 5–115 of the Uniform Commercial Code makes plain sense in referring to remedies provided under Article 2 of the Uniform Commercial Code. However, such is not the case in the present lawsuit. The letters of credit issued by NOB were procured for the purpose of securing a mortgage construction loan and not for the purpose

of insuring payment under a contract for the sale of goods. In addition, tho collateral used to secure the letters of credit also involved mortgages. Under such circumstances, this court is of the opinion that it should defer to the more general principles of law in supplementing the provisions of Article 5 of the Uniform Commercial Code. This view is expressly permitted by [§ 1–103 of] the Uniform Commercial Code itself * * *.

The court awarded more than $925,000 in damages. The face amount of the letter of credit was $275,000. The significance of the decision is not clear, however, because in addition to repudiating the letter of credit the issuer unreasonably delayed releasing the collateral which the customer gave to the issuer. Since testimony established that prompt release of the collateral would have allowed the plaintiff to obtain substitute letters of credit that would have avoided any delays in completing the project, it appears that the damages were caused by the delay in releasing the collateral rather than by the repudiation of the letter of credit.

COLORADO NATIONAL BANK OF DENVER v. BOARD OF COUNTY COMMISSIONERS

Supreme Court of Colorado, 1981.
634 P.2d 32.

HODGES, CHIEF JUSTICE. We granted certiorari to review the court of appeals' decision affirming a district court's judgment holding the petitioner, the Colorado National Bank of Denver (the Bank), liable for the face amounts of three letters of credit it issued to secure the completion of road improvements by its customer, the Woodmoor Corporation (Woodmoor). Board of County Commissioners of Routt County v. The Colorado National Bank of Denver, Colo.App., 607 P.2d 1010 (1979). We reverse the judgment as to letters of credit No. 1156 and No. 1157, and affirm the judgment as to letter of credit No. 1168.

Woodmoor planned to develop a mountain recreation community in Routt County, Colorado (the County), to be known as Stagecoach. Early in 1973, Woodmoor obtained plat approval from the Routt County Board of County Commissioners (the Commissioners) for several Stagecoach subdivisions. Pursuant to section 30–28–137, C.R.S.1973 (1977 Repl.Vol. 12), and county subdivision regulations, approval of three of these subdivision plats was conditioned upon Woodmoor's agreement to provide a bond or other undertaking to ensure the completion of roads in accordance with the subdivision design specifications. Accordingly, subdivision improvements agreements were executed between Woodmoor and the County.

At Woodmoor's request, the Bank issued three letters of credit to secure Woodmoor's obligations under the agreements. The first two letters of credit, No. 1156 and No. 1157, were issued January 23, 1973 in the respective amounts of $158,773 and $77,330 bearing expiry dates of December 31, 1975. The third letter of credit No. 1168 was issued March 7, 1973 in the amount of $113,732 bearing an expiry date of December 31, 1976. The face amounts of the letters of credit were identical to the estimated costs of the road and related improvements in the respective subdivision improvements agreements. The County was authorized by each letter of credit to draw directly on the Bank, for the account of Woodmoor, up to the face amount of each letter of credit. Each letter of credit required the County, in order to draw on the letters of credit, to submit fifteen-day sight drafts accompanied by:

> "A duly-signed statement by the Routt County Board of Commissioners that improvements have not been made in compliance with a Subdivision Improvements Agreement between Routt County and the Woodmoor Corporation dated [either January 9, 1973 or March 7, 1973] and covering the [respective subdivisions] at Stagecoach and that payment is therefore demanded hereunder."

Woodmoor never commenced construction of the roads and related improvements. On December 31, 1975, the expiry date of letters of credit No. 1156 and No. 1157, the County presented two demand drafts to the Bank for the face amounts of $158,773 and $77,330. The demand drafts were accompanied by a resolution of the Commissioners stating that Woodmoor had failed to comply with the terms of the subdivision improvements agreements and demanded payment of the face amounts of the letters of credit. On January 5, 1976, within three banking days of the demand,[1] the Bank dishonored the drafts. The Bank did not specifically object to the County's presentation of demand drafts rather than fifteen-day sight drafts as required by the letters of credit.

---

1. Under [UCC §] 5–112(1)(a), a bank called upon to honor drafts under a letter of credit may defer until the close of the third banking day following receipt of the documents.

On December 22, 1976, the County presented the Bank with a demand draft on letter of credit No. 1168 which was accompanied by the required resolution of the Commissioners. The Bank dishonored this draft because of the County's nonconforming demand, viz., that a demand draft was submitted rather than a fifteen-day sight draft. On December 29, 1976, the County presented a fifteen-day sight draft to the Bank. This draft was not accompanied by the resolution of the Commissioners. On December 31, 1976, the Bank dishonored this draft.

The County sued to recover the face amounts of the three letters of credit plus interest from the dates of the demands. The Bank answered the County's complaints alleging several affirmative defenses. The fundamental premise of the Bank's defenses was the assertion that the County would receive a windfall since it had not expended or committed to spend any funds to complete the road improvements specified in the subdivision improvements agreements.

The County filed a motion in limine seeking a determination by the trial court to exclude evidence concerning matters beyond the four corners of the letters of credit and demands made on the letters of credit. The Bank replied by filing a cross-motion in limine seeking a ruling that it would not be precluded at trial from offering evidence outside the four corners of the letters of credit. The trial court, after extensive briefing by the parties and a hearing, granted the County's motion to limit the admissibility of evidence to the letters of credit, documents and drafts presented thereunder, the demands on the letters of credit, and the Bank's refusals to honor the County's demands for payment.

The remaining issues were whether the County's demands conformed to the letters of credit or, if not, whether the Bank had waived nonconforming demands, and whether interest ought to be awarded. The parties agreed on a stipulated set of facts concerning these remaining issues. The Bank did, however, make an offer of proof as to the rejected affirmative defenses. The Bank would have attempted to prove that the subdivisions in question remained raw, undeveloped mountain property for which there was no viable market and that the County had neither constructed, made commitments to construct, nor planned to construct the roads or other improvements described in the subdivision improvements agreements secured by the letters of credit. These allegations were disputed by the County.

The trial court entered judgment against the Bank for the face amounts of the letters of credit plus accrued interest at the

statutory rate from the date of the County's demands. Costs
were awarded in favor of the County. The Bank's motion for
new trial was denied, and the Bank appealed.

The court of appeals affirmed the judgment of the trial court
ruling that standby letters of credit are governed by article 5 of
the Uniform Commercial Code　*　*　*　and that an issuer
must honor a draft or demand for payment which complies with
the terms of the relevant credit regardless of whether the goods
or documents conform to the underlying contract. The court of
appeals affirmed the trial court's refusal to consider any evidence regarding the County's alleged windfall. The court of appeals also held that any defects in the form of the County's demands were waived by the Bank.

I.

We first address the question whether the trial court properly limited the evidence to be presented at trial to the letters of
credit, the demands by the County, and the Bank's replies to the
demands. The Bank has continually asserted during each stage
of this action that it ought to be permitted to show that the
County will receive a windfall if the County is permitted to recover against the letters of credit. The Bank requested an opportunity to prove that the County will utilize the funds it would
receive in a manner other than that specified in the road improvements agreements. Fundamentally, the Bank seeks to litigate the question of the completion of the purpose of the underlying performance agreements between Woodmoor and the
County. This the Bank cannot do.

An overview of the history and law concerning letters of
credit is useful in the consideration of this issue. The letter of
credit arose to facilitate international commercial transactions
involving the sale of goods.　*　*　*　Today the commercial
utility of the letter of credit in both international and domestic
sale of goods transactions is unquestioned and closely guarded.
*　*　*　In recent years, the use of the letter of credit has ex-
panded to include guaranteeing or securing a bank's customer's
promised performance to a third party in a variety of situations.
*　*　*　This use is referred to as a standby letter of credit.
Article five of the Uniform Commercial Code governs both traditional commercial letters of credit and standby letters of credit.
*　*　*

Three contractual relationships exist in a letter of credit
transaction.　*　*　*　Underlying the letter of credit transac-

tion is the contract between the bank's customer and the beneficiary of the letter of credit, which consists of the business agreement between these parties. Then there is the contractual arrangement between the bank and its customer whereby the bank agrees to issue the letter of credit, and the customer agrees to repay the bank for the amounts paid under the letter of credit. See also [UCC §] 5–114(3). Finally, there is the contractual relationship between the bank and the beneficiary of the letter of credit created by the letter of credit itself. The bank agrees to honor the beneficiary's drafts or demands for payment which conform to the terms of the letter of credit. See generally [UCC §] 5–103(1)(a) and [UCC §] 5–114(1); White and Summers, Uniform Commercial Code § 18–6 (2d Ed. 1980).

It is fundamental that the letter of credit is separate and independent from the underlying business transaction between the bank's customer and the beneficiary of the letter of credit. * * * "The letter of credit is essentially a contract between the issuer and the beneficiary and is recognized by [article 5 of the Uniform Commercial Code] as independent of the underlying contract between the customer and the beneficiary. * * * In view of this independent nature of the letter of credit engagement the issuer is under a duty to honor the drafts for payment which in fact conform with the terms of the credit without reference to their compliance with the terms of the underlying contract." [UCC §] 5–114, Official Comment 1.

The independence of the letter of credit from the underlying contract has been called the key to the commercial vitality of the letter of credit. * * * The bank must honor drafts or demands for payment under the letter of credit when the documents required by the letter of credit appear on their face to comply with the terms of the credit. [UCC §] 5–114(2). An exception to the bank's obligation to honor an apparently conforming draft or demand for payment, * * * is when a required document is, *inter alia*, forged or fraudulent, or there is fraud in the transaction. [UCC §] 5–114(2). The application of this narrow exception is discussed in detail later in this opinion.

As mentioned above, letters of credit have recently come to be used to secure a bank's customer's performance to a third party. When a letter of credit is used to secure a bank's customer's promised performance to a third party, in whatever capacity that might be, the letter of credit is referred to as a "guaranty letter of credit," * * * Standby letters of credit are closely akin to a suretyship or guaranty contract. The bank promises to pay when there is a default on an obligation by the bank's customer. "If for any reason performance is not made, or is made defectively, the bank is liable without regard to the underlying rights of the contracting parties." Verkuil, Bank Solvency and Guaranty Letters of Credit, [25 Stan.L.Rev. 716, 723 (1973)].

While banks cannot, as a general rule, act as a surety or guarantor of another party's agreed performance, see generally Lord, The No-Guaranty Rule and the Standby Letter of Credit Controversy, 96 Banking L.J. 46 (1979), the legality of standby letters of credit has been uniformly recognized. * * * What distinguishes a standby letter of credit from a suretyship or guaranty contract is that the bank's liability rests upon the letter of credit contract rather than upon the underlying performance contract between the bank customer and the beneficiary of the letter of credit. * * *

The utilization by banks of standby letters of credit is now wide-spread, although some commentators suggest that bankers may not appreciate the legal obligations imposed by the standby letter of credit. Where the bank issues a standby letter of credit, the bank naturally expects that the credit will not be drawn on in the normal course of events, i.e., if the customer of the bank fulfills its agreed-upon performance, then the credit will not be drawn upon. This expectation of the bank must be compared to the bank's expectation with respect to a traditional letter of credit issued as a means of financing a sale of goods. In the latter situation, the bank expects that the credit will always be drawn upon.

* * *

We now turn to a discussion of the present case, and why the Bank cannot introduce evidence beyond that directly relating to its contract with the County. As discussed above, the letters of credit, and the Bank's obligations thereunder, are separate and independent from the underlying subdivision improvements agreements between Woodmoor and the County. The fact that the letters of credit issued by the Bank are standby letters of credit does not alter this general rule. The Bank is bound by its own contracts with the County.

Each of the letters of credit prepared and issued by the Bank in this case sets forth specifically the condition for payment, i.e., that Woodmoor failed to make the improvements in conformance with the respective subdivision improvements agreements. Had the Bank desired additional conditions for payment, such as the actual completion of the road improvements prior to payment under the letters of credit, it could have incorporated such a condition in the letters of credit. * * * To demand payment under the letters of credit, the County was only required to submit a "duly-designed statement by the [Commissioners] that improvements have not been made in compliance with [the] Subdivision Improvements Agreement[s]. * * * "

The Bank cannot litigate the performance of the underlying performance contracts. "[P]erformance of the underlying contract is irrelevant to the Bank's obligations under the letter of credit." West Virginia Housing Development Fund v. Sroka, [415 F.Supp. 1107] at 1114 (W.D.Pa.1976). * * * Likewise, the question of whether the beneficiary of the letter of credit has suffered any damage by the failure of the bank's customer to perform as agreed is of no concern. * * * Further, a bank cannot challenge the utilization of funds paid under a letter of credit. * * *

The Bank argues that it is entitled to dishonor the County's drafts under [UCC §] 5–114(2). * * * Under this section, the issuer of a letter of credit may in good faith honor a draft or demand for payment notwithstanding notice from its customer that documents are forged, or fraudulent, or there is fraud in the transaction. The issuer may, however, be enjoined from honoring such drafts or demands for payment. Impliedly, the issuer may also refuse to honor such drafts or demands for payment when it has been notified by its customer of these defects. [UCC §] 5–114, Official Comment 2.

In this case, the Bank has not argued, nor can it reasonably assert, that the documents presented by the County are forged or fraudulent. The Bank has not challenged the authenticity of the drafts and demands for payment by the County or the truthfulness of the statements that the requirements of the underlying subdivision improvements agreements have not been fulfilled. The Bank does assert, however, that there has been fraud in the transaction on the basis that the funds the County would receive would be utilized by the County other than to pay for the completion of the road improvements.

Fundamentally, "fraud in the transaction," as referred to in [UCC §] 5–114(2), must stem from conduct by the beneficiary of the letter of credit as against the customer of the bank. See generally White and Summers, Uniform Commercial Code § 18–6 (2d ed. 1980). It must be of such an egregious nature as to vitiate the entire underlying transaction so that the legitimate purposes of the independence of the bank's obligation would no longer be served. Intraworld Industries, Inc. v. Girard Trust Co., [461 Pa. 343, 336 A.2d 316 (1975)]; New York Life Insurance Co. v. Hartford National Bank & Trust Co., 173 Conn. 492, 378 A.2d 562 (1977); Sztejn v. Henry Schroder Banking Corp., [31 N.Y.Supp.2d 631 (Sup.Ct.1941)]. "[I]t is generally thought to include an element of intentional misrepresentation in order to profit from another. * * *" West Virginia Housing Development Fund v. Sroka, supra. This fraud is manifested in the documents themselves, and the statements therein, presented under the letter of credit. Dynamics Corporation of America v. Citizens & Southern National Bank, [356 F.Supp. 991 (N.D.Ga. 1973)]; Shaffer v. Brooklyn Park Garden Apartments, 311 Minn. 452, 250 N.W.2d 172 (1977). See generally Harfield, Enjoining Letter of Credit Transactions, 95 Banking L.J. 596 (1978); Verkuil, Bank Solvency and Guaranty Letters of Credit, supra. One court has gone so far as to say that only some defect in these documents would justify a bank's dishonor. O'Grady v. First Union National Bank of North Carolina, 296 N.C. 212, 250 S.E.2d 587 (1978).

In this case, the Bank has not asserted that there is fraud in the transaction between Woodmoor and the County, nor can it reasonably make such an argument. No facts have been pled to establish fraud which vitiated the entire agreement between the County and Woodmoor. No fraud has been asserted by the Bank's offer of proof which would entitle it to dishonor the County's drafts and demands for payment. * * * Thus, the trial court properly granted the County's motion in limine excluding all evidence beyond the four corners of the letters of credit, the demands thereunder, and the Bank's replies.

II.

We next consider whether the drafts and demands for payment by the County complied with the terms of the letters of credit, or if not, whether the Bank waived any nonconforming demands.

The Bank was obligated to examine the documents "with care so as to ascertain that on their face they appear[ed] to comply with the terms of the credit. * * *" [UCC §] 5–109(2). To maintain the commercial vitality of the letter of credit device, strict compliance with the terms of the letter of credit is required. * * * If the drafts or demands for payment on their face complied with the terms of the letters of credit, the Bank was obligated to honor the drafts. [UCC §] 5–114(1).

In this case, the Bank promised to pay the County, for the account of Woodmoor, upon the County's presentation of fifteen-day sight drafts accompanied by a "duly signed statement by the Routt County Board of Commissioners that improvements have not been made in compliance with [the respective Subdivision Improvements Agreements.]" In order to determine whether the County's drafts and demands for payment complied with the terms of the letters of credit, we must analyze the drafts on the first two letters of credit numbers 1156 and 1157 separately from the drafts on the third letter of credit number 1168.

Letters of credit No. 1156 and 1157 bore expiry dates of December 31, 1975. On that date, the County presented two demand drafts to the Bank in the full face amounts of the respective letters of credit. The drafts were accompanied by, as required by the letters of credit, a resolution of the Commissioners stating that Woodmoor failed to comply with the terms of the underlying subdivision improvements agreements and demanded payment under the terms of the respective letters of credit. On January 5, 1976, within three banking days of the demand, the Bank dishonored the drafts. The Bank did not object to the County's presentation of demand drafts as opposed to fifteen-day sight drafts.

A demand draft is not the same as a fifteen-day sight draft. A fifteen-day sight draft provides the issuer an additional period of time not conferred by a demand instrument to examine the draft and determine whether the conditions of payment, if any, have been fulfilled. Thus, the County's demand did not strictly conform to the terms of the letters of credit. * * *

The Bank did not, however, object to the form of the demands by the County. As a general rule, when an issuer of a letter of credit formally places its refusal to pay upon specified grounds, it is held to have waived all other grounds for dishonor. * * * "However, the application of the rule confining an issuer to its stated grounds for dishonor is limited to situations where the statements have misled the beneficiary who could have cured the defect but relied on the stated grounds to its injury * * *." Siderius, Inc. v. Wallace Co., [583 S.W.2d 852, 862 (Tex.Civ.App.1979)]. * * *

In this case, the County did not present its drafts and demands for payment on the letters of credit until the final day of their vitality. The Bank then had three banking days before it was required to honor or dishonor the drafts and demands for payment. Within this period the Bank dishonored the drafts. The County could not have cured the defect since the presentment would have then been untimely. * * * Consequently, the County did not detrimentally rely on the Bank's failure to state as one ground for its dishonor of the drafts that the County presented demand instruments rather than fifteen-day sight drafts. Accordingly, since the County could not have cured its nonconforming demand, we therefore hold that the Bank did not waive its objections to the County's nonconforming demands on letter of credit numbers 1156 and 1157. Therefore, the Bank is not liable on these letters of credit.

Letter of credit number 1168 bore an expiry date of December 31, 1976. On December 22, 1976, the County presented the Bank with a demand draft on this letter of credit accompanied by a resolution by the Commissioners that Woodmoor had not fulfilled its obligations on the underlying subdivision improvements agreement. The Bank timely dishonored this draft on the basis, *inter alia*, that the County submitted a demand draft rather than a fifteen-day sight draft. The County cured this defect by presenting a fifteen-day sight draft to the Bank on December 29, 1976. This fifteen-day sight draft was not accompanied by the required resolution of the Commissioners. On December 31, 1976, the Bank sent the County a letter notifying the County that this draft had also been dishonored.

The same rules of strict compliance discussed above must be applied to determine whether the County's drafts and demands for payment complied with the terms of letter of credit number 1168. The County's first draft on letter of credit number 1168 was nonconforming, since it was submitted as a demand instrument rather than a fifteen-day sight draft. On December 29, 1976, the County presented a fifteen-day sight draft which cured this defect. While the County failed to attach the required statement and demand for payment by the Commissioners with the fifteen-day sight draft, it was not required to do so. The County was merely curing a prior nonconforming demand. The two demands, taken together, consequently strictly complied with the terms of the letter of credit. The Bank therefore wrongfully dishonored this draft and demand for payment.

We reverse the judgment as to letters of credit No. 1156 and No. 1157, and affirm the judgment as to letter of credit No. 1168. This case is returned to the court of appeals for remand to the trial court for the entry of judgment in consonance with the views expressed in this opinion.

ROVIRA and LOHR, JJ., concur in part and dissent in part.

LOHR, JUSTICE, concurring in part and dissenting in part.

I concur in part I of the majority opinion and in that portion of part II which treats letter of credit number 1168 and affirms the court of appeals' opinion upholding the district court's judgment against the Colorado National Bank of Denver (Bank) on that letter of credit. I dissent to that portion of part II which reverses the judgment against the Bank on letters of credit numbers 1156 and 1157. I would affirm the decision of the court of appeals in its entirety.

The majority finds that the Bank justifiably dishonored letters of credit numbers 1156 and 1157 because the draft presented by Routt County (County) did not strictly comply with the terms of the credit. See [UCC §] 5–114(1). Because I conclude that this was an improper application of the rule of strict compliance to a non-material term of the letters of credit, I respectfully dissent.

As the majority indicates, the prevailing rule requires strict compliance with the terms of a letter of credit. * * * But the rule of strict compliance is not dictated by the language of the controlling statute, Uniform Commercial Code—Letters of Credit, * * * [UCC §] 5–114(1), merely requires that the issuer honor a draft or demand for payment "which complies with the terms of the relevant [letter of] credit * * * " Specifically, the code does not state whether strict compliance is necessary or "substantial performance" is sufficient. It was apparently a conscious decision of the drafters of the uniform act which is the source of our statute to leave this question unresolved. See J. White and R. Summers, Uniform Commercial Code, section 18–6 at 729 (1980).

The prevailing view stated by the majority not only lacks statutory mandate but also has not been uniformly accepted. A minority position has been adopted by a number of courts, rejecting a formalistic application of the rule of strict compliance where this would not be consistent with the policies underlying the use of letters of credit. As stated by Judge Coffin in Banco Espanol de Credito v. State Street Bank and Trust Co., 385 F.2d

230 (1st Cir. 1967), cert. denied 390 U.S. 1013, 88 S.Ct. 1263, 20 L.Ed.2d 163 (1968):

> But we note some leaven in the loaf of strict construction. Not only does *haec verba* not control absolutely [citation omitted], but some courts now cast their eyes on a wider scene than a single document. We are mindful, also, of the admonition of several legal scholars that the integrity of international transactions (i.e., rigid adherence to material matters) must somehow strike a balance with the requirement of their fluidity (i.e., a reasonable flexibility as to ancillary matters) if the objective of increased dealings to the mutual satisfaction to all interested parties is to be enhanced. See e.g., Mentschicoff, How to Handle Letters of Credit, 19 Bus. Lawyer 107, 111 (1963).

Banco Espanol de Credito v. State Street Bank and Trust Co., supra, at 234.

Other cases have also recognized that non-material variations from the terms of a letter of credit do not justify the issuer in dishonoring a draft or demand for payment.

* * *

In the instant case, the majority found that the County's submission of a demand draft rather than the fifteen-day sight draft required by the letters of credit rendered the presentment defective.[2] In my opinion this is the sort of non-material, technical condition which should properly be treated under a standard of substantial rather than strict compliance.[3]

There is no danger that the Bank would be misled by the use of the demand draft, nor did the use of that draft place the Bank at risk by providing a basis for its customer Woodmoor to refuse reimbursement. In this context, the Bank's contention is no more than a technical defense which frustrates equity without furthering the policies and purposes underlying the use of letters of credit.

---

2. Although I conclude that substitution of a demand draft for the fifteen-day sight draft required by the letters of credit does not excuse the Bank from all liability, this is not to suggest that the County could demand immediate payment. As noted infra, the Bank had a right to insist upon the fifteen-day review period, and the County could not unilaterally impair that right.

3. It is of interest on the issue of materiality that the Bank made no mention of the fact that the drafts were demand drafts in its letter of January 5, 1976, dishonoring the drafts and stating its reasons.

I am not unmindful of the need for certainty in letter of credit transactions, where a bank's function is designed to be primarily ministerial * * *. However, I believe that upholding the county's claim in this case would require only a limited but beneficial exception to the general rule of strict compliance. The alleged nonconformance did not relate to the underlying transaction. Rather, the nonconformity concerned only a provision designed to assure the Bank adequate time to review and consider the adequacy of the demand for payment. Thus, I would hold only that non-material defects, independent of any requirements relating to the underlying transaction, do not excuse the duty to honor a letter of credit.[4] This would avoid placing the issuer in the undesirable position of choosing between a suit by the beneficiary of a letter of credit and the risk of refusal of reimbursement by the customer who obtained that letter, while simultaneously avoiding the assertion of a technical defense to defeat payment where that payment would not place the issuer at risk.

Of course, the Bank was free in this case to inform the County that the demand draft was improper and that payment would be made as if a fifteen-day sight draft had been submitted. The County could not unilaterally deprive the Bank of the fifteen-day period for payment prescribed by the letter of credit. But the Bank should not be able to elevate a minor nonconformance into a total exoneration from liability. Neither existing law nor sound policy requires this result.

I would affirm the decision of the court of appeals.

ROVIRA, J., joins in this opinion.

4. That holding would not be inconsistent with those cases requiring strict compliance with letter of credit requirements necessary to ensure that a substantive condition precedent to payment has been met. See, e.g., Courtaulds North America, Inc. v. North Carolina Nat. Bank, [528 F.2d 802 (4th Cir. 1975)] (*packing lists* which were attached to invoices accompanying draft by beneficiary and which stated that the shipment was 100% acrylic yarn did not satisfy requirement that *invoices* specify shipment was 100% acrylic yarn); Far Eastern Textile, Ltd. v. City National Bank and Trust, [430 F.Supp. 193 (E.D.Ohio 1977)] (requirement that principal sign purchase orders evidencing underlying transaction not satisfied by the signature of an agent on those orders). When the disputed condition relates to the underlying transaction, a standard of strict compliance may well be preferable. Thus, if the nonconformance had related to the requirement that the County certify Woodmoor's failure to construct the agreed-upon improvements a different question would be presented. In this respect, it is not necessary to apply the rule of substantial compliance as broadly as some courts have. See, e.g., U.S. Industries, Inc. v. Second New Haven Bank, [462 F.Supp. 662 (D.Conn.1978)] (failure to certify expressly that payment for goods had been demanded as required by letter of credit excused where other documents satisfied the purpose of this requirement).

NOTE

As the principal case indicates the strict compliance rule has often allowed the issuer bank to avoid its liability under the letter of credit, but the cases are not uniform. Sometimes the beneficiary has won in spite of technical noncompliance. Several recent cases illustrate the problem.

Seller in accord with instructions from Buyer shipped goods to Columbus, Indiana. Payment was to be made under a letter of credit issued by Bank. The letter of credit mistakenly stated the place of delivery as Scottsdale, Arizona. Bank had issued the letter of credit without checking the financial status of Buyer. When Seller presented its demand for payment Bank refused on the ground that shipment was not made to the destination stated in the letter of credit. At that time Bank had reason to believe that Buyer would not be able to reimburse Bank for any payment made under the letter of credit. Both Buyer and Seller requested Bank to amend the letter of credit to reflect the correct destination point. Bank refused. The court stated: "In this action, [Seller] plainly relied upon the letter of credit issued by [Bank]. The point of delivery, [Seller] alleges, is of no concern to [Bank]. [Bank] did not have a security interest in the goods, and [Bank's] ability to collect from its customer will not be prejudiced by changing delivery from Arizona to Indiana. [Bank's] sole reason for refusal to amend the letter of credit was simply to rescue itself from its poor judgment when the letter was issued. On these facts, the conduct of [Bank] is inequitable." Nevertheless, the court found that Bank had no duty to amend the letter of credit and could refuse payment because the terms of the letter of credit had not been satisfied. AMF Head Sports Wear, Inc. v. Ray Scott's All-American Sports Club, 448 F.Supp. 222 (D.Ariz.1978).

In Board of Trade of San Francisco v. Swiss Credit Bank, 597 F.2d 146, 25 U.C.C.Rep. 1132 (U.S. Ct. of Appeals, 9th Cir. 1979), a letter of credit called for presentment of various documents including a "full set clean on board bills of lading" which according to expert testimony referred to ocean shipment. An initial shipment was made by air and an air way bill (bill of lading) was presented in support of the draft which was paid. Two subsequent shipments were also made by air and air way bills were again presented in support of the draft. This time the issuing bank refused to pay stating that the letter of credit required ocean shipment. The court held that if the expert testimony was correct the letter of credit required ocean shipment and the issuing bank did not wrongfully dishonor the credit.

In United States Industries, Inc. v. Second New Haven Bank, 462 F.Supp. 662 (D.Conn.1978), the letter of credit required a certificate that the demand for payment represented money owing for goods duly shipped to Buyer for which payment was demanded and not received within seven days of shipment. Seller, on the morning of the last day of the term of the credit, presented a certificate that the demand for payment represented money owing for goods duly shipped to Buyer for which payment was not received within seven days of shipment. The certificate did not expressly state that payment had been demanded; however, invoices accompanying the certificate clearly evidenced that demand had been made. (Compare *Courtaulds* discussed in footnote 4 to the dissenting opinion in *Colorado National Bank.*) When the certificate was received an officer of Issuer stated that "there did not appear to be any problems" with the documents and that if any problems arose Seller would be notified. Two days after the credit expired Issuer refused payment on the ground that the certificate did not state that demand was made. The court held that the documents presented complied with the credit because on their face they put Issuer "on notice that [Seller] had made the required demand for payment." The court also held that even if the documents did not meet the strict compliance rule Issuer was estopped to assert the noncompliance. "In the present case, [Seller], based on [Issuer's] assurances, reasonably assumed that Issuer would honor its obligation under the letter of credit. Since [Seller] acted in reliance and to its detriment, Issuer is estopped from asserting any defense it may have had concerning nonconformity of the documentary demand for payment without calling the discrepancy to the attention of [Seller] prior to the expiration of the letter of credit." The court found that Issuer in fact knew about the discrepancy prior to the expiration of the credit.

In First National Bank of Atlanta v. Wynne, 149 Ga.App. 811, 256 S.E.2d 383 (1979), the letter of credit required a draft marked "Drawn Under The First National Bank of Atlanta Credit No. S–3753." Beneficiary presented a draft without the quoted phrase but the letter transmitting the draft referred to Credit No. S–3753 and the original letter of credit No. S–3753 was enclosed. Issuer refused to pay. In holding in favor of Beneficiary the court stated: "Accordingly, we hold that if from all the documents presented to the issuer by the beneficiary there is substantial compliance *and* there is no possibility that the documents submitted could mislead the issuer to its detriment, there has been compliance with the letter of credit."

NMC ENTERPRISES, INC. v. COLUMBIA BROADCASTING SYSTEM, INC.

New York Supreme Court, New York County, 1974.
14 U.C.C.Rep. 1427.

FEIN, J. Plaintiff (NMC), a wholesaler of audio products and accessories seeks a preliminary injunction restraining defendant CBS from presenting for payment, enforcing or negotiating any drafts under or in accordance with a letter of credit in the sum of five hundred thousand dollars issued by the defendant bank (FNB) and further restraining FNB from honoring any draft drawn and presented for payment thereunder by CBS. Issuance of the letter in question was procured by NMC to engage the bank's credit and thus secure payment of NMC's obligations to CBS in connection with NMC's contract to purchase from CBS a large quantity of stereo receivers and related equipment. NMC has already received, accepted and paid for over two and a half million dollars worth of merchandise under this contract. NMC's obligation under two prior letters of credit has been satisfied.

In addition to seeking permanent injunctive relief with respect to the letter of credit, the complaint herein seeks substantial damages based upon, inter alia, claims of breach of warranty and fraud in the inducement of the portion of the contract relating to the sale of four different models of stereo receivers.

The affidavit of NMC's president avers that at the time the contract was negotiated NMC's representatives were provided with brochures containing the technical performance specifications for these receivers, including their continuous power output ratings. Such ratings, it is alleged, have a significant bearing upon the quality of the sound emitted and were a material factor in plaintiff's decision to purchase the models in question. It is further stated that after the receivers were marketed NMC was advised by many of its customers that the continuous power output of the receivers was substantially below that specified in the brochures. It appears that such advice has since been confirmed by a testing laboratory. Of critical significance upon this application, however, is the alleged admission by one of CBS's officers that it was aware of such non-conformity prior to the execution of the contract and failed to disclose this to plaintiff.

These allegations clearly suffice to make out a substantial prima facie case of fraud in the inducement of the contract. The opposing affidavit submitted by the aforesaid CBS officer is vague and evasive. He fails to make any unequivocal denial that he made the admission in question. Indeed, the crux of the CBS defense seems to be that, though there may have been some degree of non-conformity, it was insubstantial and, in any event, NMC agreed to buy the receivers on the basis of samples previously provided to and tested by it and placed no reliance on the power specifications contained in the accompanying literature.

The papers demonstrate that (1) plaintiff's present financial status is precarious; (2) if CBS is permitted to draw upon or negotiate the letter of credit and thereby obtain payment at the contract price for receivers having a market value to NMC substantially less than it had originally counted on, NMC will be unable to realize sufficient profit from sale of the receivers to meet its obligations to reimburse the bank for the credit thus extended; and (3) in all likelihood NMC will be forced into bankruptcy. On the other hand, it is unlikely that a temporary restraint upon CBS's access to such credit will defeat or impair any of its rights to payment or have any serious impact upon its financial structure.

Plaintiff makes a sufficient showing to obtain temporary injunctive relief. Concededly, a commercial letter of credit is usually independent of the underlying sales contract between the issuing bank's customer and the beneficiary. As a general rule, the responsibility of the bank to honor the draft is not affected by an ordinary breach of warranty on the part of the seller as to the quality or condition of the goods involved (Maurice O'Meara Co. v. Nat. Park Bank, 239 N.Y. 386). In the usual course, the issuing bank must honor a draft or demand for payment which complies with the terms of the relevant credit, regardless of whether the goods or documents conform to such contract of sale (UCC § 5–114[1]). However, where no innocent third parties are involved and where the documents or the underlying transaction are tainted with intentional fraud, the draft need not be honored by the bank, even though the documents conform on their face (UCC § 5–114[2][b]; Sztejn v. Schroder Banking Corp., 177 Misc. 719; Banco Tornquist v. American Bank & Trust Co., 71 Misc.2d 874) and the court may grant injunctive relief restraining such honor (UCC § 5–114[2][b]; Sztejn v. Schroder Banking Corp., supra; Merchants Corp. of America v. Chase Manhattan Bank, N. A., NYLJ, Sup.Ct.N.Y.Co., March 5,

1968, p. 2, col. 7; Dynamics Corp. of America v. Citizens & Southern Nat. Bank, 356 F.Supp. 991.

On the papers plaintiff has made a sufficient prima facie showing of fraud in the transaction underlying the letter of credit and has further shown that it may be irreparably injured if an injunction restraining honor of the drafts is not granted. This is all that is required to justify preliminary equitable relief (Sztejn v. Schroder Banking Corp., supra; Tornquist v. Amer. Bank & Tr. Co., supra).

CBS's argument that the fraud referred to in *Sztejn* (supra), is "fraud intrinsic to the documents and not as to the sales contract between the buyer and seller" is specious. If the sales contract is tainted with fraud in its inducement, then any document or signed certificate which the letter of credit requires CBS to submit, as a condition to FNB's honoring the draft, that the amount covered by the draft "is due and owing to (CBS) under Agreement of Sale and Purchase made as of the 9th day of August, 1973, between (CBS) and N. M. C. Enterprises, Inc., as amended" is equally tainted.

Accordingly, the motion is granted * * *.

* * *

PROBLEM

Buyer contracted to purchase fifty cases of bristles from Seller and arranged to have Bank issue an irrevocable letter of credit in favor of Seller. The credit required that the draft of Seller be accompanied by an invoice and bill of lading with respect to fifty cases of bristles. Seller had fifty cases of merchandise loaded on a steamship and obtained a bill of lading describing the merchandise as bristles. Seller then drew a draft and presented it, along with the bill of lading and invoices for 50 cases of bristles, to Bank. Before Bank paid the draft Buyer discovered that the fifty cases covered by the bill of lading did not contain bristles but "cowhair and other worthless material." Buyer immediately notified Bank of the fraud and demanded that the draft not be paid. You, as counsel for Bank, are notified that the documents presented by Seller are all regular on their face and comply with the letter of credit. Bank wants to know (1) whether it is required to pay the draft; (2) whether it is required to refuse payment of the draft; or (3) whether it has discretion to pay or not pay; and (4) in the last case what course of conduct is most advisable. Give the requested advice. If you were counsel to Buyer what action would you advise on his behalf? See UCC § 5–114(1) and (2). This problem is based on the facts of Sztejn v. J. Henry Schroder Banking Corp., 177 Misc. 719, 31 N.Y.S.2d 631 (1941). For a detailed discussion of *Sztejn* and UCC § 5–114, see Note, Letters of Credit: Injunction as a Remedy for Fraud in UCC Section 5–114, 63 Minn.L.Rev. 487–516 (1979).

AMERICAN BELL INTERNATIONAL, INC. v. ISLAMIC REPUBLIC OF IRAN

United States District Court, S.D.New York, 1979.
474 F.Supp. 420.

MacMahon, District Judge. Plaintiff American Bell International, Inc. ("Bell") moves for a preliminary injunction pursuant to Rule 65(a), Fed.R.Civ.P. and the All Writs Act, 28 U.S.C. § 1651, enjoining defendant Manufacturers Hanover Trust Company ("Manufacturers") from making any payment under its Letter of Credit No. SC 170027 to defendants the Islamic Republic of Iran or Bank Iranshahr or their agents, instrumentalities, successors, employees and assigns. We held an evidentiary hearing and heard oral argument on August 3, 1979. The following facts appear from the evidence presented:

The action arises from the recent revolution in Iran and its impact upon contracts made with the ousted Imperial Government of Iran and upon banking arrangements incident to such contracts. Bell, a wholly-owned subsidiary of American Telephone & Telegraph Co. ("AT & T"), made a contract on July 23, 1978 (the "Contract") with the Imperial Government of Iran— Ministry of War ("Imperial Government") to provide consulting services and equipment to the Imperial Government as part of a program to improve Iran's international communications system.

The Contract provides a complex mechanism for payment to Bell totalling approximately $280,000,000, including a down payment of $38,800,000. The Imperial Government had the right to demand return of the down payment at any time. The amount so callable, however, was to be reduced by 20% of the amounts invoiced by Bell to which the Imperial Government did not object. Bell's liability for return of the down payment was reduced by application of this mechanism as the Contract was performed, with the result that approximately $30,200,000 of the down payment now remains callable.

In order to secure the return of the down payment on demand, Bell was required to establish an unconditional and irrevocable Letter of Guaranty, to be issued by Bank Iranshahr in the amount of $38,800,000 in favor of the Imperial Government. The Contract provides that it is to be governed by the laws of Iran and that all disputes arising under it are to be resolved by the Iranian courts.

Bell obtained a Letter of Guaranty from Bank Iranshahr. In turn, as required by Bank Iranshahr, Bell obtained a standby Letter of Credit, No. SC 170027, issued by Manufacturers in favor of Bank Iranshahr in the amount of $38,800,000 to secure reimbursement to Bank Iranshahr should it be required to pay the Imperial Government under its Letter of Guaranty.

The standby Letter of Credit provided for payment by Manufacturers to Bank Iranshahr upon receipt of:

"Your [Bank Iranshahr's] dated statement purportedly signed by an officer indicating name and title or your Tested Telex Reading: (A) 'Referring Manufacturers Hanover Trust Co. Credit No. SC170027, the amount of our claim $ represents funds due us as we have received a written request from the Imperial Government of Iran Ministry of War to pay them the sum of   under our Guarantee No.   issued for the account of American Bell International Inc. covering advance payment under Contract No. 138 dated July 23, 1978 and such payment has been made by us' *   *   * .' "

In the application for the Letter of Credit, Bell agreed—guaranteed by AT & T—immediately to reimburse Manufacturers for all amounts paid by Manufacturers to Bank Iranshahr pursuant to the Letter of Credit.

Bell commenced performance of its Contract with the Imperial Government. It provided certain services and equipment to update Iran's communications system and submitted a number of invoices, some of which were paid.

In late 1978 and early 1979, Iran was wreaked with revolutionary turmoil culminating in the overthrow of the Iranian government and its replacement by the Islamic Republic. In the wake of this upheaval, Bell was left with substantial unpaid invoices and claims under the Contract and ceased its performance in January 1979. Bell claims that the Contract was breached by the Imperial Government, as well as repudiated by the Islamic Republic, in that it is owed substantial sums for services rendered under the Contract and its termination provisions.

On February 16, 1979, before a demand had been made by Bank Iranshahr for payment under the Letter of Credit, Bell and AT & T brought an action against Manufacturers in the Supreme Court, New York County, seeking a preliminary injunction prohibiting Manufacturers from honoring any demand for payment under the Letter of Credit. The motion for a preliminary injunction was denied in a thorough opinion by Justice Dontzin on March 26, 1979, and the denial was unanimously affirmed on appeal by the Appellate Division, First Department.

On July 25 and 29, 1979, Manufacturers received demands by Tested Telex from Bank Iranshahr for payment of $30,220,724 under the Letter of Credit, the remaining balance of the down payment. Asserting that the demand did not conform with the Letter of Credit, Manufacturers declined payment and so informed Bank Iranshahr. Informed of this, Bell responded by filing this action and an application by way of order to show cause for a temporary restraining order bringing on this motion for a preliminary injunction. Following argument, we granted a temporary restraining order on July 29 enjoining Manufacturers from making any payment to Bank Iranshahr until forty-eight hours after Manufacturers notified Bell of the receipt of a conforming demand, and this order has been extended pending decision of this motion.

On August 1, 1979, Manufacturers notified Bell that it had received a conforming demand from Bank Iranshahr. At the request of the parties, the court held an evidentiary hearing on August 3 on this motion for a preliminary injunction.

Criteria for Preliminary Injunctions

The current criteria in this circuit for determining whether to grant the extraordinary remedy of a preliminary injunction are set forth in Caulfield v. Board of Education, 583 F.2d 605, 610 (2d Cir. 1978):

> "[T]here must be a showing of possible irreparable injury *and* either (1) probable success on the merits *or* (2) sufficiently serious questions going to the merits to make them a fair ground for litigation *and* a balance of hardships tipping decidedly toward the party requesting the preliminary relief."

We are not persuaded that the plaintiff has met the criteria and therefore deny the motion.

A. *Irreparable Injury*

Plaintiff has failed to show that irreparable injury may possibly ensue if a preliminary injunction is denied. Bell does not even claim, much less show, that it lacks an adequate remedy at law if Manufacturers makes a payment to Bank Iranshahr in violation of the Letter of Credit. It is too clear for argument that a suit for money damages could be based on any such violation, and surely Manufacturers would be able to pay any money judgment against it.

Bell falls back on a contention that it is without any effective remedy unless it can restrain payment. This contention is based on the fact that it agreed to be bound by the laws of Iran and to submit resolution of any disputes under the Contract to the courts of Iran. Bell claims that it now has no meaningful access to those courts.

There is credible evidence that the Islamic Republic is xenophobic and anti-American and that it has no regard for consulting service contracts such as the one here. Although Bell has made no effort to invoke the aid of the Iranian courts, we think the current situation in Iran, as shown by the evidence, warrants the conclusion that an attempt by Bell to resort to those courts would be futile. Cf. Stromberg-Carlson Corp. v. Bank Melli, 467 F.Supp. 530 (Weinfeld, J.) (S.D.N.Y.1979). However, Bell has not demonstrated that it is without adequate remedy in this court against the Iranian defendants under the Sovereign Immunity Act which it invokes in this very case. 28 U.S.C. §§ 1605(a)(2), 1610(b)(2) (Supp.1979).

Accordingly, we conclude that Bell has failed to demonstrate irreparable injury.

B. *Probable Success on the Merits*

Even assuming that plaintiff has shown possible irreparable injury, it has failed to show probable success on the merits. Caulfield v. Board of Education, supra, 583 F.2d at 610.

In order to succeed on the merits, Bell must prove, by a preponderance of the evidence, that either (1) a demand for payment of the Manufacturers Letter of Credit conforming to the terms of that Letter has not yet been made, see e.g., Venizelos, S.A. v. Chase Manhattan Bank, 425 F.2d 461, 465 (2d Cir. 1970); North American Foreign Trading Corp. v. General Electronics Ltd., App.Div., 413 N.Y.S.2d 700 (1st dep't 1979), or (2) a demand, even though in conformity, should not be honored because of fraud in the transaction, see, e.g., N.Y. UCC § 5–114(2); United Bank Ltd. v. Cambridge Sporting Goods Corp., 41 N.Y.2d 254, 392 N.Y.S.2d 265, 360 N.E.2d 943 (1976); Dynamics Corp. v. Citizens & Southern Nat'l Bank, 356 F.Supp. 991 (N.D.Ga.1973). It is not probable, in the sense of a greater than 50% likelihood, that Bell will be able to prove either nonconformity or fraud.

As to nonconformity, the August 1 demand by Bank Iranshahr is identical to the terms of the Manufacturers Letter of Credit in every respect except one: it names as payee the "Government of Iran Ministry of Defense, Successor to the Imperial Government of Iran Ministry of War" rather than the "Imperial Government of Iran Ministry of War." Compare defendants' Exhibit A with Complaint Exhibit C. It is, of course, a bedrock principle of letter of credit law that a demand must strictly comply with the letter in order to justify payment. See, e.g., Key Appliance, Inc. v. First Nat'l City Bank, 46 A.D.2d 622, 359 N.Y.S.2d 866 (1st dep't 1974), aff'd, 37 N.Y.2d 826, 377 N.Y.S.2d 482, 339 N.E.2d 888 (1975). Nevertheless, we deem it less than probable that a court, upon a full trial, would find nonconformity in the instant case.

At the outset, we notice, and the parties agree, that the United States now recognizes the present Government of Iran as the legal successor to the Imperial Government of Iran. That recognition is binding on American courts. Guaranty Trust Co. v. United States, 304 U.S. 126, 137–38, 58 S.Ct. 785, 82 L.Ed. 1224 (1938). Though we may decide for ourselves the consequences of such recognition upon the litigants in this case, id., we point out that American courts have traditionally viewed contract rights as vesting not in any particular government but in the state of which that government is an agent. Id.

Accordingly, the Government of Iran is the successor to the Imperial Government under the Letter of Guaranty. As legal successor, the Government of Iran may properly demand payment even though the terms of the Letter of Guaranty only provide for payment to the Government of Iran's predecessor, see Pastor v. National Republic Bank, 56 Ill.App.3d 421, 14 Ill.Dec. 74, 371 N.E.2d 1127 (1977), aff'd, 76 Ill.2d 139, 28 Ill.Dec. 535, 390 N.E.2d 894 (1979), and a demand for payment under the Letter of Credit reciting that payment has been made by Bank Iranshahr to the new government is sufficient. * * *

If conformity is established, as here, the issuer of an irrevocable, unconditional letter of credit, such as Manufacturers normally has an absolute duty to transfer the requisite funds. This duty is wholly independent of the underlying contractual relationship that gives rise to the letter of credit. Shanghai Commercial Bank, Ltd. v. Bank of Boston Int'l, 53 A.D.2d 830, 385 N.Y.S.2d 548 (1st dep't 1976). Nevertheless, both the Uniform Commercial Code of New York, which the parties concede governs here, and the courts state that payment is enjoinable where a germane document is forged or fraudulent or there is "fraud in the transaction." N.Y.U.C.C. § 5–114(2); United Bank Ltd. v. Cambridge Sporting Goods Corp., supra. Bell does not contend that any documents are fraudulent by virtue of misstatements or omissions. Instead, it argues there is "fraud in the transaction."

The parties disagree over the scope to be given as a matter of law to the term "transaction." Manufacturers, citing voluminous authorities, argues that the term refers only to the Letter of Credit transaction, not to the underlying commercial transaction or to the totality of dealings among the banks, the Iranian government and Bell. On this view of the law, Bell must fail to establish a probability of success, for it does not claim that the Imperial Government or Bank Iranshahr induced Manufacturers to extend the Letter by lies or half-truths, that the Letter contained any false representations by the Imperial Government or Bank Iranshahr, or that they intended misdeeds with it. Nor does Bell claim that the demand contains any misstatements.

Bell argues, citing equally voluminous authorities, that the term "transaction" refers to the totality of circumstances. On this view, Bell has some chance of success on the merits, for a court can consider Bell's allegations that the Government of Iran's behavior in connection with the consulting contract suffices to make its demand on the Letter of Guaranty fraudulent and that the ensuing demand on the Letter of Credit by Bank Iranshahr is tainted with the fraud.

There is some question whether these divergent understandings of the law are wholly incompatible since it would seem impossible to keep the Letter of Credit transaction conceptually distinct. A demand which facially conforms to the Letter of Credit and which contains no misstatements may, nevertheless, be considered fraudulent if made with the goal of mulcting the party who caused the Letter of Credit to be issued. Be that as it may, we need not decide this thorny issue of law. For, even on the construction most favorable to Bell, we find that success on the merits is not probable. Many of the facts alleged, even if proven, would not constitute fraud. As to others, the proof is insufficient to indicate a probability of success on the merits.

Bell, while never delineating with precision the contours of the purported fraud, sets forth five contentions which, in its view, support the issuance of an injunction. Bell asserts that (1) both the old and new Governments failed to approve invoices for services fully performed; (2) both failed to fund contracted-for independent Letters of Credit in Bell's favor; (3) the new Government has taken steps to renounce altogether its obligations under the Contract; (4) the new Government has made it impossible to assert contract rights in Iranian courts; and (5) the new Government has caused Bank Iranshahr to demand payment on the Manufacturers Letter of Credit, thus asserting rights in a transaction it has otherwise repudiated. Plaintiff's Memorandum (Aug. 2, 1979) at 17–18.

As to contention (4), it is not immediately apparent how denial of Bell's opportunity to assert rights under the Contract makes a demand on an independent letter of credit fraudulent.

Contentions (1), (2), (3) and the latter part of (5) all state essentially the same proposition—that the Government of Iran is currently repudiating all its contractual obligations with American companies, including those with Bell. Again, the evidence on this point is uncompelling.

Bell points to (1) an intragovernmental order of July 2, 1979 ordering the termination of Iran's contract with Bell, and (2) hearsay discussions between Bell's president and Iranian officials to the effect that Iran would not pay on the Contract until it had determined whether the services under it had benefited the country. Complaint Exhibit E; Kerts Affidavit ¶ 3. Manufacturers, for its part, points to a public statement in the Wall Street Journal of July 16, 1979, under the name of the present Iranian Government, to the effect that Iran intends to honor all legitimate contracts. Defendant's Exhibit C. Taken together, this evidence does not suggest that Iran has finally and irrevocably decided to repudiate the Bell contract. It suggests equally that Iran is still considering the question whether to perform that contract.

Even if we accept the proposition that the evidence does show repudiation, plaintiff is still far from demonstrating the kind of evil intent necessary to support a claim of fraud. Surely, plaintiff cannot contend that every party who breaches or repudiates his contract is for that reason culpable of fraud. The law of contract damages is adequate to repay the economic harm caused by repudiation, and the law presumes that one who repudiates has done so because of a calculation that such damages are cheaper than performance. Absent any showing that Iran would refuse to pay damages upon a contract action here or in Iran, much less a showing that Bell has even attempted to obtain such a remedy, the evidence is ambivalent as to whether the purported repudiation results from nonfraudulent economic calculation or from fraudulent intent to mulct Bell.

Plaintiff contends that the alleged repudiation, viewed in connection with its demand for payment on the Letter of Credit, supplies the basis from which only one inference—fraud—can be drawn. Again, we remain unpersuaded.

Plaintiff's argument requires us to presume bad faith on the part of the Iranian government. It requires us further to hold that that government may not rely on the plain terms of the consulting contract and the Letter of Credit arrangements with Bank Iranshahr and Manufacturers providing for immediate repayment of the down payment upon demand, without regard to cause. On the evidence before us, fraud is no more inferable than an economically rational decision by the government to recoup its down payment, as it is entitled to do under the consulting contract and still dispute its liability under that Contract.

While fraud in the transaction is doubtless a possibility, plaintiff has not shown it to be a probability and thus fails to satisfy this branch of the *Caulfield* test.

C. *Serious Questions and Balance of Hardships*

If plaintiff fails to demonstrate probable success, he may still obtain relief by showing, in addition to the possibility of irreparable injury, both (1) sufficiently serious questions going to the merits to make them a fair ground for litigation, and (2) a balance of hardships tipping decidedly toward plaintiff. Caulfield v. Board of Education, supra. Both Bell and Manufacturers appear to concede the existence of serious questions, and the complexity and novelty of this matter lead us to find they exist. Nevertheless, we hold that plaintiff is not entitled to relief under this branch of the *Caulfield* test because the balance of hardships does not tip *decidedly* toward Bell, if indeed it tips that way at all.

To be sure, Bell faces substantial hardships upon denial of its motion. Should Manufacturers pay the demand, Bell will immediately become liable to Manufacturers for $30.2 million, with no assurance of recouping those funds from Iran for the services performed. While counsel represented in graphic detail the other losses Bell faces at the hands of the current Iranian government, these would flow regardless of whether we ordered the relief sought. The hardship imposed from a denial of relief is limited to the admittedly substantial sum of $30.2 million.

But Manufacturers would face at least as great a loss, and perhaps a greater one, were we to grant relief. Upon Manufacturers' failure to pay, Bank Iranshahr could initiate a suit on the Letter of Credit and attach $30.2 million of Manufacturers' assets in Iran. In addition, it could seek to hold Manufacturers liable for consequential damages beyond that sum resulting from the failure to make timely payment. Finally, there is not guarantee that Bank Iranshahr or the government, in retaliation for Manufacturers' recalcitrance, will not nationalize additional Manufacturers' assets in Iran in amounts which counsel, at oral argument, represented to be far in excess of the amount in controversy here.

Apart from a greater monetary exposure flowing from an adverse decision, Manufacturers faces a loss of credibility in the international banking community that could result from its failure to make good on a letter of credit.

Conclusion

Finally, apart from questions of relative hardship and the specific criteria of the *Caulfield* test, general considerations of equity counsel us to deny the motion for injunctive relief. Bell, a sophisticated multinational enterprise well advised by competent counsel, entered into these arrangements with its corporate eyes open. It knowingly and voluntarily signed a contract allowing the Iranian government to recoup its down payment on demand, without regard to cause. It caused Manufacturers to enter into an arrangement whereby Manufacturers became obligated to pay Bank Iranshahr the unamortized down payment balance upon receipt of conforming documents, again without regard to cause.

Both of these arrangements redounded tangibly to the benefit of Bell. The Contract with Iran, with its prospect of designing and installing from scratch a nationwide and international communications system, was certain to bring to Bell both monetary profit and prestige and good will in the global communications industry. The agreement to indemnify Manufacturers on its Letter of Credit provided the means by which these benefits could be achieved.

One who reaps the rewards of commercial arrangements must also accept their burdens. One such burden in this case, voluntarily accepted by Bell, was the risk that demand might be made without cause on the funds constituting the down payment. To be sure, the sequence of events that led up to that demand may well have been unforeseeable when the contracts were signed. To this extent, both Bell and Manufacturers have been made the unwitting and innocent victims of tumultuous events beyond their control. But, as between two innocents, the party who undertakes by contract the risk of political uncertainty and governmental caprice must bear the consequences when the risk comes home to roost.

Manufacturers also contends that, in view of the action apparently still pending in the state courts, we should abstain from deciding the issues before us and that Bell is engaging in forum-shopping which dirties its hands so as to require a denial of injunctive relief. In view of our findings and conclusions based on the *Caulfield* test, we find it unnecessary to consider these contentions.

The foregoing opinion constitutes this court's findings of fact and conclusions of law, pursuant to Rule 52(a), Fed.R.Civ.P.

Accordingly, plaintiff's motion for a preliminary injunction, pursuant to Rule 65(a), Fed.R.Civ.P., is denied. However, Manufacturers Hanover Trust Company, its officers and agents are hereby enjoined from making any payments to Bank Iranshahr or the Islamic Republic of Iran, pursuant to the subject Letter of Credit, until August 6, 1979, at 3:00 P.M., to permit plaintiff to apply to the Court of Appeals for a stay pending appeal, if it is so advised.

So ordered.

*

INDEX

477

†